■ For Students

MyAccountingLab provides students with a personalized interactive learning environment, where they can learn at their own pace and measure their progress.

Interactive Tutorial Exercises ▼

MyAccountingLab's homework and practice questions are correlated to the textbook, and they regenerate algorithmically to give students unlimited opportunity for practice and mastery. Questions include guided solutions, DemoDoc examples, and learning aids for extra help at point-of-use, and they offer helpful feedback when students enter incorrect answers.

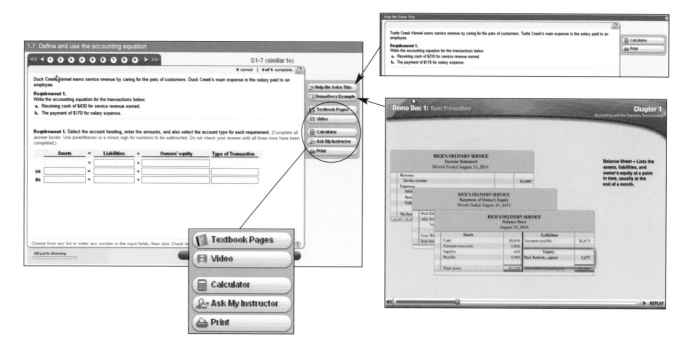

Study Plan for Self-Paced Learning ▶

MyAccountingLab's study plan helps students monitor their own progress, letting them see at a glance exactly which topics they need to practice. MyAccountingLab generates a personalized study plan for each student based on his or her test results, and the study plan links directly to interactive, tutorial exercises for topics the student hasn't yet mastered. Students can regenerate these exercises with new values for unlimited practice, and the exercises include guided solutions and multimedia learning aids to give students the extra help they need.

View a guided tour of **MyAccountingLab** at http://www.myaccountinglab.com/support/tours.

Managerial Accounting

M. Suzanne Oliver
University of West Florida

Charles T. Horngren
Stanford University

Prentice Hall
Boston Columbus Indianapolis New York San Francisco Upper Saddle River
Amsterdam Cape Town Dubai London Madrid Milan Munich Paris Montreal Toronto
Delhi Mexico City Sao Paulo Sydney Hong Kong Seoul Singapore Taipei Tokyo

VP/Publisher: Natalie E. Anderson
AVP/Executive Editor: Jodi McPherson
Director of Marketing, Intro Markets: Kate Valentine
AVP/Executive Editor, Media: Richard Keaveny
AVP/Executive Producer, Media: Lisa Strite
Director, Product Development: Pamela Hersperger
Editorial Project Manager: Rebecca Knauer
Editorial Media Project Manager: Allison Longley
Development Editor: Mignon Tucker, J.D.
 Brava 360° Publishing Solutions
Supplements Development Editor: Claire Hunter
Editorial Assistant: Christina Rumbaugh
Marketing Manager: Maggie Moylan
Marketing Assistant: Justin Jacob
Senior Managing Editor, Production:
 Cynthia Zonneveld
Production Project Manager: Lynne Breitfeller

Production Media Project Manager: John Cassar
Permissions Coordinator: Charles Morris
Senior Operations Supervision: Natacha Moore
Cover Design: Anthony Gemmellaro
Director, Image Resource Center: Melinda Patelli
Manager, Rights and Permissions: Zina Arabia
Manager, Visual Research: Beth Brenzel
Manager, Cover Visual Research & Permissions:
 Karen Sanatar
Image Permission Coordinator: Craig A. Jones
Photo Researcher: Kathy Ringrose
Composition: GEX Publishing Services
Full-Service Project Management: GEX Publishing
 Services
Printer/Binder: Courier
Typeface: 10/12 Sabon

Credits and acknowledgments borrowed from other sources and reproduced, with permission, in this textbook appear on appropriate page within text.

Dreamtime.com, pp. ix, x, xii; Chapter 1: istockphoto.com, p. 1; Chapter 2: istockphoto.com, p. 46; Chapter 3: Jupiter Unlimited, p. 97; Chapter 4: © Frank Conlon/Star Ledger/CORBIS. All Rights Reserved, p. 148; Chapter 5: Paul Sakuma/AP Wide World Photos, p. 214; Chapter 6: Scott/The Image Works, p. 263; Chapter 7: Thinkstock/Getty Images – Creative Express Royalty Free, p. 295; Chapter 8: © Thomas Pflaum/VISUM/The Image Works, p. 363; Chapter 9: Comstock Images, p. 415; Chapter 10: Sherwin Crasto/CORBIS – NY, p. 458; Chapter 11: Comstock Images/Getty Images - Creative Express Royalty Free, p. 511; Chapter 12: Ric Feld/AP Wide World Photos, p. 559; Chapter 13: © John Van Hasselt/CORBIS SYGMA, p. 604; Chapter 14: © Viviane Moos/Corbis, All Rights Reserved, p. 679.

Library of Congress Cataloging-in-Publication Data
Oliver, M. Suzanne.
 Managerial accounting / M. Suzanne Oliver, Charles T. Horngren. -- 1st ed.
 p. cm.
 Includes index.
 ISBN 978-0-13-611889-3 (0-13-611889-5 : alk. paper) 1. Managerial accounting. I. Title.
HF5657.4.O45 2010
658.15'11--dc22   2009021180

10 9 8 7 6 5 4 3 2 1

Prentice Hall
is an imprint of

www.pearsonhighered.com

ISBN-13: 978-0-13-611889-3
ISBN-10: 0-13-611889-5

Brief Contents

Contents

With
Managerial Accounting
Student Text, Study Resources,
and MyAccountingLab
students will have more
"I get it!"
moments.

Students will "get it" anytime, anywhere

Students understand (or "get it") right after the instructor does a problem in class. Once they leave the classroom, however, students often struggle to complete the homework on their own. This frustration can cause them to give up on the material altogether and fall behind in the course, resulting in an entire class falling behind as the instructor attempts to keep everyone on the same page.

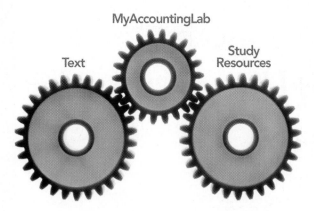

MyAccountingLab

Text

Study Resources

With the ***Managerial Accounting*** Student Learning System, all the features of the student textbook, study resources, and online homework system are designed to work together to provide students with the consistency, repetition, and high level of detail that will keep both the instructor and students on track, providing more "I get it!" moments inside and outside the classroom.

Replicating the Classroom Experience with Demo Doc Examples

The Demo Doc examples consist of entire problems, worked through step-by-step, from start to finish, narrated with the kind of comments that instructors would say in class. The Demo Docs are available in specific chapters of the text and for every chapter in the study guide. In addition to the printed Demo Docs, Flash-animated versions are available so that students can watch the problems as they are worked through while listening to the explanations and details. Demo Docs will aid students when they are trying to solve exercises and problems on their own, duplicating the classroom experience outside of class.

Chapter 2: Demo Doc

■ Allocating Manufacturing Overhead

Learning Objectives 3, 4

Macho Mike's Machine Shop manufactures specialized metal products per its customer's specifications. Macho Mike's uses direct labor cost to allocate its manufacturing overhead. Macho Mike's expects to incur $160,000 of manufacturing overhead costs and to use $400,000 of direct labor cost during 2010.

During November 2010, Macho Mike's Machine Shop had the following selected transactions:

a. Actual indirect manufacturing labor incurred was $4,200.

b. Actual indirect materials used, $3,000.

c. Other manufacturing overhead incurred, $2,800 (credit accounts payable).

d. Allocated overhead for November (the machine shop incurred $36,000 of direct labor cost during the month).

e. Finished jobs that totaled $6,500 on their job cost records.

f. Sold inventory for $70,000 (on account) that cost $42,000 to produce.

Requirements

1. Compute the predetermined manufacturing overhead rate for Macho Mike's.

2. Journalize the transactions.

3. Prepare the journal entry to close the ending balance of manufacturing overhead.

with the Student Learning System!

Consistency, Repetition, and a High Level of Detail Throughout the Learning Process

The concepts, materials, and practice problems are presented with clarity and consistency across all mediums—textbook, study resources, and online homework system. No matter which platform students use they will continually experience the same look, feel, and language, minimizing confusion and ensuring clarity.

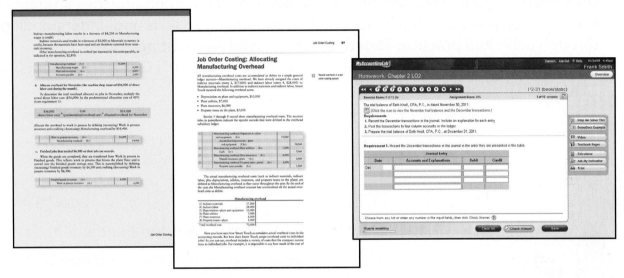

Experiencing the Power of Practice with MyAccountingLab: www.myaccountinglab.com
MyAccountingLab is an online homework system that gives students more "I get it!" moments through the power of practice. With **MyAccountingLab,** students can do the following:

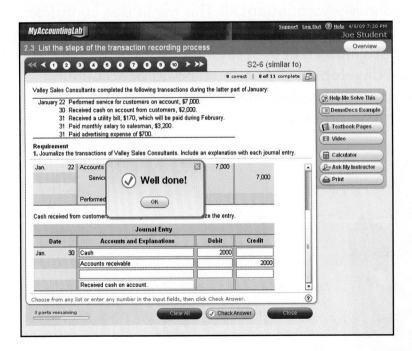

- Work on the exact end-of-chapter material and/or similar problems assigned by the instructor.
- Use the Study Plan for self-assessment and customized study outlines.
- Use the Help Me Solve This tool for a step-by-step tutorial.
- View the Demo Docs example to see an animated demonstration of where the numbers came from.
- Watch a video to see additional information pertaining to the lecture.
- Open textbook pages to find the material they need to get help on specific problems.

www.pearsonhighered.com/oliver

Oliver, *Managerial Accounting*

Learning the basic concepts through a business context, and with ample practice, is essential for building a solid foundation in managerial accounting. To help students achieve this goal, *Managerial Accounting* presents core concepts first, followed by an immediate explanation of the business implications the concept will have. **MyAccountingLab**, the text's online homework system, then provides students with a learning environment that tests and strengthens their skills and understanding through unlimited practice. Together, *Managerial Accounting* and **MyAccountingLab** will help students have more of those "I Get It!" moments.

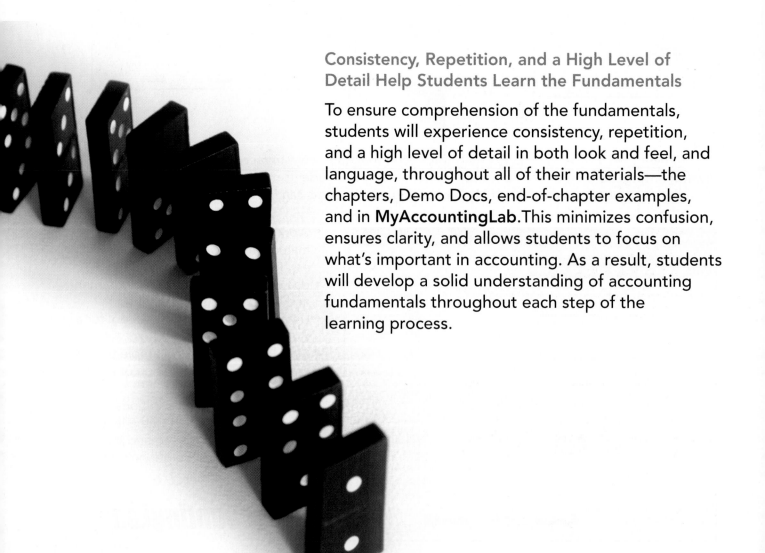

Consistency, Repetition, and a High Level of Detail Help Students Learn the Fundamentals

To ensure comprehension of the fundamentals, students will experience consistency, repetition, and a high level of detail in both look and feel, and language, throughout all of their materials—the chapters, Demo Docs, end-of-chapter examples, and in **MyAccountingLab**.This minimizes confusion, ensures clarity, and allows students to focus on what's important in accounting. As a result, students will develop a solid understanding of accounting fundamentals throughout each step of the learning process.

Developing fundamental skills in perspective!

Consistent Examples

The same two companies are used consistently in most chapters so that students can focus on learning new concepts, rather than spend time learning about a new company.

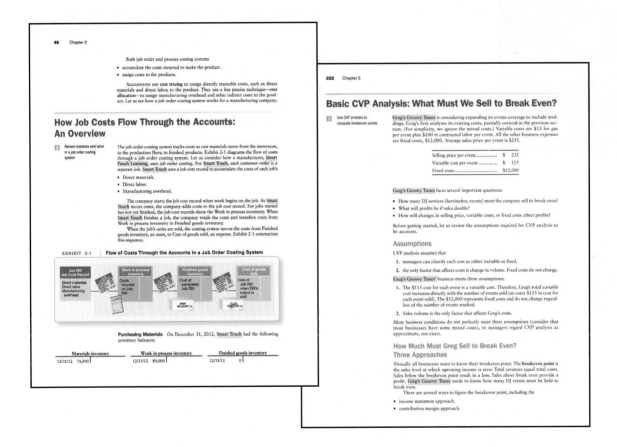

Introduction of Concepts

With *Managerial Accounting*, students are consistently looking at the big picture while learning the fundamentals. The core concepts are introduced first, followed by an explanation of the business implications the concept will have. Students then return to the original concept where it is explained with both clarity and depth. This process is continued throughout the text.

www.pearsonhighered.com/oliver

Oliver, *Managerial Accounting*

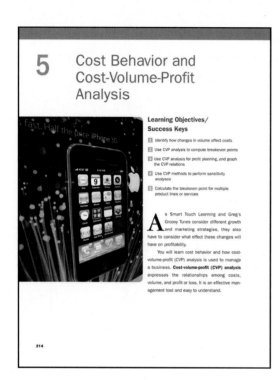

5 Cost Behavior and Cost-Volume-Profit Analysis

Learning Objectives/ Success Keys

1. Identify how changes in volume affect costs
2. Use CVP analysis to compute breakeven points
3. Use CVP analysis for profit planning, and graph the CVP relations
4. Use CVP methods to perform sensitivity analyses
5. Calculate the breakeven point for multiple product lines or services

As Smart Touch Learning and Greg's Groovy Tunes consider different growth and marketing strategies, they also have to consider what effect these changes will have on profitability.

You will learn cost behavior and how cost-volume-profit (CVP) analysis is used to manage a business. **Cost-volume-profit (CVP) analysis** expresses the relationships among costs, volume, and profit or loss. It is an effective management tool and easy to understand.

214

Reinforcing the Business Context

As students are introduced to the fundamentals throughout the text, they are also given a preview of each concept's business implications. Consistently showing students the decision-making process provides context for the fundamentals *and* works as an explanation of why the information is important and relevant.

Matching Equations

Key equations are highlighted in a blue box. Corresponding examples showing the application of the equation are highlighted in green. This distinction runs throughout the chapter and into the end-of-chapter material. By color-coding the material in this way, students can clearly identify important equations and examples.

$$\text{Predetermined manufacturing overhead rate} = \frac{\text{Total estimated manufacturing overhead costs}}{\text{Total estimated quantity of the manufacturing overhead allocation base}}$$

$$= \frac{\text{Total estimated manufacturing overhead costs}}{\text{Total estimated direct labor cost}}$$

$$= \frac{\$68,000}{\$170,000} = \$0.40$$

Developing fundamental skills in perspective!

Stop & Think sections, which appear periodically throughout the text, pull students out of the reading to show them how a concept relates to everyday life—providing immediate relevancy of the material.

Stop & Think...

Have you ever set up a special savings account to save for something you wanted to purchase in the future, or maybe saved for Spring vacation? Maybe you set aside 10% of each of your paychecks into this special account. Allocating overhead to jobs is very similar. We estimate how much total overhead will be and divide that number by the estimated cost driver (such as labor) and allocate overhead to jobs based on this rate. Special savings accounts work the same way. You decide how much you need in the future and then allocate a percentage of your paychecks to reach your goal.

Demo Docs

Bringing it all together at the end of the chapter are the Demo Docs. Demo Docs are fully worked-through problems that weave computation and concepts together in a step-by-step format for guided reinforcement of chapter concepts and skills. The worked-through problems reflect the chapter content and are available for all chapters within the text. Additional Demo Docs, including animated versions, are available in the study guide and in **MyAccountingLab**.

Chapter 2: Demo Doc

■ Allocating Manufacturing Overhead

Learning Objectives 3, 4

Macho Mike's Machine Shop manufactures specialized metal products per its customer's specifications. Macho Mike's uses direct labor cost to allocate its manufacturing overhead. Macho Mike's expects to incur $160,000 of manufacturing overhead costs and to use $400,000 of direct labor cost during 2010.

During November 2010, Macho Mike's Machine Shop had the following selected transactions:

a. Actual indirect manufacturing labor incurred was $4,200.
b. Actual indirect materials used, $3,000.
c. Other manufacturing overhead incurred, $2,800 (credit accounts payable).
d. Allocated overhead for November (the machine shop incurred $36,000 of direct labor cost during the month).
e. Finished jobs that totaled $6,500 on their job cost records.
f. Sold inventory for $70,000 (on account) that cost $42,000 to produce.

Requirements

1. Compute the predetermined manufacturing overhead rate for Macho Mike's.
2. Journalize the transactions.
3. Prepare the journal entry to close the ending balance of manufacturing overhead.

Practicing the Fundamentals

Although it's crucial for students to have a clear and thorough explanation of the fundamentals, it's in the practice where understanding is achieved.

Solidifying Chapter Concepts: After reading the fundamentals, it's important for students to have the opportunity to implement the concepts they have just learned. ***Managerial Accounting*** offers a robust and accessible selection of end-of-chapter material that allows students to practice and identify the context of what they've read, seeing how it all fits together.

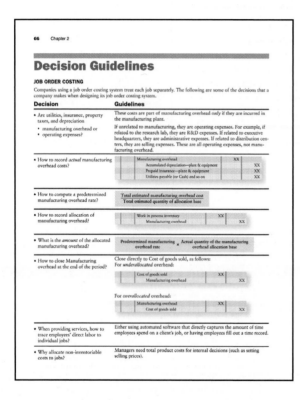

Decision Guidelines appear at the end of each chapter and provide a summary of the chapter's key terms, concepts, and formulas in the context of business decisions. These guidelines reinforce how the information students are learning is used to make decisions in a business setting.

Big Picture Summary provides an overview of the concepts as they unfold by showing students the progression of everything they have learned from Chapter 1 to the current chapter.

Continuing Exercise

This practice feature follows a single company, adding transactions or questions in each chapter to the existing fact pattern. As students move through the text, they complete additional steps in this comprehensive exercise. Students, again, see the big picture and learn how the topics build on one another. The Continuing Exercise can be assigned and completed within **MyAccountingLab**.

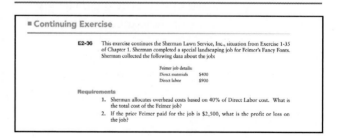

Continuing Problem

The Continuing Problem is a more comprehensive version of the Continuing Exercise. Once again, students are learning how accounting is a process and the continuing problem allows students to put it all together.

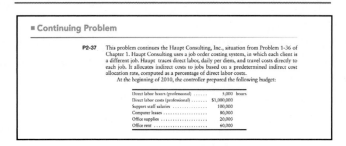

Accommodating Practice for Students. This text pays careful attention to the gradual progression of homework problems from basic practice to conceptual, or a mixture of the two. The end-of-chapter materials are designed to gradually lead students from understanding the fundamental concepts to applying them as managerial accountants would.

The End-of-Chapter Material continues to enhance students' understanding of the topics and material covered in the chapter. All material includes time estimates for completion.

- Accounting Vocabulary
- Quick Checks—in multiple choice format covering both concepts and computation
- Short Exercises
- Exercises—with four alternate sets available online in **MyAccountingLab**
- "A" and "B" Problems—each with three alternate sets available online in **MyAccountingLab**
- Continuing Exercise
- Continuing Problem
- Comprehensive Problem where applicable
- Decision Case
- Financial Statement Case
- Ethical Issues Case
- Team Projects

 NEW! End-of-Chapter Material Integrated with MyAccountingLab

Students need practice and repetition in order to successfully learn the fundamentals of accounting. In **MyAccountingLab** we offer the questions from the book, and algorithmic versions, all auto-graded for unlimited practice. For more information, visit www.myaccountinglab.com.

www.pearsonhighered.com/oliver

Student Study Aids

MyAccountingLab ®

www.myaccountinglab.com

MyAccountingLab is Web-based tutorial and assessment software for accounting that gives students more "I get it!" moments. **MyAccountingLab** provides students with a personalized interactive learning environment where they can complete their course assignments with immediate tutorial assistance, learn at their own pace, and measure their progress.

In addition to completing assignments and reviewing tutorial help, students have access to the following resources in **MyAccountingLab**:

- Pearson eText
- Study Guide
- Animated Demo Docs
- Excel in Practice

- Videos
- Audio and Student PowerPoints
- Working Papers in both Excel and PDF
- MP3 Files with Chapter Objectives and Summaries
- Flashcards

Study Guide and Study Guide CD with Demo Docs

This chapter-by-chapter learning aid helps students learn managerial accounting while getting the maximum benefit from study time. Animated Demo Docs are available on the accompanying study guide CD in Flash so students can easily refer to them when they need them.

Student Resource Website: www.pearsonhighered.com/oliver

- Excel in Practice
- Working Papers in both Excel and PDF

Student Reference Cards

International Financial Reporting Standards Student Reference Card

This four-page laminated reference card includes an overview of IFRS, why it matters and how it compares to U.S. standards, and highlights key differences between IFRS and U.S. GAAP.

Math for Accounting Student Reference Card

This six-page laminated reference card provides students with a study tool for the basic math they will need to be successful in accounting, such as rounding, fractions, converting decimals, calculating interest, break-even analysis, and more!

Instructor Supplements

The primary goal of the Instructor Resources is to help instructors deliver their course with ease, using any delivery method—traditional, self-paced, or online. *Every instructor and student resource has been either written or reviewed by the author team.*

MyAccountingLab®

www.myaccountinglab.com

MyAccountingLab is Web-based tutorial and assessment software for accounting that not only gives students more "I get it!" moments, but also provides instructors the flexibility to make technology an integral part of their course or a supplementary resource for students. And, because practice makes perfect, **MyAccountingLab** offers exactly the same end-of-chapter material found in the text along with algorithmic options that can be assigned for homework. **MyAccountingLab** also features the same look and feel for exercises and problems so that students are familiar and comfortable working with the material.

Instructor's Manual

The Instructor's Manual, available electronically or in print, offers course-specific content including a guide to available resources, a road map for using **MyAccountingLab**, a first-day handout for students, sample syllabi, guidelines for teaching an online course, and content-specific material including chapter overviews, teaching outlines, student summary handouts, lecture outline tips, assignment grids, ten-minute quizzes, and more!

Instructor Resource Center: www.pearsonhighered.com/oliver

For the instructor's convenience, many of the instructor resources are available for download from the textbook's catalog page or from **MyAccountingLab**. Available resources include the following:

- **Solutions Manual** contains the fully worked-through and accuracy-checked solutions for every question, exercise, and problem in the text.
- **Author-Written Test Item File with TestGen Software** offers over 1,600 multiple choice, true/false, and problem-solving questions that are correlated by Learning Objective and difficulty level as well as AACSB and AICPA standards.
- **Four Sets of Author-Reviewed Instructor PowerPoints** give instructors flexibility and choices for their courses. There are 508 Compliant Instructor PowerPoints with extensive notes for on-campus or online classes, Student PowerPoints, Clicker Response System (CRS) PowerPoints, and Audio Narrated PowerPoints.
- **Excel in Practice**
- **Image Library**
- **Working Papers and Solutions in Excel and PDF formats**
- **Instructor's Manual**

Course Cartridges

Course Cartridges for Blackboard, WebCT, CourseCompass, and other learning management systems are available upon request.

EXHIBIT 1-9

Financial Statements of Smart Touch Learning, Inc.

SMART TOUCH LEARNING, INC.
Income Statement
Month Ended April 30, 2010

Revenue:		
Service revenue		$8,500
Expenses:		
Salary expense	$1,200	
Rent expense, office	1,100	
Rent expense, computer	600	
Utilities expense	400	
Total expenses		3,300
Net income		$5,200

1

SMART TOUCH LEARNING, INC.
Statement of Retained Earnings
Month Ended April 30, 2010

Retained earnings, April 1, 2010	$ 0
Add: Net income for the month	5,200
	5,200
Less: Dividends	(2,000)
Retained earnings, April 30, 2010	$3,200

2

SMART TOUCH LEARNING, INC.
Balance Sheet
April 30, 2010

Assets		Liabilities	
Cash	$19,900	Accounts payable	$ 200
Accounts receivable	2,000	**Stockholders' Equity**	
Office supplies	500	Common stock	30,000
Land	11,000	Retained earnings	3,200
		Total stockholders' equity	33,200
Total assets	$33,400	Total liabilities and stockholders' equity	$33,400

3

SMART TOUCH LEARNING, INC.
Statement of Cash Flows*
Month Ended April 30, 2010

Cash flows from operating activities:		
Receipts:		
Collections from customers ($5,500 + $1,000)		$ 6,500
Payments:		
To suppliers ($600 + $1,100 + $400 + $300)	$ (2,400)	
To employees	(1,200)	(3,600)
Net cash provided by operating activities		2,900
Cash flows from investing activities:		
Acquisition of land	$(20,000)	
Sale of land	9,000	
Net cash used for investing activities		(11,000)
Cash flows from financing activities:		
Issuance of stock	$ 30,000	
Dividends	(2,000)	
Net cash provided by financing activities		28,000
Net increase in cash		19,900
Cash balance, April 1, 2010		0
Cash balance, April 30, 2010		$19,900

*Chapter 13 shows how to prepare this statement.

Color-Coded Financial Statements

Each financial statement is identified by a unique color. You will see these colors throughout the chapters when we present a financial statement.

1 The **income statement**, enclosed in the red box, provides the details of revenues earned and expenses incurred.

2 The revenue and expense transactions are then condensed into one number—net income—that becomes part of the **statement of retained earnings**, which appears in the yellow box.

3 Information from the statement of retained earnings flows into the **balance sheet**, shown in the blue box.

4 The **statement of cash flows**, as indicated by the green box, provides details of how a company got its cash and how it spent cash during the accounting period.

Acknowledgments

We'd like to thank the following contributors:

Florence McGovern *Bergen Community College*
Sherry Mills *New Mexico State University*
Helen Brubeck *San Jose State University*

We'd like to extend a special thank you to the following members of our advisory panel:

Jim Ellis *Bay State College, Boston*
Mary Ann Swindlehurst *Carroll Community College*
Andy Williams *Edmonds Community College*
Donnie Kristof-Nelson *Edmonds Community College*
Joan Cezair *Fayetteville State University*
David Baglia *Grove City College*

Anita Ellzey *Harford Community College*
Cheryl McKay *Monroe County Community College*
Todd Jackson *Northeastern State University*
Margaret Costello Lambert *Oakland Community College*
Al Fagan *University of Richmond*

We'd also like to thank the following text and supplements reviewers:

Shi-Mu (Simon) Yang *Adelphi University*
Brenda Fowler *Alamance Community College*
Thomas Stolberg *Alfred State University*
Brent Darwin *Allan Hancock College*
Thomas Branton *Alvin Community College*
Maria Lehoczky *American Intercontinental University*
Suzanne Bradford *Angelina College*
Judy Lewis *Angelo State University*
Candice Heino *Anoka Ramsey Community College*
Roy Carson *Anne Arundel Community College*
Paulette Ratliff-Miller *Arkansas State University*
Joseph Foley *Assumption College*
Jennifer Niece *Assumption College*
Bill Whitley *Athens State University*
Shelly Gardner *Augustana College*

Jeffrey Hillard *Baltimore City Community College*
Mehmet Ozbilgin *Baruch College—City University of New York*
Igor Vaysman *Baruch College—City University of New York*
Becky Jones *Baylor University*
Betsy Willis *Baylor University*
Michael Robinson *Baylor University*
Kay Walker-Hauser *Beaufort County Community College, Washington*
Joe Aubert *Bemidji State University*
Calvin Fink *Bethune Cookman College*
Michael Blue *Bloomsburg University*
Scott Wallace *Blue Mountain College*
Lloyd Carroll *Borough Manhattan Community College*
Ken Duffe *Brookdale Community College*
Chuck Heuser *Brookdale Community College*
Shafi Ullah *Broward Community College South*
Lois Slutsky *Broward Community College South*
Ken Koerber *Bucks County Community College*

Julie Browning *California Baptist University*
Richard Savich *California State University—San Bernardino*
David Bland *Cape Fear Community College*
Robert Porter *Cape Fear Community College*
Vickie Campbell *Cape Fear Community College*
Cynthia Thompson *Carl Sandburg College—Carthage*
Liz Ott *Casper College*
Joseph Adamo *Cazenovia College*
Norma Montague *Central Carolina Community College*
Julie Dailey *Central Virginia Community College*
Cynthia White *Central Texas College*
Debbie Schmidt *Cerritos College*
Janet Grange *Chicago State University*
Yvonne Baker *Cincinnati State Technical & Community College*
Bruce Leung *City College of San Francisco*
Paul Holbrook *Coconino Community College*
Pamela Legner *College of DuPage*
Jeannie Folk *College of DuPage*
Lawrence Steiner *College of Marin*
Dennis Kovach *Community College Allegheny County—Allegheny*
Bruce McMurrey *Community College of Denver*
Martin Sabo *Community College of Denver*
Jeffrey Jones *Community College of Southern Nevada*
Tom Nohl *Community College of Southern Nevada*
Christopher Kelly *Community College of Southern Nevada*
Patrick Rogan *Cosumnes River College*
Kimberly Smith *County College of Morris*

Jerold Braun *Daytona State College*
Greg Carlton *Davidson County Community College*
Irene Bembenista *Davenport University*

Thomas Szczurek *Delaware County Community College*
Charles Betts *Delaware Technical and Community College*
Patty Holmes *Des Moines Area Community College—Ankeny*
Tim Murphy *Diablo Valley College*

Phillipe Sammour *Eastern Michigan University*
Saturnino (Nino) Gonzales *El Paso Community College*
Lee Cannell *El Paso Community College*
John Eagan *Erie Community College*
Michele Berube *Everest University*

Ron O'Brien *Fayetteville Technical Community College*
Patrick McNabb *Ferris State University*
John Stancil *Florida Southern College*
Lynn Clements *Florida Southern College*
Alice Sineath *Forsyth Technical Community College*
James Makofske *Fresno City College*
Marc Haskell *Fresno City College*
Nichole Pendleton *Friends University*
Karlene Sanborn *Friends University*
James Kelly *Ft. Lauderdale City College*

Christine Jonick *Gainesville State College*
Bruce Lindsey *Genesee Community College*
Constance Hylton *George Mason University*
James Weisel *Georgia Gwinnett College*
Cody King *Georgia Southwestern State University*
Lolita Keck *Globe College*
Kay Carnes *Gonzaga University, Spokane*
Carol Pace *Grayson County College*
Susan Davis *Green River Community College*
Rebecca Floor *Greenville Technical College*
Geoffrey Heriot *Greenville Technical College*
Jackie Richards *Grossmont College*
Judith Zander *Grossmont College*
Jeffrey Patterson *Grove City College*
Lanny Nelms *Gwinnet Technical College*
Chris Cusatis *Gwynedd Mercy College*

Bridgette Mahan *Harold Washington College*
Nicole Smith *Harold Washington College*
Patrick Geer *Hawkeye Community College*
Craig Pence *Highland Community College*
Tim Griffin *Hillsborough Community College*
Clair Helms *Hinds Community College*
Michelle Powell *Holmes Community College*
Greg Bischoff *Houston Community College*
Donald Bond *Houston Community College*
Marina Grau *Houston Community College*
Carolyn Fitzmorris *Hutchinson Community College*

Susan Koepke *Illinois Valley Community College*
William Alexander *Indian Hills Community College—Ottumwa*

Dale Bolduc *Intercoast College*
Thomas Carr *International College of Naples*
Lecia Berven *Iowa Lakes Community College*
Nancy Schendel *Iowa Lakes Community College*
Chuck Smith *Iowa Western Community College*
Michelle Cannon *Ivy Tech*
Vicki White *Ivy Tech*
Robert Jackson *Ivy Tech Community College*
Jennifer Morton *Ivy Tech Community College of Indiana*
David Clifton *Ivy Tech Community College, Southern Indiana*

Stephen Christian *Jackson Community College*
Susan Cordes *Johnson County Community College*
David Krug *Johnson County Community College*
DeeDee Daughtry *Johnston Community College*
Richard Bedwell *Jones County Junior College*

John Babich *Kankakee Community College*
Ken Mark *Kansas City Kansas Community College*
Ken Snow *Kaplan Education Centers*
Charles Evans *Keiser College*
Bunney Schmidt *Keiser College*
Amy Haas *Kingsborough Community College*

Mark Dawson *La Roche College*
Cynthia Phipps *Lake Land College*
Joseph Botana *Lakeland College*
Jim Racic *Lakeland Community College*
Doug Clouse *Lakeland Community College*
Jan Ivansek *Lakeland Community College*
Patrick Haggerty *Lansing Community College*
Patricia Walczak *Lansing Community College*
Humberto M. Herrera *Laredo Community College*
Robert Everett *Lewis & Clark Community College*
Christie Comunale *Long Island University*
Ariel Markelevich *Long Island University*
Randy Kidd *Longview Community College*
John Blahnik *Lorain County Community College*
Kathy Heltzel *Luzerne County Community College*
Lori Major *Luzerne County Community College*

Fred Jex *Macomb Community College*
Dana Carpenter *Madison Area Technical College*
Patricia Cook *Manchester Community College*
Glenn Owen *Marymount College*
Behnaz Quigley *Marymount College*
Josephine Mathias *Mercer County Community College*
Penny Hanes *Mercyhurst College, Erie*
Peg Johnson *Metropolitan Community College*
John Miller *Metropolitan Community College*
Idalene Williams *Metropolitan Community College*
Jose Hortensi *Miami Dade College, Homestead Campus*
Martha Cavalaris *Miami Dade College, North Campus*

Denise Leggett *Middle Tennessee State University*
William Huffman *Missouri Southern State College*
Mary Ewanechko *Monroe Community College*
Ted Crosby *Montgomery County Community College*
Beth Engle *Montgomery County Community College*
David Candelaria *Mount San Jacinto College*
Linda Bolduc *Mount Wachusett Community College*
Richard J. Pettit *Mountain View College*

Barbara Gregorio *Nassau Community College*
James Hurat *National College of Business and Technology*
Denver Riffe *National College of Business and Technology*
Asokan Anandarajan *New Jersey Institute of Technology*
Robert Schoener *New Mexico State University*
Stanley Carroll *New York City Technical College of CUNY*
Audrey Agnello *Niagara County Community College*
Catherine Chiang *North Carolina Central University*
Karen Russom *North Harris College*
Sandra Copa *North Hennepin Community College*
Ulises Arcos-Castrejon *North Shore Community College*
Dan Bayak *Northampton Community College*
Sara Barritt *Northeast Community College*
Elizabeth Lynn Locke *Northern Virginia Community College*
Roberta Wheeler *Northwest Florida State College*
Donald Wilke *Northwest Florida State College*
Debra Prendergast *Northwestern Business College*
Nat Briscoe *Northwestern State University*
Tony Scott *Norwalk Community College*

Deborah Niemer *Oakland Community College*
Diane King *Ohio State University, Newark*
John Boyd *Oklahoma City Community College*
Kathleen O'Donnell *Onondaga Community College*
J.T. Ryan *Onondaga Community College*

Toni Clegg *Palm Beach Atlantic College*
Glenn Pate *Palm Beach Community College*
David Forsyth *Palomar College*
Robert Meyer *Parkland College*
John Graves *PCDI*
Carla Rich *Pensacola Junior College*
Judy Grotrian *Peru State College*
Ray Kreiner *Piedmont College*
Judy Daulton *Piedmont Technical College*
Koon Kwok *Pierce College, Puyallup*
Cheryl Clark *Point Park University*
John Stone *Potomac State College*
Betty Habershon *Prince George's Community College*

Kathi Villani *Queensborough Community College*

William Black *Raritan Valley Community College*
Verne Ingram *Red Rocks Community College*
Paul Juriga *Richland Community College*
Patty Worsham *Riverside Community College*
Margaret Berezewski *Robert Morris College*
Phil Harder *Robert Morris College*
Robin Turner *Rowan-Cabarrus Community College*
Shifei Chung *Rowan University of New Jersey*

Charles Fazzi *Saint Vincent College*
Lynnette Yerbuy *Salt Lake Community College*
Gloria Grayless *Sam Houston State University*
Margaret Quarles *Sam Houston State University*
Linda Serres Sweeny *Sam Houston State University*
Susan Blizzard *San Antonio College*
Hector Martinez *San Antonio College*
Audrey Voyles *San Diego Miramar College*
Margaret Black *San Jacinto College*
Merrily Hoffman *San Jacinto College*
Randall Whitmore *San Jacinto College*
Carroll Buck *San Jose State University*
Cynthia Coleman *Sandhills Community College*
Barbara Crouteau *Santa Rosa Junior College*
Pat Novak *Southeast Community College*
Susan Pallas *Southeast Community College*
Cathy Lumbattis *Southern Illinois University, Carbondale*
Al Case *Southern Oregon University*
Gloria Worthy *Southwest Tennessee Community College*
Melody Ashenfelter *Southwestern Oklahoma State University*
Douglas Ward *Southwestern Community College*
Brandi Shay *Southwestern Community College*
John May *Southwestern Oklahoma State University*
Jeffrey Waybright *Spokane Community College*
Renee Goffinet *Spokane Community College*
Susan Anders *St. Bonaventure University*
Anna Boulware *St. Charles Community College*
Anne Wessely *St. Louis Community College, Meramec*
Sue Counte *St. Louis Community College*
Elida Kraja *St. Louis Community College*
Charles Fazzi *St. Vincent College*
John Olsavsky *SUNY at Fredonia*
Peter Van Brunt *SUNY College of Technology at Delhi*

David L. Davis *Tallahassee Community College*
Nina Brown *Tarrant County Community College, Northwest Campus*
Kathy Crusto-Way *Tarrant County Community College*
Robert Elmore *Tennessee Technological University*
Sally Cook *Texas Lutheran University*
Bea Chiang *The College of New Jersey*
Matt Hightower *Three Rivers Community College*
Walter Theefs *Triton College*

About the Authors

M. Suzanne Oliver is an assistant professor of accounting at University of West Florida in Pensacola, Florida. She received her BA in Accounting Information Systems and her master's degree in accountancy from the University of West Florida.

Professor Oliver began her career in accounting in the tax department of a regional accounting firm, specializing in benefit plan administration. She has served as a software analyst for a national software development firm (CPASoftware) and as the Oracle fixed assets analyst for Spirit Energy, formerly part of Union Oil of California (Unocal). A Certified Public Accountant, Oliver is a member of the Florida Institute of Certified Public Accountants.

Professor Oliver has taught financial accounting, managerial accounting, intermediate accounting, tax accounting, accounting software applications, payroll accounting, auditing, accounting systems, advanced accounting, managerial finance, business math, and supervision. She has also taught pension continuing education classes for CPAs and has developed and instructed online courses using MyAccountingLab, WebCT, and other proprietary software.

Professor Oliver lives in Niceville where she is a member of the First United Methodist Church with her husband, Greg and son, C.J.

Charles T. Horngren is the Edmund W. Littlefield professor of accounting, emeritus, at Stanford University. A graduate of Marquette University, he received his MBA from Harvard University and his PhD from the University of Chicago. He is also the recipient of honorary doctorates from Marquette University and DePaul University.

A certified public accountant, Horngren served on the Accounting Principles Board for six years, the Financial Accounting Standards Board Advisory Council for five years, and the Council of the American Institute of Certified Public Accountants for three years. For six years he served as a trustee of the Financial Accounting Foundation, which oversees the Financial Accounting Standards Board and the Government Accounting Standards Board.

Horngren is a member of the Accounting Hall of Fame.

A member of the American Accounting Association, Horngren has been its president and its director of research. He received its first annual Outstanding Accounting Educator Award.

The California Certified Public Accountants Foundation gave Horngren its Faculty Excellence Award and its Distinguished Professor Award. He is the first person to have received both awards.

The American Institute of Certified Public Accountants presented its first Outstanding Educator Award to Horngren.

Horngren was named Accountant of the Year, in Education, by the national professional accounting fraternity, Beta Alpha Psi.

Professor Horngren is also a member of the Institute of Management Accountants, from whom he has received its Distinguished Service Award. He was a member of the institute's Board of Regents, which administers the Certified Management Accountant examinations.

Horngren is the author of these other accounting books published by Pearson Prentice Hall: *Cost Accounting: A Managerial Emphasis*, thirteenth edition, 2008 (with Srikant Datar and George Foster); *Introduction to Financial Accounting*, ninth edition, 2006 (with Gary L. Sundem and John A. Elliott); *Introduction to Management Accounting*, fourteenth edition, 2008 (with Gary L. Sundem and William Stratton); *Financial & Managerial Accounting*, second edition, 2009 and *Accounting*, eighth edition, 2009 (with Walter T. Harrison, Jr. and M. Suzanne Oliver).

Horngren is the consulting editor for Pearson Prentice Hall's Charles T. Horngren Series in Accounting.

1 Introduction to Management Accounting

Learning Objectives/Success Keys

1 Distinguish management accounting from financial accounting

2 Identify trends in the business environment and the role of management accountability

3 Classify costs and prepare an income statement for a service company

4 Classify costs and prepare an income statement for a merchandising company

5 Classify costs and prepare an income statement and statement of cost of goods manufactured for a manufacturing company

6 Use reasonable standards to make ethical judgments

Y ou got a 40% discount on your new mp3 player, and you are relaxing after a day of listening to good tunes. As you sit there, you wonder how Greg's Groovy Tunes, Inc., was able to sell the mp3 player at such a low price. Management accounting information helped Greg's Groovy Tunes design the player to maximize performance while holding down costs. Managing costs helps a company sell the right product for the right price.

Your financial accounting course laid your foundation in the building blocks of accounting:

- Accounts in the ledger for accumulating information
- Journals for recording transactions
- Financial statements for reporting operating results, financial position, and cash flows

What you have learned so far is called *financial accounting* because its main products are the financial statements.

1

This text shifts the focus to the accounting tools that managers use to run a business. As you can imagine, it is called *management (or managerial) accounting*. If you have ever dreamed of having your own business, you will find management accounting fascinating.

Before launching into how managers use accounting, let us see some of the groups to whom managers must answer. We call these groups the **stakeholders** of the company because each group has an interest of some sort in the business.

Management Accountability

1 Distinguish management accounting from financial accounting

Accountability is responsibility for one's actions. **Management accountability** is the manager's responsibility to the various stakeholders of the company. Many different stakeholders have an interest in an organization, as shown in Exhibit 1-1. Keep in mind that managers are the employees of the owners.

EXHIBIT 1-1 | **Management Accountability and the Stakeholders of a Company**

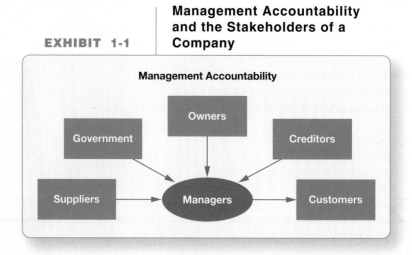

Exhibit 1-2 on the following page shows the links between management and the various stakeholders of a company. The exhibit is organized by the three main categories of cash-flow activities: operating, investing, and financing. For each activity we list the stakeholders and what they provide to the organization. The far-right column then shows how managers are accountable to the stakeholders.

To earn the stakeholders' trust, managers provide information about their decisions and the results of those decisions. Thus, management accountability requires two forms of accounting:

- Financial accounting for *external* reporting

- Management (or managerial) accounting for *internal* planning and control
  This chapter launches your study of management accounting.

Financial accounting provides financial statements that report results of operations, financial position, and cash flows both to managers and to external stakeholders: owners, creditors, suppliers, customers, the government, and society. Financial accounting satisfies management's accountability to

- Owners and creditors for their investment decisions

- Regulatory agencies, such as the Securities Exchange Commission, the Federal Trade Commission, and the Internal Revenue Service

- Customers and society to ensure that the company acts responsibly

EXHIBIT 1-2 | **Management Accountability to Stakeholders**

Stakeholders	Provide	and Management is accountable for
Operating activities		
Suppliers	Products and services	Using the goods and services to earn a profit
Employees	Time and expertise	Providing a safe and productive work environment
Customers	Cash	Providing products and services for a reasonable price
Investing activities		
Suppliers	Long-term assets	Purchasing the most productive assets
Financing activities		
Owners	Cash or other assets	Providing a return on the owners' investment
Creditors	Cash	Repaying principal and interest
Actions that affect society		
Governments	Permission to operate	Obeying laws and paying taxes
Communities	Human and physical resources	Providing jobs and operating in an ethical manner to support the community

The financial statements that you studied in your financial accounting class focused on reporting on the company as a whole.

Management accounting, on the other hand, provides information to help managers plan and control operations as they lead the business. This includes managing the company's plant, equipment, and human resources. Management accounting often requires forward-looking information because of the futuristic nature of business decisions.

Stop & Think...

You speak differently when you are speaking to your friends than when you are speaking to your boss or parents. This is the gist of managerial and financial accounting—the accounting data is formatted differently so that it "speaks" to the correct audience (stakeholders).

Managers are responsible to external stakeholders, so they must plan and control operations carefully.

- **Planning** means choosing goals and deciding how to achieve them. For example, a common goal is to increase operating income (profits). To achieve this goal, managers may raise selling prices or advertise more in the hope of increasing sales. The **budget** is a mathematical expression of the plan that managers use to coordinate the business's activities. The budget shows the expected financial impact of decisions and helps identify the resources needed to achieve goals.

- **Controlling** means implementing the plans and evaluating operations by comparing actual results to the budget. For example, managers can compare actual costs to budgeted costs to evaluate their performance. If actual costs fall below budgeted costs, that is usually good news. But if actual costs exceed the budget, managers may need to make changes. Cost data help managers make these types of decisions.

Exhibit 1-3 on the following page highlights the differences between management accounting and financial accounting. Both management accounting and financial accounting use the accrual basis of accounting. But management accounting is not required to meet external reporting requirements, such as generally accepted accounting principles. Therefore, managers have more leeway in preparing management accounting reports, as you can see in points 1–4 of the exhibit.

EXHIBIT 1-3 | **Management Accounting Versus Financial Accounting**

	Management Accounting	Financial Accounting
1. Primary users	Internal—the company's managers	External—investors, creditors, and government authorities
2. Purpose of information	Help managers plan and control operations	Help investors and creditors make investment and credit decisions
3. Focus and time dimension of the information	Relevance of the information and focus on the future—example: 2012 budget prepared in 2011	Relevance and reliability of the information and focus on the past—example: 2011 actual performance reported in 2012
4. Type of report	Internal reports are restricted only by cost/benefit analysis; no audit required	Financial statements are restricted by GAAP and audited by independent CPAs
5. Scope of information	Detailed reports on parts of the company (products, departments, territories), often on a daily or weekly basis	Summary reports primarily on the company as a whole, usually on a quarterly or annual basis
6. Behavioral	Concern about how reports will affect employee behavior	Concern about adequacy of disclosures; behavioral implications are secondary

Managers tailor their management accounting system to help them make wise decisions. Managers weigh the *benefits* of the system (better information leads to higher profits) against the *costs* to develop and run the system. Weighing the costs against the benefits is called **cost/benefit analysis**. To remain in service, a management accounting system's benefits must exceed its costs.

Point 5 of Exhibit 1-3 indicates that management accounting provides more detailed and timely information than does financial accounting. On a day-to-day basis, managers identify ways to cut costs, set prices, and evaluate employee performance. Company intranets and handheld computers provide this information with the click of a mouse. While detailed information is important to managers, summary information is more valuable to external users of financial data.

Point 6 of Exhibit 1-3 reminds us that management accounting reports affect people's behavior. Accountability is created through measuring results. Therefore, employees try to perform well on the parts of their jobs that the accounting system measures. For example, if a manufacturing company evaluates a plant manager based only on costs, the manager may use cheaper materials or hire less experienced workers. These actions will cut costs, but they can hurt profits if product quality drops and sales fall as a result. Therefore, managers must consider how their decisions will motivate company employees and if that motivation will achieve the overall results the company desires.

Today's Business Environment

2 Identify trends in the business environment and the role of management accountability

In order to be successful, managers of both large corporations and mom-and-pop businesses must consider recent business trends, such as the following:

- **Shift Toward a Service Economy.** **Service companies** provide health care, communication, banking, and other important benefits to society. **FedEx, Google,** and

Citibank do not sell products; they sell their services. In the last century, many developed economies shifted their focus from manufacturing to service, and now service companies employ more than 55% of the workforce. The U.S. Census Bureau expects services, such as technology and health care, to grow especially fast.

- **Global Competition.** To be competitive, many companies are moving operations to other countries to be closer to new markets. Other companies are partnering with foreign companies to meet local needs. For example, **Ford, General Motors,** and **DaimlerChrysler** all built plants in Brazil to feed Brazil's car-hungry middle class.

- **Time-Based Competition.** The Internet, electronic commerce (e-commerce), and express delivery speed the pace of business. Customers who instant message around the world will not wait two weeks to receive DVDs purchased online. Time is the new competitive turf for world-class business. To compete, companies have developed the following three time-saving responses:

  1. **Advanced Information Systems.** Many companies use **enterprise resource planning (ERP)** systems to integrate all their worldwide functions, departments, and data. ERP systems help to streamline operations, and enable companies to respond quickly to changes in the marketplace.

  2. **E-Commerce.** Companies use the Internet in everyday operations of selling and customer service. The internet allows the "online sales clerk" to sell to thousands of customers around the world by providing every product the company offers 24/7.

  3. **Just-in-time Management.** Inventory held too long becomes obsolete. Storing goods takes space and must be insured—that costs money. The just-in-time philosophy helps managers cut costs by speeding the transformation of raw materials into finished products. **Just-in-time (JIT)** means producing *just in time* to satisfy needs. Ideally, suppliers deliver materials for today's production in exactly the right quantities *just in time* to begin production, and finished units are completed *just in time* for delivery to customers.

- **Total Quality Management.** Companies must deliver high-quality goods and services in order to be successful. **Total quality management (TQM)** is a philosophy designed to provide customers with superior products and services. Companies achieve this goal by continuously improving quality and reducing or eliminating defects and waste. In TQM, each business function sets higher and higher goals. With TQM, **General Motors** was able to cut warranty cost from $1,600 to $548 per vehicle (as of 2007).

Now let us see how different types of companies use management accounting.

Service Companies

Service companies, such as **eBay** (online auction), **Verizon** (cell phone service), and your local bank (financial services), sell services. As with other types of businesses, service companies seek to provide services with the following three characteristics:

3 Classify costs and prepare an income statement for a service company

- High quality
- Reasonable prices
- Timely delivery

Financial accounting focuses on financial statements for service companies. Service companies have the simplest accounting, since they carry no inventories of products for sale. All of their costs are **period costs,** those costs that are incurred and expensed in the same accounting *period*.

Let us look first at Smart Touch Learning as it originally started out in early 2011 as a service company. This business sold e-learning services and software. Smart Touch's income statement for the month ended May 31, 2011, as shown in Exhibit 1-4, follows:

EXHIBIT 1-4 | **Income Statement—Service Company**

SMART TOUCH LEARNING, INC.
Income Statement
Month Ended May 31, 2011

Revenue:			
Service revenue		$7,600	100%
Expenses:			
Salary expense	$1,800		24%
Rent expense	1,000		13%
Utilities expense	400		5%
Depreciation expense—furniture	300		4%
Depreciation expense—building	200		3%
Interest expense	100		1%
Supplies expense	100		1%
Total expenses		3,900	51%
Net income		$3,700	49%

Smart Touch had no inventory in May, so the company's income statement has no Cost of goods sold. The largest expense is for the salaries of personnel who work for the company. Salary expense was 24% of Smart Touch's revenue in May. However, the company still had a 49% profit margin.

Service companies need to know which services are most profitable, and that means evaluating both revenues and costs. Knowing the cost per service helps managers to set the price of each and then to calculate operating income. In May, 2011, Smart Touch Learning provided 1,950 e-learning services. What is the cost per service? Use the following formula to calculate the unit cost:

Unit cost per service = Total service costs ÷ Total number of services provided
= $3,900 ÷ 1,950
= $2 per e-learning service

Merchandising Companies

4 Classify costs and prepare an income statement for a merchandising company

Merchandising companies, such as **Amazon.com, Wal-Mart,** and **Footlocker,** resell products they buy from suppliers. Merchandisers keep an inventory of products, and managers are accountable for the purchasing, storage, and sale of the products. You learned about merchandising companies in your financial accounting class.

In contrast with service companies, merchandisers' income statements report Cost of goods sold as the major expense. The cost of goods sold section of the income statement shows the flow of the product costs through the inventory. These product costs are **inventoriable product costs** because the products are held in inventory until sold. For *external reporting,* Generally Accepted Accounting Principles (GAAP) require companies to treat inventoriable product costs as an asset until the product is sold, at which time the costs are expensed.

Merchandising companies' inventoriable product costs include *only* the cost to purchase the goods plus freight in—the cost to get the goods *in* the warehouse. The activity in the Inventory account provides the information for the cost of goods sold section of the income statement as shown in the following formula:

> Beginning Inventory + Purchases + Freight In − Ending Inventory = Cost of Goods Sold

To highlight the roles of beginning inventory, purchases, and ending inventory, we use the periodic inventory system. However, the concepts in this chapter apply equally to companies that use perpetual inventory systems.

In management accounting we distinguish inventoriable product costs from period costs. As noted previously, *period costs* are those operating costs that are expensed in the period in which they are incurred. Therefore, period costs are the expenses that are not part of inventoriable product cost.

Greg's Groovy Tunes' December 31, 2012, results are presented as our merchandising example. Greg's Groovy Tunes first started as a service company selling musical services. Then, the company began selling music CDs and DVDs produced by other companies. At that point the company became a merchandiser. Exhibit 1-5 shows the income statement of Greg's Groovy Tunes for the year ended December 31, 2012.

EXHIBIT 1-5 | **Income Statement—Merchandising Company**

GREG'S GROOVY TUNES
Income Statement
Year Ended December 31, 2012

Sales revenue		$169,300	102.0%
Less: Sales returns and allowances	$ (2,000)		−1.2%
Sales discounts	(1,400)		−0.8%
		(3,400)	−2.0%
Net sales revenue		165,900	100.0%
Cost of goods sold:			
Beginning inventory	$ 0		
Purchases and freight in	131,000		
Cost of goods available for sale	131,000		
Ending inventory	(40,200)		
Cost of goods sold		90,800	54.7%
Gross profit		75,100	45.3%
Operating expenses			0.0%
Wage expense	$ 10,200		6.1%
Rent expense	8,400		5.1%
Insurance expense	1,000		0.6%
Depreciation expense	600		0.4%
Supplies expense	500		0.0%
Total operating expenses		20,700	12.5%
Operating income		54,400	32.8%
Other income and (expense):			
Interest expense		(1,300)	−0.8%
Net income		$ 53,100	32.0%

Greg's was not selling DVDs and CDs in 2011, so the beginning inventory at December 31, 2011, was $0. During 2012, Greg's purchased DVDs and CDs at a total cost of $131,000. At the end of 2012, Greg's ending inventory was $40,200. Of the $131,000 available for sale, the cost of DVDs and CDs sold in 2012 was

$90,800. Notice that cost of goods sold is 54.7% of sales (cost of goods sold divided by net sales revenue of $165,900). Managers watch the gross profit percentage (45.3% for Greg's) to make sure it does not change too much. A large decrease in the gross profit percentage may indicate that the company has a problem with inventory theft or shrinkage (waste). It may also indicate a problem with retail pricing of the products. The company's profit margin (net income divided by net sales revenue) is 32% for the year ended December 31, 2012.

Merchandising companies need to know which products are most profitable. Knowing the unit cost per product helps managers to set appropriate selling prices. During the year Greg's sold 10,000 CDs and DVDs. What is the cost of each item sold? Use the following formula to calculate the unit cost per item:

Unit cost per item = Total cost of goods sold ÷ Total number of items sold
= $90,800   ÷   10,000
= $9.08 per item

Now practice what you have learned by solving Summary Problem 1.

Summary Problem 1

Jackson, Inc., a retail distributor of futons, provided the following information for 2012:

Merchandise inventory, January 1.................	$ 20,000
Merchandise inventory, December 31	30,000
Selling expense	50,000
Delivery expense	18,000
Purchases of futons	265,000
Rent expense...	15,000
Utilities expense	3,000
Freight in..	15,000
Administrative expense	64,000
Sales revenue..	500,000
Units sold during the year	2,500 futons

Requirements

1. Calculate the cost of goods sold. What is the cost per futon sold?
2. Calculate the total period costs.
3. Prepare Jackson's income statement for the year ended December 31, 2012. What is the gross profit percentage? What is the profit margin percentage?

Solution

1.

> Cost of goods sold = Beginning inventory + Purchases + Freight in − Ending inventory
>
> $270,000   = $20,000   + $265,000 + $15,000 − $30,000
>
> The cost per futon sold = Cost of goods sold ÷ Number of futons sold
>
> $108   = $270,000   ÷   2,500 futons

2. Total period costs include all expenses not included in inventory:

Selling expense	$ 50,000
Delivery expense	18,000
Rent expense.............................	15,000
Utilities expense	3,000
Administrative expense	64,000
Total period costs.....................	$150,000

3. The Income Statement follows:

<table>
<thead>
<tr><th colspan="5" style="text-align:center">JACKSON, INC.
Income Statement
Year Ended December 31, 2012</th></tr>
</thead>
<tbody>
<tr><td>Sales revenue</td><td></td><td></td><td>$500,000</td><td>100%</td></tr>
<tr><td>Cost of goods sold:</td><td></td><td></td><td></td><td></td></tr>
<tr><td>Merchandise inventory, January 1</td><td></td><td>$ 20,000</td><td></td><td></td></tr>
<tr><td>Purchases and freight in ($265,000 + $15,000)</td><td></td><td>280,000</td><td></td><td></td></tr>
<tr><td>Cost of goods available for sale</td><td></td><td>300,000</td><td></td><td></td></tr>
<tr><td>Merchandise inventory, December 31</td><td></td><td>30,000</td><td></td><td></td></tr>
<tr><td>Cost of goods sold</td><td></td><td></td><td>270,000</td><td>54%</td></tr>
<tr><td>Gross profit</td><td></td><td></td><td>230,000</td><td>46%</td></tr>
<tr><td>Operating expenses:</td><td></td><td></td><td></td><td></td></tr>
<tr><td>Administrative expense</td><td></td><td>$ 64,000</td><td></td><td></td></tr>
<tr><td>Selling expense</td><td></td><td>50,000</td><td></td><td></td></tr>
<tr><td>Delivery expense</td><td></td><td>18,000</td><td></td><td></td></tr>
<tr><td>Rent expense</td><td></td><td>15,000</td><td></td><td></td></tr>
<tr><td>Utilities expense</td><td></td><td>3,000</td><td>150,000</td><td>30%</td></tr>
<tr><td>Operating income</td><td></td><td></td><td>$ 80,000</td><td>16%</td></tr>
</tbody>
</table>

Gross profit % = $230,000 / $500,000 × 100 = 46%
Profit margin % = $80,000 / $500,000 × 100 = 16%

Manufacturing Companies

Manufacturing companies use labor, equipment, supplies, and facilities to convert raw materials into finished products. Managers in manufacturing companies must use these resources to create a product that customers want. They are responsible for generating profits and maintaining positive cash flows.

In contrast with service and merchandising companies, manufacturing companies have a broad range of production activities. This requires tracking costs on three kinds of inventory:

1. **Materials inventory** includes raw materials used in making a product. For example, a baker's raw materials include flour, sugar, and eggs. Materials to manufacture a DVD include casings, colored insert label, blank DVD, and software program.

2. **Work in process inventory** includes goods that are in the manufacturing process but not yet complete. Some production activities have transformed the raw materials, but the product is not yet finished or ready for sale. A baker's work in process inventory includes dough ready for cooking. A DVD manufacturer's work in process could include the DVD and software program, but not the casing and labeling.

3. **Finished goods inventory** includes completed goods that have not yet been sold. Finished goods are the products that the manufacturer sells to a merchandiser (or to other customers), such as a finished cake or boxed DVD.

> 5   Classify costs and prepare an income statement and statement of cost of goods manufactured for a manufacturing company

Types of Costs

A **direct cost** is a cost that can be directly traced to a cost object, such as a product. Direct materials and direct labor are examples of direct costs. A **cost object** is anything for which managers want a separate measurement of cost. Managers may want to know the cost of a product, a department, a sales territory, or an activity. Costs that cannot be traced directly to a cost object, such as manufacturing overhead, are **indirect costs**. In manufacturing companies, product costs include both direct and indirect costs.

Inventoriable Product Costs

The completed product in finished goods inventory is an *inventoriable product cost*. The inventoriable product cost includes three components of manufacturing costs:

- **Direct materials** become a physical part of the finished product. The cost of direct materials (purchase cost plus freight in) can be traced directly to the finished product.
- **Direct labor** is the labor of employees who convert materials into the company's products. The cost of direct labor can be traced *directly* to the finished products.
- **Manufacturing overhead** includes all manufacturing costs other than direct materials and direct labor. These costs are created by all of the supporting production activities, including storing materials, setting up machines, and cleaning the work areas. These activities incur costs of indirect materials, indirect labor, repair and maintenance, utilities, rent, insurance, property taxes, and depreciation on manufacturing plant buildings and equipment. Manufacturing overhead is also called **factory overhead** or **indirect manufacturing cost**.

Exhibit 1-6 summarizes a manufacturer's inventoriable product costs.

EXHIBIT 1-6 | **Manufacturer's Inventoriable Product Costs**

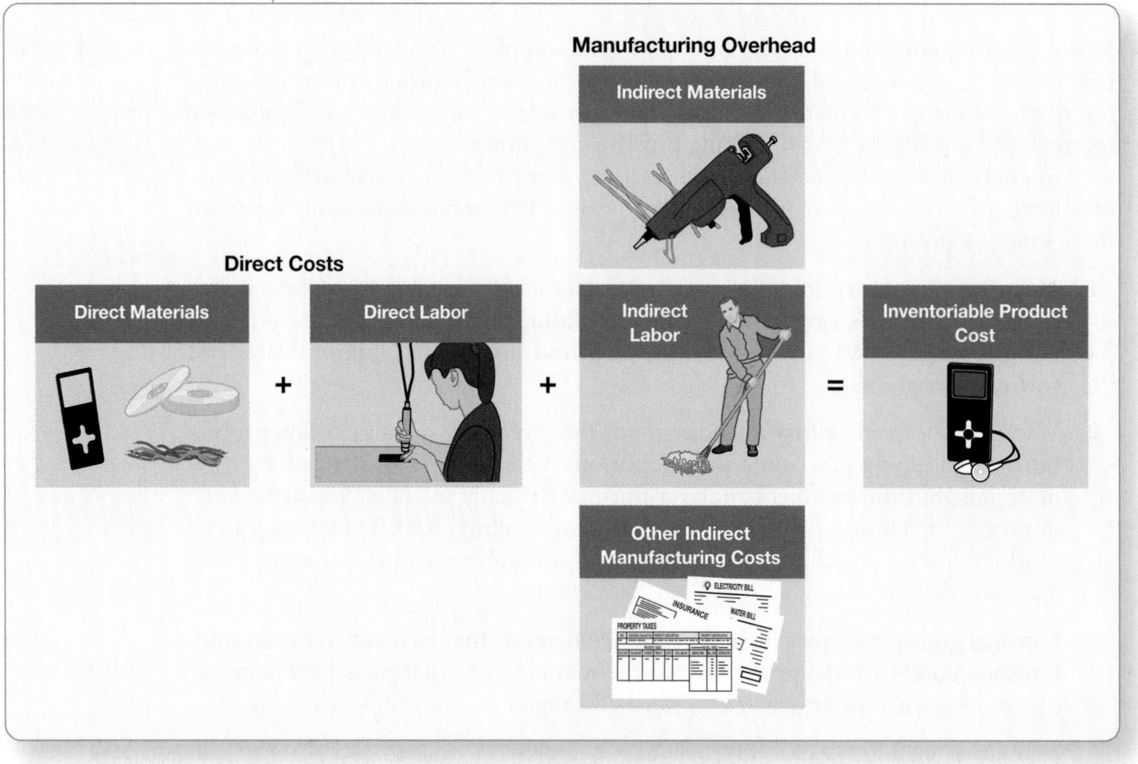

A Closer Look at Manufacturing Overhead

- Manufacturing overhead includes only those indirect costs that are related to the manufacturing operation. Insurance and depreciation on the *manufacturing plant's* building and equipment are indirect manufacturing costs, so they are part of manufacturing overhead. In contrast, depreciation on *delivery trucks* is not part of manufacturing overhead. Instead, depreciation on delivery trucks is a cost of moving the product to the customer. Its cost is delivery expense (a period cost), not an inventoriable product cost. Similarly, the cost of auto insurance for the sales force vehicles is a marketing expense (a period cost), not manufacturing overhead.

- *Manufacturing overhead includes indirect materials and indirect labor.* The spices used in cakes become physical parts of the finished product. But these costs are minor compared with the flour and sugar for the cake. Similarly, the label is necessary but minor in relation to the DVD, case, and software. Since those low-priced materials' costs cannot conveniently be traced to a particular cake or DVD, these costs are called **indirect materials** and become part of manufacturing overhead.

Like indirect materials, **indirect labor** is difficult to trace to specific products so it is part of manufacturing overhead. Examples include the pay of forklift operators, janitors, and plant managers.

Now assume that Smart Touch Learning has decided in 2013 to manufacture its own brand of learning DVDs. The company's first year of operations as a manufacturer of learning DVDs is presented in the income statement in Exhibit 1-7 for the year ended December 31, 2013.

Smart Touch's cost of goods sold represents 60% of the net sales revenue. This is the inventoriable product cost of the DVDs that Smart Touch sold in 2013. Smart Touch's balance sheet at December 31, 2013, reports the inventoriable product costs of the finished DVDs that are still on hand at the end of that year. The cost of the ending inventory, $50,000, will become the beginning inventory of next year and will then be included as part of the Cost of goods sold on next year's income statement as the DVDs are sold. The operating expenses that represent 24.1% of net sales revenue are period costs.

EXHIBIT 1-7	Income Statement—Manufacturing Company

SMART TOUCH LEARNING, INC.
Income Statement
Year Ended December 31, 2013

Sales revenue		$1,200,000	120.0%
Less: Sales returns and allowances	(120,000)		–12.0%
Sales discounts	(80,000)		–8.0%
		(200,000)	–20.0%
Net sales revenue		1,000,000	100.0%
Cost of goods sold:			
Beginning finished goods inventory	$ 0		
Cost of goods manufactured*	650,000		
Cost of goods available for sale	650,000		
Ending finished goods inventory	(50,000)		
Cost of goods sold		600,000	60.0%
Gross profit		400,000	40.0%
Operating expenses			0.0%
Wage expense	$ 120,000		12.0%
Rent expense	100,000		10.0%
Insurance expense	10,000		1.0%
Depreciation expense	6,000		0.6%
Supplies expense	5,000		0.0%
Total operating expenses		241,000	24.1%
Operating income		159,000	15.9%
Other income and (expense):			
Interest expense		(7,500)	–0.8%
Net income		$ 151,500	15.2%

Exhibit 1-8 summarizes the differences between inventoriable product costs and period costs for service, merchandising, and manufacturing companies. This is a reference tool that will help you determine how to categorize costs.

EXHIBIT 1-8	Inventoriable Product Costs and Period Costs for Service, Merchandising, and Manufacturing Companies

Type of Company	Inventoriable Product Costs—Initially an asset (Inventory), and expensed (Cost of Goods Sold) when the inventory is sold	Period Costs—Expensed in the period incurred; never considered an asset
Service company	None	Salaries, depreciation, utilities, insurance, property taxes, advertising expenses
Merchandising company	Purchases plus freight in	Salaries, depreciation, utilities, insurance, property taxes, advertising, delivery expenses
Manufacturing company	Direct materials, direct labor, and manufacturing overhead (including indirect materials; indirect labor; depreciation on the manufacturing plant and equipment; plant insurance, utilities, and property taxes)	Delivery expense; depreciation expense, utilities, insurance, and property taxes on executive headquarters (separate from the manufacturing plant); advertising; CEO's salary

Compare Smart Touch's manufacturing income statement in Exhibit 1-7 with Greg's Groovy Tunes' merchandising income statement in Exhibit 1-5. The only difference is that the merchandiser (Greg's) uses *purchases* in computing cost of goods sold, while the manufacturer (Smart Touch) uses the *cost of goods manufactured*. Notice that the term **cost of goods manufactured** is in the past tense. It is the manufacturing cost of the goods that Smart Touch *completed during 2013*. The following is the difference between a manufacturer and a merchandiser:

- The manufacturer *made* the product that it later sold.
- The merchandiser *purchased* a pre-manufactured product that was complete and ready for sale.

Calculating the Cost of Goods Manufactured The cost of goods manufactured summarizes the activities and the costs that take place in a manufacturing plant over the period. Begin by reviewing these activities. Exhibit 1-9 reminds us that the manufacturer starts by buying materials. Then the manufacturer uses direct labor and manufacturing plant and equipment (overhead) to transform these materials into work in process inventory. When inventory is completed, it becomes finished goods inventory. These are all inventoriable product costs because they are related to the inventory production process.

EXHIBIT 1-9 | **Manufacturing Company: Inventoriable Product Costs and Period Costs**

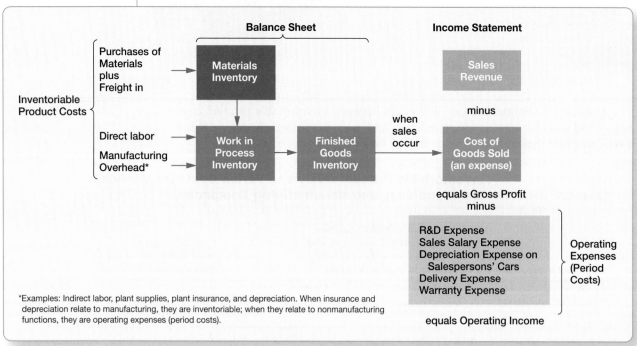

*Examples: Indirect labor, plant supplies, plant insurance, and depreciation. When insurance and depreciation relate to manufacturing, they are inventoriable; when they relate to nonmanufacturing functions, they are operating expenses (period costs).

Finished goods are the only category of inventory that is ready to sell. The cost of the finished goods that the manufacturer sells becomes its cost of goods sold on the income statement. Costs the manufacturer incurs in nonmanufacturing activities, such as sales salaries, are operating expenses—period costs—that are expensed in the period incurred. Exhibit 1-9 shows that these operating costs are deducted from gross profit to compute operating income.

You now have a clear understanding of the flow of activities and costs in the plant, and you are ready to figure the cost of goods manufactured. Exhibit 1-10 shows how Smart Touch computed its cost of goods manufactured for 2013 of

$650,000. This is the cost of making 15,000 custom DVDs that Smart Touch *finished* during 2013.

EXHIBIT 1-10 | **Schedule of Cost of Goods Manufactured**

SMART TOUCH LEARNING, INC.
Schedule of Cost of Goods Manufactured
Year Ended December 31, 2013

A	Beginning work in process inventory			$ 80,000
	Add: Direct materials used:			
B	Beginning direct materials	$ 70,000		
C	Purchases of direct materials (including freight in)	350,000		
D	Available for use	420,000		
E	Ending materials inventory	(65,000)		
F	Direct materials used		$355,000	
G	Direct labor		169,000	
	Manufacturing overhead:			
H	Indirect materials	$ 17,000		
I	Indirect labor	28,000		
J	Depreciation—plant and equipment	10,000		
K	Plant utilities, insurance, and property taxes	18,000		
L			73,000	
M	Total manufacturing costs incurred during the year			597,000
N	Total manufacturing costs to account for			$677,000
O	Less: Ending work in process inventory			(27,000)
P	Cost of goods manufactured			$650,000

$$B + C = D$$
$$D - E = F$$
$$H + I + J + K = L$$
$$F + G + L = M$$
$$A + M = N$$
$$N - O = P$$

Cost of goods manufactured summarizes the activities and related costs incurred to produce inventory during the year. As of December 31, 2012, Smart Touch had just started up manufacturing and had not completed the first custom learning DVD yet. However, the company had started several in production and had spent a total of $80,000 to partially complete them. This 2012 ending work in process inventory became the beginning work in process inventory for 2013.

Exhibit 1-10 shows that during the year, Smart Touch Learning used $355,000 of direct materials, $169,000 of direct labor, and $73,000 of manufacturing overhead.

Total manufacturing costs incurred during the year are the sum of the following three amounts:

Total Manufacturing Costs	
Direct materials used...	$355,000
Direct labor...	169,000
Manufacturing overhead	73,000
Total manufacturing costs incurred during the year	$597,000 **M**

Adding total manufacturing cost for the year, $597,000 to the beginning Work in process inventory of $80,000 gives the total manufacturing cost to account for, $677,000. At December 31, 2013, unfinished DVDs costing only $27,000 remained in Work in process (WIP) inventory. The company finished 130,000 DVDs and sent them to Finished goods (FG) inventory. Cost of goods manufactured for the year was $650,000. The following is the computation of the cost of goods manufactured:

Beginning + WIP	Direct materials used	+ Direct labor +	Manufacturing overhead	– Ending WIP	= Cost of goods manufactured
$80,000 +	355,000	+ 169,000 +	73,000	– 27,000 =	$650,000

If you refer back to Smart Touch's December, 2013, income statement in Exhibit 1-7, you will find the $650,000 listed as the cost of goods manufactured.

Flow of Costs Through the Inventory Accounts Exhibit 1-11 diagrams the flow of costs through Smart Touch's inventory accounts. The format is the same for all three stages:

- Direct materials
- Work in process
- Finished goods

EXHIBIT 1-11 | **Flow of Costs Through a Manufacturer's Inventory Accounts**

Direct Materials Inventory		Work in Process Inventory			Finished Goods Inventory	
Beginning inventory	$ 70,000	Beginning inventory		$ 80,000	Beginning inventory	$ 0
+ Purchases and freight in	350,000	+ Direct materials used	$355,000		+ Cost of goods	
		+ Direct labor	169,000		manufactured	650,000
		+ Manufacturing overhead	73,000			
		Total manufacturing costs incurred during the year	597,000			
= Direct materials available for use	420,000	= Total manufacturing costs to account for		677,000	= Cost of goods available for sale	650,000
– Ending inventory	(65,000)	– Ending inventory		(27,000)	– Ending inventory	(50,000)
= Direct materials used	$355,000	= Cost of goods manufactured		$650,000	= Cost of goods sold	$600,000

Source: The author is indebted to Judith Cassidy for this presentation.

The final amount at each stage flows into the beginning of the next stage. Take time to see how the schedule of cost of goods manufactured in Exhibit 1-11 uses the flows of the direct materials and work in process stages for Smart Touch's year ended December 31, 2013. Then examine the income statement for Greg's Groovy Tunes in Exhibit 1-5 on page 7. Because Greg's is a merchandising company, it uses only a single Inventory account.

Calculating Unit Product Cost

Manufacturing companies need to know which products are most profitable. Knowing the unit product cost helps managers decide on the prices to charge for each product. They can then measure operating income and determine the cost of finished goods inventory. Smart Touch produced 130,000 DVDs during 2013. What did it cost to make each DVD?

Cost of goods manufactured ÷	Total units produced	= Unit product cost
$650,000 ÷	130,000	= $5

During 2013, Smart Touch sold 120,000 DVDs, and the company knows each DVD cost $5 to produce. With this information Smart Touch can compute its cost of goods sold as a manager would, as follows:

Number of units sold	×	Unit product cost	=	Cost of goods sold
120,000	×	$5		$600,000

Stop & Think...

It seems lately that every time we go to the gas pump to fill up our cars, the price per gallon has changed. This change causes us to rethink our expected fuel expense each month. Similarly, the unit cost to make a product will change over time because the cost of the inputs to the production process changes over time. This is why the cost of goods manufactured statement is prepared more than once—to update management's cost data about the products the company is producing and selling.

Ethical Standards

The **WorldCom** and **Enron** scandals underscore that ethical behavior is a critical component of quality. Unfortunately, the ethical path is not always clear. You may want to act ethically and do the right thing, but the consequences can make it difficult to decide what to do. Consider the following examples:

6   Use reasonable standards to make ethical judgments

- Sarah Baker is examining the expense reports of her staff, who counted inventory at Top-Flight's warehouses in Arizona. She discovers that Mike Flinders has claimed travel expenses of $1,000 for hotel bills. Flinders could not show the paid receipts. Another staff member, who also claimed $1,000, did attach hotel receipts. When asked about the receipt, Mike admits that he stayed with an old friend, not in the hotel, but he believes he deserves the money he saved. After all, the company would have paid his hotel bill.

- As the accountant of Casey Computer, Co., you are aware of Casey's weak financial condition. Casey is close to signing a lucrative contract that should ensure its future. To do so, the controller states that the company *must* report a profit this year. He suggests the following: "Two customers have placed orders that are to be shipped in early January. Ask production to fill and ship those orders on December 31, so we can record them in this year's sales."

These situations pose ethical challenges for a manager. The Institute of Management Accountants (IMA) has developed standards to help management accountants meet the ethical challenge. The IMA standards remind us that society expects professional accountants to exhibit the highest level of ethical behavior. An excerpt from the *Statement of Ethical Profession Practice* appears in Exhibit 1-12 on the following page. These standards require management accountants to

- Maintain their professional competence
- Preserve the confidentiality of the information they handle
- Act with integrity and objectivity

EXHIBIT 1-12 | **IMA's Statement of Ethical Professional Practice (excerpt)**

Members of IMA shall behave ethically. A commitment to ethical professional practice includes overarching principles that express our values, and standards that guide our conduct.

I. COMPETENCE

Each member has a responsibility to:
1. Maintain an appropriate level of professional expertise by continually developing knowledge and skills.
2. Perform professional duties in accordance with relevant laws, regulations, and technical standards.
3. Provide decision support information and recommendations that are accurate, clear, concise, and timely.
4. Recognize and communicate professional limitations or other constraints that would preclude responsible judgment or successful performance of an activity.

II. CONFIDENTIALITY

Each member has a responsibility to:
1. Keep information confidential except when disclosure is authorized or legally required.
2. Inform all relevant parties regarding appropriate use of confidential information. Monitor subordinates' activities to ensure compliance.
3. Refrain from using confidential information for unethical or illegal advantage.

III. INTEGRITY

Each member has a responsibility to:
1. Mitigate actual conflicts of interest, regularly communicate with business associates to avoid apparent conflicts of interest. Advise all parties of any potential conflicts.
2. Refrain from engaging in any conduct that would prejudice carrying out duties ethically.
3. Abstain from engaging in or supporting any activity that might discredit the profession.

IV. CREDIBILITY

Each member has a responsibility to:
1. Communicate information fairly and objectively.
2. Disclose all relevant information that could reasonably be expected to influence an intended user's understanding of the reports, analyses, or recommendations.
3. Disclose delays or deficiencies in information, timeliness, processing, or internal controls in conformance with organization policy and/or applicable law.

RESOLUTION OF ETHICAL CONFLICT

In applying the Standards of Ethical Professional Practice, you may encounter problems identifying unethical behavior or resolving an ethical conflict. When faced with ethical issues, you should follow your organization's established policies on the resolution of such conflict. If these policies do not resolve the ethical conflict, you should consider the following courses of action:
1. Discuss the issue with your immediate supervisor except when it appears that the supervisor is involved. In that case, present the issue to the next level. If you cannot achieve a satisfactory resolution, submit the issue to the next management level. If your immediate superior is the chief executive officer or equivalent, the acceptable reviewing authority may be a group such as the audit committee, executive committee, board of directors, board of trustees, or owners. Contact with levels above the immediate superior should be initiated only with your superior's knowledge, assuming he or she is not involved. Communication of such problems to authorities or individuals not employed or engaged by the organization is not considered appropriate, unless you believe there is a clear violation of the law.
2. Clarify relevant ethical issues by initiating a confidential discussion with an IMA Ethics Counselor or other impartial advisor to obtain a better understanding of possible courses of action.
3. Consult your own attorney as to legal obligations and rights concerning the ethical conflict.

Source: © Adapted with permission from Institute of Management Accountants, www.imanet.org.

Return to the two ethical dilemmas. By asking to be reimbursed for hotel expenses he did not incur, Mike Flinders violated the IMA's integrity standards (conflict of interest in which he tried to enrich himself at the company's expense). Because Sarah Baker discovered the inflated expense report, she would not be fulfilling her ethical responsibilities (integrity and objectivity) if she allowed the reimbursement and did not take disciplinary action.

The second dilemma, in which the controller asked you to accelerate the shipments, is less clear-cut. You should discuss the available alternatives and their consequences with others. Many people believe that following the controller's suggestion to manipulate the company's income would violate the standards of competence, integrity, and objectivity. Others would argue that because Casey Computer already has the customer order, shipping the goods and recording the sale in December is still ethical behavior. If you refuse to ship the goods in December and you simply resign without attempting to find an alternative solution, you might only hurt yourself and your family.

Decision Guidelines

BUILDING BLOCKS OF MANAGEMENT ACCOUNTING

Hewlett-Packard (HP) engages in *manufacturing* when it assembles its computers, *merchandising* when it sells them on its Web site, and support *services* such as start-up and implementation services. HP had to make the following decisions in designing its management accounting system to provide managers with the information they need to run the manufacturing, merchandising, and service operations efficiently and effectively.

Decision	Guidelines
• What information should management accountants provide? What is the primary focus of management accounting?	Management accounting provides information that helps managers make better decisions; it has a • focus on *relevance* to business decisions. • *future* orientation.
• How do you decide on a company's management accounting system, which is not regulated by GAAP?	Use cost/benefit analysis: Design the management accounting system so that benefits (from helping managers make wise decisions) outweigh the costs of the system.

• How do you distinguish among service, merchandising, and manufacturing companies? How do their balance sheets differ?	*Service companies:*
	• Provide customers with intangible services
	• Have no inventories on the balance sheet
	
	Merchandising companies:
	• Resell tangible products purchased ready-made from suppliers
	• Have only one category of inventory
	
	Manufacturing companies:
	• Use labor, plant, and equipment to transform raw materials into new finished products
	• Have three categories of inventory:
	
	  • Materials inventory
	  • Work in process inventory
	  • Finished goods inventory

• How do you compute the cost of goods sold?	• *Service companies:* No cost of goods sold, because they do not sell tangible goods • *Merchandising companies:*

Beginning *merchandise* inventory
+ Purchases and freight in
– Ending *merchandise* inventory
= Cost of goods sold

• *Manufacturing companies:*

Beginning *finished goods* inventory
+ Cost of goods manufactured
– Ending *finished goods* inventory
= Cost of goods sold

Decision	Guidelines
• How do you compute the cost of goods manufactured for a manufacturer?	Beginning *work in process* inventory + Current period manufacturing costs (direct materials used + direct labor + manufacturing overhead) <u>− Ending *work in process* inventory</u> = Cost of goods manufactured
• Which costs are initially treated as assets for external reporting? When are these costs expensed?	*Inventoriable product costs* are initially treated as assets (Inventory); these costs are expensed (as Cost of goods sold) when the products are sold.
• What costs are inventoriable under GAAP?	• *Service companies:* No inventoriable product costs • *Merchandising companies:* Purchases and freight in • *Manufacturing companies:* Direct materials used, direct labor, and manufacturing overhead
• Which costs are never inventoriable product costs?	Period costs. These are never assets. They are always expenses.

Summary Problem 2

Requirements

1. For a manufacturing company, identify the following as either an inventoriable product cost or a period cost:
   a. Depreciation on plant equipment
   b. Depreciation on salespersons' automobiles
   c. Insurance on plant building
   d. Marketing manager's salary
   e. Raw materials
   f. Manufacturing overhead
   g. Electricity bill for home office
   h. Production employee wages

2. Compute cost of goods manufactured. Use the following amounts: direct materials used ($24,000); direct labor ($9,000); manufacturing overhead ($17,000); beginning work in process inventory ($5,000); and ending work in process inventory ($4,000).

Solution

Requirement 1

Inventoriable product cost: a, c, e, f, h
Period cost: b, d, g

Requirement 2

Cost of goods manufactured:

Beginning work in process inventory.....................................		$ 5,000
Add: Direct materials used	$24,000	
Direct labor	9,000	
Manufacturing overhead	17,000	
Total manufacturing costs incurred during the period ...		50,000
Total manufacturing costs to account for............................		55,000
Less: Ending work in process inventory...............................		(4,000)
Cost of goods manufactured		$51,000

Review *Introduction to Management Accounting*

■ Accounting Vocabulary

Budget (p. 3)
A mathematical expression of the plan that managers use to coordinate the business's activities.

Controlling (p. 3)
Implementing plans and evaluating the results of business operations by comparing the actual results to the budget.

Cost/Benefit Analysis (p. 4)
Weighing costs against benefits to help make decisions.

Cost Object (p. 11)
Anything for which managers want a separate measurement of cost.

Cost of Goods Manufactured (p. 14)
The manufacturing or plant-related costs of the goods that finished the production process in a given period.

Direct Cost (p. 11)
A cost that can be traced to a cost object.

Direct Labor (p. 11)
The compensation of employees who physically convert materials into finished products.

Direct Materials (p. 11)
Materials that become a physical part of a finished product and whose costs are traceable to the finished product.

Enterprise Resource Planning (ERP) (p. 5)
Software systems that can integrate all of a company's worldwide functions, departments, and data into a single system.

Factory Overhead (p. 11)
All manufacturing costs other than direct materials and direct labor. Also called **manufacturing overhead** or **indirect manufacturing costs**.

Finished Goods Inventory (p. 11)
Completed goods that have not yet been sold.

Indirect Costs (p. 11)
Costs that cannot be traced to a cost object.

Indirect Labor (p. 12)
Labor costs that are difficult to trace to specific products.

Indirect Manufacturing Cost (p. 11)
All manufacturing costs other than direct materials and direct labor. Also called **factory overhead** or **manufacturing overhead**.

Indirect Materials (p. 12)
Materials whose costs cannot conveniently be directly traced to particular finished products.

Inventoriable Product Costs (p. 6)
All costs of a product that the GAAP require companies to treat as an asset for external financial reporting. These costs are not expensed until the product is sold.

Just-in-Time (JIT) (p. 5)
A system in which a company produces just in time to satisfy needs. Suppliers deliver materials just in time to begin production and finished units are completed just in time for delivery to the customer.

Management Accountability (p. 2)
The manager's fiduciary responsibility to manage the resources of an organization.

Manufacturing Company (p. 11)
A company that uses labor, plant, and equipment to convert raw materials into new finished products.

Manufacturing Overhead (p. 11)
All manufacturing costs other than direct materials and direct labor. Also called **factory overhead** or **indirect manufacturing costs**.

Materials Inventory (p. 11)
Raw materials for use in manufacturing.

Merchandising Company (p. 6)
A company that resells products previously bought from suppliers.

Period Costs (p. 5)
Operating costs that are expensed in the period in which they are incurred.

Planning (p. 3)
Choosing goals and deciding how to achieve them.

Service Companies (p. 4)
Companies that sell intangible services, rather than tangible products.

Stakeholders (p. 2)
Groups that have a stake in a business.

Total Quality Management (TQM) (p. 5)
A philosophy of delighting customers by providing them with superior products and services. Requires improving quality and eliminating defects and waste throughout the value chain.

Work in Process Inventory (p. 11)
Goods that are partway through the manufacturing process but not yet complete.

■ Quick Check

1. Which is *not* a characteristic of management accounting information?
   a. Focuses on the future
   b. Emphasizes the external financial statements
   c. Emphasizes relevance
   d. Provides detailed information about individual parts of the company

2. World-class businesses must compete based on time. To compete effectively many companies have developed
   a. enterprise resource planning.
   b. cost standards.
   c. just-in-time management.
   d. All of the above

3. Today's business environment is characterized by
   a. a shift toward a service economy.
   b. time-based competition.
   c. global competition.
   d. All of the above

4. Which account does a manufacturing company, but not a service company, have?
   a. Retained earnings
   b. Advertising expense
   c. Cost of goods sold
   d. Salary payable

5. In computing cost of goods sold, which of the following is the manufacturer's counterpart to the merchandiser's purchases?
   a. Total manufacturing costs to account for
   b. Cost of goods manufactured
   c. Total manufacturing costs incurred during the period
   d. Direct materials used

6. Which is a direct cost of manufacturing a sport boat?
   a. Cost of customer hotline
   b. Cost of boat engine
   c. Salary of engineer who rearranges plant layout
   d. Depreciation on plant and equipment

7. Which of the following is *not* part of manufacturing overhead for producing a computer?
   a. Manufacturing plant property taxes
   b. Manufacturing plant utilities
   c. Depreciation on delivery trucks
   d. Insurance on plant and equipment

Questions 8 and 9 use the data that follow. Suppose a bakery reports this information (in thousands of dollars):

Beginning materials inventory	$ 4
Ending materials inventory	3
Beginning work in process inventory . . .	3
Ending work in process inventory	2
Beginning finished goods inventory . . .	2
Ending finished goods inventory	4
Direct labor	31
Purchases of direct materials	105
Manufacturing overhead	22

8. If the cost of direct materials used is $106, what is cost of goods manufactured?

    a. $159

    b. $157

    c. $160

    d. $158

9. If the cost of goods manufactured were $156, what is cost of goods sold?

    a. $159

    b. $151

    c. $156

    d. $154

10. A management accountant who avoids conflicts of interest meets the ethical standard of

    a. integrity.

    b. confidentiality.

    c. objectivity.

    d. competence.

Answers are given after Apply Your Knowledge (p. 40).

Assess Your Progress

■ Short Exercises

S1-1   *(L. OBJ. 1)* **Management accounting vs. financial accounting [5–10 min]**
Managerial and financial accounting differ in many aspects.

Requirement

1. For each of the following, indicate whether the statement relates to management accounting (MA) or financial accounting (FA):

    _____ a. Helps investors make investment decisions

    _____ b. Provides detailed reports on parts of the company

    _____ c. Helps in planning and controlling operations

    _____ d. Reports can influence employee behavior

    _____ e. Reports must follow Generally Accepted Accounting Principles (GAAP)

    _____ f. Reports audited annually by independent certified public accountants

S1-2   *(L. OBJ. 1)* **Management accountability and the stakeholders [10 min]**
Management has the responsibility to manage the resources of an organization in a responsible manner.

Requirement

1. For each of the following management responsibilities, indicate the primary stakeholder group to whom management is responsible. In the space provided, write the letter corresponding to the appropriate stakeholder group.

_____ 1. Providing high-quality, reliable products/services for a reasonable price in a timely manner

_____ 2. Paying taxes in a timely manner

_____ 3. Providing a safe, productive work environment

_____ 4. Generating a profit

_____ 5. Repaying principal plus interest in a timely manner

a. Owners
b. Creditors
c. Suppliers
d. Employees
e. Customers
f. Government
g. Community

S1-3 *(L. OBJ. 2)* **Business trends terminology [10 min]**
Consider the terms and definitions that follow:

_____ 1. A philosophy of delighting customers by providing them with superior products and services. Requires improving quality and eliminating defects and waste.

_____ 2. Use of the Internet for such business functions as sales and customer service. Enables companies to reach thousands of customers around the world.

_____ 3. Software systems that integrate all of a company's worldwide functions, departments, and data into a single system.

_____ 4. A system in which a company produces just in time to satisfy needs. Suppliers deliver materials just in time to begin production, and finished units are completed just in time for delivery to customers.

a. ERP
b. Just-in-time (JIT)
c. E-commerce
d. Total quality management

Requirement

1. Match the term with the correct definition.

S1-4 *(L. OBJ. 3)* **Calculating income and cost per unit for a service organization [5–10 min]**
Martin and Reynolds provides hair cutting services in the local community. In January, the business incurred the following operating costs to cut the hair of 220 clients:

Hair supplies expense	$ 700
Building rent expense	1,400
Utilities	100
Depreciation on equipment	60

Martin and Reynolds earned $4,900 in revenues from haircuts for the month of January.

Requirements

1. What is the net operating income for the month?
2. What is the cost of one haircut?

S1-5 *(L. OBJ. 4)* **Computing cost of goods sold [5 min]**

The Glass Pro, a retail merchandiser of auto windshields, has the following information:

Web site maintenance	$ 6,900
Delivery expense	800
Freight in	2,800
Purchases	41,000
Ending inventory	5,000
Revenues	60,000
Marketing expenses	10,200
Beginning inventory	8,200

Requirement

1. Compute The Glass Pro's cost of goods sold.

S1-6 *(L. OBJ. 4)* **Computing cost of goods sold [5–10 min]**

Consider the following partially completed Income Statements:

	Rustic Gear	Fit Apparel
Sales	$ 102,000	(d)
Cost of goods sold		
Beginning inventory	(a)	$ 31,000
Purchases and freight in	51,000	(e)
Cost of goods available for sale	(b)	91,000
Ending inventory	1,800	1,800
Cost of goods sold	61,000	(f)
Gross margin	$ 41,000	$ 114,000
Selling and administrative expenses	(c)	83,000
Operating income	$ 11,000	(g)

Requirement

1. Compute the missing amounts.

S1-7 *(L. OBJ. 5)* **Match type of company with product and period costs [5 min]**

Consider the following costs:

<u>S, Mer, Man</u> Example: Advertising costs

_____ 1. Cost of goods manufactured

_____ 2. The CEO's salary

_____ 3. Cost of goods sold

_____ 4. Building rent expense

_____ 5. Customer service expense

Requirement

1. For each of the costs, indicate if the cost would be found on the income statement of a service company (S), a merchandising company (Mer), and/or a manufacturing company (Man). Some costs can be found on the income statements of more than one type of company.

S1-8 *(L. OBJ. 5)* **Computing direct materials used [5 min]**

You are a new accounting intern at 101 Cookies. Your boss gives you the following information:

Purchases of direct materials	$ 6,700
Freight in	100
Property taxes	800
Ending inventory of direct materials	1,600
Beginning inventory of direct materials	4,200

Requirement

1. Compute direct materials used.

S1-9 *(L. OBJ. 5)* **Distinguishing between direct and indirect costs [5–10 min]**
Consider Maher Cards' manufacturing plant.

Requirement

1. Match one of the following terms with each example of a manufacturing cost given below:

1. Direct materials   _____ a. Artists' wages

2. Direct labor   _____ b. Wages of warehouse workers

3. Indirect materials   _____ c. Paper

4. Indirect labor   _____ d. Depreciation on equipment

5. Other manufacturing overhead   _____ e. Manufacturing plant manager's salary

                                                    _____ f. Property taxes on manufacturing plant

                                                    _____ g. Glue for envelopes

S1-10 *(L. OBJ. 5)* **Computing manufacturing overhead [5–10 min]**
Sun Pro Company manufactures sunglasses. Suppose the company's October records include the following items:

Glue for frames	$ 400	Company president's salary	$ 26,000
Depreciation expense on company		Plant foreman's salary	3,000
cars used by sales force	2,000	Plant janitor's wages	1,100
Plant depreciation expense	6,500	Oil for manufacturing equipment	150
Interest expense	2,500	Lenses	48,000

Requirements

1. List the items and amounts that are manufacturing overhead costs.
2. Calculate Sun Pro's total manufacturing overhead cost in October.

S1-11 *(L. OBJ. 5)* **Compute cost of goods manufactured [5 min]**
Max-Fli Golf Company had the following inventory data for the year ended December 31, 2010:

Direct materials used	$ 15,000
Manufacturing overhead	18,000
Work in process inventory:	
Beginning	6,000
Ending	3,000
Direct labor	7,000
Finished goods inventory	11,000

Requirement

1. Compute Max-Fli's cost of goods manufactured for 2010.

S1-12 *(L. OBJ. 5)* **Inventoriable product costs vs. period costs [5–10 min]**
Manufacturer's costs are either inventoriable product costs or period costs.

Requirement

1. Classify each of a paper manufacturer's costs as either an inventoriable product cost or a period cost:

   a. Salaries of scientists studying ways to speed forest growth
   b. Cost of computer software to track inventory
   c. Cost of electricity at a paper mill
   d. Salaries of the company's top executives
   e. Cost of chemicals to treat paper
   f. Cost of TV ads
   g. Depreciation on the gypsum board plant
   h. Cost of lumber to be cut into boards
   i. Life insurance on CEO

S1-13 *(L. OBJ. 6)* **Ethical decisions [5 min]**
The Institute of Management Accountants' *Statement of Ethical Professional Practice* (Exhibit 1-12) require management accountants to meet standards regarding the following:

- Competence
- Confidentiality
- Integrity
- Credibility

Requirement

1. Consider the following situations. Which guidelines are violated in each situation?

   a. You tell your brother that your company will report earnings significantly above financial analysts' estimates.
   b. You see that others take home office supplies for personal use. As an intern, you do the same thing, assuming that this is a "perk."
   c. At a conference on e-commerce, you skip the afternoon session and go sightseeing.
   d. You failed to read the detailed specifications of a new general ledger package that you asked your company to purchase. After it is installed, you are surprised that it is incompatible with some of your company's older accounting software.
   e. You do not provide top management with the detailed job descriptions they requested because you fear they may use this information to cut a position from your department.

■ Exercises

E1-14 *(L. OBJ. 1)* **Management vs. financial accounting and managers' use of information [5 min]**
The following statements consider how managers use information.

   a. Companies must follow GAAP in their ____ systems.
   b. Financial accounting develops reports for external parties, such as ____ and ____.
   c. When managers compare the company's actual results to the plan, they are performing the ____ role of management.
   d. ____ are decision makers inside a company.
   e. ____ provides information on a company's past performance.
   f. ____ systems are not restricted by GAAP but are chosen by comparing the costs versus the benefits of the system.
   g. Choosing goals and the means to achieve them is the ____ function of management.

Requirement

1. Complete the statements with one of the terms listed here. You may use a term more than once, and some terms may not be used at all.

Budget	Creditors	Managers	Planning
Controlling	Financial accounting	Management accounting	Shareholders

E1-15 *(L. OBJ. 2)* **Understanding today's business environment [5 min]**
The following statements relate to understanding today's business environment.

    a. ____ is a management philosophy that focuses on producing products as needed by the customer.

    b. The goal of ____ is to please customers by providing them with superior products and services by eliminating defects and waste.

    c. ____ can integrate all of a company's worldwide functions, departments, and data.

    d. Firms adopt ____ to conduct business on the Internet.

Requirement

1. Complete the statements with one of the terms listed here. You may use a term more than once, and some terms may not be used at all.

E-commerce	Just-in-time (JIT) manufacturing
Enterprise Resource Planning (ERP)	Total quality management (TQM)

E1-16 *(L. OBJ. 3)* **Calculating income and cost per unit for a service company [5–10 min]**
Buddy Grooming provides grooming services in the local community. In November, Isaac Smith, the owner, incurred the following operating costs to groom 690 dogs:

Wages	$ 4,300
Grooming supplies expense . . .	1,700
Building rent expense	1,400
Utilities	260
Depreciation on equipment . . .	150

Buddy Grooming earned $15,600 in revenues from grooming for the month of November.

Requirements

1. What is Buddy's net operating income for November?
2. What is the cost to groom one dog?

E1-17 *(L. OBJ. 3)* **Preparing an income statement and computing the unit cost for a service company [5–10 min]**
Georgie's Grooming is a competitor of Buddy Grooming. Georgie Oliver, owner, incurred the following operating costs to groom 2,700 dogs for the first quarter of 2011 (January, February, and March):

Wages	$ 16,700
Grooming supplies expense	4,000
Building rent expense	2,500
Utilities	1,100
Depreciation on furniture and equipment . . .	300

Georgie's Grooming earned $46,300 in revenues for the first quarter of 2011.

Requirements

1. Prepare an income statement for the first quarter of 2011. Compute the ratio of operating expense to total revenue and operating income to total revenue.
2. Compute Georgie's unit cost to groom one dog.

E1-18 *(L. OBJ. 4)* **Preparing an income statement and computing the unit cost for a merchandising company [15 min]**

Gonzales Brush Company sells standard hair brushes. The following information summarizes Gonzales's operating activities for 2011:

Selling and administrative expenses	$ 45,400
Purchases	62,800
Sales revenue	128,500
Merchandise inventory, January 1, 2011	7,400
Merchandise inventory, December 31, 2011	6,000

Requirements

1. Prepare an income statement for 2011. Compute the ratio of operating expense to total revenue and operating income to total revenue.
2. Gonzales sold 5,700 brushes in 2011. Compute the unit cost for one brush.

E1-19 *(L. OBJ. 5)* **Computing cost of goods manufactured [15–20 min]**

Consider the following partially completed cost of goods manufactured statements.

	Flynt Corp.	White Corp.	Fit Apparel
Beginning work in process inventory	(a)	$ 40,000	$ 2,100
Direct materials used	$ 14,900	$ 35,000	(g)
Direct labor	10,100	20,100	1,100
Manufacturing overhead	(b)	10,700	900
Total manufacturing costs incurred during year ...	45,700	(d)	(h)
Total manufacturing costs to account for	$ 56,400	(e)	$ 7,700
Less: Ending work in process inventory	(c)	(25,700)	(2,800)
Cost of goods manufactured	$ 51,900	(f)	(i)

Requirement

1. Complete the missing amounts.

E1-20 *(L.OBJ. 5)* **Preparing a statement of cost of goods manufactured [15–20 min]**

Clarkson, Corp., a lamp manufacturer, provided the following information for the year ended December 31, 2012:

Inventories:	Beginning	Ending
Materials	$ 55,000	$ 25,000
Work in process	105,000	61,000
Finished goods	43,000	44,000

Other information:			
Depreciation: plant building and equipment	$ 18,000	Repairs and maintenance–plant	$ 7,000
Materials purchases	150,000	Indirect labor	33,000
Insurance on plant	28,000	Direct labor	127,000
Sales salaries expense	49,000	Administrative expenses	51,000

3. How does the format of the income statement for Denim Bones differ from the income statement of a merchandiser?

4. Denim Bones manufactured 17,400 units of its product in 2011. Compute the company's unit product cost for the year.

P1-26A *(L. OBJ. 5)* **Preparing financial statements for a manufacturer [25–35 min]**
Certain item descriptions and amounts are missing from the monthly schedule of cost of goods manufactured and the income statement of Webber Manufacturing Company.

_____ MANUFACTURING COMPANY			
_____ June 30, 2012			
Beginning _____			$ 20,000
Direct _____:			
Beginning materials inventory	$ X		
Purchase of materials	56,000		
_____	77,000		
Ending materials inventory	(27,000)		
Direct _____		$ X	
Direct _____		X	
Manufacturing overhead:		44,000	
Total _____ costs _____			$ 171,000
Total _____ costs _____			X
Ending _____			(22,000)
_____			X
Sales revenue		$ X	
Cost of goods sold:			
Beginning _____	$ 114,000		
_____	X		
Cost of goods _____	X		
Ending _____	X		
Cost of goods sold		222,000	
Gross profit		238,000	
_____ expenses:			
Marketing expenses	96,000		
Administrative expenses	X	156,000	
_____ income		$ X	

Requirement

1. Fill in the missing items.

P1-27A *(L. OBJ. 5)* **Flow of costs through a manufacturer's inventory accounts [20–25 min]**
West Shoe Company makes loafers. During the most recent year, West incurred total manufacturing costs of $25.8 M. Of this amount, $2.3 M was direct materials used

Requirements

1. Prepare a schedule of cost of goods manufactured.

2. What is the unit product cost if Clarkson manufactured 3,200 lamps for the year?

E1-21 *(L. OBJ. 5)* **Flow of costs through a manufacturer's inventory accounts [15–20 min]**
Consider the following data for a manufacturer:

	Beginning of Year	End of Year
Direct materials inventory	$ 21,000	$ 31,000
Work in process inventory	43,000	29,000
Finished goods inventory	15,000	26,000
Purchases of direct materials ...		72,000
Direct labor		89,000
Manufacturing overhead		46,000

Requirement

1. Compute cost of goods manufactured and cost of goods sold.

E1-22 *(L. OBJ. 6)* **Ethical decisions [15 min]**
Mary Gonzales is the controller at Automax, a car dealership. Cory Loftus recently has been hired as bookkeeper. Cory wanted to attend a class on Excel spreadsheets, so Mary temporarily took over Cory's duties, including overseeing a fund for topping-off a car's gas before a test drive. Mary found a shortage in this fund and confronted Cory when he returned to work. Cory admitted that he occasionally uses this fund to pay for his own gas. Mary estimated that the amount involved is close to $300.

Requirements

1. What should Mary Gonzales do?

2. Would you change your answer to the previous question if Mary Gonzales was the one recently hired as controller and Cory Loftus was a well-liked longtime employee who indicated that he always eventually repaid the fund?

■ Problems (Group A)

P1-23A *(L. OBJ. 1, 2, 3)* **Calculating income and cost per unit for a service company [15–20 min]**
The Tree Doctors provide tree-spraying services in the company's home county. Ivan Peters, the owner, incurred the following operating costs for the month of January 2012:

Salaries and wages	$ 8,000
Chemicals	4,400
Depreciation on truck	400
Depreciation on building and equipment	1,200
Supplies expense	400
Gasoline and utilities	1,400

The Tree Doctors earned $28,000 in revenues for the month of January by spraying trees totaling 35,000 feet in height.

Requirements

1. Prepare an income statement for the month of January. Co[...]
   total operating expense to total revenue and operating incom[...]
2. Compute the unit operating cost of spraying one foot of tree [...]
3. The manager of The Tree Doctors must keep unit operating co[...]
   foot in order to get his bonus. Did he meet the goal?
4. What kind of system could The Tree Doctors use to integrate [...]

P1-24A *(L. OBJ. 4)* **Preparing an income statement for a merchar**
[45–55 min]
In 2011 Clyde Conway opened Clyde's Pets, a small retail shop s[...]
On December 31, 2011, Clyde's accounting records showed the fo[...]

Inventory on December 31, 2011	$	10,700
Inventory on January 1, 2011		15,300
Sales revenue		55,000
Utilities for shop		3,200
Rent for shop		4,300
Sales commissions		2,850
Purchases of merchandise		25,000

Requirement

1. Prepare an income statement for Clyde's Pets, a merchandiser,
   December 31, 2011.

P1-25A *(L. OBJ. 5)* **Preparing cost of goods manufactured sched**
statement for a manufacturing company [30–45 min]
Clyde's Pets succeeded so well that Clyde decided to manufacture
chewing bone—Denim Bones. At the end of December 2011, his a[...]
showed the following:

Inventories:	Beginning	
Materials	$ 13,900	
Work in process	0	
Finished goods	0	

Other information:			
Direct material purchases	$ 39,000	Utilities for plant	
Plant janitorial services	200	Rent of plant	
Sales salaries expense	5,800	Customer service hotline expense	
Delivery expense	1,300	Direct labor	
Sales revenue	108,000		

Requirements

1. Prepare a schedule of cost of goods manufactured for Denim [...]
   ended December 31, 2011.
2. Prepare an income statement for Denim Bones for [...]
   December 31, 2011.

and $18.8 M was direct labor. Beginning balances for the year were Direct Materials Inventory, $.9 M; Work in Process Inventory, $1.2 M; and Finished Goods Inventory, $.4 M. At the end of the year, inventory accounts showed these amounts:

	Materials	Direct Labor	Manufacturing Overhead
Direct Materials Inventory	$ 0.60 M	$ 0	$ 0
Work in Process Inventory	0.60 M	0.65 M	0.45 M
Finished Goods Inventory	0.10 M	0.35 M	0.05 M

Requirements

1. Compute West Shoe Company's cost of goods manufactured for the year.
2. Compute West's cost of goods sold for the year.
3. Compute the cost of materials purchased during the year.

P1-28A *(L. OBJ. 6)* **Making ethical decisions [20–25 min]**
Lee Reinhardt is the new controller for Night Software, Inc., which develops and sells education software. Shortly before the December 31 fiscal year-end, Robert Tau, the company president, asks Reinhardt how things look for the year-end numbers. He is not happy to learn that earnings growth may be below 15% for the first time in the company's five-year history. Tau explains that financial analysts have again predicted a 15% earnings growth for the company and that he does not intend to disappoint them. He suggests that Reinhardt talk to the assistant controller, who can explain how the previous controller dealt with such situations. The assistant controller suggests the following strategies:

a. Persuade suppliers to postpone billing $15,000 in invoices until January 1.
b. Record as sales $100,000 in certain software awaiting sale that is held in a public warehouse.
c. Delay the year-end closing a few days into January of the next year, so that some of next year's sales are included as this year's sales.
d. Reduce the allowance for bad debts from 2% to 1% (and bad debts expense), given the company's continued strong performance.
e. Postpone routine monthly maintenance expenditures from December to January.

Requirements

1. Which of these suggested strategies are inconsistent with IMA standards?
2. What should Reinhardt do if Tau insists that she follow all of these suggestions?

■ Problems (Group B)

P1-29B *(L. OBJ. 1, 2, 3)* **Calculating income and cost per unit for a service company**
[15–20 min]
The Tree People provide tree-spraying services in the company's home county. George Renkas, owner, incurred the following operating costs for the month of March 2012:

Salaries and wages	$ 7,000
Chemicals	4,900
Depreciation on truck	250
Depreciation on building and equipment	1,100
Supplies expense	600
Gasoline and utilities	1,000

The Tree People earned $22,000 in revenues for the month of March by spraying trees totaling 20,000 feet in height.

Requirements

1. Prepare an income statement for the month of March. Compute the ratio of total operating expense to total revenue and operating income to total revenue.
2. Compute the unit operating cost of spraying one foot of tree height.
3. The manager of The Tree People must keep unit operating cost below $0.60 per foot in order to get his bonus. Did he meet the goal?
4. What kind of system could The Tree People use to integrate all its data?

P1-30B *(L. OBJ. 4)* **Preparing an income statement for a merchandising company [45–55 min]**

In 2011 Cam Snyder opened Cam's Pets, a small retail shop selling pet supplies. On December 31, 2011, Cam's accounting records showed the following:

Inventory on December 31, 2011	$	10,400
Inventory on January 1, 2011		15,900
Sales revenue		55,000
Utilities for shop		3,800
Rent for shop		4,100
Sales commissions		2,550
Purchases of merchandise		24,000

Requirement

1. Prepare an income statement for Cam's Pets, a merchandiser, for the year ended December 31, 2011.

P1-31B *(L. OBJ. 5)* **Preparing cost of goods manufactured scheduled and income statement for a manufacturing company [30–45 min]**

Cam's Pets succeeded so well that Cam decided to manufacture his own brand of chewing bone—Chewy Bones. At the end of December 2011, his accounting records showed the following:

Inventories:	Beginning		Ending
Materials	$ 13,300		$ 9,500
Work in process	0		3,500
Finished goods	0		5,700

Other information:			
Direct material purchases	$ 33,000	Utilities for plant	$ 1,100
Plant janitorial services	300	Rent on plant	8,000
Sales salaries expense	5,200	Customer service hotline expense	1,600
Delivery expense	1,300	Direct labor	25,000
Sales revenue	106,000		

Requirements

1. Prepare a schedule of cost of goods manufactured for Chewy Bones for the year ended December 31, 2011.
2. Prepare an income statement for Chewy Bones for the year ended December 31, 2011.
3. How does the format of the income statement for Chewy Bones differ from the income statement of a merchandiser?
4. Chewy Bones manufactured 17,300 units of its product in 2011. Compute the company's unit product cost for the year.

P1-32B *(L. OBJ. 5)* **Preparing financial statements for a manufacturer [25–35 min]**
Certain item descriptions and amounts are missing from the monthly schedule of cost of goods manufactured and the income statement of Nelly Manufacturing Company.

_____ MANUFACTURING COMPANY			
_____ June 30, 2012			
Beginning _____			$ 28,000
Direct _____ :			
Beginning materials inventory	$ X		
Purchase of materials	51,000		
_____	78,000		
Ending materials inventory	(28,000)		
Direct _____		$ X	
Direct _____		X	
Manufacturing overhead:		44,000	
Total _____ costs _____			$ 173,000
Total _____ costs _____			X
Ending _____			(22,000)
_____			$ X
Sales revenue		$ X	
Cost of goods sold:			
Beginning _____	$ 115,000		
_____	X		
Cost of goods _____	X		
Ending _____	X		
Cost of goods sold		232,000	
Gross profit		238,000	
_____ expenses:			
Marketing expenses	92,000		
Administrative expenses	X	159,000	
_____ income		$ X	

Requirement

1. Fill in the missing items.

P1-33B *(L. OBJ. 5)* **Flow of costs through a manufacturer's inventory accounts [20–25 min]**
Happy Feet Shoe Company makes loafers. During the most recent year, Happy Feet incurred total manufacturing costs of $25.8 M. Of this amount, $2.7 M was direct materials used and $11.8 M was direct labor. Beginning balances for the year were Direct Materials Inventory, $.5 M; Work in Process Inventory, $1.8 M; and Finished Goods Inventory, $1.1 M. At the end of the year, inventory accounts showed these amounts:

	Materials		Direct Labor		Manufacturing Overhead	
Direct Materials Inventory	$ 0.60	M	$ 0		$ 0	
Work in Process Inventory	0.90	M	0.65	M	0.45	M
Finished Goods Inventory	0.50	M	0.15	M	0.05	M

Requirements

1. Compute Happy Feet Shoe Company's cost of goods manufactured for the year.
2. Compute Happy Feet's cost of goods sold for the year.
3. Compute the cost of materials purchased during the year.

P1-34B *(L. OBJ. 6)* **Making ethical decisions [20–25 min]**

Mary Hajjar is the new controller for Sun Software, Inc., which develops and sells education software. Shortly before the December 31 fiscal year-end, William Cauvet, the company president, asks Hajjar how things look for the year-end numbers. He is not happy to learn that earnings growth may be below 15% for the first time in the company's five-year history. Cauvet explains that financial analysts have again predicted a 15% earnings growth for the company and that he does not intend to disappoint them. He suggests that Hajjar talk to the assistant controller, who can explain how the previous controller dealt with such situations. The assistant controller suggests the following strategies:

   a. Persuade suppliers to postpone billing $10,000 in invoices until January 1.
   b. Record as sales $140,000 in certain software awaiting sale that is held in a public warehouse.
   c. Delay the year-end closing a few days into January of the next year so that some of next year's sales are included as this year's sales.
   d. Reduce the allowance for bad debts from 9% to 8% (and bad debts expense), given the company's continued strong performance.
   e. Postpone routine monthly maintenance expenditures from December to January.

Requirements

1. Which of these suggested strategies are inconsistent with IMA standards?
2. What should Hajjar do if Cauvet insists that she follow all of these suggestions?

■ Continuing Exercise

E1-35   This exercise is the first exercise in a series and is continued throughout the textbook. Sherman Lawn Service, Inc. is considering manufacturing a weed eater. Sherman expects to incur the following manufacturing costs:

     Shaft and handle of weed eater

     Motor of weed eater

     Factory labor for workers assembling weed eaters

     Nylon thread in weed eater

     Glue to hold housing together

     Plant janitorial wages

     Depreciation on factory equipment

     Rent on plant

     Sales commission expense

     Administrative salaries

     Plant utilities

     Shipping costs to deliver finished weed eaters to customers

Requirement

1. Classify each cost as either direct materials, direct labor, factory overhead, or period costs.

P1-36 This problem is the first problem in a series and is continued throughout the textbook. Haupt Consulting, Inc., is going to manufacture billing software. During its first month of manufacturing, Haupt incurred the following manufacturing costs:

Inventories:	Beginning		Ending
Materials	$ 10,000		$ 9,000
Work in process	0		22,000
Finished goods	0		30,000

Other information:				
Direct material purchases	$ 15,000	Utilities for plant		$ 12,000
Plant janitorial services	300	Rent of plant		8,000
Sales salaries expense	7,000	Customer service hotline expense		15,000
Delivery expense	2,000	Direct labor		300,000
Sales revenue	1,000,000			

Requirement

1. Prepare a Schedule of Cost of Goods Manufactured for Haupt for the month ended January 31, 2010.

Apply Your Knowledge

■ Decision Cases

Case 1. PowerSwitch, Inc., designs and manufactures switches used in telecommunications. Serious flooding throughout North Carolina affected PowerSwitch's facilities. Inventory was completely ruined, and the company's computer system, including all accounting records, was destroyed.

Before the disaster, recovery specialists clean the buildings. Stephen Plum, the company controller, is anxious to salvage whatever records he can to support an insurance claim for the destroyed inventory. He is standing in what is left of the accounting department with Paul Lopez, the cost accountant.

"I didn't know mud could smell so bad," Paul says. "What should I be looking for?"

"Don't worry about beginning inventory numbers," responds Stephen, "we'll get them from last year's annual report. We need first-quarter cost data."

"I was working on the first-quarter results just before the storm hit," Paul says. "Look, my report's still in my desk drawer. All I can make out is that for the first quarter, material purchases were $476,000 and direct labor, manufacturing overhead, and total manufacturing costs to account for were $505,000, $245,000, and $1,425,000, respectively. Wait! Cost of goods available for sale was $1,340,000."

"Great," says Stephen. "I remember that sales for the period were approximately $1.7 million. Given our gross profit of 30%, that's all you should need."

Paul is not sure about that, but decides to see what he can do with this information. The beginning inventory numbers are as follows:

- Direct materials, $113,000
- Work in process, $229,000
- Finished goods, $154,000

He remembers a schedule he learned in college that may help him get started.

1. Exhibit 1-11 resembles the schedule Paul has in mind. Use it to determine the ending inventories of direct materials, work in process, and finished goods.

2. Draft an insurance claim letter for the controller, seeking reimbursement for the flood damage to inventory. PowerSwitch's insurance representative is Gary Ogleby, at Industrial Insurance, Co., 1122 Main Street, Hartford, CT 06268. The policy number is #3454340-23. PowerSwitch's address is 5 Research Triangle Way, Raleigh, NC 27698.

Case 2. IMA's *Statement of Ethical Professional Practice* can be applied to more than just management accounting. They are also relevant to college students.

Requirement

1. Explain at least one situation that shows how each IMA standard in Exhibit 1-12 is relevant to your experiences as a student. For example, the ethical standard of competence would suggest not cutting classes!

▪ Ethical Issue

Becky Knauer recently resigned from her position as controller for Shamalay Automotive, a small, struggling foreign car dealer in Upper Saddle River, New Jersey. Becky has just started a new job as controller for Mueller Imports, a much larger dealer for the same car manufacturer. Demand for this particular make of car is exploding, and the manufacturer cannot produce enough to satisfy demand. The manufacturer's regional sales managers are each given a certain number of cars. Each sales manager then decides how to divide the cars among the independently owned dealerships in the region. Because most dealerships can sell every car they receive, the key is getting a large number of cars from the manufacturer's regional sales manager.

Becky's former employer, Shamalay Automotive, receives only about 25 cars a month. Consequently, the dealership was not very profitable.

Becky is surprised to learn that her new employer, Mueller Imports, receives over 200 cars a month. Becky soon gets another surprise. Every couple of months, a local jeweler bills the dealer $5,000 for "miscellaneous services." Franz Mueller, the owner of the dealership, personally approves payment of these invoices, noting that each invoice is a "selling expense." From casual conversations with a salesperson, Becky learns that Mueller frequently gives Rolex watches to the manufacturer's regional sales manager and other sales executives. Before talking to anyone about this, Becky decides to work through his ethical dilemma using the framework from this chapter.

Requirement

1. Put yourself in Becky's place and complete the framework.
    a. What is the ethical issue?
    b. What are my options?
    c. What are the possible consequences?
    d. What shall I do?

▪ Financial Statement Case—Amazon.com

This case is based on the **Amazon.com** annual report in Appendix A at the end of the book. Use it to answer the following questions.

Requirements

1. Review the description of **Amazon.com**'s business. Is the company primarily a service, merchandiser, or manufacturing company? Explain your reasons for your answer.

2. Assume that you are the VP of daily operations at **Amazon.com**. Review the consolidated income statement provided. Will this give you the information you need to manage operations? Is the detail sufficient? Explain the reasons for your answer.

Search the Internet for a nearby company that also has a Web page. Arrange an interview with a management accountant, a controller, or other accounting/finance officer of the company.

Requirements

Before you conduct the interview, answer the following questions:

1. Is this a service, merchandising, or manufacturing company? What is its primary product or service?

2. Is the primary purpose of the company's Web site to provide information about the company and its products, to sell online, or to provide financial information for investors?

3. Are parts of the company's Web site restricted so that you need password authorization to enter? What appears to be the purpose of limiting access?

4. Does the Web site provide an e-mail link for contacting the company?

At the interview, begin by clarifying your answers to questions 1 through 4, and ask the following additional questions:

5. If the company sells over the Web, what benefits has the company derived? Did the company perform a cost-benefit analysis before deciding to begin Web sales?

Or

If the company does not sell over the Web, why not? Has the company performed a cost-benefit analysis and decided not to sell over the Web?

6. What is the biggest cost of operating the Web site?

7. Does the company make any purchases over the Internet? What percentage?

8. How has e-commerce affected the company's management accounting system? Have the management accountant's responsibilities become more or less complex? More or less interesting?

9. Does the company use Web-based accounting applications, such as accounts receivable or accounts payable?

10. Does the company use an ERP system? If so, do managers view the system as a success? What have been the benefits? The costs?

Quick Check Answers

1. *b* 2. *c* 3. *d* 4. *c* 5. *b* 6. *b* 7. *c* 8. *c* 9. *d* 10. *a*

 For online homework, exercises, and problems that provide you immediate feedback, please visit www.myaccountinglab.com.

Big Picture

Ch 1   Introduction to Management Accounting

⚬⊓ Distinguish management accounting from financial accounting

⚬⊓ The role and responsibilities of management accountants

⚬⊓ Classify costs and prepare income statements for merchandising companies

⚬⊓ Classify costs and prepare income statements and statements of cost of goods manufactured for manufacturing companies

Chapter 1: Demo Doc

▪ Manufacturing Companies

Learning Objectives 5, 6

Chase Toys produces toys for dogs. The following information was available for the month ended November 30, 2010 (assume no beginning or ending raw materials inventory):

Sales revenue	$106,500
Direct materials used	32,000
Direct labor	16,000
Manufacturing overhead*	17,000
Beginning work in process	8,000
Ending work in process	6,000
Operating expenses	32,000
Finished goods, Nov 1, 2010	4,000
Finished goods, Nov 30, 2010	7,200

* All indirect production costs are included in manufacturing overhead.

Requirements

1. Prepare a schedule of cost of goods manufactured for the month ended November 30, 2010.

2. Prepare an income statement for the month ended November 30, 2010.

3. At an internal Chase Toys meeting, you learned that Chase Toys has developed a new product that is expected to produce record profits. Before Chase Toys went public with this product, you advised your girlfriend to invest in Chase Toys. Which standard of ethical conduct for management accountants did you violate? Explain.

Demo Doc Solution

Requirement 1

5 Classify costs and prepare an income statement and statement of cost of goods manufactured for a manufacturing company

Prepare a schedule of cost of goods manufactured for the month ended November 30, 2010.

Part 1	Part 2	Part 3	Demo Doc Complete

The cost of goods manufactured summarizes the manufacturing activities that took place for the month of November 2010.

The three manufacturing costs—direct materials, direct labor, and manufacturing overhead—are added together to get the total manufacturing costs incurred during November ($32,000 + $16,000 + $17,000 = $65,000). These are added to beginning inventory to yield the total accountable manufacturing costs. Ending inventory is then subtracted from total accountable manufacturing costs to get cost of goods manufactured. Consider the following formula:

> Beginning work in process
> + Direct materials used
> + Direct labor used
> + Factory / Manufacturing overhead applied
> Current manufacturing costs
> − Ending work in process
> Cost of goods manufactured

So for Chase Toys

Beginning work in process	$ 8,000
+ Direct materials used	32,000
+ Direct labor used	16,000
+ Factory / Manufacturing overhead applied	17,000
Current manufacturing costs	73,000
− Ending work in process	(6,000)
Cost of goods manufactured	$67,000

Here is Chase Toys' schedule of cost of goods manufactured for the month ended November 30, 2010:

CHASE TOYS
Schedule of Cost of Goods Manufactured
Month Ended November 30, 2010

Beginning work in process inventory		$ 8,000
Add: Direct materials used	$32,000	
Direct labor	16,000	
Manufacturing overhead	17,000	
Total manufacturing costs incurred during the period		65,000
Total accountable manufacturing costs		73,000
Less: Ending work in process		(6,000)
Cost of goods manufactured		$67,000

Notice the similarity between calculating cost of goods manufactured and calculating cost of goods sold for a merchandiser: Start with the beginning inventory balance, increase it for the additions during the period, and subtract the ending inventory balance.

The cost of goods manufactured becomes part of the finished goods inventory, which will be shown as an asset until the period in which it is sold, when it flows to cost of goods sold.

Note that the inventoriable product costs in Finished goods for a manufacturing company include the elements of cost required to make the goods. These include the following:

- **Direct materials**—Physical components required to manufacture the product and that can be traced directly to the finished good.

- **Direct labor**—Labor of employees who work directly on the finished product.

- **Manufacturing overhead**—Includes all of the manufacturing costs other than direct materials and direct labor. These typically include factory costs such as insurance, depreciation, and utilities. Overhead also includes **indirect materials** (low value materials that cannot be traced directly to a finished product) and **indirect labor** (supportive factory labor of janitors, managers, and equipment operators that cannot be traced directly to a finished product).

Requirement 2

Prepare an income statement for the month ended November 30, 2010.

5   Classify costs and prepare an income statement and statement of cost of goods manufactured for a manufacturing company

Part 1	**Part 2**	Part 3	Demo Doc Complete

The Cost of goods manufactured account summarizes the activities that take place in a manufacturing plant over a period of time. It represents the manufacturing cost of goods that Chase Toys finished during November.

Cost of goods sold is computed as follows:

	Beginning inventory	$ 4,000
+	Cost of goods manufactured	67,000
	Cost of goods available for sale	71,000
−	Ending inventory	(7,200)
	Cost of goods sold	$63,800

Following is Chase Toys' income statement for the month of November:

CHASE TOYS
Income Statement
Month Ended November 30, 2010

Sales revenue		$106,500	100%
Cost of goods sold:			
Beginning finished goods inventory	$ 4,000		
Cost of goods manufactured	67,000		
Cost of goods available for sale	71,000		
Ending finished goods inventory	(7,200)		
Cost of goods sold		63,800	60%
Gross profit		42,700	40%
Operating expenses		32,000	30%
Operating income		$ 10,700	10%

Notice how the cost of goods manufactured amount computed on the schedule in requirement 1 is part of finished goods here—the only inventory that is ready to sell. It becomes part of cost of goods sold on the income statement.

Note that Finished goods for a manufacturer is like the Inventory account for a merchandiser. In both cases, these accounts represent the inventory that is complete and available to be sold.

Requirement 3

At an internal Chase Toys meeting, you learned that Chase Toys has developed a new product that is expected to produce record profits. Before Chase Toys went public with this product, you advised your girlfriend to invest in Chase Toys. Which standard of ethical conduct for management accountants did you violate? Explain.

6 Use reasonable standards to make ethical judgments

Part 1	Part 2	**Part 3**	Demo Doc Complete

Providing confidential company information to your girlfriend is a clear violation of the **confidentiality standard**. Employees must refrain from disclosing confidential information acquired in the course of work except when authorized, unless legally obligated to do so.

Part 1	Part 2	Part 3	**Demo Doc Complete**

2 Job Order Costing

Learning Objectives/ Success Keys

1 Distinguish between job order costing and process costing

2 Record materials and labor in a job order costing system

3 Record overhead in a job order costing system

4 Record completion and sales of finished goods and the adjustment for under- or overallocated overhead

5 Calculate unit costs for a service company

Many schools use fundraising events to finance extracurricular activities. Let us say that you are responsible for organizing a spaghetti dinner to finance new equipment for the school playground. You have to decide how many dinners you expect to sell, what price to charge, and the ingredients needed. Knowing the cost to prepare one spaghetti dinner is important. You want to set a price low enough to draw a crowd and high enough to generate a profit so that the needed equipment can be purchased.

This chapter shows how to measure cost in situations similar to the spaghetti dinner. This type of cost accounting system is called job order costing because production is arranged by the job.

Businesses face the same situation. They must draw a crowd—sell enough goods and services to earn a profit. So, regardless of the type of business you own or manage, you need to know how much it costs to produce your product or service. This applies regardless of the type of career you plan to have.

For example, marketing managers must consider their unit product cost in order to set the selling price high enough to cover costs. Engineers study the materials, labor, and overhead that go into a product to pinpoint ways to cut costs. Production managers then decide whether it is more profitable to make the product or to *outsource* it (buy from an outside supplier). The Finance Department arranges financing for the venture. The Accounting Department provides all the cost data for making these decisions.

You can see that it is important for managers in all areas to know how much it costs to make a product. This chapter shows you how to figure these costs for Smart Touch Learning.

How Much Does It Cost to Make a Product? Two Approaches

Cost accounting systems accumulate cost information so that managers can measure how much it costs to produce each unit of merchandise. For example, **Intel** must know how much each processor costs to produce. **FedEx** knows its cost of flying each pound of freight one mile. These unit costs help managers

1 Distinguish between job order costing and process costing

- set selling prices that will lead to profits.
- compute cost of goods sold for the income statement.
- compute the cost of inventory for the balance sheet.

If a manager knows the cost to produce each product, then the manager can plan and control the cost of resources needed to create the product and deliver it to the customer. A cost accounting system assigns these costs to the company's product or service.

Job Order Costing

Some companies manufacture batches of unique products or specialized services. A **job order costing** system accumulates costs for each batch, or job. Accounting firms, music studios, health-care providers, building contractors, and furniture manufacturers are examples of companies that use job order costing systems. For example, **Dell** makes personal computers based on customer orders (see the "Customize" button on **Dell's** Web site). As we move to a more service-based economy and with the advent of ERP systems, job order costing has become more prevalent.

Process Costing

Other companies, such as **Procter & Gamble** and **Coca-Cola** produce identical units through a series of production steps or processes. A **process costing** system accumulates the costs of each *process* needed to complete the product. **Chevron, General Motors,** and **Kraft Foods** are additional examples of companies that use process costing systems. This method is used primarily by large producers of similar goods. Process costing is covered in Chapter 4 of this textbook.

Both job order and process costing systems

- accumulate the costs incurred to make the product.
- assign costs to the products.

Accountants use **cost tracing** to assign directly traceable costs, such as direct materials and direct labor, to the product. They use a less precise technique—**cost allocation**—to assign manufacturing overhead and other indirect costs to the product. Let us see how a job order costing system works for a manufacturing company.

How Job Costs Flow Through the Accounts: An Overview

2 Record materials and labor in a job order costing system

The job order costing system tracks costs as raw materials move from the storeroom, to the production floor, to finished products. Exhibit 2-1 diagrams the flow of costs through a job order costing system. Let us consider how a manufacturer, Smart Touch Learning, uses job order costing. For Smart Touch, each customer order is a separate job. Smart Touch uses a job cost record to accumulate the costs of each job's

- Direct materials.
- Direct labor.
- Manufacturing overhead.

The company starts the job cost record when work begins on the job. As Smart Touch incurs costs, the company adds costs to the job cost record. For jobs started but not yet finished, the job cost records show the Work in process inventory. When Smart Touch finishes a job, the company totals the costs and transfers costs from Work in process inventory to Finished goods inventory.

When the job's units are sold, the costing system moves the costs from Finished goods inventory, an asset, to Cost of goods sold, an expense. Exhibit 2-1 summarizes this sequence.

EXHIBIT 2-1	**Flow of Costs Through the Accounts in a Job Order Costing System**

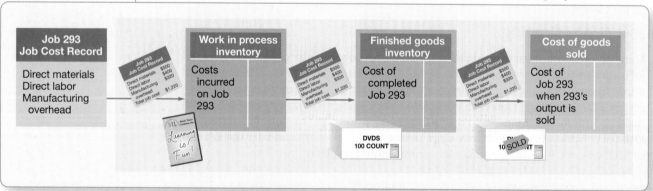

Purchasing Materials   On December 31, 2012, Smart Touch had the following inventory balances:

Materials inventory	Work in process inventory	Finished goods inventory
12/31/12 70,000	12/31/12 80,000	12/31/12 0

During the year, Smart Touch purchased direct materials of $350,000 and indirect materials of $17,000 on account. We record the purchase of materials as follows:

(1)	Materials inventory (direct) (A+)	350,000	
	Materials inventory (indirect) (A+)	17,000	
	Accounts payable (L+)		367,000

Materials inventory

12/31/12	70,000
(1) Purchased	350,000
(1) Purchased	17,000

Materials inventory is a general ledger account. Smart Touch Learning also uses a subsidiary ledger for materials. The subsidiary materials ledger includes a separate record for each type of material, so there is a subsidiary ledger for the software, the blank DVDs, the paper inserts, and the casings. Exhibit 2-2 shows the subsidiary ledger of one type of casing that Smart Touch uses. The balance of the Materials inventory account in the general ledger should always equal the sum of the balances in the subsidiary materials ledger.

EXHIBIT 2-2 | **Example Subsidiary Materials Ledger Record**

SUBSIDIARY MATERIALS LEDGER RECORD

Item No. C–101   Description   5 × 6 Casings   Smart Touch Learning, Inc.

	Received			Used				Balance		
Date	Units	Cost	Total Cost	Mat. Req. No.	Units	Cost	Total Cost	Units	Cost	Total Cost
2013										
1–20								20	$14	$280
1–23	**20**	**$14**	**$280**					40	14	560
7–24				334	10	$14	$140	30	14	420

Using Materials Smart Touch Learning works on many jobs during the year. In 2013 the company used materials costing $355,000, including DVDs, $80,000, software, $200,000, and casings, $75,000. The DVDs, software, and casings can be traced to a specific job(s), so these are all *direct materials*. Direct material costs go directly into the Work in process inventory account.

By contrast, the cost of paper inserts, $17,000, is difficult to trace to a specific job, so paper inserts are an *indirect material*. The cost of indirect material is recorded first as Manufacturing overhead. The following journal entry then records the use of materials in production:

(2)	Work in process inventory (for direct materials)	(A+)	355,000	
	Manufacturing overhead (for indirect materials)	(E+)	17,000	
	Materials inventory (A−)			372,000

We can summarize the flow of materials costs through the T-accounts as follows:

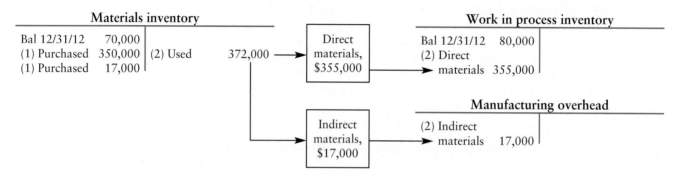

For both direct materials and indirect materials, the production team completes a document called a **materials requisition** to request the transfer of materials to the production floor. Exhibit 2-3 shows Smart Touch Learning's materials requisition for the 10 units of casings needed to make 10 Excel DVDs for Job 16.

EXHIBIT 2-3 | **Materials Requisition**

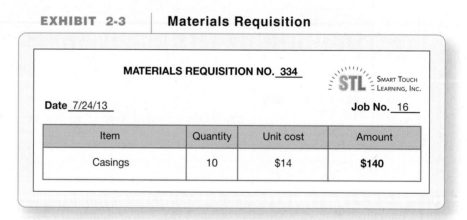

Exhibit 2-4 (on the next page) is a **job cost record**. It assigns the cost of the direct material (casings) to Job 16. Follow the $140 cost of the casings from the materials inventory record (Exhibit 2-2), to the materials requisition (Exhibit 2-3), and to the job cost record in Exhibit 2-4. Notice that all the dollar amounts in these exhibits show Smart Touch's *costs*—not the prices at which Smart Touch sells its products.

EXHIBIT 2-4 | **Direct Materials on Job Cost Record**

JOB COST RECORD

STL SMART TOUCH LEARNING, INC.

Job No. _16_

Customer Name and Address _Macy's New York City_

Job Description _10 Excel DVDs_

Date Promised	7–31	Date Started	7–24	Date Completed		

Date	Direct Materials		Direct Labor		Manufacturing Overhead Allocated		
	Requisition Numbers	Amount	Labor Time Record Numbers	Amount	Date	Rate	Amount
7–24	334	$140					
					Overall Cost Summary		
					Direct Materials.......$		
					Direct Labor.............		
					Manufacturing Overhead Allocated		
Totals					Total Job Cost.......$		

Next, we'll review how to account for labor costs.

Accounting for Labor

Smart Touch incurred labor costs of $197,000 during 2013. We record manufacturing wages as follows:

(3)	Manufacturing wages	(E+)	197,000	
	Wages payable	(L+)		197,000

This entry includes the costs of both direct labor and indirect labor.

Each employee completes a labor time record for each job he or she works on. The **labor time record** in Exhibit 2-5 on the following page identifies the employee (Ryan Oliver), the amount of time he spent on Job 16 (5 hours), and the labor cost charged to the job ($60 = 5 hours × $12 per hour).

Smart Touch Learning totals the labor time records for each job. Exhibit 2-6 on the following page shows how Smart Touch adds the direct labor cost to the job cost record. The "Labor Time Record Numbers" show that on July 24, three employees worked on Job 16. Labor time record 251 is Ryan Oliver's, from Exhibit 2-5. Labor

EXHIBIT 2-5 | **Labor Time Record**

LABOR TIME RECORD		No. 251
Employee Ryan Oliver		Date 7–24
Job 16		

TIME:

Started	1:00	Rate	$12.00
Stopped	6:00	Cost of Labor	
Elapsed	5:00	Charged to Job	**$60.00**

Employee _RO_   Supervisor _GDC_

time records 236 and 258 (not shown) indicate that two other employees also worked on Job 16. The job cost record shows that Smart Touch assigned Job 16 a total of $200 of direct labor costs for the three employees' work.

During 2013 Smart Touch incurred $169,000 for direct labor and $28,000 for indirect labor (overhead). These amounts include the labor costs for Job 16 that we have been working with plus all the company's other jobs worked on during the year.

Smart Touch Learning's accounting for labor cost requires the company to:

- Assign labor cost to individual jobs, as we saw for Ryan Oliver's work on Job 16
- Transfer labor cost out of the Manufacturing wages account and into Work in process inventory (for direct labor) and into Manufacturing overhead (for indirect labor)

EXHIBIT 2-6 | **Direct Labor on Job Cost Record**

JOB COST RECORD   STL SMART TOUCH LEARNING, INC.

Job No. 16
Customer Name and Address Macy's New York City
Job Description 10 Excel DVDs

Date Promised		7–31	Date Started	7–24	Date Completed		
	Direct Materials		Direct Labor		Manufacturing Overhead Allocated		
Date	Requisition Numbers	Amount	Labor Time Record Numbers	Amount	Date	Rate	Amount
7–24	334	$140	236, 251, 258	$200			
					Overall Cost Summary		
					Direct Materials..........$		
					Direct Labor.................		
					Manufacturing Overhead Allocated............		
Totals					Total Job Cost..........$		

The following journal entry zeroes out the Manufacturing wages account and shifts the labor cost to Work in process and the overhead account.

(4)	Work in process inventory (for direct labor) (A+)	169,000	
	Manufacturing overhead (for indirect labor) (E+)	28,000	
	Manufacturing wages (E–)		197,000

This entry brings the balance in Manufacturing wages to zero. Its transferred balance is now divided between Work in process inventory ($169,000 of direct labor) and Manufacturing overhead ($28,000 of indirect labor), as shown in the following T-accounts:

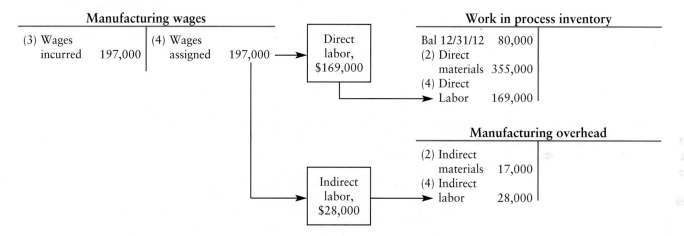

Many companies have automated these accounting procedures. The addition of labor and manufacturing overhead to materials is called **conversion costs** because the labor and overhead costs *convert* materials into a finished product.

Study the Decision Guidelines to summarize the first half of the chapter. Then work the summary problem that follows.

Decision Guidelines

JOB ORDER COSTING: TRACING DIRECT MATERIALS AND DIRECT LABOR

Smart Touch Learning uses a job order costing system that assigns manufacturing costs to each individual job for DVDs. These guidelines explain some of the decisions Smart Touch made in designing its system.

Decision	Guidelines
• Should we use job costing or process costing?	Use *job order costing* when the company produces unique products (DVDs) in small batches (usually a "batch" contains a specific learning program). Use *process costing* (covered in Chapter 4) when the company produces identical products in large batches, often in a continuous flow.
• How to record:	
• Purchase and use of materials?	*Purchase of materials:*

Materials inventory	XX	
Accounts payable (or Cash)		XX

Use of materials:

Work in process inventory (direct materials)	XX	
Manufacturing overhead (indirect materials)	XX	
Materials inventory		XX

• Incurrence and assignment of labor to jobs?

Incurrence of labor cost:

Manufacturing wages	XX	
Wages payable (or Cash)		XX

Assignment of labor cost to jobs:

Work in process inventory (direct labor)	XX	
Manufacturing overhead (indirect labor)	XX	
Manufacturing wages		XX

Summary Problem 1

Tom Baker manufactures custom teakwood patio furniture. Suppose Baker has the following transactions:

  a. Purchased raw materials on account, $135,000.
  b. Materials costing $130,000 were requisitioned (used) for production. Of this total, $30,000 were indirect materials.
  c. Labor time records show that direct labor of $22,000 and indirect labor of $5,000 were incurred (but not yet paid).
  d. Assigned labor cost to work in process and manufacturing overhead.

Requirement

  1. Prepare journal entries for each transaction. Then explain each journal entry in terms of what got increased and what got decreased.

Solution

a.

Materials inventory (A+)	135,000	
Accounts payable (L+)		135,000

When materials are purchased on account

  - debit (increase) Materials inventory for the *cost* of the materials purchased.
  - credit (increase) Accounts payable to record the liability for the materials.

b.

Work in process inventory (A+)	100,000	
Manufacturing overhead (E+)	30,000	
Materials inventory (A–)		130,000

When materials are requisitioned (used) in production, we record the movement of materials out of materials inventory and into production, as follows:

  - debit (increase) Work in process inventory for the cost of the *direct* materials (in this case, $100,000—the $130,000 total materials requisitioned less the $30,000 indirect materials).
  - debit (increase) Manufacturing overhead for the *indirect* materials cost.
  - credit (decrease) Materials inventory for the cost of both direct materials and indirect materials moved into production from the materials storage area.

c.

Manufacturing wages ($22,000 + $5,000) (E+)	27,000	
Wages payable (L+)		27,000

To record total labor costs actually incurred,

  - debit (increase) Manufacturing wages.
  - credit (increase) Wages payable to record the liability for wages not paid.

d.

Work in process inventory	(A+)	22,000	
Manufacturing overhead	(E+)	5,000	
Manufacturing wages	(E–)		27,000

To assign the labor costs,

- debit (increase) Work in process inventory for the cost of the *direct* labor.
- debit (increase) Manufacturing overhead for the cost of the *indirect* labor.
- credit (decrease) Manufacturing wages to zero out its balance.

Job Order Costing: Allocating Manufacturing Overhead

All manufacturing overhead costs are *accumulated* as debits to a single general ledger account—Manufacturing overhead. We have already assigned the costs of indirect materials (entry 2, $17,000) and indirect labor (entry 4, $28,000) to Manufacturing overhead. In addition to indirect materials and indirect labor, Smart Touch incurred the following overhead costs:

- Depreciation on plant and equipment, $10,000
- Plant utilities, $7,000
- Plant insurance, $6,000
- Property taxes on the plant, $5,000

Entries 5 through 8 record these manufacturing overhead costs. The account titles in parentheses indicate the specific records that were debited in the overhead subsidiary ledger.

(5)	Manufacturing overhead (Depreciation—plant and equipment) (E+)	10,000	
	Accumulated depreciation—plant and equipment (CA+)		10,000
(6)	Manufacturing overhead (Plant utilities) (E+)	7,000	
	Cash (A–)		7,000
(7)	Manufacturing overhead (Plant insurance) (E+)	6,000	
	Prepaid insurance—plant (A–)		6,000
(8)	Manufacturing overhead (Property taxes—plant) (E+)	5,000	
	Property taxes payable (L+)		5,000

The actual manufacturing overhead costs (such as indirect materials, indirect labor, plus depreciation, utilities, insurance, and property taxes on the plant) are debited to Manufacturing overhead as they occur throughout the year. By the end of the year, the Manufacturing overhead account has accumulated all the actual overhead costs as debits:

Manufacturing overhead	
(2) Indirect materials	17,000
(4) Indirect labor	28,000
(5) Depreciation—plant and equipment	10,000
(6) Plant utilities	7,000
(7) Plant insurance	6,000
(8) Property taxes—plant	5,000
Total overhead cost	73,000

Now you have seen how Smart Touch *accumulates* actual overhead costs in the accounting records. But how does Smart Touch *assign* overhead costs to individual jobs? As you can see, overhead includes a variety of costs that the company cannot trace to individual jobs. For example, it is impossible to say how much of the cost of

3 Record overhead in a job order costing system

plant utilities is related to Job 16. Yet manufacturing overhead costs are as essential as direct materials and direct labor, so Smart Touch must find some way to assign overhead costs to specific jobs. Otherwise, each job would not bear its fair share of the total cost. Smart Touch may then set unrealistic prices for some of its DVDs and wind up losing money on some of its hard-earned sales.

1. **Compute the predetermined overhead rate.** The **predetermined manufacturing overhead rate** is computed as follows:

$$\text{Predetermined manufacturing overhead rate} = \frac{\text{Total estimated manufacturing overhead costs}}{\text{Total estimated quantity of the manufacturing overhead allocation base}}$$

The most accurate allocation can be made only when total overhead cost is known—and that is not until the end of the year. But managers cannot wait that long for product cost information. So the predetermined overhead rate is calculated before the year begins. Then throughout the year, companies use this predetermined rate to allocate estimated overhead cost to individual jobs. The predetermined overhead rate is based on two factors:

- Total *estimated* manufacturing overhead costs for the year
- Total *estimated* quantity of the manufacturing overhead allocation base

The key to assigning indirect manufacturing costs to jobs is to identify a workable manufacturing overhead allocation base. The **allocation base** is a common denominator that links overhead costs to the products. Ideally, the allocation base is the primary cost driver of manufacturing overhead—that is the more "allocation base," the more overhead costs and vice-versa. As the phrase implies, a **cost driver** is the primary factor that causes (drives) a cost. Traditionally, manufacturing companies have used the following:

- Direct labor hours (for labor-intensive production environments)
- Direct labor cost (for labor-intensive production environments)
- Machine hours (for machine-intensive production environments)

Smart Touch uses only one allocation base, direct labor cost, to assign manufacturing overhead to jobs. Later in the textbook, we will look at other ways to assign overhead to jobs.

2. **Allocate manufacturing overhead costs to jobs as the company makes its products.** Allocate manufacturing overhead cost to jobs as follows:

$$\text{Allocated manufacturing overhead cost} = \text{\textit{Predetermined} manufacturing overhead rate (from Step 1)} \times \text{\textit{Actual} quantity of the allocation base used by each job}$$

As we have seen, Smart Touch traces direct costs directly to each job. Now let us see how it allocates overhead cost to jobs. Recall that indirect manufacturing costs include plant depreciation, utilities, insurance, and property taxes, plus indirect materials and indirect labor.

1. Smart Touch uses direct labor cost as the allocation base. In 2012, Smart Touch estimated that total overhead costs for 2013 would be $68,000 and direct labor cost would total $170,000. Using this information, we can compute the predetermined manufacturing overhead rate as follows:

$$\text{Predetermined manufacturing overhead rate} = \frac{\text{Total estimated manufacturing overhead costs}}{\text{Total estimated quantity of the manufacturing overhead allocation base}}$$

$$= \frac{\text{Total estimated manufacturing overhead costs}}{\text{Total estimated direct labor cost}}$$

$$= \frac{\$68,000}{\$170,000} = \$0.40$$

As jobs are completed in 2013, Smart Touch will allocate $0.40 of overhead cost for each $1 of labor cost incurred for the job ($0.40 = 40% × $1). Smart Touch uses the same predetermined overhead rate (40% of direct labor cost) to allocate manufacturing overhead to all jobs worked on throughout the year. Now back to Job 16.

2. The total direct labor cost for Job 16 is $200 (from Exhibit 2-6) the predetermined overhead allocation rate is 40% of direct labor cost. Therefore, Smart Touch allocates $80 ($200 × 0.40) of manufacturing overhead to Job 16.

The completed job cost record for the **Macy's** order (Exhibit 2-7) shows that Job 16 cost Smart Touch a total of $420: $140 for direct materials, $200 for direct labor, and $80 of allocated manufacturing overhead. Job 16 produced 10 DVDs, so Smart Touch's cost per DVD is $42 ($420 ÷ 10).

EXHIBIT 2-7 | **Manufacturing Overhead on Job Cost Record**

JOB COST RECORD

STL SMART TOUCH LEARNING, INC.

Job No. 16
Customer Name and Address Macy's New York City
Job Description 10 Excel DVDs

| Date Promised | 7–31 | Date Started | 7–24 | Date Completed | 7–29 |

Date	Direct Materials		Direct Labor		Manufacturing Overhead Allocated		
	Requisition Numbers	Amount	Labor Time Record Numbers	Amount	Date	Rate	Amount
7–24	334	$140	236, 251, 258	$200	7–29	40% of Direct Labor Cost	$80
					Overall Cost Summary		
					Direct Materials $140		
					Direct Labor....................200		
					Manufacturing Overhead Allocated 80		
Totals		$140		$200	Total Job Cost.............$420		

Smart Touch worked on many jobs, including Job 16, during 2013. The company allocated manufacturing overhead to each of these jobs. Smart Touch's direct labor cost for 2013 was $169,000, so total overhead allocated to all jobs is 40% of the $169,000 direct labor cost, or $67,600. The journal entry to allocate manufacturing overhead cost for the entire year to Work in process inventory is as follows:

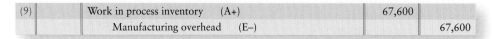

(9)	Work in process inventory (A+)	67,600	
	Manufacturing overhead (E–)		67,600

The flow of manufacturing overhead through the T-accounts follows:

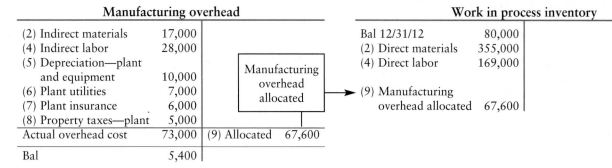

Manufacturing overhead	
(2) Indirect materials	17,000
(4) Indirect labor	28,000
(5) Depreciation—plant and equipment	10,000
(6) Plant utilities	7,000
(7) Plant insurance	6,000
(8) Property taxes—plant	5,000
Actual overhead cost	73,000
Bal	5,400

(9) Allocated 67,600

Work in process inventory	
Bal 12/31/12	80,000
(2) Direct materials	355,000
(4) Direct labor	169,000
(9) Manufacturing overhead allocated	67,600

Manufacturing overhead allocated

After allocation, a $5,400 debit balance remains in the Manufacturing overhead account. This means that Smart Touch's actual overhead costs ($73,000) exceeded the overhead allocated to Work in process inventory ($67,600). We say that Smart Touch's Manufacturing overhead is *underallocated* because the company allocated only $67,600 to jobs but actually incurred $73,000 of manufacturing overhead. We will show how to correct this problem later in the chapter.

Stop & Think...

Have you ever set up a special savings account to save for something you wanted to purchase in the future, or maybe saved for Spring vacation? Maybe you set aside 10% of each of your paychecks into this special account. Allocating overhead to jobs is very similar. We estimate how much total overhead will be and divide that number by the estimated cost driver (such as labor) and allocate overhead to jobs based on this rate. Special savings accounts work the same way. You decide how much you need in the future and then allocate a percentage of your paychecks to reach your goal.

Accounting for Completion and Sale of Finished Goods and Adjusting Manufacturing Overhead

4 Record completion and sales of finished goods and the adjustment for under- or overallocated overhead

Now you know how to accumulate and assign the cost of direct materials, direct labor, and overhead to jobs. To complete the process, we must do the following:

• Account for the completion and sale of finished goods
• Adjust manufacturing overhead at the end of the period

Accounting for the Completion and Sale of Finished Goods

Study Exhibit 2-1 on page 48 to review the flow of costs as a job goes from work in process to finished goods to cost of goods sold. Smart Touch Learning reported the following inventory balances one year ago, back on December 31, 2012:

Materials inventory........................	$70,000
Work in process inventory	80,000
Finished goods inventory...............	0

The following transactions occurred in 2013:

Cost of goods manufactured	$ 644,600
Sales on account...........................	1,200,000
Cost of goods sold........................	594,600

The $644,600 cost of goods manufactured is the cost of the jobs Smart Touch completed during 2013. The cost of goods manufactured goes from Work in process inventory to Finished goods inventory as completed products move into the finished goods storage area. Smart Touch records goods completed in 2013 as follows:

(10)	Finished goods inventory (A+)	644,600	
	Work in process inventory (A−)		644,600

As the DVDs are sold, Smart Touch records sales revenue and accounts receivable, as follows:

(11)	Accounts receivable (A+)	1,200,000	
	Sales revenue (R+)		1,200,000

The goods have been shipped to customers, so Smart Touch must also decrease the Finished goods inventory account and increase Cost of goods sold (perpetual inventory) with the following journal entry:

(11)	Cost of goods sold (E+)	594,600	
	Finished goods inventory (A−)		594,600

The key T-accounts for Smart Touch Learning's manufacturing costs now show:

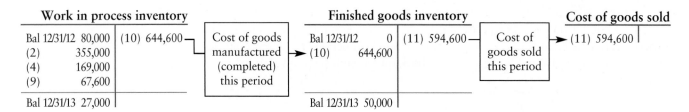

Work in process inventory				
Bal 12/31/12	80,000	(10) 644,600		
(2)	355,000			
(4)	169,000			
(9)	67,600			
Bal 12/31/13	27,000			

Some jobs are completed, and their costs are transferred out to Finished goods inventory, $644,600. We end the period with other jobs started but not finished ($27,000 ending balance of Work in process inventory) and jobs completed and not sold ($50,000 ending balance of Finished goods inventory).

During the year, Smart Touch Learning

- debits Manufacturing overhead for actual overhead costs.
- credits Manufacturing overhead for amounts allocated to Work in process inventory.

The total debits to the Manufacturing overhead account rarely equal the total credits. Why? Because Smart Touch allocates overhead to jobs using a *predetermined* allocation rate that is based on *estimates*. The predetermined allocation rate represents the *expected* relationship between overhead costs and the allocation base. In our example, the $5,400 remaining debit balance of Manufacturing overhead is called **underallocated overhead** because the manufacturing overhead allocated to Work in process inventory is *less* than actual overhead cost. (If it had been **overallocated** instead, **Manufacturing overhead** would have a credit balance.)

Accountants adjust underallocated and overallocated overhead at year-end when closing the Manufacturing overhead account. Closing the account means zeroing it out, so when overhead is underallocated, as in our example, a credit to Manufacturing overhead of $5,400 is needed to bring the account balance to zero. What account should we debit?

Because Smart Touch *undercosted* jobs during the year, the correction should increase (debit) Cost of goods sold:

(12)	Cost of goods sold (E+)	5,400	
	Manufacturing overhead (E−)		5,400

The Manufacturing overhead balance is now zero and the Cost of goods sold is up to date.

Manufacturing overhead				Cost of goods sold		
Actual	73,000	Allocated (9)	67,600	(11)	594,600	
		Closed (12)	5,400	(12)	5,400	
	0				600,000	

Exhibit 2-8 summarizes the accounting for manufacturing overhead:

EXHIBIT 2-8 | **Summary of Accounting for Manufacturing Overhead**

Before the Period

$$\text{Compute predetermined manufacturing overhead rate} = \frac{\text{Total estimated manufacturing overhead cost}}{\text{Total estimated quantity of allocation base}}$$

During the Period

$$\text{Allocate the overhead} = \begin{array}{c}\text{Predetermined}\\\text{manufacturing}\\\text{overhead rate}\end{array} \times \begin{array}{c}\text{Actual quantity of}\\\text{the manufacturing}\\\text{overhead allocation}\\\text{base}\end{array}$$

At the End of the Period

Close the Manufacturing overhead account:

Jobs are *undercosted*

If actual > allocated → *Underallocated* manufacturing overhead

Need to *increase* Cost of goods sold, as follows:

Cost of goods sold	XXX	
Manufacturing overhead		XXX

Jobs are *overcosted*

If allocated > actual → *Overallocated* manufacturing overhead

Need to *reduce* Cost of goods sold, as follows:

Manufacturing overhead	XXX	
Cost of goods sold		XXX

Job Order Costing in a Service Company

As we have seen, service firms have no inventory. These firms incur only noninventoriable costs. But their managers still need to know the costs of different jobs in order to set prices for their services as follows (amounts assumed):

5 Calculate unit costs for a service company

Cost of Job 19...	$6,000
Add standard markup of 50% ($6,000 × .50).........	3,000
Sale price of Job 19	$9,000

A merchandising company can set the selling price of its products this same way.

We now illustrate how service firms assign costs to jobs. The law firm of Walsh Associates considers each client a separate job. Walsh's most significant cost is direct labor—attorney time spent on clients' cases. How do service firms trace direct labor to individual jobs?

Suppose Walsh's accounting system is not automated. Walsh employees can fill out a weekly **time record**. Software totals the amount of time spent on each job. For example, attorney Lois Fox's time record in Exhibit 2-9 on the following page shows that she devoted 14 hours to client 367 during the week of June 10, 2010.

EXHIBIT 2-9 | **Employee Time Record**

Walsh Associates		M	T	W	Th	F
Name _Lois Fox_	8:00 – 8:30	367	520	415	367	415
	8:30 – 9:00					
Employee Time Record	9:00 – 9:30					
Week of _6/10/10_	9:30 – 10:00					
	10:00 – 10:30			367		
Weekly Summary	10:30 – 11:00					
Client # Total hours	11:00 – 11:30	520				
367 14	11:30 – 12:00	520				
415 13	12:00 – 1:00					
520 13	1:00 – 1:30	520	367	415	520	415
	1:30 – 2:00					
	2:00 – 2:30					
	2:30 – 3:00					
	3:00 – 3:30					
	3:30 – 4:00					
	4:00 – 4:30			367		
	4:30 – 5:00					

Fox's salary and benefits total $100,000 per year. Assuming a 40-hour work-week and 50 workweeks in each year, Fox has 2,000 available work hours per year (50 weeks × 40 hours per week). Fox's hourly pay rate is as follows:

$$\frac{\text{Hourly rate}}{\text{to the employer}} = \frac{\$100,000 \text{ per year}}{2,000 \text{ hours per year}} = \$50 \text{ per hour}$$

Fox worked 14 hours for client 367, so the direct labor cost traced to client 367 is 14 hours × $50 per hour = $700.

For automated services like Web site design, employees enter the client number when they start on the client's job. Software records the time elapsed until the employee signs off on that job.

Founding partner John Walsh wants to know the total cost of serving each client, not just the direct labor cost. Walsh Associates also allocates indirect costs to individual jobs (clients). The law firm develops a predetermined indirect cost allocation rate, following the same approach that Smart Touch used. In December 2009, Walsh estimates that the following indirect costs will be incurred in 2010:

Office rent...	$200,000
Office support staff...	70,000
Maintaining and updating law library for case research.......	25,000
Advertisements in the yellow pages	3,000
Sponsorship of the symphony...	2,000
Total indirect costs..	$300,000

Walsh uses direct labor hours as the allocation base, because direct labor hours are the main driver of indirect costs. He estimates that Walsh attorneys will work 10,000 direct labor hours in 2010.

STEP 1: **Compute the predetermined indirect cost allocation rate.**

$$\text{Predetermined indirect cost allocation rate} = \frac{\$300,000 \text{ expected indirect costs}}{10,000 \text{ expected direct labor hours}}$$

$$= \$30 \text{ per direct labor hour}$$

STEP 2: **Allocate indirect costs to jobs by multiplying the predetermined indirect cost rate (Step 1) by the actual quantity of the allocation base used by each job.** Client 367, for example, required 14 direct labor hours, so the indirect costs are allocated as follows:

$$14 \text{ direct labor hours} \times \$30/\text{hour} = \$420$$

To summarize, the total costs assigned to client 367 are as follows:

Direct labor: 14 hours × $50/hour............	$ 700
Indirect costs: 14 hours × $30/hour.........	420
Total costs..	$1,120

You have now learned how to use a job order cost system and assign costs to jobs.

Stop & Think...

When you have a toothache, you probably go to your dentist and ask him or her to give you an estimate of what it will cost to fix it. That estimated cost is based on the time the dentist thinks it will take to fix your tooth. The dentist has overhead, such as the dental chairs, equipment, and building. When you receive the final bill for fixing your tooth, that bill will be based on both the time it actually took the dentist to fix your tooth and an hourly rate that includes the dentist's overhead. This is an example of service job costing. Your tooth is the job for the dentist.

Review the Decision Guidelines to solidify your understanding.

Decision Guidelines

JOB ORDER COSTING

Companies using a job order costing system treat each job separately. The following are some of the decisions that a company makes when designing its job order costing system.

Decision	Guidelines

• Are utilities, insurance, property taxes, and depreciation
  • manufacturing overhead or
  • operating expenses?
	These costs are part of manufacturing overhead *only* if they are incurred in the manufacturing plant.
	
	If unrelated to manufacturing, they are operating expenses. For example, if related to the research lab, they are R&D expenses. If related to executive headquarters, they are administrative expenses. If related to distribution centers, they are selling expenses. These are all operating expenses, not manufacturing overhead.

• How to record *actual* manufacturing overhead costs?			
	Manufacturing overhead	XX	
	Accumulated depreciation—plant & equipment		XX
	Prepaid insurance—plant & equipment		XX
	Utilities payable (or Cash) and so on		XX

• How to compute a predetermined manufacturing overhead rate?	$$\dfrac{\text{Total estimated manufacturing overhead cost}}{\text{Total estimated quantity of allocation base}}$$

• How to record allocation of manufacturing overhead?			
	Work in process inventory	XX	
	Manufacturing overhead		XX

• What is the *amount* of the allocated manufacturing overhead?	$$\begin{array}{c}\text{Predetermined manufacturing}\\\text{overhead rate}\end{array} \times \begin{array}{c}\text{Actual quantity of the manufacturing}\\\text{overhead allocation base}\end{array}$$

• How to close Manufacturing overhead at the end of the period?	Close directly to Cost of goods sold, as follows: For *underallocated* overhead:

Cost of goods sold	XX	
Manufacturing overhead		XX

For *overallocated* overhead:

Manufacturing overhead	XX	
Cost of goods sold		XX

• When providing services, how to trace employees' direct labor to individual jobs?	Either using automated software that directly captures the amount of time employees spend on a client's job, or having employees fill out a time record.
• Why allocate non-inventoriable costs to jobs?	Managers need total product costs for internal decisions (such as setting selling prices).

Summary Problem 2

Skippy Scooters manufactures motor scooters. The company has automated production, so it allocates manufacturing overhead based on machine hours. Skippy expects to incur $240,000 of manufacturing overhead costs and to use 4,000 machine hours during 2012.

At the end of 2011, Skippy reported the following inventories:

Materials inventory.......................	$20,000
Work in process inventory	17,000
Finished goods inventory..............	11,000

During January 2012, Skippy actually used 300 machine hours and recorded the following transactions:

a. Purchased materials on account, $31,000
b. Used direct materials, $39,000
c. Manufacturing wages incurred totaled $40,000
d. Manufacturing labor was 90% direct labor and 10% indirect labor
e. Used indirect materials, $3,000
f. Incurred other manufacturing overhead, $13,000 (credit Accounts payable)
g. Allocated manufacturing overhead for January 2012
h. Cost of completed motor scooters, $100,000
i. Sold motor scooters on account, $175,000; cost of motor scooters sold, $95,000

Requirements

1. Compute Skippy's predetermined manufacturing overhead rate for 2012.
2. Record the transactions in the general journal.
3. Enter the beginning balances and then post the transactions to the following accounts:

Materials inventory	Work in process inventory	Finished goods inventory

Manufacturing wages	Manufacturing overhead	Cost of goods sold

4. Close the ending balance of Manufacturing overhead. Post your entry to the T-accounts.
5. What are the ending balances in the three inventory accounts and in Cost of goods sold?

Solution

Requirement 1

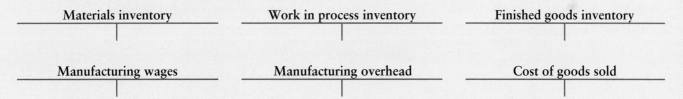

$$\text{Predetermined manufacturing overhead rate} = \frac{\text{Total estimated manufacturing overhead cost}}{\text{Total estimated quantity of allocation base}}$$

$$= \frac{\$240,000}{4,000 \text{ machine hours}}$$

$$= \$60/\text{machine hour}$$

Requirement 2

Journal entries:

a.

Materials inventory (A+)		31,000	
Accounts payable (L+)			31,000

b.

Work in process inventory (A+)		39,000	
Materials inventory (A–)			39,000

c.

Manufacturing wages (E+)		40,000	
Wages payable (L+)			40,000

d.

Work in process inventory ($40,000 × 0.90) (A+)		36,000	
Manufacturing overhead ($40,000 × 0.10) (E+)		4,000	
Manufacturing wages (E–)			40,000

e.

Manufacturing overhead (E+)		3,000	
Materials inventory (A–)			3,000

f.

Manufacturing overhead (E+)		13,000	
Accounts payable (L+)			13,000

g.

Work in process inventory (300 × $60) (A+)		18,000	
Manufacturing overhead (E–)			18,000

h.

Finished goods inventory (A+)		100,000	
Work in process inventory (A–)			100,000

i.

Accounts receivable (A+)		175,000	
Sales revenue (R+)			175,000

j.

Cost of goods sold (E+)		95,000	
Finished goods inventory (A–)			95,000

Requirement 3

Post the transactions:

Materials inventory

Bal	20,000	(b)	39,000
(a)	31,000	(e)	3,000
Bal	9,000		

Work in process inventory

Bal	17,000	(h)	100,000
(b)	39,000		
(d)	36,000		
(g)	18,000		
Bal	10,000		

Finished goods inventory

Bal	11,000	(j)	95,000
(h)	100,000		
Bal	16,000		

Manufacturing wages

(c)	40,000	(d)	40,000

Manufacturing overhead

(d)	4,000	(g)	18,000
(e)	3,000		
(f)	13,000		
Bal	2,000		

Cost of goods sold

(j)	95,000	

Requirement 4

Close Manufacturing overhead:

k.				
	Cost of goods sold (E+)		2,000	
	Manufacturing overhead (E−)			2,000

Manufacturing overhead

(d)	4,000	(g)	18,000
(e)	3,000	(k)	2,000
(f)	13,000		

Cost of goods sold

(j)	95,000	
(k)	2,000	
Bal	97,000	

Requirement 5

Ending Balances:

Materials inventory (from requirement 3)........................	$ 9,000
Work in process inventory (from requirement 3).............	10,000
Finished goods inventory (from requirement 3)...............	16,000
Cost of goods sold (from requirement 4)........................	97,000

Review *Job Order Costing*

■ Accounting Vocabulary

Allocation Base (p. 58)
A common denominator that links indirect costs to cost objects. Ideally, the allocation base is the primary cost driver of the indirect costs.

Conversion Costs (p. 53)
Direct labor plus manufacturing overhead.

Cost Allocation (p. 48)
Assigning indirect costs (such as manufacturing overhead) to cost objects (such as jobs or production processes).

Cost Driver (p. 58)
The primary factor that causes a cost.

Cost Tracing (p. 48)
Assigning direct costs (such as direct materials and direct labor) to cost objects (such as jobs or production processes) that used those costs.

Job Cost Record (p. 50)
Document that accumulates the direct materials, direct labor, and manufacturing overhead costs assigned to an individual job.

Job Order Costing (p. 47)
A system that accumulates costs for each job. Law firms, music studios, health-care providers, mail-order catalog companies, building contractors, and custom furniture manufacturers are examples of companies that use job order costing systems.

Labor Time Record (p. 51)
Identifies the employee, the amount of time spent on a particular job, and the labor cost charged to the job; a record used to assign direct labor cost to specific jobs.

Materials Requisition (p. 50)
Request for the transfer of materials to the production floor, prepared by the production team.

Overallocated (Manufacturing) Overhead (p. 62)
Occurs when the manufacturing overhead allocated to Work in process inventory is more than the amount of manufacturing overhead costs actually incurred.

Predetermined Manufacturing Overhead Rate (p. 58)
Estimated manufacturing overhead cost per unit of the allocation base, computed at the beginning of the year.

Process Costing (p. 47)
System for assigning costs to large numbers of identical units that usually proceed in a continuous fashion through a series of uniform production steps or processes.

Time Record (p. 63)
Source document used to trace direct labor to specific jobs.

Underallocated (Manufacturing) Overhead (p. 62)
Occurs when the manufacturing overhead allocated to Work in process inventory is less than the amount of manufacturing overhead costs actually incurred.

■ Quick Check

1. Would an advertising agency use job or process costing? What about a paper mill?
   a. Advertising agency—job order costing; Paper mill—process costing
   b. Advertising agency—process costing; Paper mill—process costing
   c. Advertising agency—job order costing; Paper mill—job order costing
   d. Advertising agency—process costing; Paper mill—job order costing

2. When a manufacturing company *uses* direct materials, it *traces* the cost by debiting
   a. Manufacturing overhead.
   b. Direct materials.
   c. Work in process inventory.
   d. Materials inventory.

3. When a manufacturing company *uses* indirect materials, it *assigns* the cost by debiting
   a. Indirect materials.
   b. Materials inventory.
   c. Manufacturing overhead.
   d. Work in process inventory.

4. When a manufacturing company *uses* direct labor, it *traces* the cost by debiting
   a. Work in process inventory.
   b. Manufacturing overhead.
   c. Manufacturing wages.
   d. Direct labor.

Questions 5, 6, 7, and 8 are based on the following information about Well Corporation's manufacturing of computers. Assume that Well

- allocates manufacturing overhead based on machine hours.
- budgeted 11 million machine hours and $91 million of manufacturing overhead costs.
- actually used 14 million machine hours and incurred the following actual costs (in millions):

Indirect labor	$ 10
Depreciation on plant	44
Machinery repair	15
Direct labor	76
Plant supplies	3
Plant utilities	9
Advertising	33
Sales commissions	25

5. What is Well's predetermined manufacturing overhead rate?
   a. $8.27/machine hour
   b. $5.79/machine hour
   c. $7.36/machine hour
   d. $6.50/machine hour

6. What is Well's actual manufacturing overhead cost?
   a. $157
   b. $81
   c. $215
   d. $114

7. How much manufacturing overhead would Well allocate?
   a. $91
   b. $220
   c. $84
   d. $116

8. What entry would Well make to close the manufacturing overhead account?

a.

Cost of goods sold	10	
Manufacturing overhead		10

b.

Manufacturing overhead	10	
Cost of goods sold		10

c.

Cost of goods sold	35	
Manufacturing overhead		35

d.

Manufacturing overhead	35	
Cost of goods sold		35

9. A manufacturing company's management can use product cost information to
   a. set prices of its products.
   b. identify ways to cut production costs.
   c. decide which products to emphasize.
   d. All of the above

10. For which of the following reasons would John Walsh, owner of the Walsh Associates law firm, want to know the total costs of a job (serving a particular client)?
    a. To determine the fees to charge clients
    b. For inventory valuation
    c. For external reporting
    d. All of the above

Answers are given after Apply Your Knowledge (p. 92).

Assess Your Progress

■ Short Exercises

S2-1 *(L. OBJ. 1)* **Distinguishing between job costing and process costing [5 min]**
Job costing and process costing track costs differently.

Requirement

1. Would the following companies use job order costing or process costing?

   a. A manufacturer of plywood
   b. A manufacturer of wakeboards
   c. A manufacturer of luxury yachts
   d. A professional services firm
   e. A landscape contractor

S2-2 *(L. OBJ. 2)* **Flow of costs in job order costing [10 min]**
For a manufacturer that uses job order costing, there is a correct order that the costs flow through the accounts.

Requirement

1. Order the following from 1–4. Item 1 has been completed for you.

   __1__ a. Materials inventory

   _____ b. Finished goods inventory

   _____ c. Cost of goods sold

   _____ d. Work in process inventory

S2-3 *(L. OBJ. 2)* **Accounting for materials [5–10 min]**
Gear Packs manufactures backpacks. Its plant records include the following materials-related transactions:

Purchases of canvas (on account)	$ 75,000
Purchases of thread (on account)	1,400
Materials requisitions:	
Canvas	63,000
Thread	450

Requirements

1. What journal entries record these transactions?
2. Post these transactions to the Materials inventory account.
3. If the company had $35,000 of Materials inventory at the beginning of the period, what is the ending balance of Materials inventory?

S2-4 *(L. OBJ. 2)* **Accounting for materials [10 min]**

Consider the following T-accounts:

Materials inventory					Work in process inventory			
Bal	30				Bal	40		
Purchases	210	Used			Direct materials		Cost of goods	630
Bal	70				Direct labor	320	manufactured	
					Manufacturing overhead	140		
					Bal	20		

Requirement

1. Use the T-accounts to determine direct materials used and indirect materials used.

S2-5 *(L. OBJ. 2)* **Accounting for labor [5 min]**

Seattle Creations reports the following labor-related transactions at its plant in Seattle, Washington:

Plant janitor's wages	$ 550
Furnace operator's wages	940
Glass blower's wages	77,000

Requirement

1. Journalize the entries for the incurrence and assignment of these wages.

S2-6 *(L. OBJ. 2)* **Accounting for materials and labor [5 min]**

Boston Enterprises produces LCD touch screen products. The company reports the following information at December 31, 2010:

Materials inventory		Work in process inventory		Finished goods inventory	
51,000	32,000	29,500	126,000	126,000	115,000
		60,000			
		52,500			

Manufacturing wages		Manufacturing overhead	
71,000	71,000	2,500	52,500
		11,000	
		37,000	

Boston began operations on January 30, 2010.

Requirements

1. What is the cost of direct materials used? The cost of indirect materials used?
2. What is the cost of direct labor? The cost of indirect labor?

S2-7 *(L. OBJ. 3)* **Accounting for overhead [5 min]**

Evergreen Furniture manufactures wood patio furniture. The company reports the following costs for June 2011:

Wood	$ 260,000
Nails, glue, and stain	21,000
Depreciation on saws	4,500
Indirect manufacturing labor	41,000
Depreciation on delivery truck	2,100
Assembly-line workers' wages	59,000

Requirement

1. What is the balance in the Manufacturing overhead account?

S2-8 *(L. OBJ. 3)* **Allocating overhead [5 min]**

Job 303 includes a direct materials cost of $470 and direct labor costs of $350.

Requirement

1. If the manufacturing overhead allocation rate is 60% of direct labor cost, what is the total cost assigned to Job 303?

Note: Short Exercise 2-6 must be completed before attempting Short Exercise 2-9.

S2-9 *(L. OBJ. 4)* **Comparing actual to allocated overhead [10 min]**

Refer to the data in S2-6.

Requirements

1. What is the actual manufacturing overhead of Boston Enterprises?
2. What is the allocated manufacturing overhead?
3. Is manufacturing overhead underallocated or overallocated? By how much?

S2-10 *(L. OBJ. 4)* **Under/overallocated overhead [10 min]**

The T-account showing the manufacturing overhead activity for Edith, Corp., for 2011 is as follows:

Manufacturing overhead	
199,000	215,000

Requirements

1. What is the actual manufacturing overhead?
2. What is the allocated manufacturing overhead?
3. What is the predetermined manufacturing overhead rate as a percentage of direct labor cost, if actual direct labor costs were $170,000?
4. Is manufacturing overhead underallocated or overallocated? By how much?
5. Is Cost of goods sold too high or too low?

Note: Short Exercise 2-10 must be completed before attempting Short Exercise 2-11.

S2-11 *(L. OBJ. 4)* **Closing out under/overallocated overhead [5 min]**

Refer to the data in S2-10.

Requirement

1. Journalize the entry to close out the company's Manufacturing overhead account.

S2-12 *(L. OBJ. 5)* **Job order costing in a service company [5 min]**
Blake Advertising pays Amanda Hilton $108,000 per year. Hilton works 2,000 hours per year.

Requirements

1. What is the hourly cost to Blake Advertising of employing Hilton?
2. What direct labor cost would be traced to client 507 if Hilton works 18 hours to prepare client 507's magazine ad?

Note: Short Exercise 2-12 must be completed before attempting Short Exercise 2-13.

S2-13 *(L. OBJ. 5)* **Job order costing in a service company [5 min]**
Refer to the data in S2-12. Assume that Blake's Advertising agents are expected to work a total of 12,000 direct labor hours in 2011. Blake's estimated total indirect costs are $360,000.

Requirements

1. What is Blake's indirect cost allocation rate?
2. What indirect costs will be allocated to client 507 if Hilton works 18 hours to prepare the magazine ad?

■ Exercises

E2-14 *(L. OBJ. 1)* **Distinguishing between job order costing and process costing [5–10 min]**
Consider the following incomplete statements:

a. _____ is used by companies that produce small quantities of many different products.
b. Georgia-Pacific pulverizes wood into pulp to manufacture cardboard. The company uses a _____ system.
c. To record costs of maintaining thousands of identical mortgage files, financial institutions like Money Tree use a _____ system.
d. Companies that produce large numbers of identical products use _____ systems for product costing.
e. The computer repair service that visits your home and repairs your computer uses a _____ system.

Requirement

1. Complete each of the statements with the term job order costing or the term process costing.

E2-15 *(L. OBJ. 2, 3, 4)* **Accounting for job costs [15 min]**
Great Quality Trailers' job cost records yielded the following information:

| Job | Date | | | Total Cost of Job |
No.	Started	Finished	Sold	at May 31
1	April 21	May 16	May 17	$ 3,800
2	April 29	May 21	May 26	13,700
3	May 3	June 11	June 13	6,500
4	May 7	May 29	June 1	4,200

Requirement

1. Using the dates above to identify the status of each job; compute Great Quality's cost of (a) Work in process inventory at May 31, (b) Finished goods inventory at May 31, and (c) Cost of goods sold for May.

E2-16 *(L. OBJ. 2, 3, 4)* **Job order costing journal entries [20–25 min]**
Consider the following transactions for Sleek's Furniture:

a. Incurred and paid Web site expenses, $2,100
b. Incurred and paid manufacturing wages, $17,000
c. Purchased materials on account, $15,000
d. Used in production: direct materials, $9,000; indirect materials, $1,500
e. Assigned $17,000 of manufacturing labor to jobs, 55% of which was direct labor and 45% of which was indirect labor
f. Recorded manufacturing overhead: depreciation on plant, $11,000; plant insurance, $1,000; plant property tax, $4,100 (credit Property Tax Payable)
g. Allocated manufacturing overhead to jobs, 160% of direct labor costs
h. Completed production, $32,000
i. Sold inventory on account, $24,000; cost of goods sold, $16,000

Requirement

1. Journalize the transactions in Sleek's general journal.

E2-17 *(L. OBJ. 2, 3, 4)* **Identifying job order costing journal entries [15 min]**
Consider the following:

Materials inventory		Work in process inventory		Finished goods inventory	
(a)	(b)	(b)	(g)	(g)	(h)
		(d)			
		(f)			

Manufacturing wages		Manufacturing overhead		Cost of goods sold	
(c)	(d)	(b)	(f)	(h)	
		(d)	(i)	(i)	
		(e)			

Requirement

1. Describe the letter transactions in the above accounts.

E2-18 *(L. OBJ. 2, 3, 4)* **Using the Work in process inventory account [15–20 min]**
April production generated the following activity in Premier Chassis Company's Work in process inventory account:

Work in process inventory	
Apr 1 Bal	18,000
Direct materials used	29,000
Direct labor assigned to jobs	31,000
Manufacturing overhead allocated to jobs	9,000

Additionally, Premier completed production, but has not recorded Jobs 142 and 143, with total costs of $37,000 and $35,000, respectively.

Requirements

1. Compute the cost of work in process at April 30.

2. Prepare the journal entry for production completed in April.

3. Prepare the journal entry to record the sale (on credit) of Job 143 for $45,000. Also, make the Cost of goods sold entry.

4. What is the gross profit on Job 143? What other costs must gross profit cover?

E2-19 *(L. OBJ. 3, 4)* **Allocating manufacturing overhead [15–20 min]**
Selected cost data for European Print, Co., are as follows:

Requirements

1. Compute the predetermined manufacturing overhead rate per direct labor dollar.

Estimated manufacturing overhead cost for the year	$ 93,000
Estimated direct labor cost for the year	75,000
Actual manufacturing overhead cost for the year	84,000
Actual direct labor cost for the year	64,000

2. Prepare the journal entry to allocate overhead cost for the year.

3. Use a T-account to determine the amount of underallocated or overallocated manufacturing overhead.

4. Prepare the journal entry to close the balance of the Manufacturing overhead account.

E2-20 *(L. OBJ. 3, 4)* **Allocating manufacturing overhead [15–20 min]**
Patel Foundry uses a predetermined manufacturing overhead rate to allocate overhead to individual jobs, based on the machine hours required. At the beginning of 2011, the company expected to incur the following:

Manufacturing overhead costs	$ 730,000
Direct labor costs	1,450,000
Machine hours	66,000

At the end of 2011, the company had actually incurred:

Direct labor cost	$ 1,250,000
Depreciation on manufacturing property, plant, and equipment	440,000
Property taxes on plant	18,000
Sales salaries	30,000
Delivery drivers' wages	22,500
Plant janitor's wages	9,000
Machine hours	58,000 hours

1. Compute Patel's predetermined manufacturing overhead rate.
2. Record the summary journal entry for allocating manufacturing overhead.
3. Post the manufacturing overhead transactions to the Manufacturing overhead T-account. Is manufacturing overhead underallocated or overallocated? By how much?
4. Close the Manufacturing overhead account to Cost of goods sold. Does your entry increase or decrease cost of goods sold?

E2-21 *(L. OBJ. 3, 4)* **Allocating manufacturing overhead [10–15 min]**
Refer to the data in E2-20. Patel's accountant found an error in her 2011 cost records. Depreciation on manufacturing property, plant, and equipment was actually $570,000, not the $440,000 she originally reported. Unadjusted balances at the end of 2011 include:

Finished goods inventory	$ 127,000
Cost of goods sold	610,000

Requirements

1. Use a T-account to determine whether manufacturing overhead is underallocated or overallocated, and by how much.
2. Record the entry to close out the underallocated or overallocated manufacturing overhead.
3. What is the adjusted ending balance of Cost of goods sold?

E2-22 *(L. OBJ. 3, 4)* **Allocating manufacturing overhead [15–20 min]**
The manufacturing records for Smooth Canoes at the end of the 2010 fiscal year show the following information about manufacturing overhead:

Overhead allocated to production	$ 402,000
Actual manufacturing overhead costs	$ 432,000
Overhead allocation rate for the year	$ 43 per machine hour

Requirements

1. How many machine hours did Smooth Canoes use in 2010?
2. Was manufacturing overhead over- or underallocated for the year and by how much?
3. Record the entry to close out the over- or underallocated overhead.

E2-23 *(L. OBJ. 5)* **Job order costing in a service company [15–20 min]**
Simms Realtors, a real estate consulting firm, specializes in advising companies on potential new plant sites. The company uses a job order costing system with a predetermined indirect cost allocation rate, computed as a percentage of direct labor costs. At the beginning of 2011, managing partner Debra Simms prepared the following budget for the year:

Direct labor hours (professionals)	14,000 hours
Direct labor costs (professionals)	$ 2,150,000
Office rent	260,000
Support staff salaries	850,000
Utilities	350,000

Maynard Manufacturing, Inc., is inviting several consultants to bid for work. Debra Simms estimates that this job will require about 260 direct labor hours.

Requirements

1. Compute Simms Realtors' (a) hourly direct labor cost rate and (b) indirect cost allocation rate.

2. Compute the predicted cost of the Maynard Manufacturing job.

3. If Simms wants to earn a profit that equals 55% of the job's cost, how much should she bid for the Maynard Manufacturing job?

■ Problems (Group A)

P2-24A *(L. OBJ. 1, 2, 3, 4)* **Analyzing cost data [25–35 min]**
Huntley Manufacturing makes carrying cases for portable electronic devices. Its costing records yield the following information:

Job No.	Date Started	Date Finished	Sold	Total Cost of Job at November 30	Total Manufacturing Costs Added in December
1	11/3	11/12	11/13	$ 1,300	
2	11/3	11/30	12/1	1,200	
3	11/17	12/24	12/27	600	$ 700
4	11/29	12/29	1/3	1,100	1,400
5	12/8	12/12	12/14		650
6	12/23	1/6	1/9		900

Requirements

1. Which type of costing system is Huntley using? What piece of data did you base your answer on?

2. Using the dates above to identify the status of each job, compute Huntley's account balances at November 30 for Work in process inventory, Finished goods inventory, and Cost of goods sold. Compute account balances at December 31 for Work in process inventory, Finished goods inventory, and Cost of goods sold.

3. Record summary journal entries for the transfer of completed units from work in process to finished goods for November and December.

4. Record the sale of Job 3 for $2,400.

5. What is the gross profit for Job 3? What other costs must this gross profit cover?

P2-25A *(L. OBJ. 2, 3, 4)* **Accounting for construction transactions [30–45 min]**
Sherborn Construction, Inc., is a home builder in New Mexico. Sherborn uses a job order costing system in which each house is a job. Because it constructs houses, the

company uses accounts titled Construction wages and Construction overhead. The following events occurred during August:

a. Purchased materials on account, $470,000
b. Incurred construction wages of $230,000
c. Requisitioned direct materials and used direct labor in construction as follows:

	Direct Materials	Direct Labor
House 402	$ 58,000	$ 40,000
House 403	63,000	34,000
House 404	60,000	52,000
House 405	89,000	51,000

d. Depreciation of construction equipment, $6,800
e. Other overhead costs incurred on houses 402 through 405:

Indirect labor	$ 53,000
Equipment rentals paid in cash	33,000
Worker liability insurance expired ..	7,000

f. Allocated overhead to jobs at the predetermined rate of 40% of direct labor cost
g. Houses completed: 402, 404
h. House sold: 404 for $220,000

Requirements

1. Record the events in the general journal.

2. Open T-accounts for Work in process inventory and Finished goods inventory. Post the appropriate entries to these accounts, identifying each entry by letter. Determine the ending account balances, assuming that the beginning balances were zero.

3. Add the costs of the unfinished houses, and show that this total amount equals the ending balance in the Work in process inventory account.

4. Add the cost of the completed house that has not yet been sold, and show that this equals the ending balance in Finished goods inventory.

5. Compute gross profit on the house that was sold. What costs must gross profit cover for Sherborn Construction?

P2-26A *(L. OBJ. 2, 3, 4)* **Preparing and using a job cost record [30–35 min]**
Classic Technology, Co., manufactures CDs and DVDs for computer software and entertainment companies. Classic uses job order costing and has a perpetual inventory system.

On November 2, Classic began production of 5,100 DVDs, Job 423, for Cheetah Pictures for $1.30 each. Classic promised to deliver the DVDs to Cheetah by November 5. Classic incurred the following costs:

Date	Labor Time Record No.	Description	Amount
11/2	655	10 hours @ $20	$ 200
11/3	656	20 hours @ $12	240

Date	Materials Requisition No.	Description	Amount
11/2	63	31 lbs. polycarbonate plastic @ $10	$ 310
11/2	64	25 lbs. acrylic plastic @ $26	650
11/3	74	3 lbs. refined aluminum @ $40	120

Classic Technology allocates manufacturing overhead to jobs based on the relation between estimated overhead ($520,000) and estimated direct labor costs ($450,000). Job 423 was completed and shipped on November 3.

Requirements

1. Prepare a job cost record similar to Exhibit 2-7 for Job 423. Calculate the predetermined overhead rate; then apply manufacturing overhead to the job.

2. Journalize in summary form the requisition of direct materials and the assignment of direct labor and manufacturing overhead to Job 423.

3. Journalize completion of the job and the sale of the 5,100 DVDs.

P2-27A *(L. OBJ. 2, 3, 4)* **Comprehensive accounting for manufacturing transactions [90–120 min]**

Sneeches' Stars produces stars for elementary teachers to reward their students. Sneeches' Stars' trial balance on April 1 follows:

			Balance	
	Account Title		**Debit**	**Credit**
	Cash		$ 18,000	
	Accounts receivable		170,000	
	Inventories:			
	Materials		5,300	
	Work in process		41,300	
	Finished goods		21,300	
	Plant assets		250,000	
	Accumulated depreciation			$ 68,000
	Accounts payable			129,000
	Wages payable			2,800
	Common stock			140,000
	Retained earnings			166,100
	Sales revenue			—
	Cost of goods sold		—	
	Manufacturing wages		—	
	Manufacturing overhead		—	
	Marketing and general expenses		—	
			$505,900	$505,900

SNEECHES' STARS
Trial Balance
April 1, 2010

April 1 balances in the subsidiary ledgers were as follows:

- Materials subledger: Paper, $4,800; indirect materials, $500
- Work in progress subledger: Job 120, $41,300
- Finished goods subledger: Large Stars, $9,300; Small Stars, $12,000

April transactions are summarized as follows:

a. Collections on account, $149,000
b. Marketing and general expenses incurred and paid, $25,000
c. Payments on account, $38,000
d. Materials purchases on credit: Paper, $24,500; indirect materials, $4,600
e. Materials used in production (requisitioned):
   - Job 120: paper, $750
   - Job 121: paper, $7,800
   - Indirect materials, $2,000
f. Manufacturing wages incurred during April, $38,000, of which $36,000 was paid. Wages payable at March 31 were paid during April, $2,800
g. Labor time records for the month: Job 120, $4,000; Job 121, $18,000; indirect labor, $16,000
h. Depreciation on plant and equipment, $2,400
i. Manufacturing overhead was allocated at the predetermined rate of 70% of direct labor cost
j. Jobs completed during the month: Job 120, 400,000 Large Stars at total cost of $48,850
k. Credit sales on account: all of Job 120 for $110,000
l. Closed the Manufacturing overhead account to Cost of goods sold

Requirements

1. Open T-accounts for the general ledger, the Materials ledger, the Work in process ledger, and the Finished goods ledger. Insert each account balance as given, and use the reference *Bal.*

2. Record the April transactions directly in the accounts, using the letters as references. Sneeches uses a perpetual inventory system.

3. Prepare a trial balance at April 30.

4. Use the Work in process T-account to prepare a schedule of cost of goods manufactured for the month of April. (You may want to review Exhibit 1-10.)

5. Prepare an income statement for the month of April. To calculate cost of goods sold, you may want to review Exhibit 1-7. (*Hint*: In transaction l you closed any under/overallocated manufacturing overhead to Cost of goods sold. In the income statement, show this correction as an adjustment to Cost of goods sold. If manufacturing overhead is underallocated, the adjustment will increase Cost of goods sold. If overhead is overallocated, the adjustment will decrease Cost of goods sold.)

P2-28A *(L. OBJ. 3, 4)* **Accounting manufacturing overhead [25–35 min]**
Weiters Woods manufactures jewelry boxes. The primary materials (wood, brass, and glass) and direct labor are traced directly to the products. Manufacturing overhead costs are allocated based on machine hours. Data for 2010 follow:

	Budget	Actual
Machine hours	24,000 hours	32,000 hours
Maintenance labor (repairs to equipment) . .	11,000	24,500
Plant supervisor's salary	42,000	45,000
Screws, nails, and glue	29,000	44,000
Plant utilities	48,000	92,850
Freight out	34,000	49,500
Depreciation on plant and equipment	82,000	81,000
Advertising expense	42,000	58,000

Requirements

1. Compute the predetermined manufacturing overhead rate.
2. Post actual and allocated manufacturing overhead to the Manufacturing overhead T-account.
3. Close the under- or overallocated overhead to Cost of goods sold.
4. The predetermined manufacturing overhead rate usually turns out to be inaccurate. Why don't accountants just use the actual manufacturing overhead rate?

P2-29A *(L. OBJ. 5)* **Job order costing in a service company [20–25 min]**

Robin Design, Inc., is a Web site design and consulting firm. The firm uses a job order costing system, in which each client is a different job. Robin Design traces direct labor, licensing costs, and travel costs directly to each job. It allocates indirect costs to jobs based on a predetermined indirect cost allocation rate, computed as a percentage of direct labor costs.

At the beginning of 2011, managing partner Judi Jacquin prepared the following budget:

Direct labor hours (professional)	10,000 hours
Direct labor costs (professional)	$1,400,000
Support staff salaries	170,000
Computer leases	49,000
Office supplies	29,000
Office rent	60,000

In November 2011, Robin Design served several clients. Records for two clients appear here:

	Dining Coop	Root Chocolates
Direct labor hours	740 hours	65 hours
Software licensing costs	$ 2,100	$ 300
Travel costs	9,000	—

Requirements

1. Compute Robin Design's predetermined indirect cost allocation rate for 2011.
2. Compute the total cost of each job.
3. If Jacquin wants to earn profits equal to 20% of service revenue, how much (what fee) should she charge each of these two clients?
4. Why does Robin Design assign costs to jobs?

P2-30B *(L. OBJ. 1, 2, 3, 4)* **Analyzing cost data [25–35 min]**

Hartley Manufacturing makes carrying cases for portable electronic devices. Its costing records yield the following information:

Job No.	Date Started	Date Finished	Sold	Total Cost of Job at October 31	Total Manufacturing Costs Added in November
1	10/3	10/12	10/13	$ 1,400	
2	10/3	10/30	11/1	1,500	
3	10/17	11/24	11/27	1,000	$ 1,200
4	10/29	11/29	12/3	1,100	1,000
5	11/8	11/12	11/14		550
6	11/23	12/6	12/9		200

Requirements

1. Which type of costing system is Hartley using? What piece of data did you base your answer on?

2. Using the dates above to identify the status of each job, compute Hartley's account balances at October 31 for Work in process inventory, Finished goods inventory, and Cost of goods sold. Compute account balances at November 30 for Work in process inventory, Finished goods inventory, and Cost of goods sold.

3. Record summary journal entries for the transfer of completed units from work in process to finished goods for October and November.

4. Record the sale of Job 3 for $3,000.

5. What is the gross profit for Job 3? What other costs must this gross profit cover?

P2-31B *(L. OBJ. 2, 3, 4)* **Accounting for construction transactions [30–45 min]**

Superior Construction, Inc., is a home builder in New Mexico. Superior uses a job order costing system in which each house is a job. Because it constructs houses, the company uses accounts titled Construction wages and Construction overhead. The following events occurred during August:

a. Purchased materials on account, $470,000

b. Incurred construction wages of $260,000

c. Requisitioned direct materials and used direct labor in construction as follows:

	Direct materials	Direct labor
House 402	$ 59,000	$ 40,000
House 403	68,000	32,000
House 404	61,000	58,000
House 405	83,000	57,000

d. Depreciation of construction equipment, $6,200

e. Other overhead costs incurred on houses 402 through 405:

Indirect labor	$	73,000
Equipment rentals paid in cash		30,000
Worker liability insurance expired ..		9,000

f. Allocated overhead to jobs at the predetermined rate of 40% of direct labor costs

g. Houses completed: 402, 404

h. House sold: 404 for $260,000

1. Record the events in the general journal.

2. Open T-accounts for Work in process inventory and Finished goods inventory. Post the appropriate entries to these accounts, identifying each entry by letter. Determine the ending account balances, assuming that the beginning balances were zero.

3. Add the costs of the unfinished houses, and show that this total amount equals the ending balance in the Work in process inventory account.

4. Add the cost of the completed house that has not yet been sold, and show that this equals the ending balance in Finished goods inventory.

5. Compute gross profit on the house that was sold. What costs must gross profit cover for Superior Construction?

P2-32B *(L. OBJ. 2, 3, 4)* **Preparing and using a job cost record [30–35 min]**

True Technology, Co., manufactures CDs and DVDs for computer software and entertainment companies. True uses job order costing and has a perpetual inventory system.

On April 2, True began production of 5,400 DVDs, Job 423, for Stick People Pictures for $1.10 each. True promised to deliver the DVDs to Stick People by April 5. True incurred the following costs:

Date	Labor Time Record No.	Description	Amount
4/2	655	10 hours @ $16	$ 160
4/3	656	20 hours @ $15	300

Date	Materials Requisition No.	Description	Amount
4/2	63	31 lbs. polycarbonate plastic @ $13	$ 403
4/2	64	25 lbs. acrylic plastic @ $26	650
4/3	74	3 lbs. refined aluminum @ $40	120

True Technology allocates manufacturing overhead to jobs based on the relation between estimated overhead ($560,000) and estimated direct labor costs ($450,000). Job 423 was completed and shipped on April 3.

Requirements

1. Prepare a job cost record similar to Exhibit 2-7 for Job 423. Calculate the predetermined overhead rate, then apply manufacturing overhead to the job.

2. Journalize in summary form the requisition of direct materials and the assignment of direct labor and manufacturing overhead to Job 423.

3. Journalize completion of the job and the sale of the 5,400 DVDs.

P2-33B *(L. OBJ. 2, 3, 4)* **Comprehensive accounting for manufacturing transactions [90–120 min]**

Mighties' Stars produces stars for elementary teachers to reward their students.

Mighties' Stars' trial balance on September 1 follows:

			Balance	
	Account Title		**Debit**	**Credit**
		MIGHTIES' STARS **Trial Balance** **September 1, 2010**		
	Cash		$ 15,000	
	Accounts receivable		185,000	
	Inventories:			
	Materials		6,000	
	Work in process		39,500	
	Finished goods		20,200	
	Plant assets		270,000	
	Accumulated depreciation			$ 76,000
	Accounts payable			129,000
	Wages payable			2,900
	Common stock			145,000
	Retained earnings			182,800
	Sales revenue			—
	Cost of goods sold		—	
	Manufacturing wages		—	
	Manufacturing overhead		—	
	Marketing and general expenses		—	
			$535,700	$535,700

September 1 balances in the subsidiary ledgers were:

- Materials subledger: $4,600 paper and $1,400 indirect
- WIP subledger — job 120 $39,500; $0 for job 121
- Finished goods subledger — $7,900 large stars and $12,300 small stars

September transactions are summarized as follows:

a. Collections on account, $153,000
b. Marketing and general expenses incurred and paid, $28,000
c. Payments on account, $41,000
d. Materials purchases on credit: paper, $4,600; indirect materials, $4,600
e. Materials used in production (requisitioned):
   - Job 120: paper, $800
   - Job 121: paper, $7,650
   - Indirect materials, $1,800
f. Manufacturing wages incurred during September, $37,000, of which $34,300 was paid. Wages payable at August 31 were paid during September, $2,900
g. Labor time records for the month: Job 120, $3,700; Job 121, $18,800; indirect labor, $14,500
h. Depreciation on plant and equipment, $3,300
i. Manufacturing overhead was allocated at the predetermined rate of 80% of direct labor cost
j. Jobs completed during the month: Job 120, 800,000 Large Stars at total cost of $46,960
k. Credit sales on account: all of Job 120 for $105,000
l. Closed the Manufacturing overhead account to Cost of goods sold

Requirements

1. Open T-accounts for the general ledger, the Materials ledger, the Work in process ledger, and the Finished goods ledger. Insert each account balance as given, and use the reference *Bal.*

2. Record the September transactions directly in the accounts, using the letters as references. Mighties' uses a perpetual inventory system.

3. Prepare a trial balance at September 30.

4. Use the Work in process T-account to prepare a schedule of cost of goods manufactured for the month of September. (You may want to review Exhibit 1-10.)

5. Prepare an income statement for the month of September. To calculate cost of goods sold, you may want to review Exhibit 1-7. (*Hint*: In transaction 1 you closed any under/overallocated manufacturing overhead to Cost of goods sold. In the income statement, show this correction as an adjustment to Cost of goods sold. If manufacturing overhead is underallocated, the adjustment will increase Cost of goods sold. If overhead is overallocated, the adjustment will decrease Cost of goods sold.)

P2-34B *(L. OBJ. 3, 4)* **Accounting manufacturing overhead [25–35 min]**
Regal Woods manufactures jewelry boxes. The primary materials (wood, brass, and glass) and direct labor are traced directly to the products. Manufacturing overhead costs are allocated based on machine hours. Data for 2010 follow:

	Budget	Actual
Machine hours	26,000 hours	32,500 hours
Maintenance labor (repairs to equipment) ..	14,000	28,500
Plant supervisor's salary	43,000	49,000
Screws, nails, and glue	25,000	45,000
Plant utilities	47,000	97,850
Freight out	37,000	44,500
Depreciation on plant and		
equipment	85,000	83,000
Advertising expense	43,000	55,000

Requirements

1. Compute the predetermined manufacturing overhead rate.

2. Post actual and allocated manufacturing overhead to the Manufacturing overhead T-account.

3. Close the under- or overallocated overhead to Cost of goods sold.

4. The predetermined manufacturing overhead rate usually turns out to be inaccurate. Why don't accountants just use the actual manufacturing overhead rate?

P2-35B *(L. OBJ. 5)* **Job order costing in a service company [20–25 min]**
Crow Design, Inc., is a Web site design and consulting firm. The firm uses a job order costing system, in which each client is a different job. Crow Design traces direct labor, licensing costs, and travel costs directly to each job. It allocates indirect costs to jobs based on a predetermined indirect cost allocation rate, computed as a percentage of direct labor costs.

At the beginning of 2011, managing partner Sheila Biggs prepared the following budget:

Direct labor hours (professional)	6,250 hours
Direct labor costs (professional)	$1,000,000
Support staff salaries	120,000
Computer leases	45,000
Office supplies	25,000
Office rent	60,000

In October 2011, Crow Design served several clients. Records for two clients appear here:

	Dining Coop	Mesilla Chocolates
Direct labor hours	770 hours	40 hours
Software licensing costs	$ 2,000	$ 300
Travel costs	10,000	—

Requirements

1. Compute Crow Design's predetermined indirect cost allocation rate for 2011.
2. Compute the total cost of each job.
3. If Biggs wants to earn profits equal to 20% of sales revenue, how much (what fee) should she charge each of these two clients?
4. Why does Crow Design assign costs to jobs?

■ Continuing Exercise

E2-36 This exercise continues the Sherman Lawn Service, Inc., situation from Exercise 1-35 of Chapter 1. Sherman completed a special landscaping job for Feimer's Fancy Fonts. Sherman collected the following data about the job:

Feimer job details:
Direct materials $400
Direct labor $900

Requirements

1. Sherman allocates overhead costs based on 40% of Direct Labor cost. What is the total cost of the Feimer job?
2. If the price Feimer paid for the job is $2,500, what is the profit or loss on the job?

■ Continuing Problem

P2-37 This problem continues the Haupt Consulting, Inc., situation from Problem 1-36 of Chapter 1. Haupt Consulting uses a job order costing system, in which each client is a different job. Haupt traces direct labor, daily per diem, and travel costs directly to each job. It allocates indirect costs to jobs based on a predetermined indirect cost allocation rate, computed as a percentage of direct labor costs.

At the beginning of 2010, the controller prepared the following budget:

Direct labor hours (professional)	5,000 hours
Direct labor costs (professional)	$1,000,000
Support staff salaries	100,000
Computer leases	80,000
Office supplies	20,000
Office rent	60,000

In November, 2010, Haupt served several clients. Records for two clients appear here:

	Owen's Trains	Caleigh's Cookies
Direct labor hours	700 hours	100 hours
Meal—per diem	$ 2,200	$ 500
Travel costs	9,000	0

Requirements

1. Compute Haupt's predetermined indirect cost allocation rate for 2010.
2. Compute the total cost of each job.
3. If Haupt wants to earn profits equal to 25% of sales revenue, how much (what fee) should it charge each of these two clients?
4. Why does Haupt assign costs to jobs?

Apply Your Knowledge

■ Decision Cases

Case 1. Hiebert Chocolate, Ltd., is located in Memphis. The company prepares gift boxes of chocolates for private parties and corporate promotions. Each order contains a selection of chocolates determined by the customer, and the box is designed to the customer's specifications. Accordingly, Hiebert uses a job order costing system and allocates manufacturing overhead based on direct labor cost.

One of Hiebert's largest customers is the Goforth and Leos law firm. This organization sends chocolates to its clients each Christmas and also provides them to employees at the firm's gatherings. The law firm's managing partner, Bob Goforth, placed the client gift order in September for 500 boxes of cream-filled dark chocolates. But Goforth and Leos did not place its December staff-party order until the last week of November. This order was for an additional 100 boxes of chocolates identical to the ones to be distributed to clients.

Hiebert budgeted the cost per box for the original 500-box order as follows:

Chocolate, filling, wrappers, box	$14.00
Employee time to fill and wrap the box (10 min.)	2.00
Manufacturing overhead	1.00
Total manufacturing cost	$17.00

Ben Hiebert, president of Hiebert Chocolate, Ltd., priced the order at $20 per box.

In the past few months, Hiebert has experienced price increases for both dark chocolate and direct labor. All other costs have remained the same. Hiebert budgeted the cost per box for the second order as:

Chocolate, filling, wrappers, box	$15.00
Employee time to fill and wrap the box (10 min.)	2.20
Manufacturing overhead	1.10
Total manufacturing cost	$18.30

Requirements

1. Do you agree with the cost analysis for the second order? Explain your answer.

2. Should the two orders be accounted for as one job or two in Hiebert's system?

3. What sale price per box should Ben Hiebert set for the second order? What are the advantages and disadvantages of this price?

Case 2. Nature's Own manufactures organic fruit preserves sold primarily through health food stores and on the Web. The company closes for two weeks each December to enable employees to spend time with their families over the holiday season. Nature's Own's manufacturing overhead is mostly straight-line depreciation on its plant and air-conditioning costs for keeping the berries cool during the summer months. The company uses direct labor hours as the manufacturing overhead allocation base. President Cynthia Ortega has just approved new accounting software and is telling Controller Jack Strong about her decision.

"I think this new software will be great," Ortega says. "It will save you time in preparing all those reports."

"Yes, and having so much more information just a click away will help us make better decisions and help control costs," replies Strong. "We need to consider how we can use the new system to improve our business practices."

"And I know just where to start," says Ortega. "You complain each year about having to predict the weather months in advance for estimating air-conditioning costs and direct labor hours for the denominator of the predetermined manufacturing overhead rate, when professional meteorologists can't even get tomorrow's forecast right! I think we should calculate the predetermined overhead rate on a monthly basis."

Controller Strong is not so sure this is a good idea.

Requirements

1. What are the advantages and disadvantages of Ortega's proposal?

2. Should Nature's Own compute its predetermined manufacturing overhead rate on an annual basis or monthly basis? Explain.

■ Ethical Issue

Farley, Inc., is a contract manufacturer that produces customized computer components for several well-known computer-assembly companies. Farley's latest contract with CompWest.com calls for Farley to deliver sound cards that simulate surround sound from two speakers. Farley spent several hundred thousand dollars to design the sound card to meet CompWest.com's specifications.

Farley's president, Bryon Wilson, has stipulated a pricing policy that requires the bid price for a new job to be based on Farley's estimated costs to design, manufacture, distribute, and provide customer service for the job, plus a profit margin. Upon reviewing the contract figures, Farley's controller, Paul York, was startled to find that the cost estimates, developed by Farley's cost accountant Tony Hayes for the CompWest.com bid, were based on only the manufacturing costs. York is upset with Hayes. He is not sure what to do next.

Requirements

1. How did using manufacturing cost only rather than all costs associated with the CompWest.com job affect the amount of Farley's bid for the job?

2. Identify the parties involved in Paul York's ethical dilemma. What are his alternatives? How would each party be affected by each alternative? What should York do next?

■ Financial Statement Case—Amazon.com

This case is based on the **Amazon.com** annual report in Appendix A at the end of the book. Use it to answer the following questions.

Requirements

1. Review the description of **Amazon.com**'s business. Do you think the company uses job costing or process costing? Explain your reasons for your answer.

2. What is the amount of inventory the company holds at 12/31/2008? What are the components of the total inventory number. Explain by relating the data to what you learned in this chapter.

■ Team Project

Major airlines like **American, Delta,** and **Continental** are struggling to meet the challenges of budget carriers such as **Southwest** and **JetBlue**. Suppose the **Delta** CFO has just returned from a meeting on strategies for responding to competition from budget carriers. The vice president of operations suggested doing nothing: "We just need to wait until these new airlines run out of money. They cannot be making money with their low fares." In contrast, the vice president of marketing, not wanting to lose market share, suggests cutting **Delta**'s fares to match the competition. "If **JetBlue** charges only $75 for that flight from New York, so must we!" Others, including the CFO, emphasized the potential for cutting costs. Another possibility is starting a new budget airline within **Delta**. The CEO cut the meeting short, and directed the CFO to "get some hard data."

As a start, the CFO decides to collect cost and revenue data for a typical **Delta** flight, and then compare it to the data for a competitor. Assume she prepares the following schedule:

	Delta	JetBlue
Route: New York to Tampa..................	Flight 1247	Flight 53
Distance	1,000 miles	1,000 miles
Seats per plane	142	162
One-way ticket price	$80–$621*	$75
Food and beverage	Meal	Snack

*The highest price is first class airfare.

Excluding food and beverage, the CFO estimates that the cost per available seat mile is 8.4 cents for **Delta**, compared to 5.3 cents for **JetBlue**. (That is, the cost of flying a seat for one mile—whether or not the seat is occupied—is 8.4 cents for **Delta**, and 5.3 cents for **JetBlue**.) Assume the average cost of food and beverage is $5 per passenger for snacks and $10 for a meal.

Split your team into two groups. Group 1 should prepare its response to requirement 1 and group 2 should prepare its response to requirement 2 before the entire team meets to consider requirements 3 and 4.

Requirements

1. Use the data to determine for **Delta**
   a. the total cost of Flight 1247, assuming a full plane (100% load factor).
   b. the revenue generated by Flight 1247, assuming a 100% load factor and average revenue per one-way ticket of $102.
   c. the profit per Flight 1247, given the responses to a. and b.

2. Use the data to determine for **JetBlue**
   a. the total cost of Flight 53, assuming a full plane (100% load factor).
   b. the revenue generated by Flight 53, assuming a 100% load factor.
   c. the profit per Flight 53, given the responses to a. and b.

3. Based on the responses to requirements 1 and 2, carefully evaluate each of the four alternative strategies discussed in **Delta**'s executive meeting.

4. The analysis in this project is based on several simplifying assumptions. As a team, brainstorm factors that your quantitative evaluation does not include, but that may affect a comparison of **Delta**'s operations to budget carriers.

Quick Check Answers

1. *a* 2. *c* 3. *c* 4. *a* 5. *a* 6. *b* 7. *d* 8. *d* 9. *d* 10. *a*

 For online homework, exercises, and problems that provide you immediate feedback, please visit www.myaccountinglab.com.

Big Picture

Ch 1 Introduction to Management Accounting

- Distinguish management accounting from financial accounting
- The role and responsibilities of management accountants
- Classify costs and prepare income statements for merchandising companies
- Classify costs and prepare income statements and statements of cost of goods manufactured for manufacturing companies

Ch 2 Job Order Costing

- Distinguish between job order and process costing
- Record materials, labor, and overhead in a job order costing system
- Record completion and sales of finished goods and adjust for under-/overallocated overhead
- Calculate unit costs for service companies

Chapter 2: Demo Doc

■ Allocating Manufacturing Overhead

Learning Objectives 3, 4

Macho Mike's Machine Shop manufactures specialized metal products per its customer's specifications. Macho Mike's uses direct labor cost to allocate its manufacturing overhead. Macho Mike's expects to incur $160,000 of manufacturing overhead costs and to use $400,000 of direct labor cost during 2010.

During November 2010, Macho Mike's Machine Shop had the following selected transactions:

a. Actual indirect manufacturing labor incurred was $4,200.

b. Actual indirect materials used, $3,000.

c. Other manufacturing overhead incurred, $2,800 (credit accounts payable).

d. Allocated overhead for November (the machine shop incurred $36,000 of direct labor cost during the month).

e. Finished jobs that totaled $6,500 on their job cost records.

f. Sold inventory for $70,000 (on account) that cost $42,000 to produce.

Requirements

1. Compute the predetermined manufacturing overhead rate for Macho Mike's.

2. Journalize the transactions.

3. Prepare the journal entry to close the ending balance of manufacturing overhead.

Demo Doc Solution

Requirement 1

3   Record overhead in a job order costing system

Compute the predetermined manufacturing overhead rate for Macho Mike's.

Part 1	Part 2	Part 3	Demo Doc Complete

Because Macho Mike's uses direct labor cost to allocate overhead to jobs, the predetermined manufacturing overhead rate is computed as follows:

$$\frac{\text{Total estimated manufacturing overhead costs}}{\text{Total estimated direct labor cost}}$$

In this case, the estimated manufacturing overhead cost equals $160,000/estimated direct labor cost of $400,000 = 0.40, or a predetermined manufacturing overhead rate = 40% of *actual* direct labor cost. Another way to think of this is for every $1 spent on direct labor, we incur $0.40 of manufacturing overhead.

It's important to remember that this rate is determined at the beginning of the period, *before* any production has started. This is because actual overhead costs and the actual quantity of the allocation base are not known until the end of the period, so managers need this estimate to make decisions and allocate overhead to individual jobs throughout the period.

Because the allocation base used may be direct labor hours, direct labor cost, machine hours, and other bases, it's important to label this rate accordingly. The predetermined manufacturing overhead rate is multiplied by the allocation base activity to determine the amount of overhead applied to each of the jobs.

Requirement 2

3   Record overhead in a job order costing system

4   Record completion and sales of finished goods and the adjustment for under- or overallocated overhead

Journalize the transactions.

Part 1	Part 2	Part 3	Demo Doc Complete

a. Actual indirect manufacturing labor incurred was $4,200.

b. Actual indirect materials used, $3,000.

c. Other manufacturing overhead incurred, $2,800 (credit accounts payable).

In this case, all actual manufacturing overhead costs incurred during the period are debited to Manufacturing overhead because they cannot be traced to any specific job (that is, they are indirect costs). So Manufacturing overhead is debited (increased) by

$$\$4,200 + \$3,000 + \$2,800 = \$10,000$$

Indirect manufacturing labor results in a decrease of $4,200 to Manufacturing wages (a credit).

Indirect materials used results in a decrease of $3,000 to Materials inventory (a credit), because the materials have been used and are therefore removed from materials inventory.

Other manufacturing overhead is credited (an increase) to Accounts payable, as indicated in the question, $2,800.

Manufacturing overhead	(E+)		10,000	
Manufacturing wages	(E–)			4,200
Materials inventory	(A–)			3,000
Accounts payable	(L+)			2,800

d. **Allocate overhead for November (the machine shop incurred $36,000 of direct labor cost during the month).**

To determine the total overhead allocated to jobs in November, multiply the actual direct labor cost ($36,000) by the predetermined allocation rate of 40% (from requirement 1):

$$\underset{\text{(direct labor cost)}}{\$36,000} \times \underset{\text{(predetermined overhead rate)}}{0.40} = \underset{\text{allocated overhead for November}}{\$14,400}$$

Allocate the overhead to work in process by debiting (increasing) Work in process inventory and crediting (decreasing) Manufacturing overhead by $14,400.

Work in process inventory	(A+)		14,400	
Manufacturing overhead	(E–)			14,400

e. **Finished jobs that totaled $6,500 on their job cost records.**

When the goods are completed, they are transferred from Work in process to Finished goods. This reflects work in process that leaves the plant floor and is moved into the finished goods storage area. This is accomplished by debiting (increasing) Finished goods inventory by $6,500 and crediting (decreasing) Work in process inventory by $6,500.

Finished goods inventory	(A+)		6,500	
Work in process inventory	(A–)			6,500

f. Sold inventory for $70,000 (on account) that cost $42,000 to produce.

Debit the asset Accounts receivable to record the increased amount of $70,000 that is owed to Macho Mike's. Credit (increase) the revenue account, Sales revenue, by the same amount.

Debit (increase) the expense Cost of goods sold to record the cost of the sale. Because the goods are no longer in the finished goods inventory, we must credit Finished goods inventory to reduce that asset account.

Accounts receivable	(A+)	70,000	
Sales revenue	(R+)		70,000
Cost of goods sold	(E+)	42,000	
Finished goods inventory	(A–)		42,000

Requirement 3

4 Record completion and sales of finished goods and the adjustment for under- or overallocated overhead

Prepare the journal entry to close the ending balance of manufacturing overhead.

Part 1	Part 2	**Part 3**	Demo Doc Complete

The balance of the Manufacturing overhead account should be zero at the end of the accounting period. To achieve this, if Manufacturing overhead has a debit balance, then you would credit Manufacturing overhead and debit Cost of goods sold. If Manufacturing overhead has a credit balance, then you would debit Manufacturing overhead and credit Cost of goods sold.

In this case, manufacturing overhead was overallocated, because the overhead allocated to Work in process inventory ($14,400 from requirement 2, transaction **d**) is *more* than the amount actually incurred ($4,200 + $3,000 + $2,800 = $10,000— from transactions **a**, **b**, and **c**).

This results in a credit balance of $4,400 remaining in Manufacturing overhead. To close the ending balance, we then debit Manufacturing overhead by $4,400 and credit Cost of goods sold by $4,400.

Manufacturing overhead	(E+)	4,400	
Cost of goods sold	(E–)		4,400

Why? Because Macho Mike's allocated too much manufacturing overhead to each job, resulting in cost of goods sold being too high (meaning the jobs were charged too much overhead during the period). To close the balance in Manufacturing overhead, Macho Mike's applies a decrease to Cost of goods sold.

Part 1	Part 2	Part 3	**Demo Doc Complete**

3 Activity-Based Costing and Other Cost Management Tools

Learning Objectives/Success Keys

1 Develop activity-based costs (ABC)

2 Use activity-based management (ABM) to achieve target costs

3 Describe a just-in-time (JIT) production system, and record its transactions

4 Use the four types of quality costs to make decisions

David Larimer, Matt Sewell, and Brian Jobe are college friends who share an apartment. They split the monthly costs equally as shown below:

Each roommate's share is $300 ($900/3).

Rent and utilities	$570
Cable TV	50
High-speed Internet access	40
Groceries	240
Total monthly costs	$900

Things go smoothly the first few months. But then David calls a meeting: "Since I started having dinner at Amy's, I shouldn't have to pay a full share for the groceries." Matt then pipes in: "I'm so busy surfing the Net that I never have time to watch TV. I don't want to pay for the cable TV any more. And Brian, since your friend Jennifer eats here most evenings, you should pay a double share of the grocery bill." Brian retorts, "Matt, then you should pay for the Internet access, since you're the only one around here who uses it!"

What happened? The friends originally shared the costs equally. But they are not participating equally in eating, watching TV, and surfing the Net. Splitting these costs equally is not the best arrangement.

The roommates could better match their costs with the people who participate in each activity. This means splitting cable TV between David and Brian, letting Matt pay for Internet access, and allocating the grocery bill 1/3 to Matt and 2/3 to Brian. Exhibit 3-1 compares the results of this refined system with the original system.

EXHIBIT 3-1	More-Refined Versus Original Cost Allocation System		
	David	**Matt**	**Brian**
More-refined cost allocation system:			
Rent and utilities	$190	$190	$190
Cable TV	25	—	25
High-speed Internet access	—	40	—
Groceries	—	80	160
Total costs allocated	$215	$310	$375
Original cost allocation system	$300	$300	$300
Difference	$ (85)	$ 10	$ 75

No wonder David called the meeting! The original system cost him $300 a month, but under the refined system David pays only $215.

Large companies such as **Microsoft** or **Sony**, as well as smaller companies like Smart Touch Learning, face situations like this every day. What is the best way to allocate our costs to the things we do? Fair allocations have high stakes: friendships for David, Matt, and Brian; and profits and losses for companies.

Refining Cost Systems

1	Develop activity-based costs (ABC)

Sharpening the Focus: Assigning Costs Based on the Activities That Caused the Costs

We will illustrate cost refinement by looking at Smart Touch Learning. In today's competitive market, Smart Touch needs to know what it costs to make a DVD. The cost information helps Smart Touch set a selling price to cover costs and provide a profit. To remain competitive with other learning DVD manufacturers, Smart Touch must hold costs down.

We have seen that direct costs (materials and labor) are easy to assign to products. But indirect costs (utilities, supervisor salaries, and plant depreciation) are another story. It is the indirect costs—and they are significant—that must be allocated somehow. One way to manage costs is to refine the way indirect costs are allocated. Exhibit 3-2 provides an example. The first column of Exhibit 3-2 starts with Smart Touch's production function—making the DVDs. Production is where most companies begin refining their cost systems.

Before business got so competitive, managers could limit their focus to a broad business function such as production, and use a single plant-wide rate to allocate manufacturing overhead cost to their inventory, as we demonstrated in Chapter 2. But today's environment calls for more refined cost accounting. Managers need better data to set prices and identify the most profitable products. They drill down to focus on the costs incurred by each activity within the production function, as shown in the lower right of Exhibit 3-2. This has led to a better way to allocate indirect cost to production, and it is called activity-based costing.

EXHIBIT 3-2 | **Focus on the Activities That Cause the Costs—Smart Touch Learning**

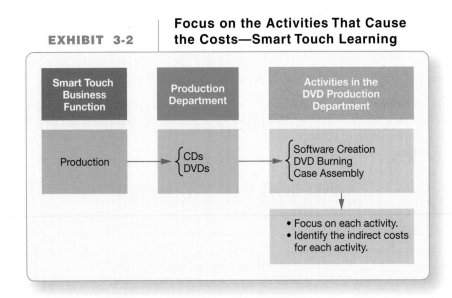

Activity-based costing (ABC) focuses on *activities*. The costs of those activities become the building blocks for measuring (allocating) the costs of products and services. Companies like **Dell**, **Coca-Cola**, and **American Express** use ABC.

Each activity has its own (usually unique) cost driver. For example, Smart Touch allocates indirect assembly costs to DVDs based on the number of inserts a worker must put in the DVD case. DVDs that require more inserts cost more to manufacture. Exhibit 3-3 shows some representative activities and cost drivers for manufacturing companies.

EXHIBIT 3-3 | **Examples of Activities and Cost Drivers**

Stop & Think...

You go to a restaurant with three of your friends and the waiter brings one bill for $100. How do you split it up? The meal you ordered only cost $20 of the total bill. Do you pay ¼ of the bill, or $25, or do you pay based on the cost of what you ordered, $20? Paying based on what you ordered is the gist of activity-based costing. Production costs get allocated based on the amount of each activity of production that the products use.

Developing an Activity-Based Costing System

The main difference between ABC and traditional systems is that ABC uses a separate allocation rate for each activity. Traditional systems, as demonstrated in Chapter 2, usually use one rate. ABC requires four steps, as outlined in Exhibit 3-4, using Smart Touch's data.

EXHIBIT 3-4 | Activity-Based Costing in Four Easy Steps

ABC Step	Application
1. Identify each activity and estimate its total indirect cost.	Activity .... Case Assembly Estimated total indirect cost per year $10,000
2. Identify the cost driver for each activity and estimate the total quantity of each driver's allocation base.	Cost driver for case assembly ...... Number of inserts Estimated total number of inserts each year 100,000
3. Compute the cost allocation rate for each activity. $$\text{Cost allocation rate} = \frac{\text{Estimated total indirect cost}}{\text{Estimated total quantity of the allocation base}}$$	$$\text{Cost allocation rate} = \frac{\$10,000}{100,000 \text{ inserts}} = \$0.10 \text{ per insert}$$
4. Allocate indirect costs to the cost object— in this case, all the inserts put in DVD cases during January. $$\text{Allocated activity cost} = \text{Cost allocation rate} \times \text{Actual quantity of the allocation base}$$	Cost of DVD Assembly for January $= \$0.10 \times 8,000 \text{ inserts during January}$ $= \underline{\$800}$

The first step in developing an activity-based costing system is to identify the activities. Analyzing all the activities required for a product or service forces managers to think about how each activity might be improved—or whether it is necessary at all.

Traditional Versus Activity-Based Costing Systems: Smart Touch Learning

To illustrate an ABC system, we use Smart Touch Learning. Smart Touch produces hundreds of different learning DVDs, including mass quantities of large audience DVDs and small quantities of "specialty" learning DVDs for specific companies.

We begin with a traditional cost system to show its weakness. You will see shortly that the ABC system that follows is clearly superior.

A Traditional Cost System

Smart Touch Learning's cost system allocates all manufacturing overhead the traditional way—based on a single allocation rate: 40% of direct labor cost. Smart Touch's controller, James Kolen, gathered data for two of the company's products:

- Microsoft Excel Training DVD (Multiple customers use this DVD)
- Specialty DVD created for a company's custom software application (A single customer uses this DVD)

Based on Smart Touch's traditional cost system, Kolen computed each product's gross profit as shown in Exhibit 3-5.

EXHIBIT 3-5 | **Smart Touch's Manufacturing Cost and Gross Profit Using Traditional Overhead Allocation**

	Excel DVD	Specialty DVD
Sale price per DVD	$12.00	$70.00
Less: Manufacturing cost per DVD:		
Direct materials	2.40	2.40
Direct labor	4.00	34.00
Manufacturing overhead (40% of Direct Labor Cost)	1.60	13.60
Total manufacturing cost per DVD	8.00	50.00
Gross profit per DVD	$ 4.00	$20.00

The gross profit for the specialty DVD is $20 per DVD—five times as high as the gross profit for the Excel DVD ($4). Smart Touch CEO Sheena Bright is surprised that the specialty DVD appears so much more profitable. She asks Kolen to check this out. Kolen confirms that the gross profit per DVD is five times as high for the specialty DVD. Bright wonders whether Smart Touch should produce more specialty DVDs.

Key Point: Because direct labor cost is the single allocation base for all products, Smart Touch allocates far more total overhead cost to the Excel DVDs than to the specialty DVDs. This costing is accurate only if direct labor really is the overhead cost driver, and only if the Excel DVD really does cause more overhead than the specialty DVD.

CEO Sheena Bright calls a meeting with production foreman Ryan Oliver and controller Kolen. Sheena is perplexed: The accounting numbers show that the specialty DVD is much more profitable than the Excel DVD. She expected the Excel DVD to be more efficiently produced and, therefore, more profitable because it is produced in a few large batches. By contrast, the specialty DVD is produced in many small batches.

Kolen fears that the problem could be Smart Touch's cost accounting system. Kolen suggests that foreman Oliver work with him to develop a pilot ABC system. Exhibit 3-6 compares the traditional single-allocation-base system (Panel A) to the new ABC system that Kolen's team developed (Panel B).

EXHIBIT 3-6 | **Overview of Smart Touch's Traditional and ABC Systems**

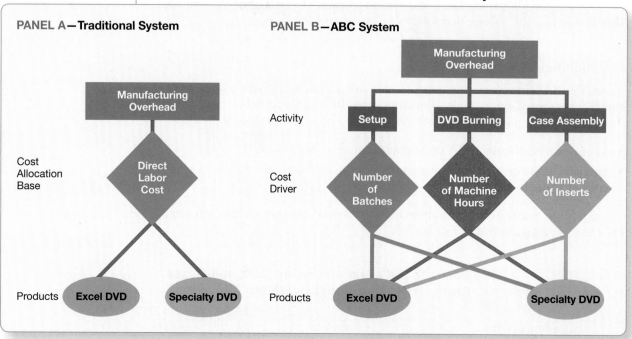

Activity-Based Cost System

Panel B of Exhibit 3-6 shows that Smart Touch's ABC team identifies three activities: setup, DVD burning, and case assembly. Each activity has its own cost driver. But exactly how does ABC work? The ABC team develops the new system by following the four steps described in Exhibit 3-4.

Let us see how an ABC system works, with a focus on the setup activity. Exhibit 3-7 develops Smart Touch's ABC system. Follow the details of each step. Make sure you understand exactly how each ABC step applies to Smart Touch's setup process.

Controller Kolen then uses the ABC costs allocated from Exhibit 3-7 to recompute manufacturing overhead costs, as shown in Exhibit 3-8. For each product, Kolen adds the total costs of setup, DVD burning, and assembly. He then divides each product's total manufacturing overhead cost by the number of DVDs produced to get the overhead cost per DVD.

Activity-based costs are more accurate because ABC considers the resources each product actually uses. Focus on the bottom line of Exhibit 3-8. Manufacturing overhead costs of

- Excel DVDs are $0.60 per DVD, which is less than the $1.60 cost allocated under the old system (shown in color in Exhibit 3-5).
- specialty DVDs are $33.70 per DVD, which far exceeds the $13.60 cost under the old system (shown in color in Exhibit 3-5).

Now that we know the indirect costs of Excel and specialty DVDs under ABC, next we will see how Smart Touch's managers *use* the ABC cost information to make better decisions.

EXHIBIT 3-7 | **Smart Touch's ABC System**

Step 1: Identify activities and estimate their total indirect costs.

Controller Kolen's team identifies all the manufacturing activities. Focus on setup.

Foreman Oliver estimates total setup costs for all production at $600,000. This cost is for all products that Smart Touch produces.

Step 2: Identify the cost driver for each activity.
Then estimate the total quantity of each driver's allocation base.

The allocation base for each activity should be its cost driver. The number of batches drive setup costs.

Kolen and Oliver estimate the setup department will have 40 batches.

Step 3: Compute the allocation rate for each activity.

Kolen computes the allocation rate for setup as follows:

$$\text{Cost allocation rate} = \frac{\$600,000}{40 \text{ batches}} = \$15,000 \text{ per batch}$$

Step 4: Allocate indirect costs to the cost object—batches of DVDs in this case.*

Kolen allocates setup costs as follows:

Excel DVD:	3 batches	×	$15,000 per batch	= $45,000
Specialty DVD:	1 batch	×	$15,000 per batch	= $15,000

*Other Smart Touch products represent the remaining 36 batches.

EXHIBIT 3-8 | **Smart Touch's Manufacturing Overhead Costs Under ABC**

Manufacturing Overhead Costs	Excel DVD	Specialty DVD
Setup (from Exhibit 3-7)	$45,000	$15,000
DVD Burning (amounts assumed)	5,000	1,500
Case Assembly (from Exhibit 3-4, based on $0.10 per insert): Each Excel DVD has 1 insert. Each specialty DVD has 7 inserts.	10,000	350
Total manufacturing overhead cost	60,000	16,850
Divide by number of DVDs produced	100,000	500
Manufacturing overhead cost per DVD under ABC	$ 0.60	$ 33.70

Activity-Based Management: Using ABC for Decision Making

Activity-based management (ABM) uses activity-based costs to make decisions that increase profits while meeting customer needs. In this section, we show how Smart Touch can use ABC in two kinds of decisions:

2 Use activity-based management (ABM) to achieve target costs

1. Pricing and product mix

2. Cost cutting

Pricing and Product Mix Decisions

Controller Kolen now knows the ABC manufacturing overhead cost per DVD (Exhibit 3-8). To determine which products are the most profitable, he recomputes each product's total manufacturing cost and gross profit. Panel A of Exhibit 3-9 shows that the total manufacturing cost per DVD for the Excel DVDs is $7.00 under the ABC system. Contrast this with the $8.00 cost per DVD under Smart Touch's traditional cost system, as shown in Panel B. More important, the ABC data in Panel A show that the specialty DVDs cost $70.10 per DVD, rather than the $50.00 per DVD indicated by the old system (Panel B). Smart Touch has been losing $0.10 on each specialty DVD—and this is *before* R&D, marketing, and distribution expenses! It seems that specialty DVDs are not currently profitable for Smart Touch.

EXHIBIT 3-9 | **Smart Touch's Cost Comparison— ABC Versus Traditional Allocation**

PANEL A—Total Manufacturing Cost and Gross Profit Under ABC

	Excel DVD	Specialty DVD
Sale price per DVD	$12.00	$70.00
Less: Manufacturing cost per DVD:		
Direct materials	2.40	2.40
Direct labor	4.00	34.00
Manufacturing overhead (from Exhibit 3-8)	0.60	33.70
Total manufacturing cost per DVD	7.00	70.10
Gross profit per DVD	$ 5.00	$ (0.10)

PANEL B—Total Manufacturing Cost and Gross Profit Under Traditional Allocation of Costs

	Excel DVD	Specialty DVD
Sale price per DVD	$12.00	$70.00
Less: Manufacturing cost per DVD:		
Direct materials	2.40	2.40
Direct labor	4.00	34.00
Manufacturing overhead (40% of Direct Labor Cost)	1.60	13.60
Total manufacturing cost per DVD	8.00	50.00
Gross profit per DVD	$ 4.00	$20.00

This illustration shows that ABC is often the best way to measure the cost of manufacturing a product. As a result, ABC helps businesses set the selling prices of their products. The selling price must cover *all* costs—both manufacturing costs and operating expenses—plus provide a profit.

As you will see in the next section, Smart Touch may be able to use ABC to cut costs. If Smart Touch cannot cut costs enough to earn a profit on the specialty DVDs, then the company may have to raise the sale price. If customers will not pay more, Smart Touch may have to drop the specialty DVDs. *This is the exact opposite of the strategy suggested by cost data from the traditional system. That system favored specialty DVDs.*

Cutting Costs

Most companies adopt ABC to get better product costs for pricing and product-mix decisions. However, they often benefit more by cutting costs. ABC and value engineering can work together. **Value engineering** means reevaluating activities to reduce costs. It requires the following cross-functional teams:

- Marketers to identify customer needs
- Engineers to design more efficient products
- Accountants to estimate costs

Why are managers turning to value engineering? Because it gets results! Companies like **General Motors** and **Carrier Corporation** are following Japanese automakers **Toyota** and **Nissan** and setting sale prices based on **target prices**—what customers are willing to pay for the product or service. Exhibit 3-10 provides an example. Study each column separately.

EXHIBIT 3-10	Target Pricing Versus Traditional Cost-Based Pricing

Instead of starting with product cost and then adding a profit to determine the sale price (right column of the exhibit), target pricing (left column) does just the opposite. Target pricing starts with the price that customers are willing to pay and then subtracts the company's desired profit to determine the **target cost**. Then the company works backward to develop the product at the target cost. The target cost is a goal for which the company must aim.

Now return to our Smart Touch illustration. The ABC analysis in Exhibit 3-9, Panel A, prompts CEO Sheena Bright to push Excel DVDs because it appears that the specialty DVD is losing money. The marketing department says the selling price of the Excel DVDs is likely to fall to $10.00 per DVD. Bright wants to earn a profit equal to 20% of the sale price.

Full-product costs consider *all* costs, including nonmanufacturing costs, when determining target costs and target profits. What is Smart Touch's target full-product cost per Excel DVD? The following is the computation:

Target sale price per Excel DVD	$10.00
− Desired profit ($10.00 × 20%)	(2.00)
= Target cost per Excel DVD	$ 8.00

Does Smart Touch's current full-product cost meet this target? See below.

Current total manufacturing cost per Excel DVD	$7.00
+ Nonmanufacturing costs (operating expenses—amount assumed)	1.10
= Current full-product cost per Excel DVD	$8.10

Smart Touch's current cost does not meet the target cost.

Because Smart Touch's current full-product cost, $8.10, exceeds the target cost of $8.00, Bright assembles a value-engineering team to identify ways to cut costs. The team analyzes each production activity. For each activity, the team considers how to

- cut costs, given Smart Touch's current production process.
- redesign the production process to further cut costs.

Of the team's several proposals, Bright decides to *Redesign Setup to reduce the setup cost per batch* by grouping raw materials that are used together to reduce the time required to assemble the materials for each setup. Estimated cost saving is $160,000, and the number of batches remains unchanged at 40.

Will this change allow Smart Touch to reach the target cost? Exhibit 3-11 shows how controller Kolen recomputes the cost of Setup based on the value-engineering study.

EXHIBIT 3-11 | **Recomputing Activity Costs After a Value-Engineering Study**

		Setup	DVD Burning	Assembly	Total Cost
			Manufacturing Overhead		
Estimated total indirect costs of activity:					
Setup ($600,000 − $160,000)		$440,000			
Estimated total quantity of each allocation base		40 batches			
Compute the cost allocation rate for each activity:					
(Divide estimated indirect cost by estimated		$440,000	Amounts	Amounts	
quantity of the allocation base)	÷	40 batches	From	From	
Cost allocation rate for each activity	=	$ 11,000	Exhibit	Exhibit	
Actual quantity of each allocation base used			3-8	3-8	
by Excel DVDs:					
Setup	×	3 batches			
Allocated Costs	=	$ 33,000 +	$5,000 +	$10,000 =	$48,000

Exhibit 3-12 shows that value engineering cuts total manufacturing overhead cost of the Excel DVDs to $48,000 from $60,000 (in Exhibit 3-8). Now Kolen totals the revised cost estimates for Excel DVDs.

EXHIBIT 3-12	**ABC Costs After Value-Engineering Study**

PANEL A—Manufacturing Cost Under ABC After Value-Engineering Study

	Excel DVD
Manufacturing Overhead Costs	
Setup (from Exhibit 3-11)	$33,000
DVD Burning (amounts assumed)	5,000
Case Assembly (from Exhibit 3-4, based on $0.10 per insert): Each Excel DVD has 1 insert. Each specialty DVD has 7 inserts.	10,000
Total manufacturing overhead cost	48,000
Divide by number of DVDs produced	100,000
Manufacturing overhead cost per DVD under ABC after Value-Engineering Study	$ 0.48

PANEL B—Total Manufacturing Cost and Full Product Cost Under ABC After Value-Engineering Study

	Excel DVD
Manufacturing cost per DVD:	
Direct materials	2.40
Direct labor	4.00
Manufacturing overhead (from Panel A)	0.48
Total manufacturing cost per DVD after Value-Engineering Study	6.88
Non manufacturing costs (assumed)	$1.10
Full product cost-after Value-Engineering Study	$7.98

Cost of $6.88 is quite an improvement from the prior manufacturing cost of $7.00 per DVD (Exhibit 3-9, Panel A). Now Smart Touch's full cost of $7.98 is less than its target full product cost of $8.00. Value engineering worked.

Decision Guidelines

ACTIVITY-BASED COSTING

Several years ago **Dell** refined its cost system. Starting with an Excel spreadsheet, **Dell** developed a simple ABC system to focus on its 10 most critical activities. Here are some of the decisions **Dell** faced as it began refining its cost system.

Decision	Guidelines
• How to develop an ABC system?	1. Identify each activity and estimate its total indirect costs. 2. Identify the cost driver for each activity. Then estimate the total quantity of each driver's allocation base. 3. Compute the cost allocation rate for each activity. 4. Allocate indirect costs to the cost object.
• How to compute a cost allocation rate for an activity?	$$\dfrac{\text{Estimated total indirect cost of the activity}}{\text{Estimated total quantity of the allocation base}}$$
• How to allocate an activity's cost to the cost object?	$$\begin{array}{c}\text{Cost allocation} \\ \text{rate for the activity}\end{array} \times \begin{array}{c}\text{Actual quantity of the allocation} \\ \text{base used by the cost object}\end{array}$$
• For what kinds of decisions do managers use ABC?	Managers use ABC data to decide on the following: • Pricing and product mix • Cost cutting
• How to set target costs?	Target sale price (based on market research) − Desired profit = Target cost
• How to achieve target costs?	Use value engineering to cut costs by improving product design and production processes.
• What are the main benefits of ABC?	• More accurate product cost information • More detailed information on the costs of activities and their cost drivers helps managers control costs

Summary Problem 1

Indianapolis Auto Parts (IAP) has a Seat Manufacturing Department that uses activity-based costing. IAP's system has the following features:

Activity	Allocation Base	Cost Allocation Rate
Purchasing	Number of purchase orders	$50.00 per purchase order
Assembling	Number of parts	$0.50 per part
Packaging	Number of finished seats	$1.00 per finished seat

Each auto seat has 20 parts. Direct materials cost per seat is $11. Suppose **Ford** has asked IAP for a bid on 50,000 built-in baby seats that would be installed as an option on some **Ford** SUVs. IAP will use a total of 200 purchase orders if **Ford** accepts IAP's bid.

Requirements

1. Compute the total cost IAP will incur to (a) purchase the needed materials and then (b) assemble and (c) package 50,000 baby seats. Also compute the average cost per seat.
2. For bidding, IAP adds a 30% markup to total cost. What total price will IAP bid for the entire **Ford** order?
3. Suppose that instead of an ABC system, IAP has a traditional product costing system that allocates all costs other than direct materials at the rate of $65 per direct labor hour. The baby-seat order will require 10,000 direct labor hours. What price will IAP bid using this system's total cost?
4. Use your answers to requirements 2 and 3 to explain how ABC can help IAP make a better decision about the bid price to offer **Ford**.

Solution

Requirement 1

Total Cost of Order and Average Cost per Seat:

Direct materials, 50,000 × $11.00....................	$ 550,000
Activity costs:	
Purchasing, 200 × $50.00	10,000
Assembling, 50,000 × 20 × $0.50	500,000
Packaging, 50,000 × $1.00	50,000
Total cost of order	$1,110,000
Divide by number of seats...............................	÷ 50,000
Average cost per seat......................................	$ 22.20

Requirement 2

Bid Price (ABC System):

Bid price ($1,110,000 × 130%).............	$1,443,000

Requirement 3

Bid Price (Traditional System):

Direct materials, 50,000 × $11.00.............	$ 550,000
Other product costs, 10,000 × $65............	650,000
Total cost of order............................	$1,200,000
Bid price ($1,200,000 × 130%)................	$1,560,000

Requirement 4

IAP's bid would be $117,000 higher using the traditional system than using ABC ($1,560,000 − $1,443,000). Assuming the ABC system more accurately captures the costs caused by the order, the traditional system over costs the order. This leads to a higher bid price and reduces IAP's chance of winning the bid. The ABC system can increase IAP's chance of getting the order by bidding a lower price.

Just-In-Time (JIT) Systems

Competition is fierce, especially in manufacturing and technology-related services. Chinese and Indian companies are producing high-quality goods at very low costs. As we saw in the discussion of activity-based costing, there is a never-ending quest to cut costs.

The cost of buying, storing, and moving inventory can be significant for **Home Depot**, **Toyota**, and **Dell**. To lower inventory costs, many companies use a just-in-time (JIT) system.

Companies with JIT systems buy materials and complete finished goods *just in time* for delivery to customers. Production is completed in self-contained work cells as shown in Exhibit 3-13 on the following page. Each cell includes the machinery and labor resources to manufacture a product. Employees work in a team and are empowered to complete the work without supervision. Workers complete a small batch of units and are responsible for inspecting for quality throughout the process. As the completed product moves out of the work cell, the suppliers deliver more materials just in time to keep production moving along.

By contrast, traditional production systems separate manufacturing into various processing departments that focus on a single activity. Work in process moves from one department to another. That wastes time, and wasted time is wasted money.

Under JIT, a customer's order—customer demand—triggers manufacturing. The sales order "pulls" materials, labor, and overhead into production. This "demand–pull" system extends back to the suppliers of materials. Suppliers make frequent deliveries of defect-free materials *just in time* for production. Purchasing only what customers demand reduces inventory. Less inventory frees floor space for more productive use. Thus, JIT systems help to reduce waste. Exhibit 3-13 shows a traditional production system in Panel B. The traditional system requires more inventory, more workers, and usually costs more to operate than a JIT system.

Companies like **Toyota**, **Carrier**, and **Dell** credit JIT for saving the companies millions. But JIT systems are not without problems. With no inventory buffers, JIT users lose sales when they cannot get materials on time, or when poor-quality materials arrive just in time. There is no way to make up for lost time. As a result, strong relationships with quality raw materials vendors are very important to JIT. Additionally, many JIT companies still maintain small inventories of critical materials.

3 Describe a just-in-time (JIT) production system, and record its transactions

EXHIBIT 3-13 | **Production Flow Comparison: Just-in-Time Versus Traditional Production**

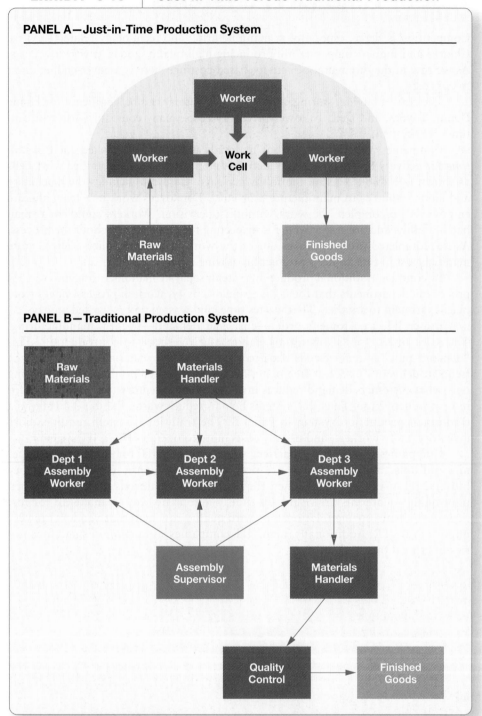

PANEL A—Just-in-Time Production System

PANEL B—Traditional Production System

Just-in-Time Costing

JIT costing leads many companies to simplify their accounting. **Just-in-time costing,** sometimes called **backflush costing,** seems to work backwards. JIT costing starts with output that has been completed and then assigns manufacturing costs to units sold and to inventories. There are three major differences between JIT costing and traditional standard costing as shown in Exhibit 3-14:

1. JIT systems do not track the cost of products from Raw materials inventory to Work in process inventory to Finished goods inventory. Instead, JIT costing waits until the units are completed to record the cost of production.

2. JIT systems combine raw materials and work in process inventories into a single account called **Raw and in-process inventory.**

3. Under the JIT philosophy, workers perform many tasks. Most companies using JIT combine labor and manufacturing overhead costs into a single account called Conversion costs. *Conversion costs* is a temporary account that works just like the Manufacturing overhead account. Actual conversion costs accumulate as debits in the Conversion costs account. This account is credited when conversion costs are allocated to completed units. Accountants close any under- or overallocated conversion costs to Cost of goods sold at the end of the year, just like they do for under- or overallocated manufacturing overhead.

EXHIBIT 3-14 | **Comparison of Traditional and Just-in-Time Costing**

	Traditional	Just-in-Time
Recording production activity	Build the costs of products as they move from raw materials into work in process and on to finished goods inventory	Record the costs of products when units are completed
Inventory accounts	Materials inventory Work in process inventory Finished goods inventory	Raw and in-process inventory Finished goods inventory
Manufacturing costs	Direct materials Direct labor Manufacturing overhead	Direct materials Conversion costs

JIT Costing Illustrated: Smart Touch Learning

To illustrate JIT costing, let us continue with our Smart Touch Learning example. Smart Touch has only one direct material cost: blank DVDs. This cost is recorded in the Raw and in-process inventory account. All other manufacturing costs—including labor, various materials, and overhead—are indirect costs of converting the "raw" DVDs into finished goods (DVD learning systems). All these indirect costs are collected in the Conversion costs account.

JIT does not use a separate Work in process inventory account. Instead, it uses only two inventory accounts:

- Raw and in-process inventory, which combines direct materials with work in process
- Finished goods inventory

Assume that on January 31, Smart Touch had $100,000 of beginning Raw and in-process inventory, and $200,000 of beginning Finished goods inventory. During February, Smart Touch uses JIT costing to record the following transactions:

1. Smart Touch purchased $240,000 of direct materials (blank DVDs) on account.

1.				
	Raw and in-process inventory (A+)		240,000	
	Accounts payable (L+)			240,000
	Purchased direct materials on account.			

2. Smart Touch spent $590,000 on labor and overhead.

2.				
	Conversion costs (E+)		590,000	
	Wages payable, Accumulated depreciation, etc.			590,000
	Incurred conversion costs.			

3. Smart Touch completed 115,000 Excel DVDs that it moved to Finished goods. Recall that the standard cost of each Excel DVD in Exhibit 3-9 is $7 ($2.40 direct materials + $4.60 conversion costs). The debit (increase) to Finished goods inventory is a standard cost of $805,000 (115,000 completed Excel DVDs × $7). There is no work in process inventory in JIT costing, so Smart Touch credits the following:

3.				
	Finished goods inventory (115,000 × $7) (A+)		805,000	
	Raw and in-process inventory (115,000 × $2.40) (A–)			276,000
	Conversion costs (115,000 × $4.60) (E–)			529,000
	Completed production.			

- Raw and in-process inventory for the blank DVDs, $276,000 (115,000 completed Excel DVDs × $2.40 standard raw material cost per DVD)
- Conversion costs for the labor and other indirect costs allocated to the finished circuits, $529,000 (115,000 completed Excel DVDs × $4.60 standard conversion cost per DVD)

This is the essence of JIT costing. The system does not track costs as the DVDs move through manufacturing. Instead, *completion* of the DVDs triggers the accounting system to go back and pull costs from Raw and in-process inventory and to allocate conversion costs to the finished products.

4. Smart Touch sold 110,000 Excel DVDs (110,000 DVDs × cost of $7 per DVD = $770,000). The cost of goods sold entry is as follows:

4.				
	Cost of goods sold (E+)		770,000	
	Finished goods inventory (A–)			770,000
	Cost of sales.			

Exhibit 3-15 shows Smart Touch's relevant accounts. Combining raw materials with work in process to form the single Raw and in-process inventory account eliminates detail.

EXHIBIT 3-15 | **Smart Touch Learning's JIT Costing Accounts**

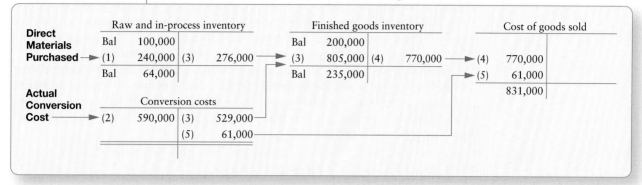

5. You can see from Exhibit 3-15 that conversion costs are underallocated by $61,000 (actual cost of $590,000 – applied cost of $529,000). Under- and overallocated conversion costs are treated just like under- and overallocated manufacturing overhead and closed to Cost of goods sold, as follows:

5.	Cost of goods sold (E+)	61,000	
	Conversion costs (E–)		61,000
	Closed conversion costs on account.		

In the final analysis, cost of goods sold for February is $831,000, as shown in the T-account in Exhibit 3-15.

Stop & Think...

If you were to go to the grocery store today, you could either buy just the ingredients you need to make dinner tonight or you could purchase enough groceries to last you two weeks. If you purchase for two weeks, can you be sure you will use all the groceries you buy or will some of it "go bad" before you eat it? Choosing to purchase just enough to get you through a short period (today) is like Just-In-Time costing. Companies purchase just enough raw materials for the production needs of the next day or two, rather than purchasing large amounts of raw materials that have to be stored.

Continuous Improvement and the Management of Quality

Companies using just-in-time production systems strive for high-quality production. Poor-quality materials or defective products shut down production, and that runs counter to the JIT philosophy.

4 Use the four types of quality costs to make decisions

To meet this challenge, many companies adopt *total quality management (TQM)*. The goal of TQM is to provide customers with superior products and services. In TQM, each business function monitors its activities to improve quality and eliminate defects and waste. Continuous improvement is the goal. Take a break, or miss a beat, and another manufacturer will put you out of business.

Well-designed products reduce inspections, rework, and warranty claims. Investing in research and development (R&D) can generate savings in marketing and customer service. World-class companies like **Toyota** and **Dell** *design* and *build* quality into their products rather than having to *inspect* and *repair* later. Let us see how they achieve the goal of high quality.

The Four Types of Quality Costs

The four types of quality-related costs are as follows:

1. **Prevention costs** are costs spent to *avoid* poor-quality goods or services.

2. **Appraisal costs** are costs spent to *detect* poor-quality goods or services.

3. **Internal failure costs** are costs spent to avoid poor-quality goods or services *before* delivery to customers.

4. **External failure costs** are costs spent after the company *delivers poor-quality goods or services* to customers and then has to make things right with the customer.

Exhibit 3-16 gives examples of the four types of quality costs. Most prevention costs occur in the R&D stage of the value chain. In contrast, most appraisal and internal failure costs occur in production. External failure occurs in customer service or, worse, it results from lost sales due to an unhappy customer. Prevention is much cheaper than external failure.

EXHIBIT 3-16 | **Four Types of Quality Costs**

Prevention Costs	Appraisal Costs
Training personnel	Inspection at various stages of production
Improved materials	Inspection of final products or services
Preventive maintenance	Product testing
Internal Failure Costs	**External Failure Costs**
Production loss caused by downtime	Lost profits due to unhappy customers
Rework	Warranty costs
Rejected product units	Service costs at customer sites
	Sales returns due to product defects

Stop & Think...

Do you go to the dentist every six months to have your teeth cleaned? The cost of the cleaning is a prevention cost. By investing in the care of your teeth, not only do your teeth look nice, but you hope to *prevent* decay in your teeth. Preventing that decay helps you to avoid a bigger dentist bill for repairing your teeth in the future. The same is true for producing products. Monies spent on improving quality are much cheaper than monies spent to repair defective products in the future.

Deciding Whether to Adopt a New Quality Program

Let us revisit Smart Touch Learning. CEO Sheena Bright is considering spending the following on a new quality program:

Inspect raw materials	$100,000
Reengineer to improve product quality	750,000
Inspect finished goods	150,000
Preventive maintenance of equipment	100,000

Smart Touch expects this quality program to reduce costs by the following amounts:

Avoid lost profits due to unhappy customers	$800,000
Fewer sales returns	50,000
Decrease the cost of rework	250,000
Lower warranty costs..	100,000

Bright asks controller Kolen to

1. classify each cost into one of the four categories (prevention, appraisal, internal failure, external failure). Total the estimated cost for each category.

2. recommend whether Smart Touch should undertake the quality program. Kolen uses Exhibit 3-17 to compare the costs to

- undertake the quality program, or

- not undertake the quality program.

EXHIBIT 3-17	**Analysis of Smart Touch's Proposed Quality Program**

Undertake the Quality Program		Do Not Undertake the Quality Program	
Prevention		**Internal Failure**	
Reengineer to improve product quality	$ 750,000	Cost of rework	$ 250,000
Preventive maintenance of equipment	100,000	Total internal failure costs	$ 250,000
Total prevention costs	$ 850,000		
		External Failure	
		Lost profits due to unhappy customers	$ 800,000
Appraisal		Sales returns	50,000
Inspect raw materials	$ 100,000	Warranty costs	100,000
Inspect finished goods	150,000	Total external failure costs	$ 950,000
Total appraisal costs	$ 250,000	**Total costs of not undertaking the**	
Total costs of the quality program	$1,100,000	**quality program**	$1,200,000

Decision: Undertake the Quality Program and Save $100,000.

These estimates suggest that Smart Touch would save $100,000 ($1,200,000 – $1,100,000) by undertaking the quality program.

Quality costs can be hard to measure. For example, it is very hard to measure external failure costs. Lost profits due to unhappy customers do not appear in the accounting records! Therefore, TQM uses lots of nonfinancial measures such as the number of customer complaints and the volume of incoming customer-service phone calls as a means to measure success or failure.

Decision Guidelines

JUST-IN-TIME AND QUALITY COSTS

Dell is famous for using just-in-time production and total quality management. **Dell's** managers made the following decisions.

Decision	Guidelines	
• How to change from traditional production to JIT?	*Traditional*	*JIT*
	Similar machines grouped together	Production cells
	Larger batches	Smaller batches
	Higher inventories	Lower inventories
	Each worker does a few tasks	Each worker does a wide range of tasks
	Many suppliers	Fewer, but well-coordinated suppliers
• How does costing work under JIT?	Under JIT costing, 　1. raw materials and work in process are combined into a single Raw and in-process inventory account. 　2. labor and overhead are combined into a Conversion costs account. 　3. summary journal entries are recorded *after* units are completed.	
• What are the four types of quality costs?	Prevention Appraisal Internal failure External failure	
• How to manage the four types of quality costs?	Invest up front in prevention and appraisal to reduce internal and external failure costs.	

Summary Problem 2

Flores Company manufactures cell phones and uses JIT costing. The standard unit cost is $30: $20 direct materials and $10 conversion costs. Direct materials purchased on account during June totaled $2,500,000. Actual conversion costs totaled $1,100,000. Flores completed 100,000 cell phones in June and sold 98,000.

Requirements

1. Journalize these transactions.
2. Were conversion costs under- or overallocated? Explain your answer and then make the entry to close the Conversion costs account.
3. How much Cost of goods sold did Flores have in June?

Solution

Requirement 1

Raw and in-process inventory (A+)		2,500,000	
Accounts payable (L+)			2,500,000
Conversion costs (E+)		1,100,000	
Wages payable, Accumulated depreciation, etc.			1,100,000
Finished goods inventory (A+)		3,000,000	
Raw and in-process inventory (100,000 × $20) (A–)			2,000,000
Conversion costs (100,000 × $10) (E–)			1,000,000
Cost of goods sold (98,000 × $30) (E+)		2,940,000	
Finished goods inventory (A–)			2,940,000

Requirement 2

Conversion costs were underallocated. Actual costs ($1,100,000)			
exceeded the cost allocated to inventory ($1,000,000).			
Cost of goods sold (E+)		100,000	
Conversion costs (E–)			100,000

Requirement 3

COGS = $3,040,000 ($2,940,000 + $100,000)

Review *Activity-Based Costing and Other Cost Management Tools*

■ Accounting Vocabulary

Activity-Based Costing (ABC) (p. 99)
Focuses on activities as the fundamental cost objects. The costs of those activities become building blocks for compiling the indirect costs of products, services, and customers.

Activity-Based Management (ABM) (p. 103)
Using activity-based cost information to make decisions that increase profits while satisfying customer needs.

Appraisal Costs (p. 116)
Costs incurred to detect poor-quality goods or services.

Backflush Costing (p. 112)
A standard costing system that starts with output completed and then assigns manufacturing costs to units sold and to inventories. Also called **just-in-time costing**.

External Failure Costs (p. 116)
Costs incurred when the company does not detect poor-quality goods or services until after delivery to customers.

Internal Failure Costs (p. 116)
Costs incurred when the company detects and corrects poor-quality goods or services before delivery to customers.

Just-in-Time (JIT) Costing (p. 112)
A standard costing system that starts with output completed and then assigns manufacturing costs to units sold and to inventories. Also called **backflush costing**.

Prevention Costs (p. 116)
Costs incurred to avoid poor-quality goods or services.

Raw and In-Process Inventory (p. 113)
Combined account for raw materials and work in process inventories under JIT systems.

Target Cost (p. 105)
Allowable cost to develop, produce, and deliver the product or service. Equals target price minus desired profit.

Target Price (p. 105)
What customers are willing to pay for the product or service.

Value Engineering (p. 105)
Reevaluating activities to reduce costs while satisfying customer needs.

■ Quick Check

1. Which statement is *false*?
   a. Information technology makes it feasible for most companies to adopt ABC.
   b. An ABC system is more refined than one that uses a companywide overhead rate.
   c. ABC focuses on indirect costs.
   d. ABC is primarily for manufacturing companies.

Use the following information for questions 2–4. Two of Keyboard's production activities are *kitting* (assembling the raw materials needed for each computer in one kit) and *boxing* the completed products for shipment to customers. Assume that Keyboard spends $8 million a month on kitting and $16 million a month on boxing. Keyboard allocates the following:

- Kitting costs based on the number of parts used in the computer
- Boxing costs based on the cubic feet of space the computer requires

Suppose Keyboard estimates it will use 700 million parts a month and ship products with a total volume of 25 million cubic feet.

Assume that each desktop computer requires 100 parts and has a volume of 5 cubic feet.

2. What is the activity cost allocation rate?

	Kitting	Boxing
a.	$0.01/part	$0.02/cubic foot
b.	$0.01/part	$0.64/cubic foot
c.	$0.32/part	$0. 02/cubic foot
d.	$87.50/part	$1.56/cubic foot

3. What are the kitting and boxing costs assigned to one desktop computer?

	Kitting	Boxing
a.	$1.92	$0.26
b.	$3.20	$4.00
c.	$0.50	$0.16
d.	$1.00	$3.20

4. Keyboard contracts with its suppliers to pre-kit certain component parts before delivering them to Keyboard. Assume this saves $1.0 million of the kitting cost and reduces the total number of parts by 300 million (because Keyboard considers each pre-kit as one part). If a desktop now uses 80 parts, what is the new kitting cost assigned to one desktop?

a. $1.00

b. $1.60

c. $0.80

d. $4.00

5. Keyboard can use ABC information for what decisions?

a. Product mix

b. Cost cutting

c. Pricing

d. All of the above

6. Which of the following is true for **Dell**, the computer company?

a. Most of **Dell's** costs are for direct materials and direct labor. Indirect costs are a small proportion of total costs.

b. ABC helps **Dell** keep costs low and remain competitive.

c. **Dell** uses only a few activities, so a companywide overhead allocation rate would serve **Dell** quite well.

d. All the above are true.

7. Companies enjoy many benefits from using JIT. Which is *not* a benefit of adopting JIT?

a. More space available for production

b. Ability to continue production despite disruptions in deliveries of raw materials

c. Ability to respond quickly to changes in customer demand

d. Lower inventory carrying costs

8. Which account is *not* used in JIT costing?

a. Finished goods inventory

b. Raw and in-process inventory

c. Work in process inventory

d. Conversion costs

9. The cost of lost future sales after a customer finds a defect in a product is which type of quality cost?

a. Internal failure cost

b. Prevention cost

c. External failure cost

d. Appraisal cost

10. Spending on testing a product before shipment to customers is which type of quality cost?

    a. Appraisal cost

    b. External failure cost

    c. Prevention cost

    d. None of the above

Answers are given after Apply Your Knowledge (p. 142).

Assess Your Progress

▪ Short Exercises

S3-1 *(L. OBJ. 1)* **Activity-based costing [5–10 min]**
Activity-based costing requires four steps.

Requirement

1. Rank the following steps in the order in which they would be completed. Number the first step as "1" until you have ranked all four steps.
   a. Compute the cost allocation rate for each activity.
   b. Identify the cost driver for each activity and estimate the total quantity of each driver's allocation base.
   c. Allocate indirect costs to the cost object.
   d. Identify each activity and estimate its total indirect cost.

S3-2 *(L. OBJ. 1)* **Calculating costs using Traditional and ABC [10 min]**
Blake and Roscoe are college friends planning a skiing trip to Aspen before the New Year. They estimated the following costs for the trip:

	Estimated Costs	Cost Driver	Activity Allocation Blake	Activity Allocation Roscoe
Food	$ 600	Pounds of food eaten	20	30
Skiing	210	# of lift tickets	3	0
Lodging	400	# of nights	2	2
	$ 1,210			

Requirements

1. Blake suggests that the costs be shared equally. Calculate the amount each person would pay.

2. Roscoe does not like the idea because he plans to stay in the room rather than ski. Roscoe suggests that each type of cost be allocated to each person based on the above listed cost driver. Using the activity allocation for each person, calculate the amount that each person would pay based on his own consumption of the activity.

S3-3   *(L.OBJ. 1)* **Computing indirect manufacturing costs per unit [15 min]**

Durkin, Corp., is considering the use of activity-based costing. The following information is provided for the production of two product lines:

Activity	Cost	Cost Driver
Setup	$ 107,000	Number of setups
Machine maintenance	50,000	Machine hours
Total indirect manufacturing costs	$ 157,000	

	Product A	Product B	Total
Direct labor hours	7,000	3,000	10,000
Number of setups	30	70	100
Number of machine hours	1,200	3,800	5,000

Durkin plans to produce 350 units of Product A and 225 units of Product B.

Requirement

1. Compute the ABC indirect manufacturing cost per unit for each product.

S3-4   *(L.OBJ. 1)* **Computing indirect manufacturing costs per unit [15 min]**

The following information is provided for the Asteroid Antenna, Corp., which manufactures two products: Lo-Gain antennas, and Hi-Gain antennas for use in remote areas.

Activity	Cost	Cost Driver
Setup	$ 55,000	Number of setups
Machine maintenance	39,000	Machine hours
Total indirect manufacturing costs	$ 94,000	

	Lo-Gain	Hi-Gain	Total
Direct labor hours	1,700	5,800	7,500
Number of setups	25	25	50
Number of machine hours	2,100	1,400	3,500

Asteroid plans to produce 200 Lo-Gain antennas and 325 Hi-Gain antennas.

Requirements

1. Compute the ABC indirect manufacturing cost per unit for each product.
2. Compute the indirect manufacturing cost per unit using direct labor hours from the single-allocation-base system.

S3-5   *(L.OBJ. 1)* **Using ABC to compute product costs per unit [15 min]**

Daily, Corp., makes two products: C and D. The following data have been summarized:

	Product C	Product D
Direct materials cost per unit	$ 900	$ 2,100
Direct labor cost per unit	400	200
Indirect manufacturing cost per unit	?	?

Indirect manufacturing cost information includes the following:

		Allocation Base Units	
Activity	Allocation Rate	Product C	Product D
Setup	$ 1,000	37	77
Machine maintenance	$ 11	1,350	3,850

The company plans to manufacture 225 units of each product.

Requirement

1. Calculate the product cost per unit for Products C and D using activity-based costing.

S3-6 *(L.OBJ. 1)* **Using ABC to compute product costs per unit [15 min]**
Johnstone, Corp., manufactures mid-fi and hi-fi stereo receivers. The following data have been summarized:

	Mid-Fi	Hi-Fi
Direct materials cost per unit	$ 500	$ 1,200
Direct labor cost per unit	300	200
Indirect manufacturing cost per unit	?	?

Indirect manufacturing cost information includes:

		Allocation Base Units	
Activity	Allocation Rate	Mid–Fi	Hi–Fi
Setup	$ 1,000	36	36
Inspections	$ 600	35	20
Machine maintenance	$ 14	1,650	1,450

The company plans to manufacture 75 units of the mid-fi receivers and 325 units of the hi-fi receivers.

Requirement

1. Calculate the product cost per unit for both products using activity-based costing.

S3-7 *(L.OBJ. 1)* **Allocating indirect costs and computing income [10 min]**
Antics, Inc., is a technology consulting firm focused on Web site development and integration of Internet business applications. The president of the company expects to incur $719,600 of indirect costs this year, and she expects her firm to work 8,000 direct labor hours. Antics' systems consultants earn $350 per hour. Clients are billed at 150% of direct labor cost. Last month Antics' consultants spent 100 hours on Crickett's engagement.

Requirements

1. Compute Antics' indirect cost allocation rate per direct labor hour.
2. Compute the total cost assigned to the Crickett engagement.
3. Compute the operating income from the Crickett engagement.

Note: Short Exercise 3-7 must be completed before attempting Short Exercise 3-8.

S3-8   *(L.OBJ. 1)* **Computing ABC allocation rates [5 min]**
Refer to Short Exercise 3-7. The president of Antics suspects that her allocation of indirect costs could be giving misleading results, so she decides to develop an ABC system.
She identifies three activities: documentation preparation, information technology support, and training. She figures that documentation costs are driven by the number of
pages, information technology support costs are driven by the number of software
applications used, and training costs are driven by the number of direct labor hours
worked. Estimates of the costs and quantities of the allocation bases follow:

Activity	Estimated Cost	Allocation Base	Estimated Quantity of Allocation Base
Documentation preparation	$ 100,000	Pages	3,125 pages
Information technology support	159,600	Applications used	760 applications
Training	460,000	Direct labor hours	4,600 hours
Total indirect costs	$ 719,600		

Requirement

1.   Compute the cost allocation rate for each activity.

Note: Short Exercises 3-7 and 3-8 must be completed before attempting Short Exercise 3-9.

S3-9   *(L.OBJ. 1)* **Using ABC to allocate costs and compute profit [10–15 min]**
Refer to Short Exercises 3-7 and 3-8. Suppose Antics' direct labor rate was $350 per
hour, the documentation cost was $32 per page, the information technology support
cost was $210 per application, and training costs were $100 per direct labor hour.
The Crickett engagement used the following resources last month:

Cost Driver	Crickett
Direct labor hours	100
Pages	300
Applications used	74

Requirements

1.   Compute the cost assigned to the Crickett engagement, using the ABC system.
2.   Compute the operating income from the Crickett engagement, using the ABC
     system.

Note: Short Exercise 3-9 must be completed before attempting Short Exercise 3-10.

S3-10   *(L.OBJ. 2)* **Using ABC to achieve target profit [10–15 min]**
Refer to Short Exercise 3-9. Antics desires a 20% target profit after covering
all costs.

Requirement

1.   Considering the total costs assigned to the Crickett engagement in 3-9, what
     would Antics have to charge the customer to achieve that profit?

S3-11 *(L.OBJ. 3)* **Just-in-time characteristics [5–10 min]**
Consider the following characteristics of either a JIT production system or a traditional production system.

    a. Products produced in large batches.
    b. Large stocks of finished goods protect against lost sales if customer demand is higher than expected.
    c. Suppliers make frequent deliveries of small quantities of raw materials.
    d. Long setup times.
    e. Employees do a variety of jobs, including maintenance and setups as well as operating machines.
    f. Machines are grouped into self-contained production cells or production lines.
    g. Machines are grouped according to function. For example, all cutting machines are located in one area.
    h. Suppliers can access the company's intranet.
    i. The final operation in the production sequence "pulls" parts from the preceding operation.
    j. Each employee is responsible for inspecting his or her own work.
    k. Management works with suppliers to ensure defect-free raw materials.

Requirement

    1. Indicate whether each is characteristic of a JIT production system or a traditional production system.

S3-12 *(L.OBJ. 3)* **Recording JIT costing journal entries [10 min]**
Prized Products uses a JIT system to manufacture trading pins for the **Hard Rock Café**. The standard cost per pin is $1 for raw materials and $2 for conversion costs. Last month Prized recorded the following data:

Number of pins completed	4,100 pins	Raw material purchases	$ 7,500
Number of pins sold	3,700 pins	Conversion costs	$ 12,000

Requirement

    1. Use JIT costing to prepare journal entries for the month, including the entry to close the Conversion costs account.

S3-13 *(L.OBJ. 4)* **Matching cost-of-quality examples to categories [5–10 min]**
Harry, Inc., manufactures motor scooters. Consider each of the following examples of quality costs.

    _____ **1.** Preventive maintenance on machinery

    _____ **2.** Direct materials, direct labor, and manufacturing overhead costs incurred to rework a defective scooter that is detected in-house through inspection

    _____ **3.** Lost profits from lost sales if company's reputation was hurt because customers previously purchased a poor-quality scooter

    _____ **4.** Costs of inspecting raw materials, such as chassis and wheels

    _____ **5.** Working with suppliers to achieve on-time delivery of defect-free raw materials

    _____ **6.** Cost of warranty repairs on a scooter that malfunctions at customer's location

    _____ **7.** Costs of testing durability of vinyl

    _____ **8.** Cost to re-inspect reworked scooters

Requirement

1. Indicate which of the following quality cost categories each example represents.
   - P   Prevention costs
   - A   Appraisal costs
   - IF Internal failure costs
   - EF External failure costs

■ Exercises

E3-14   *(L.OBJ. 1)* **Product costing in an activity-based costing system [15–20 min]**

Farragut, Inc., uses activity-based costing to account for its chrome bumper manufacturing process. Company managers have identified four manufacturing activities: materials handling, machine setup, insertion of parts, and finishing. The budgeted activity costs for 2010 and their allocation bases are as follows:

Activity	Total Budgeted Cost	Allocation Base
Materials handling	$ 6,000	Number of parts
Machine setup	3,300	Number of setups
Insertion of parts	54,000	Number of parts
Finishing	80,000	Finishing direct labor hours
Total	$ 143,300	

Farragut expects to produce 1,000 chrome bumpers during the year. The bumpers are expected to use 3,000 parts, require 20 setups, and consume 2,000 hours of finishing time.

Requirements

1. Compute the cost allocation rate for each activity.
2. Compute the indirect manufacturing cost of each bumper.

E3-15   *(L.OBJ. 1)* **Product costing in an activity-based costing system [15–20 min]**

Tyler Champs Corp. uses activity-based costing to account for its motorcycle manufacturing process. Company managers have identified three supporting manufacturing activities: inspection, machine setup, and machine maintenance. The budgeted activity costs for 2011 and their allocation bases are as follows:

Activity	Total Budgeted Cost	Allocation Base
Inspection	$ 6,600	Number of inspections
Machine setup	26,000	Number of setups
Machine maintenance	8,000	Maintenance hours
Total	$ 40,600	

Tyler Champs expects to produce 10 custom-built motorcycles for the year. The motorcycles are expected to require 30 inspections, 10 setups, and 200 maintenance hours.

Requirements

1. Compute the cost allocation rate for each activity.
2. Compute the indirect manufacturing cost of each motorcycle.

E3-16 *(L.OBJ. 1)* **Product costing in an activity-based costing system [20–30 min]**

Erickson Company manufactures wheel rims. The controller budgeted the following ABC allocation rates for 2010:

Activity	Allocation Base	Cost Allocation Rate	
Materials handling	Number of parts	$ 6.00	per part
Machine setup	Number of setups	600.00	per setup
Insertion of parts	Number of parts	24.00	per part
Finishing	Finishing direct labor hours	30.00	per hour

The number of parts is now a feasible allocation base because Erickson recently purchased bar-coding technology. Erickson produces two wheel rim models: standard and deluxe. Budgeted data for 2010 are as follows:

	Standard	Deluxe
Parts per rim	5.0	7.0
Setups per 1,000 rims	15.0	15.0
Finishing direct labor hours per rim	3.0	4.5
Total direct labor hours per rim	5.0	8.0

The company expects to produce 1,000 units of each model during the year.

Requirements

1. Compute the total budgeted indirect manufacturing cost for 2010.
2. Compute the ABC indirect manufacturing cost per unit of each model. Carry each cost to the nearest cent.
3. Prior to 2010, Erickson used a direct labor hour single-allocation-base system. Compute the (single) allocation rate based on direct labor hours for 2010. Use this rate to determine the indirect manufacturing cost per wheel rim for each model, to the nearest cent.

E3-17 *(L.OBJ. 1, 2)* **Using activity-based costing to make decisions [10 min]**

Fetch Dog Collars uses activity-based costing. Fetch's system has the following features:

Activity	Allocation Base	Cost Allocation Rate
Purchasing	Number of purchase orders	$57 per purchase order
Assembling	Number of parts	0.50 per part
Packaging	Number of finished collars	0.15 per collar

Each collar has 2 parts; direct materials cost per collar is $10. Suppose PetStart has asked for a bid on 20,000 dog collars. Fetch will issue a total of 175 purchase orders if PetStart accepts Fetch's bid.

Requirements

1. Compute the total cost Fetch will incur to purchase the needed materials and then assemble and package 20,000 dog collars. Also compute the cost per collar.
2. For bidding, Fetch adds a 35% markup to total cost. What total price will the company bid for the entire PetStart order?
3. Suppose that instead of an ABC system, Fetch has a traditional product costing system that allocates all costs other than direct materials at the rate of $9.20 per direct labor hour. The dog collar order will require 10,000 direct labor hours. What total price will Fetch bid using this system's total cost?
4. Use your answers to requirements 2 and 3 to explain how ABC can help Fetch make a better decision about the bid price it will offer PetStart.

Note: Exercise 3-16 must be completed before attempting Exercise 3-18.

E3-18   *(L.OBJ. 2)* **Using activity-based costing to make decisions [15–20 min]**

Refer to Exercise 3-16. For 2011, Erickson's managers have decided to use the same indirect manufacturing costs per wheel rim that they computed in 2010. In addition to the unit indirect manufacturing costs, the following data are budgeted for the company's standard and deluxe models for 2011:

	Standard	Deluxe
Sales price	900.00	1,040.00
Direct materials	34.00	51.00
Direct labor	48.00	54.00

Because of limited machine-hour capacity, Erickson can produce *either* 2,000 standard rims *or* 2,000 deluxe rims.

Requirements

1. If Erickson's managers rely on the ABC unit cost data computed in 3-16, which model will they produce? Carry each cost to the nearest cent. (All nonmanufacturing costs are the same for both models.)

2. If the managers rely on the single-allocation-base cost data, which model will they produce?

3. Which course of action will yield more income for Erickson?

Note: Exercises 3-16 and 3-18 must be completed before attempting Exercise 3-19.

E3-19   *(L.OBJ. 2)* **Activity-based management and target cost [10 min]**

Refer to Exercises 3-16 and 3-18. Controller Michael Bender is surprised by the increase in cost of the deluxe model under ABC. Market research shows that for the deluxe rim to provide a reasonable profit, Erickson will have to meet a target manufacturing cost of $454 per rim. A value engineering study by Erickson's employees suggests that modifications to the finishing process could cut finishing cost from $30 to $20 per hour and reduce the finishing direct labor hours per deluxe rim from 4.5 hours to 4 hours. Direct materials would remain unchanged at $51 per rim, as would direct labor at $54 per rim. The materials handling, machine setup, and insertion of parts activity costs also would remain the same.

Requirement

1. Would implementing the value engineering recommendation enable Erickson to achieve its target cost for the deluxe rim?

E3-20   *(L.OBJ. 3)* **Recording manufacturing costs in a JIT costing system [15–20 min]**

Lally, Inc., produces universal remote controls. Lally uses a JIT costing system. One of the company's products has a standard direct materials cost of $7 per unit and a standard conversion cost of $26 per unit.

During January 2011, Lally produced 575 units and sold 570. It purchased $6,800 of direct materials and incurred actual conversion costs totaling $14,000.

Requirements

1. Prepare summary journal entries for January.

2. The January 1, 2011, balance of the Raw and in-process inventory account was $40. Use a T-account to find the January 31 balance.

3. Use a T-account to determine whether Conversion costs are over- or underallocated for the month. By how much? Give the journal entry to close the Conversion costs account.

E3-21 *(L.OBJ. 3)* **Recording manufacturing costs in a JIT costing system [10–15 min]**
Smith produces electronic calculators. Suppose Smith's standard cost per calculator is $26 for materials and $65 for conversion costs. The following data apply to July production:

Materials purchased	$ 7,200	
Conversion costs incurred	18,500	
Number of calculators produced		250 calculators
Number of calculators sold		245 calculators

Requirements

1. Prepare summary journal entries for July using JIT costing, including the entry to close the Conversion costs account.
2. The beginning balance of Finished goods inventory was $1,400. Use a T-account to find the ending balance of Finished goods inventory.

E3-22 *(L.OBJ. 4)* **Classifying quality costs [5–10 min]**
Millan & Co. makes electronic components. Mike Millan, the president, recently instructed vice president Steve Bensen to develop a total quality control program. "If we don't at least match the quality improvements our competitors are making," he told Bensen, "we'll soon be out of business." Bensen began by listing various "costs of quality" that Millan incurs. The first six items that came to mind were:

a. Costs incurred by Millan customer representatives traveling to customer sites to repair defective products
b. Lost profits from lost sales due to reputation for less-than-perfect products
c. Costs of inspecting components in one of Millan's production processes
d. Salaries of engineers who are designing components to withstand electrical overloads
e. Costs of reworking defective components after discovery by company inspectors
f. Costs of electronic components returned by customers

Requirement

1. Classify each item as a prevention cost, an appraisal cost, an internal failure cost, or an external failure cost.

E3-23 *(L.OBJ. 4)* **Classifying quality costs and using these costs to make decisions [15–20 min]**
Cleary, Inc., manufactures door panels. Suppose Cleary is considering spending the following amounts on a new total quality management (TQM) program:

Strength–testing one item from each batch of panels	$ 70,000
Training employees in TQM	27,000
Training suppliers in TQM	32,000
Identifying suppliers who commit to on-time delivery of perfect-quality materials	55,000

Cleary expects the new program would save costs through the following:

Avoid lost profits from lost sales due to disappointed customers	$ 92,000
Avoid rework and spoilage	66,000
Avoid inspection of raw materials	56,000
Avoid warranty costs	25,000

Requirements

1. Classify each cost as a prevention cost, an appraisal cost, an internal failure cost, or an external failure cost.
2. Should Cleary implement the new quality program? Give your reason.

E3-24 *(L.OBJ. 4)* **Classifying quality costs and using these costs to make decisions [10–15 min]**

Kelley manufactures high-quality speakers. Suppose Kelley is considering spending the following amounts on a new quality program:

Additional 20 minutes of testing for each speaker	$ 675,000
Negotiating with and training suppliers to obtain higher-quality materials and on-time delivery	430,000
Redesigning the speakers to make them easier to manufacture	1,100,000

Kelley expects this quality program to save costs, as follows:

Reduce warranty repair costs	$ 310,000
Avoid inspection of raw materials	510,000
Avoid rework because of fewer defective units	780,000

It also expects this program to avoid lost profits from the following:

Lost sales due to disappointed customers	$ 850,000
Lost production time due to rework	279,000

Requirements

1. Classify each of these costs into one of the four categories of quality costs (prevention, appraisal, internal failure, external failure).
2. Should Kelley implement the quality program? Give your reasons.

■ Problems (Group A)

P3-25A *(L.OBJ. 1)* **Product costing in an ABC system [15–20 min]**

The Alright Manufacturing Company in Hondo, Texas, assembles and tests electronic components used in handheld video phones. Consider the following data regarding component T24:

Direct materials cost	$ 84.00
Activity costs allocated	?
Manufacturing product cost	$?

The activities required to build the component follow:

Activity	Allocation Base	Cost Allocated to Each Unit				
Start station	Number of raw component chasis	2	× $	1.40	= $	2.80
Dip insertion	Number of dip insertions	?	× $	0.40	=	12.00
Manual insertion	Number of manual insertions	12	× $	0.60	=	?
Wave solder	Number of components soldered	2	× $	1.40	=	2.80
Backload	Number of backload insertions	6	× $	?	=	5.40
Test	Testing hours	0.38	× $	80.00	=	?
Defect analysis	Defect analysis hours	0.12	× $	?	= $	3.60
Total					$	?

1. Fill in the blanks in both the opening schedule and the list of activities.

2. How is labor cost assigned to products under this ABC product costing system?

3. Why might managers favor this ABC system instead of Alright's older system, which allocated all conversion costs on the basis of direct labor?

P3-26A *(L.OBJ. 1, 2)* **Product costing in an ABC system [20–30 min]**

Allen, Inc., manufactures bookcases and uses an activity-based costing system. Allen's activity areas and related data follow:

Activity	Budgeted Cost of Activity	Allocation Base	Cost Allocation Rate
Materials handling	$ 22,000	Number of parts	$ 0.90
Assembly	3,000,000	Direct labor hours	12.00
Finishing	170,000	Number of finished units	3.90

Allen produced two styles of bookcases in April: the standard bookcase and an unfinished bookcase, which has fewer parts and requires no finishing. The totals for quantities, direct materials costs, and other data follow:

Product	Total Units Produced	Total Direct Materials Costs	Total Number of Parts	Total Assembling Direct Labor Hours
Standard bookcase	2,000	$ 29,600	82,000	3,300
Unfinished bookcase	2,600	28,600	86,000	2,000

Requirements

1. Compute the manufacturing product cost per unit of each type of bookcase.

2. Suppose that premanufacturing activities, such as product design, were assigned to the standard bookcases at $5 each, and to the unfinished bookcases at $4 each. Similar analyses were conducted of postmanufacturing activities such as distribution, marketing, and customer service. The postmanufacturing costs were $21 per standard bookcase and $18 per unfinished bookcase. Compute the full product costs per unit.

3. Which product costs are reported in the external financial statements? Which costs are used for management decision making? Explain the difference.

4. What price should Allen's managers set for unfinished bookcases to earn a unit profit of $19?

P3-27A *(L.OBJ. 1, 2)* **Comparing costs from ABC and single-rate systems [30–40 min]**

Willitte Pharmaceuticals manufactures an over-the-counter allergy medication. The company sells both large commercial containers of 1,000 capsules to health-care facilities and travel packs of 20 capsules to shops in airports, train stations, and hotels. The following information has been developed to determine if an activity-based costing system would be beneficial:

Activity	Estimated Indirect Activity Costs	Allocation Base	Estimated Quantity of Allocation Base
Materials handling	$ 115,000	Kilos	23,000 kilos
Packaging	204,000	Machine hours . .	2,125 hours
Quality assurance	118,000	Samples	2,000 samples
Total indirect costs	$ 437,000		

Other production information includes the following:

	Commerical Containers		Travel Packs	
Units produced	2,400	containers	41,000	packs
Weight in kilos	8,000		6,000	
Machine hours	1,500		500	
Number of samples	200		300	

Requirements

1. Compute the cost allocation rate for each activity.

2. Use the activity-based cost allocation rates to compute the activity costs per unit of the commercial containers and the travel packs. (*Hint*: First compute the total activity costs allocated to each product line, and then compute the cost per unit.)

3. Willitte's original single-allocation-base costing system allocated indirect costs to products at $158 per machine hour. Compute the total indirect costs allocated to the commercial containers and to the travel packs under the original system. Then compute the indirect cost per unit for each product.

4. Compare the activity-based costs per unit to the costs from the single-allocation-base system. How have the unit costs changed? Explain why the costs changed.

P3-28A (*L. OBJ. 3*) **Recording manufacturing costs for a JIT costing system [15–25 min]**
Low Range produces fleece jackets. The company uses JIT costing for its JIT production system.

Low Range has two inventory accounts: Raw and in-process inventory and Finished goods inventory. On February 1, 2010, the account balances were Raw and in-process inventory, $13,000; Finished goods inventory, $2,000.

The standard cost of a jacket is $45: $18 direct materials plus $27 conversion costs. Data for February's activities follow:

Number of jackets completed	16,000	Direct materials purchased	$ 283,000
Number of jackets sold	15,600	Conversion costs incurred	$ 533,000

Requirements

1. What are the major features of a JIT production system such as that of Low Range?

2. Prepare summary journal entries for February. Under- or overallocated conversion costs are closed to Cost of goods sold monthly.

3. Use a T-account to determine the February 28, 2010, balance of Raw and in-process inventory.

P3-29A (L.OBJ. 4) Analyzing costs of quality [20–30 min]

Lori, Inc., is using a costs-of-quality approach to evaluate design engineering efforts for a new skateboard. Lori's senior managers expect the engineering work to reduce appraisal, internal failure, and external failure activities. The predicted reductions in activities over the 2-year life of the skateboards follow. Also shown are the cost allocation rates for each activity.

Activity	Predicted Reduction in Activity Units	Activity Cost Allocation Rate Per Unit
Inspection of incoming materials	380	$ 46
Inspection of finished goods	380	25
Number of defective units		
discovered in-house	1,200	50
Number of defective units		
discovered by customers	275	74
Lost sales to dissatisfied customers	175	101

Requirements

1. Calculate the predicted quality cost savings from the design engineering work.

2. Lori spent $102,000 on design engineering for the new skateboard. What is the net benefit of this "preventive" quality activity?

3. What major difficulty would Lori's managers have in implementing this costs-of-quality approach? What alternative approach could they use to measure quality improvement?

■ Problems (Group B)

P3-30B (L.OBJ. 1) Product costing in an ABC system [15–20 min]

The Arial Manufacturing Company in Hondo, Texas, assembles and tests electronic components used in handheld video phones. Consider the following data regarding component T24:

Direct materials cost	$	82.00
Activity costs allocated		?
Manufacturing product cost	$	?

The activities required to build the component follow:

Activity	Allocation Base		Cost Allocated to Each Unit
Start station	Number of raw component chasis	3 × $ 1.30 =	$ 3.90
Dip insertion	Number of dip insertions	? × $ 0.25 =	6.75
Manual insertion	Number of manual insertions	13 × $ 0.70 =	?
Wave solder	Number of components soldered	3 × $ 1.30 =	3.90
Backload	Number of backload insertions	6 × ? =	2.40
Test	Testing hours	0.40 × $ 60.00 =	?
Defect analysis	Defect analysis hours	0.15 × ? =	$ 7.50
Total			$?

Requirements

1. Fill in the blanks in both the opening schedule and the list of activities.
2. How is labor cost assigned to products under this ABC product costing system?
3. Why might managers favor this ABC system instead of Arial's older system, which allocated all conversion costs on the basis of direct labor?

P3-31B *(L.OBJ. 1, 2)* **Product costing in an ABC system [20–30 min]**

Johnston, Inc., manufactures bookcases and uses an activity-based costing system. Johnston's activity areas and related data follow:

Activity	Budgeted Cost of Activity	Allocation Base	Cost Allocation Rate
Materials handling	$ 210,000	Number of parts	$ 0.90
Assembly	3,200,000	Direct labor hours	13.00
Finishing	180,000	Number of finished units	4.00

Johnston produced two styles of bookcases in May: the standard bookcase and an unfinished bookcase, which has fewer parts and requires no finishing. The totals for quantities, direct materials costs, and other data follow:

Product	Total Units Produced	Total Direct Materials Costs	Total Number of Parts	Total Assembling Direct Labor Hours
Standard bookcase	7,000	$ 29,500	80,500	3,200
Unfinished bookcase	7,600	28,700	84,500	2,100

Requirements

1. Compute the manufacturing product cost per unit of each type of bookcase.
2. Suppose that premanufacturing activities, such as product design, were assigned to the standard bookcases at $6 each, and to the unfinished bookcases at $2 each. Similar analyses were conducted of postmanufacturing activities such as distribution, marketing, and customer service. The postmanufacturing costs were $23 per standard bookcase and $14 per unfinished bookcase. Compute the full product costs per unit.
3. Which product costs are reported in the external financial statements? Which costs are used for management decision making? Explain the difference.
4. What price should Johnston's managers set for unfinished bookcases to earn a unit profit of $15?

P3-32B *(L.OBJ. 1, 2)* **Comparing costs from ABC and single-rate systems [30–40 min]**

Corbertt Pharmaceuticals manufactures an over-the-counter allergy medication. The company sells both large commercial containers of 1,000 capsules to health-care facilities and travel packs of 20 capsules to shops in airports, train stations, and hotels. The following information has been developed to determine if an activity-based costing system would be beneficial:

Activity	Estimated Indirect Activity Costs	Allocation Base	Estimated Quantity of Allocation Base
Materials handling	$ 98,000	Kilos	24,500 kilos
Packaging	200,000	Machine hours . .	2,000 hours
Quality assurance	118,000	Samples	2,000 samples
Total indirect costs	$ 416,000		

Other production information includes the following:

	Commerical Containers		Travel Packs	
Units produced	2,800	containers	43,000	packs
Weight in kilos	8,000		6,000	
Machine hours	1,800		600	
Number of samples	100		200	

Requirements

1. Compute the cost allocation rate for each activity.
2. Use the activity-based cost allocation rates to compute the activity costs per unit of the commercial containers and the travel packs. (*Hint*: First compute the total activity costs allocated to each product line, and then compute the cost per unit.)
3. Corbertt's original single-allocation-base costing system allocated indirect costs to products at $152 per machine hour. Compute the total indirect costs allocated to the commercial containers and to the travel packs under the original system. Then compute the indirect cost per unit for each product.
4. Compare the activity-based costs per unit to the costs from the single-allocation-base system. How have the unit costs changed? Explain why the costs changed as they did.

P3-33B *(L.OBJ. 3)* **Recording manufacturing costs for a JIT costing system [15–25 min]**
High Range produces fleece jackets. The company uses JIT costing for its JIT production system.

High Range has two inventory accounts: Raw and in-process inventory and Finished goods inventory. On March 1, 2010, the account balances were Raw and in-process inventory, $13,000; Finished goods inventory, $2,100.

The standard cost of a jacket is $34: $12 direct materials plus $22 conversion costs. Data for March's activities follow:

Number of jackets completed	17,000	Direct materials purchased	$ 196,500
Number of jackets sold	16,600	Conversion costs incurred	$ 469,000

Requirements

1. What are the major features of a JIT production system such as that of High Range?
2. Prepare summary journal entries for March. Under- or overallocated conversion costs are closed to Cost of goods sold monthly.
3. Use a T-account to determine the March 31, 2010, balance of Raw and in-process inventory.

P3-34B *(L.OBJ. 4)* **Analyzing costs of quality [20–30 min]**
Rachael, Inc., is using a costs-of-quality approach to evaluate design engineering efforts for a new wakeboard. Rachael's senior managers expect the engineering work to reduce appraisal, internal failure, and external failure activities. The predicted reductions in activities over the 2-year life of the wakeboards follow. Also shown are the cost allocation rates for each activity.

	Predicted Reduction in Activity Units	Activity Cost Allocation Rate Per Unit
Inspection of incoming materials	400	$ 43
Inspection of finished goods	400	25
Number of defective units discovered in-house	1,000	53
Number of defective units discovered by customers	325	74
Lost sales to dissatisfied customers	175	99

Requirements

1. Calculate the predicted quality cost savings from the design engineering work.
2. Rachael spent $101,000 on design engineering for the new wakeboard. What is the net benefit of this "preventive" quality activity?
3. What major difficulty would Rachael's managers have in implementing this costs-of-quality approach? What alternative approach could they use to measure quality improvement?

▪ Continuing Exercise

E3-35   This exercise continues the Sherman Lawn Service, Inc., situation from Exercise 2-36 of Chapter 2. Recall that Sherman completed a special landscaping job for Feimer's Fancy Fonts. If Sherman had used activity-based costing, Sherman's data about the job, including ABC information, would be as follows:

Feimer Job details:
Direct Materials $400
Direct Labor $900

ABC Costing Rates:
$350 per setup
$10 per plant

Requirements

1. Sherman uses one setup for the Feimer job and installs 20 plants. What is the total cost of the Feimer job?
2. If Feimer paid $2,500 for the job, what is the profit or loss under ABC?

▪ Continuing Problem

P3-36   This problem continues the Haupt Consulting, Inc., situation from Problem 2-37 of Chapter 2. Recall that Haupt allocated indirect costs to jobs based on a predetermined indirect cost allocation rate, computed as a percentage of direct labor costs. Haupt is now considering using an ABC system. Information about ABC costs follows:

Activity	Budgeted Cost of Activity	Allocation Base	Cost Allocation Rate
Design	$ 300,000	Number of designs	$ 10,000
Programming	760,000	Direct labor hours	200
Testing	200,000	Number of tests	5,000

Records for two clients appear here:

Job	Total Direct Costs	Total Number of Designs	Total Programming Direct Labor Hours	Number of Tests
Owen's Trains	$ 11,200	1	700	4
Caleigh's Cookies	500	2	100	5

Requirements

1. Compute the total cost of each job.
2. Is the job cost greater or less than that computed in Problem 2-37 for each job? Why?
3. If Haupt wants to earn profits equal to 25% of sales revenue, how much (what fee) should it charge each of these two clients?

Apply Your Knowledge

■ Decision Cases

Case 1. Harris Systems specializes in servers for workgroup, e-commerce, and ERP applications. The company's original job costing system has two direct cost categories: direct materials and direct labor. Overhead is allocated to jobs at the single rate of $22 per direct labor hour.

A task force headed by Harris's CFO recently designed an ABC system with four activities. The ABC system retains the current system's two direct cost categories. Thus, it budgets only overhead costs for each activity. Pertinent data follow:

Activity	Allocation Base	Cost Allocation Rate
Materials handling	Number of parts	$ 0.85
Machine setup	Number of setups	500.00
Assembling	Assembling hours	80.00
Shipping	Number of shipments	1,500.00

Harris Systems has been awarded two new contracts, which will be produced as Job A and Job B. Budget data relating to the contracts follow:

	Job A	Job B
Number of parts.............................	15,000	2,000
Number of setups............................	6	4
Number of assembling hours............	1,500	200
Number of shipments.......................	1	1
Total direct labor hours	8,000	600
Number of output units	100	10
Direct materials cost........................	$220,000	$30,000
Direct labor cost..............................	$160,000	$12,000

Requirements

1. Compute the product cost per unit for each job, using the original costing system (with two direct cost categories and a single overhead allocation rate).

2. Suppose Harris Systems adopts the ABC system. Compute the product cost per unit for each job using ABC.

3. Which costing system more accurately assigns to jobs the costs of the resources consumed to produce them? Explain.

4. A dependable company has offered to produce both jobs for Harris for $5,400 per output unit. Harris may outsource (buy from the outside company) either Job A only, Job B only, or both jobs. Which course of action will Harris's managers take if they base their decision on (a) the original system? (b) ABC system costs? Which course of action will yield more income? Explain.

Case 2. To remain competitive, Harris Systems' management believes the company must produce Job B-type servers (from Decision Case 1) at a target cost of $5,400. Harris Systems has just joined a B2B e-market site that management believes will enable the firm to cut direct materials costs by 10%. Harris's management also believes that a value-engineering team can reduce assembly time.

Requirement

1. Compute the assembling cost savings per Job B-type server required to meet the $5,400 target cost. (*Hint*: Begin by calculating the direct materials, direct labor, and allocated activity costs per server.)

■ Ethical Issue

Cassidy Manning is assistant controller at LeMar Packaging, Inc., a manufacturer of cardboard boxes and other packaging materials. Manning has just returned from a packaging industry conference on activity-based costing. She realizes that ABC may help LeMar meet its goal of reducing costs by 5% over each of the next three years.

LeMar Packaging's Order Department is a likely candidate for ABC. While orders are entered into a computer that updates the accounting records, clerks manually check customers' credit history and hand-deliver orders to shipping. This process occurs whether the sales order is for a dozen specialty boxes worth $80, or 10,000 basic boxes worth $8,000.

Manning believes that identifying the cost of processing a sales order would justify (1) further computerization of the order process and (2) changing the way the company processes small orders. However, the significant cost savings would arise from elimination of two positions in the Order Department. The company's sales order clerks have been with the company many years. Manning is uncomfortable with the prospect of proposing a change that will likely result in terminating these employees.

Requirement

1. Use the IMA's ethical standards to consider Manning's responsibility when cost savings come at the expense of employees' jobs.

■ Financial Statement Case—Amazon.com

This case is based on the **Amazon.com** annual report in Appendix A at the end of the book. Use it to answer the following questions.

Requirement

1. Review the description of **Amazon.com**'s business. Describe the benefits **Amazon.com** might derive from using JIT. Do you think it uses JIT? If so, for what part of its business? Explain your reasons for your answer.

■ Team Project

Bronson Shrimp Farms, in Brewton, Alabama, has a Processing Department that processes raw shrimp into two products:

- Headless shrimp
- Peeled and deveined shrimp

Bronson recently submitted bids for two orders: (1) headless shrimp for a cruise line and (2) peeled and deveined shrimp for a restaurant chain. Bronson won the first bid, but lost the second. The production and sales managers are upset. They believe that Bronson's state-of-the-art equipment should have given the company an edge in the peeled and deveined market. Consequently, production managers are starting to keep their own sets of product cost records.

Bronson is reexamining both its production process and its costing system. The existing costing system has been in place since 1991. It allocates all indirect costs based on direct labor hours. Bronson is considering adopting activity-based costing. Controller Heather Barefield and a team of production managers performed a preliminary study. The team identified six activities, with the following (department-wide) estimated indirect costs and cost drivers for 2010:

Activity	Estimated Total Cost of Activity	Allocation Base
Redesign of production process (costs of changing process and equipment)	$ 5,000	Number of design changes
Production scheduling (production scheduler's salary)..	6,000	Number of batches
Chilling (depreciation on refrigerators).............................	1,500	Weight (in pounds)
Processing (utilities and depreciation on equipment)	20,675	Number of cuts
Packaging (indirect labor and depreciation on equipment)	1,425	Cubic feet of surface exposed
Order filling (order-takers' and shipping clerks' wages)	7,000	Number of orders
Total indirect costs for the entire department	$41,600	

The raw shrimp are chilled and then cut. For headless shrimp, employees remove the heads, then rinse the shrimp. For peeled and deveined shrimp, the headless shrimp are further processed—the shells are removed and the backs are slit for deveining. Both headless shrimp and peeled and deveined shrimp are packaged in foam trays and covered with shrink wrap. Order-filling personnel assemble orders of headless shrimp as well as peeled and deveined shrimp.

Barefield estimates that Bronson will produce 10,000 packages of headless shrimp and 50,000 packages of peeled and deveined shrimp in 2010. The two products incur the following costs per package:

	Costs per Package	
	Headless Shrimp	Peeled and Deveined Shrimp
Shrimp	$3.50	$4.50
Foam trays	$0.05	$0.05
Shrink wrap	$0.05	$0.02
Number of cuts	12 cuts	48 cuts
Cubic feet of exposed surface ...	1 cubic foot	0.75 cubic foot
Weight (in pounds)	2.5 pounds	1 pound
Direct labor hours	0.01 hour	0.05 hour

Bronson pays direct laborers $20 per hour. Barefield estimates that each product line also will require the following *total* resources:

	Headless Shrimp		Peeled and Deveined Shrimp	
Design changes	1 change	for all	4 changes	for all
Batches	40 batches	10,000	20 batches	50,000
Sales orders	90 orders	packages	110 orders	packages

Requirements

Form groups of four students. All group members should work together to develop the group's answers to the three requirements.

(Carry all computations to at least four decimal places.)

1. Using the original costing system with the single indirect cost allocation base (direct labor hours), compute the total budgeted cost per package for the headless shrimp and then for the peeled and deveined shrimp. (*Hint*: First, compute the indirect cost allocation rate—that is, the predetermined overhead rate. Then, compute the total budgeted cost per package for each product.)

2. Use activity-based costing to recompute the total budgeted cost per package for the headless shrimp and then for the peeled and deveined shrimp. (*Hint*: First, calculate the budgeted cost allocation rate for each activity. Then, calculate the total indirect costs of (a) the entire headless shrimp product line and (b) the entire peeled and deveined shrimp product line. Next, compute the indirect cost per package of each product. Finally, calculate the total cost per package of each product.)

3. Write a memo to Bronson CEO Gary Pololu explaining the results of the ABC study. Compare the costs reported by the ABC system with the costs reported by the original system. Point out whether the ABC system shifted costs toward headless shrimp or toward peeled and deveined shrimp, and explain why. Finally, explain whether Pololu should feel more comfortable making decisions using cost data from the original system or from the new ABC system.

Quick Check Answers

1. *d* 2. *b* 3. *d* 4. *b* 5. *d* 6. *b* 7. *b* 8. *c* 9. *c* 10. *a*

 For online homework, exercises, and problems that provide you immediate feedback, please visit www.myaccountinglab.com.

Big Picture

Ch 1 Introduction to Management Accounting

- ⚷ Distinguish management accounting from financial accounting
- ⚷ The role and responsibilities of management accountants
- ⚷ Classify costs and prepare income statements for merchandising companies
- ⚷ Classify costs and prepare income statements and statements of cost of goods manufactured for manufacturing companies

Ch 2 Job Order Costing

- ⚷ Distinguish between job order and process costing
- ⚷ Record materials, labor, and overhead in a job order costing system
- ⚷ Record completion and sales of finished goods and adjust for under-/overallocated overhead
- ⚷ Calculate unit costs for service companies

Ch 3 Activity-Based Costing and Other Cost Management Tools

- ⚷ Develop activity-based costs and used activity-based management to determine target product costs
- ⚷ Record transactions in JIT systems
- ⚷ Use the four types of quality costs to make management decisions

Chapter 3: Demo Doc

■ Activity-Based Costing

Learning Objectives 1, 2

Home Beauty uses activity-based costing to account for its concrete countertop manufacturing process. Company managers have identified three manufacturing activities: mold assembly, mixing, and finishing. The budgeted activity costs for the year and their allocation bases are as follows:

Activity	Total Budgeted cost	Allocation Base
Mold assembly	$14,000	Number of parts
Mixing	$32,000	Number of batches
Finishing	$27,000	Number of direct labor hours

Home Beauty expects to produce 2,500 countertops during the year. The countertops are expected to use 10,000 parts, require 8,000 batches, and use 3,750 finishing hours.

Direct material cost is expected to be $40 per countertop and direct labor cost is expected to be $37.50 per countertop.

Requirements

1. Compute the cost allocation rate for each activity.

2. Compute the indirect manufacturing cost of each countertop.

3. Home Beauty would like to bid on selling 50 countertops to Ben Jones Builder. Assuming that Home Beauty requires a 30% markup on total costs, what bid price should Home Beauty use on the Ben Jones proposal?

Demo Doc Solution

Requirement 1

1 Develop activity-based costs (ABC)

Compute the cost allocation rate for each activity.

Part 1	Part 2	Part 3	Demo Doc Complete

For Home Beauty, we have the first few steps in developing an ABC system based on the information given in the question:

Home Beauty identifies three manufacturing activities:	Home Beauty estimates the total budgeted cost for each activity:	The allocation base for each activity is the primary cost driver for each. Home Beauty identifies these:	Home Beauty estimates the quantities of each cost driver allocation base:
Mold assembly	$14,000	# of parts	10,000 parts
Mixing	$32,000	# of batches	8,000 batches
Finishing	$27,000	# of direct labor hours	3,750 direct labor hours

To compute the cost allocation rate for each activity, divide the total budgeted cost of each activity by the estimated total quantity of the cost driver's allocation base:

$$\text{Mold assembly cost allocation rate} = \frac{\$14,000}{10,000 \text{ parts}} = \$1.40 \text{ per part}$$

$$\text{Mixing cost allocation rate} = \frac{\$32,000}{8,000 \text{ batches}} = \$4.00 \text{ per batch}$$

$$\text{Finishing cost allocation rate} = \frac{\$27,000}{3,750 \text{ direct labor hours}} = \$7.20 \text{ DL hour}$$

We will use the cost allocation *rate* for each activity to compute the indirect manufacturing cost of each countertop in the next requirement.

Requirement 2

1 Develop activity-based costs (ABC)

Compute the indirect manufacturing cost of each countertop.

Part 1	Part 2	Part 3	Demo Doc Complete

To calculate the indirect cost of manufacturing each countertop, we must calculate the average *quantity* of each cost allocation base used per countertop. The average quantity of each cost allocation base used per countertop is calculated by dividing the expected total used for each base by the number of countertops Home Beauty expects to produce.

We know from the question that Home Beauty expects to produce 2,500 countertops during the year, requiring 10,000 parts, 8,000 mixing batches, and 3,750 direct labor hours per countertop. Calculations are as follows:

$$\text{Parts per countertop} = \frac{10,000}{2,500} = 4 \text{ parts per countertop}$$

$$\text{Batches per countertop} = \frac{8,000}{2,500} = 3.2 \text{ batches per countertop}$$

$$\text{Finishing hours per countertop} = \frac{3,750}{2,500} = 1.5 \text{ DL hours per countertop}$$

To compute the indirect manufacturing cost of each countertop, multiply the average quantity of each activity cost allocation base used per countertop by the cost allocation rate (as determined in requirement 1).

Activity	Actual Quantity of Cost Allocation Base Used per Countertop		Activity Cost Allocation Rate		Standard Activity Cost per Countertop
Mold assembly	4	×	$1.40	=	$ 5.60
Mixing	3.2	×	$4.00	=	$12.80
Finishing	1.5	×	$7.20	=	$10.80
Total indirtect cost per countertop					$29.20

Shown another way, you can also solve this using total costs. We know that:

Total assembly cost	= $14,000
Total mixing cost	= $32,000
Total finishing cost	= $27,000
Total indirect manufacturing cost	= $73,000

You can calculate the indirect manufacturing cost per countertop by summing the total costs and dividing by the number of countertops produced during the year:

Indirect manufacturing cost of each countertop = $73,000/2,500
= $29.20 per countertop

This is also a good way to check your work.

So, Home Beauty estimates that each countertop will incur $29.20 in indirect manufacturing costs. This cost will help us compute the total cost of producing each countertop in the next requirement, which, among other decisions, helps management determine a sales price for each countertop.

Requirement 3

2 Use activity-based management (ABM) to achieve target costs

Home Beauty would like to bid on selling 50 countertops to Ben Jones Builder. Assuming that Home Beauty requires a 30% markup on total costs, what bid price should Home Beauty use on the Ben Jones proposal?

Part 1	Part 2	**Part 3**	Demo Doc Complete

To determine the bid price, Home Beauty must first determine the cost of producing one countertop. The cost would be direct materials + direct labor + indirect cost.

We know from the question that direct materials are expected to be $40 per countertop and direct labor is expected to be $37.50 per countertop. In requirement 2, we determined that indirect manufacturing costs amount to $29.20 per countertop. So, Home Beauty's cost of producing one countertop is:

$$\$40 + \$37.50 + \$29.20 = \$106.70 \text{ cost per countertop}$$

Because they require a 30% markup, the price that Home Beauty would charge per countertop is 130% of the cost:

$$\text{Price per countertop} = \$106.70 \times 130\% = \$138.71$$

Home Beauty is bidding on a job of 50 countertops, so the total bid price would be as follows:

$$\$138.71 \times 50 = \$6,935.50$$

Again, shown another way, we can reach the same computation using total costs. We know from the question that direct material cost is expected to be $40 per countertop and direct labor cost is expected to be $37.50 per countertop. For 2,500 countertops, direct material costs = 2,500 × $40 = $100,000, and direct labor cost = 2,500 × $37.50 = $93,750. So our total costs are:

Total assembly cost	= $ 14,000
Total mixing cost	= $ 32,000
Total finishing cost	= $ 27,000
Direct material cost	= $100,000
Direct labor cost	= $ 93,750
Total cost	= $266,750

We then determine the cost per unit as total cost divided by the number of units:

$$\text{Cost per unit} = \$266{,}750/2{,}500$$
$$= \$106.70 \text{ cost per countertop}$$

This matches the cost per countertop computed earlier in this requirement. Calculations would continue as before:

Price per countertop	$= \$106.70 \times 130\%$ markup
	$= \$138.71$
Total bid price	$= \$138.71 \times 50$ countertops
	$= \$6{,}935.50$

This is also a good way to check your work.

Part 1	Part 2	Part 3	**Demo Doc Complete**

4 Process Costing

Learning Objectives/ Success Keys

1 Prepare cost of production reports using the weighted-average costing method and prepare related journal entries

2 Prepare cost of production reports using the FIFO costing method and prepare related journal entries

In some instances, due to the type of manufacturing process required, manufactured products are incomplete or partially finished at the end of the period. To ensure accurate reporting, companies must assign costs to products that are partially and fully completed during a period. Tracing costs is different for a process costing system than that of a job order costing system (Chapter 2).

This chapter shows how to allocate production costs between partially and fully completed units in production. This occurs through preparation of a cost of production report prepared for a specific period of time. This report summarizes necessary calculations required in process costing through a four step process:

STEP 1: **Summarize the flow of physical units.**

- Record the physical flow of goods through the production process by determining the units to account for. Separate goods that are completely finished and transferred out from those partially complete that remain in ending work in process inventory.

STEP 2: **Compute output in terms of equivalent units.**

- Track the number of goods flowing through production separating calculations for transferred-in work, direct materials work and conversion work through the calculation of equivalent units of production.

STEP 3: **Compute the cost per equivalent unit.**

- Accumulate all costs incurred by cost category and calculate the cost per unit for producing one unit.

STEP 4: **Assign costs to units completed and to units still in ending Work in process inventory.**

- Allocate the total cost of production by assigning costs to either ending work in process (for partially completed units) or products transferred out (those products completed and either transferred out to another department or moved to finished goods).

There are two methods by which accountants allocate these costs: weighted average and FIFO. We cover weighted average first.

Process Costing—Weighted-Average Method

Process Costing: An Overview

We saw in Chapter 2 that companies like **Dell Computer, Boeing,** and Smart Touch Learning use job order costing to determine the cost of their custom goods and services. In contrast, **Shell Oil, Crayola,** and **Sony** use a series of steps (called *processes*) to make large quantities of similar products, called **process costing** systems. There are two methods for handling process costing: weighted average and FIFO. We will focus on the weighted-average method first.

To introduce process costing, we will look at the crayon manufacturing process. Let us separate **Crayola**'s manufacturing into three processes: Mixing, Molding, and Packaging. **Crayola** accumulates the costs of each process. The company then assigns these costs to the crayons passing through that process.

Suppose **Crayola**'s production costs incurred to make 10,000 crayons and the costs per crayon are as follows:

	Total Costs	Cost per Crayon
Mixing.............................	$200	$0.02
Molding...........................	100	0.01
Packaging.........................	300	0.03
Total cost........................	$600	$0.06

The total cost to produce 10,000 crayons is the sum of the costs incurred for the three processes. The cost per crayon is the total cost divided by the number of crayons, or

$$\$600/10{,}000 = \$0.06 \text{ per crayon}$$

Crayola Company uses the cost per unit of each process to

- control costs. The company will work on finding ways to cut costs if the actual process costs are more than planned process costs.
- set selling prices. The company wants the selling price to cover the costs of making the crayons and it also wants to earn a profit.
- calculate the ending inventory of crayons for the balance sheet and the cost of goods sold for the income statement.

As crayons are made, they move through the manufacturing process from one stage to another: Some crayons are in the Mixing process, some are in the Molding process, and others are in the Packaging Department at any point in time. Computing the crayons' cost becomes more complicated when units are still in

1   Prepare cost of production reports using the weighted-average costing method and prepare related journal entries

process. In this chapter, you will learn how to use process costing to calculate the cost of homogeneous products, using crayons as an example.

Exhibit 4-1 compares cost flows in

- a job order costing system for **Dell Computer**, and
- a process costing system for **Crayola**.

EXHIBIT 4-1 | **Comparison of Job Order Costing and Process Costing**

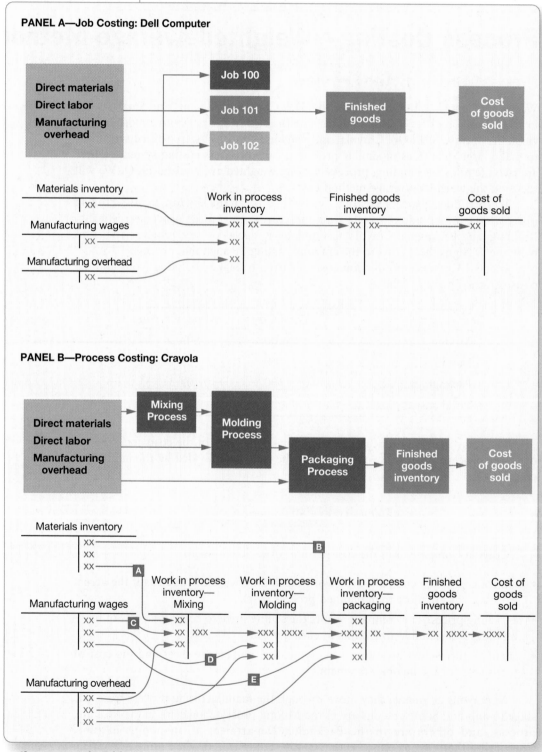

*Letters correspond to Exhibit 4-2

Panel A shows that **Dell**'s job order costing system has a single Work in process inventory control account. The Work in process inventory account in **Dell**'s general ledger is supported by an individual subsidiary cost record for each job (for example, each custom-built computer). Panel B summarizes the flow of costs for **Crayola**. Notice that

1. each process (Mixing, Molding, and Packaging) is a separate department and each department has its own Work in process inventory account.

2. direct materials, direct labor (manufacturing wages), and manufacturing overhead are assigned to Work in process inventory for each process that uses them.

3. when the Mixing Department's process is complete, the wax moves out of mixing and into the Molding Department. The Mixing Department's cost is also transferred out of the account titled Work in process inventory—Mixing into the account titled Work in process inventory—Molding.

4. when the Molding Department's process is complete, the finished crayons move from Molding into the Packaging Department. The cost of the crayons flows out of the account titled Work in process inventory—Molding and into another account called Work in process inventory—Packaging.

5. when production is complete, the boxes of crayons go into finished goods storage. The combined costs from all departments then flow into Finished goods inventory, but only from the Work in process inventory account of the *last manufacturing process*. (For **Crayola**, Packaging is the last department.)

6. Note that the letters in the charts correspond to the letters in the process costing reports you will see in future exhibits in this chapter.

Exhibit 4-2 on the next page illustrates this cost flow for **Crayola**.

Stop & Think...

When you make cookies, you may divide the production into two processes: Mixing and Baking. This is the same thought process manufacturing companies go through when dividing a manufacturing process into separate departments. Once separated, production costs are more easily allocated to each department through the resulting work in process account.

EXHIBIT 4-2 | **Flow of Costs in Production of Crayons**

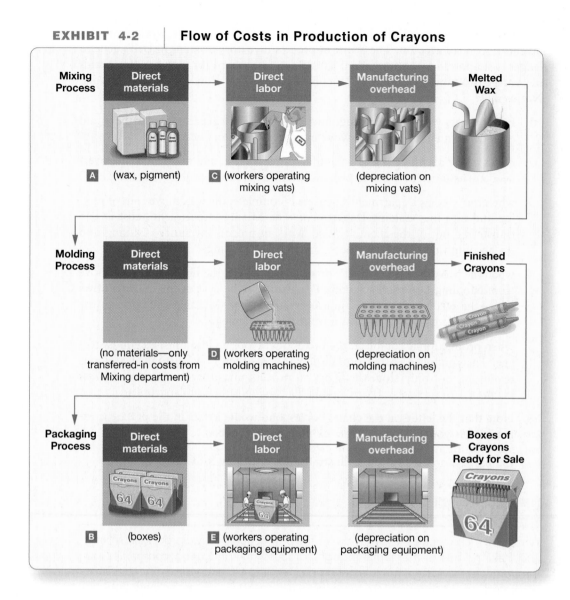

Building Blocks of Process Costing

Chapter 1 introduced the three types of manufacturing costs for any product: direct materials, direct labor, and manufacturing overhead. Recall that direct labor and manufacturing overhead together are called conversion costs, because by applying labor and overhead to materials we *convert* the materials into a product. These are the same cost components, whether we are using weighted-average or FIFO costing. Additionally, we use two building blocks for process costing:

• Conversion costs
• Equivalent units of production

However, many companies are highly automated, so direct labor is a small part of total manufacturing costs. Such companies often use only two categories:

- Direct materials
- Conversion costs (direct labor plus manufacturing overhead)

Combining direct labor and manufacturing overhead in a single category simplifies the accounting.

Completing most products takes time, so the **Crayola Company** may have Work in process inventories for crayons that are only partially completed. The concept of **equivalent units** allows us to measure the amount of work done on partially finished products during a period and to express it in terms of fully complete units of output. To simplify the concept, think of the idea that two halves make a whole. Therefore, two products that are 50% complete are the equivalent of one whole product, and six products that are 50% complete would be the equivalent of three whole products.

Equivalent units must be calculated at the end of the accounting period in a process costing system so that costs can be determined for each unit. Conversion costs and materials are often added differently to a product, which makes the calculations complex. In many instances, conversion costs are added equally throughout production but materials are added either at the beginning or at the end of the process. Therefore equivalent units must be calculated for each component and time frame. As an example, assume **Crayola**'s production plant has 10,000 crayons in ending Work in process inventory—Packaging. Each of the 10,000 crayons is 80% complete. If conversion costs are incurred evenly throughout the process, then getting 10,000 crayons 80% of the way through production is the same amount of work as getting 8,000 crayons 100% of the way through the process (10,000 × 80%). So, ending Work in process inventory—Packaging, has 8,000 equivalent units.

Number of partially complete units	×	Percentage of process completed	=	Number of equivalent units
10,000	×	80%	=	8,000

Use this formula when costs are incurred evenly throughout production. This is usually true for conversion costs. However, direct materials are often added at a specific point in the process. For example, **Crayola**'s wax is added at the beginning of production in the Mixing Department, and packaging materials are added at the end in the Packaging Department. How many equivalent units of wax, conversion costs, and packaging materials are in the ending inventory of 10,000 crayons?

Look at the time line in Exhibit 4-3.

The 10,000 crayons in Ending work in process inventory have

- 100% of their wax because wax was added at the very beginning. So, they have 10,000 equivalent units of wax. (10,000 × 100% have the wax material.)
- They have none of their boxes because that is the very last thing that happens in the Packaging Department. So, they have zero equivalent units of packaging materials. (The crayons have not been packaged yet.)
- 8,000 equivalent units of conversion costs that we completed earlier.

This example emphasizes an important point:

We must compute separate equivalent units for the following:
- Transferred-in costs (but not for the first department)
- Materials
- Conversion costs

EXHIBIT 4-3 | **Crayola Production Plant Time Line**

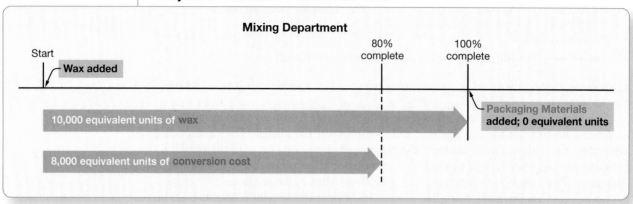

Process Costing in the First Department with No Beginning Inventory—Weighted-Average Method

To illustrate process costing, we will use Puzzle Me, a division of Smart Touch Learning that recycles calendars into educational jigsaw puzzles. Exhibit 4-4 illustrates the two major production processes:

- The Assembly Department applies the glue to cardboard and then presses a calendar page with various education plans onto the cardboard.
- The Cutting Department cuts the board into puzzle pieces and packages the puzzles in a box. The box is then moved to finished goods storage.

EXHIBIT 4-4 | **Flow of Costs in Producing Puzzles**

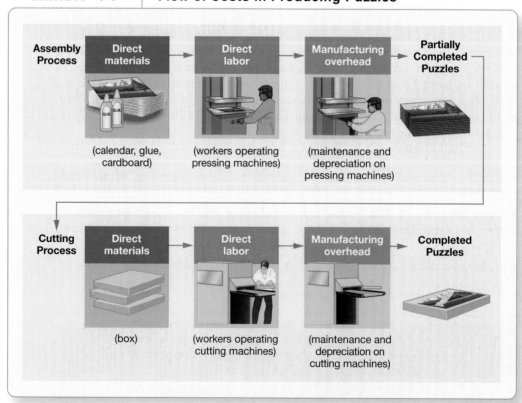

The production process uses materials, machines, and labor in both departments, and there are two Work in process inventory accounts: one for the Assembly Department and one for the Cutting Department.

During July, Puzzle Me incurred the following costs as shown in Exhibit 4-5:

EXHIBIT 4-5 | **Puzzle Me's Production Costs for July**

	Assembly Dept	Cutting Dept
Units:		
Beginning WIP-units	0	5,000
Started in production	50,000	must calculate
Transferred out in July	40,000	38,000
Beginning WIP-% complete (conversion)	N/A	60%
Ending WIP-% complete (conversion)	25%	30%
Costs:		
Beginning WIP-Transferred-in costs	$ 0	$22,000
Beginning WIP-Materials costs	$ 0	$ 0
Beginning WIP-Conversion costs	$ 0	$ 1,200
Direct materials	$140,000	$19,000
Conversion costs:		
Direct labor	$ 20,000	$ 3,840
Manufacturing overhead	$ 48,000	$11,000
Total conversion costs	$ 68,000	$14,840

The accounting period ends before all of the puzzle boards are made. Exhibit 4-6 shows a time line for the Assembly Department.

EXHIBIT 4-6 | **Puzzle Me's Assembly Department Time Line**

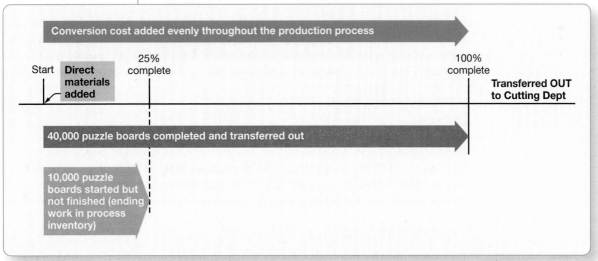

The four steps to process costing are as follows:

- Step 1: Summarize the flow of physical units.
- Step 2: Compute output in terms of equivalent units.
- Step 3: Compute the cost per equivalent unit.
- Step 4: Assign costs to units completed and to units still in ending Work in process inventory.

- "Units to account for" include the number of puzzle boards still in process at the beginning of July plus the number of puzzle boards started during July.
- "Units accounted for" shows what happened to the puzzle boards in process during July. We want to take the July costs incurred in each department and allocate them to the puzzle boards completed and to the puzzle boards still in process at the end of July.

EXHIBIT 4-7 | **Step 1: Summarize the Flow of Physical Units**

PUZZLE ME
Cost of Production Report—ASSEMBLY DEPT—Weighted Average
Month Ended July 31, 2010

Flow of Production		
1 Step 1: PHYSICAL FLOW	Whole Units	
Units to account for:		
Beginning work in process, June 30	0	
Started in production during July	50,000	
Total physical units to account for	50,000 A	

Of the 50,000 puzzle boards started by the Assembly Department in July, 40,000 were completed and transferred out to the Cutting Department. The remaining 10,000 are only partially completed. These partially complete units are the Assembly Department's Ending work in process inventory on July 31.

The Assembly Department time line in Exhibit 4-6 on the previous page shows that all direct materials are added at the beginning of the process. In contrast, conversion costs are incurred evenly throughout the process. This is because labor and overhead production activities occur daily. Thus, we must compute equivalent units separately for the following:

- Direct materials
- Conversion costs

The Assembly Department worked on 50,000 puzzle boards during July, as shown in Exhibit 4-7. As Exhibit 4-8 shows, 40,000 puzzle boards are now complete for both materials and conversion costs. Another 10,000 puzzle boards are only 25% complete. How many equivalent units did Assembly produce during July?

Stop & Think...

Think about those cookies we referred to in the previous Stop & Think. You can either make 50 cookies 60% of the way through the process or you can make 30 cookies 100% of the way through the process. Making 30 cookies 100% of the way is equivalent to 50 cookies 60% of the way through the process.

Equivalent Units for Materials

Equivalent units for materials total 50,000 because they are 100% through the process: All the direct materials have been added to all 50,000 units worked on during July.

Equivalent Units for Conversion Costs

Equivalent units for conversion costs total 42,500. Conversion costs are complete for the 40,000 puzzle boards completed and transferred out (B and E). But only 25% of the conversion work has been done on the 10,000 puzzle boards in Ending work in process inventory. Therefore, ending inventory represents only 2,500 equivalent units for conversion costs (**F**).

Exhibit 4-8 summarizes steps 1 and 2.

EXHIBIT 4-8 | **Step 2: Calculate Number of Equivalent Units**

PUZZLE ME
Cost of Production Report—ASSEMBLY DEPT—Weighted Average
Month Ended July 31, 2010

Flow of Production	Whole Units			
1 Step 1: PHYSICAL FLOW				
Units to account for:				
Beginning work in process, June 30	0			
Started in production during July	50,000			
Total physical units to account for	50,000 **A**			

2			Step 2: EQUIVALENT UNITS	
	Whole Units	Transferred-In	Direct Materials	Conversion Costs
Units accounted for:				
Completed and transferred out during July	40,000	N/A—first department	40,000 **B**	40,000 **E**
Ending work in process, July 31	10,000	N/A	10,000 **C**	10,000 × 25% = 2,500 **F**
Total physical units to be assigned costs	50,000 **A**	N/A	50,000 **D**	42,500 **G**

Our ultimate goal is to determine the cost per unit. This is a simple calculation of total cost divided by number of units. However in process costing, where there are partially finished goods, the denominator is equivalent units instead of total whole units as found in job order costing.

The cost per equivalent unit requires information about total costs and equivalent units. This information must be separated by direct materials and conversion costs. The computations are as follows:

$$\text{Cost per equivalent unit for direct materials} = \frac{\text{Total direct materials cost}}{\text{Equivalent units of materials}}$$

$$\text{Cost per equivalent unit for conversion costs} = \frac{\text{Total conversion cost}}{\text{Equivalent units for conversion}}$$

Exhibit 4-5, presented earlier, summarizes the total costs to account for in the Assembly Department. The Assembly Department has 50,000 physical units and $208,000 of costs to account for. Our next task is to split these costs between the following:

- 40,000 puzzle boards transferred out to the Cutting Department
- 10,000 partially complete puzzle boards that remain in the Assembly Department's Ending work in process inventory

In step 2, we computed equivalent units for direct materials (50,000) (**D**) and conversion costs (42,500) (**G**). Because the equivalent units differ, we must compute a separate cost per unit for direct materials and for conversion costs. Exhibit 4-5 shows that the direct materials costs are $140,000. Conversion costs are $68,000, which is the sum of direct labor ($20,000) and manufacturing overhead ($48,000).

The cost per equivalent unit of material is $2.80 (**K**), and the cost per equivalent unit of conversion cost is $1.60 (**O**), as shown in Exhibit 4-9.

EXHIBIT 4-9 | Step 3: Calculate Cost per Equivalent Unit

PUZZLE ME
Cost of Production Report—ASSEMBLY DEPT—Weighted Average
Month Ended July 31, 2010

Flow of Production					
1 Step 1: PHYSICAL FLOW	Whole Units				
Units to account for:					
Beginning work in process, June 30	0				
Started in production during July	50,000				
Total physical units to account for	50,000 A				

2			Step 2: EQUIVALENT UNITS		
	Whole Units	Transferred-In	Direct Materials	Conversion Costs	
Units accounted for:					
Completed and transferred out during July	40,000	N/A-first department	40,000 B	40,000 E	
Ending work in process, July 31	10,000	N/A	10,000 C	10,000 × 25% = 2,500 F	
Total physical units to be assigned costs	50,000 A	N/A	50,000 D	42,500 G	

3 Step 3: COST PER EQUIVALENT UNIT	Transferred-In	Direct Materials	Conversion Costs	Total Costs	
Units costs:					
Beginning work in process, June 30	N/A	$ 0 H	$ 0 L	$ 0 H+L=P	
Costs added during July (from Exhibit 4-5)	N/A	$140,000 I	$68,000 M	$208,000 I+M=Q	
Total costs to account for		$140,000 H+I=J	$68,000 L+M=N	$208,000 J+N=R	
Total equivalent units	N/A	÷ 50,000 D	÷ 42,500 G		
Cost per equivalent unit	N/A	$ 2.80 J÷D=K	$ 1.60 N÷G=O	$ 4.40 K+O=S	

We must determine how much of the $208,000 total costs to be accounted for by the Assembly Department should be assigned to

- the 40,000 completed puzzle boards that have been transferred out to the Cutting Department.
- the 10,000 partially completed puzzle boards remaining in the Assembly Department's Ending work in process inventory.

Exhibit 4-10 shows how to assign costs and depicts the completed cost of production report.

EXHIBIT 4-10 | Step 4: Assign Costs

PUZZLE ME
Cost of Production Report—ASSEMBLY DEPT—Weighted Average

Flow of Production					
1 Step 1: PHYSICAL FLOW	Whole Units				
Units to account for:					
Beginning work in process, June 30	0				
Started in production during July	50,000				
Total physical units to account for	50,000 A				

2			Step 2: EQUIVALENT UNITS		
	Whole Units	Transferred-In	Direct Materials	Conversion Costs	
Units accounted for:					
Completed and transferred out during July	40,000	N/A-first department	40,000 B	40,000 E	
Ending work in process, July 31	10,000	N/A	10,000 C	10,000 × 25% = 2,500 F	
Total physical units to be assigned costs	50,000 A	N/A	50,000 D	42,500 G	

3 Step 3: COST PER EQUIVALENT UNIT	Transferred-In	Direct Materials	Conversion Costs	Total Costs	
Units costs:					
Beginning work in process, June 30	N/A	$ 0 H	$ 0 L	$ 0 H+L=P	
Costs added during July (from Exhibit 4-5)	N/A	$140,000 I	$68,000 M	$208,000 I+M=Q	
Total costs to account for		$140,000 H+I=J	$68,000 L+M=N	$208,000 J+N=R	
Total equivalent units	N/A	÷ 50,000 D	÷ 42,500 G		
Cost per equivalent unit	N/A	$ 2.80 J÷D=K	$ 1.60 N÷G=O	$ 4.40 K+O=S	

4 Step 4: ASSIGN COSTS		Direct Materials	Conversion Costs	Total Costs	
Completed and transferred out during July		40,000 × $2.80 = $112,000 B×K	40,000 × $1.60 = $64,000 E×O	$176,000 T	
Ending work in process, July 31		10,000 × $2.80 = $ 28,000 C×K	2,500 × $1.60 = $ 4,000 F×O	$ 32,000 U	
Total costs accounted for				$208,000 R	

The total cost of completed puzzle boards for the Assembly Department is $176,000, as shown in Exhibit 4-10 (**T**). This amount will be reflected as transferred-in costs in the Work in process-Cutting account. The cost of the 10,000 partially completed puzzle boards in Ending work in process inventory is $32,000 (**U**), which is the sum of direct material costs ($28,000) (**C** × **K**) and conversion costs ($4,000) (**F** × **O**) allocated in Exhibit 4-10. This will be reflected as the ending balance in the Work in process-Assembly account.

Exhibit 4-10 has accomplished our goal of splitting the $208,000 total costs between the following:

The 40,000 puzzles completed and transferred out to the Cutting Department	$176,000 **T**
The 10,000 puzzles remaining in the Assembly Department's ending work in process inventory on July 31 ($28,000 + $4,000)......	32,000 **U**
Total costs of the Assembly Department	$208,000 **R**

Journal entries to record July costs placed into production in the Assembly Department follow (data from Exhibit 4-5):

(1) Work in process inventory—Assembly	208,000	
Materials inventory		140,000
Manufacturing wages		20,000
Manufacturing overhead		48,000
To assign materials, labor, and overhead cost to Assembly.		

The entry to transfer the cost of the 40,000 completed puzzles out of the Assembly Department and into the Cutting Department follows (Item **T** from Exhibit 4-10):

T Work in process inventory—Cutting	176,000	
Work in process inventory—Assembly		176,000
To transfer costs from Assembly to Cutting.		

After these entries are posted, the Work in process inventory—Assembly account appears as follows:

Work in process inventory—Assembly

Balance, June 30	—	Transferred to Cutting	176,000 **T**
(1) Direct materials	140,000		
(1) Direct labor	20,000		
(1) Manufacturing overhead	48,000		
U Balance, July 31	32,000		

Note that the ending balance is the same, $32,000, as item **U** on Exhibit 4-10's cost of production report.

See Exhibit 4-10 for the entire production report for the assembly department using weighted average for Puzzle Me.

Process Costing in a Second Department— Weighted-Average Method

Most products require a series of processing steps. In this section, we consider a second department—Puzzle Me's Cutting Department for July—to complete the picture of process costing.

EXHIBIT 4-11 | **Puzzle Me's Cutting Department Time Line—July**

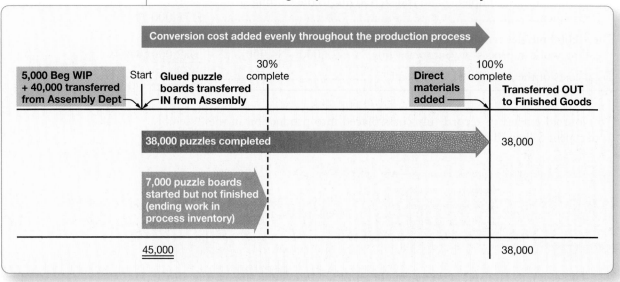

The Cutting Department receives the puzzle boards and cuts the board into puzzle pieces before inserting the pieces into the box at the end of the process. Exhibit 4-11 shows the following:

- Glued puzzle boards are transferred in from the Assembly Department at the beginning of the Cutting Department's process: 40,000 boards were transferred in (items **B**, **E**, and **T** from Exhibit 4-10) and 5,000 were already in process (Exhibit 4-5).
- The Cutting Department's conversion costs are added evenly throughout the process.
- The Cutting Department's direct materials (box) are added at the end of the process.

The cost of materials and conversion costs accumulated in the Assembly Department that are *transferred into* the Cutting Department are called **transferred-in costs**. Keep in mind that *direct materials* in the Cutting Department refers to the boxes added *in that department* and not to the materials (cardboard and glue) added in the Assembly Department, which are transferred-in costs. Likewise, *conversion costs* in the Cutting Department refer to the direct labor and manufacturing overhead costs incurred only in the Cutting Department.

Exhibit 4-5, presented earlier in the chapter, lists July information for both of Puzzle Me's departments. We will be referring to this data as we complete our Cutting Department allocation for July. Remember that Work in process inventory at the close of business on June 30 is both of the following:

- Ending inventory for June
- Beginning inventory for July

Exhibit 4-5 shows that Puzzle Me's Cutting Department started the July period with 5,000 puzzle boards partially completed through work done in the Cutting Department in June. During July, the Cutting Department started work on 40,000 additional puzzle boards that were received from the Assembly Department (which we calculated earlier in Exhibits 4-7 through 4-10, items **B**, **E**, and **T** from Exhibit 4-10).

The weighted-average method combines the Cutting Department's

- work done last month—Beginning work in process, containing 5,000 partially completed puzzle boards —to start the Cutting process
- work done in July to complete the 5,000 puzzle boards in Beginning work in process and to work on the 40,000 additional puzzle boards that were transferred in from the Assembly Department during July.

Thus, the **weighted-average process costing method** determines the average cost of all the Cutting Department's equivalent units of work on these 45,000 puzzle boards (5,000 Beginning work in process inventory + 40,000 transferred in from the previous department).

Just as we did for the Assembly Department, our goal is to split the total cost in the Cutting Department between the following:

- 38,000 puzzles that the Cutting Department completed and transferred out to Finished goods inventory. These products were completely converted and had all direct materials added. They are 100% complete.
- 7,000 partially completed puzzles remaining in the Cutting Department's ending Work in process inventory at the end of July. These puzzles had all their transferred-in costs and were 30% converted but had no materials added as this will occur at the end of the process.

We use the same four-step costing procedure that we used for the Assembly Department.

> **STEP 1: Summarize the Flow of Physical Units.** Let us account for July production, using the data about Physical units given in Exhibit 4-5 and the results from Exhibit 4-10 for the Assembly Department.

We must account for these 45,000 units **A** (beginning inventory of 5,000 plus 40,000 started). Exhibit 4-12 shows this:

EXHIBIT 4-12 | **Step 1: Summarize the Flow of Physical Units**

PUZZLE ME
Cost of Production Report—CUTTING DEPT—Weighted Average
Month Ended July 31, 2010

	Flow of Production	Whole Units
1	Step 1: PHYSICAL FLOW	
	Units to account for:	
	Beginning work in process, June 30 (from Exhibit 4-5)	5,000
	Started in production during July (from Exhibit 4-10, items **B** and **E**)	40,000
	Total physical units to account for	45,000 **A**

Exhibit 4-13 on the next page shows that, of the 45,000 units to account for **A**, Puzzle Me completed and transferred out 38,000 units. That left 7,000 units as Ending work in process in the Cutting Department on July 31.

Steps 2 and 3 will help us determine the costs of these units.

STEP 2: **Compute output in terms of Equivalent Units.** Exhibit 4-13 computes the Cutting Department's equivalent units of work. Under the weighted-average method, Puzzle Me computes the equivalent units for the total work done to date. This includes all the work done in the current period (July), plus the work done last period (June) on the Beginning work in process inventory.

| EXHIBIT 4-13 | Step 2: Calculate Number of Equivalent Units |

PUZZLE ME
Cost of Production Report—CUTTING DEPT—Weighted Average
Month Ended July 31, 2010

Flow of Production					
1 Step 1: PHYSICAL FLOW	Whole Units				
Units to account for:					
Beginning work in process,					
June 30 (from Exhibit 4-5)	5,000				
Started in production during					
July (from Exhibit 4-10, items B and E)	40,000				
Total physical units to account for	45,000 A				

			Step 2: EQUIVALENT UNITS		
2	Whole Units	Transferred-In	Direct Materials	Conversion Costs	
Units accounted for:					
Completed and transferred out during					
July (from Exhibit 4-5)	38,000	38,000 B	38,000 E	38,000 H	
Ending work in process, July 31	7,000	7,000 × 100% = 7,000 C	7,000 × 0% = 0 F	7,000 × 30% = 2,100 I	
Total physical units to be assigned costs	45,000 A	45,000 D	38,000 G	40,100 J	

We can see in Exhibit 4-13 that the total equivalent units with respect to

- transferred-in costs include all 45,000 units (D) because they are complete with respect to work done in the Assembly Department. The equivalent units for transferred-in costs will always be 100% of the units to account for, because these units must be 100% complete on previous work before coming to the Cutting Department.
- direct materials include only the 38,000 (G) finished puzzles because Cutting Department materials (boxes) are added at the end.
- conversion costs include the 38,000 (H) finished puzzles plus the 2,100 (I) puzzles (7,000 puzzle boards × 30%) that are still in process at the end of the month, or total of 40,100 equivalent units (J). Conversion work occurs evenly throughout the cutting process.

STEP 3: **Compute the Cost per Equivalent Unit.**

Exhibit 4-14 accumulates the Cutting Department's total costs to account for so that cost per equivalent unit can be calculated. In addition to direct material and conversion costs, the Cutting Department must account for transferred-in costs. Transferred-in costs are those costs that were incurred in a previous process (the Assembly Department, in this case) and brought into a later process (the Cutting Department) as part of the product's cost.

EXHIBIT 4-14 | **Step 3: Calculate Cost per Equivalent Unit**

PUZZLE ME
Cost of Production Report—CUTTING DEPT—Weighted Average
Month Ended July 31, 2010

Flow of Production					
1 Step 1: PHYSICAL FLOW	Whole Units				
Units to account for:					
Beginning work in process,					
June 30 (from Exhibit 4-5)	5,000				
Started in production during					
July (from Exhibit 4-10, items B and E)	40,000				
Total physical units to account for	45,000 A				

2		Step 2: EQUIVALENT UNITS			
	Whole Units	Transferred-In	Direct Materials	Conversion Costs	
Units accounted for:					
Completed and transferred out during					
July (from Exhibit 4-5)	38,000	38,000 B	38,000 E	38,000 H	
Ending work in process, July 31	7,000	7,000 × 100% = 7,000 C	7,000 × 0% = 0 F	7,000 × 30% = 2,100 I	
Total physical units to be assigned costs	45,000 A	45,000 D	38,000 G	40,100 J	

3 Step 3: COST PER EQUIVALENT UNIT	Transferred-In	Direct Materials	Conversion Costs	Total Costs
Units costs:				
Beginning work in process, June 30 (from Exhibit 4-5)	$ 22,000 K	$ 0 N	$ 1,200 S	$ 23,200 K+N+S=X
Costs added during July (from Exhibit 4-5)	$176,000 L (T from Exh. 4-10)	$19,000 O	$14,840 T	$209,840 L+O+T=Y
Total costs to account for	$198,000 K+L	$19,000 N+O=P	$16,040 S=T=U	$233,040 X+Y=Z
Total equivalent units	÷ 45,000 D	÷ 38,000 G	÷ 40,100 J	
Cost per equivalent unit	$ 4.40 K÷D=M	$ 0.50 P÷G=R	$ 0.40 U÷J=W	$ 5.30 M+R+W=t

Exhibit 4-14 shows that the Cutting Department's total cost to account for ($233,040) (Z) is the sum of the following:

- The cost incurred in June to start the Cutting process on the 5,000 puzzles in Cutting's Beginning work in process inventory ($22,000 (K) transferred in from the Assembly Department + $1,200 (S) conversion costs added in the Cutting Department to complete the 5,000 puzzles for a total cost of $23,200 (X)

- The costs added to Work in process inventory—Cutting during July {$176,000 L (T from Exh 4-10) transferred in from the Assembly Department + $19,000 (O) direct materials added in the Cutting Department + $14,840 (T) conversion costs added in the Cutting Department for a total cost of $ 209,840 (Y)}

The final part of step 3 is to calculate the cost per equivalent unit. For each cost category, we divide total cost by the number of equivalent units. Perform this computation for all cost categories: transferred-in costs, direct materials, and conversion costs. In this illustration the total cost per equivalent unit is $5.30 ($4.40 + $0.50 + $0.40) (t).

STEP 4: Assign Costs completed and to units still in ending Work in process inventory.

This step is illustrated in Exhibit 4-15 on the next page. This shows how Puzzle Me assigns the total Cutting Department costs ($233,040, from Exhibit 4-15) to

- units completed and transferred out to Finished goods inventory in July ($201,400) (U).
- units remaining in the Cutting Department's Ending work in process inventory, July 31 ($31,640) (V).

EXHIBIT 4-15 | **Step 4: Assign Costs**

PUZZLE ME
Cost of Production Report—CUTTING DEPT—Weighted Average
Month Ended July 31, 2010

Flow of Production					
1 Step 1: PHYSICAL FLOW	Whole Units				
Units to account for:					
Beginning work in process,					
June 30 (from Exhibit 4-5)	5,000				
Started in production during					
July (from Exhibit 4-10, items B and E)	40,000				
Total physical units to account for	45,000 A				

2			Step 2: EQUIVALENT UNITS		
	Whole Units	Transferred-In	Direct Materials	Conversion Costs	
Units accounted for:					
Completed and transferred out during					
July (from Exhibit 4-5)	38,000	38,000 B	38,000 E	38,000 H	
Ending work in process, July 31	7,000	7,000 × 100% = 7,000 C	7,000 × 0% = 0 F	7,000 × 30% = 2,100 I	
Total physical units to be assigned costs	45,000 A	45,000 D	38,000 G	40,100 J	

3 Step 3: COST PER EQUIVALENT UNIT	Transferred-In	Direct Materials	Conversion Costs	Total Costs
Units costs:				
Beginning work in process, June 30 (from Exhibit 4-5)	$ 22,000 K	$ 0 N	$ 1,200 S	$ 23,200 K+N+S=X
Costs added during July (from Exhibit 4-5)	$176,000 L (T from Exh. 4-10)	$19,000 O	$14,840 T	$209,840 L+O+T=Y
Total costs to account for	$198,000 K+T	$19,000 N+O=P	$16,040 S=T=U	$233,040 X+Y=Z
Total equivalent units	÷ 45,000 D	÷ 38,000 G	÷ 40,100 J	
Cost per equivalent unit	$ 4.40 K÷D=M	$ 0.50 P÷G=R	$ 0.40 U÷J=W	$ 5.30 M+R+W=t

4 Step 4: ASSIGN COSTS				
Completed and transferred out during July	38,000 × $4.40 = $167,200 B × M	38,000 × $0.50 = $19,000 E × R	38,000 × $0.40 = $15,200 H × W	$201,400 u
Ending work in process, July 31	7,000 × $4.40 = $ 30,800 C × M	0 × $0.50 = $ 0 F × R	2,100 × $0.40 = $ 840 I × W	$ 31,640 V
Total costs accounted for				$233,040 u+v

We use the same approach as we used for the Assembly Department in Exhibit 4-10. Multiply the number of equivalent units from step 2 by the cost per equivalent unit from step 3.

Exhibit 4-16 shows how Exhibit 4-15 divided the Cutting Department's costs.

EXHIBIT 4-16 | **Assigning Cutting Department Costs to Units Completed and Transferred Out, and to Ending Work in Process Inventory**

Total Cutting Department Costs

$233,040 Z

Puzzles Completed and Transferred Out to Finished Goods

Cutting Dept to Finished Goods Inventory

$201,400 u

Puzzles Still in Process on July 31

Cutting Dept, Work in Process Inventory

$31,640 v

The Cutting Department's journal entries previously recorded the $176,000 in transferred-in costs of puzzle boards from the Assembly Department into the Cutting Department on page 159.

The following entry records the Cutting Department's other costs during July (data from Exhibit 4-15):

(2) Work in process inventory—Cutting	33,840	
Materials inventory		19,000
Manufacturing wages		3,840
Manufacturing overhead		11,000
To assign materials and conversion costs to the		
Cutting Department.		

The entry to transfer the cost of completed puzzles out of the Cutting Department and into Finished goods inventory is based on the dollar amount in Exhibit 4-15:

u Finished goods inventory	201,400	
Work in process inventory—Cutting		201,400
To transfer costs from Cutting to Finished Goods.		

After posting, the key accounts appear as follows:

Work in process inventory—Assembly

Balance, June 30	—	Transferred to Cutting	176,000 T
(1) Direct materials	140,000		
Direct labor	20,000		
Manufacturing overhead	48,000		
U Balance, July 31	32,000		

Work in process inventory—Cutting

Balance, June 30	23,200	Transferred to Finished	
T Transferred in from Assembly	176,000	goods inventory	201,400 u
(2) Direct materials	19,000		
Direct labor	3,840		
Manufacturing overhead	11,000		
v Balance, July 31	31,640		

Finished goods inventory

Balance, June 30	0	
u Transferred in from Cutting	201,400	

Summary Problem 1

Process Costing Using the Weighted-Average Method

Stevie's Scissors had the following information about its Stamping and Assembly Departments:

	Stamping Dept	Assembly Dept
Units:		
Beginning WIP-units	0	5,000
Started in production	12,000	must calculate
Transferred out in June	10,000	11,000
Beginning WIP-% complete	N/A	40%
Ending WIP-% complete	20%	70%
Costs:		
Beginning WIP-Transferred-in costs	$ 0	$11,000
Beginning WIP-Materials costs	$ 0	$ 0
Beginning WIP-Conversion costs	$ 0	$ 1,290
Direct materials	$ 6,000	$ 2,750
Conversion costs:		
Direct labor	$ 6,800	$ 1,540
Manufacturing overhead	$14,000	$ 2,000
Total conversion costs	$20,800	$ 3,540

Materials are added at the beginning of the Stamping Department and at the end in the Assembly Department.

Requirements:

1. Prepare the cost of production report using the weighted-average method for the Stamping Department for the month of June.
2. Prepare the cost of production report using the weighted-average method for the Assembly Department.

Solutions

Requirement 1: Stamping Department

As discussed in the chapter, we must complete the four steps to prepare the cost of production report for each department. Since the Stamping Department is the first department, there are no transferred-in costs.

STEP 1: Summarize the Flow of Physical Units.

The company had no beginning WIP, so only the 12,000 units started in production must be accounted for. **A**

STEP 2: Compute output in terms of Equivalent Units. Of the total 12,000 units, 10,000 were completed and transferred to the Assembly Department in June. So, the 10,000 units received 100% of their materials and conversion costs in June. The 2,000 units remaining in WIP received all their materials, since materials are added at the beginning of this department. They are 20% complete, so they received only 20% equivalent work for conversion costs (2,000 units times 20% equals 400 units). **F**

STEP 3: Compute the Cost per Equivalent Unit.

For Direct materials, $6,000 in cost divided by 12,000 equivalent units from step 2 equals $0.50 per unit. **K**

For Conversion costs, $20,800 in cost divided by 10,400 equivalent units from step 2 equals $2.00 per unit. **O**

STEP 4: Assign Costs.

The calculations are shown in the following final production report.

STEVIE'S SCISSORS
Cost of Production Report—STAMPING DEPT
Month Ended June 30, 2010

Flow of Production					
1 Step 1: PHYSICAL FLOW	Whole Units				
Units to account for:					
Beginning work in process, May 31	0				
Started in production during June	12,000				
Total physical units to account for	12,000 **A**				

2		Step 2: EQUIVALENT UNITS			
	Whole Units	Transferred-In	Direct Materials	Conversion Costs	
Units accounted for:					
Completed and transferred out during June	10,000	N/A-first department	10,000 **B**	10,000 **E**	
Ending work in process, June 30	2,000	N/A	2,000 **C**	2,000 × 20% = 400 **F**	
Total physical units to be assigned costs	12,000 **A**	N/A	12,000 **D**	10,400 **G**	

3 Step 3: COST PER EQUIVALENT UNIT	Transferred-In	Direct Materials	Conversion Costs	Total Costs
Units costs:				
Beginning work in process, May 31	N/A	$ 0 **H**	$ 0 **L**	$ 0
Costs added during June	N/A	$6,000 **I**	$20,800 **M**	$26,800
Total costs to account for		$6,000 **H+I=J**	$20,800 **L+M=N**	$26,800
Total equivalent units	N/A	÷ 12,000 **D**	÷ 10,400 **G**	
Cost per equivalent unit	N/A	$ 0.50 **J÷D=K**	$ 2.00 **N÷G=O**	$ 2.50

4 Step 4: ASSIGN COSTS		Direct Materials	Conversion Costs	Total Costs
Completed and transferred out during June		10,000 × 0.50 = $5,000 **B×K**	10,000 × $2.00 = $20,000 **E×O**	$25,000 **P**
Ending work in process, June 30		2,000 × 0.50 = $1,000 **C×K**	400 × $2.00 = $ 800 **F×O**	$ 1,800 **Q**
Total costs accounted for				$26,800

Note that of the total costs incurred of $26,800 during June in the Stamping Department, $25,000 **P** of those costs have moved to the Assembly Department during June with the 10,000 units transferred. Therefore, $1,800 **Q** in costs remains with the 2,000 incomplete units in the Stamping Department.

Requirement 2: Assembly Department

For the Assembly Department we must also complete the four steps to prepare the cost of production report for each department. Since the Assembly Department is the second department, there are transferred-in costs from the Stamping Department to account for.

STEP 1: Summarize the physical flow of goods.

The company had 5,000 units of beginning WIP and 10,000 units were transferred in from the Stamping Department; a total of 15,000 units to account for in the Assembly Department in June **A**

STEP 2: Compute output in terms of Equivalent Units.

Of the total 15,000 units, 11,000 were completed and transferred to finished goods during June. So, the 11,000 units have 100% of their transferred-in materials, and conversion costs in June. The 4,000 units remaining in WIP received all their transferred-in costs, since the prior department's transferred-in work is added at the beginning of this department. These units have none of their materials because materials are added at the END of this department. They are 70% complete, so they received only 70% equivalent work for conversion costs (2,800 units). Material equivalent units and conversion cost equivalent units are totaled in Step 2 of the cost of production report.

STEP 3: Compute the Cost per Equivalent Unit.

For Transferred-in costs, $36,000 in costs divided by 15,000 equivalent units equals $2.40 per unit. **M**

For Direct materials, $2,750 in cost divided by 11,000 equivalent units from step 2 equals $0.25 per unit. **R**

For Conversion costs, $4,830 in cost divided by 13,800 equivalent units from step 2 equals $0.35 per unit. **W**

The cost to manufacture one unit is $3.00.

STEP 4: Assign costs.

The calculations are shown in the following final production report.

STEVIE'S SCISSORS
Cost of Production Report—ASSEMBLY DEPT
Month Ended June 30, 2010

	Flow of Production	Whole Units			
1	Step 1: PHYSICAL FLOW				
	Units to account for:				
	Beginning work in process, May 31	5,000			
	Started in production during June	10,000			
	Total physical units to account for	15,000 **A**			

2			Step 2: EQUIVALENT UNITS		
		Whole Units	Transferred-In	Direct Materials	Conversion Costs
	Units accounted for:				
	Completed and transferred out during June	11,000	11,000 **B**	11,000 **E**	11,000 **H**
	Ending work in process, June 30	4,000	4,000 × 100% = 4,000 **C**	4,000 × 0% = 0 **F**	4,000 × 70% = 2,800 **I**
	Total physical units to be assigned costs	15,000 **A**	15,000 **D**	11,000 **G**	13,800 **J**

3	Step 3: COST PER EQUIVALENT UNIT	Transferred-In	Direct Materials	Conversion Costs	Total Costs
	Units costs:				
	Beginning work in process, May 31	$11,000 **K**	$ 0 **N**	$1,290 **S**	$12,290
	Costs added during June	25,000 **L P from Stamping dept.**	$2,750 **O**	$3,540 **T**	$31,290
	Total costs to account for	$36,000 **K+L**	$2,750 **N+O=P**	$4,830 **S=T=U**	$43,580
	Total equivalent units	÷ 15,000 **D**	÷ 11,000 **Q**	÷ 13,800 **V**	
	Cost per equivalent unit	$ 2.40 **K÷D=M**	$ 0.25 **P÷Q=R**	$ 0.35 **U÷V=W**	$ 3.00

4	Step 4: ASSIGN COSTS				
	Completed and transferred out during June	11,000 × $2.40 = $26,400 **B×M**	11,000 × $0.25 = $2,750 **E×R**	11,000 × $0.35 = $3,850 **H×W**	$33,000 **X**
	Ending work in process, June 30	4,000 × $2.40 = $ 9,600 **C×M**	0 × $0.25 = $ 0 **F×R**	2,800 × $0.35 = $ 980 **I×W**	$10,580 **Y**
	Total costs accounted for				$43,580

Note that of the total costs incurred of $43,580 during June in the Assembly Department, $33,000 (**X**) of those costs have moved to finished goods during June with the 11,000 units transferred. The remaining $10,580 (**Y**) in costs remains with the 4,000 partially completed units in the Work in process ending inventory for the Assembly Department.

Process Costing in the First Department with No Beginning Inventory—FIFO Method

FIFO process costing differs from weighted average process costing in that it weights the cost of beginning inventory separately from the cost of goods started and finished during a period. We will now illustrate the difference in Puzzle Me's results using FIFO process costing. To refresh your memory, review the flow of costs listed in Exhibit 4-4 on page 154.

2 Prepare cost of production reports using the FIFO costing method and prepare related journal entries

The production process uses materials, machines, and labor in both departments, and there are two Work in process inventory accounts: one for the Assembly Department and one for the Cutting Department.

Puzzle Me's July costs are reproduced from Exhibit 4-5 below in Exhibit 4-17:

EXHIBIT 4-17 | **Puzzle Me's Production Costs for July**

	Assembly Dept	Cutting Dept
Units:		
Beginning WIP-units	0	5,000
Started in production	50,000	must calculate
Transferred out in July	40,000	38,000
Beginning WIP-% complete (conversion)	N/A	60%
Ending WIP-% complete (conversion)	25%	30%
Costs:		
Beginning WIP-Transferred-in costs	$ 0	$22,000
Beginning WIP-Materials costs	$ 0	$ 0
Beginning WIP-Conversion costs	$ 0	$ 1,200
Direct materials	$140,000	$19,000
Conversion costs:		
Direct labor	$ 20,000	$ 3,840
Manufacturing overhead	$ 48,000	$11,000
Total conversion costs	$ 68,000	$14,840

reproduced from Exhibit 4-5 on page 155.

The accounting period ends before all of the puzzle boards are made, so there are partially completed puzzle boards in ending inventory. Exhibit 4-18 shows an exact reproduction of the Exhibit 4-6 time line for the Assembly Department. Note again that direct materials are added at the beginning of the process.

EXHIBIT 4-18 | **Puzzle Me's Assembly Department Time Line**

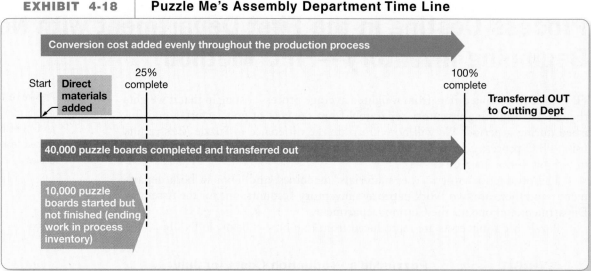

reproduced from Exhibit 4-6 on page 155.

Recall the four steps to process costing are as follows:

- Step 1: Summarize the flow of physical units.
- Step 2: Compute output in terms of equivalent units.
- Step 3: Compute the cost per equivalent unit.
- Step 4: Assign costs to units completed and to units still in ending Work in process inventory.

- "Units to account for" include the number of puzzle boards still in process at the beginning of July plus the number of puzzle boards started during July.
- "Units accounted for" shows what happened to the puzzle boards in process during July. The July costs incurred in each department need to be allocated to two accounts: the puzzle boards completed and transferred out to the next processing department and to puzzle boards partially completed in ending inventory.

Puzzle Me had no beginning inventory in the Assembly department on July 1. Of the 50,000 puzzle boards started by the Assembly Department in July, 40,000 were completed and transferred out to the Cutting Department. The remaining 10,000 were only partially completed. These partially complete units are the Assembly Department's Ending work in process inventory on July 31.

The materials and conversion costs are added to the process separately, as before. The Assembly Department time line in Exhibit 4-18 shows that all direct materials are added at the beginning of the process. In contrast, conversion costs are incurred evenly throughout the process. This is because labor and overhead production activities occur daily. Thus, we must compute equivalent units separately for the following:

- Direct materials
- Conversion costs

The Assembly Department worked on 50,000 (**A**) puzzle boards during July, as shown in Exhibit 4-19.

EXHIBIT 4-19 | **Step 1: Summarize the Flow of Physical Units**

PUZZLE ME
Cost of Production Report—ASSEMBLY DEPT—FIFO
Month Ended July 31, 2010

Flow of Production		
Step 1: PHYSICAL FLOW	Whole Units	
Units to account for:		
Beginning work in process, June 30	0	
Started in production during July	50,000	
Total physical units to account for	50,000 A	

As Exhibit 4-20 shows, 40,000 (B and E) puzzle boards are now complete for both materials and conversion costs. Another 10,000 (C and F) puzzle boards are only 25% complete. How many equivalent units did Assembly produce during July?

Equivalent Units for Materials

Equivalent units for materials total 50,000 because all direct materials are added at the beginning of the process in July.

Equivalent Units for Conversion Costs

Equivalent units for conversion costs total 42,500:

- Conversion costs are complete for the 40,000 (B and E) puzzle boards started and completed during July. But only 25% of the conversion work has been done on the 10,000 puzzle boards in Ending work in process inventory. Therefore, ending inventory represents only 2,500 (F) equivalent units for conversion costs.

Exhibit 4-20 summarizes steps 1 and 2.

EXHIBIT 4-20 | **Step 2: Calculate Number of Equivalent Units**

PUZZLE ME
Cost of Production Report—ASSEMBLY DEPT—FIFO
Month Ended July 31, 2010

Flow of Production				
1 Step 1: PHYSICAL FLOW	Whole Units			
Units to account for:				
Beginning work in process, June 30	0			
Started in production during July	50,000			
Total physical units to account for	50,000 A			

2		Step 2: EQUIVALENT UNITS		
	Whole Units	Transferred-In	Direct Materials	Conversion Costs
Units accounted for:				
Beginning work in process, June 30	0	0	0	0
Started and completed during July	40,000	N/A-first department	40,000	40,000
Completed and transferred out during July	40,000	N/A-first department	40,000 B	40,000 E
Ending work in process, July 31	10,000	N/A	10,000 C	10,000 × 25% = 2,500 F
Total physical units to be assigned costs	50,000 A	N/A	50,000 D	42,500 G

The cost per equivalent unit requires information about total costs and equivalent units. The computations are as follows:

$$\text{Cost per equivalent unit for direct materials} = \frac{\text{Total direct materials cost}}{\text{Equivalent units of materials}}$$

$$\text{Cost per equivalent unit for conversion costs} = \frac{\text{Total conversion cost}}{\text{Equivalent units for conversion}}$$

Exhibit 4-17 summarizes the total costs to account for in the Assembly Department. The Assembly Department has 50,000 physical units and $208,000 (Q) of costs to account for.

EXHIBIT 4-21 | **Step 3: Calculate Cost per Equivalent Unit**

PUZZLE ME					
Cost of Production Report—ASSEMBLY DEPT—FIFO					
Month Ended July 31, 2010					

Flow of Production					
1 Step 1: PHYSICAL FLOW	Whole Units				
Units to account for:					
Beginning work in process, June 30	0				
Started in production during July	50,000				
Total physical units to account for	50,000 A				

2			Step 2: EQUIVALENT UNITS		
	Whole Units	Transferred-In	Direct Materials	Conversion Costs	
Units accounted for:					
Beginning work in process, June 30	0	0	0	0	
Started and completed during July	40,000	N/A-first department	40,000	40,000	
Completed and transferred out during July	40,000	N/A-first department	40,000 B	40,000 E	
Ending work in process, July 31	10,000	N/A	10,000 C	10,000 × 25% = 2,500 F	
Total physical units to be assigned costs	50,000 A	N/A	50,000 D	42,500 G	

3 Step 3: COST PER EQUIVALENT UNIT	Transferred-In	Direct Materials	Conversion Costs	Total Costs	
Units costs:					
Beginning work in process, June 30	N/A	$ 0 H	$ 0 L	$ 0 H+L=P	
Costs added during July (from Exhibit 4-5)	N/A	$140,000 I	$68,000 M	$208,000 I+M=Q	
Total costs to account for		$140,000 H+I=J	$68,000 L+M=N	$208,000 J+N=R	
Total equivalent units	N/A	÷ 50,000 D	÷ 42,500 G		
Cost per equivalent unit	N/A	$ 2.80 J÷D=K	$ 1.60 N÷G=O	$ 4.40 K+O=S	

Our next task is to split these costs between the following:

- 40,000 (B and E) puzzle boards transferred out to the Cutting Department (recall zero beginning inventory)
- 10,000 (C and F) partially complete puzzle boards that remain in the Assembly Department's Ending work in process inventory

In step 2, we computed equivalent units for direct materials (50,000) (D) and conversion costs (42,500) (G). Because the equivalent units differ, we must compute a separate cost per unit for direct materials and for conversion costs. Exhibit 4-17 shows that the direct materials costs are $140,000 (I). Conversion costs are $68,000 (M), which is the sum of direct labor ($20,000) and manufacturing overhead ($48,000).

The cost per equivalent unit of material is $2.80 (K), and the cost per equivalent unit of conversion cost is $1.60 (O), as shown in Exhibit 4-21.

We must determine how much of the $208,000 total costs to be accounted for by the Assembly Department should be assigned to

- the 40,000 completed puzzle boards that have been transferred out to the Cutting Department.
- the 10,000 partially completed puzzle boards remaining in the Assembly Department's Ending work in process inventory.

Exhibit 4-22 on the following page shows how to assign costs.

EXHIBIT 4-22 | Step 4: Assign Costs

PUZZLE ME
Cost of Production Report—ASSEMBLY DEPT—FIFO
Month Ended July 31, 2010

Flow of Production

1 Step 1: PHYSICAL FLOW

Units to account for:	Whole Units	
Beginning work in process, June 30	0	
Started in production during July	50,000	
Total physical units to account for	50,000	A

2 Step 2: EQUIVALENT UNITS

Units accounted for:	Whole Units	Transferred-In	Direct Materials	Conversion Costs
Beginning work in process, June 30	0	0	0	0
Started and completed during July	40,000	N/A–first department	40,000	40,000
Completed and transferred out during July	40,000	N/A–first department	40,000 **B**	40,000 **E**
Ending work in process, July 31	10,000	N/A	10,000 **C**	10,000 × 25% = 2,500 **F**
Total physical units to be assigned costs	50,000 **A**	N/A	50,000 **D**	42,500 **G**

3 Step 3: COST PER EQUIVALENT UNIT

Units costs:	Transferred-In	Direct Materials	Conversion Costs	Total Costs
Beginning work in process, June 30	N/A	$ 0 **H**	$ 0 **L**	$ 0 **H+L=P**
Costs added during July (from Exhibit 4-5)	N/A	$140,000 **I**	$68,000 **M**	$208,000 **I+M=Q**
Total costs to account for		$140,000 **H+I=J**	$68,000 **L+M=N**	$208,000 **J+N=R**
Total equivalent units	N/A	÷ 50,000 **D**	÷ 42,500 **G**	
Cost per equivalent unit	N/A	$ 2.80 **J÷D=K**	$ 1.60 **N÷G=O**	$ 4.40 **K+O=S**

4 Step 4: ASSIGN COSTS

	Direct Materials	Conversion Costs	Total Costs
Beginning work in process, June 30	0	0	0
Costs to complete June 30 inventory	0 × $2.80 = 0	0 × $1.60 = 0	0
Started and completed during July	40,000 × $2.80 = $112,000 **B×K**	40,000 × $1.60 = $64,000 **E×O**	$176,000
Completed and transferred out during July	$112,000	$64,000	$176,000 **T**
Ending work in process, July 31	10,000 × $2.80 = $ 28,000 **C×K**	2,500 × $1.60 = $ 4,000 **F×O**	$ 32,000 **U**
Total costs accounted for			$208,000 **R**

The total cost of completed puzzle boards for the Assembly Department is $176,000 **T**, as shown in Exhibit 4-22. The cost of the 10,000 partially completed puzzle boards in Ending work in process inventory is $32,000 (see letter **U**), which is the sum of direct material costs ($28,000) (**C** × **K**) and conversion costs ($4,000) (**F** × **O**) allocated in Exhibit 4-22.

Exhibit 4-22 has accomplished our goal of splitting the $208,000 total cost between the following:

The 40,000 puzzles started, completed, and transferred out to the Cutting Department...	$176,000 **T**
The 10,000 puzzles remaining in the Assembly Department's ending work in process inventory on July 31 ($28,000 + $4,000)......	32,000 **U**
Total costs of the Assembly Department	$208,000 **R**

Journal entries to record July costs placed into production in the Assembly Department follow (data from Exhibit 4-17):

(1) Work in process inventory—Assembly		208,000	
Materials inventory			140,000
Manufacturing wages			20,000
Manufacturing overhead			48,000
To assign materials, labor, and overhead cost to Assembly.			

The entry to transfer the cost of the 40,000 completed puzzles out of the Assembly Department and into the Cutting Department follows (Item **T** from Exhibit 4-22):

T	Work in process inventory—Cutting	176,000	
	Work in process inventory—Assembly		176,000
	To transfer costs from Assembly to Cutting.		

After these entries are posted, the Work in process inventory—Assembly account appears as follows:

Work in process inventory—Assembly

	Balance, June 30	—	Transferred to Cutting	176,000	**T**
	Direct materials	140,000			
(1)	Direct labor	20,000			
	Manufacturing overhead	48,000			
U	Balance, July 31	32,000			

Note that the ending balance is the same, $32,000, as item **U** on Exhibit 4-22's cost of production report. Also note that the results are EXACTLY the same as the weighted-average method (see Exhibit 4-10). Why are they the same? There was no beginning inventory in the Assembly Department. If there was, the results would likely differ, as they do in the Cutting Department (see the next section).

Process Costing in a Second Department—FIFO Method

Most products require a series of processing steps. In this section, we consider a second department—Puzzle Me's Cutting Department for July—to complete the picture of process costing under the FIFO method of handling costs in a process costing system.

EXHIBIT 4-23 | **Puzzle Me's Cutting Department Time Line**

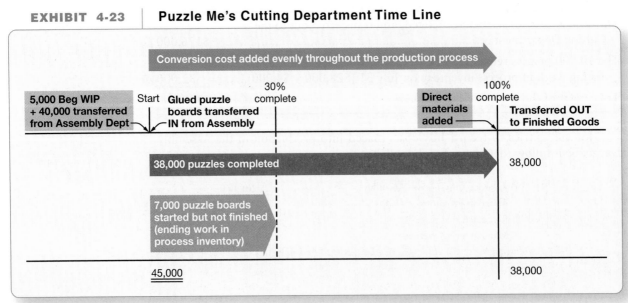

The Cutting Department receives the puzzle boards from the Assembly Department and cuts the board into puzzle pieces before inserting the pieces into the box (packaging) at the end of the process. Exhibit 4-23 shows the following:

- Glued puzzle boards are transferred in from the Assembly Department at the beginning of the Cutting Department's process.
- The Cutting Department's conversion costs are added evenly throughout the process.
- The Cutting Department's direct materials (box) are added at the end of the process.

Keep in mind that *direct materials* in the Cutting Department refers to the boxes added *in that department* and not to the materials (cardboard and glue) added in the Assembly Department(*transferred-in costs*). The materials from Assembly that are *transferred into* the Cutting Department are called *transferred-in costs*. Likewise, *conversion costs* in the Cutting Department refers to the direct labor and manufacturing overhead costs incurred only in the Cutting Department.

Exhibit 4-17 on page 169 lists July information for both of Puzzle Me's departments. We will be referring to this data as we complete our Cutting Department allocation for July. Remember that Work in process inventory at the close of business on June 30 is both of the following:

- Ending inventory for June
- Beginning inventory for July

Exhibit 4-17 shows that Puzzle Me's Cutting Department started the July period with 5,000 puzzle boards partially completed through work done in the Cutting Department in June. During July, the Cutting Department started work on 40,000 additional puzzle boards that were received from the Assembly Department (which we calculated earlier in Exhibits 4-19 through 4-22).

The FIFO method separates the Cutting Department work into three categories:

- work done last month—Beginning work in process—to start the Cutting process on the 5,000 puzzle boards that were in Beginning work in process inventory.
- work done in July to complete the 5,000 puzzle boards in Beginning inventory.
- work on the 40,000 additional puzzle boards that were transferred in from the Assembly Department during July.

Thus, the **FIFO method** determines the cost of each part of the Cutting Department's equivalent units of work on these 45,000 puzzle boards.

Just as we did for the Assembly Department, our goal is to split the total cost in the Cutting Department among the following:

- 5,000 puzzles that the Cutting Department completed from the June ending inventory
- 33,000 puzzles that the Cutting Department started, completed, and transferred out to Finished goods inventory
- 7,000 partially completed puzzles remaining in the Cutting Department's ending Work in process inventory at the end of July

We use the same four-step costing procedure that we used for the Assembly Department.

STEP 1: **Summarize the Flow of Physical Units.** Let us account for July production, using the data about Physical units given in Exhibit 4-17 and the results from Exhibit 4-20 for the Assembly Department.

We must account for these 45,000 units (A) (beginning inventory of 5,000 (June's ending inventory) plus 40,000 started). Exhibit 4-24 shows this.

EXHIBIT 4-24 | **Step 1: Summarize the Flow of Physical Units**

	PUZZLE ME Cost of Production Report—CUTTING DEPT—FIFO Month Ended July 31, 2010	
Flow of Production		
1 Step 1: PHYSICAL FLOW	Whole Units	
Units to account for:		
Beginning work in process, June 30 (from Exhibit 4-5)	5,000	
Started in production during July (from Exhibit 4-20)	40,000	
Total physical units to account for	45,000 A	

Exhibit 4-25 shows that, of the 45,000 units to account for (A), Puzzle Me completed and transferred out 38,000 units by first finishing the 5,000 units that were left over from June. Then, it started and finished another 33,000 (b d f) that were transferred in during July from the Assembly Department. That left 7,000 (C F I) units as Ending work in process in the Cutting Department on July 31. Steps 2 and 3 will help us determine the costs of these units.

EXHIBIT 4-25 | **Step 2: Calculate Number of Equivalent Units**

	PUZZLE ME Cost of Production Report—CUTTING DEPT—FIFO Month Ended July 31, 2010			
Flow of Production				
1 Step 1: PHYSICAL FLOW	Whole Units			
Units to account for:				
Beginning work in process, June 30 (from Exhibit 4-5)	5,000			
Started in production during July (from Exhibit 4-20)	40,000			
Total physical units to account for	45,000 A			

		Step 2: EQUIVALENT UNITS		
2	Whole Units	Transferred-In	Direct Materials	Conversion Costs
Units accounted for:				
Beginning work in process, June 30 (from Exhibit 4-5)	5,000	0 a	$5,000 \times 100\% = 5,000$ c	$5,000 \times (100\% - 60\%) = 2,000$ e
Started and completed during July	33,000	$33,000 \times 100\% = 33,000$ b	$33,000 \times 100\% = 33,000$ d	$33,000 \times 100\% = 33,000$ f
Completed and transferred out during July (from Exhibit 4-5)	38,000	33,000 B	38,000 E	35,000 H
Ending work in process, July 31	7,000	$7,000 \times 100\% = 7,000$ C	$7,000 \times 0\% = 0$ F	$7,000 \times 30\% = 2,100$ I
Total physical units to be assigned costs	45,000 A	40,000 D	38,000 G	37,100 J

STEP 2: **Compute Equivalent Units.** Exhibit 4-25 computes the Cutting Department's equivalent units of work. Under the FIFO method Puzzle Me computes the equivalent units for the total work done to date. This includes all the work done in the current period (July), plus the work done last period (June) on the Beginning work in process inventory.

We can see in Exhibit 4-25 that the total equivalent units with respect to

- transferred-in costs include only 40,000 units (D) because they are complete with respect to work that is the amount of units that were transferred in during July (see Exhibit 4-17) done in the Assembly Department. The equivalent units for transferred-in costs will always be 100% of the units started in production, because these units must be 100% complete on previous work before coming to the Cutting Department.

- direct materials include only the 38,000 (G) finished puzzles (the total completed and transferred out) because Cutting Department materials (boxes) are added at the end of the process.
- conversion cost equivalent units includes three components:
  - 2,000 (e) equivalent units to finish the June ending inventory (5,000 units requiring 40% conversion to complete them**)
  - 33,000 (f) units started and completed during July
  - 2,100 (I) puzzles (7,000 puzzle boards × 30% completion) that are still in process at the end of July.

Again recall that conversion work occurs evenly throughout the cutting process.

**It is important to note that the 5,000 units of June inventory were already 60% complete. Therefore they require 40% conversion to finish them (100% less 60% completed in June).

STEP 3: Compute Cost per Equivalent Unit.

Exhibit 4-26 on the following page accounts for the Cutting Department's total costs. In addition to direct material and conversion costs, the Cutting Department must account for transferred-in costs. Transferred-in costs are those costs that were incurred in a previous process (the Assembly Department, in this case) and brought into a later process (the Cutting Department) as part of the product's cost.

Exhibit 4-26 shows that the Cutting Department's total cost accounts for ($233,040) is the sum of the following:

- The cost incurred in June to start the Cutting process on the 5,000 puzzles in Cutting's Beginning work in process inventory ($22,000 + $1,200) (X)
- The costs added to Work in process inventory—Cutting during July ($209,840 (Y) = $176,000 (L T from Exh. 4-22) transferred in from the Assembly Department + $19,000 (O) direct materials added in the Cutting Department + $14,840 (T) conversion costs added in the Cutting Department)

This is summarized in Exhibit 4-26. Again, dollar amounts for costs can be found in Exhibit 4-5.

For each cost category, we divide total cost by the number of equivalent units calculated in step 2. Perform this computation for all cost categories: transferred-in costs, direct materials, and conversion costs. In this illustration the total cost per equivalent unit during July is $5.30 (t) ($4.40 + $0.50 + $0.40).

STEP 4: Assign Costs.

Exhibit 4-27 on the following page shows how Puzzle Me assigns the total Cutting Department costs ($233,040 (Z), from Exhibit 4-27) to:

- 5,000 units from beginning inventory completed and transferred to Finished Goods ($23,200 (u) beginning work in process + $3,300 (V) cost to complete beginning work in process = $26,500).
- Units started, completed, and transferred out to Finished goods inventory ($174,900 (W) consisting of 33,000 units @ $5.30 per unit).
- Units remaining in the Cutting Department's Ending work in process inventory ($30,800 (C × M) costs transferred in + $840 (I × W) conversion costs = $31,640 (x)).

The Cutting Department's journal entries previously recorded the $176,000 (L T from Exh. 4-22) in transferred-in costs of puzzle boards from the Assembly Department into the Cutting Department on page 173.

EXHIBIT 4-26 | Step 3: Calculate Cost per Equivalent Unit

PUZZLE ME
Cost of Production Report—CUTTING DEPT—FIFO
Month Ended July 31, 2010

Flow of Production

1	Step 1: PHYSICAL FLOW	Whole Units
	Units to account for:	
	Beginning work in process, June 30	
	(from Exhibit 4-5)	5,000
	Started in production during July	
	(from Exhibit 4-20)	40,000
	Total physical units to account for	45,000 **A**

2		Whole Units	Step 2: EQUIVALENT UNITS		
			Transferred-In	Direct Materials	Conversion Costs
	Units accounted for:				
	Beginning work in process, June 30				
	(from Exhibit 4-5)	5,000	0 **a**	5,000 × 100% = 5,000 **c**	5,000 × (100% − 60%) = 2,000 **e**
	Started and completed during July	33,000	33,000 × 100% = 33,000 **b**	33,000 × 100% = 33,000 **d**	33,000 × 100% = 33,000 **f**
	Completed and transferred out during July				
	(from Exhibit 4-5)	38,000	33,000 **B**	38,000 **E**	35,000 **H**
	Ending work in process, July 31	7,000	7,000 × 100% = 7,000 **C**	7,000 × 0% = 0 **F**	7,000 × 30% = 2,100 **I**
	Total physical units to be assigned costs	45,000 **A**	40,000 **D**	38,000 **G**	37,100 **J**

3	Step 3: COST PER EQUIVALENT UNIT	Transferred-In	Direct Materials	Conversion Costs	Total Costs
	Units costs:				
	Beginning work in process, June 30 (from Exhibit 4-5)	**K**	$ 0 **N**	**S**	$ 23,200 **K+N+S=X**
	Costs added during July (from Exhibit 4-5)	$176,000 **L** (T from Exh 4-22)	$19,000 **O**	$14,840 **T**	$209,840 **L+O+T=Y**
	Total costs to account for	$176,000 **K+L**	$19,000 **N+O=P**	$14,840 **S+T=U**	$233,040 **X+Y=Z**
	Total equivalent units	÷ $ 40,000 **D**	÷ 38,000 **Q**	÷ 37,100 **V**	
	Cost per equivalent unit	$ 4.40 **K÷D=M**	$ 0.50 **P÷Q=R**	$ 0.40 **U÷V=W**	$ 5.30 **M+R+W=t**

EXHIBIT 4-27 | Step 4: Assign Costs

PUZZLE ME
Cost of Production Report—CUTTING DEPT—FIFO
Month Ended July 31, 2010

Flow of Production

1	Step 1: PHYSICAL FLOW	Whole Units
	Units to account for:	
	Beginning work in process, June 30	
	(from Exhibit 4-5)	5,000
	Started in production during July	
	(from Exhibit 4-20)	40,000
	Total physical units to account for	45,000 **A**

2		Whole Units	Step 2: EQUIVALENT UNITS		
			Transferred-In	Direct Materials	Conversion Costs
	Units accounted for:				
	Beginning work in process, June 30				
	(from Exhibit 4-5)	5,000	0 **a**	5,000 × 100% = 5,000 **c**	5,000 × (100% − 60%) = 2,000 **e**
	Started and completed during July	33,000	33,000 × 100% = 33,000 **b**	33,000 × 100% = 33,000 **d**	33,000 × 100% = 33,000 **f**
	Completed and transferred out during July				
	(from Exhibit 4-5)	38,000	33,000 **B**	38,000 **E**	35,000 **H**
	Ending work in process, July 31	7,000	7,000 × 100% = 7,000 **C**	7,000 × 0% = 0 **F**	7,000 × 30% = 2,100 **I**
	Total physical units to be assigned costs	45,000 **A**	40,000 **D**	38,000 **G**	37,100 **J**

3	Step 3: COST PER EQUIVALENT UNIT	Transferred-In	Direct Materials	Conversion Costs	Total Costs
	Units costs:				
	Beginning work in process, June 30 (from Exhibit 4-5)	**K**	$ 0 **N**	**S**	$ 23,200 **K+N+S=X**
	Costs added during July (from Exhibit 4-5)	$176,000 **L** (T from Exh 4-22)	$19,000 **O**	$14,840 **T**	$209,840 **L+O+T=Y**
	Total costs to account for	$176,000 **K+L**	$19,000 **N+O=P**	$14,840 **S+T=U**	$233,040 **X+Y=Z**
	Total equivalent units	÷ $ 40,000 **D**	÷ 38,000 **Q**	÷ 37,100 **V**	
	Cost per equivalent unit	$ 4.40 **K÷D=M**	$ 0.50 **P÷Q=R**	$ 0.40 **U÷V=W**	$ 5.30 **M+R+W=t**

4	Step 4: ASSIGN COSTS	Transferred-In	Direct Materials	Conversion Costs	Total Costs
	Beginning work in process, June 30 (from Exhibit 4-5)	$22,000 (Exh 4-5)	$ 0 (Exh 4-5)	$ 1,200 (Exh 4-5)	$ 23,200 **u**
	Costs to complete June 30 inventory	0 × $4.40 = $ 0 **a × M**	5,000 × $0.50 = $ 2,500 **c × R**	2,000 × $0.40 = $ 800 **e × W**	$ 3,300 **v**
	Started and transferred out during July	33,000 × $4.40 = $145,200 **b × M**	33,000 × $0.50 = $15,500 **d × R**	33,000 × $0.40 = $13,200 **f × W**	$174,900 **w**
	Ending work in process, July 31	7,000 × $4.40 = $ 30,800 **C × M**	0 × $0.50 = $ 0 **F × R**	2,100 × $0.40 = $ 840 **I × W**	$ 31,640 **x**
	Total costs accounted for				$233,040

The following entry records the Cutting Department's materials labor and overhead during July (data from Exhibit 4-17):

(2) Work in process inventory—Cutting	33,840	
Materials inventory		19,000
Manufacturing wages		3,840
Manufacturing overhead		11,000
To assign materials and conversion costs to the		
Cutting Department.		

The entry to transfer the cost of completed puzzles out of the Cutting Department and into Finished goods inventory is based on the dollar amount in Exhibit 4-27 ($23,200 **u** + $3,300 **v** + $174,900 **w**):

u + v + w Finished goods inventory ($23,200 + $3,300 + $174,900)	201,400	
Work in process inventory—Cutting		201,400
To transfer costs from Cutting to Finished Goods.		

After posting, the key accounts appear as follows:

Work in process inventory—Assembly

Balance, June 30	—	Transferred to Cutting	176,000 **T**
(1) { Direct materials	140,000		
Direct labor	20,000		
Manufacturing overhead	48,000		
U Balance, July 31	32,000		

Work in process inventory—Cutting

Balance, June 30	23,200	Transferred to Finished	
T Transferred in from Assembly	176,000	goods inventory	201,400 **u + v + w**
(2) { Direct materials	19,000		
Direct labor	3,840		
Manufacturing overhead	11,000		
x Balance, July 31	31,640		

Finished goods inventory

Balance, June 30	0
u + v + w Transferred in from Cutting	201,400

See Exhibit 4-27 for the entire production report for the cutting department of Puzzle Me.

So, why are the results exactly the same between weighted average and FIFO for Puzzle Me? The answer is the company had NO change in costs from June to July for any of the materials or conversion costs. This is not normally the case, but it was done intentionally to help simplify these examples.

Accountants prepare cost reports to help production managers evaluate the efficiency of their manufacturing operations. Both job order and process costing are similar in that they

- *accumulate* costs as the product moves through production.
- *assign* costs to the units (such as gallons of gasoline or number of crayons) passing through that process.

The difference between job order costing and process costing lies in the way costs are accumulated. Job order costing uses a *job cost sheet* and process costing uses a *production cost report*. (See Exhibits 4-10 and 4-15 that we completed for the Assembly and Cutting Departments.)

The **production cost report** in Exhibit 4-15 (weighted-average method)and Exhibit 4-27 (FIFO method) summarizes Puzzle Me's Cutting Department operations during July. The report combines the costs to account for and the cost per equivalent unit. It shows how those costs were assigned to the puzzles completed and transferred out of the Cutting Department ($201,400) and to Ending work in process inventory remaining in the department ($31,640).

How do managers use the production cost report?

- Controlling cost: Puzzle Me uses product cost data to reduce costs. A manager may decide that the company needs to change either suppliers or a certain component to reduce the cost of its materials. To reduce labor costs, it may need either different employee job requirements or new production equipment. An increase in overhead costs in the current year may require closer scrutiny to determine if corrective action should be taken.

- Evaluating performance: Managers are often rewarded based on how well they meet the budget. Puzzle Me can use the per-unit information from the production cost report to compare the actual direct materials and conversion costs with expected amounts. If actual unit costs are too high, managers look for ways to cut them. If actual costs are less than expected due to exemplary management, the Cutting Department's managers may receive a pay raise.

- Pricing products: Puzzle Me must set its selling price high enough to cover the manufacturing cost of each puzzle. The sales price should be greater than the cost of $5.30 per unit to ensure overhead costs are covered plus a reasonable profit is made.

- Identifying the most profitable products: Selling price and cost data help managers figure out which products are most profitable so that the company can maximize net income.

- Preparing the financial statements: Finally, the production cost report aids financial reporting. It provides inventory data for the balance sheet and cost of goods sold for the income statement.

Decision Guidelines

PROCESS COSTING

Process costing helps managers determine the cost to produce products. Here are some questions you will ask, and guidelines for answering them.

Decision	Guidelines
• What type of company uses process costing?	Companies that use a series of steps (called processes) to make large quantities of similar products use process costing. Some examples are manufacturers of crayons, iPods, and gasoline.

• Which of the two methods should a company use to account for its production costs?
  – Weighted-average
 	
  – FIFO
	
	• The company only needs to distinguish the cost of completed products from the cost of products still in process.
	• The company distinguishes production cost into three pools:
	  – The cost of beginning inventory that was finished during the period
	  – The cost of products that were started and completed during the period
	  – The cost of products still in process at the end of the period

What are the four steps a company follows in process costing?	The four steps are as follows:
	  1. Summarize the flow of physical units.
	  2. Compute output in terms of equivalent units.
	  3. Compute the cost per equivalent unit.
	  4. Assign costs to units completed and to units still in ending Work in process inventory.

What is an equivalent unit?	• Measure of work done on partially finished products • Expressed in terms of complete units • Example: 3 products that are 1/3 complete = 1 equivalent unit

Summary Problem 2

Process Costing Using the FIFO Method

Using the data from Summary Problem 1 on page 166 you should be able to do the following:

1. Prepare the cost of production report using FIFO for the Stamping Department.
2. Prepare the cost of production report using FIFO for the Assembly Department.

Solutions

Requirement 1: Stamping Department

As discussed in the chapter, we must complete the four steps to prepare the cost of production report for each department. Since the Stamping Department is the first department, there are no transferred-in costs.

STEP 1: Summarize the Flow of Physical Units.

The company had no beginning WIP, so only the 12,000 units started in production must be accounted for. **A**

STEP 2: Compute output in terms of Equivalent Units.

Of the total 12,000 units, 10,000 units were completed and transferred to the Assembly Department in June. So, the 10,000 units received 100% of their materials and conversion costs in June. The 2,000 units remaining in WIP received all their materials, since materials are added at the beginning of this department. They are 20% complete, so they received only 20% equivalent work for conversion costs (400 units). **F**

STEP 3: Compute the Cost per Equivalent Unit.

For Direct materials, $6,000 in cost divided by 12,000 equivalent units from step 2 equals $0.50 per unit. **K**

For Conversion costs, $20,800 in cost divided by 10,400 equivalent units from step 2 equals $2.00 per unit. **O**

STEP 4: Assign Costs.

The calculations are shown in the following final production report.

	Flow of Production				
1	Step 1: PHYSICAL FLOW	Whole Units			
	Units to account for:				
	Beginning work in process, May 31	0			
	Started in production during June	12,000			
	Total physical units to account for	12,000 **A**			

			Step 2: EQUIVALENT UNITS		
2		Whole Units	Transferred-In	Direct Materials	Conversion Costs
	Units accounted for:				
	Beginning work in process, May 31	0	0	0	0
	Started and completed during June	10,000	N/A–first department	10,000	10,000
	Completed and transferred out during June	10,000	N/A–first department	10,000 **B**	10,000 **E**
	Ending work in process, July 30	2,000	N/A	2,000 **C**	2,000 × 20% = 400 **F**
	Total physical units to be assigned costs	12,000 **A**	N/A	12,000 **D**	10,400 **G**

		Transferred-In	Direct Materials	Conversion Costs	Total Costs
3	Step 3: COST PER EQUIVALENT UNIT				
	Units costs:				
	Beginning work in process, May 31	N/A	$ 0 **H**	$ 0 **L**	$ 0
	Costs added during June	N/A	$6,000 **I**	$20,800 **M**	$26,800
	Total costs to account for		$6,000 **H + I = J**	$20,800 **L + M = N**	$26,800
	Total equivalent units	N/A	÷ 12,000 **D**	÷ 10,400 **G**	
	Cost per equivalent unit	N/A	$ 0.50 **J ÷ D = K**	$ 2.00 **N ÷ G = O**	$ 2.50

			Direct Materials	Conversion Costs	Total Costs
4	Step 4: ASSIGN COSTS				
	Beginning work in process, May 31		0	0	0
	Costs to complete May 31 inventory		0 × $0.50 = 0	0 × $2.00 = 0	0
	Started and completed during June		10,000 × $0.50 = $5,000 **B × K**	10,000 × $2.00 = $20,000 **B × O**	$25,000
	Completed and transferred out during June		$5,000	$20,000	$25,000 **P**
	Ending work in process, June 30		2,000 × $0.50 = $1,000 **C × K**	400 × $2.00 = $ 800 **F × O**	$ 1,800 **Q**
	Total costs accounted for				$26,800

Note that of the total costs incurred of $26,800 during June in the Stamping Department, $25,000 **P** of those costs have moved to the Assembly Department during June with the 10,000 units transferred. In addition, $1,800 **Q** in costs remains with the 2,000 incomplete units in the Stamping Department.

Notice that these results are exactly the same as in Summary Problem 1, which used the weighted-average method because there was no beginning inventory in the Stamping Department.

Requirement 2: Assembly Department

Again, we must complete the four steps to prepare the cost of production report for each department. Since the Assembly Department is the second department, there are transferred-in costs from the Stamping Department to account for. (The Stamping Department's Cost of Production Report is on the following page.)

STEP 1: Summarize the Physical Flow of Goods.

The company had 5,000 units of beginning WIP and 10,000 units were transferred in from the Stamping Department, or a total of 15,000 units to account for in the Assembly Department in June. **A**

STEP 2: Compute Output in Terms of Equivalent Units.

The 5,000 units in beginning WIP inventory were completed during June. All the transferred-in costs were already there as of the end of May, so zero equivalent units of transferred-in work were done on these units in June. All the direct materials were added, since the materials are added at the end of the process. We know, from the original data provided about the company on page 166, that the beginning 5,000 units in inventory already have 40% of there conversion costs completed. The remaining work for conversion (100% – 40%) or 60% was completed on the 5,000 units during June, for 3,000 equivalent units. **e**

Of the total 11,000 units transferred to finished goods, 6,000 were started and completed during June. So, the 6,000 units have 100% of their transferred-in costs, materials, and conversion costs in June. **d** The 4,000 units remaining in WIP received all their transferred-in costs, since the prior department's transferred-in work is added at the beginning of this department. These units have none of their materials because materials are added at the END of this department. They are 70% complete, so they received only 70% equivalent work for conversion costs (2,800 units). **I**

STEP 3: Compute the Cost per Equivalent Unit.

For Transferred-in costs, $25,000 in costs divided by 10,000 equivalent units equals $2.50 per unit. **M**

For Direct materials, $2,750 in cost divided by 11,000 equivalent units from step 2 equals $0.25 per unit. **R**

For Conversion costs, $3,540 in cost divided by 11,800 equivalent units from step 2 equals $0.30 per unit. **W**

STEP 4: Assign Costs.

The calculations are shown in the following final production report.

STEVIE'S SCISSORS
Cost of Production Report—ASSEMBLY DEPT—FIFO
Month Ended June 30, 2010

Flow of Production					
1 Step 1: PHYSICAL FLOW	Whole Units				
Units to account for:					
Beginning work in process, May 31	5,000				
Started in production during June	10,000				
Total physical units to account for	10,000 **A**				

2		Step 2: EQUIVALENT UNITS			
	Whole Units	Transferred-In	Direct Materials	Conversion Costs	
Units accounted for:					
Beginning work in process, May 31	5,000	0 **a**	5,000 × 100% = 5,000 **C**	5,000 × (100%–40%) = 3,000 **e**	
Started and completed during June	6,000	6,000 × 100% = 6,000 **b**	6,000 × 100% = 6,000 **d**	6,000 × 100% = 6,000 **f**	
Completed and transferred out during June	11,000	6,000 **B**	11,000 **E**	9,000 **H**	
Ending work in process, July 30	4,000	4,000 × 100% = 4,000 **C**	4,000 × 0% = 0 **F**	4,000 × 70% = 2,800 **I**	
Total physical units to be assigned costs	15,000 **A**	10,000 **D**	11,000 **G**	11,800 **J**	

3 Step 3: COST PER EQUIVALENT UNIT	Transferred-In	Direct Materials	Conversion Costs	Total Costs
Units costs:				
Beginning work in process, May 31	$ - **K**	$ - **N**	$ - **S**	$12,290
Costs added during June	$25,000 **L** P from Stamping dept.	$ 2,750 **O**	$ 3,540 **T**	$31,290
Total costs to account for	$25,000 **K+L**	$ 2,750 **N+O=P**	$ 3,540 **S=T=U**	$43,580
Total equivalent units	÷10,000 **D**	÷11,000 **Q**	÷11,800 **V**	
Cost per equivalent unit	$ 2.50 **K÷D=M**	$ 0.25 **P÷Q=R**	$ 0.30 **U÷V=W**	$ 3.05

4 Step 4: ASSIGN COSTS	Transferred-In	Direct Materials	Conversion Costs	Total Costs
Beginning work in process, May 31	$11,000	$ 0	$1,290	$12,290
Costs to complete May 31 ending inventory	0 × $2.50 = $ 0 **a×M**	5,000 × $0.25 = $1,250 **c×R**	3,000 × $0.30 = $ 900 **e×W**	$ 2,150 **g**
Completed and transferred out during June	6,000 × $2.50 = $26,400 **b×M**	6,000 × $0.25 = $1,500 **d×R**	6,000 × $0.30 = $1,800 **f×W**	$18,300 **X**
Ending work in process, June 30	4,000 × $2.50 = $10,000 **c×M**	0 × $0.25 = $ 0 **F×R**	2,800 × $0.30 = $ 840 **i×W**	$10,840 **Y**
Total costs accounted for				$43,580

Note that of the total costs incurred of $43,580 during June in the Assembly Department, $32,740 (12,290 + 2,150 **g** + 18,300 **X**) of those costs have moved to finished goods during June with the 11,000 units transferred. Further, $10,840 **Y** in costs remains with the 4,000 incomplete units in the Assembly Department.

Review *Process Costing*

■ Accounting Vocabulary

Equivalent Units (p. 153)
Allows us to measure the amount of work done on a partially finished group of units during a period and to express it in terms of fully complete units of output.

FIFO Method (p. 169)
Determines the cost of all of a specific department's equivalent units of work based on flow of the goods through the process.

Process Costing (p. 149)
System for assigning costs to large numbers of identical units that usually proceed in a continuous fashion through a series of uniform production steps or processes.

Production Cost Report (p. 180)
Summarizes operations for one department for a month. Combines the costs to account for and the cost per equivalent unit and shows how those costs were assigned to the goods completed and transferred out.

Transferred-in Costs (p. 160)
Costs that were incurred in a previous process and brought into a later process as part of the product's cost.

Weighted-Average Method (p. 161)
Determines the average cost of all of a specific department's equivalent units of work.

■ Quick Check

1. Would a CPA firm use job or process costing? What about a paper mill?
   a. CPA firm—job order costing; Paper mill—process costing
   b. CPA firm—process costing; Paper mill—process costing
   c. CPA firm—job order costing; Paper mill—job order costing
   d. CPA firm—process costing; Paper mill—job order costing

2. A manufacturing company that separates work completed on last month's ending inventory from work started and finished during the month uses
   a. job order costing.
   b. weighted-average process costing.
   c. FIFO process costing.
   d. LIFO process costing.

3. A calculation that tells the accountant how many units could have been started and completely finished is called
   a. equivalent units.
   b. finished goods.
   c. work in process.
   d. completed units.

Questions 4 through 10 are based on the following information about Aledia Corporation. Aledia manufactures multivitamins in a two stage process: Mixing and Packaging.

Materials are added at the beginning of the Mixing Process. Conversion costs occur evenly throughout the department. Packaging materials are added at the end of the Packaging process and conversion costs occur evenly throughout the department. June data follow:

Mixing Dept	Packaging Dept
Beg WIP Inventory, 10,000 units, 20%	Beg WIP Inventory, 4,000 units, 60%
Started in production, 30,000 units	Started in production, 38,000 units
End WIP Inventory, 2,000 units, 30%	End WIP Inventory, 1,000 units, 55%

Assume Aledia uses the weighted-average method.

4. What are the total equivalent units for direct materials for the Mixing Department for June?
    a. 38,000
    b. 28,000
    c. 2,000
    d. 40,000

5. What are the total equivalent units for conversion costs for the Mixing Department for June?
    a. 28,000
    b. 38,600
    c. 30,000
    d. 30,600

6. What are the total equivalent units for direct materials for the Packaging Department for June?
    a. 2,200
    b. 30,000
    c. 36,200
    d. 41,000

7. What are the total equivalent units for transferred-in costs for the Packaging Department for June?
    a. 38,000
    b. 34,000
    c. 36,200
    d. 42,000

8. What are the total equivalent units for conversion costs for the Packaging Department for June?
    a. 550
    b. 38,000
    c. 42,000
    d. 41,550

9. If the amount transferred from the Mixing Department to packaging is $100,000 and the amount transferred from packaging to finished goods is $180,000, which of the following journal entries would be correct?

a.	Work in process—Packaging	100,000	
	Work in process—Mixing		100,000
b.	Work in process—Packaging	180,000	
	Work in process—Mixing		180,000
c.	Work in process—Packaging	180,000	
	Finished goods inventory		180,000
d.	Finished goods inventory	280,000	
	Work in process—Packaging		180,000
	Work in process—Mixing		100,000

10. Assume instead that Aledia uses the FIFO method. What is the amount of Equivalent units for Direct Materials and Conversion costs for the Mixing Department?

   a. Materials – 36,000 EU; Conversion Costs – 36,600

   b. Materials – 32,600 EU; Conversion Costs – 32,600

   c. Materials – 30,000 EU; Conversion Costs – 36,600

   d. Materials – 32,600 EU; Conversion Costs – 38,600

Answers are given after Apply Your Knowledge (p. 208).

Assess Your Progress

■ Short Exercises

S4-1 **(L. OBJ. 1) Calculating conversion costs and unit cost—weighted average [5–10 min]**

Cold Spring produces premium bottled water. Cold Spring purchases artesian water, stores the water in large tanks, and then runs the water through two processes: Filtration and Bottling.

During February, the Filtration process incurred the following costs in processing 190,000 liters:

Wages of workers operating the filtration equipment	$ 21,950
Manufacturing overhead allocated to filtration	25,050
Water	150,000

Cold Spring had no beginning inventory in the Filtration Department in February.

Requirements

   1. Compute the February conversion costs in the Filtration Department.

   2. The Filtration Department completely processed 190,000 liters in February. What was the filtration cost per liter using the weighted-average method?

Note: Short Exercise 4-1 must be completed before attempting Short Exercise 4-2.

S4-2 *(L. OBJ. 1)* **Drawing a time line, and computing equivalent units—weighted average [10 min]**

Refer to S4-1. At Cold Spring, water is added at the beginning of the Filtration process. Conversion costs are added evenly throughout the process. Assume that in February, 125,000 liters were completed and transferred out of the Filtration Department into the Bottling Department. The 65,000 units remaining in Filtration's Ending work in process inventory were 80% of the way through the Filtration process. Recall that Cold Spring has no beginning inventories.

Requirements

1. Draw a time line for the Filtration process.
2. Compute the equivalent units of direct materials and conversion costs for the Filtration Department using the weighted-average method.

S4-3 *(L. OBJ. 1)* **Computing equivalent units—weighted average [5 min]**

The Mixing Department of Best Foods had 52,000 units to account for, all of which began production in October. Of the 52,000 units, 8,000 units were in beginning inventory and were 60% complete, 44,000 units were started in process during October and 26,000 units were 30% complete. All of the materials are added at the beginning of the process. Conversion costs are added equally throughout the Filtration process.

Requirement

1. Compute the total equivalent units of direct materials and conversion costs for October using the weighted-average method.

Note: Short Exercise 4-3 must be completed before attempting Short Exercise 4-4.

S4-4 *(L. OBJ. 1)* **Computing the cost per equivalent unit—weighted average [5 min]**

Refer to the data in S4-3 and your results for equivalent units. The Mixing Department of Best Foods had Beginning WIP of $10,600 for direct materials and $4,090 for conversion costs. During October, the mixing department added direct materials costs of $44,000 and conversion costs of $14,500 for October.

Requirement

1. Compute the cost per equivalent unit for direct materials and for conversion costs using the weighted-average method.

Note: Short Exercises 4-3 and 4-4 must be completed before attempting Short Exercise 4-5.

S4-5 *(L. OBJ. 1)* **Computing cost of units transferred out and units in ending work in process—weighted average [5 min]**

Refer to S4-3 and S4-4. Use Best Foods' costs per equivalent unit for direct materials and conversion costs that you calculated in S4-4.

Requirement

1. Calculate the cost of the 26,000 units completed and transferred out and the 26,000 units, 30% complete, in the Ending work in process inventory using the weighted-average method.

S4-6 **(L. OBJ. 1) Compute the physical flow—weighted average [15–20 min]**
Consider the following incomplete data:

Units to account for:	Dept A	Dept 33	Dept Z17
Beginning work in process, 40% complete	97	(c)	45
Started in production during month	253	113	(g)
Total physical units to account for	350	172	(f)
Units accounted for:			
Completed and transferred out during month	(b)	117	121
Ending work in process, 20% complete	119	(d)	26
Total physical units accounted for	(a)	172	(e)

Requirement

1. Calculate the missing items.

S4-7 **(L. OBJ. 2) Calculating conversion costs and unit cost—FIFO [5–10 min]**
Use the data from S4-1 to answer the questions using the FIFO method.

Requirements

1. Compute the February conversion costs in the Filtration Department.
2. The Filtration Department completely processed 190,000 liters in February. What was the filtration cost per liter using the FIFO method?

Note: Short Exercise 4-7 must be completed before attempting Short Exercise 4-8.

S4-8 **(L. OBJ. 2) Drawing a time line, and computing equivalent units—FIFO [10 min]**
Refer to S4-7. At Cold Spring, water is added at the beginning of the Filtration process. Conversion costs are added evenly throughout the process. Now assume that in February, 125,000 liters were completed and transferred out of the Filtration Department into the Bottling Department. The 65,000 units remaining in Filtration's Ending work in process inventory were 80% of the way through the Filtration process. Recall that Cold Spring has no beginning inventories.

Requirements

1. Draw a time line for the Filtration process.
2. Compute the equivalent units of direct materials and conversion costs for the Filtration Department using the FIFO method.

S4-9 **(L. OBJ. 2) Computing equivalent units—FIFO [5 min]**
Using the data from S4-3, answer the questions using the FIFO method.

Requirement

1. Compute the total equivalent units of direct materials and conversion costs for October using the FIFO method.

Note: Short Exercise 4-9 must be completed before attempting Short Exercise 4-10.

S4-10 **(L. OBJ. 2) Computing the cost per equivalent unit—FIFO [5 min]**
Refer to the data in S4-9 and your results for equivalent units. The Mixing Department of Best Foods has direct materials costs of $44,000 and conversion costs of $14,500 for October.

Requirement

1. Compute the cost per equivalent unit for direct materials and for conversion costs using the FIFO method.

Note: Short Exercises 4-9 and 4-10 must be completed before attempting Short Exercise 4-11.

S4-11 *(L. OBJ. 2)* **Computing cost of units transferred out and units in ending work in process—FIFO [5 min]**
Refer to S4-9 and S4-10. Use Best Foods' costs per equivalent unit for direct materials and conversion costs that you calculated in S4-10.

Requirement

1. Calculate the cost of the units completed and transferred out and the units remaining in the Ending work in process inventory using the FIFO method.

S4-12 *(L. OBJ. 2)* **Compute the physical flow—FIFO [15–20 min]**
Consider the following incomplete data:

	Dept A	Dept 33	Dept Z17
Units to account for:			
Beginning work in process, 40% complete	97	(e)	45
Started in production during month	253	113	(i)
Total physical units to account for	350	172	(j)
Units accounted for:			
Beginning work in process, 40% complete	(a)	(f)	(k)
Started and completed during the month	(b)	(g)	(l)
Completed and transferred out during month	(c)	117	121
Ending work in process, 20% complete	119	(h)	26
Total physical units accounted for	(d)	172	(m)

Requirement

1. Calculate the missing items.

■ Exercises

E4-13 *(L. OBJ. 1)* **Drawing a time line, computing equivalent units, and assigning cost to completed units and ending work in process; no beginning inventory or cost transferred-in—weighted average [20 min]**
Paint My World prepares and packages paint products. Paint My World has two departments: (1) Blending and (2) Packaging. Direct materials are added at the beginning of the Blending process (dyes) and at the end of the Packaging process (cans).

Conversion costs are added evenly throughout each process. Data from the month of May for the Blending Department are as follows:

Gallons:		
Beginning work in process inventory	0	
Started in production	9,200	gallons
Completed and transferred out to Packaging in May	6,300	gallons
Ending work in process inventory (30% of the way through Blending process)	2,900	gallons
Costs:		
Beginning work in process inventory	$ 0	
Costs added during May:		
Direct materials	4,500	
Direct labor	1,050	
Manufacturing overhead	2,400	
Total costs added during May	$ 7,950	

Requirements

1. Fill in the time line for the Blending Department.
2. Use the time line to help you compute the Blending Department's equivalent units for direct materials and for conversion costs using the weighted-average method.
3. Compute the total costs of the units (gallons):
   a. completed and transferred out to the Packaging Department.
   b. in the Blending Department Ending work in process inventory.

Note: Exercise 4-13 must be completed before attempting Exercise 4-14.

E4-14 *(L. OBJ. 1)* **Preparing journal entries and posting to work in process T-accounts – weighted average [15 min]**
Refer to your answers from E4-13.

Requirements

1. Present the journal entries to record the assignment of direct materials and direct labor, and the allocation of manufacturing overhead to the Blending Department. Also, give the journal entry to record the costs of the gallons completed and transferred out to the Packaging Department using the weighted-average method.
2. Post the journal entries to the Work in process inventory—Blending T-account. What is the ending balance?
3. What is the average cost per gallon transferred out of Blending into Packaging? Why would the company managers want to know this cost?

E4-15 *(L. OBJ. 1)* **Drawing a time line, computing equivalent units, and assigning cost to completed units and ending work in process; beginning inventory without cost transferred-in—weighted average [20 min]**

Paulson Winery in Napa Valley, California, has two departments: Fermenting and Packaging. Direct materials are added at the beginning of the Fermenting process (grapes) and at the end of the Packaging process (bottles). Conversion costs are added evenly throughout each process. Data from the month of March for the Fermenting Department are as follows:

Gallons:	
Beginning work in process inventory (70% of the way through Fermenting process)	1,000
Started production	7,800 gallons
Completed and transferred out to Packaging in March	6,400 gallons
Ending work in process inventory (75% of the way through Fermenting process)	2,400 gallons
Costs:	
Beginning work in process inventory ($1,000 materials, $10,420 conversion costs)	$11,420
Costs added during March:	
Direct materials	7,800
Direct labor	5,000
Manufacturing overhead	10,000
Total costs added during March	$22,800

Requirements

1. Draw a time line for the Fermenting Department.
2. Use the time line to help you compute the equivalent units for direct materials and for conversion costs using the weighted-average method.
3. Compute the total costs of the units (gallons)
   a. completed and transferred out to the Packaging Department.
   b. in the Fermenting Department Ending work in process inventory.

Note: Exercise 4-15 must be completed before attempting Exercise 4-16.

E4-16 *(L. OBJ. 1)* **Preparing journal entries and posting to work in process T-accounts—weighted average [15 min]**
Refer to the data and your answers from E4-15.

Requirements

1. Present the journal entries to record the assignment of Direct materials and Direct labor and the allocation of Manufacturing overhead to the Fermenting Department. Also give the journal entry to record the cost of the gallons completed and transferred out to the Packaging Department.
2. Post the journal entries to the Work in process inventory—Fermenting T-account. What is the ending balance?
3. What is the average cost per gallon transferred out of Fermenting into Packaging? Why would Paulson Winery's managers want to know this cost?

E4-17 *(L. OBJ. 1)* **Drawing a time line, computing equivalent units, computing cost per equivalent unit; assigning costs; journalizing; second department— weighted-average method [25–30 min]**
Clear Water Company produces premium bottled water. In the second department, the Bottling Department, conversion costs are incurred evenly throughout the bottling process, but packaging materials are not added until the end of the

process. Costs in Beginning work in process inventory include transferred-in costs of $4,700, and conversion costs of $2,760. February data for the Bottling Department follow:

CLEAR WATER COMPANY
Work in Process Inventory—Bottling
Month Ended February 28, 2011

	Physical Units	Dollars		Physical Units	Dollars
Beginning inventory, January 31 (40% complete)	8,000	$ 7,460	Transferred out	150,000	$?
Production started:					
Transferred-in	162,000	129,600			
Direct materials		30,000			
Conversion costs:					
Direct labor		33,500			
Manufacturing overhead		22,780			
Total to account for	170,000	223,340			
Ending inventory, February 28 (70% complete)	20,000	$?			

Requirements

1. Draw a time line.
2. Compute the Bottling Department equivalent units for the month of February. Use the weighted-average method.
3. Compute the cost per equivalent unit for February.
4. Assign the costs to units completed and transferred out and to Ending inventory.
5. Prepare the journal entry to record the cost of units completed and transferred out.
6. Post all transactions to the Work in process inventory—Bottling Department T-account. What is the ending balance?

E4-18 *(L. OBJ. 2)* **Drawing a time line, computing equivalent units, and assigning cost to completed units and ending work in process; no beginning inventory or cost transferred-in—FIFO [20 min]**
Use the data for Exercise 4-13 to answer the requirements using the FIFO method.

Requirements

1. Fill in the time line for the Blending Department.
2. Use the time line to help you compute the Blending Department's equivalent units for direct materials and for conversion costs using the FIFO method.
3. Compute the total costs of the units (gallons)
   a. completed and transferred out to the Packaging Department.
   b. in the Blending Department Ending work in process inventory.

Note: Exercise 4-18 must be completed before attempting Exercise 4-19.

E4-19 *(L. OBJ. 2)* **Preparing journal entries and posting to work in process T-accounts—FIFO [15 min]**
Refer to your answers from E4-18.

Requirements

1. Present the journal entries to record the assignment of direct materials and direct labor, and the allocation of manufacturing overhead to the Blending Department. Also, give the journal entry to record the costs of the gallons completed and transferred out to the Packaging Department using the FIFO method.

2. Post the journal entries to the Work in process inventory—Blending T-account. What is the ending balance?

3. What is the average cost per gallon transferred out of Blending into Packaging? Why would the company managers want to know this cost?

E4-20 *(L. OBJ. 2)* **Drawing a time line, computing equivalent units, and assigning cost to completed units and ending work in process; beginning inventory without cost transferred-in—FIFO [20 min]**

Use the data provided in Exercise 4-15 to answer the requirements using the FIFO method.

Requirements

1. Draw a time line for the Fermenting Department.

2. Use the time line to help you compute the equivalent units for direct materials and for conversion costs using the FIFO method.

3. Compute the total costs of the units (gallons)
   a. completed and transferred out to the Packaging Department.
   b. in the Fermenting Department Ending work in process inventory.

Note: Exercise 4-20 must be completed before attempting Exercise 4-21.

E4-21 *(L. OBJ. 2)* **Preparing journal entries and posting to work in process T-accounts—FIFO [15 min]**

Refer to the data and your answers from E4-20.

Requirements

1. Present the journal entries to record the assignment of Direct materials and Direct labor and the allocation of Manufacturing overhead to the Fermenting Department. Also give the journal entry to record the cost of the gallons completed and transferred out to the Packaging Department.

2. Post the journal entries to the Work in process inventory—Fermenting T-account. What is the ending balance?

3. What is the average cost per gallon transferred out of Fermenting into Packaging? Why would Paulson Winery's managers want to know this cost?

E4-22 *(L. OBJ. 2)* **Drawing a time line, computing equivalent units, computing cost per equivalent unit; assigning costs; journalizing; second department—FIFO [25–30 min]**

Use the data from Exercise 4-17 to answer the requirements using the FIFO method.

Requirements

1. Draw a time line.

2. Compute the Bottling Department equivalent units for the month of February. Use the FIFO method.

3. Compute the cost per equivalent unit for February.

4. Assign the costs to units completed and transferred out and to Ending inventory.

5. Prepare the journal entry to record the cost of units completed and transferred out.

6. Post all transactions to the Work in process inventory—Bottling Department T-account. What is the ending balance?

P4-23A *(L. OBJ. 1)* **Computing equivalent units and assigning costs to completed units and ending work in process; beginning inventory without cost transferred-in—weighted average [30–45 min]**

Beth Electronics makes CD players in three processes: Assembly, Programming, and Packaging. Direct materials are added at the beginning of the Assembly process. Conversion costs are incurred evenly throughout the process. The Assembly Department had 10,000 units that were 60% complete in beginning Work in process on May 31. In mid-June, Beth Electronics started production on 101,000 CD players. Of this number, 75,000 CD players were assembled during June and transferred out to the Programming Department. The June 30 Work in process in the Assembly Department was 35% of the way through the Assembly process. Beginning WIP had materials cost of $34,950 and conversion cost of $21,780. During June, direct materials costing $409,050 were placed in production in Assembly, and Direct labor of $135,740 and Manufacturing overhead of $100,900 were assigned to that department.

Requirements

1. Draw a time line for the Assembly Department.
2. Use the time line to help you compute the number of equivalent units and the cost per equivalent unit in the Assembly Department for June.
3. Assign total costs in the Assembly Department using the weighted-average method to (a) units completed and transferred to Programming during June and (b) units still in process at June 30.
4. Prepare a T-account for Work in process inventory—Assembly to show its activity during June, including the June 30 balance.

P4-24A *(L. OBJ. 1)* **Computing equivalent units and assigning costs to completed units and ending work in process; beginning inventory without cost transferred-in—weighted average [30–45 min]**

Smith Paper, Co., produces the paper used by wallpaper manufacturers. Smith's four-stage process includes Mixing, Cooking, Rolling, and Cutting. Smith started August with 1,000 rolls of paper that were 40% complete with $1,524 of materials and $1,112 of conversion associated with them. During August, the Mixing Department started 5,000 rolls of paper. The department did not finish the mixing for 600 rolls, which were 20% complete with respect to both direct materials and conversion work at the end of August. Direct materials and conversion costs are incurred evenly throughout the Mixing process. The Mixing Department incurred the following costs during August:

Work in process inventory—Mixing

Bal, Aug 1	$2,636	
Direct materials	5,376	
Direct labor	1,383	
Manufacturing overhead	5,785	

Requirements

1. Draw a time line for the Mixing Department.
2. Use the time line to help you compute the number of equivalent units and the cost per equivalent unit in the Mixing Department for August using the weighted-average method.

3. Show that the sum of (a) cost of goods transferred out of the Mixing Department and (b) ending Work in process inventory—Mixing equals the total cost accumulated in the department during August.

4. Journalize all transactions affecting the company's Mixing process during August, including those already posted.

P4-25A *(L. OBJ. 1)* **Computing equivalent units and assigning costs to completed units and ending WIP inventory; two materials, added at different points; beginning inventory without cost transferred-in—weighted average [30–45 min]**

Hall's Exteriors produces exterior siding for homes. The Preparation Department begins with wood, which is chopped into small bits. At the end of the process, an adhesive is added. Then the wood/adhesive mixture goes on to the Compression Department, where the wood is compressed into sheets. Conversion costs are added evenly throughout the preparation process. The beginning WIP inventory is composed of $832 of wood costs and $300 of conversion costs.

January data for the Preparation Department are as follows (in millions):

Sheets		Costs	
Beginning work in process inventory,		Beginning work in process inventory	$1,132
(30% of the way through Preparation process)	1,000 sheets		
Started in production	3,600 sheets	Costs added during January:	
Completed and transferred out to		Wood	2,664
Compression in January	1,910 sheets	Adhesives	1,337
		Direct labor	750
Ending work in process inventory (40%		Manufacturing overhead	1,936
of the way through Preparation process)	2,690 sheets	Total costs	$7,819

Requirements

1. Draw a time line for the Preparation Department.

2. Use the time line to help you compute the equivalent units using the weighted-average method. (*Hint*: Each direct material added at a different point in the Production process requires its own equivalent-unit computation.)

3. Compute the total costs of the units (sheets)
   a. completed and transferred out to the Compression Department.
   b. in the Preparation Department's Ending work in process inventory.

4. Prepare the journal entry to record the cost of the sheets completed and transferred out to the Compression Department.

5. Post the journal entries to the Work in process inventory—Preparation T-account. What is the ending balance?

P4-26A *(L. OBJ. 1)* **Computing equivalent units for a second department with beginning inventory; preparing a production cost report and recording transactions on the basis of the report's information—weighted-average method [45–60 min]**

Casey Carpet manufactures broadloom carpet in seven processes: Spinning, Dyeing, Plying, Spooling, Tufting, Latexing, and Shearing. In the Dyeing Department, direct materials (dye) are added at the beginning of the process. Conversion costs are incurred evenly throughout the process. Casey uses weighted-average process costing. Information for March 2011 follows:

Units:	
Beginning work in process inventory, 40% complete as to conversion work	75 rolls
Transferred-in from Spinning Department during March	560 rolls
Completed during March	500 rolls
Ending work in process (80% complete as to conversion work)	135 rolls
Costs:	
Beginning work in process (transferred-in cost, $1,852	
materials cost, $3,075 conversion costs, $2,212	$ 7,139
Transferred-in from Spinning Department during March	12,880
Materials cost added during March	22,960
Conversion costs added during March (manufacturing wages,	
$8,445; manufacturing overhead, $45,887)	54,332

Requirements

1. Prepare a time line for Casey's Dyeing Department.
2. Use the time line to help you compute the equivalent units, cost per equivalent unit, and total costs to account for in Casey's Dyeing Department for March using the weighted-average method.
3. Prepare the March production cost report for Casey's Dyeing Department.
4. Journalize all transactions affecting Casey's Dyeing Department during March, including the entries that have already been posted.

P4-27A *(L. OBJ. 1)* **Computing equivalent units for a second department with beginning inventory; assigning costs to completed units and ending work in process— weighted-average method [50–60 min]**

SeaWorthy uses three processes to manufacture lifts for personal watercraft: forming a lift's parts from galvanized steel, assembling the lift, and testing the completed lifts. The lifts are transferred to finished goods before shipment to marinas across the country.

    SeaWorthy's Testing Department requires no direct materials. Conversion costs are incurred evenly throughout the Testing process. Other information follows:

Units:	
Beginning work in process inventory, 70% complete as to conversion work	2,100 units
Transferred-in from Assembling Dept during the period	7,300 units
Completed during the period	4,300 units
Ending work in process (40% complete as to conversion work)	5,100 units
Costs:	
Beginning work in process (transferred-in cost, $142,000	
conversion costs, $17,180)	$159,180
Transferred-in from Assembling Dept during the period	657,000
Conversion costs added during the period	77,920

The cost transferred into Finished goods inventory is the cost of the lifts transferred out of the Testing Department. SeaWorthy uses weighted-average process costing.

Requirements

1. Draw a time line for the Testing Department.
2. Use the time line to compute the number of equivalent units of work performed by the Testing Department during the period using the weighted-average method.

3. Compute SeaWorthy's transferred-in and conversion costs per equivalent unit. Use the unit costs to assign total costs to (a) units completed and transferred out of Testing and (b) units in Testing's Ending work in process inventory.

4. Compute the cost per unit for lifts completed and transferred out to Finished goods inventory. Why would management be interested in this cost?

P4-28A *(L. OBJ. 2)* **Computing equivalent units and assigning costs to completed units and ending work in process; beginning inventory without cost transferred-in—FIFO [30–45 min]**

Use the data from P4-23A to answer the requirements using the FIFO method.

Requirements

1. Draw a time line for the Assembly Department.

2. Use the time line to help you compute the number of equivalent units and the cost per equivalent unit in the Assembly Department for June.

3. Assign total costs in the Assembly Department using the FIFO method to (a) units completed and transferred to Programming during June and (b) units still in process at June 30.

4. Prepare a T-account for Work in process inventory—Assembly to show its activity during June, including the June 30 balance.

P4-29A *(L. OBJ. 2)* **Computing equivalent units and assigning costs to completed units and ending work in process; beginning inventory without cost transferred-in—FIFO [30–45 min]**

Use the data from P4-24A to answer the requirements using the FIFO method.

Requirements

1. Draw a time line for the Mixing Department.

2. Use the time line to help you compute the number of equivalent units and the cost per equivalent unit in the Mixing Department for August using the FIFO method.

3. Show that the sum of (a) cost of goods transferred out of the Mixing Department and (b) ending Work in process inventory—Mixing equals the total cost accumulated in the department during August.

4. Journalize all transactions affecting the company's Mixing process during August, including those already posted.

P4-30A *(L. OBJ. 2)* **Computing equivalent units and assigning costs to completed units and ending WIP inventory; two materials, added at different points; beginning inventory without cost transferred-in—FIFO [30–45 min]**

Use the data from P4-25A to answer the requirements using the FIFO method.

Requirements

1. Draw a time line for the Preparation Department.

2. Use the time line to help you compute the equivalent units using the FIFO method. (*Hint*: Each direct material added at a different point in the Production process requires its own equivalent-unit computation.)

3. Compute the total costs of the units (sheets)
   a. completed and transferred out to the Compression Department.
   b. in the Preparation Department's Ending work in process inventory.

4. Prepare the journal entry to record the cost of the sheets completed and transferred out to the Compression Department.

5. Post the journal entries to the Work in process inventory—Preparation T-account. What is the ending balance?

P4-31A *(L. OBJ. 2)* **Computing equivalent units for a second department with beginning inventory; preparing a production cost report and recording transactions on the basis of the report's information—FIFO method [45–60 min]**

Use the data from P4-26A to answer the requirements using the FIFO method.

Requirements

1. Prepare a time line for Casey's Dyeing Department.

2. Use the time line to help you compute the equivalent units, cost per equivalent unit, and total costs to account for in Casey's Dyeing Department for March using the FIFO method.

3. Prepare the March production cost report for Casey's Dyeing Department.

4. Journalize all transactions affecting Casey's Dyeing Department during March, including the entries that have already been posted.

P4-32A *(L. OBJ. 2)* **Computing equivalent units for a second department with beginning inventory; assigning costs to completed units and ending work in process—FIFO method [50–60 min]**

Use the data from P4-27A to answer the requirements using the FIFO method.

Requirements

1. Draw a time line for the Testing Department.

2. Use the time line to compute the number of equivalent units of work performed by the Testing Department during the period.

3. Compute SeaWorthy's transferred-in and conversion costs per equivalent unit using the FIFO method. Use the unit costs to assign total costs to (a) units completed and transferred out of Testing and (b) units in Testing's Ending work in process inventory.

4. Compute the cost per unit for lifts completed and transferred out to Finished goods inventory. Why would management be interested in this cost?

■ Problems (Group B)

P4-33B *(L. OBJ. 1)* **Computing equivalent units and assigning costs to completed units and ending work in process; beginning inventory without cost transferred-in— weighted average [30–45 min]**

Liz Electronics makes CD players in three processes: Assembly, Programming, and Packaging. Direct materials are added at the beginning of the Assembly process. Conversion costs are incurred evenly throughout the process. The Assembly Department had 8,000 units that were 50% complete in Work in process on May 31. In mid-June, Liz Electronics started production on 100,000 CD players. Of this number 85,000 CD players were assembled during June and transferred out to the Programming Department. The June 30 Work in process in the Assembly Department was 25% of the way through the Assembly process. Beginning Work in Process had materials cost of $23,000 and conversion costs of $18,675. During June, direct materials costing $355,000 were placed in production in Assembly during June, and Direct labor of $103,600 and Manufacturing overhead of $104,600 were assigned to that department.

Requirements

1. Fill-in the time line for Liz Electronics.

2. Use the time line to help you compute the number of equivalent units and the cost per equivalent unit in the Assembly Department for June.

3. Assign total costs in the Assembly Department using the weighted-average method to (a) units completed and transferred to Programming during June and (b) units still in process at June 30.

4. Prepare a T-account for Work in process inventory Assembly to show activity during June, including the June 30 balance.

P4-34B *(L. OBJ. 1)* **Computing equivalent units and assigning costs to completed units and ending work in process; beginning inventory without cost transferred-in—weighted average [30–45 min]**

Neal Paper, Co., produces the paper used by wallpaper manufacturers. Neal's four-stage process includes Mixing, Cooking, Rolling, and Cutting. Neal started August with 1,500 rolls of paper that were 60% complete with $2,407 of materials and $2,587 of conversion costs associated with them. During August, the Mixing Department started mixing for an additional 4,400 rolls of paper. The department did not finish 300 rolls of paper, which were 45% complete with respect to both direct materials and conversion work at the end of August. Direct materials and conversion costs are incurred evenly throughout the Mixing process. The Mixing Department incurred the following costs during August:

Work in process inventory-Mixing

Bal, Aug 1	4,994
Direct materials	6,769
Direct labor	1,597
Manufacturing overhead	6,139

Requirements

1. Fill-in the time line for the Mixing Department.

2. Use the time line to help you compute the number of equivalent units and the cost per equivalent unit in the Mixing Department for August using the weighted-average method.

3. Does the sum of (a) cost of goods transferred out of the Mixing Department and (b) ending Work in process inventory—Mixing equal the total cost accumulated in the department during August? Explain your answer.

4. Journalize all transactions affecting the company's Mixing process during August, including those already posted.

P4-35B *(L. OBJ. 1)* **Computing equivalent units and assigning costs to completed units and ending WIP inventory; two materials, added at different points; beginning inventory without cost transferred-in—weighted average [30–45 min]**

White's Exteriors produces exterior siding for homes. The Preparation Department begins with wood, which is chopped into small bits. At the end of the process, an adhesive is added. Then the wood/adhesive mixture goes on to the Compression Department, where the wood is compressed into sheets. Conversion costs are added evenly throughout the preparation process. The beginning Work in process inventory is composed of $930 of wood costs and $864 of conversion costs. January data for the Preparation Department are as follows (in millions):

Sheets		Costs	
Beginning work in process inventory,		Beginning work in process inventory	$ 1,794
(40% of the way through Preparation process)	1,800 sheets	Costs added during January:	
Started in production	4,200 sheets	Wood	3,150
Completed and transferred out to		Adhesives	3,010
Compression in January	3,500 sheets	Direct labor	1,300
Ending work in process inventory (35%		Manufacturing overhead	3,086
of the way through Preparation process)	2,500 sheets	Total costs	$12,340

Requirements

1. Fill-in the time line for the Preparation Department.

2. Use the time line to help you compute the equivalent units using the weighted-average method. (*Hint:* Each direct material added at a different point in the Production process requires its own equivalent-unit computation.)

3. Compute the total costs of the units (sheets)
   a. completed and transferred out to the Compression Department.
   b. in the Preparation Department's Ending work in process inventory.

4. Prepare the journal entry to record the cost of the sheets completed and transferred out to the Compression Department.

5. Post the journal entries to the Work in process inventory Preparation T-account. What is the ending balance?

P4-36B *(L. OBJ. 1)* **Computing equivalent units for a second department with beginning inventory; preparing a production cost report and recording transactions on the basis of the report's information—weighted-average method [45–60 min]**

Claudia Carpet manufactures broadloom carpet in seven processes: Spinning, Dyeing, Plying, Spooling, Tufting, Latexing, and Shearing. In the Dyeing Department the direct materials (dye) are added at the beginning of the process. Conversion costs are incurred evenly throughout the process. Claudia uses weighted-average process costing. Information for March 2011 follows:

Units:	
Beginning work in process inventory, (20% complete as to conversion work)	55 rolls
Transferred-in from Spinning Department during March	890 rolls
Completed during March	870 rolls
Ending work in process (60% complete as to conversion work)	75 rolls
Costs:	
Beginning work in process (transferred-in cost, $1,770; materials cost, $2,365; conversion costs, $2,710)	$ 6,845
Transferred-in from Spinning Department during March	13,350
Materials cost added during March	38,270
Conversion costs added during March (manufacturing wages, $7,225; manufacturing overhead, $65,095)	72,320

Requirements

1. Fill in the time line for Claudia's Dyeing Department.

2. Use the time line to help you compute the equivalent units, cost per equivalent unit, and total costs to account for in Claudia's Dyeing Department for March using the weighted-average method.

3. Prepare the March production cost report for Claudia's Dyeing Department.

4. Journalize all transactions affecting Claudia's Dyeing Department during March, including the entries that have already been posted.

P4-37B *(L. OBJ. 1)* **Computing equivalent units for a second department with beginning inventory; assigning costs to completed units and ending work in process—weighted average method [50–60 min]**

WaterWorthy uses three processes to manufacture lifts for personal watercraft: forming a lift's parts from galvanized steel, assembling the lift, and testing the completed lifts. The lifts are transferred to finished goods before shipment to marinas across the country. WaterWorthy's Testing Department requires no direct materials. Conversion costs are incurred evenly throughout the testing process. Other information follows:

Units:	
Beginning work in process inventory (50% complete as to conversion work)	1,500 units
Transferred-in from Assembling Dept during the period	9,000 units
Completed during the period	6,500 units
Ending work in process (30% complete as to conversion work)	4,000 units
Costs:	
Beginning work in process (transferred-in cost, $63,000; conversion costs, $2,050)	$ 65,050
Transferred-in from Assembling Dept during the period	756,000
Conversion costs added during the period	90,350

The costs transferred into Finished goods inventory is the cost of the lifts transferred out of the Testing Department. WaterWorthy uses weighted-average process costing.

Requirements

1. Fill in the time line for the Testing Department.
2. Use the time line to compute the number of equivalent units of work performed by the Testing Department during the period using the weighted-average method.
3. Compute WaterWorthy's transferred-in and conversion costs per equivalent unit. Use the unit costs to assign total costs to (a) units completed and transferred out of Testing and (b) units in Testing's Ending work in process inventory.
4. Compute the cost per unit for lifts completed and transferred out to Finished goods inventory. Why would management be interested in this cost?

P4-38B *(L. OBJ. 2)* **Computing equivalent units and assigning costs to completed units and ending work in process; beginning inventory without cost transferred-in—FIFO [30–45 min]**
Use the data from P4-33B to answer the requirements using the FIFO method.

Requirements

1. Fill-in the time line for Liz Electronics.
2. Use the time line to help you compute the number of equivalent units and the cost per equivalent unit in the Assembly Department for June.
3. Assign total costs in the Assembly Department using the FIFO method to (a) units completed and transferred to Programming during June and (b) units still in process at June 30.
4. Prepare a T-account for Work in process inventory—Assembly to show activity during June, including the June 30 balance.

P4-39B *(L. OBJ. 2)* **Computing equivalent units and assigning costs to completed units and ending work in process; beginning inventory without cost transferred-in—FIFO [30–45 min]**
Use the data from P4-34B to answer the requirements using the FIFO method.

Requirements

1. Fill-in the time line for the Mixing Department.
2. Use the time line to help you compute the number of equivalent units and the cost per equivalent unit in the Mixing Department for August using the FIFO method.

3. Does the sum of (a) cost of goods transferred out of the Mixing Department and (b) ending Work in process inventory—Mixing equal the total cost accumulated in the department during August? Explain your answer.

4. Journalize all transactions affecting the company's Mixing process during August, including those already posted.

P4-40B *(L. OBJ. 2)* **Computing equivalent units and assigning costs to completed units and ending WIP inventory; two materials, added at different points; beginning inventory without cost transferred-in—FIFO [30–45 min]**

Use the data from P4-35B to answer the requirements using the FIFO method.

Requirements

1. Fill-in the time line for the Preparation Department.

2. Use the time line to help you compute the equivalent units using the FIFO method. (*Hint:* Each direct material added at a different point in the production process requires its own equivalent-unit computation.)

3. Compute the total costs of the units (sheets)
    a. completed and transferred out to the Compression Department.
    b. in the Preparation Department's Ending work in process inventory.

4. Prepare the journal entry to record the cost of the sheets completed and transferred out to the Compression Department.

5. Post the journal entries to the Work in process inventory-Preparation T-account. What is the ending balance?

P4-41B *(L. OBJ. 2)* **Computing equivalent units for a second department with beginning inventory; preparing a production cost report and recording transactions on the basis of the report's information—FIFO method [45–60 min]**

Use the data from P4-36B to answer the requirements using the FIFO method.

Requirements

1. Fill in the time line for Claudia's Dyeing Department.

2. Use the time line to help you compute the equivalent units, cost per equivalent unit, and total costs to account for in Claudia's Dyeing Department for March using the FIFO method.

3. Prepare the March production cost report for Claudia's Dyeing Department.

4. Journalize all transactions affecting Claudia's Dyeing Department during March, including the entries that have already been posted.

P4-42B *(L. OBJ. 2)* **Computing equivalent units for a second department with beginning inventory; assigning costs to completed units and ending work in process— FIFO method [50–60 min]**

Use the data from P4-37B to answer the requirements using the FIFO method.

Requirements

1. Fill in the time line for the Testing Department.

2. Use the time line to compute the number of equivalent units of work performed by the Testing Department during the period using the FIFO method.

3. Compute WaterWorthy's transferred-in and conversion costs per equivalent unit. Use the unit costs to assign total costs to (a) units completed and transferred out of Testing and (b) units in Testing's Ending work in process inventory.

4. Compute the cost per unit for lifts completed and transferred out to Finished goods inventory. Why would management be interested in this cost?

Continuing Exercise

E4-43 This exercise continues the Sherman Lawn Service, Inc., situation from Exercise 3-35 of Chapter 3. Sherman manufactures mulch in a two stage process: Chopping and Mixing. Wood is added at the beginning of the Chopping Department. After chopping, the material is moved to the Mixing Department. In the Mixing Department, dirt is added to the chopped wood mixture; it is stirred and then bagged in one pound bags. The Chopping Department has the following data for June:

	March Chopping Dept	N/A
Units:		
Beginning WIP-units	10,000	pounds
Started in production	100,000	pounds
Transferred out	75,000	pounds
Ending WIP	35,000	pounds
Beginning WIP-% complete	60%	
Ending WIP-% complete	35%	
Costs:		
Beginning WIP-Materials costs	$ 20,000	
Beginning WIP-Conversion costs	$ 10,000	
Direct materials	$200,000	
Conversion costs:		
Direct labor	$ 10,000	
Manufacturing overhead	$ 67,250	
Total conversion costs	$ 77,250	

Requirements

1. Prepare the cost of production report using the weighted-average method for the Chopping Department for March.

2. Prepare the journal entry to transfer 75,000 pounds from the Chopping Department to the Mixing Department.

Continuing Problem

P4-44 This problem continues the Haupt Consulting, Inc., situation from Problem 3-36 of Chapter 3. Haupt Consulting uses a FIFO process costing system to track production of its new software, Fix-IT. Fix-IT is processed in three departments: The first, Encoding Department, encodes software onto the CD; the second, Casing Department, places the CD into a plastic case; and the last, Packaging Department, shrink wraps the CD and operating manual with the software before the product is sent to finished goods. Conversion occurs equally in all departments.

Haupt has the following data for the Casing Department:

	September Casing
Units:	
Beginning WIP	20,000
Transferred in from the Encoding Department	50,000
Transferred out	60,000
Ending WIP	10,000
Beginning WIP-% complete	70%
Ending WIP-% complete	20%
Costs:	
Beginning WIP-Transferred-in costs	$12,000
Beginning WIP-Materials costs	$20,000
Beginning WIP-Conversion costs	$13,000
Cost transferred from the Encoding Department	$20,000
Direct materials	$30,000
Conversion costs:	
Direct labor	$ 8,600
Manufacturing overhead	$ 3,400
Total conversion costs	$12,000

Requirements

1. The cases are added immediately in the Casing Department. Prepare the cost of production report using the FIFO method for the Casing Department for September.

2. Prepare all journal entries that affect the Work in process—Casing Department account for September.

Apply Your Knowledge

■ Decision Cases

Case 1. Hiebert Chocolate, Ltd., is located in Memphis. The company prepares gift boxes of chocolates for private parties and corporate promotions. Each order contains a pre-determined selection of chocolates that are distributed and sold by various retail stores. The chocolate gift boxes are made in a three stage production process: Mixing, Drying, and Packaging. In the Mixing Department, chocolate is melted and mixed with other ingredients. The Drying Department takes the melted mixture, forms it into various shapes, and dries the chocolates. The Packaging Department takes the dried chocolates and boxes them, just before they are sent to finished goods. Accordingly, Hiebert uses a process costing system.

One of Hiebert's largest customers is **Wal-Mart**. This organization purchases roughly 80% of all Hiebert's products.

The following data for the Packaging Department for March are available:

	Packaging Department
Units:	
Beginning WIP-Units	10,000
Started in production	80,000
Transferred out	75,000
Ending WIP-Units	15,000
Beginning WIP-% complete	40%
Ending WIP-% complete	80%
Costs:	
Beginning WIP-Transferred-in costs	$ 3,000
Beginning WIP-Materials costs	$ -
Beginning WIP-Conversion costs	$ 1,630
Transferred-in costs	$ 9,600
Direct materials-Packaging	$21,000
Conversion costs:	
Direct labor	$ 8,470
Manufacturing overhead	$ 7,300
Total conversion costs	$15,770

Ben Hiebert, president of Hiebert Chocolate, Ltd, is trying to determine whether to use a weighted-average or FIFO product costing system, since Hiebert's contract with Wal-Mart allows for a sales price of cost per department + 15%.

Requirements

1. Consider only the Packaging Department data. Prepare cost of production reports using both weighted-average and FIFO process costing.
2. Which method should Heibert use and why?

■ Ethical Issue

Farley, Inc., is a coffee bean manufacturer that produces whole bean coffee for retailers. Farley uses weighted-average costing to account for production costs. Farley's has experienced significant cost increases over the past few months in its production costs. Significantly, materials input into the process have increased in cost from $100.00 to $175.00 per ton. Farley has significant stores to last for approximately six months of production.

Farley's production manager gets a bonus based on profit made on each one pound bag of coffee sold and is advocating Farley switch to a FIFO process costing for production costs for the product.

Requirements

1. How would the increase in direct materials affect the final cost per bag? Consider both weighted-average and FIFO costing.
2. Would Farley's production manager benefit from this switch to the FIFO costing method?

Financial Statement Case—Amazon.com

This case is based on the **Amazon.com** annual report in Appendix A at the end of the book. Use it to answer the following questions.

Requirement

1. Review the description of **Amazon.com**'s business. Give some examples of business segments or departments where they might benefit from using process costing. Explain your reasons for your answer.

Team Project

Major airlines like **American, Delta,** and **Continental** are struggling to meet the challenges of budget carriers such as **Southwest** and **JetBlue.** Suppose the **Delta** CFO has just returned from a meeting on strategies for responding to competition from budget carriers. The vice president of operations suggested doing nothing: "We just need to wait until these new airlines run out of money. They cannot be making money with their low fares." In contrast, the vice president of marketing, not wanting to lose market share, suggests cutting **Delta**'s fares to match the competition. "If **JetBlue** charges only $75 for that flight from New York, so must we!" Others, including the CFO, emphasized the potential for cutting costs. Another possibility is starting a new budget airline within **Delta.** The CEO cut the meeting short, and directed the CFO to "get some hard data."

Quickly, the CFO zones in on beverage costs. The current beverages are provided by various manufacturers at an average cost of $0.50 per beverage. **Delta** budgets annual beverages used of 80 million for all flights.

The CFO suggests that Delta acquire a facility and manufacture its own beverages for use in flights. They could be manufactured in a simple one stage process where sugar, flavors, and water are added at the beginning, mixed, and then placed in cans at the end of the process. Data estimates for the first year of production are shown next:

	Soda Dept
Units:	
Beginning WIP-Units	-
Started in production	100,000,000
Transferred out	80,000,000
Ending WIP-Units	20,000,000
Beginning WIP-% complete	N/A
Ending WIP-% complete	60%
Costs:	
Direct materials-Sugar, flavoring and water	$ 8,500,000
Direct materials-Cans	$16,000,000
Conversion costs:	
Direct labor	$19,100,000
Manufacturing overhead	$ 3,900,000
Total conversion costs	$23,000,000

Requirements

1. Use the data to determine for **Delta** the weighted-average cost per can based on the first year's production estimates. Is it better for Delta to consider manufacturing its own beverage brand?

2. If Delta anticipates that its manufacturing facility can double annual production without affecting average production costs and Delta can sell the excess for $0.47 per can to various retailers, would it want to do so and why?

Quick Check Answers

1. *a* 2. *c* 3. *a* 4. *d* 5. *b* 6. *d* 7. *d* 8. *d* 9. *a* 10. *c*

For online homework, exercises, and problems that provide you immediate feedback, please visit www.myaccountinglab.com.

Big Picture

Ch 1   Introduction to Management Accounting

- ○⊓ Distinguish management accounting from financial accounting
- ○⊓ The role and responsibilities of management accountants
- ○⊓ Classify costs and prepare income statements for merchandising companies
- ○⊓ Classify costs and prepare income statements and statements of cost of goods manufactured for manufacturing companies

Ch 2   Job Order Costing

- ○⊓ Distinguish between job order and process costing
- ○⊓ Record materials, labor, and overhead in a job order costing system
- ○⊓ Record completion and sales of finished-goods and adjust for under-/overallocated overhead
- ○⊓ Calculate unit costs for service companies

Ch 3   Activity-Based Costing and Other Cost Management Tools

- ○⊓ Develop activity-based costs and used activity-based management to determine target product costs
- ○⊓ Record transactions in JIT systems
- ○⊓ Use the four types of quality costs to make management decisions

Ch 4   Process Costing

- ○⊓ Calculate equivalent units and conversion costs
- ○⊓ Prepare cost of production reports and the related journal entries using the weighted-average costing method
- ○⊓ Prepare cost of production reports and the related journal entries using the FIFO costing method

Chapter 4: Demo Doc

■ Illustrating Process Costing

Clear Bottled Water produces packaged water. Clear has two production departments: blending and packaging. In the blending department, materials are added at the beginning of the process. Conversion costs are added throughout the process for blending. Data for the month of April for the blending department are as follows:

Blending Department Data for April:

Units:

Beginning work in process	0 units
Started in production during April	116,000 units
Completed and transferred out to Packaging in April	98,000 units
Ending work in process inventory (70% completed)	18,000 units

Costs:

Beginning work in process	$ 0
Costs added during April:	
Direct materials	54,520
Conversion costs	32,074
Total costs added during April	$86,594

Requirement

1. Use the four-step process to calculate (1) the cost of the units completed and transferred out to the packaging department, and (2) the total cost of the units in the blending department ending work in process inventory. Use the weighted-average method.

Demo Doc Solution

Requirement 1

Use the four-step process to calculate (1) the cost of the units completed and transferred out to the packaging department, and (2) the total cost of the units in the blending department ending work in process inventory. Use the weighted-average method.

Steps 1 and 2: Summarize the flow of physical units and compute output in terms of equivalent units.

Part 1	Part 2	Part 3	Demo Doc Complete

1 Prepare cost of production reports using the weighted-average costing method and prepare related journal entries

Total units to account for is the equivalent of units completed and transferred out of packaging in April (98,000) plus the ending work in process inventory of April 30 (18,000):

	Step 1 Flow of Physical Units	Step 2: Equivalent Units	
CLEAR BOTTLED WATER Blending Department Month Ended April 30, 2010		Direct Materials	Conversion Costs
Flow of Production			
Units to account for:			
Beginning work in process, March 31	0		
Started in production during April	116,000		
Total physical units to account for	116,000		

Materials are added at the beginning of the blending production process, so equivalent units for materials is the same as the total units.

Completed units have 100% of their conversion costs (98,000).

Conversion costs are added evenly throughout the blending process, so the conversion equivalent units for ending work in process inventory are the total units in ending work in process, 18,000, times the percent complete, 70% = 12,600.

Remember, conversion costs include both direct labor and manufacturing overhead.

CLEAR BOTTLED WATER
Blending Department
Month Ended April 30, 2010

Flow of Production	Step 1 Flow of Physical Units	Step 2: Equivalent Units Direct Materials	Conversion Costs
Units to account for:			
Beginning work in process, March 31	0		
Started in production during April	116,000		
Total physical units to account for	116,000		
Units accounted for:			
Completed and transferred out during April	98,000	98,000	98,000
Ending work in process, April 30	18,000	18,000	12,600
Total physical units accounted for	116,000		
Equivalent units		116,000	110,600

From this, we can see that the total units accounted for is 116,000 units, with 98,000 completed units + 18,000 work in process units = 116,000 equivalent units for direct materials, and 98,000 completed units + 12,600 work in process units = 110,600 equivalent units for conversion costs.

Step 3: Compute the cost per equivalent unit.

Part 1	Part 2	Part 3	Demo Doc Complete

The cost per equivalent unit is computed by dividing the costs added during the period by the equivalent units:

$$\text{Cost per equivalent unit for direct materials} = \frac{\text{Total direct material cost}}{\text{Equivalent units for direct material cost}}$$

$$\text{Cost per equivalent unit for conversion cost} = \frac{\text{Total conversion cost}}{\text{Equivalent units for conversion cost}}$$

We know from Step 1 that Clear has 116,000 accountable units. From the question, we know that Clear has $54,520 of total accountable direct materials costs in April.

Using the formula for cost per equivalent unit for direct materials, we divide the total direct materials costs of $54,520 by the equivalent units of materials, determined in Step 2 as 116,000 units = $0.47 per equivalent units for direct materials.

By using equivalent units, we are indicating that $32,074 of conversion costs will blend 110,600 units from the start of the blending process to the end of the blending process. To calculate costs per equivalent unit for conversion costs, we must divide the total conversion costs of $32,074 by the number of equivalent units for conversion, determined in Step 2 to be 110,600 = $0.29 per equivalent units for conversion costs.

CLEAR BOTTLED WATER
Blending Department
Month Ended April 30, 2010

| | Step 3: Cost per Equivalent Unit | |
	Direct Materials	Conversion Costs
Beginning work in process, March 31	$ 0	$ 0
Costs added during April	54,520	32,074
Total costs for April	$ 54,520	$ 32,074
Divide by equivalent units	÷ 116,000	÷ 110,600
Cost per equivalent unit	$ 0.47	$ 0.29

Step 4: Assign costs to units completed and to units still in ending Work in process inventory.

Part 1	Part 2	**Part 3**	Demo Doc Complete

Because the units completed and transferred out were started and finished in the month of April, their cost is the full unit cost of $0.76. Shown another way

$98,000 \times \$0.47 = \$46,060$ (direct materials) (100%)
$98,000 \times \underline{\$0.29} = \underline{\$28,420}$ (conversion costs) (100%)
$98,000 \times \underline{\$0.76} = \underline{\$74,480}$

The ending work in process is complete regarding materials because they are added in their entirety at the beginning of the blending process.

The conversion costs in ending work in process are only 70% complete because conversion costs occur evenly throughout the blending process. Multiplying each by their respective per-unit cost

$$18,000 \times \$0.47 = \$ \ 8,460 \text{ (direct materials) (100\%)}$$
$$12,600 \times \$0.29 = \underline{\$ \ 3,654} \text{ (conversion costs) (70\%)}$$
$$\underline{\$12,114}$$

The solution to the problem is (1) the $74,480 cost of the goods completed and transferred out of the blending department to the packaging department during April added to (2) the $12,114 cost of the ending work in process in the blending department as of April 30 = total costs accounted for of $86,594.

CLEAR BOTTLED WATER
Blending Department
Month Ended April 30, 2010

		Step 4: Assign Costs		
		Direct Materials	Conversion Costs	Total
Units completed and transferred out to Packaging in April	[98,000 ×	($0.47 +	$0.29)]	= $74,480
Ending work in process, April 30:				
Direct materials	18,000 ×	0.47		= 8,460
Conversion costs	12,600 ×		0.29	= 3,654
Total ending work in process, March 31				$12,114
Total costs accounted for				$86,594

Part 1	Part 2	Part 3	Demo Doc Complete

5 Cost Behavior and Cost-Volume-Profit Analysis

Learning Objectives/ Success Keys

1. Identify how changes in volume affect costs

2. Use CVP analysis to compute breakeven points

3. Use CVP analysis for profit planning, and graph the CVP relations

4. Use CVP methods to perform sensitivity analyses

5. Calculate the breakeven point for multiple product lines or services

As Smart Touch Learning and Greg's Groovy Tunes consider different growth and marketing strategies, they also have to consider what effect these changes will have on profitability.

You will learn cost behavior and how cost-volume-profit (CVP) analysis is used to manage a business. **Cost-volume-profit (CVP) analysis** expresses the relationships among costs, volume, and profit or loss. It is an effective management tool and easy to understand.

Cost Behavior

Some costs increase as the volume of activity increases. Other costs are not affected by volume changes. Managers need to know how a business's costs are affected by changes in its volume of activity. Let us look at the three different types of costs:

1   Identify how changes in volume affect costs

- Variable costs
- Fixed costs
- Mixed costs

Variable Costs

Total variable costs change in direct proportion to changes in the volume of activity. For our purposes, an activity is a business action that affects costs. Those activities include selling, producing, driving, and calling. The activities can be measured by units sold, units produced, miles driven, and the number of phone calls placed. So **variable costs** are those costs that increase or decrease in total as the volume of activity increases or decreases.

As you may recall, Greg's Groovy Tunes offers DJ services for parties, weddings, and other events. For each event, Greg's spends $15 for equipment rental. Greg's can perform for 15 to 30 events per month. To calculate total variable costs Natalie Blanding, the office manager, would show the following:

Number of Events per Month	Equipment Rental Cost per Event	Total Equipment Rental Cost per Month
15	$15	$225
20	$15	$300
30	$15	$450

As you can see, the total variable cost of equipment rental increases as the number of events increases. But the equipment rental cost per event does not change. Exhibit 5-1 graphs total variable costs for equipment rental as the number of events increases from 0 to 30.

EXHIBIT 5-1 | **Variable Costs**

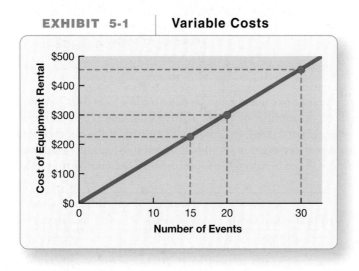

If there are no events, Greg's incurs no equipment rental costs, so the total variable cost line begins at the bottom left corner. This point is called the *origin*, and it represents zero volume and zero cost. The *slope* of the variable cost line is the change in equipment rental cost (on the vertical axis) divided by the change in the number of events (on the horizontal axis). The slope of the graph equals the variable cost per unit. In Exhibit 5-1, the slope of the variable cost line is 15 because Greg's spends $15 on equipment rental for each event.

If Greg's Groovy Tunes performs at 15 events during the month, it will spend a total of $225 (15 events × $15 each) for equipment rental. Follow this total variable cost line to the right to see that doubling the number of events to 30 likewise doubles the total variable cost to $450 (30 × $15 = $450). Exhibit 5-1 shows how the *total variable cost* of equipment rental varies with the number of events. But note that *the per-event cost remains constant* at $15.

Remember this important fact about *variable costs*:

> Total variable costs fluctuate with changes in volume, but the variable cost per unit remains constant.

Fixed Costs

In contrast, **total fixed costs** are costs that do not change over wide ranges of volume. Greg's fixed costs include depreciation on the cars, as well as the DJs' salaries. Greg's has these fixed costs regardless of the number of events—15, 20, or 30.

Suppose Greg's incurs $12,000 of fixed costs each month, and the number of monthly events is between 15 and 30. Exhibit 5-2 graphs total fixed costs as a flat line that intersects the cost axis at $12,000, because Greg's will incur the same $12,000 of fixed costs regardless of the number of events.

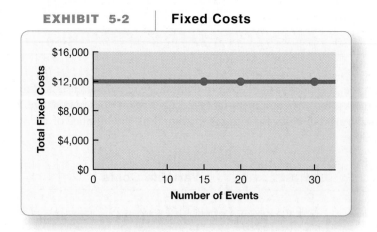

EXHIBIT 5-2 | **Fixed Costs**

Total fixed cost does not change, as shown in Exhibit 5-2. But the *fixed cost per event* depends on the number of events. If Greg's Groovy Tunes performs at 15 events, the fixed cost per event is $800 ($12,000 ÷ 15 events). If the number of events doubles to 30, the fixed cost per event is cut in half to $400 ($12,000 ÷ 30 events). Therefore, the fixed cost per event is *inversely* proportional to the number of events, as follows:

Total Fixed Costs	Number of Events	Fixed Cost per Event
$12,000	15	$800
$12,000	20	$600
$12,000	30	$400

Remember the following important fact about **fixed costs:**

> Total fixed costs remain constant, but the fixed cost per unit is inversely proportional to volume.

Mixed Costs

Costs that have both variable and fixed components are called **mixed costs**. For example, Greg's Groovy Tunes' cell-phone company charges $10 a month to provide the service and $0.15 for each minute of use. If the cell phone is used for 100 minutes, the company will bill Greg's $25 [$10 + (100 minutes × $0.15)].

Exhibit 5-3 shows how Greg's can separate its cell-phone bill into fixed and variable components. The $10 monthly charge is a fixed cost because it is the same no matter how many minutes the company uses the cell phone. The $0.15-per-minute charge is a variable cost that increases in direct proportion to the number of minutes of use. If Greg's uses the phone for 100 minutes, its total variable cost is $15 (100 minutes × $0.15). If it doubles the use to 200 minutes, total variable cost also doubles to $30 (200 minutes × $0.15), and the total bill rises to $40 ($10 + $30).

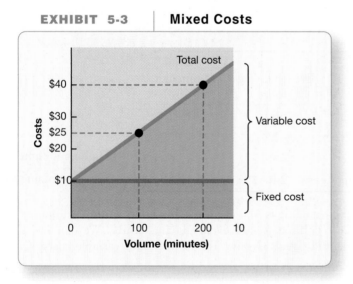

EXHIBIT 5-3 | **Mixed Costs**

Stop & Think...

Think about your costs related to taking this class. Which ones are fixed? Which ones are variable? The cost of your tuition and books are fixed costs, because you pay one price for the class and your books, no matter how many days you come to class. If you drive to class, the cost of gas put in your car is variable, because you only incur gas costs when you come to class. Are there any mixed costs associated with your class? Maybe your Internet service provider charges you a flat fee each month plus a rate for every hour you are online. Your time using myaccountinglab would be a mixed cost associated with this class.

High-Low Method to Separate Fixed Cost from Variable Cost

An easy method to separate mixed costs into variable and fixed components is the **high-low method**. This method requires you to identify the highest and lowest levels of activity over a period of time. Using this information, complete the following three steps:

STEP 1: Calculate the variable cost per unit.

Variable cost per unit = Change in total cost ÷ Change in volume of activity

STEP 2: Calculate the total fixed costs.

Total fixed cost = Total mixed cost − Total variable cost

STEP 3: Create and use an equation to show the behavior of a mixed cost.

Total mixed cost = (Variable cost per unit × number of units) + Total fixed costs

Let us revisit the Greg's Groovy Tunes illustration. A summary of Greg's Groovy Tunes' music equipment maintenance costs for the past year shows the following costs for each quarter:

	Event-Playing Hours	Total Maintenance Cost	
1st Quarter	360	$1,720	
2nd Quarter	415	1,830	
3rd Quarter	480	1,960	◀── Highest Volume and Cost
4th Quarter	240	1,480	◀── Lowest Volume and Cost

The highest volume is 480 event-playing hours in the 3rd quarter of the year, and the lowest volume is 240 event-playing hours. We can use the high-low method to identify Greg's Groovy Tunes' fixed and variable costs of music equipment maintenance.

STEP 1: Calculate the variable cost per unit.

Variable cost per unit = Change in total cost ÷ Change in volume of activity
= ($1,960 − $1,480) ÷ (480 hours − 240 hours)
= $480 ÷ 240 hours
= $2 per event-playing hour

STEP 2: Calculate the total fixed costs.

Total fixed cost = Total mixed cost − Total variable cost
= $1,960 − ($2 × 480)
= $1,960 − $960
= $1,000

This example uses the highest cost and volume to calculate the total fixed costs, but you can use any volume and calculate the same $1,000 total fixed cost.

> STEP 3:   Create and use an equation to show the behavior of a mixed cost.

Total mixed cost   = (Variable cost per unit × number of units) + Total fixed costs
Total equipment maintenance cost = ($2 per event-playing hour × No. of hours) + $1,000

Using this equation, the estimated music equipment maintenance cost for 400 event-playing hours would be as follows:

($2 × 400 event-playing hours) + $1,000 = $1,800

This method provides a rough estimate of fixed and variable costs for cost-volume-profit analysis. The high and low volumes become the relevant range, which we discuss in the next section. Managers find the high-low method to be quick and easy, but regression analysis provides the most accurate estimates and is discussed in cost accounting textbooks.

Least Squares Regression Analysis to Separate Fixed Cost from Variable Cost

The **least squares regression method** provides an alternate way to separate mixed costs into variable and fixed components. This method uses all the available cost and activity data to form a regression line that minimizes the deviations. The data is entered into an Excel or other computer model to form the equation that symbolizes the mixed cost. The equation is basically the same as what we saw in the high-low formula, but is represented by letters.

High-low: Total mixed cost = (Variable cost per unit × number of units) + Total fixed costs
Least squares: Y   = bX   + a

Let us revisit the Greg's Groovy Tunes illustration. A summary of Greg's Groovy Tunes' music equipment maintenance costs for the past year shows the following costs for each quarter as well as some of the totals we will need for our least squares formula.

	Event-Playing Hours (X)	Total Maintenance Cost (Y)	XY	X^2	Y^2
1st Quarter	360	$1,720	619,200	129,600	2,958,400
2nd Quarter	415	1,830	759,450	172,225	3,348,900
3rd Quarter	480	1,960	940,800	230,400	3,841,600
4th Quarter	240	1,480	355,200	57,600	2,190,400
Total	1,495	6,990	2,674,650	589,825	12,339,300

The formulas used to calculate least squares are:

$$b = \frac{n(\Sigma XY) - (\Sigma X)(\Sigma Y)}{n(\Sigma X^2) - (\Sigma X)^2}$$

$$a = \frac{(\Sigma Y) - b(\Sigma X)}{n}$$

where

X = The level of activity (event-playing hours)

Y = The total mixed cost (total maintenance cost)

a = The total fixed cost

b = The variable cost per unit of activity (variable cost per event-playing hours)

n = Number of observations (four in our example)

Σ = The sum of

STEP 1:   Calculate b, the variable cost per event hour of playing.

$$b = \frac{n(\Sigma XY) - (\Sigma X)(\Sigma Y)}{n(\Sigma X^2) - (\Sigma X)^2}$$

$$b = \frac{4(2,674,650) - (1,495)(6,990)}{4(589,825) - (1,495)^2}$$

$$b = \frac{248,550}{124,275}$$

$$b = 2$$

This example uses the highest cost and volume to calculate the total fixed costs, but you can use any volume and calculate the same $1,000 total fixed cost.

STEP 2:   Calculate the fixed cost portion of the maintenance costs.

$$a = \frac{(\Sigma Y) - b(\Sigma X)}{n}$$

$$a = \frac{(6,990) - 2(1,495)}{4}$$

$$a = 1,000$$

STEP 3:   Create and use an equation to show the behavior of a mixed cost. The formula for Total mixed cost then is:

Total mixed cost   = (Variable cost per unit × number of units) + Total fixed costs

Total equipment maintenance cost = ($2 per event-playing hour × No. of hours) + $1,000

Using this equation, the estimated music equipment maintenance cost for 400 event-playing hours would be as follows:

($2 × 400 event-playing hours) + $1,000 = $1,800

Now we can show our least squares regression equation that calculates total maintenance costs based on even playing hours for Greg's Groovy Tunes

$$Y = 1,000 + 2(X)$$

Relevant Range

The **relevant range** is the band of volume where total fixed costs remain constant and the variable cost *per unit* remains constant. To estimate costs, managers need to know the relevant range. Why? Because,

- total "fixed" costs can differ from one relevant range to another.
- the variable cost *per unit* can differ in various relevant ranges.

Exhibit 5-4 shows fixed costs for Greg's Groovy Tunes over three different relevant ranges. If the company expects to offer 15,000 event-playing hours next year, the relevant range is between 10,000 and 20,000 event-playing hours, and managers budget fixed costs of $80,000.

To offer 22,000 event-playing hours, Greg's will have to expand the company. This will increase total fixed costs for added rent and equipment costs. Exhibit 5-4 shows that total fixed costs increase to $120,000 as the relevant range shifts to this higher band of volume. Conversely, if Greg's expects to offer only 8,000 event-playing hours, the company will budget only $40,000 of fixed costs. Managers will have to lay off employees or take other actions to cut fixed costs.

EXHIBIT 5-4 | **Relevant Range**

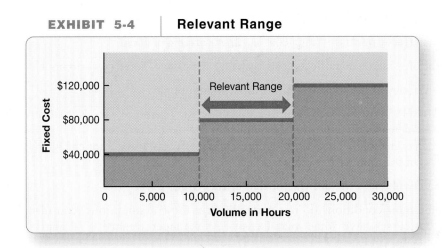

Variable cost per unit can also change outside the relevant range. For example, Greg's Groovy Tunes may get a quantity discount for equipment maintenance if it can provide more than 20,000 event-playing hours.

We have now covered the basics of CVP analysis. Let us apply CVP analysis to answer some interesting management questions.

Basic CVP Analysis: What Must We Sell to Break Even?

Greg's Groovy Tunes is considering expanding its events coverage to include weddings. Greg's first analyzes its existing costs, partially covered in the previous section. (For simplicity, we ignore the mixed costs.) Variable costs are $15 for gas per event plus $100 in contracted labor per event. All the other business expenses are fixed costs, $12,000. Average sales price per event is $235.

Selling price per event.................	$ 235
Variable cost per event...............	$ 115
Fixed costs	$12,000

Greg's Groovy Tunes faces several important questions:

- How many DJ services (hereinafter, events) must the company sell to break even?
- What will profits be if sales double?
- How will changes in selling price, variable costs, or fixed costs affect profits?

Before getting started, let us review the assumptions required for CVP analysis to be accurate.

Assumptions

CVP analysis assumes that

1. managers can classify each cost as either variable or fixed.

2. the only factor that affects costs is change in volume. Fixed costs do not change.

Greg's Groovy Tunes' business meets these assumptions:

1. The $115 cost for each event is a variable cost. Therefore, Greg's *total variable cost* increases directly with the number of events sold (an extra $115 in cost for each event sold). The $12,000 represents fixed costs and do not change regardless of the number of events worked.

2. Sales volume is the only factor that affects Greg's costs.

Most business conditions do not perfectly meet these assumptions (consider that most businesses have some mixed costs), so managers regard CVP analysis as approximate, not exact.

How Much Must Greg Sell to Break Even?
Three Approaches

Virtually all businesses want to know their breakeven point. The **breakeven point** is the sales level at which operating income is zero: Total revenues equal total costs. Sales below the breakeven point result in a loss. Sales above break even provide a profit. Greg's Groovy Tunes needs to know how many DJ events must be held to break even.

There are several ways to figure the breakeven point, including the

- income statement approach.
- contribution margin approach.

We start with the income statement approach because it is the easiest method to remember. You are already familiar with the income statement.

The Income Statement Approach

Start by expressing income in equation form:

Sales revenue – Total costs = Operating income

Sales revenue – Variable costs – Fixed costs = Operating income

Sales revenue equals the unit sale price ($235 per event in this case) multiplied by the number of units (events) sold. Variable costs equal variable cost per unit ($115 in this case) times the number of units sold. Greg's fixed costs total $12,000. At the breakeven point, operating income is zero. We use this information to solve the income statement equation for the number of DJ events Greg's must sell to break even.

Sales revenue	–	Variable costs	– Fixed costs = Operating income
$\left(\dfrac{\text{Sale price}}{\text{per unit}} \times \text{Units sold}\right)$ –		$\left(\dfrac{\text{Variable cost}}{\text{per unit}} \times \text{Units sold}\right)$	– Fixed costs = Operating income
($235 × Units sold) –		($115 × Units sold) – $12,000 =	$0
($235 –		$115) × Units sold – $12,000 =	$0
		$120 × Units sold =	$12,000
		Units sold =	$12,000 ÷ 120
		Breakeven sales in units =	100 events

Greg's Groovy Tunes must sell 100 events to break even. The breakeven sales level in dollars is $23,500 (100 events × $235).

Be sure to check your calculations. "Prove" the breakeven point by substituting the breakeven number of units into the income statement. Then check to ensure that this level of sales results in zero profit.

Proof	Sales revenue – Variable cost – Fixed costs = Operating income
	($235 × 100) – ($115 × 100) – $12,000 = $0
	$23,500 – $11,500 – $12,000 = $0

The Contribution Margin Approach: A Shortcut

This shortcut method of computing the breakeven point uses Greg's contribution margin. The **contribution margin** is sales revenue minus variable costs. It is called the *contribution margin* because the excess of sales revenue over variable costs contributes to covering fixed costs and then to providing operating income.

The **contribution margin income statement** shows costs by cost behavior—variable costs and fixed costs—and highlights the contribution margin. The format shows the following:

Sales revenue
– Variable costs
= Contribution margin
– Fixed costs
= Operating income

Now let us rearrange the income statement formula and use the contribution margin to develop a shortcut method for finding the number of DJ events Greg's must hold to break even.

$$\text{Sales revenue} \quad - \quad \text{Variable costs} \quad - \text{Fixed costs} = \text{Operating income}$$

$$\left(\frac{\text{Sale price}}{\text{per unit}} \times \text{Units sold}\right) - \left(\frac{\text{Variable cost}}{\text{per unit}} \times \text{Units sold}\right) - \text{Fixed costs} = \text{Operating income}$$

$$\left(\frac{\text{Sale price}}{\text{per unit}} - \frac{\text{Variable cost}}{\text{per unit}}\right) \times \text{Units sold} \qquad = \text{Fixed costs} + \text{Operating income}$$

$$\text{Contribution margin per unit} \times \text{Units sold} \qquad = \text{Fixed costs} + \text{Operating income}$$

Dividing both sides of the equation by the contribution margin per unit yields the cost-volume-profit equation:

$$\text{Units sold} = \frac{\text{Fixed costs} + \text{Operating income}}{\text{Contribution margin per unit}}$$

Greg's Groovy Tunes can use this contribution margin approach to find its breakeven point. Fixed costs total $12,000. Operating income is zero at break even. The contribution margin per event is $120 ($235 sale price – $115 variable cost). Greg's breakeven computation is as follows:

$$\text{Breakeven sales in units} = \frac{\$12,000}{\$120}$$
$$= 100 \text{ events}$$

Why does this shortcut method work? Each event Greg's Groovy Tunes sells provides $120 of contribution margin. To break even, Greg's must generate enough contribution margin to cover $12,000 of fixed costs. At the rate of $120 per event, Greg's must sell 100 events ($12,000/$120) to cover fixed costs. You can see that the contribution margin approach just rearranges the income statement equation, so the breakeven point is the same under both methods.

To "prove" the breakeven point, you can also use the contribution margin income statement format:

GREG'S GROOVY TUNES, INC. Income Statement For one month	
Sales revenue ($235 × 100 events)	$ 23,500
Less: Variable costs ($115 × 100 events)	(11,500)
Contribution margin ($120 × 100 events)	12,000
Less: Fixed costs	(12,000)
Operating income	$ 0

Using the Contribution Margin Ratio to Compute the Breakeven Point in Sales Dollars

Companies can use the contribution margin ratio to compute their breakeven point in terms of *sales dollars*. The **contribution margin ratio** is the ratio of contribution margin to sales revenue. For Greg's Groovy Tunes, we have the following:

$$\text{Contribution margin ratio} = \frac{\text{Contribution margin}}{\text{Sales revenue}} = \frac{\$120}{\$235} = 51.06\%$$

The 51% contribution margin ratio means that each dollar of sales revenue contributes $0.51 toward fixed costs and profit.

The contribution margin *ratio* approach differs from the shortcut contribution margin approach we have just seen in only one way: Here we use the contribution margin *ratio* rather than the dollar amount of the contribution margin.

$$\text{Breakeven sales in dollars} = \frac{\text{Fixed costs}}{\text{Contribution margin ratio}}$$

Using this ratio formula, Greg's breakeven point in sales dollars is as follows:

$$\text{Breakeven sales in dollars} = \frac{\$12,000}{0.5106}$$
$$= \$23,502$$

This is $2 larger than the breakeven sales revenue we calculated in the contribution margin approach, due to rounding. Therefore, it is basically the same.

Why does the contribution margin ratio formula work? Each dollar of Greg's sales contributes 51.06% to fixed costs and profit. To break even, Greg's must generate enough contribution margin at the rate of 51.06% of sales to cover the $12,000 fixed costs ($12,000 ÷ 0.5106 = $23,502).

Now, we have seen how companies use *contribution margin* to estimate breakeven points in CVP analysis. But managers use the contribution margin for other purposes too, such as motivating the sales force. Salespeople who know the contribution margin of each product can generate more profit by emphasizing high-margin products over low-margin products. This is why many companies base sales commissions on the contribution margins produced by sales rather than on sales revenue alone.

Using CVP to Plan Profits

For established products and services, managers are more interested in the sales level needed to earn a target profit than in the breakeven point. Managers of new business ventures are also interested in the profits they can expect to earn. For example, now that Greg's Groovy Tunes knows it must sell 100 events to break even, Natalie Blanding, the controller for Greg's, wants to know how many more events must be sold to earn a monthly operating profit of $6,000.

3   Use CVP analysis for profit planning, and graph the CVP relations

How Much Must Greg's Sell to Earn a Profit?

What is the only difference from our prior analysis? Here, Greg's wants to know how many events must be sold to earn a $6,000 profit. We can use the income statement approach or the shortcut contribution margin approach to find the answer. Let us start with the income statement approach.

	Sales revenue	−	Variable cost	− Fixed costs	= Operating income
	($235 × units sold)	−	($115 × units sold) −	$12,000 =	$ 6,000
		[($235 − 115) × units sold]		− $12,000 =	$ 6,000
		$120 × units sold		=	$18,000
				units sold =	$18,000 ÷ $120
				units sold =	150 events
Proof	($235 × 150)	−	($115 × 150)	− $12,000	= Operating income
	$35,250	−	$17,250	− $12,000 =	$6,000

This analysis shows that Greg's must sell 150 events each month to earn an operating profit of $6,000. This is 150 − 100 = 50 more events than the breakeven sales level (100 events).

The proof shows that Greg's needs sales revenues of $35,250 to earn a profit of $6,000. Alternatively, we can compute the dollar sales necessary to earn a $6,000 profit directly, using the contribution margin ratio form of the CVP formula:

$$\text{Target sales in dollars} = \frac{\text{Fixed costs} + \text{Operating income}}{\text{Contribution margin ratio}}$$

$$= \frac{\$12,000 + \$6,000}{0.5106}$$

$$= \frac{\$18,000}{0.5106}$$

$$= \$35,253$$

This shows that Greg's needs $35,253 in sales revenue, which is $3 off due to rounding. Essentially, this is the same result.

Graphing Cost-Volume-Profit Relations

Controller Natalie Blanding can graph the CVP relations for Greg's Groovy Tunes. A graph provides a picture that shows how changes in the levels of sales will affect profits. As in the variable-, fixed-, and mixed-cost graphs of Exhibits 5-1, 5-2, and 5-3, Blanding shows the volume of units (events) on the horizontal axis and dollars on the vertical axis. Then she follows four steps to graph the CVP relations for Greg's Groovy Tunes, as illustrated in Exhibit 5-5.

STEP 1: Choose a sales volume, such as 200 events. Plot the point for total sales revenue at that volume: 200 events × $235 per event = sales of $47,000. Draw the *sales revenue line* from the origin (0) through the $47,000 point. Why start at the origin? If Greg's sells no events, there is no revenue.

STEP 2: Draw the *fixed cost line*, a horizontal line that intersects the dollars axis at $12,000. The fixed cost line is flat because fixed costs are the same, $12,000, no matter how many events are sold.

EXHIBIT 5-5	Cost-Volume-Profit Graph

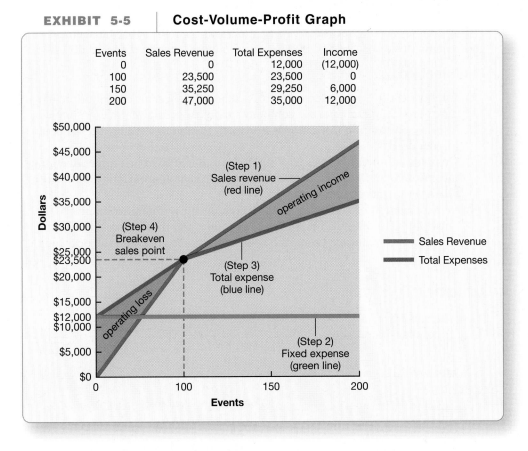

Events	Sales Revenue	Total Expenses	Income
0	0	12,000	(12,000)
100	23,500	23,500	0
150	35,250	29,250	6,000
200	47,000	35,000	12,000

STEP 3: Draw the *total cost line*. Total cost is the sum of variable cost plus fixed expenses. Thus, total cost is *mixed*. So the total cost line follows the form of the mixed cost line in Exhibit 5-3. Begin by computing variable cost at the chosen sales volume: 200 events × $115 per event = variable cost of $23,000. Add variable cost to fixed cost: $23,000 + $12,000 = $35,000. Plot the total cost point ($35,000) for 200 events. Then draw a line through this point from the $12,000 fixed cost intercept on the dollars vertical axis. This is the *total cost line*. The total cost line starts at the fixed cost line because even if Greg's Groovy Tunes sells no events, the company still incurs the $12,000 fixed cost.

STEP 4: Identify the *breakeven point* and the areas of operating income and loss. The breakeven point is where the sales revenue line intersects the total cost line. This is where revenue exactly equals total costs—at 100 events, or $23,500 in sales.

Mark the *operating loss* area on the graph. To the left of the breakeven point, total costs exceed sales revenue—leading to an operating loss, indicated by the orange zone.

Mark the *operating income* area on the graph. To the right of the breakeven point, the business earns a profit because sales revenue exceeds total cost, as shown by the green zone.

Why bother with a graph? Why not just use the income statement approach or the shortcut contribution margin approach? Graphs like Exhibit 5-5 help managers quickly estimate the profit or loss earned at different levels of sales. The income statement and contribution margin approaches indicate income or loss for only a single sales amount.

Summary Problem 1

Happy Feet buys hiking socks for $6 a pair and sells them for $10. Management budgets monthly fixed costs of $10,000 for sales volumes between 0 and 12,000 pairs.

Requirements

1. Use both the income statement approach and the shortcut contribution margin approach to compute the company's monthly breakeven sales in units.
2. Use the contribution margin ratio approach to compute the breakeven point in sales dollars.
3. Compute the monthly sales level (in units) required to earn a target operating income of $6,000. Use either the income statement approach or the shortcut contribution margin approach.
4. Prepare a graph of Happy Feet's CVP relationships, similar to Exhibit 5-5. Draw the sales revenue line, the fixed cost line, and the total cost line. Label the axes, the breakeven point, the operating income area, and the operating loss area.

Solution

Requirement 1

Income statement approach:

Sales revenue	–	Variable costs	– Fixed costs = Operating income
$\left(\dfrac{\text{Sale price}}{\text{per unit}} \times \text{Units sold}\right)$	–	$\left(\dfrac{\text{Variable cost}}{\text{per unit}} \times \text{Units sold}\right)$	– Fixed costs = Operating income
($10 × Units sold) –		($6 × Units sold)	– $10,000 = $0
($10 –		$6) × Units sold	= $10,000
		$4 × Units sold	= $10,000
		Units sold	= $10,000 ÷ $4
		Breakeven sales in units	= 2,500 units

Shortcut contribution margin approach:

$$\text{Units sold} = \frac{\text{Fixed costs} + \text{Operating income}}{\text{Contribution margin per unit}}$$

$$\text{Breakeven sales in units} = \frac{\$10,000 + \$0}{\$10 - \$6}$$

$$= \frac{\$10,000}{\$4}$$

$$= 2,500 \text{ units}$$

Requirement 2

$$\text{Breakeven sales in dollars} = \frac{\text{Fixed costs} + \text{Operating income}}{\text{Contribution margin ratio}}$$

$$= \frac{\$10,000 + \$0}{0.40^*}$$

$$= \$25,000$$

$$^*\text{Contribution margin ratio} = \frac{\text{Contribution margin per unit}}{\text{Sale price per unit}} = \frac{\$4}{\$10} = 0.40$$

Requirement 3

Income statement equation approach:

Sales revenue   –   Variable costs   – Fixed costs = Operating income

$$\left(\frac{\text{Sale price}}{\text{per unit}} \times \text{Units sold}\right) - \left(\frac{\text{Variable cost}}{\text{per unit}} \times \text{Units sold}\right) - \text{Fixed costs} = \text{Operating income}$$

($10 × Units sold) –	($6 × Units sold)	– $10,000 = $6,000
($10 –	$6) × Units sold	= $10,000 + $6,000
	$4 × Units sold	= $16,000
	Units sold	= $16,000 ÷ $4
	Units sold	= 4,000 units

Shortcut contribution margin approach:

$$\text{Units sold} = \frac{\text{Fixed costs} + \text{Operating income}}{\text{Contribution margin per unit}}$$

$$= \frac{\$10,000 + \$6,000}{(\$10 - \$6)}$$

$$= \frac{\$16,000}{\$4}$$

$$= 4{,}000 \text{ units}$$

Requirement 4

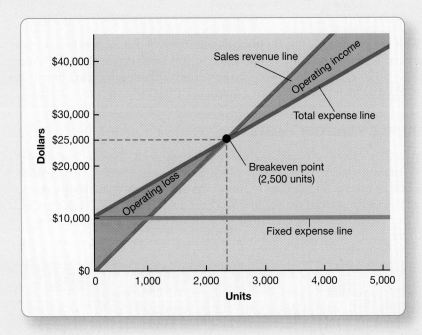

Using CVP for Sensitivity Analysis

4 Use CVP methods to perform sensitivity analyses

Managers often want to predict how changes in sale price, costs, or volume affect their profits. Managers can use CVP relationships to conduct sensitivity analysis. **Sensitivity analysis** is a "what if" technique that asks what results are likely if selling price or costs change, or if an underlying assumption changes. Let us see how Greg's Groovy Tunes can use CVP analysis to estimate the effects of some changes in its business environment.

Changing the Selling Price

Competition in the DJ event services business is so fierce that Greg's Groovy Tunes believes it must cut the selling price to $215 per event to maintain market share. Suppose Greg's Groovy Tunes' variable costs remain $115 per event and fixed costs stay at $12,000. How will the lower sale price affect the breakeven point?

Using the income statement approach, the results are as follows:

Sales revenue	−	Variable cost	−	Fixed costs	= Operating income
($215 × units sold)	−	($115 × units sold) −		$12,000	= $0
	[($215 − 115) × units sold]		−	$12,000	= $0
	$100 × units sold				= $12,000
				units sold	= $12,000 ÷ $100
				units sold	= 120 events

Proof	($215 × 120)	−	($115 × 120)	−	$12,000	= Operating income
	$25,800	−	$13,800	−	$12,000	= $0

With the original $235 sale price, Greg's Groovy Tunes' breakeven point was 100 events. With the new lower sale price of $215 per event, the breakeven point increases to 120 events. The lower sale price means that each event contributes less toward fixed costs, so Greg's Groovy Tunes must sell 20 more events to break even.

Changing Variable Costs

Return to Greg's Groovy Tunes' original data on page 219. Assume that one of Greg's Groovy Tunes' suppliers raises prices, which increases the cost for each event to $155 (instead of the original $115). Greg's cannot pass this increase on to its customers, so the company holds the price at the original $235 per event. Fixed costs remain at $12,000. How many events must Greg's sell to break even after the supplier raises prices?

Using the income statement approach:

Sales revenue	−	Variable cost	−	Fixed costs	= Operating income
($235 × units sold)	−	($155 × units sold) −		$12,000	= $0
	[($235 − 155) × units sold]		−	$12,000	= $0
	$80 × units sold				= $12,000
				units sold	= $12,000 ÷ $80
				units sold	= 150 events

Proof	($235 × 150)	−	($155 × 150)	−	$12,000	= Operating income
	$35,250	−	$23,250	−	$12,000	= $0

Higher variable costs per event reduce Greg's Groovy Tunes' per-unit contribution margin from $120 per event to $80 per event. As a result, Greg's must sell more events to break even—150 rather than the original 100. This analysis shows why managers are particularly concerned with controlling costs during an economic downturn. Increases in cost raise the breakeven point, and a higher breakeven point can lead to problems if demand falls due to a recession.

Of course, a decrease in variable costs would have the opposite effect. Lower variable costs increase the contribution margin on each event and, therefore, lower the breakeven point.

Changing Fixed Costs

Return to Greg's original data on page 219. Controller Natalie Blanding is considering spending an additional $3,000 on Web site banner ads. This would increase fixed costs from $12,000 to $15,000. If the events are sold at the original price of $235 each and variable costs remain at $115 per event, what is the new breakeven point?

Using the income statement approach:

Sales revenue	–	Variable cost	–	Fixed costs	= Operating income
($235 × units sold)	–	($115 × units sold) –		$15,000	= $0
[($235 – 115) × units sold]			–	$15,000	= $0
$120 × units sold					= $15,000
				units sold	= $15,000 ÷ $120
				units sold	= 125 events

Proof	($235 × 125)	–	($115 × 125)	–	$15,000	= Operating income
	$29,375	–	$14,375	–	$15,000	= $0

Higher fixed costs increase the total contribution margin required to break even. In this case, increasing the fixed costs from $12,000 to $15,000 increases the breakeven point to 125 events (from the original 100 events).

Managers usually prefer a lower breakeven point to a higher one. But do not overemphasize this one aspect of CVP analysis. Even though investing in the Web banner ads increases Greg's Groovy Tunes' breakeven point, the company should pay the extra $3,000 if that would increase both sales and profits.

Exhibit 5-6 shows how all of these changes affect the contribution margin and break even.

EXHIBIT 5-6 | **How Changes in Selling Price, Variable Costs, and Fixed Costs Affect the Contribution Margin per Unit and the Breakeven Point**

Cause	Effect	Result
Change	Contribution Margin per Unit	Breakeven Point
Selling Price per Unit Increases	Increases	Decreases
Selling Price per Unit Decreases	Decreases	Increases
Variable Cost per Unit Increases	Decreases	Increases
Variable Cost per Unit Decreases	Increases	Decreases
Total Fixed Cost Increases	Is not affected	Increases
Total Fixed Cost Decreases	Is not affected	Decreases

Stop & Think...

The sensitivity analysis can be applied to many types of situations. For example, consider that you are deciding between purchasing a hybrid SUV and a subcompact car. In your decision, you consider the gas mileage, maintenance costs, insurance, and the price of the cars. You compare these factors and purchase the car that is most economical to use (least costly).

Margin of Safety

The **margin of safety** is the excess of expected sales over breakeven sales. The margin of safety is therefore the "cushion" or drop in sales that the company can absorb without incurring a loss.

Managers use the margin of safety to evaluate the risk of both their current operations and their plans for the future. Let us apply the margin of safety to Greg's Groovy Tunes.

Greg's Groovy Tunes' original breakeven point was 100 events. Suppose the company expects to sell 170 events. The margin of safety is as follows:

Expected sales	–	Breakeven sales	=	Margin of safety in units
170 events	–	100 events	=	70 events

Margin of safety in units	×	Sales price	=	Margin of safety in dollars
70 events	×	$235	=	$16,450

Sales can drop by 70 events, or $16,450, before Greg's incurs a loss. This margin of safety (70 events) is 41.2% of total expected sales (170 events). That is a comfortable margin of safety.

Stop & Think...

If you have done really well on all your assignments in a particular course for the semester, you have created a sort of "margin of safety" for your grade. That is, by performing above the minimum (break even), you have a cushion to help you maintain a good grade even if you happen to perform poorly on a future assignment.

Information Technology and Sensitivity Analysis

Information technology allows managers to perform lots of sensitivity analyses before launching a new product or shutting down a plant. Excel spreadsheets are useful for sensitivity analyses like those we just did for Greg's Groovy Tunes. Spreadsheets can show how one change (or several changes simultaneously) affects operations. Managers can plot basic CVP data to show profit-planning graphs similar to the one shown in Exhibit 5-5.

Large companies use enterprise resource planning software—**SAP, Oracle,** and **Peoplesoft**—for their CVP analysis. For example, after **Sears** stores lock their doors at 9:00 P.M., records for each individual transaction flow into a massive database. From a Diehard battery sold in California to a Trader Bay polo shirt sold in New Hampshire, the system compiles an average of 1.5 million transactions a day. With the click of a mouse, managers can conduct breakeven or profit planning analysis on any product they choose.

Effect of Sales Mix on CVP Analysis

Most companies sell more than one product. Selling price and variable costs differ for each product, so each product line makes a different contribution to profits. The same CVP formulas we used earlier apply to a company with multiple products.

To calculate breakeven point for each product line, we must compute the *weighted-average contribution margin* of all the company's products. The sales mix provides the weights. **Sales mix** is the combination of products that make up total sales. For example, Fat Cat Furniture sold 6,000 cat beds and 4,000 scratching posts during the past year. The sales mix of 6,000 beds and 4,000 posts creates a ratio of 3:2 or a percentage of 60% for the beds and 40% for the posts. For every three cat beds, Fat Cat expects to sell two scratching posts, so Fat Cat expects 3/5 of the sales to be cat beds and 2/5 to be scratching posts.

Fat Cat's total fixed costs are $40,000. The cat bed's unit selling price is $44 and variable costs per bed are $24. The scratching post's unit selling price is $100 and variable cost per post is $30. To compute breakeven sales in units for both product lines, Fat Cat completes the following three steps.

STEP 1: Calculate the weighted-average contribution margin per unit, as follows:

	Cat Beds	Scratching Posts	Total
Sale price per unit	$ 44	$100	
Deduct: Variable cost per unit	(24)	(30)	
Contribution margin per unit	$ 20	$ 70	
Sales mix in units	× 3	× 2	5
Contribution margin	$ 60	$140	$200
Weighted-average contribution margin per unit ($200 ÷ 5)			$ 40

STEP 2: Calculate the breakeven point in units for the "package" of products:

$$\text{Breakeven sales in total units} = \frac{\text{Fixed costs} + \text{Operating income}}{\text{Weighted-average contribution margin per unit}}$$

$$= \frac{\$40,000 + \$0}{\$40}$$

$$= 1,000 \text{ items}$$

STEP 3: Calculate the breakeven point in units for each product line. Multiply the "package" breakeven point in units by each product line's proportion of the sales mix.

Breakeven sales of cat beds (1,000 × 3/5) .... 600 cat beds
Breakeven sales of scratching posts (1,000 × 2/5) .... 400 scratching posts

In this example the calculations yield round numbers. When the calculations do not yield round numbers, round your answer up to the next whole number.

The overall breakeven point in sales dollars is $66,400:

600 cat beds at $44 selling price each..............................	$26,400
400 scratching posts at $100 selling price each	40,000
Total revenues...	$66,400

5 Calculate the breakeven point for multiple product lines or services

We can prove this breakeven point by preparing a contribution margin income statement:

		Cat Beds	Scratching Posts	Total
Sales revenue:				
	Cat beds (600 × $44)	$26,400		
	Scratching posts (400 × $100)		$40,000	$ 66,400
Variable costs:				
	Cat beds (600 × $24)	14,400		
	Scratching posts (400 × $30)		12,000	26,400
Contribution margin		$12,000	$28,000	$ 40,000
Fixed costs				(40,000)
Operating income				$ 0

If the sales mix changes, then Fat Cat can repeat this analysis using new sales mix information to find the breakeven points for each product line.

In addition to finding the breakeven point, Fat Cat can also estimate the sales needed to generate a certain level of operating profit. Suppose Fat Cat would like to earn operating income of $20,000. How many units of each product must Fat Cat now sell?

$$\text{Breakeven sales in total units} = \frac{\text{Fixed costs} + \text{Operating income}}{\text{Weighted-average contribution margin per unit}}$$

$$= \frac{\$40,000 + \$20,000}{\$40}$$

$$= 1,500 \text{ items}$$

Breakeven sales of cat beds (1,500 × 3/5) .... 900 cat beds
Breakeven sales of scratching posts (1,500 × 2/5) .... 600 scratching posts

We can prove this planned profit level by preparing a contribution margin income statement:

		Cat Beds	Scratching Posts	Total
Sales revenue:				
	Cat beds (900 × $44)	$39,600		
	Scratching posts (600 × $100)		$60,000	$ 99,600
Variable costs:				
	Cat beds (900 × $24)	21,600		
	Scratching posts (600 × $30)		18,000	39,600
Contribution margin		$18,000	$42,000	$ 60,000
Fixed costs				(40,000)
Operating income				$ 20,000

You have learned how to use CVP analysis as a managerial tool. Review the CVP Analysis Decision Guidelines to make sure you understand these basic concepts.

Decision Guidelines

COST BEHAVIOR AND COST-VOLUME-PROFIT ANALYSIS

As a manager, you will find CVP very useful. Here are some questions you will ask, and guidelines for answering them.

Decision	Guidelines
• How do changes in volume of activity affect	
• total costs?	Total *variable* costs → Change in proportion to changes in volume (number of products or services sold) Total *fixed* costs → No change
• cost per unit?	Variable cost per unit → No change
• Fixed cost per unit:	• Decreases when volume rises (Fixed costs are spread over *more* units) • Increases when volume drops (Fixed costs are spread over *fewer* units)
• How do I calculate the sales needed to break even or earn a target operating income	
• in units?	*Income Statement Method:*

$$\text{Sales revenue} - \text{Variable costs} - \text{Fixed costs} = \text{Operating income}$$

$$\left(\frac{\text{Sale price}}{\text{per unit}} \times \text{Units sold}\right) - \left(\frac{\text{Variable cost}}{\text{per unit}} \times \text{Units sold}\right) - \text{Fixed costs} = \text{Operating income}$$

$$\underbrace{\left(\frac{\text{Sale price}}{\text{per unit}} - \frac{\text{Variable cost}}{\text{per unit}}\right)}_{\text{Contribution margin per unit}} \times \text{Units sold} = \text{Fixed costs} + \text{Operating income}$$

$$\text{Contribution margin per unit} \times \text{Units sold} = \text{Fixed costs} + \text{Operating income}$$

$$\text{Units sold} = \frac{\text{Fixed Costs} + \text{Operating income}}{\text{Contribution margin per unit}}$$

Shortcut Contribution Margin Method:

$$\frac{\text{Fixed costs} + \text{Operating income}}{\text{Contribution margin per unit}}$$

• in dollars?

Shortcut Contribution Margin Ratio Method:

$$\frac{\text{Fixed costs} + \text{Operating income}}{\text{Contribution margin ratio}}$$

Decision	Guidelines

Cause	Effect	Result
Change	**Contribution Margin per Unit**	**Breakeven Point**
Selling Price per Unit Increases	Increases	Decreases
Selling Price per Unit Decreases	Decreases	Increases
Variable Cost per Unit Increases	Decreases	Increases
Variable Cost per Unit Decreases	Increases	Decreases
Total Fixed Cost Increases	Is not affected	Increases
Total Fixed Cost Decreases	Is not affected	Decreases

- How will changes in sale price, or variable, or fixed costs affect the breakeven point?

- How do I use CVP analysis to measure risk?

Margin of safety = Expected sales − Breakeven sales

- How do I calculate my breakeven point when I sell more than one product or service?

STEP 1: Compute the weighted-average contribution margin per unit.
STEP 2: Calculate the breakeven point in units for the "package" of products.
STEP 3: Calculate breakeven point in units for each product line. Multiply the "package" breakeven point in units by each product line's proportion of the sales mix.

Summary Problem 2

Happy Feet buys hiking socks for $6 a pair and sells them for $10. Management budgets monthly fixed costs of $12,000 for sales volumes between 0 and 12,000 pairs.

Requirements

Consider each of the following questions separately by using the foregoing information each time.

1. Calculate the breakeven point in units.
2. Happy Feet reduces its selling price from $10 a pair to $8 a pair. Calculate the new breakeven point in units.
3. Happy Feet finds a new supplier for the socks. Variable costs will decrease by $1 a pair. Calculate the new breakeven point in units.
4. Happy Feet plans to advertise in hiking magazines. The advertising campaign will increase total fixed costs by $2,000 per month. Calculate the new breakeven point in units.
5. In addition to selling hiking socks, Happy Feet would like to start selling sports socks. Happy Feet expects to sell one pair of hiking socks for every three pairs of sports socks. Happy Feet will buy the sports socks for $4 a pair and sell them for $8 a pair. Total fixed costs will stay at $12,000 per month. Calculate the breakeven point in units for both hiking socks and sports socks.

Solution

Requirement 1

$$\text{Units sold} = \frac{\text{Fixed costs}}{\text{Contribution margin per unit}}$$

$$\text{Breakeven sales in units} = \frac{\$12,000}{\$10 - \$6}$$

$$= \frac{\$12,000}{\$4}$$

$$= 3,000 \text{ units}$$

Requirement 2

$$\text{Units sold} = \frac{\text{Fixed costs}}{\text{Contribution margin per unit}}$$

$$\text{Breakeven sales in units} = \frac{\$12,000}{\$8 - \$6}$$

$$= \frac{\$12,000}{\$2}$$

$$= 6,000 \text{ units}$$

Requirement 3

$$\text{Units sold} = \frac{\text{Fixed costs}}{\text{Contribution margin per unit}}$$

$$\text{Breakeven sales in units} = \frac{\$12,000}{\$10 - \$5}$$

$$= \frac{\$12,000}{\$5}$$

$$= 2,400 \text{ units}$$

Requirement 4

$$\text{Units sold} = \frac{\text{Fixed costs}}{\text{Contribution margin per unit}}$$

$$\text{Breakeven sales in units} = \frac{\$14,000}{\$10 - \$6}$$

$$= \frac{\$14,000}{\$4}$$

$$= 3,500 \text{ units}$$

Requirement 5

STEP 1: Calculate the weighted-average contribution margin:

	Hiking	Sports	
Sale price per unit	$10.00	$ 8.00	
Variable expenses per unit	6.00	4.00	
Contribution margin per unit	$ 4.00	$ 4.00	
Sales mix in units	× 1	× 3	4
Contribution margin per unit	$ 4.00	$12.00	$16.00
Weighted-average CM ($16 ÷ 4)			$ 4.00

STEP 2: Calculate breakeven point for "package" of products:

$$\text{Breakeven sales in units} = \frac{\text{Fixed costs}}{\text{Contribution margin per unit}}$$

$$= \frac{\$12,000}{\$4}$$

$$= 3,000 \text{ units}$$

STEP 3: Calculate breakeven point for each product line:

Number of hiking socks (3,000 × (1/4)) 750
Number of sport socks (3,000 × (3/4)) 2,250

Review Cost Behavior and Cost-Volume-Profit Analysis

■ Accounting Vocabulary

Breakeven Point (p. 222)
The sales level at which operating income is zero: Total revenues equal total expenses.

Contribution Margin (p. 223)
Sales revenue minus variable expenses.

Contribution Margin Income Statement (p. 223)
Income statement that groups costs by behavior—variable costs or fixed costs—and highlights the contribution margin.

Contribution Margin Ratio (p. 225)
Ratio of contribution margin to sales revenue.

Cost-Volume-Profit (CVP) Analysis (p. 214)
Expresses the relationships among costs, volume, and profit or loss.

Fixed Costs (p. 217)
Costs that tend to remain the same in amount, regardless of variations in level of activity.

High-Low Method (p. 218)
A method used to separate mixed costs into variable and fixed components, using the highest and lowest total cost.

Least Squares Regression Method (p. 219)
A method used to separate mixed costs into variable and fixed portions that minimize the effect of cost deviations.

Margin of Safety (p. 232)
Excess of expected sales over breakeven sales. A drop in sales that a company can absorb without incurring an operating loss.

Mixed Costs (p. 217)
Costs that have both variable and fixed components.

Relevant Range (p. 221)
The band of volume where total fixed costs remain constant and the variable cost per unit remains constant.

Sales Mix (p. 233)
Combination of products that make up total sales.

Sensitivity Analysis (p. 230)
A "what if" technique that asks what results will be if actual prices or costs change, or if an underlying assumption changes.

Total Fixed Costs (p. 216)
Costs that do not change in total despite wide changes in volume.

Total Variable Costs (p. 215)
Costs that change in total in direct proportion to changes in volume.

Variable Costs (p. 215)
Costs that increase or decrease in total as the volume of activity increases or decreases.

■ Quick Check

1. For Greg's Groovy Tunes, straight-line depreciation on the trucks is
   a. fixed cost.
   b. mixed cost.
   c. variable cost.
   d. None of the above

2. Assume Cape Cod Railway is considering hiring a reservations agency to handle passenger reservations. The agency would charge a flat fee of $7,000 per month, plus $2 per passenger reservation. What is the total reservation cost if 100,000 passengers take the trip next month?
   a. $200,000
   b. $207,000
   c. $2.07
   d. $7,000

3. If Cape Cod's fixed costs total $40,000 per month, the variable cost per passenger is $10, and tickets sell for $50, what is the breakeven point in units?
   a. 1,000 passengers
   b. 686 passengers
   c. 100 passengers
   d. 8,100 passengers

4. Suppose Cape Cod Railway's total revenues are $4,900,000, its variable costs are $2,900,000, and its fixed costs are $1,300,000. Compute the breakeven point in dollars.

a. $410,000

b. $4,200,000

c. $3,170,732

d. $4,900,000

5. If Cape Cod Railway's fixed costs total $40,000 per month, the variable cost per passenger is $10, and tickets sell for $59, how much revenue must the Railway have to generate to earn $150,000 in operating income per month? (*Hint:* Begin by calculating contribution margin in whole units.)

a. $268,802

b. $228,802

c. $188,802

d. $190,022

6. On a CVP graph, the total cost line intersects the vertical (dollars) axis at

a. the level of the variable costs.

b. the breakeven point.

c. the level of the fixed costs.

d. the origin.

7. If a company increases its selling price per unit for Product A, then the new breakeven point will

a. increase.

b. decrease.

c. remain the same.

8. If a company increases its fixed costs for Product B, then the contribution margin per unit will

a. increase.

b. decrease.

c. remain the same.

9. Telluride Railway had the following revenue over the past five years:

2005	$ 400,000
2006	500,000
2007	700,000
2008	600,000
2009	800,000

To predict revenues for 2010, Telluride uses the average for the past five years. The company's breakeven revenue is $600,000 per year. What is Telluride's margin of safety?

a. $100,000

b. $50,000

c. $0

d. $110,000

10. Intervale Railway sells half of its tickets for the regular price of $65. The other half go to senior citizens and children for the discounted price of $45. Variable cost per passenger is $10 for both groups, and fixed costs total $45,000 per month. What is Intervale's breakeven point in total passengers? Regular passengers? Discount passengers?

    a. 1,000/500/500

    b. 600/300/300

    c. 1,500/750/750

    d. 1,250/625/625

Answers are given after Apply Your Knowledge (p. 255).

Assess Your Progress

■ Short Exercises

S5-1   *(L. OBJ. 1)* **Variable and fixed costs [5–10 min]**
Chicago Acoustics builds innovative loudspeakers for music and home theater systems. Consider the following costs:

    ☐   **1.** Depreciation on routers used to cut wood enclosures

    ☐   **2.** Wood for speaker enclosures

    ☐   **3.** Patents on crossover relays

    ☐   **4.** Crossover relays

    ☐   **5.** Grill cloth

    ☐   **6.** Glue

    ☐   **7.** Quality inspector's salary

Requirement

    1. Identify the costs as variable or fixed. Indicate V for variable costs and F for fixed costs.

S5-2   *(L. OBJ. 1)* **Variable and fixed costs [5–10 min]**
Sally's DayCare has been in operation for several years. Consider the following costs:

    ☐   **1.** Building rent

    ☐   **2.** Toys

    ☐   **3.** Playground equipment

    ☐   **4.** Afternoon snacks

    ☐   **5.** Sally's salary

    ☐   **6.** Wages of afterschool employees

    ☐   **7.** Drawing paper

    ☐   **8.** Tables and chairs

Requirement

    1. Identify the costs as variable or fixed. Indicate V for variable costs and F for fixed costs.

S5-3   *(L. OBJ. 1)* **Mixed costs [5–10 min]**

Suppose Worldwide-Link offers an international calling plan that charges $10.00 per month plus $0.30 per minute for calls outside the United States.

Requirements

1. Under this plan, what is your monthly international long-distance cost if you call Europe for
   a. 20 minutes?
   b. 50 minutes?
   c. 95 minutes?

2. Draw a graph illustrating your total cost under this plan. Label the axes, and show your costs at 20, 50, and 95 minutes.

S5-4   *(L. OBJ. 1)* **Mixed costs [5–10 min]**

Mel owns a machine shop. In reviewing his utility bill for the last 12 months he found that his highest bill of $2,400 occurred in August when his machines worked 1,000 machine hours. His lowest utility bill of $2,200 occurred in December when his machines worked 500 machine hours.

Requirement

1. Calculate (a) the variable rate per machine hour and (b) Mel's total fixed utility cost.

S5-5   *(L. OBJ. 2)* **Computing breakeven point in sales units [5–10 min]**

Storytime Park competes with Daisy World by providing a variety of rides. Storytime sells tickets at $70 per person as a one-day entrance fee. Variable costs are $15 per person, and fixed costs are $371,250 per month.

Requirement

1. Compute the number of tickets Storytime must sell to break even. Perform a numerical proof to show that your answer is correct.

Note: Short Exercise 5-5 must be completed before attempting Short Exercise 5-6.

S5-6   *(L. OBJ. 2)* **Computing breakeven point in sales dollars [5 min]**

Refer to Short Exercise 5-5.

Requirements

1. Compute Storytime Park's contribution margin ratio. Carry your computation to five decimal places.

2. Use the contribution margin ratio CVP formula to determine the sales revenue Storytime Park needs to break even.

S5-7   *(L. OBJ. 3)* **Computing contribution margin, breakeven point, and units to achieve operating income [10–15 min]**

Consider the following facts:

	A	B	C
Number of units	1,100	3,000	8,000
Sale price per unit	$ 12	$ 16	$ 30
Variable costs per unit	6	8	21
Total fixed costs	50,000	21,000	180,000
Target operating income	50,000	70,000	90,000
Calculate:			
Contribution margin per unit	_____	_____	_____
Contribution margin ratio	_____	_____	_____
Breakeven points in units	_____	_____	_____
Breakeven point in sales dollars	_____	_____	_____
Units to achieve target operating income	_____	_____	_____

Requirement

1. Compute the missing information.

Note: Short Exercise 5-5 must be completed before attempting Short Exercise 5-8.

S5-8 *(L. OBJ. 4)* **Sensitivity analysis of changing sale price and variable costs on breakeven point [10 min]**
Refer to Short Exercise 5-5.

Requirements

1. Suppose Storytime Park cuts its ticket price from $70 to $60 to increase the number of tickets sold. Compute the new breakeven point in tickets and in sales dollars. Carry your computations to five decimal places.

2. Ignore the information in requirement 1. Instead, assume that Storytime Park reduces the variable cost from $15 to $10 per ticket. Compute the new breakeven point in tickets and in dollars. Carry your computations to five decimal places.

Note: Short Exercise 5-5 must be completed before attempting Short Exercise 5-9.

S5-9 *(L. OBJ. 4)* **Sensitivity analysis of changing fixed cost on breakeven point [5–10 min]**
Refer to Short Exercise 5-5. Suppose Storytime Park reduces fixed costs from $371,250 per month to $343,750 per month.

Requirement

1. Compute the new breakeven point in tickets and in sales dollars.

Note: Short Exercise 5-5 must be completed before attempting Short Exercise 5-10.

S5-10 *(L. OBJ. 4)* **Computing margin of safety [5–10 min]**
Refer to Short Exercise 5-5.

Requirement

1. If Storytime Park expects to sell 6,900 tickets, compute the margin of safety in tickets and in sales dollars.

S5-11 *(L. OBJ. 5)* **Calculating weighted average contribution margin [5–10 min]**
SoakNSun Swim Park sells individual and family tickets, which include a meal, three beverages, and unlimited use of the swimming pools. SoakNSun has the following ticket prices and variable costs for 2010:

	Individual	Family
Sale price per ticket	$ 35	$ 105
Variable cost per ticket . . .	25	100

SoakNSun expects to sell one individual ticket for every three family tickets.

Requirement

1. Compute the weighted-average contribution margin per ticket.

Note: Short Exercise 5-11 must be completed before attempting Short Exercise 5-12.

S5-12 *(L. OBJ. 5)* **Calculating breakeven point for two product lines [5–10 min]**
Refer to Short Exercise 5-11. For 2011, SoakNSun expects a sales mix of two individual tickets for every three family tickets. In this mix, the weighted-average contribution margin per ticket is $7. SoakNSun's total fixed costs are $21,000.

Requirements

1. Calculate the total number of tickets SoakNSun must sell to break even.

2. Calculate the number of individual tickets and the number of family tickets the company must sell to break even.

E5-13 *(L. OBJ. 1)* **CVP definitions [15 min]**
Consider the following terms and definitions.

_____ 1. Costs that do not change in total despite wide changes in volume

_____ 2. The sales level at which operating income is zero: Total revenues equal total costs

_____ 3. Drop in sales a company can absorb without incurring an operating loss

_____ 4. Combination of products that make up total sales

_____ 5. Sales revenue minus variable costs

_____ 6. Describes how costs change as volume changes

_____ 7. Costs that change in total in direct proportion to changes in volume

_____ 8. The band of volume where total fixed costs remain constant and the variable cost *per unit* remains constant

a. Breakeven
b. Contribution margin
c. Cost behavior
d. Margin of safety
e. Relevant range
f. Sales mix
g. Fixed costs
h. Variable costs

Requirement

1. Match the terms with the correct definitions.

E5-14 *(L. OBJ. 1)* **Mixed costs; the high-low method and least squares [10–15 min]**
The manager of Swift Car Inspection reviewed his monthly operating costs for the past year. His costs range and additional least squares information follows.

	Number of Inspections	Operating Costs			
	X	Y	XY	X^2	Y^2
	1,400	4,400	6,160,000	1,960,000	19,360,000
	900	4,000	3,600,000	810,000	16,000,000
	950	4,040	3,838,000	902,500	16,321,600
	1,200	4,240	5,088,000	1,440,000	17,977,600
Total	4,450	16,680	18,686,000	5,112,500	69,659,200

Requirements

1. Calculate the variable cost per inspection using the high-low method.
2. Calculate the total fixed costs using the high-low method.
3. Write the equation and calculate the operating costs for 1,000 inspections using the high-low method.
4. Calculate the least squares regression equation for monthly operating costs.

E5-15 *(L. OBJ. 2)* **Preparing contribution margin income statements and calculating breakeven sales [15 min]**

For its top managers, Countrywide Travel formats its income statement as follows:

COUNTRYWIDE TRAVEL	
Contribution Margin Income Statement	
Three Months Ended March 31, 2011	
Sales revenue	$ 316,500
Variable costs	127,000
Contribution margin	189,500
Fixed costs	174,000
Operating income	$ 15,500

Countrywide's relevant range is between sales of $251,000 and $365,000.

Requirements

1. Calculate the contribution margin ratio.
2. Prepare two contribution margin income statements: one at the $251,000 level and one at the $365,000 level. (*Hint*: The proportion of each sales dollar that goes toward variable costs is constant within the relevant range. The proportion of each sales dollar that goes toward contribution margin also is constant within the relevant range.)
3. Compute breakeven sales in dollars.

E5-16 *(L. OBJ. 2)* **Computing breakeven sales by the contribution margin approach [15 min]**

Hang Ten, Co., produces sports socks. The company has fixed costs of $90,000 and variable costs of $0.90 per package. Each package sells for $1.80.

Requirements

1. Compute the contribution margin per package and the contribution margin ratio.
2. Find the breakeven point in units and in dollars, using the contribution margin approach.

E5-17 *(L. OBJ. 3)* **Computing a change in breakeven sales [10–15 min]**

Owner Shan Lo is considering franchising her Noodles restaurant concept. She believes people will pay $8 for a large bowl of noodles. Variable costs are $1.60 per bowl. Lo estimates monthly fixed costs for a franchise at $8,600.

Requirements

1. Use the contribution margin ratio approach to find a franchise's breakeven sales in dollars.
2. Lo believes most locations could generate $22,313 in monthly sales. Is franchising a good idea for Lo if franchisees want a minimum monthly operating income of $8,850?

E5-18 *(L. OBJ. 3)* **Computing breakeven sales and operating income or loss under different conditions [10–15 min]**

Gary's Steel Parts produces parts for the automobile industry. The company has monthly fixed costs of $630,000 and a contribution margin of 95% of revenues.

Requirements

1. Compute Gary's monthly breakeven sales in dollars. Use the contribution margin ratio approach.

2. Use contribution margin income statements to compute Gary's monthly operating income or operating loss if revenues are $510,000 and if they are $1,000,000.

3. Do the results in requirement 2 make sense given the breakeven sales you computed in requirement 1? Explain.

E5-19 *(L. OBJ. 3)* **Analyzing a cost-volume profit graph [15–20 min]**

Zac Hill is considering starting a Web-based educational business, e-Prep MBA. He plans to offer a short-course review of accounting for students entering MBA programs. The materials would be available on a password-protected Web site; students would complete the course through self-study. Hill would have to grade the course assignments, but most of the work is in developing the course materials, setting up the site, and marketing. Unfortunately, Hill's hard drive crashed before he finished his financial analysis. However, he did recover the following partial CVP chart:

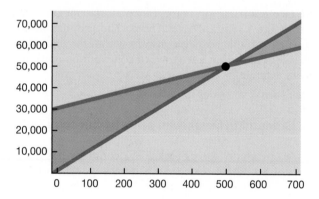

Requirements

1. Label each axis, the sales revenue line, the total costs line, the fixed costs, the operating income area, and the breakeven point.

2. If Hill attracts 400 students to take the course, will the venture be profitable?

3. What are the breakeven sales in students and dollars?

E5-20 *(L. OBJ. 4)* **Impact on breakeven point if sale price, variable costs, and fixed costs change [15 min]**

Country Road Driving School charges $230 per student to prepare and administer written and driving tests. Variable costs of $70 per student include trainers' wages, study materials, and gasoline. Annual fixed costs of $112,000 include the training facility and fleet of cars.

Requirements

1. For each of the following independent situations, calculate the contribution margin per unit and the breakeven point in units:
   a. Breakeven point with no change in information
   b. Decrease sales price to $200 per student
   c. Decrease variable costs to $50 per student
   d. Decrease fixed costs to $102,000

2. Compare the impact of changes in the sales price, variable costs, and fixed costs on the contribution margin per unit and the breakeven point in units.

E5-21 *(L. OBJ. 4)* **Computing margin of safety [15 min]**

Ronnie's Repair Shop has a monthly target operating income of $17,000. Variable costs are 80% of sales, and monthly fixed costs are $12,000.

Requirements

1. Compute the monthly margin of safety in dollars if the shop achieves its income goal.
2. Express Ronnie's margin of safety as a percentage of target sales.

E5-22 *(L. OBJ. 5)* **Calculating breakeven point for two product lines [15–20 min]**

Scotty's Scooters plans to sell a standard scooter for $40 and a chrome scooter for $50. Scotty's purchases the standard scooter for $25 and the chrome scooter for $30. Scotty expects to sell two standard scooters for every three chrome scooters. His monthly fixed costs are $18,900.

Requirements

1. How many of each type of scooter must Scotty's Scooters sell each month to break even?
2. To earn $14,400?

■ Problem (Group A)

P5-23A *(L .OBJ. 1, 2, 3)* **Calculating cost-volume profit elements [45–60 min]**

The budgets of four companies yield the following information:

	Company			
	North	South	East	West
Sales revenue	$ 710,000	$ (4)	$ 600,000	$ (10)
Variable costs	(1)	150,000	288,000	160,160
Fixed costs	(2)	121,000	139,000	(11)
Operating income (loss)	$ 13,800	$ (5)	$ (7)	$ 42,840
Units sold	190,000	10,000	(8)	(12)
Contribution margin per unit	$ 1.42	$ (6)	$ 97.50	$ 14.72
Contribution margin ratio	(3)	0.20	(9)	0.23

Requirements

1. Fill in the blanks for each missing value.
2. Which company has the lowest breakeven point in sales dollars? What causes the low breakeven point?

P5-24A *(L. OBJ. 2, 3)* **Break even sales; sales to earn a target operating income; contribution margin income statement [30–45 min]**

British Productions performs London shows. The average show sells 1,200 tickets at $50 per ticket. There are 120 shows a year. The average show has a cast of 70, each earning an average of $300 per show. The cast is paid after each show. The other variable cost is a program-printing cost of $7 per guest. Annual fixed costs total $459,000.

Requirements

1. Compute revenue and variable costs for each show.
2. Use the income statement equation approach to compute the number of shows British Productions must perform each year to break even.

3. Use the contribution margin approach to compute the number of shows needed each year to earn a profit of $3,825,000. Is this profit goal realistic? Give your reasoning.

4. Prepare British Productions' contribution margin income statement for 120 shows for 2011. Report only two categories of costs: variable and fixed.

P5-25A *(L. OBJ. 2, 3, 4)* **Analyzing CVP relationships [30–45 min]**
Allen Company sells flags with team logos. Allen has fixed costs of $588,000 per year plus variable costs of $5.50 per flag. Each flag sells for $12.50.

Requirements

1. Use the income statement equation approach to compute the number of flags Allen must sell each year to break even.

2. Use the contribution margin ratio CVP formula to compute the dollar sales Allen needs to earn $32,200 in operating income for 2011.

3. Prepare Allen's contribution margin income statement for the year ended December 31, 2011, for sales of 73,000 flags. Cost of goods sold is 60% of variable costs. Operating costs make up the rest of variable costs and all of fixed costs.

4. The company is considering an expansion that will increase fixed costs by 20% and variable costs by $0.60 cents per flag. Compute the new breakeven point in units and in dollars. Should Allen Company undertake the expansion? Give your reasoning.

P5-26A *(L. OBJ. 2, 3, 4)* **Computing breakeven sales and sales needed to earn a target operating income; graphing CVP relationships; sensitivity analysis [30–45 min]**
Big Time Investor Group is opening an office in Dallas. Fixed monthly costs are office rent ($8,200), depreciation on office furniture ($1,500), utilities ($2,300), special telephone lines ($1,300), a connection with an online brokerage service ($2,900), and the salary of a financial planner ($11,800). Variable costs include payments to the financial planner (9% of revenue), advertising (12% of revenue), supplies and postage (4% of revenue), and usage fees for the telephone lines and computerized brokerage service (5% of revenue).

Requirements

1. Use the contribution margin ratio CVP formula to compute Big Time's breakeven revenue in dollars. If the average trade leads to $800 in revenue for Big Time, how many trades must be made to break even?

2. Use the income statement equation approach to compute the dollar revenues needed to earn a target monthly operating income of $11,200.

3. Graph Big Time's CVP relationships. Assume that an average trade leads to $800 in revenue for Big Time. Show the breakeven point, the sales revenue line, the fixed cost line, the total cost line, the operating loss area, the operating income area, and the sales in units (trades) and dollars when monthly operating income of $11,200 is earned. The graph should range from 0 to 80 units.

4. Suppose that the average revenue Big Time earns increases to $900 per trade. Compute the new breakeven point in trades. How does this affect the breakeven point?

P5-27A *(L. OBJ. 4, 5)* **Calculating breakeven point for two product lines; margin of safety [20 min]**

The contribution margin income statement of Cosmic Donuts for March 2012 follows:

COSMIC DONUTS Contribution Margin Income Statement For the Month of March 2012		
Sales revenue		$ 127,000
Variable costs:		
Cost of goods sold	$ 32,400	
Marketing costs	17,300	
General and administrative cost	10,625	60,325
Contribution margin		66,675
Fixed costs:		
Marketing costs	56,700	
General and administrative cost	6,300	63,000
Operating income		$ 3,675

Cosmic sells two dozen plain donuts for every dozen custard-filled donuts. A dozen plain donuts sells for $6, with total variable cost of $2 per dozen. A dozen custard-filled donuts sells for $8, with total variable cost of $5.50 per dozen.

Requirements

1. Determine Cosmic's monthly breakeven point in dozens of plain donuts and custard-filled donuts. Prove your answer by preparing a summary contribution margin income statement at the breakeven level of sales. Show only two categories of costs: variable and fixed.

2. Compute Cosmic's margin of safety in dollars for March 2012.

3. If Cosmic can increase monthly sales volume by 10%, what will operating income be? (The sales mix remains unchanged.)

■ Problem (Group B)

P5-28B *(L. OBJ. 1, 2, 3)* **Calculating cost-volume profit elements [45–60 min]**

The budgets of four companies yield the following information:

	Company			
	Blue	Red	Green	Yellow
Sales revenue	$ 705,000	$ (4)	$ 616,000	$ (10)
Variable costs	(1)	152,100	295,680	164,320
Fixed costs	(2)	122,000	136,000	(11)
Operating income (loss)	$ 12,900	$ (5)	$ (7)	$ 35,680
Units sold	190,000	10,000	(8)	(12)
Contribution margin per unit	$ 1.41	$ (6)	$ 100.10	$ 13.44
Contribution margin ratio	(3)	0.22	(9)	0.21

Requirements

1. Fill in the blanks for each missing value.

2. Which company has the lowest breakeven point in sales dollars? What causes the low breakeven point?

P5-29B *(L. OBJ. 2, 3)* **Breakeven sales; sales to earn a target operating income; contribution margin income statement [30–45 min]**
England Productions performs London shows. The average show sells 1,100 tickets at $55 per ticket. There are 110 shows a year. The average show has a cast of 65, each earning an average of $310 per show. The cast is paid after each show. The other variable cost is program-printing cost of $7 per guest. Annual fixed costs total $522,400.

Requirements

1. Compute revenue and variable costs for each show.

2. Use the income statement equation approach to compute the number of shows England Productions must perform each year to break even.

3. Use the contribution margin approach to compute the number of shows needed each year to earn a profit of $4,113,900. Is this profit goal realistic? Give your reasoning.

4. Prepare England Productions' contribution margin income statement for 110 shows for 2011. Report only two categories of costs: variable and fixed.

P5-30B *(L. OBJ. 2, 3, 4)* **Analyzing CVP relationships [30–45 min]**
Webb company sells flags with team logos. Webb has fixed costs of $639,600 per year plus variable costs of $4.20 per flag. Each flag sells for $12.00.

Requirements

1. Use the income statement equation approach to compute the number of flags Webb must sell each year to break even.

2. Use the contribution margin ratio CVP formula to compute the dollar sales. Webb needs to earn $32,500 in operating income for 2011.

3. Prepare Webb's contribution margin income statement for the year ended December 31, 2011, for sales of 76,000 flags. Cost of goods sold is 65% of variable costs. Operating costs make up the rest of variable costs and all of fixed costs.

4. The company is considering an expansion that will increase fixed costs by 20% and variable costs by $0.30 per flag. Compute the new breakeven point in units and in dollars. Should Webb undertake the expansion? Give your reasoning.

P5-31B *(L. OBJ. 2, 3, 4)* **Computing breakeven sales and sales needed to earn a target operating income; graphing CVP relationships; sensitivity analysis [30–45 min]**
Big Time Advisor Group is opening an office in Dallas. Fixed monthly costs are office rent ($8,000), depreciation on office furniture ($1,400), utilities ($2,000), special telephone lines ($1,300), a connection with an online brokerage service ($2,600), and the salary of a financial planner ($12,700). Variable costs include payments to the financial planner (9% of revenue), advertising (12% of revenue), supplies and postage (4% of revenue), and usage fees for the telephone lines and computerized brokerage service (5% of revenue).

Requirements

1. Use the contribution margin ratio CVP formula to compute Big Time's breakeven revenue in dollars. If the average trade leads to $800 in revenue for Big Time, how many trades must be made to break even?

2. Use the income statement equation approach to compute the dollar revenues needed to earn a target monthly operating income of $10,000.

3. Graph Big Time's CVP relationships. Assume that an average trade leads to $800 in revenue for Big Time. Show the breakeven point, the sales revenue line, the fixed cost line, the total cost line, the operating loss area, the operating income area, and the sales in units (trades) and dollars when monthly operating income of $10,000 is earned. The graph should range from 0 to 80 units.

4. Suppose that the average revenue Big Time earns increases to $900 per trade. Compute the new breakeven point in trades. How does this affect the breakeven point?

P5-32B *(L. OBJ. 4, 5)* **Calculating breakeven point for two product lines; margin of safety [20 min]**

The contribution margin income statement of Krazy Kustard Donuts for October 2012 follows:

KRAZY KUSTARD DONUTS		
Contribution Margin Income Statement		
For the Month of October 2012		
Sales revenue		$ 125,020
Variable costs:		
Cost of goods sold	$ 32,000	
Marketing costs	16,556	
General and administrative cost	5,400	53,956
Contribution margin		71,064
Fixed costs:		
Marketing costs	38,880	
General and administrative cost	4,320	43,200
Operating income		$ 27,864

Krazy Kustard sells two dozen plain donuts for every dozen custard-filled donuts. A dozen plain donuts sells for $6, with a variable cost of $2 per dozen. A dozen custard-filled donuts sells for $7, with a variable cost of $4.20 per dozen.

Requirements

1. Determine Krazy Kustard's monthly breakeven point in dozens of plain donuts and custard-filled donuts. Prove your answer by preparing a summary contribution margin income statement at the breakeven level of sales. Show only two categories of costs: variable and fixed.

2. Compute Krazy Kustard's margin of safety in dollars for October 2012.

3. If Krazy Kustard can increase the monthly sales volume by 10%, what will operating income be? (The sales mix remains unchanged.)

■ Continuing Exercise

E5-33 This exercise continues the Sherman Lawn Service, Inc., situation from Exercise 4-43 of Chapter 4. Sherman Lawn Service currently charges $50 for a standard lawn service and incurs $20 in variable cost. Assume fixed costs are $1,200 per month.

Requirements

1. What is the number of lawns that must be serviced to reach break even?

2. If Sherman desires to make a profit of $1,500, how many lawns must be serviced?

P5-34 This problem continues the Haupt Consulting, Inc., situation from Problem 4-44 of Chapter 4. Haupt Consulting provides consulting service at an average price of $100 per hour and incurs variable cost of $40 per hour. Assume average fixed costs are $4,000 a month.

Requirements

1. What is the number of hours that must be billed to reach break even?
2. If Haupt desires to make a profit of $5,000, how many lawns must be serviced?
3. Haupt thinks it can reduce fixed cost to $3,000 per month, but variable cost will increase to $42 per hour. What is the new break even in hours?

Apply Your Knowledge

■ Decision Cases

Case 1. Steve and Linda Hom live in Bartlesville, Oklahoma. Two years ago, they visited Thailand. Linda, a professional chef, was impressed with the cooking methods and the spices used in the Thai food. Bartlesville does not have a Thai restaurant, and the Homs are contemplating opening one. Linda would supervise the cooking, and Steve would leave his current job to be the maitre d'. The restaurant would serve dinner Tuesday—Saturday.

Steve has noticed a restaurant for lease. The restaurant has seven tables, each of which can seat four. Tables can be moved together for a large party. Linda is planning two seatings per evening, and the restaurant will be open 50 weeks per year.

The Homs have drawn up the following estimates:

Average revenue, including beverages and dessert	$ 45 per meal
Average cost of food	$ 15 per meal
Chef's and dishwasher's salaries	$61,200 per *year*
Rent (premises, equipment)	$ 4,000 per month
Cleaning (linen and premises)	$ 800 per month
Replacement of dishes, cutlery, glasses	$ 300 per month
Utilities, advertising, telephone	$ 2,300 per month

Requirements

1. Compute the *annual* breakeven number of meals and sales revenue for the restaurant.
2. Also compute the number of meals and the amount of sales revenue needed to earn operating income of $75,600 for the year.
3. How many meals must the Homs serve each night to earn their target income of $75,600?
4. Should the couple open the restaurant?

■ Ethical Issue

You have just begun your summer internship at Omni Instruments. The company supplies sterilized surgical instruments for physicians. To expand sales, Omni is considering paying a commission to its sales force. The controller, Matthew Barnhill, asks you to compute: (1) the new breakeven sales figure, and (2) the operating profit if sales increase 15% under the new sales commission plan. He thinks you can handle this task because you learned CVP analysis in your accounting class.

You spend the next day collecting information from the accounting records, performing the analysis, and writing a memo to explain the results. The company president is pleased with your memo. You report that the new sales commission plan will lead to a significant increase in operating income and only a small increase in breakeven sales.

The following week, you realize that you made an error in the CVP analysis. You overlooked the sales personnel's $2,800 monthly salaries and you did not include this fixed marketing cost in your computations. You are not sure what to do. If you tell Matthew Barnhill of your mistake, he will have to tell the president. In this case, you are afraid Omni might not offer you permanent employment after your internship.

Requirements

1. How would your error affect breakeven sales and operating income under the proposed sales commission plan? Could this cause the president to reject the sales commission proposal?

2. Consider your ethical responsibilities. Is there a difference between: (a) initially making an error, and (b) subsequently failing to inform the controller?

3. Suppose you tell Matthew Barnhill of the error in your analysis. Why might the consequences not be as bad as you fear? Should Barnhill take any responsibility for your error? What could Barnhill have done differently?

4. After considering all the factors, should you inform Barnhill or simply keep quiet?

■ Financial Statement Case—Amazon.com

This case is based on the **Amazon.com** annual report in Appendix A at the end of the book. Use it to answer the following questions.

Requirement

1. Review the description of **Amazon.com**'s business. Describe the benefits **Amazon.com** might derive from using break even analysis. Consider its extensive product lines and its role as a reseller, not a manufacturer. How would you figure break even? By units? Product lines? Why? How might categorizing help **Amazon.com** use this technique?

■ Team Project

FASTPACK Manufacturing produces filament packaging tape. In 2009, FASTPACK produced and sold 15 million rolls of tape. The company has recently expanded its capacity, so it now can produce up to 30 million rolls per year. FASTPACK's accounting records show the following results from 2009:

Sale price per roll	$ 3.00
Variable manufacturing costs per roll..................................	$ 2.00
Variable marketing and administrative costs per roll............	$ 0.50
Total fixed manufacturing overhead costs............................	$8,400,000
Total fixed marketing and administrative costs....................	$1,100,000
Sales...	15 million rolls
Production	15 million rolls

There were no beginning or ending inventories in 2009.

In January 2010, FASTPACK hired a new president, Kevin McDaniel. McDaniel has a one-year contract that specifies he will be paid 10% of FASTPACK's 2010 absorption costing operating income, instead of a salary. In 2010, McDaniel must make two major decisions:

- Should FASTPACK undertake a major advertising campaign? This campaign would raise sales to 24 million rolls. This is the maximum level of sales FASTPACK can expect to make in the near future. The ad campaign would add an additional $2.3 million in fixed marketing and administrative costs. Without the campaign, sales will be 15 million rolls.
- How many rolls of tape will FASTPACK produce?

At the end of the year, FASTPACK Manufacturing's Board of Directors will evaluate McDaniel's performance and decide whether to offer him a contract for the following year.

Requirements

Within your group, form two subgroups. The first subgroup assumes the role of Kevin McDaniel, FASTPACK Manufacturing's new president. The second subgroup assumes the role of FASTPACK Manufacturing's Board of Directors. McDaniel will meet with the Board of Directors shortly after the end of 2010 to decide whether he will remain at FASTPACK. Most of your effort should be devoted to advance preparation for this meeting. Each subgroup should meet separately to prepare for the meeting between the Board and McDaniel. (*Hint:* Keep computations other than per-unit amounts in millions.)

Kevin McDaniel should:

1. compute FASTPACK Manufacturing's 2009 operating income.
2. decide whether to adopt the advertising campaign. Prepare a memo to the Board of Directors explaining this decision. Give this memo to the Board of Directors as soon as possible (before the joint meeting).
3. assume FASTPACK adopts the advertising campaign. Decide how many rolls of tape to produce in 2010.
4. (given the response to requirement 3) prepare an absorption costing income statement for the year ended December 31, 2010, ending with operating income before bonus. Then compute the bonus separately. The variable cost per unit and the total fixed costs (with the exception of the advertising campaign) remain the same as in 2009. Give this income statement and bonus computation to the Board of Directors as soon as possible (before the meeting with the Board).
5. decide whether he wishes to remain at FASTPACK for another year. He currently has an offer from another company. The contract with the other company is identical to the one he currently has with FASTPACK—he will be paid 10% of absorption costing operating income instead of a salary.

The Board of Directors should:

1. compute FASTPACK's 2009 operating income.
2. determine whether FASTPACK should adopt the advertising campaign.
3. determine how many rolls of tape FASTPACK should produce in 2010.
4. evaluate McDaniel's performance, based on his decisions and the information he provided the Board. (*Hint:* You may want to prepare a variable costing income statement.)
5. evaluate the contract's bonus provision. Is the Board satisfied with this provision? If so, explain why. If not, recommend how it should be changed.

After McDaniel has given the Board his memo and income statement, and after the Board has had a chance to evaluate McDaniel's performance, McDaniel and the Board should meet. The purpose of the meeting is to decide whether it is in their mutual interest for McDaniel to remain with FASTPACK, and if so, the terms of the contract FASTPACK will offer McDaniel.

For online homework, exercises, and problems that provide you immediate feedback, please visit www.myaccountinglab.com.

Big Picture

Ch 1   Introduction to Management Accounting

- Distinguish management accounting from financial accounting
- The role and responsibilities of management accountants
- Classify costs and prepare income statements for merchandising companies
- Classify costs and prepare income statements and statements of cost of goods manufactured for manufacturing companies

Ch 2   Job Order Costing

- Distinguish between job order and process costing
- Record materials, labor, and overhead in a job order costing system
- Record completion and sales of finished goods and adjust for under-/overallocated overhead
- Calculate unit costs for service companies

Ch 3   Activity-Based Costing and Other Cost Management Tools

- Develop activity-based costs and used activity-based management to determine target product costs
- Record transactions in JIT systems
- Use the four types of quality costs to make management decisions

Ch 4   Process Costing

- Calculate equivalent units and conversion costs
- Prepare cost of production reports and the related journal entries using the weighted-average costing method
- Prepare cost of production reports and the related journal entries using the FIFO costing method

Ch 5   Cost Behavior and Cost-Volume-Profit Analysis

- Identify how changes in volume affect cost
- Distinguish among variable, mixed, and fixed cost
- Split mixed cost into fixed and variable components by using the high-low method and by using regression analysis
- Use CVP to compute breakeven points, to plan profits, to graph relationships, and to perform sensitivity analysis

Chapter 5: Demo Doc

■ Using CVP for Sensitivity Analysis

Learning Objectives 2, 4, 5

Hacker Golf has developed a unique swing trainer golf club. It currently has a production company produce the golf club for it at a cost of $22. Other variable costs total $6, whereas monthly fixed costs are $16,000. Hacker currently sells the trainer golf club for $48.

Requirements

NOTE: Solve each requirement as a separate situation.

1. Calculate Hacker's breakeven point in units.

2. Hacker is considering raising its selling price to $49.95. Calculate the new breakeven in units.

3. Hacker has found a new company to produce the golf club at a lower cost of $19 each. Calculate the new breakeven in units.

4. Because many customers have requested a golf glove to go along with the trainer club, Hacker is considering selling gloves. It only expects to sell one glove for every four trainer clubs it sells. Hacker can purchase the gloves for $5 each and sell them for $9 each. Total fixed costs should remain the same at $16,000 per month. Calculate the breakeven point in units for trainer clubs and golf gloves.

5. Use a contribution margin income statement to prove the breakeven point calculated in requirement 4.

Demo Doc Solution

Requirement 1

Calculate Hacker's breakeven point in units.

2 Use CVP analysis to compute breakeven points

Part 1	Part 2	Part 3	Part 4	Part 5	Part 6	Part 7	Demo Doc Complete

To determine how changes in sales prices, costs, or volume affect profits, let us first start by calculating the current breakeven point.

To determine the breakeven point, we first must calculate the contribution margin per unit. The contribution margin per unit is calculated by subtracting variable costs from the sales revenue. Therefore:

Contribution margin per unit = Sales price per unit – Variable cost per unit

Hacker's variable cost per club (unit) is the price it pays for each club ($22) plus its additional variable costs ($6). Therefore, its unit contribution margin is

Selling price per club	$48
Variable cost per club ($22 + $6)	(28)
Contribution margin per club	$20

The contribution margin represents the amount from each unit sold that is available to recover fixed costs. That means that after variable costs are covered, Hacker earns $20 per club, which then contributes toward fixed costs until fixed costs are covered, after which point Hacker will begin to generate $20 profit per club sold.

Breakeven is the level of sales at which income is zero. To compute breakeven using the contribution margin approach:

$$\text{Breakeven} = \frac{\text{Fixed cost}}{\text{Contribution margin per unit}}$$

$$= \frac{\$16,000}{\$20}$$

$$= 800 \text{ trainer clubs}$$

Requirement 2

Hacker is considering raising its selling price to $49.95. Calculate the new breakeven point in units.

4 Use CVP methods to perform sensitivity analyses

Part 1	Part 2	Part 3	Part 4	Part 5	Part 6	Part 7	Demo Doc Complete

In this case, the selling price is changing, but Hacker's variable and fixed costs are staying the same as in the original question ($28 and $16,000, respectively). The new selling price for the club is going to be $1.95 higher than the original price: from $48.00 to $49.95.

Once we update the original data to reflect the changes, the data are then processed with the same calculations. First, calculate the new contribution margin:

Selling price per club	$49.95
Variable cost per club ($22 + 6)	(28.00)
Contribution margin per club	$21.95

Using the contribution margin approach:

$$\text{Breakeven in units} = \frac{\text{Fixed cost}}{\text{Contribution margin per unit}}$$

$$= \frac{\$16,000}{\$21.95}$$

$$= 728.93, \textbf{ rounded up to 729 } \textbf{trainer clubs}$$

Again, we round because Hacker cannot sell a partial unit (the 0.93 in the actual calculation).

With the increased selling price, breakeven has been reduced from 800 clubs to 729 clubs. The higher price means that each club contributes more to fixed costs.

You can prove this using the income statement approach:

Sales revenue (729 × $49.95)	$36,414
Less: Variable costs (729 × $28)	20,412
Total contribution margin	16,002
Less: Fixed costs	16,000
Operating income	$ 2*

*The $2 profit results from rounding 728.93 clubs to 729

Remember that as selling prices increase (provided all costs remain the same), the volume required to break even or achieve target profit goals decreases. Conversely, as selling prices decrease, the volume required to break even or achieve target profit goals increases.

Consider the following:

Selling price goes from $50 to $60, variable costs stay at $20, and total fixed costs are $60,000.

Old contribution margin was $50 − $20 = $30.

Old breakeven point in **units** was $60,000 ÷ $30 = 2,000 units.

New contribution margin is $60 − $20 = $40.

New breakeven point in **units** is $60,000 ÷ $40 = 1,500 units.

There is an *inverse* relationship between contribution margin (an increase of $10 in this case) and breakeven in units (a decrease of 500 units in this case).

Requirement 3

Hacker has found a new company to produce the golf club at a lower cost of $19 each. Calculate the new breakeven point in units.

Use CVP methods to perform sensitivity analyses

Part 1	Part 2	**Part 3**	Part 4	Part 5	Part 6	Part 7	Demo Doc Complete

Once costs begin to change, a new breakeven point must be calculated to determine the effects of the changes. In this case, the variable cost is changing, yet fixed costs and the sales price is staying the same as in the original question ($16,000 and $48, respectively).

In this case, we calculate as we normally would, except that our contribution margin will be different:

> Contribution margin per unit = Sales price per unit – Variable cost per unit

Hacker's variable cost per club (unit) is the price it pays for each club (now $19) plus its additional variable costs ($6). Therefore, its unit contribution margin is

Selling price per club	$48
Variable cost per club ($19 + $6)	(25)
Contribution margin per club	$23

Using the contribution margin approach:

$$\text{Breakeven in units} = \frac{\text{Fixed cost}}{\text{Contribution margin per unit}}$$

$$= \frac{\$16,000}{\$23}$$

$$= 695.65, \textbf{rounded up to 696 clubs}$$

With the reduced variable cost, Hacker's breakeven in units decreases from 800 clubs to 696 clubs. Using this information, Hacker's management must decide if it is worth the risk to switch to a new producer.

You can also prove this using the income statement approach:

Sales revenue (696 × $48)	$33,408
Less: Variable costs (696 × $25)	17,400
Total contribution margin	16,008
Less: Fixed costs	16,000
Operating income	$ 8*

*The $8 profit results from rounding 695.65 to 696 clubs

With both fixed and variable costs, remember that as these costs increase, so does the volume needed to break even or achieve target profits. Conversely, as these costs decrease, the volume needed to break even or achieve target profits also decreases.

Requirement 4

5 Calculate the breakeven
point for multiple product
lines or services

Because many customers have requested a golf glove to go along with the trainer club, Hacker is considering selling gloves. It only expects to sell one glove for every four trainer clubs it sells. Hacker can purchase the gloves for $5 each and sell them for $9 each. Total fixed costs should remain the same at $16,000 per month. Calculate the breakeven point in units for trainer clubs and golf gloves.

Part 1	Part 2	Part 3	**Part 4**	Part 5	Part 6	Part 7	Demo Doc Complete

Calculating the breakeven point is fairly straightforward when a company is only dealing with one product. But Hacker is now considering selling two products rather than just one. Now breakeven becomes a little more complicated. This is because different products will have different effects on the contribution margins because of different costs and selling prices. So the company needs to consider the sales mix (a combination of products that make up total sales) in figuring CVP relationships.

You can use the same formulas to determine the breakeven point considering the sales mix, but before calculating breakeven, you must calculate the weighted-average contribution margin of all the products first. You saw another weighted-average for process costing in Chapter 4. In this case, the sales mix provides the weights.

Step 1: Calculate the weighted-average contribution margin.

Hacker believes that it can sell one glove for every four trainer clubs that it sells. This would give it a 4:1 sales mix. So it expects that 4/5 (or 80%) of its sales will be trainer clubs, and 1/5 (or 20%) of its sales will be gloves.

Recall that Hacker pays $28 in variable costs for its clubs and sells them for $48, for a contribution margin of $20 per unit. The gloves will cost it $5 per pair and sell for $9, for a contribution margin of $4 per unit:

	Clubs	Gloves	Total
Sales price per unit	$48	$9	
Deduct: variable cost per unit	(28)	(5)	
Contribution margin per unit	$20	$4	

The weighted-average contribution margin is calculated by multiplying the contribution margin per unit by the sales mix expected for each. Once we have a total contribution margin ($80 + $4 = $84, in this case), we divide the total contribution margin by the total sales mix in units (5), as follows:

	Sales Mix Percentage		
	80% Clubs	20% Gloves	Total
Sales price per unit	$48	$9	
Deduct: Variable cost per unit	(28)	(5)	
Contribution margin per unit	$20	$4	
Sales mix in units	4	1	5.00
Contribution margin per product	$80	$4	$84.00
Weighted-average contribution margin ($84 ÷ 5)			

Another way to calculate this is to multiply each product's contribution margin by its sales mix percentage:

$$
\begin{array}{llll}
\text{Clubs:} & \$20 \times 80\% & = & \$16.00 \\
\text{Gloves:} & \$\ 4 \times 20\% & = & \underline{\$\ 0.80} \\
& & = & \underline{\underline{\$16.80}}
\end{array}
$$

The $16.80 represents an average contribution margin for all the products Hacker sells. The golf clubs are weighted more heavily because Hacker expects to sell four times as many clubs compared to the gloves.

The next step is to calculate the breakeven in units for the bundle of products.

Step 2: Calculate the breakeven point in units for the total of both products combined.

Part 1	Part 2	Part 3	Part 4	**Part 5**	Part 6	Part 7	Demo Doc Complete

This is calculated using the following formula:

$$
\begin{array}{l}
\text{Total sales} \\
\text{in units}
\end{array} = \frac{\text{Fixed cost}}{\text{Weighted-average contribution margin per unit}}
$$

We know from the question that fixed costs will not be affected, so they should remain at $16,000. The weighted-average contribution margin, as we just calculated, is $16.80 per unit. So we compute as follows:

$$
\begin{aligned}
\text{Total sales in unit} &= \frac{\$16,000}{\$16.80} \\
&= 952.38, \textbf{ rounded to 953}
\end{aligned}
$$

Recall that we round up because Hacker cannot sell a partial unit.

Hacker must sell a combined 953 clubs and gloves to break even. Management needs to know how many units of each product must be sold to break even.

The next step is to determine the breakeven point in units for each product.

Step 3: Calculate the breakeven in units for each product line.

Part 1	Part 2	Part 3	Part 4	Part 5	**Part 6**	Part 7	Demo Doc Complete

Because Hacker believes that it will sell four trainer clubs for every one glove, the total breakeven, 953, is multiplied by each product's respective percent of expected total sales:

Breakeven sales of clubs $(953 \times 80\%)$ = 762.4, **rounded to 763**

Breakeven sales of gloves $(953 \times 20\%)$ = 190.6, **rounded to 191**

= 954 total units

So from this analysis, we know that Hacker needs to sell 763 trainer clubs and 191 gloves to break even. The breakeven point in sales dollars is:

$$
\begin{aligned}
763 \text{ clubs} \times \$48 &= \$36,624 \\
\text{plus } 191 \text{ gloves} \times \$9 &= \underline{\$\ 1,719} \\
\text{for a total} &= \underline{\underline{\$38,343}}
\end{aligned}
$$

Requirement 5

5 Calculate the breakeven point for multiple product lines or services

Use a contribution margin income statement to prove the breakeven point calculated in requirement 4.

Part 1	Part 2	Part 3	Part 4	Part 5	Part 6	**Part 7**	Demo Doc Complete

To test the calculation of the breakeven point, you would add together the revenue generated from all sales, subtract the variable costs for each of the clubs and gloves, and then subtract the total fixed costs. The result should balance to zero (or close to zero, in cases in which rounding occurs).

HACKER GOLF
Contribution Margin Income Statement

			Clubs	Gloves	Total
	Sales revenue:				
		Trainer clubs (763 × $48)	$36,624		
		Gloves (191 × $9)		$1,719	$38,343
	Variable costs:				
		Trainer clubs (763 × $28)	21,364		
		Gloves (191 × $5)		955	$22,319
	Contribution margin		$15,260	$ 764	$16,024
	Fixed costs				(16,000)
	Operating income				$ 24

There is a slight $24 profit at the breakeven level because of rounding to whole units.

Part 1	Part 2	Part 3	Part 4	Part 5	Part 6	Part 7	**Demo Doc Complete**

6 Absorption and Variable Costing

Learning Objectives/Success Keys

1 Distinguish between absorption costing and variable costing

2 Prepare absorption costing and variable costing income statements and explain the difference in results

3 Illustrate the pros and cons of absorption and variable costing

As Smart Touch Learning considers different growth and marketing strategies, it also has to consider what information form will be most helpful to make those decisions.

This chapter will look at how income statements are prepared under absorption and variable costing. We will also compare the results under both methods, as well as the information management can glean from each statement type.

Absorption Costing

1 Distinguish between absorption costing and variable costing

Up to this point, we have focused on the income statements that companies report to the public under the generally accepted accounting principles (GAAP). GAAP requires that we assign both variable and fixed manufacturing costs to products. This approach is called **absorption costing** because products absorb both fixed and variable manufacturing costs. Supporters of absorption costing argue that companies cannot produce products without incurring fixed costs, so these costs are an important part of product costs. Financial accountants usually prefer absorption costing.

Variable Costing

The alternate method is called variable costing. **Variable costing** assigns only variable manufacturing costs to products. Thus, variable costs are product costs under this costing method. Fixed costs are considered *period costs* and are *expensed immediately* because the company incurs these fixed costs whether or not it produces any products or services. In variable costing, fixed costs are not product costs. Management accountants often prefer variable costing for their planning and control decisions.

Comparison

Absorption costing and variable costing are methods used to calculate the cost of a product. The key difference between absorption costing and variable costing is that

- absorption costing considers fixed manufacturing costs as inventoriable product costs.
- variable costing considers fixed manufacturing costs as period costs (expenses).

All other costs are treated the same way under both absorption and variable costing:

- Variable manufacturing costs are products costs that appear as inventory on the balance sheet.
- All nonmanufacturing costs—both fixed and variable—are period costs and are expensed immediately when incurred.

Recall that manufacturing costs are those costs directly related to the product being manufactured. If these costs are fixed, they do not change regardless of the amount of production that occurs during a period.

Exhibit 6-1 summarizes the difference between variable and absorption costing, with the differences shown in color.

| EXHIBIT 6-1 | Differences Between Absorption Costing and Variable Costing |

Type of Cost	Absorption Costing	Variable Costing
Product Costs (Capitalized as Inventory until expensed as Cost of Goods Sold)	Direct materials Direct labor Variable manufacturing overhead Fixed manufacturing overhead	Direct materials Direct labor Variable manufacturing overhead
Period Costs (Expensed in period incurred)	Variable nonmanufacturing costs Fixed nonmanufacturing costs	Fixed manufacturing overhead Variable nonmanufacturing costs Fixed nonmanufacturing costs
Income Statement Format	Conventional income statement	Contribution margin income statement

Stop & Think...

Think about your monthly cell phone costs. Assume you pay a flat rate of $50.00 a month for 1,000 minutes, or $0.05 per minute. Whether you use all the minutes or not, your fixed cost is still $50.00 a month. Now consider that you do not use all your minutes in a particular month and that the minutes rollover for you to use next month. The fee you pay each month does not change—just your usage of minutes changes. This analogy is the same for fixed costs related to production. How we treat those fixed costs is all that changes between absorption and variable costing—that is do we expense all $50.00 each month of the cell phone bill (variable costing) or do we attach those costs to inventory 0.05 per minute used?

To see how absorption costing and variable costing differ, take a look at Smart Touch Learning's data. Exhibit 6-2 details Smart Touch's costs for production of Excel DVDs for March and April of 2011:

2 Prepare absorption costing and variable costing income statements

| EXHIBIT 6-2 | Smart Touch Learning Costs |

	March	April
Direct materials cost per DVD	$ 2.40	$ 2.40
Direct labor cost per DVD	$ 4.00	$ 4.00
Variable manufacturing overhead cost per DVD	$ 0.60	$ 0.60
Total fixed manufacturing overhead costs	$150,000	$150,000
Total fixed selling and administrative costs	$200,000	$200,000
Number of DVDs produced	100,000	100,000
Number of DVDs sold	90,000	105,000
Sale price per DVD	$ 12.00	$ 12.00

There were no beginning inventories on March 1, 2011, so Smart Touch has 10,000 DVDs in ending inventory in March (100,000 DVDs produced in March less the 90,000 DVDs sold in March). In April there are 5,000 DVDs in ending inventory (10,000 Beginning inventory leftover from March + 100,000 DVDs produced in April – 105,000 DVDs sold in April).

What is Smart Touch's inventoriable product cost per DVD under absorption costing and variable costing? Exhibit 6-3 details the comparison.

EXHIBIT 6-3	Smart Touch Learning's Cost per Unit		
		Absorption Costing	Variable Costing
Direct materials		$2.40	$2.40
Direct labor		4.00	4.00
Variable manufacturing overhead		0.60	0.60
Fixed manufacturing overhead ($150,000/100,000 DVDs)		1.50	
Total cost per DVD		$8.50	$7.00

The only difference between absorption and variable costing is that the $150,000 monthly fixed manufacturing overhead is a product cost under absorption costing, but a period cost under variable costing. The monthly fixed manufacturing cost was divided into units or **unitized** by taking the $150,000 and dividing it by the 100,000 DVDs produced. This is why the cost per DVD is $1.50 higher under absorption (total cost of $8.50) than under variable costing (total cost of $7.00).

Exhibit 6-4 shows the March income statements using absorption costing and variable costing. The exhibit also shows the calculation for ending inventory at March 31, 2011.

Notice the absorption costing operating income is $15,000 higher than the variable costing operating income. Why? Because fixed manufacturing costs are unitized

EXHIBIT 6-4	March 2011 Income Statements for Smart Touch Learning, Inc.

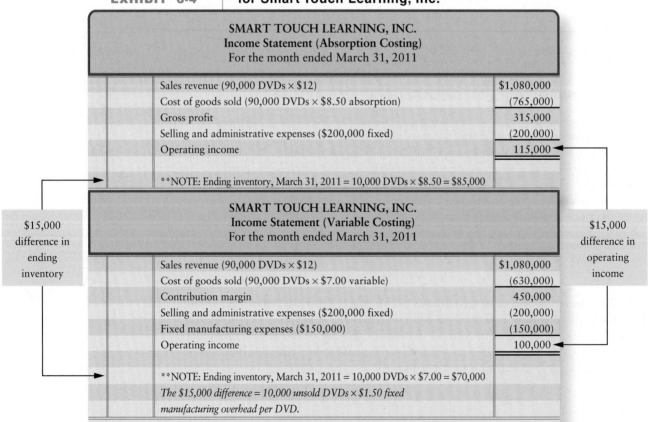

SMART TOUCH LEARNING, INC.
Income Statement (Absorption Costing)
For the month ended March 31, 2011

Sales revenue (90,000 DVDs × $12)	$1,080,000
Cost of goods sold (90,000 DVDs × $8.50 absorption)	(765,000)
Gross profit	315,000
Selling and administrative expenses ($200,000 fixed)	(200,000)
Operating income	115,000

**NOTE: Ending inventory, March 31, 2011 = 10,000 DVDs × $8.50 = $85,000

SMART TOUCH LEARNING, INC.
Income Statement (Variable Costing)
For the month ended March 31, 2011

Sales revenue (90,000 DVDs × $12)	$1,080,000
Cost of goods sold (90,000 DVDs × $7.00 variable)	(630,000)
Contribution margin	450,000
Selling and administrative expenses ($200,000 fixed)	(200,000)
Fixed manufacturing expenses ($150,000)	(150,000)
Operating income	100,000

**NOTE: Ending inventory, March 31, 2011 = 10,000 DVDs × $7.00 = $70,000
The $15,000 difference = 10,000 unsold DVDs × $1.50 fixed manufacturing overhead per DVD.

$15,000 difference in ending inventory

$15,000 difference in operating income

under absorption costing, and because Smart Touch produced more DVDs than it sold in March of 2011. Look at the two ending inventory amounts for March, 2011:

- $85,000 under absorption costing
- $70,000 under variable costing

This $15,000 difference results because ending inventory under absorption costing holds $15,000 of fixed manufacturing costs that were expensed under variable costing. The ending inventory difference of $15,000 is the same as the operating income difference, as follows:

Month	Units of ending finished goods inventory	×	Fixed manufacturing cost per unit	=	Difference in ending inventory
March 1, 2011 beginning inventory	-		$1.50		$ -
+ March 2011 production	100,000		$1.50		$ 150,000
– March 2011 sales	(90,000)		$1.50		$(135,000)
= March 31, 2011 ending inventory	10,000		$1.50		$ 15,000

Now let's look at April 2011's results for Smart Touch Learning. Exhibit 6-5 shows the April income statements using absorption costing and variable costing. The exhibit also shows the calculation for ending inventory at April 30, 2011.

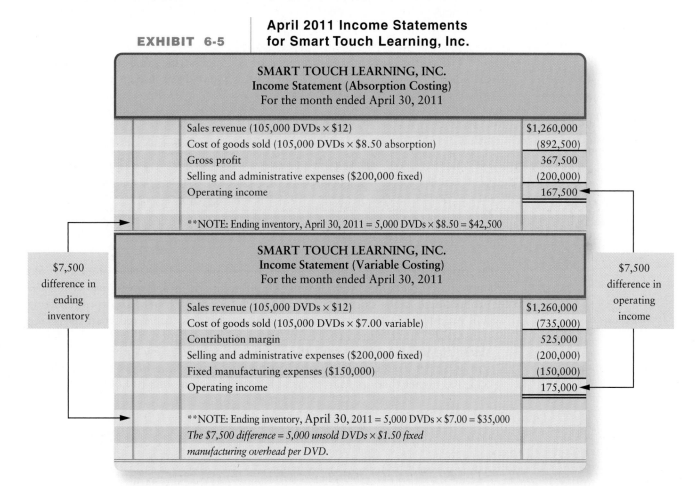

EXHIBIT 6-5 | **April 2011 Income Statements for Smart Touch Learning, Inc.**

SMART TOUCH LEARNING, INC.
Income Statement (Absorption Costing)
For the month ended April 30, 2011

Sales revenue (105,000 DVDs × $12)	$1,260,000
Cost of goods sold (105,000 DVDs × $8.50 absorption)	(892,500)
Gross profit	367,500
Selling and administrative expenses ($200,000 fixed)	(200,000)
Operating income	167,500

**NOTE: Ending inventory, April 30, 2011 = 5,000 DVDs × $8.50 = $42,500

SMART TOUCH LEARNING, INC.
Income Statement (Variable Costing)
For the month ended April 30, 2011

Sales revenue (105,000 DVDs × $12)	$1,260,000
Cost of goods sold (105,000 DVDs × $7.00 variable)	(735,000)
Contribution margin	525,000
Selling and administrative expenses ($200,000 fixed)	(200,000)
Fixed manufacturing expenses ($150,000)	(150,000)
Operating income	175,000

**NOTE: Ending inventory, April 30, 2011 = 5,000 DVDs × $7.00 = $35,000
The $7,500 difference = 5,000 unsold DVDs × $1.50 fixed manufacturing overhead per DVD.

$7,500 difference in ending inventory

$7,500 difference in operating income

Notice the absorption costing operating income is now $7,500 lower than the variable costing operating income. Why? Again, it is because of the differing treatments of fixed manufacturing costs.

Another reason for the difference in income between absorption costing and variable costing relates to number of units produced compared to the number of units sold. Smart Touch sold 5,000 more DVDs than it produced in April. How did Smart Touch sell more than they produced in April—by selling the March ending inventory. Remember also that the cost per DVD is higher under absorption costing, so the difference is shown on the two main accounts related to the product: Inventory and Cost of goods sold

Look at the two ending inventory amounts for April 2011:

- $42,500 under absorption costing
- $35,000 under variable costing

This $7,500 difference results because ending inventory under absorption costing contains $7,500 of fixed manufacturing cost that were expensed under variable costing.

Month	Units of ending finished goods inventory	× Fixed manufacturing cost per unit	= Difference in ending inventory
March 31, 2011 ending inventory	10,000	$1.50	$ 15,000
+ April 2011 production	100,000	$1.50	$ 150,000
– April 2011 sales	(105,000)	$1.50	$(157,500)
= April 30, 2011 ending inventory	5,000	$1.50	$ 7,500

The ending inventory difference of $7,500 is the same as the operating income difference because the change in sales equaled the change in ending inventory, as follows:

Month	Units of ending finished goods inventory	× Fixed manufacturing cost per unit	= Difference in operating income
+ April 2011 production	100,000	$1.50	$ 150,000
– April 2011 sales	(105,000)	$1.50	$(157,500)
= April 30, 2011 operating income	(5,000)	$1.50	$ (7,500)

Production Exceeds Sales Smart Touch produced 100,000 units and sold only 90,000 units in March, leaving 10,000 units in ending inventory. Whenever production exceeds sales, as it did in March for Smart Touch, absorption costing will produce more reported income. This occurs because fixed costs are being "absorbed" into the inventory costs (an asset) and are not included on the income statement as an expense until the product is sold. Review Exhibit 6-4, which shows Smart Touch's March absorption costing income of $115,000. This is $15,000 higher than its March variable costing income of $100,000.

Sales Exceed Production   Companies sometimes sell more units of inventory than they produced that period. How can they do that? By selling inventory produced in prior periods along with inventory produced in the current period. This is exactly what happened in April 2011 for Smart Touch. Only 100,000 units were produced, but 105,000 units were sold. Review Exhibit 6-5, which shows Smart Touch's April absorption costing income of $167,500 was $7,500 less than Smart Touch's April variable costing income of $175,000. Why? The 10,000 units in March ending inventory decreased by 5,000 units remaining in April ending inventory. Also, fixed costs in the March inventory are expensed under variable costing. This leads to the opposite result: Variable costing produced more reported income in April because sales exceeded production.

Stop & Think...

Let us revisit your monthly cell phone costs. Assume you had 100 minutes leftover at the end of a month. Under absorption costing, you would have $5.00 in value of ending inventory minutes (100 minutes × $.05 per minute). Under variable costing, you would still have the minutes, just no value would be attached to those minutes and consequently ending inventory would be zero.

Absorption Costing Pros and Cons

Absorption costing is required by GAAP, so using this method is a pro for companies required to report using GAAP. Additionally, this method clearly ties all product costs to the product, which gives a more accurate matching of income and expenses.

> **3** Illustrate the pros and cons of absorption and variable costing

Suppose Ryan Oliver, production manager, receives a bonus from Smart Touch Learning based on operating income using absorption costing. Will Ryan increase or decrease production? Ryan knows that absorption costing assigns each DVD $1.50 of fixed manufacturing overhead.

- For every DVD that is produced but not sold, absorption costing "hides" $1.50 of fixed overhead in ending inventory (an asset).
- The more DVDs added to inventory, the more fixed overhead is "hidden" in ending inventory at the end of the month.
- The more fixed overhead in ending inventory, the smaller the cost of goods sold and the higher the operating income.

To maximize the bonus under absorption costing, Ryan may be motivated to increase production to build up inventory. This in turn would increase net income, consequently increasing Ryan's bonus unfairly. As an example, refer to the March Smart Touch Learning production of 100,000 DVDs of which only 90,000 were sold. The 10,000 increase in ending inventory allowed the absorption costing operating income to report $115,000 whereas the variable costing income statement only reported $100,000 in operating income (Exhibit 6-4).

This incentive directly conflicts with the just-in-time philosophy, which emphasizes minimal inventory levels. Companies that have adopted just-in-time should either (1) evaluate their managers based on variable costing income, or (2) use strict controls to prevent inventory buildup.

Variable Costing Pros and Cons

As previously stated, variable costing is more in-line with JIT inventories. Further, its illustration of contribution margin on the income statement allows managers to make better CVP (cost-volume-profit) analyses, not available on absorption costing income statements. This allows managers to make better marketing and production decisions when multiple products are produced utilizing constrained production availability.

Additionally, fixed costs are often out of management's control. Evaluating management on their ability to control costs could be perceived as unfair if the product cost includes an unreasonable amount of per unit fixed costs.

Another advantage is that the fixed costs are itemized on the variable costing statement. This illustrates the effect inventory changes have on profit for operations managers from month to month. This could also be perceived as a disadvantage if the product sales are seasonal (such as beach chairs), but the production is not—that is beach chairs are produced all year to be ready for Summer sales. Further, variable costing income is more closely aligned to the cash flows generated, which helps with budgeting.

You have learned how to calculate absorption and variable costing income statements. Review the Decision Guidelines to make sure you understand these basic concepts.

Decision Guidelines

ABSORPTION AND VARIABLE COSTING ANALYSIS

Managers find product costing information very useful for decision making. Here are some questions you will ask, and guidelines for answering them.

Decision	Guidelines
• What is the main difference between absorption and variable costing?	Accounting for fixed manufacturing costs is the only difference: • Absorption Costing—*Attached* as a product cost (unitized) • Variable Costing—*Expensed* as a period cost
• How do changes in inventory levels affect income under • absorption costing?	• Production > Sales: fixed manufacturing costs are deferred as part of the asset, Inventory. Operating income is higher by the amount of net deferred fixed manufacturing costs. • Production < Sales: fixed manufacturing costs are expensed as part of COGS. Operating income is lower by the amount of net increase in COGS. COGS is higher because per unit fixed manufacturing costs are included in COGS.
• variable costing?	• Production > Sales: operating income is lower because all fixed overhead costs are expensed. • Production < Sales: operating income is higher because fixed overhead costs are expensed and no additional fixed overhead costs associated with the inventory sell down are expensed.

Summary Problem 1

Tucker's Tot Chairs produces activity chairs for toddlers. Tucker began production of chairs in January, 2011. In January and February, 2011, Tucker's incurred the following costs:

	January	February
Direct materials cost per chair	$ 25	$ 25
Direct labor cost per chair	$ 15	$ 15
Variable manufacturing overhead cost per chair	$ 20	$ 20
Total fixed manufacturing overhead costs	$100,000	$100,000
Total fixed selling and administrative costs	$400,000	$400,000
Number of chairs produced	20,000	20,000
Number of chairs sold	18,000	21,500
Sale price per chair	$ 100	$ 100

Requirements

1. Calculate the absorption and variable cost per unit.
2. Calculate the January 2011 absorption and variable cost operating income and ending inventory cost and explain the differences, if any.
3. Calculate the February, 2011 absorption and variable cost operating income and ending inventory cost and explain the differences, if any.

Solution

Requirement 1

Since production costs remained unchanged in January and February, the cost per unit is the same for both months.

	Absorption Costing	Variable Costing
Direct materials cost per chair	$25	$25
Direct labor cost per chair	$15	$15
Variable manufacturing overhead cost per chair	$20	$20
Fixed manufacturing overhead costs ($100,000/20,000 chairs)	$ 5	—
Total cost per chair	$65	$60

Requirement 2

Given the same product cost information above, assume Tucker's Tot Chairs produced 20,000 units, but only sold 18,000 units in January.

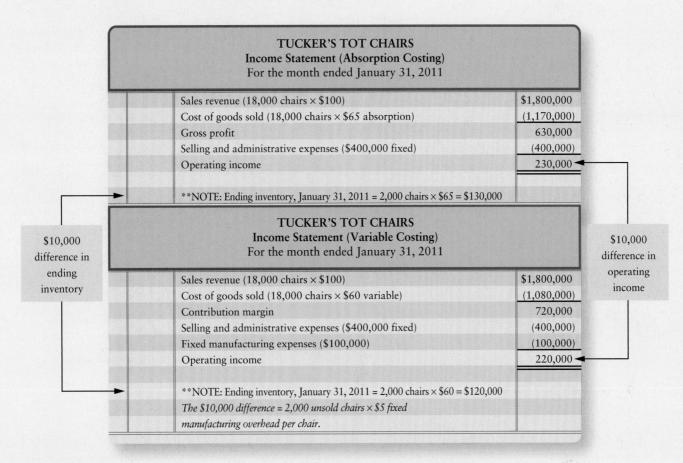

TUCKER'S TOT CHAIRS Income Statement (Absorption Costing) For the month ended January 31, 2011		
Sales revenue (18,000 chairs × $100)		$1,800,000
Cost of goods sold (18,000 chairs × $65 absorption)		(1,170,000)
Gross profit		630,000
Selling and administrative expenses ($400,000 fixed)		(400,000)
Operating income		230,000

**NOTE: Ending inventory, January 31, 2011 = 2,000 chairs × $65 = $130,000

TUCKER'S TOT CHAIRS Income Statement (Variable Costing) For the month ended January 31, 2011		
Sales revenue (18,000 chairs × $100)		$1,800,000
Cost of goods sold (18,000 chairs × $60 variable)		(1,080,000)
Contribution margin		720,000
Selling and administrative expenses ($400,000 fixed)		(400,000)
Fixed manufacturing expenses ($100,000)		(100,000)
Operating income		220,000

**NOTE: Ending inventory, January 31, 2011 = 2,000 chairs × $60 = $120,000
The $10,000 difference = 2,000 unsold chairs × $5 fixed manufacturing overhead per chair.

$10,000 difference in ending inventory

$10,000 difference in operating income

The 2,000 units in ending inventory at January 31, 2011 have $10,000 more in inventory cost under absorption costing ($130,000 versus $120,000 ending inventory), due to the application of fixed overhead of $5 per unit. The same $10,000 change in operating income for the month is reported with absorption costing reflecting an operating income of $230,000. This is $10,000 higher than the $220,000 variable costing income. Again, this is due to the 2,000 units of ending inventory that have $5 fixed overhead included, unitized by taking $100,000 in fixed overhead divided by 20,000 chairs produced.

Requirement 3

Tucker's Tot Chairs produced 20,000 chairs (units) in February, and sold 21,500 chairs during the same month.

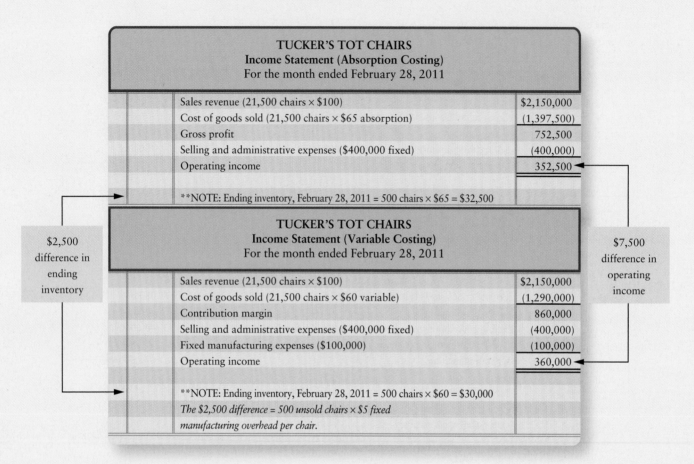

TUCKER'S TOT CHAIRS
Income Statement (Absorption Costing)
For the month ended February 28, 2011

Sales revenue (21,500 chairs × $100)	$2,150,000
Cost of goods sold (21,500 chairs × $65 absorption)	(1,397,500)
Gross profit	752,500
Selling and administrative expenses ($400,000 fixed)	(400,000)
Operating income	352,500

**NOTE: Ending inventory, February 28, 2011 = 500 chairs × $65 = $32,500

TUCKER'S TOT CHAIRS
Income Statement (Variable Costing)
For the month ended February 28, 2011

Sales revenue (21,500 chairs × $100)	$2,150,000
Cost of goods sold (21,500 chairs × $60 variable)	(1,290,000)
Contribution margin	860,000
Selling and administrative expenses ($400,000 fixed)	(400,000)
Fixed manufacturing expenses ($100,000)	(100,000)
Operating income	360,000

**NOTE: Ending inventory, February 28, 2011 = 500 chairs × $60 = $30,000
The $2,500 difference = 500 unsold chairs × $5 fixed manufacturing overhead per chair.

$2,500 difference in ending inventory

$7,500 difference in operating income

The 50 units in ending inventory at February 28, 2011 have $2,500 more in inventory cost under absorption costing ($32,500 versus $30,000 ending inventory), due to the application of fixed overhead of $5 per unit. Why? Under absorption costing, ending inventory contains $2,500 in fixed manufacturing overhead (500 units of ending inventory times $5 per chair) compared to variable costing, where all fixed manufacturing overhead was expensed in the prior period.

Month	Units of ending finished goods inventory	×	Fixed manufacturing cost per unit	=	Difference in ending inventory
January 31, 2011 ending inventory	2,000		$5.00		$ 10,000
+ February 2011 production	20,000		$5.00		$ 100,000
– February 2011 sales	(21,500)		$5.00		$(107,500)
= February 28, 2011 ending inventory	500		$5.00		$ 2,500

The difference in operating income for the month shows absorption costing having operating income of $7,500 lower than variable costing. This is caused by the change in the inventories and the absorption of fixed manufacturing overhead costs of $5 per chair (times 2,500 chairs from last month's ending overhead) that occurred between January and February as follows:

Month	Units of ending finished goods inventory	×	Fixed manufacturing cost per unit	=	Difference in operating income
+ February 2011 production	20,000		$5.00		$ 100,000
– February 2011 sales	(21,500)		$5.00		$(107,500)
= February 28, 2011 operating income	(1,500)		$5.00		$ (7,500)

Review   *Absorption and Variable Costing*

■ Accounting Vocabulary

Absorption Costing (p. 264)
A product costing method that assigns both variable and fixed manufacturing costs to products.

Unitized (p. 266)
Dividing a cost by the total number of units produced to create a per unit cost.

Variable Costing (p. 264)
A product costing method that assigns only variable manufacturing costs to products.

■ Quick Check

1. This method considers fixed manufacturing cost to be a period cost that is expensed in full, regardless of production.
   a. Absorption costing
   b. Variable costing
   c. Blended costing
   d. None of the above

2. Which method considers fixed manufacturing cost to be a product cost that is inventoriable?
   a. Absorption costing
   b. Variable costing
   c. Blended costing
   d. None of the above

Consider the following data for Jetson's Jetskis for questions 3–8:

	January
Direct materials cost per jetski	$ 1,000
Direct labor cost per jetski	$ 2,000
Variable manufacturing overhead cost per jetski	$ 3,000
Total fixed manufacturing overhead costs	$1,000,000
Total fixed selling and administrative costs	$ 400,000
Number of jetskis produced	1,000
Number of jetskis sold	900
Sale price per jetski	$ 8,000

3. What is Jetson's total absorption cost per jet ski for January?
   a. $6,000
   b. $7,000
   c. $7,111
   d. $7,400

4. What is Jetson's total variable cost per jetski for January?
   a. $6,000
   b. $7,000
   c. $7,111
   d. $7,400

5. What is Jetson's operating income for January using absorption costing?
   a. $900,000
   b. $400,000
   c. $500,000
   d. $ 1,800,000

6. What is Jetson's ending inventory for January using absorption costing?
   a. $600,000
   b. $700,000
   c. $711,100
   d. $800,000

7. What is Jetson's operating income for January using variable costing?
   a. $900,000
   b. $400,000
   c. $500,000
   d. $2,000

8. What is Jetson's ending inventory for January using variable costing?
   a. $600,000
   b. $700,000
   c. $711,100
   d. $800,000

9. Management bonuses should not be tied to operating income under which costing method?
   a. Absorption costing
   b. Variable costing
   c. Blended costing
   d. All of the above

10. Which costing method shows the contribution margin of each product on the income statement?
    a. Absorption costing
    b. Variable costing
    c. Blended costing
    d. All of the above

Answers are given after Apply Your Knowledge (p. 288).

Assess Your Progress

S6-1 *(L. OBJ. 1)* **Differentiating between absorption and variable costs [5–10 min]**
Consider each of the following costs:

Direct materials cost

Fixed manufacturing overhead

Fixed selling costs

Direct labor cost

Indirect labor cos

Indirect materials cost

Straight-line depreciation on manufacturing equipment

Salary of administrative staff

Requirement

1. Identify the costs as part of total product costs under absorption costing, variable costing, or both. Indicate A for absorption costing, V for variable costing, B for both, or N for neither.

S6-2 *(L. OBJ. 2)* **Preparing variable costing income statements [15–25 minutes]**
RefreshAde produced 12,000 cases of powdered drink mix and sold 10,000 cases in April 2011. The sale price was $27, variable costs were $10 per case ($8 manufacturing and $2 selling and administrative), and total fixed costs were $45,000 ($35,000 manufacturing and $10,000 selling and administrative). The company had no beginning inventory.

Requirement

1. Prepare the April income statement using variable costing.

Note: Short Exercise 6-2 must be completed before attempting Short Exercise 6-3.

S6-3 *(L. OBJ. 2)* **Preparing absorption costing income statements [15–25 minutes]**
Refer to Short Exercise 6-2.

Requirements

1. Prepare the April income statement under absorption costing.
2. Is absorption costing income higher or lower than variable costing income? Explain why by providing calculations to show the difference.

S6-4 *(L. OBJ. 2)* **Calculating fixed overhead cost per unit [5–10 min]**
Tinker Toys incurs $5 per toy in direct materials, labor, and variable overhead costs. Additionally, it incurs $100,000 in fixed selling and administrative expenses and $200,000 in fixed manufacturing overhead per month.

Requirement

1. If Tinker Toys produced 100,000 toys in August 2011, what is Tinker Toy's fixed overhead cost per unit?

Note: Short Exercise 6-4 must be completed before attempting Short Exercise 6-5.

S6-5   *(L. OBJ. 2)* **Calculating total variable and absorption cost per unit [5–10 min]**
Refer to Short Exercise 6-4.

Requirement

1. If Tinker produces 100,000 toys per month, calculate the total
   a. variable cost per toy.
   b. absorption cost per toy.

Note: Short Exercises 6-4 and 6-5 must be completed before attempting Short Exercise 6-6.

S6-6   *(L. OBJ. 2)* **Prepare absorption costing income statement [5–10 min]**
Refer to Short Exercises 6-4 and 6-5.

Requirement

1. If Tinker sells 95,000 of the toys it produced in August for a selling price of $10 per toy, prepare an absorption costing income statement for Tinker for the month ended August 31, 2011. Assume there is no beginning inventory.

Note: Short Exercises 6-4 and 6-5 must be completed before attempting Short Exercise 6-7.

S6-7   *(L. OBJ. 2)* **Prepare a variable costing income statement [5–10 min]**
Refer to Short Exercises 6-4 and 6-5.

Requirement

1. If Tinker sells 95,000 of the toys it produced in August for a selling price of $10 per toy, prepare a variable costing income statement for Tinker for the month ended August 31, 2011. Assume there is no beginning inventory.

Note: Short Exercises 6-6 and 6-7 must be completed before attempting Short Exercise 6-8.

S6-8   *(L. OBJ. 3)* **Identifying pros and cons of variable costing [5–10 min]**
Refer to your results from Short Exercises 6-6 and 6-7. Consider that the operations manager receives a 5% bonus based on monthly operating income.

Requirements

1. Identify which product costing method would net the largest bonus to the operations manager. Why?
2. Which costing method would most closely reflect the cash flows from operations?

■ Exercises

E6-9   *(L. OBJ. 1)* **Absorption and variable costing definitions [10 min]**
Consider the following terms and definitions.

TERMS:	DEFINITIONS:
Absorption costing	Not approved under GAAP
Fixed manufacturing overhead cost per unit	Calculated by dividing total fixed manufacturing cost by the number of units produced in a period
Variable costing	The costing method that assigns only variable manufacturing costs to products.
	Total cost per unit = Direct materials + direct labor + variable manufacturing overhead costs per unit
	Total cost per unit = Direct materials + direct labor + variable manufacturing overhead costs + fixed manufacturing overhead cost per unit
	GAAP approved method
	The costing method that assigns both variable and fixed manufacturing costs to products as part of the cost of inventory

Requirement

1. Match the terms with the correct definitions. Note you may use the terms to match multiple definitions.

E6-10 *(L. OBJ. 2)* **Calculating total absorption and variable cost per unit [10–15 min]**
Consider the following data for the first month for Basket Bonanza:

	May
Direct materials cost per basket	$ 0.50
Direct labor cost per basket	$ 1.25
Variable manufacturing overhead cost per basket	$ 0.25
Total fixed manufacturing overhead costs	$10,000
Total fixed selling and administrative costs	$40,000
Number of baskets produced	10,000
Number of baskets sold	9,800
Sale price per basket	$ 10

Requirements

1. Calculate the total absorption cost per basket.
2. Calculate the total variable cost per basket.

Note: Exercise 6-10 must be completed before attempting Exercise 6-11.

E6-11 *(L. OBJ. 2)* **Preparing absorption costing income statements and calculating ending inventory [15–20 min]**
Refer to Exercise 6-10.

Requirements

1. Prepare the May income statement using absorption costing.
2. Calculate the May ending inventory using absorption costing.

Note: Exercise 6-10 must be completed before attempting Exercise 6-12.

E6-12 *(L. OBJ. 2)* **Preparing variable costing income statements and calculating ending inventory [15-20 min]**
Refer to Exercise 6-10.

Requirements

1. Prepare the May income statement using variable costing.
2. Calculate the May ending inventory using variable costing.

E6-13 *(L. OBJ. 2)* **Calculating total absorption and variable cost per unit with beginning inventory [10–15 min]**
Noodle-Raman began manufacturing beef noodle soup in May of 2011. The noodles sell for $1 for a large package of noodle soup mix. Total variable production costs are $0.60 per package. Noodle-Raman incurs monthly fixed manufacturing overhead costs of $20,000 and fixed selling and administrative cost of $8,000. On May 31, 2011 ending inventory was 5,000 soup packages. The May ending inventory has the same cost per soup package as the June packages produced. Assume Noodle-Raman produced 200,000 soup packages in June. Noodle-Ramen sold 202,000 of the soup packages in June.

Requirements

1. Calculate the total absorption cost per soup package.
2. Calculate the total variable cost per soup package.

Note: Exercise 6-13 must be completed before attempting Exercise 6-14.

E6-14   *(L. OBJ. 2)* **Preparing absorption costing income statements and calculating ending inventory [15–20 min]**
Refer to Exercise 6-13.

Requirements

1. Prepare the June income statement using absorption costing.
2. Calculate the June ending inventory using absorption costing.

Note: Exercise 6-13 must be completed before attempting Exercise 6-15.

E6-15   *(L. OBJ. 2)* **Preparing variable costing income statements and calculating ending inventory [15–20 min]**
Refer to Exercise 6-13.

Requirements

1. Prepare the June income statement using variable costing.
2. Calculate the June ending inventory statement using variable costing.

Note: Exercises 6-10 through 6-12 must be completed before attempting Exercise 6-16.

E6-16   *(L. OBJ. 3)* **Identifying pros and cons of variable costing [5-10 min]**
Refer to your results from Exercises 6-10 through 6-12 for Basket Bonanza.

Requirements

1. Identify which method resulted in the larger operating income. Why? Show your calculations verifying the difference.
2. List three advantages to using the reporting method identified in question 1.

E6-17   *(L. OBJ. 2, 3)* **Preparing variable and absorption costing income statements, identifying pros and cons, and considering changes in costs. [25–30 minutes]**
The 2010 data that follow pertain to Swim Clearly, a manufacturer of swimming goggles. (Swim Clearly had no beginning inventories in January 2010.)

Sale price	$ 41	Fixed manufacturing overhead. . . .	$ 2,000,000
Variable manufacturing		Fixed operating expense.	250,000
expense per unit.	22	Number of goggles produced	200,000
Sales commission expense per unit . . .	6	Number of goggles sold	185,000

Requirements

1. Prepare both conventional (absorption costing) and contribution margin (variable costing) income statements for Swim Clearly for the year ended December 31, 2010.
2. Which statement shows the higher operating income? Why? Identify two reasons for your answer.
3. Swim Clearly's marketing vice president believes a new sales promotion that costs $150,000 would increase sales to 200,000 goggles. Should the company go ahead with the promotion? Give your reasoning.

P6-18A *(L. OBJ. 1, 2, 3)* **Differentiating between absorption and variable costs, preparing variable and absorption costing income statements, and identifying pros and cons [35–40 minutes]**

Clarita's Foods produces frozen meals that it sells for $12 each. The company computes a new monthly fixed manufacturing overhead rate based on the planned number of meals to be produced that month. All costs and production levels are exactly as planned. The following data are from Clarita's Foods' first month in business:

	January 2011	
Sales	850	meals
Production	1,050	meals
Variable manufacturing cost per meal	$ 5	
Sales commission cost per meal	$ 2	
Total fixed manufacturing overhead	$ 315	
Total fixed marketing and administrative costs	$ 750	

Requirements

1. Identify the costs as part of total product costs under absorption costing, variable costing, or both. Indicate A for absorption costing, V for variable costing, B for both, or N for neither.

2. Compute the product cost per meal produced under absorption costing and under variable costing.

3. Prepare income statements for January 2011 using
   a. absorption costing.
   b. variable costing.

4. Is operating income higher under absorption costing or variable costing in January? Give two reasons why.

P6-19A *(L. OBJ. 1, 2, 3)* **Differentiating between absorption and variable costs, preparing variable and absorption costing income statements, and identifying pros and cons [35–40 minutes]**

Game King manufactures video games that it sells for $36 each. The company uses a fixed manufacturing overhead rate of $3 per game. All costs and production levels are exactly as planned. The following data are from Game King's first two months in business during 2010:

	October		November	
Sales	1,600	units	3,000	units
Production	2,800	units	2,800	units
Variable manufacturing cost per game	$ 13		$ 13	
Sales commission per game	$ 6		$ 6	
Total fixed manufacturing overhead	$ 8,400		$ 8,400	
Total fixed marketing and administrative costs	$ 7,500		$ 7,500	

Requirements

1. Identify the costs as part of total product costs under absorption costing, variable costing, or both. Indicate A for absorption costing, V for variable costing, B for both, or N for neither.

2. Compute the product cost per game produced under absorption costing and under variable costing.

3. Prepare monthly income statements for November, using
   a. absorption costing.
   b. variable costing.

4. Is operating income higher under absorption costing or variable costing in November? Give two reasons why and explain the pattern of differences in operating income based on absorption costing versus variable costing.

P6-20A *(L. OBJ. 1, 2, 3)* **Differentiating between absorption and variable costs, preparing variable and absorption costing income statements, and identifying pros and cons [35–40 minutes]**

Health Nut manufactures protein drinks that it sells for $3 each. All costs and production levels are exactly as planned. Health Nut began production of its protein drinks in December of 2010. Consider the following financial data related to production and sales for the first two months of 2011:

	December 2010	January 2011	February 2011
Direct materials cost per protein drink	$ 0.25	$ 0.25	$ 0.22
Direct labor cost per protein drink	$ 0.50	$ 0.50	$ 0.50
Variable manufacturing overhead cost per protein drink	$ 0.15	$ 0.15	$ 0.18
Total fixed manufacturing overhead costs	$15,000	$15,000	$15,400
Total fixed selling and administrative costs	$27,000	$27,000	$27,500
Number of protein drinks produced	20,000	20,000	20,000
Number of protein drinks sold	19,000	21,000	19,200
Sale price per protein drink	$ 3	$ 3	$ 3

Requirements

1. Identify the costs as part of total product costs under absorption costing, variable costing, or both. Indicate A for absorption costing, V for variable costing, B for both, or N for neither.
2. Assuming a FIFO cost flow, compute the product cost per protein drink produced under absorption costing and under variable costing for each of the three months provided.
3. Prepare monthly income statements for the first two months of 2011, side by side in column form, using
   a. absorption costing.
   b. variable costing.
4. Assuming a FIFO cost flow, calculate the ending inventory values for the first two months of 2011. Compare the ending inventory under absorption costing and variable costing from your results. Explain the pattern of differences in the ending inventory based on absorption costing versus variable costing. Give two reasons why the results differ.

P6-21A *(L. OBJ. 2, 3)* **Preparing variable and absorption costing income statements, and identifying pros and cons [35–40 minutes]**

Mp3 Musico Co. manufactures mp3 players. The company had beginning inventory of 1,000 mp3 players. These players had $30 each in variable costs per player and $2 each in fixed manufacturing costs per player. The following data are from the company's production records for two months of 2011:

	June 2011	July 2011
Direct materials cost per mp3 player	$ 5.00	$ 5.00
Direct labor cost per mp3 player	$ 14.00	$ 14.00
Variable manufacturing overhead cost per mp3 player	$ 10.00	$ 10.00
Total fixed manufacturing overhead costs	$70,000	$70,000
Total fixed selling and administrative costs	$20,000	$20,000
Number of mp3 players produced	35,000	40,000
Number of mp3 players sold	34,800	40,300
Sale price per mp3 player	$ 40	$ 40

1. Assuming a FIFO cost flow, compute the product cost per mp3 player produced under absorption costing and under variable costing.

2. Prepare monthly income statements for June and July, using
   a. absorption costing.
   b. variable costing.

3. Is operating income higher under absorption costing or variable costing in June? In July? Give two reasons why and explain the pattern of differences in operating income based on absorption costing versus variable costing.

■ Problems (Group B)

P6-22B *(L. OBJ. 1, 2, 3)* **Differentiating between absorption and variable costs, preparing variable and absorption costing income statements, identifying pros and cons [35–40 minutes]**

Stella's Foods produces frozen meals that it sells for $13 each. The company computes a new monthly fixed manufacturing overhead rate based on the planned number of meals to be produced that month. All costs and production levels are exactly as planned. The following data are from Stella's Foods' first month in business:

	January 2011
Sales	1,200 meals
Production	1,500 meals
Variable manufacturing cost per meal	$ 6
Sales commission cost per meal	$ 2
Total fixed manufacturing overhead	$1,050
Total fixed marketing and administrative costs	$ 300

1. Identify the costs as part of total product costs under absorption costing, variable costing, or both. Indicate A for absorption costing, V for variable costing, B for both, or N for neither.

2. Compute the product cost per meal produced under absorption costing and under variable costing.

3. Prepare income statements for January 2011 using
   a. absorption costing.
   b. variable costing.

4. Is operating income higher under absorption costing or variable costing in January? Give two reasons why.

P6-23B *(L. OBJ. 1, 2, 3)* **Differentiating between absorption and variable costs, preparing variable and absorption costing income statements, identifying pros and cons [35–40 minutes]**

Arcade Away manufactures video games that it sells for $45 each. The company uses a fixed manufacturing overhead rate of $6 per game. All costs and production levels are exactly as planned. The following data are from Arcade Away's first two months in business during 2011:

	October	November
Sales	1,700 units	3,000 units
Production	2,700 units	2,700 units
Variable manufacturing cost per game	$ 17	$ 17
Sales commission per game	$ 6	$ 6
Total fixed manufacturing overhead	$16,200	$16,200
Total fixed marketing and administrative costs	$ 8,500	$ 8,500

1. Identify the costs as part of total product costs under absorption costing, variable costing, or both. Indicate A for absorption costing, V for variable costing, B for both, or N for neither.

2. Compute the product cost per game produced under absorption costing and under variable costing.

3. Prepare monthly income statements for November, using
   a. absorption costing.
   b. variable costing.

4. Is operating income higher under absorption costing or variable costing in November? Give two reasons why and explain the pattern of differences in operating income based on absorption costing versus variable costing.

P6-24B *(L. OBJ. 1, 2, 3)* **Differentiating between absorption and variable costs, preparing variable and absorption costing income statements, identifying pros and cons [35–40 minutes]**

Replenish manufactures protein drinks that it sells for $3.50 each. All costs and production levels are exactly as planned. Replenish began production of its protein drinks in December, 2010. Consider the following two months of financial data related to production and sales for the first two months of 2011:

	December 2010	January 2011	February 2011
Direct materials cost per protein drink	$ 0.45	$ 0.45	$ 0.45
Direct labor cost per protein drink	$ 0.60	$ 0.60	$ 0.60
Variable manufacturing overhead cost per protein drink	$ 0.20	$ 0.20	$ 0.20
Total fixed manufacturing overhead costs	$18,750	$18,750	$18,860
Total fixed selling and administrative costs	$18,000	$18,000	$19,500
Number of protein drinks produced	25,000	25,000	23,000
Number of protein drinks sold	24,000	26,000	21,000

Requirements

1. Identify the costs as part of total product costs under absorption costing, variable costing, or both. Indicate A for absorption costing, V for variable costing, B for both, or N for neither.

2. Assuming a FIFO cost flow, compute the product cost per protein drink produced under absorption costing and under variable costing for each of the three months provided.

3. Prepare monthly income statements for the first 2 months of 2011, using
   a. absorption costing.
   b. variable costing.

4. Assuming a FIFO cost flow, calculate the ending inventory values for the first two months of 2011. Compare the ending inventory under absorption costing and variable costing from your results. Explain the pattern of differences in the ending inventory based on absorption costing versus variable costing. Give two reasons why the results differ.

P6-25B *(L. OBJ. 2, 3)* **Preparing variable and absorption costing income statements, and identifying pros and cons [35–40 minutes]**

Easy Listening Co. manufactures mp3 players. The company had beginning inventory of 1,600 mp3 players. These players had $27.50 each in variable costs per player and $3.55 each in fixed manufacturing costs per player. The following data are from the company's production records for two months of 2011:

	April 2011	May 2011
Direct materials cost per mp3 player	$ 3.50	$ 3.50
Direct labor cost per mp3 player	$ 18.00	$ 18.00
Variable manufacturing overhead cost per mp3 player	$ 8.00	$ 8.00
Total fixed manufacturing overhead costs	$66,000	$66,000
Total fixed selling and administrative costs	$18,000	$18,000
Number of mp3 players produced	20,000	24,000
Number of mp3 players sold	18,700	25,500
Sale price per mp3 player	$ 45.00	$ 45.00

Requirements

1. Assuming a FIFO cost flow, compute the product cost per mp3 player produced under absorption costing and under variable costing.

2. Prepare monthly income statements for April and May, using
   a. absorption costing.
   b. variable costing.

3. Is operating income higher under absorption costing or variable costing in April? In May? Give two reasons why and explain the pattern of differences in operating income based on absorption costing versus variable costing.

Continuing Exercise

E6-26   This exercise continues the Sherman Lawn Service, Inc., situation from Exercise 5-33 of Chapter 5. Recall that Sherman Lawn Service currently charges $50 for a standard lawn service and incurs $20 in variable cost. Assume fixed costs are $1,200 per month and that Sherman averages 100 lawns a month.

Requirement

1. What is the variable cost per lawn? What is the absorption cost per lawn?

Continuing Problem

P6-27   This problem continues the Haupt Consulting, Inc., situation from Problem 5-34 of Chapter 5, a service company that calculates product costing similar to a manufacturing facility. Recall that Haupt Consulting provides consulting service at an average price of $100 per hour and incurs variable cost of $40 per hour. Assume average fixed costs are $4,000 a month for 1,000 production hours.

Requirements

1. Calculate the variable cost and absorption cost per hour for Haupt.

2. If Haupt bills (sells) 900 production hours, what is its variable costing operating income? Absorption costing operating income?

3. If unsold production hours of this service company are treated similar to unsold products of a manufacturer, what would be the value attributed to the unsold production hours using variable costing? Absorption costing?

Apply Your Knowledge

■ Decision Cases

Case 1. Chip and Maggie Moylan recently returned from a Caribbean cruise. They loved the vegan foods found on the islands and decide that they should open a factory that will produce these vegan entrees for consumers. After securing capitalization for the venture, and beginning production in August, 2013, Moylan's Vegan Delites has the following results:

	August 2013
Vegetables	$ 33,000
Tofu	$ 70,000
Sauce	$ 15,000
Hourly assembly line workers' wages	$ 50,000
Seasonings (indirect)	$ 2,000
Cooks salaries	$ 70,000
Plant janitorial	$ 20,000
Straight line depreciation on production equipment	$ 30,000
Salesperson's salaries	$ 40,000
President's salary	$ 60,000
Plant supplies (paper towels, etc.)	$ 4,000
Number of entrees produced	100,000
Number of entrees sold @ $4 sales price	99,000

Requirements

1. Classify each cost as either variable production costs (V), fixed production costs (F), or fixed selling and administrative costs (S).
2. Calculate the variable cost per entrée in August. Compute variable costing operating income for August.
3. Calculate absorption cost per entrée for August. Compute absorption costing operating income for August.
4. Describe which statement will help Maggie make the best decisions about production and why.
5. Describe which statement Maggie would want to give to the bank. Why?

■ Ethical Issue

Consider again Maggie's Vegan Delites from Decision Case 1. As the cost accountant for Maggie's, you realize that you failed to include your $50,000 salary in the analysis. You quickly realize that this changes the fixed manufacturing costs significantly.

You realize you need to tell Maggie and the bank quickly of your inadvertent error, but after calculating the affect on the August results, you are afraid your error will impact Maggie's ability to secure additional financing, which could impact Maggie's ability to continue operations—in short, you could be out of work.

Requirements

1. How does your error affect the results reported to the bank? Describe the details of the difference.
2. Consider cost reduction techniques that could help Maggie's secure the needed financing. Assume that you could reduce depreciation costs by extending the life of the equipment from 5 to 10 years, which is the actual life suggested by the equipment's manufacturer. What suggestions can you make to Maggie and the bank?
3. Draft a memo to the company president regarding this problem.

■ Financial Statement Case—Amazon.com

This case is based on the Amazon.com annual report in Appendix A at the end of the book. Use it to answer the following questions.

Requirement

1. Review the description of Amazon.com's business. Describe the benefits Amazon.com might derive from using variable costing for its operations report. Consider its extensive product lines and its role as a reseller, not a manufacturer. Consider carefully its business lines in your answer.

■ Team Project

Review the cost data from Decision Case 1 for Maggie's Vegan Delites. Consider the following cost reduction strategies that might be available to the company:

  a. Maggie can sign a one-year contract with a supplier that will allow her to reduce the monthly vegetable costs to $29,500 and the tofu costs to $62,500. This contract will require Maggie to pay for supplies two months in advance, which will require Maggie to borrow the needed funds for two months of supplies. Maggie can secure an 8% interest rate for this.
  b. Maggie can negotiate commission-only rates with her sales force. This would eliminate the $40,000 monthly costs, but would require her to pay commissions of 5% of sales revenue. Maggie anticipates that after the first six months, the company will be able to increase production and sales to an average monthly level of 120,000.
  c. Maggie can provide a training program that will train assembly-line workers to be more efficient. Currently there are 50 workers but the program will reduce this to 45. The program will cost $2,000 each month. With this new program, hourly wages will increase by 10%.

Requirement

1. Compare and contrast the value of each cost change strategy through a spreadsheet analysis. Include clear labels on each option. Recommend one or all three strategies for Maggie's Vegan Delites. Explain your data analysis, recommending implementation or not for each. Justify your responses with supporting financial information.

Quick Check Answers

1. *b* 2. *a* 3. *b* 4. *a* 5. *c* 6. *b* 7. *b* 8. *a* 9. *a* 10. *b*

For online homework, exercises, and problems that provide you immediate feedback, please visit www.myaccountinglab.com.

Big Picture

Ch 1 Introduction to Management Accounting

- Distinguish management accounting from financial accounting
- The role and responsibilities of management accountants
- Classify costs and prepare income statements for merchandising companies
- Classify costs and prepare income statements and statements of cost of goods manufactured for manufacturing companies

Ch 2 Job Order Costing

- Distinguish between job order and process costing
- Record materials, labor, and overhead in a job order costing system
- Record completion and sales of finished goods and adjust for under-/overallocated overhead
- Calculate unit costs for service companies

Ch 3 Activity-Based Costing and Other Cost Management Tools

- Develop activity-based costs and used activity-based management to determine target product costs
- Record transactions in JIT systems
- Use the four types of quality costs to make management decisions

Ch 4 Process Costing

- Calculate equivalent units and conversion costs
- Prepare cost of production reports and the related journal entries using the weighted-average costing method
- Prepare cost of production reports and the related journal entries using the FIFO costing method

Ch 5 Cost Behavior and Cost-Volume-Profit Analysis

- Identify how changes in volume affect cost
- Distinguish among variable, mixed, and fixed cost
- Split mixed cost into fixed and variable components by using the high-low method and by using regression analysis
- Use CVP to compute breakeven points, to plan profits, to graph relationships, and to perform sensitivity analysis

Ch 6 Absorption and Variable Costing

- Distinguish between absorption costing and variable costing
- Prepare absorption costing and variable costing income statements and explained the differences between the two costing techniques
- Illustrate the pros and cons of absorption and variable costing

Chapter 6: Demo Doc

■ Preparing Contribution Margin Income Statements: Manufacturing

Learning Objective 2

Eagle Eye Optics, a binocular manufacturer, started operations on June 1, 2011. During the company's first month of operations, 1,000 pairs of binoculars were produced but only 900 pairs were sold at a sales price of $280 each. Eagle Eye had no work in process at the end of June. Management has accumulated the following costs for the month of June:

Direct materials...	$92,000
Direct labor...	58,000
Variable manufacturing overhead	46,000
Fixed manufacturing overhead................................	24,000
Variable selling and administrative expense	9,000
Fixed selling and administrative expense.................	14,000

Requirements

1. Prepare Eagle Eye's June income statement using an absorption costing (traditional) format.

2. Prepare Eagle Eye's June income statement using a variable costing (contribution margin) format.

3. Reconcile the absorption costing income to the variable costing income.

Demo Doc Solution

Requirement 1

Prepare Eagle Eye's June income statement using an absorption costing (traditional) format.

Prepare absorption costing and variable costing income statements and explain the difference in results

- In order to prepare the absorption income statement for Eagle Eye, we first need to calculate the cost of goods manufactured. Following the format we learned in Chapter 1, we can calculate the cost of goods manufactured by preparing a statement of cost of goods manufactured as follows:

Beginning work in process inventory*		$ 0
Add manufacturing costs:		
Direct materials	$92,000	
Direct labor	58,000	
Manufacturing overhead** (46,000 + 24,000)	70,000	
Total manufacturing costs		220,000
Total manufacturing costs to account for		220,000
Less ending work in process inventory (given in problem)		0
Cost of goods manufactured		$220,000

*Because this is Eagle Eye's first month of operations, there is no beginning work in process inventory.
**Under absorption costing, both fixed and variable overhead are considered to be product costs.

- Now that we have the cost of goods manufactured, we can complete Eagle Eye's absorption costing format income statement by following the format that we learned in Chapter 1. The completed income statement should look like this:

<table>
<tr><td colspan="3" align="center">Eagle Eye Optics
Income Statement (Absorption Costing)
For the Month Ended June 30, 2011</td></tr>
<tr><td>Sales revenue (900 pairs sold × $280 sales price)</td><td></td><td>$252,000</td></tr>
<tr><td>Less: Cost of goods sold:</td><td></td><td></td></tr>
<tr><td> Beginning finished goods inventory*</td><td>$ 0</td><td></td></tr>
<tr><td> Cost of goods manufactured</td><td>220,000</td><td></td></tr>
<tr><td> Goods available for sale</td><td>220,000</td><td></td></tr>
<tr><td> Less ending inventory**</td><td>22,000</td><td></td></tr>
<tr><td> Cost of goods sold</td><td></td><td>198,000</td></tr>
<tr><td>Gross profit</td><td></td><td>54,000</td></tr>
<tr><td>Less: Selling and administrative expenses*** ($9,000 + $14,000)</td><td></td><td>23,000</td></tr>
<tr><td>Operating income</td><td></td><td>$ 31,000</td></tr>
</table>

*Because this is Eagle Eye's first month of operations, there is no beginning finished goods inventory.
**To calculate the value of ending inventory, we first need to calculate the cost per pair of binoculars by dividing the total cost of goods manufactured by the quantity of goods manufactured ($220,000 ÷ 1,000) to get $220. Next, we find the number of units in ending inventory by subtracting the number of units sold from the number of units manufactured (1,000 − 900) to get 100 and multiply this times the cost per unit (100 × $220) to get $22,000.
***Remember, under absorption costing, both fixed and variable selling and administrative expenses are considered to be period expenses and are deducted in the month they are incurred as operating expenses.

Requirement 2

2 Prepare absorption costing and variable costing income statements and explain the difference in results

Prepare Eagle Eye's June income statement using a variable costing (contribution margin) format.

- Remember that in order to prepare a variable costing (contribution margin format) income statement, we must first classify all of Eagle Eye's costs as either variable or fixed. Eagle Eye's variable costs will be the cost of goods sold and the variable selling and administrative expenses. The fixed costs for Eagle Eye will be the fixed manufacturing overhead as well as the fixed selling and administrative expenses.

- First, let's calculate the cost of goods manufactured. We can utilize a statement of cost of goods manufactured format that is very similar to what we used in Requirement 1, as follows:

Beginning work in process inventory*.....................		$ 0
Add variable manufacturing costs:		
Direct materials...	$92,000	
Direct labor...	58,000	
Variable manufacturing overhead**...................	46,000	
Total variable manufacturing costs......................		196,000
Total manufacturing costs to account for...............		196,000
Less ending work in process inventory....................		0
Variable cost of goods manufactured		$196,000

*Because this is Eagle Eye's first month of operations, there is no beginning work in process inventory.

**Under variable costing, only variable manufacturing overhead is considered to be a product cost. Fixed manufacturing overhead is classified as a period cost and thus is expensed in full on the income statement.

- Now that we have the cost of goods manufactured, we can complete Eagle Eye's variable costing income statement. The completed income statement should look like this:

Eagle Eye Optics
Income Statement (Variable Costing)
For the Month Ended June 30, 2011

Sales revenue (900 pairs sold × $280 sales price)....................			$252,000
Less variable expenses:			
Variable cost of goods sold:			
Beginning finished goods inventory*.............................	$ 0		
Variable cost of goods manufactured	196,000		
Goods available for sale	196,000		
Less ending finished goods inventory**........................	19,600		
Variable cost of goods sold...		$176,400	
Variable selling and administrative...................................		9,000	
Total variable expenses			185,400
Contribution margin			66,600
Less fixed expenses:			
Fixed manufacturing overhead***....................................		$ 24,000	
Fixed selling and administrative..		14,000	
Total fixed expenses			38,000
Operating income..			$ 28,600

*Because this is Eagle Eye's first month of operations, there is no beginning finished goods inventory.

**To calculate the value of ending finished goods inventory, we first need to calculate the cost per pair of binoculars by dividing the total cost of goods manufactured by the quantity of goods manufactured ($196,000 ÷ 1,000) to get $196.00. Next, we find the number of units in ending finished goods inventory by subtracting the number of units sold from the number of units manufactured (1,000 − 900) to get 100 and then multiply this times the cost per unit (100 × $196.00) to get $19,600.

***Remember, under variable costing, fixed manufacturing overhead expenses are considered to be period expenses and are deducted in the month they are incurred.

Requirement 3

Reconcile the absorption costing income to the variable costing income.

- First, let's calculate the difference between the absorption costing and the variable costing income:

Absorption costing income.............	$31,000
Variable costing income	28,600
Income difference...........................	$ 2,400

- The difference between the absorption costing income and the variable costing income is due to the treatment of the $24,000 of fixed manufacturing overhead. Under absorption costing, the fixed overhead is treated as a product cost and, therefore, a portion of it is included in the value of ending finished goods inventory since more items are produced than sold.

2   Prepare absorption costing and variable costing income statements and explain the difference in results

- Under variable costing, the entire $24,000 of fixed manufacturing overhead cost is treated as a period cost and is expensed in the month of June. Because of this, none of the $24,000 will be included in the ending finished goods inventory when using variable costing.
- If we calculate the amount of fixed manufacturing cost that is included in each unit produced under absorption costing and multiply it by the number of units in ending finished goods inventory, it should equal the difference in the income between absorption and variable costing since there was no beginning inventory. Let's see if this works:

Fixed manufacturing overhead	$24,000
Number of units produced	÷ 1,000
Fixed manufacturing included in each unit under absorption costing	= $ 24.00
Number of units in ending finished goods inventory (1,000 produced – 900 sold)	× 100
Difference in income between absorption and variable costing	$ 2,400

Yes, it works!

7

The Master Budget: Profit Planning

Learning Objectives/ Success Keys

1. Learn why managers use budgets

2. Understand the components of the master budget

3. Prepare an operating budget for a manufacturer

4. Prepare a financial budget for a manufacturer

5. Use sensitivity analysis in budgeting

If you are one of the millions of customers worldwide who point and click to buy your books and CDs (or other items) on **Amazon.com**, then you are part of **Amazon.com**'s strategy to "get big fast." This strategy increased **Amazon.com**'s sales, but at a cost. Corporate spending was out of control. There was no budget, and managers spared no expense to help the company grow. As a result, **Amazon.com** lost more than $860 *million* in 2000.

Founder and CEO Jeff Bezos had to turn this sea of red ink into income. Bezos set up a *budget* for **Amazon.com**'s plan of action. Now, each division budgets both sales and expenses. In weekly meetings, managers compare actual results to the budget, which helps them correct problems quickly.

So what happened? Between 2000 and 2002, **Amazon.com**'s sales increased 42%. With such an increase in sales, you would expect expenses to also increase proportionally. But **Amazon.com**'s new budget helped managers *cut* operating expenses. How did they decrease expenses when sales were increasing so dramatically? The budget helped **Amazon.com** reduce order-filling and distribution costs by 5%. Switching to lower-cost computer systems reduced "technical and content" operating costs by 20%. What was the result? **Amazon.com** reported its first ever income from operations in 2002. By 2008, income from operations had risen to over $842 million.[1]

Perhaps, like **Amazon.com**, you have prepared a budget to ensure that you have enough cash to pay your expenses. The budget is just a tool that forces you to plan as it projects your financial situation for future periods. If your budgeted cash inflow falls short of expenses, you have options:

- increase your cash inflow (by taking on a job or a student loan), or
- cut your expenses.

In addition to planning, your personal budget can help you control expenses. To stay within your grocery budget, you may buy macaroni and cheese instead of steak. At the end of the month, if your bank balance is less than expected, you can compare your actual cash inflows and expenses to your budget to see why. You need to know whether cash inflows are lower than expected or expenses are higher than expected to know what corrective action to take.

As **Amazon.com** learned, it is easy for spending to get out of control if you do not have a budget. That is why everyone from individuals like you to complex international organizations like **Amazon.com** to mid-size companies like Smart Touch Learning and Greg's Groovy Tunes uses budgets. Careful budgeting helps both individuals and businesses stay out of trouble by reducing the risk that they will spend more than they earn.

As you will see throughout this chapter, knowing how costs behave continues to be important when forming budgets. Total fixed costs will not change as volume changes within the relevant range. However, total variable costs must be adjusted when sales volume is expected to fluctuate.

---

[1]*Sources:* Katrina Brooker, "Beautiful Dreamer," *Fortune*, December 18, 2000, pp. 234–239; Fred Vogelstein, "Bezos," *Fortune*, September 2, 2002, pp. 186–187; Fred Vogelstein, "What Went Right 2002," *Fortune*, December 30, 2002, p. 166; Nick Wingfield, "Survival Strategy: Amazon Takes Page from Wal-Mart to Prosper on Web," *Wall Street Journal*, November 22, 2002, A1; Fred Vogelstein, "Mighty Amazon," *Fortune*, May 26, 2003, pp. 60–74; Amazon.com 2008 annual report.

Why Managers Use Budgets

Let us continue our study of budgets by moving from your personal budget to see how a small service business develops a simple budget. When Smart Touch Learning, Inc., first began, it was a small online service company that provided e-learning services to customers. Assume Smart Touch wanted to earn $50,000 a month and expected to sell 100,000 e-learning courses per month at a price of $12 each. For March, they expect total variable COGS to be $8.50 per course and monthly selling and administrative costs to be $400,000. Smart Touch expected these monthly costs to remain about the same, so these were the monthly fixed costs. Then, subtract budgeted expenses to arrive at budgeted operating income. The income statement formula is used; however, now instead of actual amounts, we are using budgeted amounts.

<table>
<tr><td>1</td><td>Learn why managers use budgets</td></tr>
</table>

EXHIBIT 7-1	**Budgeted Income Statement**

SMART TOUCH LEARNING, INC. **Budgeted Income Statement** For the month ended March 31, 2012	
Sales revenue (100,000 × $12)	$1,200,000
Less: COGS (100,000 × $8.50)	850,000
Gross margin	350,000
Less: Selling and administrative expenses	400,000
Operating income (loss)	$ (50,000)

As you can see from the figure, if business goes according to plan, Smart Touch will not meet its $550 per month operating income goal. It will have to increase revenue (perhaps through word-of-mouth advertising) or cut expenses (perhaps by finding a less expensive Internet access provider).

Using Budgets to Plan and Control

Large international for-profit companies, such as **Amazon.com**, and nonprofit organizations, such as **Habitat for Humanity**, use budgets for the same reasons as you do in your personal life or in your small business—to plan and control actions and the related revenues and expenses. Exhibit 7-2 on the next page shows how managers use budgets in fulfilling their major responsibilities. First, they develop strategies— overall business goals like **Amazon.com**'s goal to expand its international operations, or **Gateway**'s goal to be a value leader in the personal computer market, while diversifying into other markets. Companies then plan and budget for specific actions to achieve those goals. The next step is to act. For example, **Amazon.com** recently planned for and then added a grocery feature to its Web sites. And **Gateway** is leaning on its suppliers to cut costs, while at the same time it is pumping out new products like plasma TVs and audio and video gear.

After acting, managers compare actual results with the budget. This feedback allows them to determine what, if any, corrective action to take. If, for example, **Amazon.com** spent more than expected to add the grocery feature to its Web sites, managers must cut other costs or increase revenues. These decisions affect the company's future strategies and plans.

Amazon.com has a number of budgets, as its managers develop budgets for their own divisions. Software then "rolls up" the division budgets to create a

EXHIBIT 7-2 | **Managers Use Budgets to Plan and Control Business Activities**

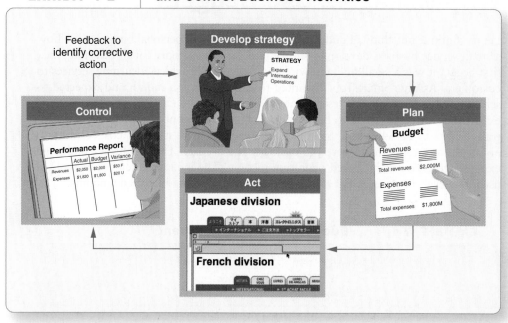

companywide budget. Managers also prepare both long-term and short-term budgets. Some of the budgets include long-term forecasts that project demand for various business segments for the next 20 years.

However, most companies budget their cash flows monthly, weekly, and even daily to ensure that they have enough cash. They also budget revenues and expenses—and operating income—for months, quarters, and years. This chapter focuses on short-term budgets of one year or less. Chapter 11 will explain how companies budget on a more long-term basis for major capital expenditures on property, plant, and equipment.

Benefits of Budgeting

There are three key benefits of budgeting. Budgeting forces managers to plan, promotes coordination and communication, and provides a benchmark for evaluating actual performance.

Planning

Exhibit 7-1 shows that the expected income from Smart Touch's online e-learning business falls short of the company's target. The sooner Smart Touch learns of the expected shortfall, the more time it has to plan how to increase revenues or cut expenses. The better Smart Touch's plan, and the more time it has to act on the plan, the more likely it will be to find a way to meet the target. **Amazon.com**'s budget required that managers plan the expansion of the Web sites tailored for customers in Germany, France, and Japan.

Coordination and Communication

The master budget coordinates a company's activities. It forces managers to consider relations among operations across the entire value chain. For example, **Amazon.com** stimulates sales by offering free shipping on orders over a specified dollar amount. The budget encourages managers to ensure that the extra profits from increased sales outweigh the revenue lost from free shipping.

Budgets also communicate a consistent set of plans throughout the company. For example, the initial **Amazon.com** budget communicated the message that all employees should help control costs.

Benchmarking

Budgets provide a benchmark that motivates employees and helps managers evaluate performance. In most companies, part of the manager's performance evaluation depends on how actual results compare to the budget. So, for example, the budgeted expenses for international expansion encourage **Amazon.com**'s employees to increase the efficiency of international warehousing operations and to find less-expensive technology to support the Web sites.

Let us return to Smart Touch's e-learning business. Suppose that comparing actual results to the budget in Exhibit 7-1 leads to the performance report in Exhibit 7-3.

EXHIBIT 7-3 | **Summary Performance Report**

SMART TOUCH LEARNING, INC.
Partial Income Statement
For the month ended March 31, 2012

	ACTUAL	BUDGET (From Exhibit 7-1)	VARIANCE (Actual – Budget)
Sales revenue	$1,250,000	$1,200,000	$50,000
Less: COGS	850,000	850,000	-
Gross margin	400,000	350,000	50,000
Less: Selling and administrative expenses	410,000	400,000	10,000
Operating income (loss)	$ (10,000)	$ (50,000)	$40,000

This report should prompt you to investigate why actual sales are $50,000 more than budgeted. There are three possibilities:

1. The budget was unrealistic.

2. The sales team performed well.

3. Uncontrollable factors (such as a robust economy) increased sales.

All three may have contributed to the results.

You will also want to know why expenses are $10,000 higher than expected. Did the Internet service provider increase rates? Did Smart Touch have to buy more reference materials than planned? Did Smart Touch spend more than 5% of its revenue on Web banner ads? Smart Touch needs to know the answers to these kinds of questions so it can make necessary changes to get its business back on track.

Understanding The Components Of The Master Budget

Now that you know *why* managers go to the trouble of developing budgets, consider the steps they take to prepare a budget.

2 Understand the components of the master budget

Components of the Master Budget

The **master budget** is the set of budgeted financial statements and supporting schedules for the entire organization. Exhibit 7-4 on the next page shows the order in which managers prepare the components of the master budget for a merchandiser such as **Amazon.com** or Smart Touch Learning.

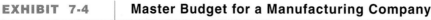

EXHIBIT 7-4 | **Master Budget for a Manufacturing Company**

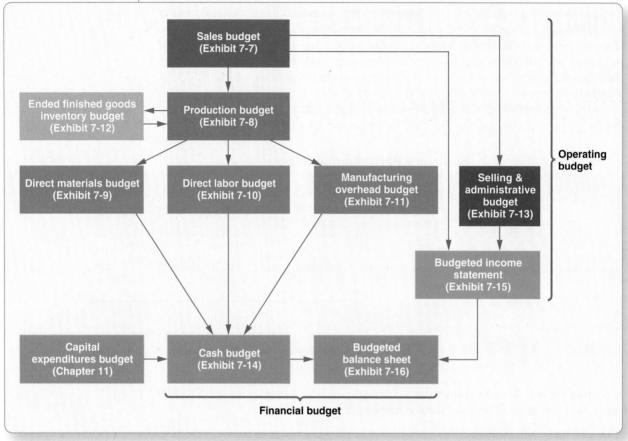

The exhibit shows that the master budget includes three types of budgets:

1. The operating budget
2. The capital expenditures budget
3. The financial budget

Let us consider each, in turn.

The first component of the **operating budget** is the sales budget, the cornerstone of the master budget. Why? Because sales affect most other components of the master budget. After projecting sales revenue, production budgets (from Exhibit 7-8 to Exhibit 7-12), and selling and administrative expense budgets, management prepares the end result of the operating budget: the **budgeted income statement** that projects operating income for the period.

The second type of budget is the **capital expenditures budget**. This budget presents the company's plan for purchasing property, plant, equipment, and other long-term assets and is covered in Chapter 11.

The third type is the **financial budget**. Prior components of the master budget, including the budgeted income statement and the capital expenditures budget, along with plans for raising cash and paying debts, provide information for the first element of the financial budget: the cash budget. The cash budget, which projects cash inflows and outflows, feeds into the budgeted balance sheet. These budgeted financial statements look exactly like ordinary statements. The only difference is that they list budgeted (projected) rather than actual amounts. The statement of cash flows may be budgeted also, however, we do not cover that until Chapter 13.

Data for Smart Touch Learning

Using projected amounts for Smart Touch Learning, we can illustrate how managers prepare operating and financial budgets. Chapter 11 will explain the capital budgeting process. The information needed is in Exhibit 7-5. We will refer back to this information as we create the operating and financial budgets.

EXHIBIT 7-5 | **Facts for Smart Touch Learning Budget Preparation**

Time period for which to budget	For the year ended December 31, 2012	
Cash collections:		
Collected in quarter of sale	60%	
Collected in quarter after sale	40%	
Bad debt percentage	1%	h
Cash disbursements:		
Paid in quarter of purchase	10%	
Paid in quarter after purchase	90%	
Ending Raw materials inventory	25% of next quarter's sales	
Ending Finished goods inventory	30% of next quarter's sales	
Estimated Beg Raw materials inventory, 12/31/2011	75,000 sq. feet	E
Estimated Beg Finished goods inventory, 12/31/2011	84,000 DVDs	B
Budgeted sales, 1st quarter 2012	300,000 DVDs	A
Budgeted sales, 2nd quarter 2012	310,000 DVDs	A
Budgeted sales, 3rd quarter 2012	270,000 DVDs	A
Budgeted sales, 4th quarter 2012	320,000 DVDs	A
Budgeted sales, 1st quarter 2013	280,000 DVDs	
Equipment purchases, 1st quarter 2012	$ 60,000	S
Equipment purchases, 2nd quarter 2012	-	
Equipment purchases, 3rd quarter 2012	-	
Equipment purchases, 4th quarter 2012	-	
Quarterly dividends declared and paid each quarter in 2012	$ 8,000	T
Expected sales price per unit	$ 12.00	
Standard cost data:		
Direct materials	$ 2.40 per sq. foot, 1 sq. foot per DVD	D
Direct labor	$ 10.00 per DL hour, .40 hours per DVD	G
Variable Manufacturing overhead	$ 1.50 per DL hour, .40 hours per DVD	H
Fixed Manufacturing overhead	$150,000 per month	I
Variable Selling	$ 2.00 per DVD	L
Fixed selling and administrative expenses:		
Insurance	$260,000 per month	j
Sales salaries	$315,000 per month	i
Depreciation expense—manufacturing	$175,000 per quarter	J
Depreciation expense—selling	$ 25,000 per quarter	M
Minimum required cash balance	10,000	
Interest rate on loans	2%	
Loans are made and repaid in $10,000 increments as soon as cash is available.		
Provision for Income tax payable is assumed to stay the same.		

1. **You are the operations manager for Smart Touch Learning, which produces various educational learning DVDs.** You are to prepare the company's 2012 master budget using the facts in Exhibit 7-5, which assumes the Excel DVD is the only product it will make in 2012.

2. **Monthly payroll is paid in the month incurred.**

3. **The company requires a minimum cash balance of $10,000 at the end of each quarter to provide for its cash flow needs.** The company can borrow money monthly on a line of credit in $10,000 increments at an annual interest rate of 2%. Management borrows no more than the amount needed to maintain the $10,000 minimum. Total interest expense will vary as the amount of borrowing varies from quarter to quarter. Notes payable are repaid in the quarter excess cash is available. Borrowing and all principal and interest payments occur at the end of the quarter.

4. **Income taxes are the responsibility of corporate headquarters, and can be ignored.**

5. **The company's balance sheet at December 31, 2011, the beginning of the budget period, appears in Exhibit 7-6.**

As you prepare the master budget, remember that you are developing the company's operating and financial plan for the next year. The steps in this process may seem mechanical, but you must think carefully about pricing, product lines, job assignments, needs for additional equipment, and negotiations with banks. Successful managers use this opportunity to make decisions that affect the future course of business.

EXHIBIT 7-6 | **Beginning Balance Sheet**

SMART TOUCH LEARNING, INC.					
Balance Sheet					
December 31, 2011					
Assets			**Liabilities**		
Current assets			Current liabilities		
W Cash		$ 110,000	Accounts payable		$ 620,000 X
V Accounts receivable		1,400,000	Income taxes payable		100,000 U
			Total current liabilities		720,000
Inventories:			Long-term liabilities		
Raw materials	180,000		Notes payable		50,000
Finished goods	714,000	894,000	Total liabilities		770,000
Total current assets		2,404,000	**Stockholders' Equity**		
Plant assets, net of accumulated depreciation		5,000,000	Common stock		6,000,000
			Retained earnings		634,000
Total assets		$7,404,000	Total liabilities and stockholders' equity		$7,404,000

Preparing The Operating Budget

3 Prepare an operating budget for a manufacturer

The first eight components of the operating budget as shown in Exhibit 7-4 are as follows:

1. Sales budget (and Budgeted cash collections from customers) (Exhibit 7-7)

2. Production budget (Exhibit 7-8)

3. Direct materials budget (and Budgeted cash disbursements for direct materials) (Exhibit 7-9)

4. Direct labor budget (Exhibit 7-10)

5. Manufacturing overhead budget (Exhibit 7-11)

6. Ending finished goods inventory budget (Exhibit 7-12)

7. Selling and administrative expenses budget (Exhibit 7-13)

8. Budgeted income statement (Exhibit 7-15)

The results of the first seven budgets feed into the eighth element of the operating budget: the budgeted income statement (Exhibit 7-15). Most companies use spreadsheets or ERP software to prepare their budgets, with built-in formulas for figures and carry-forwards. From year to year, assumptions are modified and key figures, such as estimated sales, are entered, allowing the entire budget to be prepared with a few small entries. However, the initial spreadsheet must be prepared from scratch. For Smart Touch Learning, we'll discuss a budget prepared from scratch.

The Sales Budget

The forecast of sales revenue is the cornerstone of the master budget because the level of sales affects expenses and almost all other elements of the master budget. Budgeted total sales for each product are the sales price of $12 multiplied by the expected number of units sold, given in Exhibit 7-5. The overall sales budget is in Exhibit 7-7. Trace the quarterly sales (**Z**) to the budgeted income statement in Exhibit 7-15. The Budgeted cash collections from customers (**N**) will be discussed later in the chapter when we prepare the financial budgets.

EXHIBIT 7-7 | **Sales Budget and Budgeted Cash Collected from Customers**

SMART TOUCH LEARNING, INC.
Sales Budget
For the year ended December 31, 2012

	Quarter					
	1st	2nd	3rd	4th	Annual Total	
Budgeted sales in DVD quantities	300,000	310,000	270,000	320,000	1,200,000	**A**
Budgeted sales price per DVD	$ 12.00	$ 12.00	$ 12.00	$ 12.00	$ 12.00	
Total budgeted sales	$3,600,000	$3,720,000	$3,240,000	$3,840,000	$14,400,000	**Z**

SMART TOUCH LEARNING, INC.
Budgeted Cash Collections from Customers
For the year ended December 31, 2012

	Quarter					
	1st	2nd	3rd	4th	Annual Total	
Accounts receivable, beginning balance	$1,400,000				$ 1,400,000	**V**
Collections from 1st quarter sales	2,138,400	1,425,600			3,564,000	
Collections from 2nd quarter sales		2,209,680	1,473,120		3,682,800	
Collections from 3rd quarter sales			1,924,560	1,283,040	3,207,600	
Collections from 4th quarter sales				2,280,960	2,280,960	
Budgeted cash collections from customers	$3,538,400	$3,635,280	$3,397,680	$3,564,000	$14,135,360	**N**

L Ending Accounts receivable, December 31, 2012 = $3,840,000 × (100% − 1% uncollectible) × 40% = $1,520,640

The Production Budget

This budget determines the quantity of Excel DVDs Smart Touch must produce in order to meet expected sales and Ending finished goods inventory targets from quarter to quarter. This production calculation includes Estimated beginning finished goods inventory already on hand.

Beginning Finished goods inventory + Production – Ending Finished goods inventory = Budgeted sales units

Estimated beginning inventory is known from last year's balance sheet (Exhibit 7-6), budgeted sales in units are given in Exhibit 7-5 (**A**), and Ending finished goods inventory is a computed amount (**C**). You must solve for the budgeted production figure (**C**). To do this, rearrange the previous equation to isolate production on the left side:

Production = Budgeted sales units + Ending Finished goods inventory – Beginning Finished goods inventory

This equation makes sense. How much does Smart Touch Learning have to produce? Enough to cover sales and Ending finished goods inventory, less the amount of beginning finished goods inventory already on hand at the start of the period. Exhibit 7-8 shows Smart Touch's production budget.

EXHIBIT 7-8 | **Production Budget**

SMART TOUCH LEARNING, INC.
Production Budget
For the year ended December 31, 2012

	Quarter				
	1st	2nd	3rd	4th	Annual Total
Budgeted sales in DVD quantities (from Exhibit 7-7)	300,000	310,000	270,000	320,000	1,200,000 **A**
Add: Ending Finished goods inventory	93,000	81,000	96,000	84,000 **C**	84,000
Budgeted Finished goods available	393,000	391,000	366,000	404,000	1,284,000
Less: Beginning Finished goods inventory	84,000 **B**	93,000	81,000	96,000	84,000
Budgeted Production	309,000	298,000	285,000	308,000	1,200,000 **C**

C Ending Finished goods inventory = 280,000 next quarter's sales × 30% = 84,000

A couple of key points should be noted:

- Ending finished goods inventory is estimated at 30% of next quarter's sales. Therefore, for the first quarter, ending finished goods inventory is targeted at 30% multiplied by 310,000 estimated sales for the second quarter, or 93,000 DVDs.
- The current period's ending finished goods inventory becomes the next period's beginning finished goods inventory.

Now that we know how many DVDs Smart Touch needs to produce each quarter, we can calculate its production resources needed and its ending finished goods inventory (the next four budgets).

The Direct Materials Budget

The **direct materials budget** determines the amount of direct materials needed for the desired production, ending raw materials inventory for the budgeted balance sheet, and the budgeted cash disbursements for materials for the cash budget. The familiar periodic inventory formula, shown when we calculated the production budget, specifies the relations among these items. Estimated beginning direct materials inventory is known from last year's balance sheet (E), budgeted production is known from Exhibit 7-8 (C), and Ending raw materials inventory is a computed amount (F). You must solve for the budgeted raw materials available. Exhibit 7-9 shows Smart Touch's direct materials budget. This also shows the budgeted cash disbursements for direct materials (O), which we'll use later in preparing our cash budget in Exhibit 7-14.

EXHIBIT 7-9 | **Direct Materials Budget and Budgeted Cash Disbursements for Direct Materials**

SMART TOUCH LEARNING, INC.
Direct Materials Budget
For the year ended December 31, 2012

	Quarter					
	1st	2nd	3rd	4th	Annual Total	
Budgeted production (from Exhibit 7-8)	309,000	298,000	285,000	308,000	1,200,000	C
Raw materials needed per DVD, in sq. feet	1	1	1	1	1	
Square feet of raw materials needed	309,000	298,000	285,000	308,000	1,200,000	
Add: Ending Raw materials inventory	77,500	67,500	80,000	70,000 F	70,000	
Budgeted raw materials available	386,500	365,500	365,000	378,000	1,270,000	
Less: Raw materials beginning inventory	75,000 E	77,500	67,500	80,000	75,000	
Budgeted direct materials needed to be purchased, in sq. feet	311,500	288,000	297,500	298,000	1,195,000	
Standard price per sq. foot	$ 2.40	$ 2.40	$ 2.40	$ 2.40	$ 2.40	D
Budgeted direct materials needed to be purchased, in sq. feet	$747,600	$691,200	$714,000	$715,200	$2,868,000	

F 280,000 first quarter 2013 sales * 25% = 70,000

SMART TOUCH LEARNING, INC.
Budgeted Cash Disbursements for Direct Materials
For the year ended December 31, 2012

	Quarter					
	1st	2nd	3rd	4th	Annual Total	
Accounts payable, beginning balance	$620,000				$ 620,000	X
Payments from 1st quarter purchases	74,760	672,840			747,600	
Payments from 2nd quarter purchases		69,120	622,080		691,200	
Payments from 3rd quarter purchases			71,400	642,600	714,000	
Payments from 4th quarter purchases				71,520	71,520	
Budgeted cash disbursements for direct materials	$694,760	$741,960	$693,480	$714,120	$2,844,320	O

The Direct Labor Budget

The **direct labor budget** determines the cost of labor that will be used on the budgeted income statement, and the cash budget. It is much simpler than the materials and production budget as there is no beginning or ending inventory to consider. To calculate these values, we start with budgeted production from the Production Budget in Exhibit 7-8 (C) and use information given in Exhibit 7-5 about direct labor. The production is then multiplied by the standard number of direct labor hours used for each Excel DVD, .40. The results are the total direct labor hours needed per quarter. That is then multiplied by the standard hourly rate for direct labor of $10.00 (G) given in Exhibit 7-5 to derive budgeted direct labor cost (P). This is also the amount spent for direct labor during each quarter since the assumptions given on page 302 state that direct labor is paid in the month incurred.

EXHIBIT 7-10 | **Direct Labor Budget**

SMART TOUCH LEARNING, INC.
Direct Labor Budget
For the year ended December 31, 2012

	Quarter					
	1st	2nd	3rd	4th	Annual Total	
Budgeted production (Exhibit 7-8)	309,000	298,000	285,000	308,000	1,200,000	C
Direct labor hours needed per DVD	0.40	0.40	0.40	0.40	0.40	
Hours of direct labor needed	123,600	119,200	114,000	123,200	480,000	
Standard price per hour	$ 10.00	$ 10.00	$ 10.00	$ 10.00	$ 10.00	G
Budgeted direct labor cost	$1,236,000	$1,192,000	$1,140,000	$1,232,000	$4,800,000	P

The Manufacturing Overhead Budget

The **manufacturing overhead budget** determines the amount of variable overhead projected, fixed overhead projected, and the predetermined manufacturing overhead rate. Direct labor hours calculated in Exhibit 7-10 are multiplied by the standard variable overhead rate of $1.50 per direct labor hour (**H**) given in Exhibit 7-5. This is then added to the budgeted fixed overhead amount, also given in Exhibit 7-5, to arrive at the total budgeted manufacturing overhead (**d**).

The budgeted cash disbursements for manufacturing overhead (**Q**) is calculated by subtracting the non-cash manufacturing overhead (in this example, the depreciation) (**J**) from the total budgeted manufacturing overhead (**d**). This is used later to prepare our cash budget (Exhibit 7-14). Lastly, the budget shows the calculation of the predetermined manufacturing overhead rate of $5.25 (**e**), which is the total manufacturing overhead for the year of $2,520,000 divided by the total budgeted direct labor hours for the year of 480,000.

EXHIBIT 7-11 | **Manufacturing Overhead Budget**

SMART TOUCH LEARNING, INC.
Manufacturing Overhead Budget
For the year ended December 31, 2012

	Quarter					
	1st	2nd	3rd	4th	Annual Total	
Budgeted direct labor hours (Exhibit 7-10)	123,600	119,200	114,000	123,200	480,000	
Standard variable overhead rate ($1.60 per DL hour or $.50 per DVD)	$ 1.50	$ 1.50	$ 1.50	$ 1.50	$ 1.50	H
Budgeted variable manufacturing overhead	185,400	178,800	171,000	184,800	720,000	
Fixed manufacturing overhead	450,000	450,000	450,000	450,000	1,800,000	I
Total budgeted manufacturing overhead	635,400	628,800	621,000	634,800	2,520,000	d
Less: Depreciation	(175,000)	(175,000)	(175,000)	(175,000)	(700,000)	J
Budgeted cash disbursements for manufacturing overhead	$ 460,400	$ 453,800	$ 446,000	$ 459,800	$1,820,000	Q
Total manufacturing overhead for the year					$2,520,000	d
Total budgeted direct labor hours for the year					÷ 480,000	
Predetermined manufacturing overhead rate					$ 5.25	e

The Ending Finished Goods Inventory Budget

The **ending finished goods inventory budget** summarizes the absorption cost per unit for each Excel DVD to derive the $8.50 cost per unit (**f**). This budget next calculates the budgeted cost of ending finished goods inventory of $714,000 (**K**) based on expected ending inventory on 12/31/2012 of 84,000 units (B). The $714,000 is also on the budgeted balance sheet as an asset.

EXHIBIT 7-12 | **Ending Finished Goods Inventory Budget using Absorption Costing**

SMART TOUCH LEARNING, INC.
Ending Finished Goods Inventory Budget (Absorption Costing)
For the year ended December 31, 2012

	Quantity	Cost	Quarter 1st
Production costs:			
Direct materials	1 sq. foot vinyl	D $ 2.40 per sq. foot	$ 2.40
Direct labor	.40 hours	G $10.00 per hour	$ 4.00
Manufacturing overhead	.40 hours	e $ 5.25 per hour (from Exhibit 7-11)	$ 2.10
Production cost per DVD			$ 8.50 f
Ending Finished goods inventory, quantity (from Exhibit 7-8)			84,000 c
Ending Finished goods inventory, budgeted cost			$714,000 K

The Selling and Administrative Expenses Budget

Exhibit 7-13 shows the **selling and administrative expenses budget**. The variable selling expense of $2.00 per DVD is given (L). Note that this includes the Uncollectible account expense of 1% of sales from Exhibit 7-5. Then it is multiplied by the Budgeted sales from Exhibit 7-7 (A) to calculate budgeted variable selling and administrative expenses. Next, the given fixed selling and administrative expenses (for insurance, sales salaries, and depreciation expense – selling) are added from Exhibit 7-5. The budgeted fixed selling and administrative expenses total $600,000 a quarter. The variable (k) plus the fixed (I) selling and administrative overhead add together to get the total budgeted selling and administrative expenses (a). This value will be used later when we calculate our budgeted income statement (Exhibit 7-15).

EXHIBIT 7-13 | **Selling and Administrative Expenses Budget**

SMART TOUCH LEARNING, INC.
Selling and Administrative Expenses Budget
For the year ended December 31, 2012

	Quarter				
	1st	2nd	3rd	4th	Annual Total
Budgeted sales in DVD quantities (Exhibit 7-7)	300,000	310,000	270,000	320,000	1,200,000 A
Standard variable selling and administrative expenses per DVD (includes Uncollectible account expense of 1% of sales from Exhibit 7-5)	$ 2.00	$ 2.00	$ 2.00	$ 2.00	$ 2.00 L
Budgeted variable selling and administrative expenses	600,000	620,000	540,000	640,000	2,400,000 k
Budgeted fixed selling and administrative expenses					
Sales salaries	315,000	315,000	315,000	315,000	1,260,000 i
Insurance	260,000	260,000	260,000	260,000	1,040,000 j
Depreciation	25,000	25,000	25,000	25,000	100,000 M
Total budgeted fixed selling and administrative expenses	600,000	600,000	600,000	600,000	2,400,000 I
Total budgeted selling and administrative expenses	1,200,000	1,220,000	1,140,000	1,240,000	4,800,000 a
Less: Depreciation and Uncollectible account expense	61,000	62,200	57,400	63,400	$ 244,000 g
Budgeted cash disbursements for selling and administrative expenses	$1,139,000	$1,157,800	$1,082,600	$1,176,600	$4,556,000 R

Last, the budgeted cash disbursements for selling and administrative expenses (R) is calculated by subtracting the non-cash manufacturing overhead [Depreciation and uncollectible account expense (g)] from the total budgeted selling and administrative expenses (a). To calculate non-cash manufacturing overhead for the first quarter, as an example, budgeted depreciation of $25,000 is added to budgeted Uncollectible account expense (1% of $3,600,000 sales) of $36,000. Thus, total noncash manufacturing overhead for the first quarter equals $61,000. This is used later to prepare our cash budget (Exhibit 7-14).

Stop & Think...

Why is depreciation expense and uncollectible account expense from the selling and administrative budget expenses budget (Exhibit 7-13) *excluded* from the budgeted cash payments for selling and administrative expenses that is used in the Cash Budget in Exhibit 7-14?

Answer: These expenses do not require cash outlays in the current period and therefore are not part of a cash budget. Depreciation is the periodic allocation of the cost of the equipment and fixtures that Smart Touch Learning acquired previously. Uncollectible account expense is the estimate of uncollectible sales made on account; thus, no cash was paid or received for these sales.

Preparing the Financial Budget

4 Prepare a financial budget for a manufacturer

Armed with a clear understanding of Smart Touch Learning's operating budget, you are now ready to prepare the financial budget. Review Exhibit 7-4, which shows that the financial budget includes the cash budget, the budgeted balance sheet, and the budgeted income statement (which is also part of the operating budget). We start with the cash budget.

Preparing the Cash Budget

The **cash budget**, or statement of budgeted cash receipts and payments, details how the business expects to go from the beginning cash balance to the desired ending balance. The cash budget is computed as follows:

- Beginning cash balance (Exhibit 7-6) (W)
- + Cash collections from customers (Exhibit 7-7) (N)
- – Cash payments for direct materials purchases (Exhibit 7-9) (O)
- – Cash payments for direct labor (Exhibit 7-10) (P)
- – Cash payments for manufacturing overhead (Exhibit 7-11) (Q)
- – Cash payments for selling and administrative expenses (Exhibit 7-13) (R)
- – Cash payments for capital expenditures (Exhibit 7-5) (S)
- – Cash payments for dividends (Exhibit 7-5) (T)
- = Net cash excess/deficiency
- +/– Cash financing (U)/repayments (m) and/or interest payments on notes (b)
- = Ending cash balance (Exhibit 7-14) (Y)

Besides the basic math of the preceding equation, the only value we have to calculate is the amount of borrowings or repayments on the note and the interest due on the same. If the company has excess cash, interest payments or loan repayments will be made. If the company has a deficit, additional cash financing is necessary.

The initial facts in Exhibit 7-5 told us that the company maintains a minimum cash balance of $10,000 and borrows in increments of $10,000. We also learned that interest is calculated at 2% annually. For example, at the end of the first quarter, Smart Touch had a net cash excess of only $50,240, so it was able to pay $30,000 of the loan back and still maintain minimum cash (note ending cash on line **Y** for the first quarter of $19,990). The company also paid interest of $250. Interest is calculated using the interest formula we learned in financial accounting (principal × interest rate × time) and is shown on line **b**. The remaining debt was paid off in the second quarter.

EXHIBIT 7-14 | **Cash Budget**

SMART TOUCH LEARNING, INC.
Cash Budget
For the year ended December 31, 2012

	Quarter					
	1st	2nd	3rd	4th	Annual Total	
Cash balance, beginning of quarter	$ 110,000 **W**	$ 19,990	$ 81,610	$ 109,210	$ 110,000	
Add: Cash collections from customers (Exhibit 7-7)	3,538,400	3,635,280	3,397,680	3,564,000	14,135,360	**N**
Total cash available	3,648,400	3,655,270	3,479,290	3,673,210	14,245,360	
Less: Budgeted cash disbursements for:						
Direct materials (Exhibit 7-9)	694,760	741,960	693,480	714,120	2,844,320	**O**
Direct labor (Exhibit 7-10)	1,236,000	1,192,000	1,140,000	1,232,000	4,800,000	**P**
Manufacturing overhead (Exhibit 7-11)	460,400	453,800	446,000	459,800	1,820,000	**Q**
Selling and administrative expenses (Exhibit 7-13)	1,139,000	1,157,800	1,082,600	1,176,600	4,556,000	**R**
Equipment purchases	60,000	-	-	-	60,000	**S**
Dividends	8,000	8,000	8,000	8,000	32,000	**T**
Total cash disbursements	$3,598,160	$3,553,560	$3,370,080	$3,590,520	$14,112,320	
Net cash excess (deficiency)	$ 50,240	$ 101,710	$ 109,210	$ 82,690	$ 133,040	
Financing:						
Borrowing, beginning balance	50,000					**U**
Net borrowing/repayments	(30,000)	(20,000)			(50,000)	**m**
Interest (Beg balance × 2% (Exhibit 7-5) × 3/12)	(250)	(100)			(350)	**b**
Total financing change	(30,250)	(20,100)	-	-	(50,350)	
Cash balance, end of quarter	$ 19,990	$ 81,610	$ 109,210	$ 82,690	$ 82,690	**Y**

The Budgeted Income Statement

The preparation of a budgeted income statement is no different than the preparation of a regular income statement, which you learned about in your financial accounting course. First, use the sales budget values for sales revenue from Exhibit 7-7 (**Z**) to begin your budgeted income statements. Deduct Cost of goods sold, which is calculated by multiplying the standard cost of $8.50 per DVD from Exhibit 7-12 by the number of units budgeted to be sold each quarter from Exhibit 7-7 (**A**). Gross margin equals Sales minus COGS. Next, deduct selling and administrative expenses from Exhibit 7-13 (**a**) to arrive at net operating income. Lastly, we deduct the interest expense on the notes, calculated in Exhibit 7-14 (**b**), to arrive at net income.

EXHIBIT 7-15 | **Budgeted Income Statement**

SMART TOUCH LEARNING, INC.
Budgeted Income Statement
For the year ended December 31, 2012

	Quarter				
	1st	2nd	3rd	4th	Annual Total
Sales revenue (Exhibit 7-7)	$3,600,000	$3,720,000	$3,240,000	$3,840,000	$14,400,000
Less: COGS*	2,550,000	2,635,000	2,295,000	2,720,000	10,200,000
Gross margin	1,050,000	1,085,000	945,000	1,120,000	4,200,000
Less: Selling and administrative expenses (Exhibit 7-13)	1,200,000	1,220,000	1,140,000	1,240,000	4,800,000
Net operating income (loss)	(150,000)	(135,000)	(195,000)	(120,000)	(600,000)
Less: Interest expense (Exhibit 7-14)	(250)	(100)	-	-	(350)
Net income (loss)	$ (150,250)	$ (135,100)	$ (195,000)	$ (120,000)	$ (600,350)

*COGS = sales in DVDs from Exhibit 7-7 × $8.50 standard cost from Exhibit 7-12

The Budgeted Balance Sheet

To prepare the **budgeted balance sheet**, project each asset, liability, and stockholders' equity account based on the plans outlined in the previous exhibits.

Study the budgeted balance sheet in Exhibit 7-16 to make certain you understand the computation of each figure. For example, on the budgeted balance sheet as of December 31, 2012, budgeted cash equals the ending cash balance from the cash budget in Exhibit 7-14 (Y). Accounts receivable as of December 31 equal the last quarter's credit sales that are expected to be collected in the first quarter of 2013 of $1,520,640 (L) from Exhibit 7-9. December 31 inventories are $168,000 for Raw materials (70,000 sq. feet from Exhibit 7-7 × $2.40 standard direct materials cost per square yard from Exhibit 7-5). Finished goods inventories are $714,000 from Exhibit 7-12 (K). Plant assets, net of accumulated depreciation were figured by taking the Beginning balance of $5,000,000 (Exhibit 7-6) and adding the new equipment purchased of $60,000 from Exhibit 7-5 S, subtracting the accumulated depreciation budgeted for manufacturing ($700,000 from Exhibit 7-11 J) and for selling ($100,000 from Exhibit 7-13 M) projected during 2012 to arrive at the ending Plant assets, net balance of $4,260,000 (n). The liabilities and equity values are computed as shown.

EXHIBIT 7-16 | **Budgeted Balance Sheet**

SMART TOUCH LEARNING, INC.
Budgeted Balance Sheet
December 31, 2012

Assets			Liabilities	
Current assets			**Current liabilities**	
Y Cash (from Exhibit 7-14)		$ 82,690	Accounts payable (from Exhibit 7-9,	
L Accounts receivable (from Exhibit 7-7)		1,520,640	$715,200 – 71,520)	$ 643,680
			Income taxes payable (no change)	100,000
Inventories:			Total current liabilities	743,680
Raw materials (from Exhibit 7-9,			Long-term liabilities	
70,000 * $2.40)	168,000		Notes payable (from Exhibit 7-14)	-
K Finished goods (from Exhibit 7-12)	714,000	882,000	Total liabilities	743,680
Total current assets		2,485,330	**Stockholders' Equity**	
n Plant Assets, net of accumulated depreciation		4,260,000	Common stock (no change)	6,000,000
			Retained earnings*	1,650
Total assets		$6,745,330	Total liabilities and stockholders' equity	$6,745,330

n Beg Bal of $5,000,000 from Exhibit 7-6 + Equipment purchased from Exhibit 7-5 of $60,000 – Depreciation of $700,000 from Exhibit 7-11 and Depreciation of $100,000 from Exhibit 7-13 = $4,260,000

o Retained earnings = Beg Bal of $634,000 – $600,350 net loss for 2012 – dividends declared of $32,000 = $1,650 Ending Balance

Getting Employees to Accept the Budget

What is the most important part of Smart Touch Learning's budgeting system? Despite all the numbers we have crunched, it is not the mechanics. It is getting managers and employees to accept the budget so the company can reap the planning, coordination, and control benefits described at the beginning of this chapter.

Few people enjoy having their work monitored and evaluated. If managers want to use the budget as a benchmark to evaluate employees' performance, managers must first motivate employees to accept the budget's goals. Here is how they can do it:

- Managers must support the budget themselves, or no one else will.
- Managers must show employees how budgets can help them achieve better results.
- Managers must have employees participate in developing the budget.

But these principles alone are not enough. As the manager of Smart Touch, your performance is evaluated by comparing actual results to the budget. When you develop the company's budget, you may be tempted to build in *slack*. For example, you might want to budget fewer sales and higher purchases than you expect. This increases the chance that actual performance will be better than the budget and that you will receive a good evaluation. But adding slack into the budget makes it less accurate—and less useful for planning and control. When the division manager and the head of the accounting department arrive from headquarters next week, they will scour your budget to find any slack you may have inserted.

Using Information Technology for Sensitivity Analysis and Rolling Up Unit Budgets

Exhibits 7-7 through 7-16 show that the manager must prepare many calculations to develop the master budget for just one product for Smart Touch Learning's manufacturing division. No wonder managers embrace information technology to help prepare budgets! Let us see how advances in information technology make it more cost-effective for managers to

5 Use sensitivity analysis in budgeting

- conduct sensitivity analysis on their own unit's budget, and
- roll up individual unit budgets to create the companywide budget.

Sensitivity Analysis

The master budget models the company's *planned* activities. Top management pays special attention to ensure that the results of the budgeted income statement (Exhibit 7-15), the cash budget (Exhibit 7-14), and the budgeted balance sheet (Exhibit 7-16) support key strategies.

But actual results often differ from plans so management wants to know how budgeted income and cash balances would change if key assumptions were changed. In Chapter 5, we defined *sensitivity analysis* as a *what-if* technique that asks *what* a result will be *if* a predicted amount is not achieved or *if* an underlying assumption changes. *What if* the stock market crashes? How will this affect **Amazon.com**'s sales? Will it have to postpone the planned expansion in Asia and Europe? *What* will be Smart Touch Learning's cash balance on December 31 *if* the uncollectible sales increase from 1% to 2%? Will Smart Touch have to borrow more cash? If Smart Touch increases sales revenue, can it generate net income?

Most companies use computer spreadsheet programs to prepare master budget schedules and statements. One of the earliest spreadsheet programs was developed by graduate business students who realized that computers could take the drudgery out of hand-computed master budget sensitivity analyses. Today, managers answer what-if questions simply by changing a number. At the press of a key, the computer screen flashes a revised budget that includes all the effects of the change.

Technology makes it cost-effective to perform more comprehensive sensitivity analyses. Armed with a better understanding of how changes in sales and costs are likely to affect the company's bottom line, today's managers can react quickly if key assumptions underlying the master budget (such as sales price or quantity) turn out to be wrong.

Rolling Up Individual Unit Budgets into the Companywide Budget

Smart Touch Learning's Excel products are just one of the company's many products. As Exhibit 7-17 shows, Smart Touch's headquarters must roll up the budget data from all product divisions to prepare the companywide master budget. This roll up can be difficult for companies whose units use different spreadsheets to prepare the budgets.

EXHIBIT 7-17 | **Rolling Up Individual Unit Budgets into the Companywide Budget**

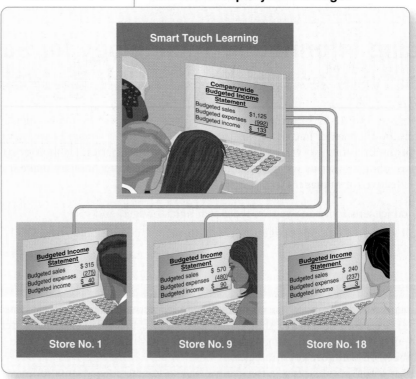

Companies like **Sunoco** turn to budget-management software to solve this problem. Often designed as a component of the company's Enterprise Resource Planning (ERP) system (or data warehouse), this software helps managers develop and analyze budgets.

Across the globe, managers sit at their desks, log into the company's budget system, and enter their budget amounts. The software allows them to conduct sensitivity analyses on their own unit's data. When the manager is satisfied with the budget, it can be entered in the companywide budget with the click of a mouse. The specific unit's budget automatically rolls up with budgets from all other units around the world.

Whether at headquarters or on the road, top executives can log into the budget system and conduct their own sensitivity analyses on individual units' budgets or on the companywide budget. Managers can spend less time compiling and summarizing data and more time analyzing it to ensure that the budget leads the company to achieve its key strategic goals.

Stop & Think...

Consider two budget situations:

(1) Smart Touch Learning's marketing analysts produce a near-certain forecast for one year's sales of $14,400,000 for the company's Excel DVDs divisions.

(2) Smart Touch Learning's marketing analysts express uncertainty regarding the period's sales. The most likely amount is $14,400,000, but marketing considers any amount between $13,400,000 and $15,400,000 to be possible.

How will the budgeting process differ in these two circumstances?

Answer: Smart Touch Learning will prepare a master budget for the expected sales level of $14,400,000 in either case. Because of the uncertainty in the second situation, executives will want a set of budgets covering the entire range of volume rather than a single level. Smart Touch's managers may prepare budgets based on sales of, for example, $13,400,000, $13,900,000, $14,400,000, $14,900,000, and $15,400,000. These budgets will help managers plan for sales levels throughout the forecasted range.

The "Decision Guidelines" review budgets and how managers use them in responsibility accounting. Study these guidelines before working on Summary Problem 1.

Decision Guidelines

THE MASTER BUDGET

Amazon.com's initial strategy was to "get big fast." But without a budget, spending got out of control. So founder and CEO Jeff Bezos added a second strategic goal—to become the world's most cost-efficient, high-quality e-tailer. Today, **Amazon.com**'s managers use budgets to help reach both the growth and cost-efficiency goals. Consider some of the decisions **Amazon.com** made as it set up its budgeting process.

Decision	Guidelines
• What benefits should **Amazon.com** expect to obtain from developing a budget?	• Requires managers to *plan* how to increase sales and how to cut costs • Promotes *coordination and communication*, such as communicating the importance of the cost-efficiency goal • Provides a *benchmark* that motivates employees and helps managers evaluate how well employees contributed to the sales growth and cost-efficiency goals
• In what order should **Amazon.com**'s managers prepare the components of the master budget?	Begin with the *operating budget*. • Start with the *sales budget*, which feeds into all other budgets. • Using the sales and *ending inventory budgets* determine the production, *direct materials, direct labor, manufacturing overhead, and ending finished goods budgets*. • The sales, and other operating budgets, and *selling and administrative expenses budgets* determine the *budgeted income statement*. Next, prepare the *capital expenditures budget* (Chapter 11). Finally, prepare the *financial budget*. • Start with the *cash budget*. • The cash budget provides the ending cash balance for the *budgeted balance sheet*.
• What extra budgeting steps should **Amazon.com** take given the uncertainty of Internet-based sales forecasts?	Prepare a *sensitivity analysis* and project budgeted results at different sales levels.

Take this opportunity to solidify your understanding of operating budgets by carefully working out Summary Problem 1.

Summary Problem 1

Review the Smart Touch Learning example. You now consider that the facts change from Exhibit 7-5 as follows (differences highlighted):

EXHIBIT 7-5SP | **Facts for Smart Touch Learning Budget Preparation**

Time period for which to budget	For the year ended December 31, 2012	
Cash collections:		
Collected in quarter of sale	60%	
Collected in quarter after sale	40%	
Bad debt percentage	1%	h
Cash disbursements:		
Paid in quarter of purchase	10%	
Paid in quarter after purchase	90%	
Ending Raw materials inventory	25% of next quarter's sales	
Ending Finished goods inventory	30% of next quarter's sales	
Beg Raw materials inventory, 12/31/2011	75,000 sq. feet	E
Beg Finished goods inventory, 12/31/2011	84,000 DVDs	B
Budgeted sales, 1st quarter 2012	320,000 DVDs	A
Budgeted sales, 2nd quarter 2012	305,000 DVDs	A
Budgeted sales, 3rd quarter 2012	285,000 DVDs	A
Budgeted sales, 4th quarter 2012	290,000 DVDs	A
Budgeted sales, 1st quarter 2013	280,000 DVDs	
Equipment purchases, 1st quarter 2012	$ 50,000	S
Equipment purchases, 2nd quarter 2012	-	
Equipment purchases, 3rd quarter 2012	-	
Equipment purchases, 4th quarter 2012	-	
Quarterly dividends declared and paid each quarter in 2012	$ 8,000	T
Expected sales price per unit	$ 12.00	
Standard cost data:		
Direct materials	$ 2.20 per sq. foot, 1 sq. foot per DVD	D
Direct labor	$ 9.80 per DL hour, .40 hours per DVD	G
Variable Manufacturing overhead	$ 1.50 per DL hour, .40 hours per DVD	H
Fixed Manufacturing overhead	$150,000 per month	I
Variable Selling	$ 2.00 per DVD	L
Fixed Selling and administrative expenses:		
Insurance	$260,000 per month	j
Sales salaries	$315,000 per month	i
Depreciation expense—manufacturing	$175,000 per quarter	J
Depreciation expense—selling	$ 25,000 per quarter	M
Minimum required cash balance	10,000	
Interest rate on loans	2%	
Loans are made and repaid in $10,000 increments as soon as cash is available.		
Provision for Income tax payable is assumed to stay the same.		

You want to see how these changes affect the budget. Note that you will use a different set of balance sheet amounts at 12/31/11 due to the cost changes in this Summary Problem.

Requirement

1. Revise all budgets to determine how the changes will affect Smart Touch's master budget.

EXHIBIT 7-6SP | **Beginning Balance Sheet**

SMART TOUCH LEARNING, INC.
Balance Sheet
December 31, 2011

Assets			Liabilities	
Current assets			Current liabilities	
W Cash		$ 110,000	Accounts payable	$ 620,000 **X**
V Accounts receivable		1,400,000	Income taxes payable	100,000 **U**
			Total current liabilities	720,000
Inventories:			Long-term liabilities	
Raw materials	165,000		Notes payable	50,000
Finished goods	690,480	855,480	Total liabilities	770,000
Total current assets		2,365,480	**Stockholders' Equity**	
Plant Assets, net of accumulated depreciation		5,000,000	Common stock	6,000,000
			Retained earnings	595,480
Total assets		$7,365,480	Total liabilities and stockholders' equity	$7,365,480

EXHIBIT 7-7SP | **Sales Budget and Budgeted Cash Collected from Customers**

SMART TOUCH LEARNING, INC.
Sales Budget
For the year ended December 31, 2012

	Quarter				
	1st	2nd	3rd	4th	Annual Total
Budgeted sales in DVD quantities	320,000	305,000	285,000	290,000	1,200,000 **A**
Budgeted sales price per DVD	$ 12.00	$ 12.00	$ 12.00	$ 12.00	$ 12.00
Total budgeted sales	$3,840,000	$3,660,000	$3,420,000	$3,480,000	$14,400,000 **Z**

SMART TOUCH LEARNING, INC.
Budgeted Cash Collections from Customers
For the year ended December 31, 2012

	Quarter				
	1st	2nd	3rd	4th	Annual Total
Accounts receivable, beginning balance	$1,400,000				$ 1,400,000 **V**
Collections from 1st quarter sales	2,280,960	1,520,640			3,801,600
Collections from 2nd quarter sales		2,174,040	1,449,360		3,623,400
Collections from 3rd quarter sales			2,031,480	1,354,320	3,385,800
Collections from 4th quarter sales				2,067,120	2,067,120
Budgeted cash collections from customers	$3,680,960	$3,694,680	$3,480,840	$3,421,440	$14,277,920 **N**

L Ending Accounts receivable, December 31, 2012 = $3,480,000 × (100% − 1% uncollectible) × 40% = $1,378,080

EXHIBIT 7-8SP | **Production Budget**

SMART TOUCH LEARNING, INC.
Production Budget
For the year ended December 31, 2012

	Quarter					
	1st	2nd	3rd	4th	Annual Total	
Budgeted sales in DVD quantities (from Exhibit 7-7SP)	320,000	305,000	285,000	290,000	1,200,000	**A**
Add: Ending Finished goods inventory	91,500 ◄	85,500 ◄	87,000 ◄	84,000 **c**	84,000	
Budgeted finished goods available	411,500	390,500	372,000	374,000	1,284,000	
Less: Beginning Finished goods inventory	84,000 **B**	► 91,500	► 85,500	► 87,000	84,000	
Budgeted Production	327,500	299,000	286,500	287,000	1,200,000	**C**

c Ending Finished goods inventory = 280,000 next quarter's sales × 30% = 84,000

SMART TOUCH LEARNING, INC.
Direct Materials Budget
For the year ended December 31, 2012

	Quarter					
	1st	2nd	3rd	4th	Annual Total	
Budgeted production (from Exhibit 7-8SP)	327,500	299,000	286,500	287,000	1,200,000	**C**
Raw materials needed per DVD, in sq. feet	1	1	1	1	1	
Square feet of raw materials needed	327,500	299,000	286,500	287,000	1,200,000	
Add: Ending Raw materials inventory	76,250	71,250	72,500	70,000 **F**	70,000	
Budgeted raw materials available	403,750	370,250	359,000	357,000	1,270,000	
Less: Raw materials beginning inventory	75,000 **E**	76,250	71,250	72,500	75,000	
Budgeted direct materials needed to be purchased, in sq. feet	328,750	294,000	287,750	284,500	1,195,000	
Standard price per sq. foot	$ 2.20	$ 2.20	$ 2.20	$ 2.20	$ 2.40	**D**
Budgeted direct materials needed to be purchased, in sq. feet	$723,250	$646,800	$633,050	$625,900	$2,629,000	

F 280,000 first quarter 2013 sales * 25% = 70,000

SMART TOUCH LEARNING, INC.
Budgeted Cash Disbursements for Direct Materials
For the year ended December 31, 2012

	Quarter					
	1st	2nd	3rd	4th	Annual Total	
Accounts payable, beginning balance	$620,000				$ 620,000	**X**
Payments from 1st quarter purchases	72,325	650,925			723,250	
Payments from 2nd quarter purchases		64,680	582,120		646,800	
Payments from 3rd quarter purchases			63,305	569,745	633,050	
Payments from 4th quarter purchases				62,590	62,590	
Budgeted cash disbursements for direct materials	$692,325	$715,605	$645,425	$632,335	$2,685,690	**O**

EXHIBIT 7-10SP | Direct Labor Budget

SMART TOUCH LEARNING, INC.
Direct Labor Budget
For the year ended December 31, 2012

	Quarter				
	1st	2nd	3rd	4th	Annual Total
Budgeted production (Exhibit 7-8SP)	327,500	299,000	286,500	287,000	1,200,000 C
Direct labor hours needed per DVD	0.40	0.40	0.40	0.40	0.40
Hours of direct labor needed	131,000	119,600	114,600	114,800	480,000
Standard price per hour	$ 9.80	$ 9.80	$ 9.80	$ 9.80	$ 9.80 G
Budgeted direct labor cost	$1,283,800	$1,172,080	$1,123,080	$1,125,040	$4,704,000 P

EXHIBIT 7-11SP | Manufacturing Overhead Budget

SMART TOUCH LEARNING, INC.
Manufacturing Overhead Budget
For the year ended December 31, 2012

	Quarter				
	1st	2nd	3rd	4th	Annual Total
Budgeted direct labor hours (Exhibit 7-10SP)	131,000	119,600	114,600	114,800	480,000
Standard variable overhead rate ($1.50 per DL hour or $0.60 per DVD)	$ 1.50	$ 1.50	$ 1.50	$ 1.50	$ 1.50 H
Budgeted variable manufacturing overhead	196,500	179,400	171,900	172,200	720,000
Fixed manufacturing overhead	450,000	450,000	450,000	450,000	1,800,000 I
Total budgeted manufacturing overhead	646,500	629,400	621,900	622,200	2,520,000 d
Less: Depreciation	(175,000)	(175,000)	(175,000)	(175,000)	(700,000) J
Budgeted cash disbursements for manufacturing overhead	$ 471,500	$ 454,400	$ 446,900	$ 447,200	$1,820,000 Q

Total manufacturing overhead for the year	$2,520,000 d
Total budgeted direct labor hours for the year	÷ 480,000
Predetermined manufacturing overhead rate	$ 5.25 e

SMART TOUCH LEARNING, INC.
Ending Finished Goods Inventory Budget (Absorption Costing)
For the year ended December 31, 2012

	Quantity	Cost	Quarter 1st
Production costs:			
Direct materials	1 sq. foot vinyl	D $2.20 per sq. foot	$ 2.20
Direct labor	.40 hours	G $9.80 per hour	$ 3.92
Manufacturing overhead	.40 hours	e $5.25 per hour (from Exhibit 7-11SP)	$ 2.10
Production cost per DVD			$ 8.22 f
Budgeted number of ending Finished goods inventory			
(from Exhibit 7-8SP)			84,000 B
Budgeted cost of ending Finished goods inventory			$690,480 K

EXHIBIT 7-13SP Selling and Administrative Expenses Budget

SMART TOUCH LEARNING, INC.
Selling and Administrative Expenses Budget
For the year ended December 31, 2012

		Quarter			
	1st	2nd	3rd	4th	Annual Total
Budgeted sales in DVD quantities (Exhibit 7-7SP)	320,000	305,000	285,000	290,000	1,200,000 **A**
Standard variable selling and administrative expenses per DVD (includes Uncollectible account expense of 1% of sales from Exhibit 7-5SP)	$ 2.00	$ 2.00	$ 2.00	$ 2.00	$ 2.00 **L**
Budgeted variable selling and administrative expenses	640,000	610,000	570,000	580,000	2,400,000 **k**
Budgeted fixed selling and administrative expenses					
Sales salaries	315,000	315,000	315,000	315,000	1,260,000 **i**
Insurance	260,000	260,000	260,000	260,000	1,040,000 **j**
Depreciation	25,000	25,000	25,000	25,000	100,000 **M**
Total budgeted fixed selling and administrative expenses	600,000	600,000	600,000	600,000	2,400,000 **l**
Total budgeted selling and administrative expenses	1,240,000	1,210,000	1,170,000	1,180,000	4,800,000 **a**
Less: Depreciation and Uncollectible account expense	63,400	61,600	59,200	59,800	$ 244,000 **g**
Budgeted cash disbursements for selling and administrative expense	$1,176,600	$1,148,400	$1,110,800	$1,120,200	$4,556,000 **R**

EXHIBIT 7-14SP Cash Budget

SMART TOUCH LEARNING, INC.
Cash Budget
For the year ended December 31, 2012

		Quarter			
	1st	2nd	3rd	4th	Annual Total
Cash balance, beginning of quarter	$ 110,000 **W**	$ 58,485	$ 254,680	$ 401,315	$ 110,000
Add: Cash collections from customers (Exhibit 7-7SP)	3,680,960	3,694,680	3,480,840	3,421,440	14,277,920 **N**
Total cash available	3,790,960	3,753,165	3,735,520	3,822,755	14,387,920
Less: Budgeted cash disbursements for:					
Direct materials (Exhibit 7-9SP)	692,325	715,605	645,425	632,335	2,685,690 **O**
Direct labor (Exhibit 7-10SP)	1,283,800	1,172,080	1,123,080	1,125,040	4,704,000 **P**
Manufacturing overhead (Exhibit 7-11SP)	471,500	454,400	446,900	447,200	1,820,000 **Q**
Selling and administrative expenses (Exhibit 7-13SP)	1,176,600	1,148,400	1,110,800	1,120,200	4,556,000 **R**
Equipment purchases	50,000	-	-	-	50,000 **S**
Dividends	8,000	8,000	8,000	8,000	32,000 **T**
Total cash disbursements	$3,682,225	$3,498,485	$3,334,205	$3,332,775	$13,847,690
Net cash excess (deficiency)	$ 108,735	$ 254,680	$ 401,315	$ 489,980	$ 540,230
Financing:					
Borrowing, beginning balance	50,000				**U**
Net borrowing/repayments	(50,000)				(50,000) **m**
Interest (Beg balance × 2% (Exhibit 7-5SP) × 3/12)	(250)	-			(250) **b**
Total financing change	(50,250)	-	-	-	(50,250)
Cash balance, end of quarter	$ 58,485	$ 254,680	$ 401,315	$ 489,980	$ 489,980 **Y**

EXHIBIT 7-15SP | **Budgeted Income Statement**

SMART TOUCH LEARNING, INC.
Budgeted Income Statement
For the year ended December 31, 2012

	Quarter					
	1st	2nd	3rd	4th	Annual Total	
Sales revenue (Exhibit 7-7SP)	$3,840,000	$3,660,000	$3,420,000	$3,480,000	$14,400,000	**z**
Less: COGS*	2,630,400	2,507,100	2,342,700	2,383,800	9,864,000	
Gross margin	1,209,600	1,152,900	1,077,300	1,096,200	4,536,000	
Less: Selling and administrative expenses (Exhibit 7-13SP)	1,240,000	1,210,000	1,170,000	1,180,000	4,800,000	**a**
Net operating income (loss)	(30,400)	(57,100)	(92,700)	(83,800)	(264,000)	
Less: Interest expense (Exhibit 7-14SP)	(250)	-	-	-	(250)	**b**
Net income (loss)	$ (30,650)	$ (57,100)	$ (92,700)	$ (83,800)	$ (264,250)	

*COGS = sales in DVDs from Exhibit 7-7SP × $8.22 standard cost from Exhibit 7-12SP

EXHIBIT 7-16SP | **Budgeted Balance Sheet**

SMART TOUCH LEARNING, INC.
Budgeted Balance Sheet
December 31, 2012

Assets			Liabilities	
Current assets			Current liabilities	
Y Cash (from Exhibit 7-14SP)		$ 489,980	Accounts payable (from Exhibit 7-9SP,	
L Accounts receivable (from Exhibit 7-7SP)		1,378,080	$625,900 – 62,590)	$ 563,310
			Income taxes payable (no change)	100,000
Inventories:			Total current liabilities	663,310
Raw materials (from Exhibit 7-9SP,			Long-term liabilities	
70,000 * $2.20)	154,000		Notes payable (from Exhibit 7-14SP)	-
K Finished goods (from Exhibit 7-12SP)	690,480	844,480	Total liabilities	663,310
Total current assets		2,712,540	**Stockholders' Equity**	
n Plant Assets, net of accumulated depreciation		4,250,000	Common stock (no change)	6,000,000
			Retained earnings*	299,230 **o**
Total assets		$6,962,540	Total liabilities and stockholders' equity	$6,962,540

n Beg Bal of $5,000,000 from Exhibit 7-6SP + Equipment purchased from Exhibit 7-5SP of $50,000 – Depreciation of $700,000 from Exhibit 7-11SP and Depreciation of $100,000 from Exhibit 7-13SP = $4,250,000
o Retained earnings = Beg Bal of $595,480 – $264,250 net loss for 2012 – dividends declared of $32,000 = $299,230 Ending Balance

Review The Master Budget

Accounting Vocabulary

Budgeted Balance Sheet (p. 310)
Projects ending assets, liabilities, and equities for a period.

Budgeted Income Statement (p. 300)
Projects operating income for a period.

Capital Expenditures Budget (p. 300)
A company's plan for purchases of property, plant, equipment, and other long-term assets.

Cash Budget (p. 308)
Details how the business expects to go from the beginning cash balance to the desired ending balance; also called the *statement of budgeted cash receipts and payments*.

Direct Materials Budget (p. 304)
The budget determines the amount of direct materials needed for the desired production, ending inventory for the budgeted balance sheet, and the budgeted cash disbursements for materials for the cash budget.

Direct Labor Budget (p. 305)
This determines the number of hours needed based on desired production, the cost of direct labor for the budgeted income statement, and cash disbursements for labor for the cash budget.

Ending Finished Goods Inventory Budget (p. 306)
This budget summarizes the number of units of ending finished goods inventory as well as the dollar value for the balance sheet.

Financial Budget (p. 300)
The cash budget (cash inflows and outflows) and the budgeted balance sheet.

Manufacturing Overhead Budget (p. 306)
This budget determines the amount of variable overhead projected based on a standard, such as direct labor and adds to that value the budgeted fixed overhead amount. It also determines required cash disbursements for overhead.

Master Budget (p. 299)
The set of budgeted financial statements and supporting schedules for the entire organization. Includes the operating budget, the capital expenditures budget, and the financial budget.

Operating Budget (p. 300)
Projects sales revenue, production budgets, and selling and administrative expenses, leading to the budgeted income statement that projects operating income for the period.

Selling and Administrative Expenses Budget (p. 307)
The budget that shows the total non-production operating expenses, and the cash disbursements for the administrative and selling expenses.

Quick Check

1. **Amazon.com** expected to receive which of the following benefits when it started its budgeting process?
   a. The budget provides **Amazon.com**'s managers with a benchmark against which to compare actual results for performance evaluation.
   b. The planning required to develop the budget helps managers foresee and avoid potential problems before they occur.
   c. The budget helps motivate employees to achieve **Amazon.com**'s sales growth and cost-reduction goals.
   d. All of the above

2. Which of the following is the cornerstone (or most critical element) of the master budget?
   a. The sales budget
   b. The direct materials budget
   c. The selling and administrative expenses budget
   d. The finished goods inventory budget

3. The balance sheet is part of which element of **Amazon.com**'s master budget?

   a. The selling and administrative expenses budget

   b. The capital expenditures budget

   c. The financial budget

   d. None of the above

Use the following information to answer Questions 4–8. Suppose Textbooks of NWF sells one million hardcover books a day at an average price of $37. Assume that its cost of production averages $22 a book. Textbooks of NWF has no beginning inventory, but it wants to have a three-day supply of books in ending inventory. Assume that operating expenses are $2 million per day.

4. Compute Textbooks of NWF's budgeted sales for the next (seven-day) week.

   a. $273 million

   b. $259 million

   c. $481 million

   d. $154 million

5. Determine Textbook's budgeted COGS for the next (seven-day) week.

   a. $154 million

   b. $68 million

   c. $160 million

   d. $266 million

6. What is Textbooks of NWF's budgeted operating income for a (seven-day) week?

   a. $85 million

   b. $31 million

   c. $91 million

   d. $191 million

7. What is Textbooks of NWF's budgeted cost of production for a (seven-day) week? (*Hint*: include the inventory reserves it needs to acquire.)

   a. $154 million

   b. $220 million

   c. $88 million

   d. $200 million

8. Assuming Textbooks of NWF receives 80% of sales in cash the day of the sale and 20% in accounts receivable that is paid in the subsequent week, what is the company's budgeted cash collections from customers for the week if it had beginning Accounts receivable of $1.8 million?

   a. $1.2 million

   b. $205.4 million

   c. $207.2 million

   d. $209 million

9. Which of the following expenses would *not* appear in Textbooks of NWF's cash budget?

   a. Wages expense

   b. Depreciation expense

   c. Marketing expense

   d. Interest expense

10. Information Technology has made it easier for Textbooks of NWF's managers to perform all of the following tasks *except*

   a. preparing performance reports that identify variances between actual and budgeted revenues and costs.

   b. sensitivity analyses.

   c. rolling up individual units' budgets into the companywide budget.

   d. removing slack from the budget.

Assess Your Progress

■ Short Exercises

S7-1 *(L.OBJ. 1)* **Why managers use budgets [5 min]**
Consider the budget for any business.

Requirement

1. Explain how a company and its management and employees benefit from preparing the budget.

S7-2 *(L.OBJ. 2)* **Understanding the components of the master budget [5–10 min]**
The following components are included in the reports of the master budget.

a. Budgeted balance sheet
b. Sales budget
c. Budgeted income statement
d. Cash budget
e. Direct materials, direct labor, manufacturing overhead, and ending finished goods inventory budgets
f. Selling and administrative budget
g. Production budget

Requirement

1. List in order of preparation the items of the master budget.

S7-3 *(L.OBJ. 3)* **Preparing an operating budget [5 min]**
Mountaineers sells its rock-climbing shoes worldwide. Mountaineers expects to sell 4,000 pairs of shoes for $165 each in January, and 2,000 pairs of shoes for $220 each in February. All sales are cash only.

Requirement

1. Prepare the sales budget for January and February.

Note: Short Exercise 7-3 must be completed before attempting Short Exercise 7-4.

S7-4 *(L.OBJ. 3)* **Preparing an operating budget [10 min]**
Review your results from S7-3. Mountaineers' production cost per pair of shoes is budgeted at $80 in direct materials cost, $50 in direct labor cost, and $20 in variable manufacturing overhead cost per shoe. Additionally, its monthly fixed overhead budget is $20,000 of which $4,000 represents depreciation, and the company expects to sell 4,600 pairs of shoes in March for $240 each. Mountaineers has no beginning finished goods inventory for the first quarter but desires ending finished goods inventory to be 40% of the following months' sales. Mountaineer maintains no direct materials inventory. April sales are projected to be 4,000 pairs of shoes. Selling and administrative expenses total $5,000 per month.

Requirement

1. Use this information and the sales budget prepared in S7-3 to prepare Mountaineers' production budget, direct materials budget, direct labor budget, and manufacturing overhead budget for January, February, and March.

Note: Short Exercise 7-3 must be completed before attempting Short Exercise 7-5.

S7-5 *(L.OBJ. 4)* **Preparing a financial budget [15–20 min]**
Refer to Mountaineers' sales budget that you prepared in S7-3. Now assume that Mountaineers' sales are 20% cash and 80% on credit. Mountaineers' collection history indicates that credit sales are collected as follows:

30% in the month of the sale
60% in the month after the sale
7% two months after the sale
3% never collected

November sales totaled $386,000 and December sales were $399,500.

Requirement

1. Prepare a schedule for the budgeted cash collections for January and February.

S7-6 *(L.OBJ. 4)* **Preparing a financial budget [5–10 min]**
Mountaineers has $8,600 cash on hand on December 1. The company requires a minimum cash balance of $7,400. December cash collections are $548,600. Total cash payments for December are $563,230.

Requirement

1. Prepare a cash budget for December. Will Mountaineers need to borrow cash by the end of December?

S7-7 *(L.OBJ. 5)* **Using sensitivity analysis in budgeting [10–15 min]**
Riverbed Sporting Goods has the following sales budget:

					April–July
RIVERBED SPORTING GOODS STORE					
Sales Budget					
	April	May	June	July	Total
Cash sales, 60%	$ 32,400	$ 51,600	$ 36,000	$ 32,400	
Credit sales, 40%	21,600	34,400	24,000	21,600	
Total sales, 100%	$ 54,000	$ 86,000	$ 60,000	$ 54,000	$ 254,000

Suppose June sales are expected to be $40,000 rather than $60,000.

Requirement

1. Revise Riverbed Sporting Goods' sales budget.

▪ Exercises

E7-8 *(L.OBJ.1)* **Why managers use budgets [15 min]**

Diego Garcia owns a chain of travel goods stores. Last year, his sales staff sold 10,000 suitcases at an average sale price of $150. Variable expenses were $120 per suitcase and the total fixed expense was $110,000. This year, the chain sold more expensive product lines. Sales were 8,000 suitcases at an average price of $200. Production cost of the more expensive line totaled $150 per suitcase. The total fixed expenses were the same both years. Garcia evaluates the chain manager by comparing this year's income with last year's income.

Requirement

1. Prepare a performance report for this year, similar to Exhibit 7-3. How would you improve Garcia's performance evaluation system to better analyze this year's results?

E7-9 *(L.OBJ. 2)* **Understanding the components of the master budget [15–20 min]**

Chloe Allred, division manager for Tires Plus, is speaking to the controller, Crystal Thayer, about the budgeting process. Chloe states, "I'm not an accountant, so can you explain the three main parts of the master budget to me and tell me their purpose?"

Requirement

1. Answer Chloe's question.

E7-10 *(L.OBJ. 3)* **Preparing an operating budget [25–30 min]**

Swenson, Inc., sells tire rims at $100 per rim. Its sales budget for the nine months ended September 30 follows:

	Quarter Ended			Nine-Month
	March 31	June 30	September 30	Total
Cash sales, 30%	$ 30,000	$ 45,000	$ 39,000	$114,000
Credits sales, 70%	70,000	105,000	91,000	266,000
Total sales, 100%	$100,000	$150,000	$130,000	$380,000

Swenson, Inc., expects the following production costs:

Direct materials	10 lbs of rubber per tire at $2 per pound
Direct labor	0.5 hours per tire at $10 per hour
Variable MOH	$1 per DL hour
Fixed MOH	$4,030 per month, including $1,000 of depreciation
Variable selling	$2 per tire
Fixed selling	$10,000 per month, no depreciation

The director of marketing and the financial vice president agree that each quarter's ending inventory should not be below 10% of sales for the following quarter. The marketing director expects sales of $200,000 during the fourth quarter. The January 1 inventory was 100 tire rims.

Requirement

1. Prepare a production budget for each of the first three quarters of the year for Swenson, Inc.

Note: Exercise 7-10 must be completed before attempting Exercise 7-11.

E7-11 *(L.OBJ. 3)* **Preparing an operating budget [15–20 min]**
Review your results from E7-10. Assume that direct materials are paid 30% in the current month and 70% in the following month. Beginning accounts payable is $14,000. Direct labor, overhead, and selling costs are all paid in the quarter incurred.

Requirements

1. Prepare a direct materials, direct labor, manufacturing overhead, and ending finished goods inventory budget for each of the first three quarters of the year for Swenson, Inc. Additionally, compute cost of goods sold for the entire nine-month period.
2. Prepare a schedule of cash disbursements for direct materials purchases for Swenson, Inc.

Note: Exercise 7-10 and 7-11 must be completed before attempting Exercise 7-12.

E7-12 *(L.OBJ. 4)* **Preparing a financial budget [15–20 min]**
Review your results from E7-10 and E7-11. Assume that credit sales are collected 40% in the current quarter and 60% in the following quarter. Beginning accounts receivable is $40,000.

Requirements

1. Prepare a sales budget for Swenson, Inc.
2. Prepare a schedule of cash collections for Swenson, Inc.
3. Prepare a cash budget for Swenson Inc. Beginning cash is $10,000.

E7-13 *(L.OBJ. 3)* **Preparing an operating budget [20–25 min]**
Posh International, Inc., is an exotic car dealership. Suppose that its Los Angeles office projects that 2011 quarterly sales will increase by 3% in Quarter 1, by 4% in Quarter 2, by 6% in Quarter 3, and by 5% in Quarter 4. Management expects COGS to be 60% of revenues during each of the first two quarters, 55% of revenues during the third quarter, and 60% during the fourth. Selling and administrative expenses are expected to be fixed at $10,000 per quarter. The office manager expects to borrow $500,000 on July 1, with quarterly principal payments of $10,000 beginning on September 30 and interest paid at an annual rate of 14%. Assume that fourth quarter 2010 sales were $7,000,000.

Requirement

1. Prepare a budgeted income statement for each of the four quarters of 2011 including a summary of entire year for Posh International, Inc.

E7-14 *(L.OBJ. 4)* **Preparing a financial budget [20–30 min]**
Agua Ole is a distributor of bottled water.

Requirement

1. For each of the Items a through c, compute the amount of cash receipts or payments Agua Ole will budget for September. The solution to one item may depend on the answer to an earlier item.

   a. Management expects to sell equipment that cost $22,000 at a gain of $4,000. Accumulated depreciation on this equipment is $7,000.

   b. Management expects to sell 7,800 cases of water in August and 9,100 in September. Each case sells for $13. Cash sales average 30% of total sales, and credit sales make up the rest. Three-fourths of credit sales are collected in the month of sale, with the balance collected the following month.

   c. The company pays rent and property taxes of $4,000 each month. Commissions and other selling expenses average 25% of sales. Agua Ole pays two-thirds of commissions and other selling expenses in the month incurred, with the balance paid in the following month.

E7-15 *(L.OBJ. 4, 5)* **Preparing a financial budget; using sensitivity analysis in budgeting [25–30 min]**
Lipman Auto Parts, a family-owned auto parts store, began January with $10,300 cash. Management forecasts that collections from credit customers will be $11,400 in January and $14,800 in February. The store is scheduled to receive $5,000 cash on a business note receivable in January. Projected cash payments include materials purchases ($3,000 in January and $3,600 in February), direct labor ($7,000 monthly) and manufacturing overhead ($2,500 in January and $2,800 in February). Selling and administrative expenses are ($2,700 each month).

Lipman Auto Parts' bank requires a $10,000 minimum balance in the store's checking account. At the end of any month when the account balance dips below $10,000, the bank automatically extends credit to the store in multiples of $1,000. Lipman Auto Parts borrows as little as possible and pays back loans in quarterly installments of $2,000, plus 4% annual interest on the entire unpaid principal. The first loan payment occurs three months after the initial loan.

Requirements

1. Prepare Lipman Auto Parts' cash budget for January and February.
2. How much cash will Lipman Auto Parts borrow, if any, in February if collections from customers that month total $13,800 instead of $14,800?

E7-16 *(L.OBJ. 4)* **Preparing a financial budget [20 min]**
You recently began a job as an accounting intern at Ralph Golf Park. Your first task was to help prepare the cash budget for April and May. Unfortunately, the computer with the budget file crashed, and you did not have a backup or even a hard copy. You ran a program to salvage bits of data from the budget file. After entering the following data in the budget, you may have just enough information to reconstruct the budget.

RALPH GOLF PARK Cash Budget April and May	April	May
Beginning cash balance	$ 16,200	$?
Cash collections	?	80,100
Cash from sale of plant assets	0	2,000
Cash available	106,300	?
Cash payments:		
Purchase of inventory	$?	$ 41,600
Operating expenses	47,400	?
Total payments	98,000	?
Ending cash balance before financing	?	27,500
Less: Minimum cash balance desired	(25,000)	(25,000)
Cash excess (deficiency)	$?	$?
Financing of cash deficiency:		
Borrowing (at end of month)	?	?
Principal repayments (at end of month)	?	?
Interest expense	?	?
Total effects of financing	?	?
Ending cash balance	$?	$?

Ralph Golf Park requires a minimum cash balance of $25,000 at the end of the month, and eliminates any cash deficiency by borrowing the exact amount needed from State Street Bank, where the current annual interest rate is 8%. Ralph Golf Park pays interest on its outstanding debt at the end of each month. The company also repays all borrowed amounts at the end of the month, as cash becomes available. There is no loan outstanding from State Street Bank at the beginning of April.

Requirement

1. Complete the cash budget.

E7-17 *(L.OBJ. 4)* **Preparing a financial budget [25–30 min]**
Consider the following information for Omas.com at March 31, 2011.

    a. February 28 inventory balance, $17,780
    b. March payments for inventory, $4,400
    c. March payments of accounts payable and accrued liabilities, $8,400
    d. February 28 accounts payable balance, $10,100
    e. February 28 furniture and fixtures balance, $34,600; accumulated depreciation balance $29,870
    f. February 28 equity, $29,040
    g. March depreciation expense, $600
    h. Cost of goods sold, 40% of sales
    i. Other March expenses, including income tax, total $7,000, paid in cash
    j. February 28 cash balance, $11,500
    k. March budgeted credit sales, $12,400
    l. February 28 accounts receivable balance, $5,130
    m. March cash receipts, $14,600

Requirement

1. Prepare a budgeted balance sheet.

P7-18A *(L.OBJ. 1, 2)* **Why managers use budgets and understanding the components of the master budget [50–60 min]**

Doggy World operates a chain of pet stores in the Midwest. The manager of each store reports to the regional manager, who, in turn, reports to the headquarters in Milwaukee, Wisconsin. The *actual* income statements for the Dayton store, the Ohio region (including the Dayton store), and the company as a whole (including the Ohio region) for July 2011 are as follows:

DOGGY WORLD
Income Statement
For the month ended July 31, 2011

	Dayton	Ohio	Companywide
Revenue	$ 158,400	$ 1,760,000	$ 4,400,000
Expenses:			
Regional manager/headquarters office	$ –	$ 58,000	$ 122,000
Cost of materials	85,536	880,000	1,760,000
Salary expense	41,184	440,000	1,100,000
Depreciation expense	7,800	91,000	439,000
Utilities expense	4,000	46,600	264,000
Rent expense	2,500	34,500	178,000
Total expenses	141,020	1,550,100	3,863,000
Operating income	$ 17,380	$ 209,900	$ 537,000

Budgeted amounts for July were as follows:

DOGGY WORLD
Budgeted Income Statement
For the month ended July 31, 2011

	Dayton	Ohio	Companywide
Revenue	$ 173,400	$ 1,883,000	$ 4,650,000
Expenses:			
Regional manager/headquarters office	$ –	$ 64,600	$ 124,000
Cost of materials	91,902	1,035,650	2,092,500
Salary expense	41,616	470,750	1,162,500
Depreciation expense	7,800	87,500	446,000
Utilities expense	4,900	54,600	274,000
Rent expense	3,400	32,700	169,000
Total expenses	149,618	1,745,800	4,268,000
Operating income	$ 23,782	$ 137,200	$ 382,000

Requirement

1. Prepare a report for July 2011 that shows the performance of the Dayton store, the Ohio region, and the company as a whole. Follow the format of Exhibit 7-3.

P7-19A *(L.OBJ. 3, 5)* **Preparing an operating budget; sensitivity analysis [60–90 min]**

Tucker's Turkey Sandwiches, Inc., manufactures and sells turkey sandwiches. Tucker's balance sheet for the year ended December 31, 2011 was as follows:

TUCKER'S TURKEY SANDWICHES					
Balance Sheet					
December 31, 2011					
Assets			**Liabilities**		
Current assets			Current liabilities		
Cash		$ 50,000	Accounts payable		$ 22,000
Accounts receivable		180,000	Income taxes payable		20,000
Inventories:			Total current liabilities		42,000
Raw materials	$ 8,000		Long-term liabilities		
Finished goods	$69,600	77,600	Notes payable		40,000
Total current assets		307,600	Total liabilities		82,000
			Stockholders' Equity		
Plant Assets, net of accumulated depreciation		2,000,000	Common stock		2,000,000
			Retained earnings		225,600
			Total equity		2,225,600
Total assets		$2,307,600	Total liabilities and stockholders' equity		$2,307,600

The following additional data about Tucker's sales, production costs, and other expenses follow:

Tucker's Turkey Sandwiches, Inc., additional data:	
Time period for which to budget	**For the year ended December 31, 2012**
Cash collections: (all sales are on account)	
Collected in the quarter of sale	30%
Collected in the quarter of sale	70%
Bad debt percentage	2%
Cash disbursements:	
Paid in quarter of purchase	80%
Paid in quarter after purchase	20%
Ending Raw materials inventory	10% of next quarter's sales
Ending Finished goods inventory	40% of next quarter's sales
Beg Raw materials inventory, 12/31/2011	10,000 pounds
Beg Finished goods inventory, 12/31/2011	40,000 Turkey sandwiches
Budgeted sales, 1st quarter, 2012	100,000 Turkey sandwiches
Budgeted sales, 2nd quarter, 2012	110,000 Turkey sandwiches
Budgeted sales, 3rd quarter, 2012	120,000 Turkey sandwiches
Budgeted sales, 4th quarter, 2012	90,000 Turkey sandwiches
Budgeted sales, 1st quarter, 2013	110,000 Turkey sandwiches
Equipment purchases, 1st quarter 2012	$ 0
Equipment purchases, 2nd quarter 2012	$30,000
Equipment purchases, 3rd quarter 2012	$ 0
Equipment purchases, 4th quarter 2012	$ 0
Note: all equipment purchased will be placed in service on 1/1/2013	
Quarterly dividends declared and paid each quarter in 2012	$ 4,000
Expected sales price per unit	$ 3.00
Standard cost data:	
Direct materials	$ 0.80 per pound, 1 pound per sandwich
Direct labor	$ 10.00 per DL hour, 0.05 hours per sandwich
Variable Manufacturing overhead	$ 1.00 per DL hour
Fixed Manufacturing overhead	$13,780 per month
Variable Selling (includes Uncollectible account expense)	$ 0.10 per sandwich
Fixed Selling and administrative expenses:	
Insurance	$45,000 per quarter
Sales salaries	$30,000 per quarter
Depreciation expense—manufacturing	$ 8,000 per quarter
Depreciation expense—selling	$ 6,000 per quarter
Minimum required cash balance	$50,000
Interest rate on loans	6%
Loans are made and repaid in $10,000 increments at the end of the quarter.	
Provision for Income tax payable is assumed to stay the same.	

Requirements

1. Prepare the selling and administrative budget for the year.
2. Prepare the sales and production budget for the year.
3. Prepare updated sales and production budgets considering a 10% increase in sales volume for the 2nd and 3rd quarters.

Note: Problem 7-19A must be completed before attempting Problem 7-20A.

P7-20A *(L.OBJ. 3)* **Preparing an operating budget [35–45 min]**
Review your results from P7-19A.

Requirement

1. Prepare the direct materials, direct labor, manufacturing overhead, and ending finished goods inventory budgets.

Note: Problems 7-19A and 7-20A must be completed before attempting Problem 7-21A.

P7-21A *(L.OBJ. 3)* **Preparing a financial budget [35–45 min]**
Review your results from P7-19A and P7-20A.

Requirements

1. Prepare a financial budget for the year, a schedule of cash collections from customers, cash payments for direct materials, and the cash budget.
2. Prepare the budgeted income statement and budgeted balance sheet.

P7-22A *(L.OBJ. 3)* **Preparing an operating budget [60–90 min]**
Randy's Kayaks, Inc., manufactures and sells one person fiberglass kayaks. Randy's balance sheet for the year ended December 31, 2011, was as follows:

RANDY'S KAYAKS, INC. **Balance Sheet** **December 31, 2011**				
Assets			**Liabilities**	
Current assets			Current liabilities	
Cash		$ 52,000	Accounts payable	$ 131,000
Accounts receivable		1,200,000	Income taxes payable	45,000
Inventories:			Total current liabilities	176,000
Raw materials	$120,000		Long-term liabilities	
Finished goods	$287,500	407,500	Notes payable	70,000
Total current assets		1,659,500	Total liabilities	246,000
			Stockholders' Equity	
Plant Assets, net of accumulated depreciation		2,250,000	Common stock	1,600,000
			Retained earnings	2,063,500
			Total equity	3,663,500
Total assets		$3,909,500	Total liabilities and stockholders' equity	$3,909,500

The following additional data about Randy's sales, production costs, and other expenses follow:

Randy's Kayaks, Inc., additional data:	
Time period for which to budget	For the year ended December 31, 2012
Cash collections: (all sales are on account)	
Collected in the quarter of sale	40%
Collected in the quarter of sale	60%
Bad debt percentage	1%
Cash disbursements:	
Paid in quarter of purchase	70%
Paid in quarter after purchase	30%
Ending Raw materials inventory	40% of next quarter's sales
Ending Finished goods inventory	10% of next quarter's sales
Beg Raw materials inventory, 12/31/2011	40,000 pounds
Beg Finished goods materials inventory, 12/31/2011	1,000 Kayaks
Budgeted sales, 1st quarter, 2012	10,000 Kayaks
Budgeted sales, 2nd quarter, 2012	15,000 Kayaks
Budgeted sales, 3rd quarter, 2012	16,000 Kayaks
Budgeted sales, 4th quarter, 2012	14,000 Kayaks
Budgeted sales, 1st quarter, 2013	10,000 Kayaks
Equipment purchases, 1st quarter 2012	$ 30,000 Purchased 1/1/12
Equipment purchases, 2nd quarter 2012	$ 0
Equipment purchases, 3rd quarter 2012	$ 0
Equipment purchases, 4th quarter 2012	$150,000 Purchased 12/30/12
Quarterly dividends declared and paid each quarter in 2012	$ 4,000
Expected sales price per unit	$ 400.00
Standard cost data:	
Direct materials	$ 3.00 per pound, 10 pounds per kayak
Direct labor	$ 20.00 per DL hour, 10.00 hours per kayak
Variable Manufacturing overhead	$ 5.00 per DL hour
Fixed Manufacturing overhead	$ 34,375 per month
Variable Selling (Includes Uncollectible account expense)	$ 25.00 per kayak
Fixed Selling and administrative expenses:	
Insurance	$ 45,000 per quarter
Sales salaries	$ 30,000 per quarter
Depreciation expense—manufacturing	$ 9,000 per quarter
Depreciation expense—selling	$ 6,000 per quarter
Minimum required cash balance	$50,000
Interest rate on loans	6%
Loans are made and repaid in $10,000 increments at the end of each quarter.	
Provision for Income tax payable is assumed to stay the same.	

Requirements

1. Prepare the selling and administrative budget for the year.
2. Prepare the sales and production budget for the year for Randy's Kayaks, Inc.

Note: Problem 7-22A must be completed before attempting Problem 7-23A.

P7-23A *(L.OBJ. 3)* **Preparing an operating budget [35–45 min]**
Review your results from P7-22A.

Requirement

1. Prepare the direct materials, direct labor, manufacturing overhead, and ending finished goods inventory budgets for Randy's Kayaks, Inc.

Note: Problems 7-22A and 7-23A must be completed before attempting Problem 7-24A.

P7-24A *(L.OBJ. 4)* **Preparing a financial budget [35–45 min]**
Review your results from P7-22A and P7-23A.

Requirements

1. Prepare a financial budget for the year, a schedule of cash collections from customers, cash payments for direct materials, and the cash budget.
2. Prepare the budgeted income statement and budgeted balance sheet.

■ Problems (Group B)

P7-25B *(L.OBJ. 1, 2)* **Why managers use budgets and understanding the components of the master budget [50–60 min]**
Cat World operates a chain of pet stores in the Midwest. The manager of each store reports to the regional manager, who, in turn, reports to the headquarters in Milwaukee, Wisconsin. The *actual* income statements for the Dayton store, the Ohio region (including the Dayton store), and the company as a whole (including the Ohio region) for July 2011 are as follows:

CAT WORLD Income Statement For the month ended July 31, 2011			
	Dayton	Ohio	Companywide
Revenue	$ 162,000	$ 1,800,000	$ 4,500,000
Expenses:			
Regional manager/headquarters office	$ –	$ 56,000	$ 110,000
Cost of materials	87,480	900,000	1,800,000
Salary expense	42,120	450,000	1,125,000
Depreciation expense	7,300	95,000	438,000
Utilities expense	4,200	46,300	264,000
Rent expense	2,500	34,900	175,000
Total expenses	143,600	1,582,200	3,912,000
Operating income	$ 18,400	$ 217,800	$ 588,000

Budgeted amounts for July were as follows:

CAT WORLD Budgeted Income Statement For the month ended July 31, 2011			
	Dayton	Ohio	Companywide
Revenue	$ 176,000	$ 1,923,000	$ 4,750,000
Expenses:			
Regional manager/headquarters office	$ –	$ 62,600	$ 112,000
Cost of materials	93,280	1,057,650	2,137,500
Salary expense	42,240	480,750	1,187,500
Depreciation expense	7,300	87,500	449,000
Utilities expense	4,700	54,800	271,000
Rent expense	3,800	32,700	173,000
Total expenses	151,320	1,776,000	4,330,000
Operating income	$ 24,680	$ 147,000	$ 420,000

Requirement

1. Prepare a report for July 2011 that shows the performance of the Dayton store, the Ohio region, and the company as a whole. Follow the format of Exhibit 7-3.

P7-26B *(L.OBJ. 3, 5)* **Preparing an operating budget; sensitivity analysis [60–90 min]**
Timothy's Turkey Sandwiches, Inc., manufactures and sells turkey sandwiches. Timothy's balance sheet for the year ended December 31, 2011, was as follows:

TIMOTHY'S TURKEY SANDWICHES Balance Sheet December 31, 2011					
Assets			**Liabilities**		
Current assets			Current liabilities		
Cash		$ 59,000	Accounts payable		$ 15,000
Accounts receivable		210,000	Income taxes payable		20,000
Inventories:			Total current liabilities		35,000
Raw materials	$16,500		Long-term liabilities		
Finished goods	$92,840	109,340	Notes payable		50,000
Total current assets		378,340	Total liabilities		85,000
			Stockholders' Equity		
Plant Assets, net of accumulated depreciation		2,150,000	Common stock		2,300,000
			Retained earnings		143,340
			Total equity		2,443,340
Total assets		$2,528,340	Total liabilities and stockholders' equity		$2,528,340

The following additional data about Timothy's sales, production costs, and other expenses follow:

Timothy's Turkey Sandwiches, Inc., additional data:	
Time period for which to budget	**For the year ended December 31, 2012**
Cash collections: (all sales are on account)	
Collected in the quarter of sale	40%
Collected in the quater after sale	60%
Bad debt percentage	5%
Cash disbursements:	
Paid in quarter of purchase	75%
Paid in quarter after purchase	25%
Ending Raw materials inventory	20% of next quarter's sales
Ending Finished goods inventory	40% of next quarter's sales
Beg Raw materials inventory, 12/31/2011	22,000 pounds
Beg Finished goods inventory, 12/31/2011	44,000 Turkey sandwiches
Budgeted sales, 1st quarter 2012	110,000 Turkey sandwiches
Budgeted sales, 2nd quarter 2012	100,000 Turkey sandwiches
Budgeted sales, 3rd quarter 2012	120,000 Turkey sandwiches
Budgeted sales, 4th quarter 2012	110,000 Turkey sandwiches
Budgeted sales, 1st quarter 2013	100,000 Turkey sandwiches
Equipment purchases, 1st quarter 2012	$ 0
Equipment purchases, 2nd quarter 2012	$55,000
Equipment purchases, 3rd quarter 2012	$ 0
Equipment purchases, 4th quarter 2012	$ 0
Note: all equipment purchased will be placed in service on 1/1/2013	
Quarterly dividends declared and paid each quarter in 2012	$ 3,000
Expected sales price per unit	$ 3.25
Standard cost data:	
Direct materials	$ .75 per pound, 1 pound per sandwich
Direct labor	$ 8.00 per DL hour, 0.50 hours per sandwich
Variable Manufacturing overhead	$ 0.50 per DL hour
Fixed Manufacturing overhead	$18,530 per month
Variable Selling (includes Uncollectible account expense)	$ 0.20 per sandwich
Fixed Selling and administrative expenses:	
Insurance	$35,000 per quarter
Sales salaries	$40,000 per quarter
Depreciation expense—manufacturing	$11,000 per quarter
Depreciation expense—selling	$ 6,000 per quarter
Minimum required cash balance	$50,000
Interest rate on loans	8%
Loans are made and repaid in $10,000 increments at the end of the quarter.	
Provision for Income tax payable is assumed to stay the same.	

Requirements

1. Prepare the selling and administrative budget for the year.
2. Prepare the sales and production budget for the year.
3. Prepare updated sales and production budgets, considering a 10% increase in sales volume for the 2nd and 3rd quarters.

Note: Problem 7-26B must be completed before attempting Problem 7-27B.

P7-27B *(L.OBJ. 3)* **Preparing an operating budget [35–45 min]**
Review your results from P7-26B.

Requirement

1. Prepare the direct materials, direct labor, manufacturing overhead, and ending finished goods inventory budgets.

Note: Problems 7-26B and 7-27B must be completed before attempting Problem 7-28B.

P7-28B *(L.OBJ. 3)* **Preparing a financial budget [35–45 min]**
Review your results from P7-26B and P7-27B.

Requirements

1. Prepare a financial budget for the year, a schedule of cash collections from customers, cash payments for direct materials, and the cash budget.
2. Prepare the budgeted income statement and budgeted balance sheet.

P7-29B *(L.OBJ. 3)* **Preparing an operating budget [60–90 min]**
Ranger's Kayaks, Inc., manufactures and sells one-person fiberglass kayaks. Ranger's balance sheet for the year ended December 31, 2011, was as follows:

RANGER'S KAYAKS, INC.
Balance Sheet
December 31, 2011

Assets			Liabilities	
Current assets			Current liabilities	
Cash		$ 58,000	Accounts payable	$ 120,000
Accounts receivable		2,500,000	Income taxes payable	15,000
Inventories:			Total current liabilities	135,000
Raw materials	$264,000		Long-term liabilities	
Finished goods	$523,600	787,600	Notes payable	220,000
Total current assets		3,345,600	Total liabilities	355,000
			Stockholders' Equity	
Plant Assets, net of accumulated depreciation		2,150,000	Common stock	2,400,000
			Retained earnings	2,740,600
			Total equity	5,140,600
Total assets		$5,495,600	Total liabilities and stockholders' equity	$5,495,600

The following additional data about Ranger's sales, production costs, and other expenses follow:

Ranger's Kayaks, Inc., additional data:	
Time period for which to budget	For the year ended December 31, 2012
Cash collections: (all sales are on account)	
Collected in the quarter of sale	45%
Collected in the quarter of sale	55%
Bad debt percentage	1%
Cash disbursements:	
Paid in quarter of purchase	90%
Paid in quarter after purchase	10%
Ending Raw materials inventory	40% of next quarter's sales
Ending Finished goods inventory	20% of next quarter's sales
Beg Raw materials inventory, 12/31/2011	66,000 pounds
Beg Finished goods inventory, 12/31/2011	2,200 Kayaks
Budgeted sales, 1st quarter 2012	11,000 Kayaks
Budgeted sales, 2nd quarter 2012	12,000 Kayaks
Budgeted sales, 3rd quarter 2012	15,000 Kayaks
Budgeted sales, 4th quarter 2012	13,000 Kayaks
Budgeted sales, 1st quarter 2013	11,000 Kayaks
Equipment purchases, 1st quarter 2012	$ 20,000 Purchased 1/1/12
Equipment purchases, 2nd quarter 2012	$ 0
Equipment purchases, 3rd quarter 2012	$ 0
Equipment purchases, 4th quarter 2012	$225,000 Purchased 12/31/12
Quarterly dividends declared and paid each quarter in 2012	$ 70,000
Expected sales price per unit	$ 300.00
Standard cost data:	
Direct materials	$ 4.00 per pound, 15 pounds per kayak
Direct labor	$ 10.00 per DL hour, 10.00 hours per kayak
Variable Manufacturing overhead	$ 7.00 per DL hour
Fixed Manufacturing overhead	$ 34,000 per month
Variable Selling (includes Uncollectible account expense)	$ 20.00 per kayak
Fixed Selling and administrative expenses:	
Insurance	$ 75,000 per quarter
Sales salaries	$ 45,000 per quarter
Depreciation expense—manufacturing	$ 8,000 per quarter
Depreciation expense—selling	$ 7,000 per quarter
Minimum required cash balance	$ 50,000
Interest rate on loans	7%
Loans are made and repaid in $10,000 increments at the end of each quarter.	
Provision for Income tax payable is assumed to stay the same.	

Requirements

1. Prepare the selling and administrative budget for the year.
2. Prepare the sales and production budget for the year.

Note: Problem 7-29B must be completed before attempting Problem 7-30B.

P7-30B *(L.OBJ. 3)* **Preparing an operating budget [35–45 min]**
Review your results from P7-29B.

Requirement

1. Prepare the direct materials, direct labor, manufacturing overhead, and ending finished goods inventory budgets.

Note: Problems 7-29B and 7-30B must be completed before attempting Problem 7-31B.

P7-31B *(L.OBJ. 4)* **Preparing a financial budget [35–45 min]**
Review your results from 7-29B and 7-30B.

Requirements

1. Prepare a financial budget for the year, a schedule of cash collections from customers, cash payments for direct materials, and the cash budget.
2. Prepare the budgeted income statement and budgeted balance sheet.

■ Continuing Exercise

E7-32 This exercise continues the Sherman Lawn Service, Inc., situation from Exercise 6-26 of Chapter 6. Sherman Lawn Service is projecting sales for April of $20,000. May's sales will be 5% higher than April's. June's sales are expected to be 6% higher than May's.

Requirement

1. Prepare a sales budget for the quarter ended June 30 for Sherman Lawn Service, Inc.

■ Continuing Problem

P7-33 This problem continues the Haupt Consulting, Inc., situation from P6-27 of Chapter 6. Assume Haupt Consulting began January with $10,000 cash. Management forecasts that collections from credit customers will be $50,000 in January and $53,500 in February. Projected cash payments include equipment purchases ($18,000 in January and $40,400 in February) and operating expenses ($5,000 each month).

Haupt's bank requires a $25,000 minimum balance in the store's checking account. At the end of any month when the account balance dips below $25,000 the bank automatically extends credit to the store in multiples of $5,000. Haupt borrows as little as possible and pays back loans at the end of each month in $1,000 increments, taking into consideration their minimum balance requirements, plus 8% annual interest on the entire unpaid principal. The first loan payment occurs one month after the initial loan.

Requirements

1. Prepare Haupt Consulting's cash budget for January and February.
2. How much cash will Haupt borrow in February if collections from customers that month total $30,000 instead of $53,500?

Apply Your Knowledge

■ Decision Case

Case 1. Donna Tse has recently accepted the position of assistant manager at Cycle World, a bicycle store in St. Louis. She has just finished her accounting courses. Cycle World's manager and owner, Jeff Towry, asks Tse to prepare a budgeted income statement for 2013 based on the information he has collected. Tse's budget follows:

CYCLE WORLD
Budgeted Income Statement
For the Year Ending July 31, 2013

Sales revenue		$244,000
Cost of goods sold		177,000
Gross profit		67,000
Operating expenses:		
Salary and commission expense	$ 46,000	
Rent expense	8,000	
Depreciation expense	2,000	
Insurance expense	800	
Miscellaneous expenses	12,000	68,800
Operating loss		(1,800)
Interest expense		(225)
Net loss		$ (2,025)

Requirement

1. Tse does not want to give Towry this budget without making constructive suggestions for steps Towry could take to improve expected performance. Write a memo to Towry outlining your suggestions, including any additional reports you might prepare to measure performance.

■ Ethical Issue

Residence Suites operates a regional hotel chain. Each hotel is operated by a manager and an assistant manager/controller. Many of the staff who run the front desk, clean the rooms, and prepare the breakfast buffet work part-time or have a second job so turnover is high.

Assistant manager/controller Terry Dunn asked the new bookkeeper to help prepare the hotel's master budget. The master budget is prepared once a year and is submitted to company headquarters for approval. Once approved, the master budget is used to evaluate the hotel's performance. These performance evaluations affect hotel managers' bonuses and they also affect company decisions on which hotels deserve extra funds for capital improvements, based both upon need and adherence to the budget.

When the budget was almost complete, Dunn asked the bookkeeper to increase amounts budgeted for labor and supplies by 15%. When asked why, Dunn responded that hotel manager Clay Murry told her to do this when she began working at the hotel. Murry explained that this budgetary cushion gave him flexibility in running the hotel. For example, because company headquarters tightly controls capital improvement funds, Murry can use the extra money budgeted for labor and supplies to replace broken televisions or pay "bonuses" to keep valued employees. Dunn initially accepted this explanation because she had observed similar behavior at the hotel where she worked previously.

Requirements

Put yourself in Dunn's position. In deciding how to deal with the situation, answer the following questions:

1. What is the ethical issue?
2. What are my options?
3. What are the possible consequences?
4. What should I do?

■ Financial Statement Case—Amazon.com

This case is based on the **Amazon.com** annual report in Appendix A at the end of the book. Use it to answer the following questions.

Requirement

1. Review the data for **Amazon.com**. Prepare a budgeted income statement for the next two years assuming two scenarios:
   a. Sales will increase 2%. Costs will remain stable.
   b. Sales will increase 5%. COGS will increase 7% and other costs will decrease 1%.
   c. Which scenario is best for the company and why?

■ Team Project

Each autumn, as a hobby, Anne Magnuson weaves cotton place mats to sell through a local craft shop. The mats sell for $20 per set of four. The shop charges a 10% commission and remits the net proceeds to Magnuson at the end of December. Magnuson has woven and sold 25 sets each of the last two years. She has enough cotton in inventory to make another 25 sets. She paid $7 per set for the cotton. Magnuson uses a four-harness loom that she purchased for cash exactly two years ago. It is depreciated at the rate of $10 per month. The accounts payable relate to the cotton inventory and are payable by September 30.

Magnuson is considering buying an eight-harness loom so that she can weave more intricate patterns in linen. The new loom costs $1,000; it would be depreciated at $20 per month. Her bank has agreed to lend her $1,000 at 18% interest, with $200 principal plus accrued interest payable each December 31. Magnuson believes she can weave 15 linen place mat sets in time for the Christmas rush if she does not weave any cotton mats. She predicts that each linen set will sell for $50. Linen costs $18 per set. Magnuson's supplier will sell her linen on credit, payable December 31.

Magnuson plans to keep her old loom whether or not she buys the new loom. The balance sheet for her weaving business at August 31, 2013, is as follows:

ANNE MAGNUSON, WEAVER
Balance Sheet
August 31, 2013

Current assets:			Current liabilities:	
Cash	$ 25		Accounts payable	$ 74
Inventory of cotton	175			
	200			
Fixed assets:				
Loom	500		Stockholders' equity	386
Accumulated depreciation	(240)			
	260			
Total assets	$ 460		Total liabilities and stockholders' equity	$460

Requirements

1. Prepare a cash budget for the four months ending December 31, 2013, for two alternatives: weaving the place mats in cotton using the existing loom, and weaving the place mats in linen using the new loom. For each alternative, prepare a budgeted income statement for the four months ending December 31, 2013, and a budgeted balance sheet at December 31, 2013.

2. On the basis of financial considerations only, what should Magnuson do? Give your team's reasons.

3. What nonfinancial factors might Magnuson consider in her decision?

4. If the bank lowers the interest rate to 10%, linen costs increase $1, and sales prices increase $2, how will that affect Anne's cash budget? Make any recommendations your team can from these changes.

Quick Check Answers

1. *d*. 2. *a*. 3. *d*. 4. *b*. 5. *a*. 6. *c*. 7. *b*. 8. *d*. 9. *b*. 10. *d*.

For online homework, exercises, and problems that provide you immediate feedback, please visit www.myaccountinglab.com.

Big Picture

Ch 1 Introduction to Management Accounting

- Distinguish management accounting from financial accounting
- The role and responsibilities of management accountants
- Classify costs and prepare income statements for merchandising companies
- Classify costs and prepare income statements and statements of cost of goods manufactured for manufacturing companies

Ch 2 Job Order Costing

- Distinguish between job order and process costing
- Record materials, labor, and overhead in a job order costing system
- Record completion and sales of finished goods and adjust for under-/overallocated overhead
- Calculate unit costs for service companies

Ch 3 Activity-Based Costing and Other Cost Management Tools

- Develop activity-based costs and used activity-based management to determine target product costs
- Record transactions in JIT systems
- Use the four types of quality costs to make management decisions

Ch 4 Process Costing

- Calculate equivalent units and conversion costs
- Prepare cost of production reports and the related journal entries using the weighted-average costing method
- Prepare cost of production reports and the related journal entries using the FIFO costing method

Ch 5 Cost Behavior and Cost-Volume-Profit Analysis

- Identify how changes in volume affect cost
- Distinguish among variable, mixed, and fixed cost
- Split mixed cost into fixed and variable components by using the high-low method and by using regression analysis
- Use CVP to compute breakeven points, to plan profits, to graph relationships, and to perform sensitivity analysis

Ch 6 Absorption and Variable Costing

- Distinguish between absorption costing and variable costing
- Prepare absorption costing and variable costing income statements and explained the differences between the two costing techniques
- Illustrate the pros and cons of absorption and variable costing

Ch 7 The Master Budget: Profit Planning

- Understand and prepare all components of the master budget for manufacturers
- Use sensitivity analysis to adjust budget preparations

Master Budget for Merchandisers

The following shows the cycle and budgets that would be prepared for a merchandiser.

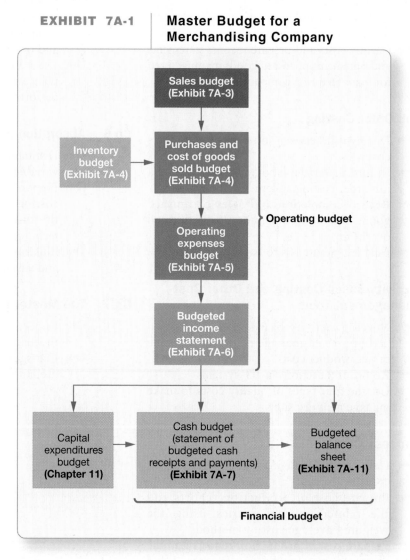

EXHIBIT 7A-1 | **Master Budget for a Merchandising Company**

The main difference between the manufacturer's and merchandiser's budget is in the operating budget: The manufacturer prepares production, direct materials, direct labor, and manufacturing overhead budgets to determine cash expenditures and COGS. The merchandiser prepares a single budget for this data: purchases and cost of goods sold budget. The facts and complete budgets for Greg's Groovy Tunes, a merchandiser, are presented next:

1. **You manage Greg's Groovy Tunes, Inc., which carries a complete line of music CDs and DVDs.** You are to prepare the store's master budget for April, May, June, and July, the main selling season. The division manager and the head of the Accounting Department will arrive from headquarters next week to review the budget with you.

2. **Cash collections follow sales because the company sells on account.**

3. Your store's balance sheet at March 31, 2011, the beginning of the budget period, appears in Exhibit 7A-2.

EXHIBIT 7A-2 | **Balance Sheet**

GREG'S GROOVY TUNES, INC.
Balance Sheet
March 31, 2011

Assets		Liabilities	
Current assets:		Current liabilities:	
Cash	$ 15,000	Accounts payable	$ 16,800
Accounts receivable	16,000	Salary and commissions	
Inventory	48,000	payable	4,250
Prepaid insurance	1,800	Total liabilities	21,050
Total current assets	80,800		
Plant assets:		**Stockholders' Equity**	
Equipment and fixtures	32,000	Stockholders' equity	78,950
Accumulated depreciation	(12,800)		
Total plant assets	19,200	Total liabilities and	
Total assets	$100,000	stockholders' equity	$100,000

4. **Sales in March were $40,000.** The sales force predicts the following future monthly sales:

April	$50,000
May	80,000
June	60,000
July	50,000

Sales are 60% cash and 40% on credit. Greg's Groovy Tunes collects all credit sales the month after the sale. The $16,000 accounts receivable at March 31 arose from credit sales in March (40% of $40,000). Uncollectible accounts are assumed to be immaterial.

5. Greg's Groovy Tunes maintains inventory equal to $20,000 plus 80% of the budgeted cost of goods sold for the following month. Ending finished goods inventory on July 31 is $42,400. Cost of goods sold averages 70% of sales. This is a variable cost. Inventory on March 31 is $48,000:

> March 31 inventory = $20,000 + {0.80 × (0.70 × April sales of $50,000)}
> = $20,000 + (0.80 × $35,000)
> = $20,000 + $28,000
> = $48,000

Greg's Groovy Tunes pays for inventory as follows: 50% during the month of purchase and 50% during the next month. Accounts payable consists of inventory purchases only. March purchases were $33,600 so accounts payable at the end of March totals $16,800 ($33,600 × 50%).

6. Monthly payroll has two parts: a salary of $2,500 plus sales commissions equal to 15% of sales. This is a mixed cost. The company pays half this amount during the month and half early in the next month. Therefore, at the end of each month, Greg's reports salary and commissions payable equal to half the month's payroll. The $4,250 liability on the March 31 balance sheet is half the March payroll of $8,500:

March payroll = Salary of $2,500 + Sales commissions of $6,000 (0.15 × $40,000)
= $8,500

March 31 salary and commissions payable = 0.50 × $8,500 = $4,250

7. Other monthly expenses are as follows:

Rent expense (fixed cost).........................	$2,000, paid as incurred
Depreciation expense, including truck (fixed cost)	500
Insurance expense (fixed cost)................	200 expiration of prepaid amount
Miscellaneous expenses (variable cost)....	5% of sales, paid as incurred

8. Greg's Groovy Tunes plans to purchase a used delivery truck in April for $3,000 cash.

9. Greg's Groovy Tunes requires each store to maintain a minimum cash balance of $10,000 at the end of each month. At the end of the month, when the cash balance is determined, the store can borrow money on six-month notes payable of $1,000 each at an annual interest rate of 12%. Management borrows no more than the amount needed to maintain the $10,000 minimum. Total interest expense will vary as the amount of borrowing varies from month to month. Notes payable require six equal monthly payments of principal, plus monthly interest on the entire unpaid principal. Borrowing and all principal and interest payments occur at the end of the month.

10. Income taxes are the responsibility of corporate headquarters, and consequently are not considered in budget preparation.

EXHIBIT 7A-3 | **Sales Budget**

GREG'S GROOVY TUNES, INC.
Sales Budget
April–July, 2011

	April	May	June	July	April–July Total
Cash sales, 60%	$30,000	$48,000	$36,000	$30,000	
Credit sales, 40%	20,000	32,000	24,000	20,000	
Total sales, 100%	$50,000	$80,000	$60,000	$50,000	$240,000

EXHIBIT 7A-4 | Inventory, Purchases, and Cost of Goods Sold Budget

GREG'S GROOVY TUNES, INC.
Inventory, Purchases, and Cost of Goods Sold Budget
April–July, 2011

	April	May	June	July	April–July Total
Cost of goods sold (0.70 × sales, from sales budget in Exhibit 7A-3)	$ 35,000	$ 56,000	$ 42,000	$ 35,000	$168,000
+ Desired ending inventory					
($20,000 + 0.80 × Cost of goods sold for the next month)	64,800*	53,600	48,000	42,400‡	
= Total inventory required	99,800	109,600	90,000	77,400	
− Beginning inventory	(48,000)†	(64,800)	(53,600)	(48,000)	
= Purchases	$ 51,800	$ 44,800	$ 36,400	$ 29,400	

*$20,000 + (0.80 × $56,000) = $64,800
†Balance at March 31 (Exhibit 7A-2)
‡Given in item 5 on page 345

EXHIBIT 7A-5 | Operating Expenses Budget

GREG'S GROOVY TUNES, INC.
Operating Expenses Budget
April–July, 2011

	April	May	June	July	April–July Total
Salary, fixed amount	$ 2,500	$ 2,500	$ 2,500	$ 2,500	
Commission, 15% of sales from sales budget (Exhibit 7A-3)	7,500	12,000	9,000	7,500	
Total salary and commissions	10,000	14,500	11,500	10,000	$46,000
Rent expense, fixed amount	2,000	2,000	2,000	2,000	8,000
Depreciation expense, fixed amount	500	500	500	500	2,000
Insurance expense, fixed amount	200	200	200	200	800
Miscellaneous expenses, 5% of sales from sales budget (Exhibit 7A-3)	2,500	4,000	3,000	2,500	12,000
Total operating expenses	$15,200	$21,200	$17,200	$15,200	$68,800

EXHIBIT 7A-6 | Budgeted Income Statement

GREG'S GROOVY TUNES, INC.
Budgeted Income Statement
Four Months Ending July 31, 2011

		Amount	Source
Sales revenue		$240,000	Sales budget (Exhibit 7A-3)
Cost of goods sold		168,000	Inventory, Purchases, and Cost of Goods
Gross profit		72,000	Sold budget (Exhibit 7A-4)
Operating expenses:			
Salary and commissions	$46,000		Operating expenses budget (Exhibit 7A-5)
Rent expense	8,000		Operating expenses budget (Exhibit 7A-5)
Depreciation expense	2,000		Operating expenses budget (Exhibit 7A-5)
Insurance expense	800		Operating expenses budget (Exhibit 7A-5)
Miscellaneous expenses	12,000	68,800	Operating expenses budget (Exhibit 7A-5)
Operating income		3,200	
Interest expense		225*	Cash budget (Exhibit 7A-9)
Net income		$ 2,975	

*$90 + $75 + $60

GREG'S GROOVY TUNES, INC.
Budgeted Cash Collections from Customers
April–July, 2011

	April	May	June	July	April–July Total
Cash sales from sales budget (Exhibit 7A-3)	$30,000	$48,000	$36,000	$30,000	
Collections of last month's credit sales, from sales budget (Exhibit 7A-3)	16,000*	20,000	32,000	24,000	
Total collections	$46,000	$68,000	$68,000	$54,000	$236,000

*March 31 accounts receivable (Exhibit 7A-2)

GREG'S GROOVY TUNES, INC.
Budgeted Cash Payments for Purchases
April–July, 2011

	April	May	June	July	April–July Total
50% of last month's purchases from inventory, purchases, and cost of goods sold budget (Exhibit 7A-4)	$16,800*	$25,900	$22,400	$18,200	
50% of this month's purchases from inventory, purchases, and cost of goods sold budget (Exhibit 7A-4)	25,900	22,400	18,200	14,700	
Total payments for purchases	$42,700	$48,300	$40,600	$32,900	$164,500

*March 31 accounts payable (Exhibit 7A-2)

Payment of 50% of March's salary and commissions (from March 31 balance sheet, Exhibit 7A-2)	$ 4,250
Payment of 50% of April's salary and commissions (50% × $10,000, Exhibit 7A-5)	5,000
Payment of rent expense (Exhibit 7A-5)	2,000
Payment of miscellaneous expenses (Exhibit 7A-5)	2,500
Total April cash payments for operating expenses	$13,750

Budgeted Cash Payments for Operating Expenses

GREG'S GROOVY TUNES, INC.
Budgeted Cash Payments for Operating Expenses
April–July, 2011

	April	May	June	July	April–July Total
Salary and commissions:					
50% of last month's expenses, from operating expenses budget (Exhibit 7A-5)	$ 4,250*	$ 5,000	$ 7,250	$ 5,750	
50% of this month's expenses, from operating expenses budget (Exhibit 7A-5)	5,000	7,250	5,750	5,000	
Total salary and commissions	9,250	12,250	13,000	10,750	
Rent expense, from operating expenses budget (Exhibit 7A-5)	2,000	2,000	2,000	2,000	
Miscellaneous expenses, from operating expenses budget (Exhibit 7A-5)	2,500	4,000	3,000	2,500	
Total payments for operating expenses	$13,750	$18,250	$18,000	$15,250	$65,250

*March 31 salary and commissions payable (page 348)

Cash Budget

GREG'S GROOVY TUNES, INC.
Cash Budget
Four Months Ending July 31, 2011

	April	May	June	July
Beginning cash balance	$ 15,000*	$ 10,550	$ 10,410	$ 18,235
Cash collections (Exhibit 7A-7)	46,000	68,000	68,000	54,000
Cash available	$ 61,000	$ 78,550	$ 78,410	$ 72,235
Cash payments:				
Purchases of inventory (Exhibit 7A-8)	$ 42,700	$ 48,300	$ 40,600	$ 32,900
Operating expenses (Exhibit 7A-9)	13,750	18,250	18,000	15,250
Purchase of delivery truck	3,000	—	—	—
Total cash payments	59,450	66,550	58,600	48,150
(1) Ending cash balance before financing	1,550	12,000	19,810	24,085
Less: Minimum cash balance desired	(10,000)	(10,000)	(10,000)	(10,000)
Cash excess (deficiency)	$ (8,450)	$ 2,000	$ 9,810	$ 14,085
Financing of cash deficiency (see notes a–c):				
Borrowing (at end of month)	$ 9,000			
Principal payments (at end of month)		$ (1,500)	$ (1,500)	$ (1,500)
Interest expense (at 12% annually)		(90)	(75)	(60)
(2) Total effects of financing	9,000	(1,590)	(1,575)	(1,560)
Ending cash balance (1) + (2)	$ 10,550	$ 10,410	$ 18,235	$ 22,525

*March 31 cash balance (Exhibit 7A-2)
Notes
[a]Borrowing occurs in multiples of $1,000 and only for the amount needed to maintain a minimum cash balance of $10,000.
[b]Monthly principal payments: $9,000 ÷ 6 = $1,500
[c]Interest expense:
  May: $9,000 × (0.12 × 1/12) = $90
  June: ($9,000 − $1,500) × (0.12 × 1/12) = $75
  July: ($9,000 − $1,500 − $1,500) × (0.12 × 1/12) = $60

GREG'S GROOVY TUNES, INC.
Budgeted Balance Sheet
July 31, 2011

Assets		
Current assets:		
Cash (Exhibit 7A-10)	$ 22,525	
Accounts receivable (sales budget, Exhibit 7A-3)	20,000	
Inventory (inventory, purchases, and cost of goods sold budget, Exhibit 7A-4)	42,400	
Prepaid insurance (beginning balance of $1,800 – $800* for four months' expiration; operating expenses budget, Exhibit 7A-5)	1,000	
Total current assets		$ 85,925
Plant assets:		
Equipment and fixtures (beginning balance of $32,000* + $3,000 truck acquisition	$ 35,000	
Accumulated depreciation (beginning balance of $12,800* + $2,000 for four months' depreciation; operating expenses budget, Exhibit 7A-5)	(14,800)	
Total plant assets		20,200
Total assets		$106,125
Liabilities		
Current liabilities:		
Account payable (0.50 × July purchases of $29,400; inventory, purchases, and cost of goods sold budget, Exhibit 7A-4)	$ 14,700	
Short-term note payable ($9,000 – $4,500 paid back; Exhibit 7A-10)	4,500	
Salary and commissions payable (0.50 × July expenses of $10,000; operating expenses budget, Exhibit 7A-5)	5,000	
Total liabilities		$ 24,200
Stockholders' Equity		
Stockholders' equity (beginning balance of $78,950* + $2,975 net income; Exhibit 7A-6)		81,925
Total liabilities and stockholders' equity		$106,125

*March 31, 2011, Balance Sheet (Exhibit 7A-2)

Problems (Group A)

P7A-1A (L.OBJ. 3) Preparing an operating budget [30 min]

The budget committee of Clipboard Office Supply has assembled the following data. As the business manager, you must prepare the budgeted income statements for May and June 2012.

Requirement

Rent expense	$2,600, paid as incurred
Depreciation expense	$300
Insurance expense	$200, expiration of prepaid amount
Income tax	20% of operating income

1. Prepare Clipboard Office Supply's budgeted income statements for May and June. Show cost of goods sold computations. Round *all* amounts to the nearest $100. (Round amounts ending in $50 or more upward, and amounts ending in less than $50 downward.) For example, budgeted May sales are $51,000 ($50,000 × 1.02), and June sales are $52,200 ($51,000 × 1.024).

Note: Problem 7A-1A must be completed before attempting Problem 7A-2A.

P7A-2A   (L.OBJ. 4) Preparing a financial budget [30 min]

Refer to P7A-1A. Clipboard Office Supply's sales are 75% cash and 25% credit. (Use the rounded sales values.) Credit sales are collected in the month after sale. Inventory purchases are paid 25% in the month of purchase and 75% the following month. Salaries and sales commissions are also paid half in the month earned and half the next month. Income tax is paid at the end of the year. If cash falls below $1,000, the company secures financing in $1,000 increments at an annual interest rate of 8%. Repayments of interest and principal are made as soon as excess cash is available.

The April 30, 2012, balance sheet showed the following balances:

Cash	$ 25,000
Accounts payable	53,000
Salaries and commissions payable	2,500

Requirements

1. Prepare schedules of (a) budgeted cash collections, (b) budgeted cash payments for purchases, and (c) budgeted cash payments for operating expenses. Show amounts for each month and totals for May and June. *Round* your computations to the nearest dollar.
2. Prepare a cash budget. If no financing activity took place, what is the budgeted cash balance on June 30, 2012?

P7A-3A   (L.OBJ. 4) Preparing a financial budget [50–60 min]

Box Printing of Baltimore has applied for a loan. **Bank of America** has requested a budgeted balance sheet at April 30, 2012, and a budgeted statement of cash flows for April. As Box Printing's controller, you have assembled the following information:

a. March 31 equipment balance, $80,900; accumulated depreciation, $12,900
b. April capital expenditures of $16,900 budgeted for cash purchase of equipment
c. April depreciation expense, $600
d. Cost of goods sold, 45% of sales
e. Other April operating expenses, including income tax, total $33,000, 40% of which will be paid in cash and the remainder accrued at the end of April
f. March 31 stockholders' equity, $136,700
g. March 31 cash balance, $50,200
h. April budgeted sales, $84,000, 60% of which is for cash; of the remaining 40%, half will be collected in April and half in May
i. April cash collections on March sales, $15,300
j. April cash payments of March 31 liabilities incurred for March purchases of inventory, $8,600
k. March 31 inventory balance, $11,800
l. April purchases of inventory, $10,800 for cash and $37,200 on credit. Half the credit purchases will be paid in April and half in May.

Requirements

1. Prepare the budgeted balance sheet for Box Printing at April 30, 2012. Show separate computations for cash, inventory, and stockholders' equity balances.
2. Prepare the budgeted statement of cash flows for April.

3. Suppose that Box Printing has become aware of more efficient (and more expensive) equipment than it budgeted for purchase in April. What is the total amount of cash available for equipment purchases in April, before financing, if the minimum desired ending cash balance is $21,000? (For this requirement, disregard the $16,900 initially budgeted for equipment purchases.)

Note: Problem 7A-3A must be completed before attempting Problem 7A-4A.

P7A-4A *(L.OBJ. 4,5)* **Preparing a financial budget, and using sensitivity analysis in budgeting [30–40 min]**

Refer to P7A-3A. Before granting a loan to Box Printing, **Bank of America** asks for a sensitivity analysis assuming April sales are only $56,000 rather than the $84,000 originally budgeted. (While the cost of goods sold will change, assume that purchases, depreciation, and the other operating expenses will remain the same as in P7A-3A.)

Requirements

1. Prepare a revised budgeted balance sheet for Box Printing, showing separate computations for cash, inventory, and owners' equity balances.
2. Suppose Box Printing has a minimum desired cash balance of $21,000. Will the company need to borrow cash in April?
3. In this sensitivity analysis, sales declined by 33 1/3% ($28,000 ÷ $84,000). Is the decline in expenses and net income more or less than 33 1/3%? Explain why.

■ Problems (Group B)

P7A-5B *(L.OBJ. 3)* **Preparing an operating budget [30 min]**

The budget committee of Omaha Office Supply has assembled the following data. As the business manager, you must prepare the budgeted income statements for May and June 2011.

  a. Sales in April were $42,000. You forecast that monthly sales will increase 2.0% in May and 2.4% in June.
  b. Omaha maintains inventory of $10,000 plus 25% of the sales revenue budgeted for the following month. Monthly purchases average 50% of sales revenue in that same month. Actual inventory on April 30 is $13,000. Sales budgeted for July are $70,000.
  c. Monthly salaries amount to $4,000. Sales commissions equal 4% of sales for that month. Combine salaries and commissions into a single figure.
  d. Other monthly expenses are as follows:

Rent expense	$2,800, paid as incurred
Depreciation expense	$600
Insurance expense	$300, expiration of prepaid amount
Income tax	20% of operating income

Requirement

1. Prepare Omaha Office Supply's budgeted income statements for May and June. Show cost of goods sold computations. Round *all* amounts to the nearest $100. (Round amounts ending in $50 or more upward, and amounts ending in less than $50 downward.) For example, budgeted May sales are $42,800 ($42,000 × 1.02), and June sales are $43,800 ($42,800 × 1.024).

Note: Problem 7A-5B must be completed before attempting Problem 7A-6B.

P7A-6B (L.OBJ. 4) **Preparing a financial budget [30 min]**

Refer to P7A-5B. Omaha Office Supply's sales are 75% cash and 25% credit. (Use the rounded sales values.) Credit sales are collected in the month after the sale. Inventory purchases are paid 25% in the month of purchase and 75% the following month. Salaries and sales commissions are also paid half in the month earned and half the next month. Income tax is paid at the end of the year.

The April 30, 2011, balance sheet showed the following balances:

Cash	$ 25,000
Accounts payable	50,000
Salaries and commissions payable	2,850

Requirements

1. Prepare schedules of (a) budgeted cash collections, (b) budgeted cash payments for purchases, and (c) budgeted cash payments for operating expenses. Show amounts for each month and totals for May and June. *Round* your computations to the nearest dollar. Sales in April were $42,000.

2. Prepare a cash budget similar to Exhibit 21-14. If no financing activity took place, what is the budgeted cash balance on June 30, 2011?

P7A-7B (L.OBJ. 4) **Preparing a financial budget [50–60 min]**

Note Printing of Baltimore has applied for a loan. **Bank of America** has requested a budgeted balance sheet at April 30, 2011, and a budgeted statement of cash flows for April. As Note Printing's controller, you have assembled the following information:

   a. March 31 equipment balance, $80,500; accumulated depreciation, $12,100

   b. April capital expenditures of $16,500, budgeted for cash purchase of equipment

   c. April depreciation expense, $600

   d. Cost of goods sold, 55% of sales

   e. Other April operating expenses, including income tax, total $35,000, 40% of which will be paid in cash and the remainder accrued at the end of April

   f. March 31 stockholders' equity, $138,600

   g. March 31 cash balance, $50,900

   h. April budgeted sales, $89,000, 60% of which is for cash; of the remaining 40%, half will be collected in April and half in May

   i. April cash collections on March sales, $15,300

   j. April cash payments of March 31 liabilities incurred for March purchases of inventory, $7,900

   k. March 31 inventory balance, $11,900

   l. April purchases of inventory, $10,700 for cash and $37,000 on credit. Half the credit purchases will be paid in April and half in May.

Requirements

1. Prepare the budgeted balance sheet for Note Printing at April 30, 2011. Show separate computations for cash, inventory, and stockholders' equity balances.

2. Prepare the budgeted statement of cash flows for April.

3. Suppose that Note Printing has become aware of more efficient (and more expensive) equipment than it budgeted for purchase in April. What is the total amount of cash available for equipment purchases in April, before financing, if the minimum desired ending cash balance is $12,000? (For this requirement, disregard the $16,500 initially budgeted for equipment purchases.)

Note: Problem 7A-7B must be completed before attempting Problem 7A-8B.

P7A-8B *(L.OBJ. 4, 5)* **Preparing a financial budget, and using sensitivity analysis in budgeting [30–40 min]**

Refer to P7A-7B. Before granting a loan to Note Printing, **Bank of America** asks for a sensitivity analysis assuming that April sales are only $59,350 rather than the $89,000 originally budgeted. (While the cost of goods sold will change, assume that purchases, depreciation, and the other operating expenses will remain the same as in P7A-7B.)

Requirements

1. Prepare a revised budgeted balance sheet for Note Printing, showing separate computations for cash, inventory, and stockholders' equity balances.

2. Suppose Note Printing has a minimum desired cash balance of $19,000. Will the company need to borrow cash in April?

3. In this sensitivity analysis, sales declined by 33 1/3% (29,650 ÷ $89,000). Is the decline in expenses and net income more or less than 33 1/3%? Explain why.

Chapter 7: Demo Doc

■ Master Budget-Merchandiser

Learning Objectives 2, 3

Manuel Mova started a company, Mova Company, that sells computer mice. Actual sales for the month ended September 30 were $30,000. Manuel expects sales to increase 7% in October and increase another 4% over October sales in November. Cash sales are expected to be 60% of total sales and credit sales about 40% of sales. Cost of goods sold should be 60% of total sales. Manuel does not want inventory to fall below $4,000 plus 10% of cost of goods sold for the next month. Sales of $35,000 are expected for December. Inventory on September 30 is $6,000.

Operating expenses include sales commission, 10% of sales; rent expense of $1,000; depreciation expense of $1,200; utility expense of $800; and insurance expense of $400.

Round all figures to the nearest dollar.

Requirement

1. Prepare the following budgets for October and November:

   a. Sales budget

   b. Inventory, purchases, and cost of goods sold budget

   c. Operating expense budget

   d. Budgeted income statement

Demo Doc Solution

2 Understand the components of the master budget

3 Prepare an operating budget-merchandiser

Requirement 1

Prepare the following budgets for October and November:

a. **Sales budget**

Part 1	Part 2	Part 3	Part 4	Demo Doc Complete

We prepare the sales budget first because sales affect most elements of the other budgets we will be preparing for this period.

In order to complete the sales budget, we start by calculating the total sales for each month. We will then compute the split between cash sales and credit sales for each month based on the company's estimation that cash sales will be 60% of the total sales for each month and credit sales will be 40% of total sales for each month.

Let's begin by calculating the total sales for October and November. The question tells us that actual sales for the month ended September 30 were $30,000, and that sales are expected to increase by 7% over that in October and another 4% over October's sales in November:

$$\text{October total sales} = \text{September sales} \times 107\%$$

$$\text{October total sales} = \$30,000 \times 107\%$$
$$= \$32,100$$

$$\text{November total sales} = \text{October sales} \times 104\%$$

$$\text{November total sales} = \$32,100 \times 104\%$$
$$= \$33,384$$

So we begin to build our sales budget with these data:

MOVA COMPANY
Sales Budget
Two Months Ended November 30

	October	November	Total
Cash sales, 60%			
Credit sales, 40%			
Total sales	$32,100	$33,384	

Now we work backwards to calculate the split between cash and credit sales for each month. In this case, cash sales are 60% of total sales and credit sales are 40% of total sales for the current months:

$$
\begin{aligned}
\text{Cash sales} &= \text{Total sales} \times 60\% \\
\text{October cash sales} &= \$32,100 \times 60\% \\
&= \$19,260 \\
\text{November cash sales} &= \$33,384 \times 60\% \\
&= \$20,030.40 \text{ (rounded to \$20,030)} \\[6pt]
\text{Credit sales} &= \text{Total sales} \times 40\% \\
\text{October credit sales} &= \$32,100 \times 40\% \\
&= \$12,840 \\
\text{November credit sales} &= \$33,384 \times 40\% \\
&= \$13,353.60 \text{ (rounded to \$13,354)}
\end{aligned}
$$

Following is the completed sales budget:

MOVA COMPANY
Sales Budget
Two Months Ended November 30

	October	November	Total
Cash sales, 60%	$19,260	$20,030	$39,290
Credit sales, 40%	12,840	13,354	26,194
Total sales	$32,100	$33,384	$65,484

The calculations give us a total sales budget for October and November of $65,484, with 60% of that ($39,290) from cash and 40% ($26,194) from credit.

Because the sales budget calculates values that you will use when preparing other budgets, it is always a good idea to check your work. These calculations can be performed in a number of ways. Here is one alternative:

$$
\begin{aligned}
\text{October total sales} &= \text{Previous month's sales} \times 107\% \\
&= \$30{,}000 \times 107\% \\
&= \$32{,}100
\end{aligned}
$$

$$
\begin{aligned}
\text{October cash sales} &= \text{October expected sales} \times 60\% \\
&= \$32{,}100 \times 60\% \\
&= \$19{,}260
\end{aligned}
$$

$$
\begin{aligned}
\text{October credit sales} &= \text{October expected sales} \times 40\% \\
&= \$32{,}100 \times 40\% \\
&= \$12{,}840
\end{aligned}
$$

$$
\begin{aligned}
\text{November total sales} &= \text{Previous month's sales} \times 104\% \\
&= \$32{,}100 \times 104\% \\
&= \$33{,}384
\end{aligned}
$$

$$
\begin{aligned}
\text{November cash sales} &= \text{November expected sales} \times 60\% \\
&= \$33{,}384 \times 60\% \\
&= \$20{,}030 \text{ (rounded)}
\end{aligned}
$$

$$
\begin{aligned}
\text{November credit sales} &= \text{November expected sales} \times 40\% \\
&= \$33{,}384 \times 40\% \\
&= \$13{,}354 \text{ (rounded)}
\end{aligned}
$$

2 Understand the components of the master budget

3 Prepare an operating budget-merchandiser

b. Inventory, purchases, and cost of goods sold budget

Part 1	**Part 2**	Part 3	Part 4	Demo Doc Complete

The inventory, purchases, and cost of goods sold budget statement takes the following format:

> Cost of goods sold
> + Desired ending inventory
> = Total inventory required
> − Beginning inventory
> = Purchases

So we first calculate the cost of goods sold. We know from the question that cost of goods sold is expected to be 60% of total sales for the period. From the sales budget, we know that total sales for October are expected to be $32,100, and total sales for November are expected to be $33,384. So we can calculate cost of goods sold as follows:

$$\text{Cost of goods sold} = 60\% \text{ of budgeted sales from the sales budget}$$
$$\text{October} = \$32,100 \times 60\%$$
$$= \$19,260$$
$$\text{November} = \$33,384 \times 60\%$$
$$= \$20,030 \text{ (rounded)}$$

So here is our budget so far:

MOVA COMPANY
Inventory, Purchases, and Cost of Goods Sold Budget
Two Months Ended November 30

	October	November
Cost of goods sold	$19,260	$20,030
+ Desired ending inventory		
= Total inventory required		
− Beginning inventory		
= Purchases		

Next, we need to add the desired ending inventory for each month. The question states that the company does not want inventory to fall below $4,000 plus 10% of cost of goods sold for the next month. In order to calculate the desired ending inventory for November, we need to know the cost of goods sold for December. The question tells us that December's sales are expected to be $35,000. Returning to our calculation for cost of goods sold:

$$\text{Cost of goods sold} = 60\% \text{ of budgeted sales from the sales budget}$$
$$\text{December} = \$35,000 \times 60\%$$
$$= \$21,000$$

Desired ending inventory is now calculated as follows:

$$\text{Desired ending inventory} = [\$4,000 + (10\% \text{ of cost of goods sold for the next month})]$$
$$\text{October} = \$4,000 + (10\% \times 20,030)$$
$$= \$6,003$$
$$\text{November} = \$4,000 + (10\% \times 21,000)$$
$$= \$6,100$$

We can now calculate the total ending inventory required:

MOVA COMPANY
Inventory, Purchases, and Cost of Goods Sold Budget
Two Months Ended November 30

	October	November
Cost of goods sold	$19,260	$20,030
+ Desired ending inventory	6,003	6,100
= Total inventory required	$25,263	$26,130
– Beginning inventory		
= Purchases		

Beginning inventory is equal to the previous month's desired ending inventory. We are told in the question that the inventory on September 30 is $6,000, so this amount becomes October's beginning inventory. Once we determine beginning inventory, we subtract it from the total inventory required to determine total purchases for the period:

MOVA COMPANY
Inventory, Purchases, and Cost of Goods Sold Budget
Two Months Ended November 30

	October	November
Cost of goods sold	$19,260	$20,030
+ Desired ending inventory	6,003	6,100
= Total inventory required	$25,263	$26,130
– Beginning inventory	6,000	6,003
= Purchases	$19,263	$20,127

2 Understand the components of the master budget

3 Prepare an operating budget-merchandiser

c. **Operating expense budget**

Part 1	Part 2	**Part 3**	Part 4	Demo Doc Complete

With the exception of the sales commission, which we know from the question to be 10% of sales, all expenses remain constant between October and November, as follows:

MOVA COMPANY
Operating Expense Budget
Two Months Ended November 30

	October	November	Total
Sales commission			
Rent expense	$1,000	$1,000	$2,000
Insurance expense	400	400	800
Depreciation expense	1,200	1,200	2,400
Utility expense	800	800	1,600
Total operating expense			

The only calculation to perform here is sales commission. We can compute sales commissions for October and November using the respective sales computations ($32,100 and $33,384) from the sales budget:

$$\text{Sales commission} = \text{Expected sales} \times 10\%$$
$$\text{October sales commission} = \$32,100 \times 10\%$$
$$= \$3,210$$

$$\text{November sales commision} = \$33,384 \times 10\%$$
$$= \$3,338.40 \text{ (rounded to } \$3,338)$$

Here is our completed operating expense budget for October and November:

MOVA COMPANY
Operating Expense Budget
Two Months Ended November 30

	October	November	Total
Sales commission	$3,210	$3,338	$ 6,548
Rent expense	1,000	1,000	2,000
Insurance expense	400	400	800
Depreciation expense	1,200	1,200	2,400
Utility expense	800	800	1,600
Total operating expense	$6,610	$6,738	$13,348

d. Budgeted income statement

Part 1	Part 2	Part 3	**Part 4**	Demo Doc Complete

2 Understand the components of the master budget

3 Prepare an operating budget-merchandiser

The results of the budgets you have created so far are carried over into the fourth element: the budgeted income statement.

Sales revenue is traced from the sales budget in part **a**.

Cost of goods sold is traced from the inventory, purchases, and cost of goods sold budget in part **b**.

We compute gross profit by subtracting the cost of goods sold from sales revenue:

MOVA COMPANY Budgeted Income Statement Two Months Ended November 30			
	October	November	Total
Sales revenue	$32,100	$33,384	$65,484
Cost of goods sold	19,260	20,030	39,290
Gross profit	12,840	13,354	26,194
Operating expenses			
Net income			

Operating expenses are traced from the operating expenses budget from part c.

We compute net income (loss) by subtracting operating expenses from gross profit. Our completed budgeted income statement looks this way:

MOVA COMPANY Budgeted Income Statement Two Months Ended November 30			
	October	November	Total
Sales revenue	$32,100	$33,384	$65,484
Cost of goods sold	19,260	20,030	39,290
Gross profit	12,840	13,354	26,194
Operating expenses	6,610	6,738	13,348
Net income	$ 6,230	$ 6,616	$12,846

For the period, our totals are as follows:

MOVA COMPANY Budgeted Income Statement Two Months Ending November 30		
Sales revenue		$65,484
Cost of goods sold		39,290
Gross profit		26,194
Operating expenses:		
Salary and commissions	$6,548	
Depreciation expense	2,400	
Rent expense	2,000	
Utility expense	1,600	
Insurance expense	800	13,348
Operating income		12,846

Part 1	Part 2	Part 3	Part 4	Demo Doc Complete

8

Flexible Budgets and Standard Costs

Learning Objectives/Success Keys

1 Prepare a flexible budget for the income statement

2 Prepare an income statement performance report

3 Identify the benefits of standard costs and learn how to set standards

4 Compute standard cost variances for direct materials and direct labor

5 Analyze manufacturing overhead in a standard cost system

6 Record transactions at standard cost and prepare a standard cost income statement

Suppose you bought soft drinks for a party. Your budget was $30, but you actually spent $35. You need to stay within your budget in the future. It would be helpful to know *why* you spent more than the $30 budget. Here are some possibilities:

1. If each case of drinks costs more than the budget, then you might

   - find a cheaper price at a place like **Wal-mart**, or wait for the drinks to go on sale.
   - buy less-expensive store-brand drinks.

2. If you bought a larger quantity of soft drinks than you budgeted, why did you need this larger quantity?

- If too many guests came to the party, next time you can restrict the invitation list.

- If each guest drank more than you budgeted, perhaps you can cut per-guest consumption, start the party later, end it earlier, or reduce the salty snacks.

3. If the budget for soft drinks was too low, you may need to increase the budget.

This chapter builds on your knowledge of budgeting. A budget variance is just the difference between an actual amount and a budgeted figure. This chapter shows how managers use variances to operate a business. It is important to know *why* actual costs differ from the budget. That will enable you to identify problems and decide what action to take.

In this chapter, you will learn how to figure out *why* actual results differ from your budget. This is the first step in correcting problems. You will also learn to use another management tool—standard costing.

How Managers Use Flexible Budgets

1 Prepare a flexible budget for the income statement

Let us revisit Smart Touch Learning, Inc. At the beginning of the year, Smart Touch's managers prepared a master budget. The master budget is a **static budget**, which means that it is prepared for only *one* level of sales volume. The static budget does not change after it is developed.

Exhibit 8-1 shows that Smart Touch's actual operating income for the month of June is $16,000. This is $4,000 higher than expected from the static budget. This is a $4,000 favorable variance for June operating income. A **variance** is the difference between an actual amount and the budget. The variances in the third column of Exhibit 8-1 are as follows:

- Favorable (F) if an actual amount increases operating income
- Unfavorable (U) if an actual amount decreases operating income

EXHIBIT 8-1 | **Actual Results Versus Static Budget**

SMART TOUCH LEARNING, INC.
Comparison of Actual Results with Static Budget
Month Ended June 30, 2011

	Actual Results	Static Budget	Variance
Output units	10,000	8,000	2,000 F
Sales revenue	$ 121,000	$ 96,000	$ 25,000 F
Cost	(105,000)	(84,000)	(21,000) U
Operating income	$ 16,000	$ 12,000	$ 4,000 F

Smart Touch Learning's variance for operating income is favorable because Smart Touch sold 10,000 learning DVDs rather than the 8,000 DVDs it budgeted to sell during June. But there is more to this story. Smart Touch needs a flexible budget to show *why* operating income was favorable during June. Let us see how to prepare and use a flexible budget.

What Is a Flexible Budget?

The report in Exhibit 8-1 is hard to analyze because the static budget is based on 8,000 DVDs, but the actual results are for 10,000 DVDs. This report raises more questions than it answers—for example,

- why did the $21,000 unfavorable cost variance occur?
- did workers waste materials?
- did the cost of materials suddenly increase?
- how much of the additional cost arose because Smart Touch sold 10,000 rather than 8,000 DVDs?

We need a flexible budget to help answer these questions.

A **flexible budget** summarizes costs and revenues for several different volume levels within a relevant range. Flexible budgets separate variable costs from fixed costs; it is the variable costs that put the "*flex*" in the flexible budget. To create a flexible budget, you need to know the following:

- Budgeted selling price per unit
- Variable cost per unit
- Total fixed costs
- Different volume levels within the relevant range

Exhibit 8-2 is a flexible budget for Smart Touch's revenues and costs that shows what will happen if sales reach 5,000, 8,000, or 10,000 DVDs during June. The budgeted sale price per DVD is $12. Budgeted variable costs (such as direct materials and direct labor) are $8 per DVD, and budgeted fixed costs total $20,000. The formula for total cost is as follows:

$$\text{Total cost} = \left(\begin{array}{c} \text{Number of} \\ \text{output units} \end{array} \times \begin{array}{c} \text{Variable cost} \\ \text{per output unit} \end{array} \right) + \text{Total fixed cost}$$

EXHIBIT 8-2 | **Flexible Budget**

SMART TOUCH LEARNING, INC.
Flexible Budget
Month Ended June 30, 2011

		Flexible Budget per Output Units	Output Units (DVDs sold)		
			5,000	8,000	10,000
Sales revenue		$12	$60,000	$96,000	$120,000
Variable costs		$ 8	40,000	64,000	80,000
Fixed costs*			20,000	20,000	20,000
Total costs			60,000	84,000	100,000
Operating income			$ 0	$12,000	$ 20,000

*Fixed costs are usually given as a total amount rather than as a cost per unit.

Notice in Exhibit 8-2 that sales revenue and variable costs increase as more DVDs are sold. But fixed costs remain constant regardless of the number of DVDs sold within the relevant range of 5,000–10,000 DVDs. Remember: *The cost formula applies only to a specific relevant range.* Why? Because fixed costs and the variable cost per DVD may change outside this range. In our example, Smart Touch's relevant range is 5,000–10,000 DVDs. If the company sells 12,000 DVDs it will have to rent additional equipment, so fixed costs will exceed $20,000. Smart Touch will also have to pay workers for overtime pay, so the variable cost per DVD will be more than $8.

Stop & Think...

Assume you are a waiter or waitress. Each night, you cannot be sure how much you will receive in tips from your customers. The more tips you receive, the more income you have to spend on gas, CDs, or possibly saving for a vacation. Informally, you probably figure in your head each night how much you receive in average tips and of that amount, how much you want to save or spend. The flexible budget is just a formalization of that same process for a business.

Using the Flexible Budget: Why Do Actual Results Differ from the Static Budget?

2 Prepare an income statement performance report

It is not enough to know that a variance occurred. That is like knowing you have a fever. The doctor needs to know *why* your temperature is above normal.

Managers must know *why* a variance occurred in order to pinpoint problems and take corrective action. As you can see in Exhibit 8-1, the static budget underestimated both sales and total costs. The variance in Exhibit 8-1 is called a static budget variance because actual activity differed from what was expected in the static budget. To develop more useful information, managers divide the static budget variance into two broad categories:

- **Sales volume variance**—arises because the number of units actually sold differed from the number of units on which the static budget was based.
- **Flexible budget variance**—arises because the company had more or less revenue, or more or less cost, than expected for the *actual* level of output.

Exhibit 8-3 diagrams these variances.

EXHIBIT 8-3 | **The Static Budget Variance: The Sales Volume Variance and the Flexible Budget Variance**

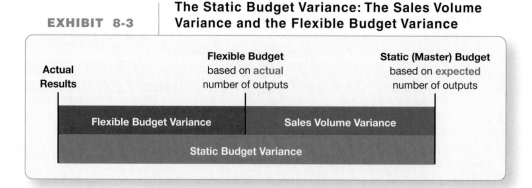

Following are the formulas for computing the two variances:

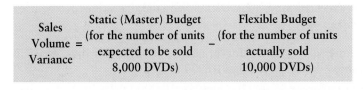

| Sales Volume Variance = | Static (Master) Budget (for the number of units expected to be sold 8,000 DVDs) | − | Flexible Budget (for the number of units actually sold 10,000 DVDs) |

| Flexible Budget Variance = | Flexible Budget (for the number of units actually sold 10,000 DVDs) | − | Actual Results (for the number of units actually sold 10,000 DVDs) |

We have seen that Smart Touch budgeted for 8,000 DVDs during June. Actual production was 10,000 DVDs. We will need to compute a sales volume variance for Smart Touch, and there may also be a flexible budget variance. Exhibit 8-4 is Smart Touch's income statement performance report for June.

EXHIBIT 8-4 | **Income Statement Performance Report**

SMART TOUCH LEARNING, INC.
Income Statement Performance Report
Month Ended June 30, 2011

	1 Actual Results at Actual Prices	2 (1) − (3) Flexible Budget Variance	3 Flexible Budget for Actual Number of Output Units*	4 (3) − (5) Sales Volume Variance	5 Static (Master) Budget*
Output Units	10,000	0	10,000	2,000 F	8,000
Sales revenue	$121,000	$1,000 F	$120,000	$24,000 F	$96,000
Variable costs	83,000	3,000 U	80,000	16,000 U	64,000
Fixed costs	22,000	2,000 U	20,000	0	20,000
Total costs	105,000	5,000 U	100,000	16,000 U	84,000
Operating income	$ 16,000	$4,000 U	$ 20,000	$ 8,000 F	$12,000

Flexible budget variance, $4,000 U   Sales volume variance, $8,000 F

Static budget variance, $4,000 F

*From Exhibit 8-2 for 10,000 output units

Column 1 of the performance report shows the actual results—based on the 10,000 DVDs actually sold. Operating income was $16,000 for June.

Column 3 is Smart Touch's flexible budget for the 10,000 DVDs actually sold. Operating income should have been $20,000.

Column 5 gives the static budget for the 8,000 DVDs expected to be sold for June. Smart Touch budgeted to earn $12,000.

The budget variances appear in columns 2 and 4 of the exhibit. Let us begin with the static budget in column 5. These data come from Exhibit 8-2.

The flexible budget for 10,000 units is in column 3. The differences between the static budget and the flexible budget—column 4—arise only because Smart Touch sold 10,000 DVDs rather than 8,000 during June. Column 4 shows the sales volume variances. Operating income is favorable by $8,000 because Smart Touch sold more DVDs than it planned to sell (10,000 sold rather than the 8,000 budgeted).

Column 1 of Exhibit 8-4 gives the actual results for June—10,000 DVDs and operating income of $16,000. Operating income is $4,000 less than Smart Touch would have expected for 10,000 DVDs. Why did operating income not measure up to the flexible budget?

- It was not because the selling price of DVDs took a dive. Sales revenue was $1,000 more than expected for 10,000 DVDs.
- Variable costs were $3,000 too high for 10,000 DVDs.
- Fixed costs were $2,000 too high for 10,000 DVDs.

Overall, expenses rose by $5,000 above the flexible budget, while sales revenue only increased by $1,000.

The static budget is developed *before* the period. The performance report in Exhibit 8-4 is developed after the *end* of the period. Why? Because flexible budgets used in performance reports are based on the actual number of outputs, and the actual outputs are not known until the end of the period.

Decision Guidelines

FLEXIBLE BUDGETS

You and your roommate have started a business that prints T-shirts (for example, for school and student organizations). How can you use flexible budgets to plan and control your costs?

Decision	Guidelines
• How do you estimate sales revenue, costs, and profits over your relevant range?	Prepare a set of flexible budgets for different sales levels, as in Exhibit 8-2.
• How do you prepare a flexible budget for total costs?	$$\text{Total cost} = \left(\begin{array}{c} \text{Number} \\ \text{of T-shirts} \end{array} \times \begin{array}{c} \text{Variable cost} \\ \text{per T-shirt} \end{array} \right) + \begin{array}{c} \text{Fixed} \\ \text{cost} \end{array}$$
• How do you use budgets to help control costs?	Prepare an income statement performance report, as in Exhibit 8-4.
• On which output level is the budget based?	Static (master) budget—*expected* number of T-shirts, estimated before the period Flexible budget—*actual* number of T-shirts, not known until the end of the period
• Why does your actual income differ from budgeted income?	Prepare an income statement performance report comparing actual results, flexible budget for the actual number of T-shirts sold, and static (master) budget, as in Exhibit 8-4.

• How much of the difference arises because the actual number of T-shirts sold does not equal budgeted sales?	Compute the sales volume variance (SVV) by comparing the flexible budget with the static budget.
	 • Favorable SVV—
	   • Actual number of T-shirts sold > Expected number of T-shirts sold
	 • Unfavorable SVV—
	   • Actual number of T-shirts sold < Expected number of T-shirts sold

• How much of the difference occurs because revenues and costs are not what they should have been for the actual number of T-shirts sold?	Compute the flexible budget variance (FBV) by comparing actual results with the flexible budget.
	 • Favorable FBV—
	   • Actual sales revenue > Flexible budget sales revenue
	   • Actual costs < Flexible budget costs
	 • Unfavorable FBV—
	   • Actual sales revenue < Flexible budget sales revenue
	   • Actual costs > Flexible budget costs

• What actions can you take to avoid an unfavorable sales volume variance?	• Design more attractive T-shirts to increase demand. • Provide marketing incentives to increase number of T-shirts sold.
• What actions can you take to avoid an unfavorable flexible budget variance?	• Avoid an unfavorable flexible budget variance for *sales revenue* by maintaining (not discounting) your selling price. • Avoid an unfavorable flexible budget variance for *costs* by controlling variable costs, such as the cost of the T-shirts, dye, and labor, and by controlling fixed costs.

Summary Problem 1

Exhibit 8-4 shows that Smart Touch sold 10,000 DVDs during June. Now assume that Smart Touch sold 7,000 DVDs (instead of 10,000) and that the actual sale price averaged $12.50 per DVD. Actual variable costs were $57,400, and actual fixed costs were $19,000.

Requirements

1. Prepare a revised income statement performance report using Exhibit 8-4 as a guide.
2. As the company owner, which employees would you praise or reprimand after you analyze this performance report?

Solution

Requirement 1

SMART TOUCH LEARNING, INC.
Income Statement Performance Report—Revised
Month Ended June 30, 2011

	1 Actual Results at Actual Prices	2 (1) – (3) Flexible Budget Variance	3 Flexible Budget for Actual Number of Output Units*	4 (3) – (5) Sales Volume Variance	5 Static (Master) Budget
Output Units (DVDs sold)	7,000	0	7,000	1,000 U	8,000
Sales revenue	$87,500	$3,500 F	$84,000	$12,000 U	$96,000
Variable costs	57,400	1,400 U	56,000	8,000 F	64,000
Fixed costs	19,000	1,000 F	20,000	—	20,000
Total costs	76,400	400 U	76,000	8,000 F	84,000
Operating income	$11,100	$3,100 F	$ 8,000	$ 4,000 U	$12,000

Flexible budget variance, $3,100 F   Sales volume variance, $4,000 U

Static budget variance, $900 U

*The Flexible Budget amounts were figured from data provided in Exhibit 8-2, adjusted to the 7,000 units of output

Requirement 2

As the company owner, you should determine the *causes* of the variances before praising or reprimanding employees. It is especially important to determine whether the variance is due to factors the manager can control. For example,

- the unfavorable sales volume variance could be due to an ineffective sales staff. Or it could be due to a long period of snow that made it difficult for employees to get to work and brought work to a standstill.
- the $1,000 favorable flexible budget variance for fixed costs could be due to an employee finding less expensive equipment. Or the savings might have come from delaying a needed overhaul of equipment that could increase the company's costs in the long run.

Smart managers use variances to raise questions and direct attention, not to fix blame.

Standard Costing

Most companies use **standard costs** to develop their flexible budgets. Think of a standard cost as a budget for a single unit. For example, Smart Touch Learning's standard variable cost is $8 per DVD (Exhibit 8-2). This $8 variable cost includes the standard cost of inputs like the direct materials, direct labor, and variable overhead needed for one DVD.

In a standard cost system, each input has both a quantity standard and a price standard. Smart Touch has a standard for the following:

- Amount of vinyl for making the DVDs
- Price it pays per square foot of vinyl (this determines the price standard)

Let us see how managers set these price and quantity standards.

3 Identify the benefits of standard costs and learn how to set standards

Price Standards

The price standard for direct materials starts with the base purchase cost of each unit of inventory. Accountants help managers set a price standard for materials after considering early-pay discounts, freight in, and receiving costs.

World-class businesses demand continuous reductions in costs. This can be achieved several ways. You can work with suppliers to cut their costs. You can use the Internet to solicit price quotes from suppliers around the world, and you can share information.

For direct labor, accountants work with human resource managers to determine standard labor rates. They must consider basic pay rates, payroll taxes, and fringe benefits. Job descriptions reveal the level of experience needed for each task.

Accountants work with production managers to estimate manufacturing overhead costs. Production managers identify an appropriate allocation base such as direct labor hours or direct labor cost, as you learned in Chapter 2. Accountants then compute the standard overhead rates. Exhibit 8-5 summarizes the setting of standard costs.

EXHIBIT 8-5 | **Summary of Standard Setting Issues**

	Price Standard	Quantity Standard
Direct Materials	Responsibility: Purchasing manager Factors: Purchase price, discounts, delivery requirements, credit policy	Responsibility: Production manager and engineers Factors: Product specifications, spoilage, production scheduling
Direct Labor	Responsibility: Human resource managers Factors: Wage rate based on experience requirements, payroll taxes, fringe benefits	Responsibility: Production manager and engineers Factors: Time requirements for the production level of experience needed
Manufacturing Overhead	Responsibility: Production managers Factors: Nature and amount of resources needed for support activities (e.g., moving materials, maintaining equipment, and inspecting output)	

Application

Let us see how Smart Touch might determine its cost standards for materials, labor, and overhead.

The manager in charge of purchasing for Smart Touch indicates that the purchase price, net of discounts, is $1.90 per square foot of vinyl. Delivery, receiving, and inspection add an average of $0.10 per square foot. Smart Touch's hourly wage for workers is $8 and payroll taxes and fringe benefits total $2.50 per direct labor hour. Variable and fixed overhead will total $6,400 and $9,600, respectively, and overhead is allocated based on 3,200 estimated direct-labor hours.

Requirement

Compute Smart Touch Learning's cost standards for direct materials, direct labor, and overhead.

Answer

Direct materials price standard for vinyl:

Purchase price, net of discounts...	$1.90 per square foot
Delivery, receiving, and inspection	0.10 per square foot
Total standard cost per square foot of vinyl.........................	$2.00 per square foot

Direct labor price (or rate) standard:

Hourly wage	$ 8.00 per direct labor hour
Payroll taxes and fringe benefits.............................	2.50 per direct labor hour
Total standard cost per direct labor hour................	$10.50 per direct labor hour

Variable overhead price (or rate) standard:

$$\frac{\text{Estimated variable overhead cost}}{\text{Estimated quantity of allocation base}}$$

$$= \frac{\$6,400}{3,200 \text{ direct labor hours}}$$

$$= \$2.00 \text{ per direct labor hour}$$

Fixed overhead price (or rate) standard:

$$\frac{\text{Estimated fixed overhead cost}}{\text{Estimated quantity of allocation base}}$$

$$= \frac{\$9,600}{3,200 \text{ direct labor hours}}$$

$$= \$3.00 \text{ per direct labor hour}$$

Quantity Standards

Production managers and engineers set direct material and direct labor *quantity standards*. To set its labor standards, **Westinghouse Air Brake's** Chicago plant analyzed every moment in the production of the brakes.

To eliminate unnecessary work, **Westinghouse** rearranged machines in tight U-shaped cells so that work could flow better. Workers no longer had to move parts all over the plant floor, as illustrated in the following diagram.

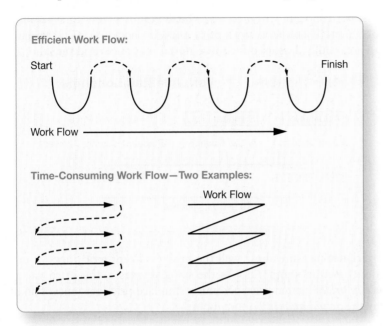

Westinghouse conducted time-and-motion studies to streamline various tasks. For example, the plant installed a conveyer at waist height to minimize bending and lifting. The result? Workers slashed one element of standard time by 90%.

Companies from the **Ritz-Carlton** to **Federal Express** develop quantity standards based on "best practices." This is often called *benchmarking*. The *best practice* may be an internal benchmark from other plants or divisions within the company or it may be an external benchmark from other companies. Internal benchmarks are easy to obtain, but managers can also purchase external benchmark data. For example, **Riverside Hospital** in Columbus, Ohio, can compare its cost of performing an appendectomy with the "best practice" cost developed by a consulting firm that compares many different hospitals' costs for the same procedure.

Why Do Companies Use Standard Costs?

U.S. surveys show that more than 80% of responding companies use standard costing. Over half of responding companies in the United Kingdom, Ireland, Sweden, and Japan use standard costing. Why? Standard costing helps managers:

- Prepare the budget
- Set target levels of performance
- Identify performance standards
- Set sales prices of products and services
- Decrease accounting costs

Standard cost systems might appear to be expensive. Indeed, the company must invest up front to develop the standards. But standards can save accounting costs. It is cheaper to value inventories at standard rather than actual costs. With standard costs, accountants avoid the LIFO, FIFO, or average-cost computations.

Variance Analysis

Once we establish standard costs, we can use the standards to assign costs to production. At least once a year, we will compare our actual production costs to the standard costs to locate variances. Exhibit 8-6 shows how to separate total variances for materials and labor into price and efficiency (quantity) variances. Study this exhibit carefully. It is used for the materials variances and the labor variances.

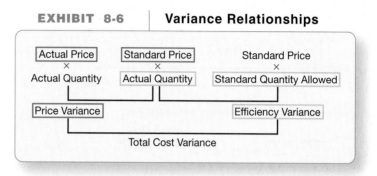

EXHIBIT 8-6 | **Variance Relationships**

A **price variance** measures how well the business keeps unit prices of material and labor inputs within standards. As the name suggests, the price variance is the *difference in prices* (actual price per unit − standard price per unit) of an input, multiplied by the *actual quantity* of the input:

Price Variance = (Actual Price × Actual Quantity) − (Standard Price × Actual Quantity)

Or, Price Variance = (Actual Price − Standard Price) × Actual Quantity

$$= (AP - SP) \times AQ$$

An **efficiency or quantity variance** measures how well the business uses its materials or human resources. The efficiency variance is the difference in quantities (actual quantity of input used − standard quantity of input allowed for the actual number of outputs) multiplied by the standard price per unit of the input:

Efficiency Variance = (Standard Price × Actual Quantity) − (Standard Price × Standard Quantity)

Or, Efficiency Variance = (Actual Quantity − Standard Quantity) × Standard Price

$$= (AQ - SQ) \times SP$$

Exhibit 8-7 illustrates these variances and emphasizes two points.

EXHIBIT 8-7 | **The Relationships Among Price, Efficiency, Flexible Budget, Sales Volume, and Static Budget Variances**

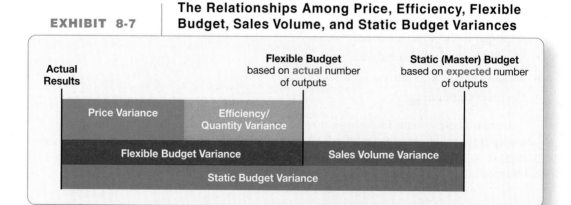

- First, the price and efficiency variances add up to the flexible budget variance.
- Second, static budgets like column 5 of Exhibit 8-4 play no role in the price and efficiency variances.

The static budget is used only to compute the sales volume variance—never to compute the flexible budget variance or the price and efficiency cost variances for materials and labor.

Stop & Think...

When you go to the gas station, do you fill up your car? How many miles per gallon does your car normally get? What is the usual price per gallon that you pay for gas? Let us assume you normally pay $4.00 per gallon and buy 10 gallons of gas. That is your standard cost for gas for your car. But what if the next time you need to fill up, you have to pay $4.25 per gallon, but you only have to buy 9.8 gallons of gas? The price variance is unfavorable because it is $0.25 more per gallon, but your car is using the gas more efficiently because you used .2 gallons less than normal.

How Smart Touch Uses Standard Costing: Analyzing the Flexible Budget Variance

Let us return to our Smart Touch Learning example. Exhibit 8-4 showed that the main cause for concern at Smart Touch is the $4,000 unfavorable flexible budget variance for total costs. The first step in identifying the causes of the cost variance is to identify the variable and fixed costs, as shown in Panel A of Exhibit 8-8.

4 Compute standard cost variances for direct materials and direct labor

Carefully study Exhibit 8-8 shown on the next page. Panel B shows how to compute the flexible budget amounts. Panel C shows how to compute actual materials and labor costs. Trace the following:

- Flexible budget amounts from Panel B to column (2) of Panel A
- Actual costs from Panel C to column (1) of Panel A

Column 3 of Panel A gives the flexible budget variances for direct materials and direct labor. For now, focus on materials and labor. We will cover overhead later.

Direct Material Variances

Direct Materials Price Variance

Let us investigate the $2,800 unfavorable variance for direct materials. Recall that the direct materials standard price was $2.00 per square foot, and 10,000 square feet are needed for 10,000 DVDs (1 square foot per DVD × 10,000 DVDs). The actual price of materials was $1.90 per square foot, and 12,000 square feet were actually used to make 10,000 DVDs. Using the formula, the materials price variance is $1,200 favorable. The calculation follows:

$$
\begin{aligned}
\text{Materials Price Variance} &= (AP - SP) \times AQ \\
&= (\$1.90 \text{ per square foot} - \$2.00 \text{ per square foot}) \times 12,000 \text{ square feet} \\
&= -\$0.10 \text{ per square foot} \times 12,000 \text{ square feet} \\
&= \$1,200 \text{ F}
\end{aligned}
$$

The $1,200 direct materials price variance is *favorable*, because the purchasing manager spent $0.10 *less* per square foot of vinyl than budgeted ($1.90 actual price − $2.00 standard price).

EXHIBIT 8-8 | **Data for Standard Costing Example**

PANEL A—Comparison of Actual Results with Flexible Budget for 10,000 DVDs

SMART TOUCH LEARNING, INC.
Data for Standard Costing Example
Month Ended June 30, 2011

	Actual Results at Actual Prices	Flexible Budget for 10,000 DVDs#	Flexible Budget Variance
Variable costs:			
Direct materials	$ 22,800*	$ 20,000†	$2,800 U
Direct labor	41,800*	42,000†	200 F
Variable overhead	9,000	8,000†	1,000 U
Marketing and administrative costs	9,400	10,000	600 F
Total variable costs	83,000	80,000	3,000 U
Fixed costs:			
Fixed overhead	12,300	9,600‡	2,700 U
Marketing and administrative expense	9,700	10,400	700 F
Total fixed costs	22,000	20,000	2,000 U
Total costs	$105,000	$100,000	$5,000 U

*amounts from Exhibit 8-2 for 10,000 units
*See Panel C.
†See Panel B.
‡Fixed overhead was budgeted at $9,600 per month (Application Answer on page 372).

PANEL B—Computation of Flexible Budget for Direct Materials, Direct Labor, and Variable Overhead for 7,000 DVDs—Based on Standard Costs

	(1) Standard Quantity of Inputs Allowed for 10,000 DVDs	(2) Standard Price per Unit of Input*	(3) (1) × (2) Flexible Budget for 10,000 DVDs
Direct materials	1 square foot per DVD × 10,000 DVDs = 10,000 square feet	$ 2.00	$20,000
Direct labor	.40 hours per DVD × 10,000 DVDs = 4,000 hours	$10.50	42,000
Variable overhead	.40 hours per DVD × 10,000 DVDs = 4,000 hours	$ 2.00	8,000

*amounts from page 372

PANEL C—Computation of Actual Costs for Direct Materials and Direct Labor for 10,000 DVDs

	(1) Actual Quantity of Inputs Used for 10,000 DVDs	(2) Actual Price per Unit of Input	(3) (1) × (2) Actual Cost for 10,000 DVDs
Direct materials	12,000 square feet actually used	$1.90 actual cost/square foot	$22,800
Direct labor	3,800 hours actually used	$11.00 actual cost/hour	41,800

Direct Materials Efficiency Variance

Now let us see what portion of the unfavorable materials variance was due to the quantity used.

The standard quantity of inputs is the *quantity that should have been used* for the actual output. For Smart Touch, the *standard quantity of inputs (vinyl) that workers should have used for the actual number of outputs* (10,000 DVDs) is 1 square foot of vinyl per DVD, or a total of 10,000 square feet. Thus, the direct materials efficiency variance is as follows:

> Direct Materials Efficiency Variance = (AQ − SQ) × SP
>
> = (12,000 square feet − 10,000 square feet) × $2.00 per square foot
>
> = + 2,000 square feet × $2.00 per square foot
>
> = $4,000 U

The $4,000 direct materials efficiency variance is *unfavorable*, because workers used 2,000 *more* square feet of vinyl than they planned (budgeted) to use for 10,000 DVDs.

Summary of Direct Material Variances   Exhibit 8-9 summarizes how Smart Touch splits the $2,800 net unfavorable direct materials flexible budget variance into price and efficiency effects.

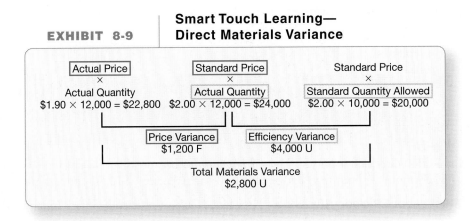

EXHIBIT 8-9 | **Smart Touch Learning— Direct Materials Variance**

In summary, Smart Touch spent $2,800 more than it should have for vinyl because

- a good price for the vinyl increased profits by $1,200, but
- inefficient use of the vinyl reduced profits by $4,000.

Let us review who is responsible for each of these variances and consider why each variance may have occurred.

1. The purchasing manager is in the best position to explain the favorable price variance. Smart Touch's purchasing manager may have negotiated a good price for vinyl.

2. The manager in charge of making DVDs can explain why workers used so much vinyl to make the 10,000 DVDs. Was the vinyl of lower quality? Did workers waste materials? Did their equipment malfunction? Smart Touch's top management needs this information to decide what corrective action to take.

These variances raise questions that can help pinpoint problems. But be careful! A favorable variance does not always mean that a manager did a good job, nor does an unfavorable variance mean that a manager did a bad job. Perhaps Smart Touch's purchasing manager got a lower price by purchasing inferior-quality materials. This would lead to waste and spoilage. If so, the purchasing manager's decision hurt the company. This illustrates why good managers

- use variances as a guide for investigation rather than merely to assign blame.
- investigate favorable as well as unfavorable variances.

Direct Labor Variances

Smart Touch uses a similar approach to analyze the direct labor flexible budget variance.

Why did Smart Touch spend $200 less on labor than it should have used for 10,000 DVDs? To answer this question, Smart Touch computes the labor price and efficiency variances, in exactly the same way as it did for direct materials. Recall that the standard price for direct labor is $10.50 per hour, and 4,000 hours were budgeted for 10,000 DVDs (.40 hours per DVD × 10,000 DVDs). But actual direct labor cost was $11.00 per hour, and it took 3,800 hours to make 10,000 DVDs.

Direct Labor Price Variance

Using the formula, the direct labor price variance was $1,900 unfavorable. The calculation follows:

$$\text{Direct Labor Price Variance} = (\text{AP} - \text{SP}) \times \text{AH}$$
$$= (\$11.00 - \$10.50) \times \$3,800 \text{ hours}$$
$$= \$1,900 \text{ U}$$

The $1,900 direct labor price variance is *unfavorable* because Smart Touch paid workers $0.50 *more* per hour than budgeted ($11.00 actual price – $10.50 standard price).

Direct Labor Efficiency Variance   Now let us see how efficiently Smart Touch used its labor. The *standard quantity of direct labor hours that workers should have used to make 10,000 DVDs* is .40 direct labor hours each or 4,000 total direct labor hours. Thus, the direct labor efficiency variance is as follows:

$$\text{Direct Labor Efficiency Variance} = (\text{AH} - \text{SH}) \times \text{SP}$$
$$= (3,800 \text{ hours} - 4,000 \text{ hours}) \times \$10.50 \text{ per hour}$$
$$= -200 \text{ hours} \times \$10.50$$
$$= \$2,100 \text{ F}$$

The $2,100 direct labor efficiency variance is *favorable* because laborers actually worked 200 *fewer* hours than the budget called for.

Summary of Direct Labor Variances   Exhibit 8-10 summarizes how Smart Touch computes the labor price and efficiency variances.

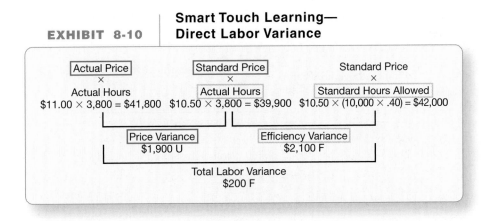

EXHIBIT 8-10 | **Smart Touch Learning—Direct Labor Variance**

The $200 favorable direct labor variance suggests that labor costs were close to expectations. But to manage Smart Touch's labor costs, we need to gain more insight:

- Smart Touch paid its employees an average of $11.00 per hour in June instead of the standard rate of $10.50—for an unfavorable price variance.
- Workers made 10,000 DVDs in 3,800 hours instead of the budgeted 4,000 hours—for a favorable efficiency variance.

This situation reveals a trade-off. Smart Touch hired more experienced (and thus more expensive) workers and had an unfavorable price variance. But the workers turned out more work than expected, and the strategy was successful. The overall effect on profits was favorable. This possibility reminds us that managers should take care in using variances to evaluate performance. Go slow, analyze the data, and then take action.

Manufacturing Overhead Variances

In this section of the chapter we use the terms *manufacturing overhead* and *overhead* interchangeably. The total overhead variance is the difference between

5 Analyze manufacturing overhead in a standard cost system

Actual overhead cost	and	Standard overhead allocated to production

Exhibit 8-8 shows that Smart Touch actually incurred $21,300 of overhead: $9,000 variable and $12,300 fixed. The next step is to see how Smart Touch allocates overhead in a standard cost system.

Allocating Overhead in a Standard Cost System

In a standard costing system, the manufacturing overhead allocated to production is as follows:

$$\text{Overhead allocated to production} = \text{(predetermined) Standard overhead rate} \times \text{Standard quantity of the allocation base allowed for } \textit{actual} \text{ output}$$

Let us begin by computing Smart Touch's standard overhead rate, as follows (data from page 372):

$$\begin{aligned}
\text{Standard overhead rate} &= \frac{\text{Budgeted manufacturing overhead cost}}{\text{Budgeted direct labor hours}} \\[6pt]
&= \frac{\text{Variable overhead + Fixed overhead}}{\text{Budgeted direct labor hours}} \\[6pt]
&= \frac{\$6,400 + \$9,600}{3,200 \text{ direct labor hours}} \\[6pt]
&= \frac{\$6,400}{3,200} + \frac{\$9,600}{3,200} \\[6pt]
&= \$2.00 \text{ variable} + \$3.00 \text{ fixed} \\[6pt]
&= \$5.00 \text{ per direct labor hour}
\end{aligned}$$

Now let us determine the standard quantity of direct labor hours that Smart Touch allowed for actual output (10,000 DVDs), as follows (data from Exhibit 8-8, Panel B):

$$\begin{aligned}
\text{Standard quantity of direct labor hours for actual output} &= .4 \text{ hours per DVD} \times 10,000 \text{ DVDs} \\[4pt]
&= 4,000 \text{ direct labor hours}
\end{aligned}$$

Thus, Smart Touch allocates the cost of overhead to production based on standard costs as follows:

$$\begin{aligned}
\textit{Standard} \text{ overhead allocated to production} &= \textit{Standard} \text{ overhead rate} \times \begin{array}{l} \textit{Standard} \text{ quantity of the allocation} \\ \text{base allowed for } \textit{actual} \text{ output} \end{array} \\[6pt]
&= \$5.00 \text{ per hour} \times 4,000 \text{ hours} \\[4pt]
&= \$20,000
\end{aligned}$$

Smart Touch computes its total overhead cost variance as follows:

$$\begin{aligned}
\text{Total overhead variance} &= \begin{array}{c}\text{Actual overhead cost}\\ \text{(Exhibit 8-8, Panel A)}\end{array} - \begin{array}{c}\text{Standard overhead allocated to production}\\ (\$4,000 \text{ hours} \times \$5.00 \text{ per hour})\end{array} \\[6pt]
&= \qquad \$21,300^* \qquad - \qquad \$20,000 \\[4pt]
&= \qquad \$1,300 \text{ U}
\end{aligned}$$

*Variable of $9,000 + fixed of $12,300 = $21,300

Smart Touch actually spent $1,300 more on overhead than it allocated to production. To see why this unfavorable variance occurred, Smart Touch "drills down" by splitting the total overhead variance into two components:

- The overhead flexible budget variance
- The production volume variance

Exhibit 8-11 shows the computation of the overhead variances, and the discussion that follows explains them.

EXHIBIT 8-11 | **Manufacturing Overhead Variances**

SMART TOUCH LEARNING, INC.
Manufacturing Overhead Variances
Month Ended June 30, 2011

	(1) Actual Overhead Cost (Exhibit 8-8)	(2) Flexible Budget Overhead for Actual Output (Exhibit 8-8)	(3) Standard Overhead Allocated to Production for Actual Output (Rates from page 372)
Variable overhead	$ 9,000	$ 8,000	$2.00 × 4,000 direct labor hours = $ 8,000
Fixed overhead	12,300	9,600	$3.00 × 4,000 direct labor hours = $12,000
Total overhead	$21,300	$17,600	$5.00 × 4,000 direct labor hours = $20,000

Flexible budget variance, $3,700 U

Production volume variance, $2,400 F

Total manufacturing overhead variance, $1,300 U

Overhead Flexible Budget Variance

The **overhead flexible budget variance** tells how well managers controlled overhead costs. Smart Touch actually spent $21,300 on overhead ($9,000 variable + $12,300 fixed from Exhibit 8-8, panel A, Actual Column) to sell the 10,000 DVDs. The flexible budget for 10,000 DVDs called for overhead of only $17,600 ($8,000 variable + $9,600 fixed from Exhibit 8-8, Panel A, Flexible Budget Column). So Smart Touch's overhead flexible budget variance is computed as follows:

Overhead Flexible Budget Variance = Actual overhead cost − Flexible budget overhead for actual output
(Exhibit 8-11, column 1) (Exhibit 8-11, column 2)

= $21,300 − $17,600

= $ 3,700 U

Why did Smart Touch spend $3,700 more on overhead than it should have spent to sell the 10,000 DVDs in June? You can see from Exhibit 8-11 that $1,000 ($9,000 − $8,000) of the variance is due to higher-than-expected spending on *variable* overhead. The remaining $2,700 ($12,300 − $9,600) is due to higher than expected spending on *fixed* overhead. Smart Touch will investigate the reason for each of these variances.

Overhead Production Volume Variance

The second component of the total overhead variance is the overhead **production volume variance**. This variance arises when actual production differs from expected production. Smart Touch expected to sell 8,000 DVDs during June, but actually sold 10,000. The overhead production volume variance is computed as follows:

Overhead Production Volume Variance = Flexible budget overhead for actual output (10,000 DVDs) − Standard overhead allocated to (actual) production
(Exhibit 8-11, column 2) (Exhibit 8-11, column 3)

= $17,600 − $20,000

= $ 2,400 F

The production volume variance is favorable because Smart Touch's actual output (10,000 DVDs) exceeded expected output (8,000 DVDs). By selling 10,000 DVDs Smart Touch used its production capacity more fully than originally planned. If Smart Touch had sold 7,000 or fewer DVDs, the production volume variance would have been unfavorable because the company would have had unused production capacity.

Summary of Overhead Variances

Most companies compile cost information for the individual items of overhead, such as indirect materials, indirect labor, and utilities. Managers drill down by comparing actual to budgeted costs for each item. For example, Smart Touch's analysis might reveal that variable overhead costs were higher than expected because utility rates increased or because workers used more power than expected. Perhaps spending on fixed overhead increased because Smart Touch purchased new equipment and its depreciation increased.

Standard Cost Accounting Systems

6 Record transactions at standard cost and prepare a standard cost income statement

Journal Entries

We use Smart Touch Learning's June transactions to demonstrate standard costing in a job costing context. Management needs to know about variances to address each problem. Therefore, Smart Touch records variances from standards as soon as possible. This means that Smart Touch records direct materials price variances when materials are purchased. It also means that Work in process inventory is debited (DVDs are costed) at standard input quantities and standard prices. The entries for the month of June follow:

1.	Materials inventory (12,000 square feet × $2.00) (A+)	24,000	
	Direct materials price variance (CE+)		1,200
	Accounts payable (12,000 × $1.90) (L+)		22,800
	To record purchase of direct materials.		

The credit to Accounts payable is for the *actual quantity* of vinyl purchased (12,000 square feet) at the *actual price* ($1.90 per square foot). In contrast, the debit to Materials inventory is recorded at the *standard price* ($2 per square foot). Maintaining Materials inventory at the *standard price* ($2.00) allows Smart Touch to record the direct materials price variance at time of purchase. Recall that Smart Touch's direct materials price variance was $1,200 favorable. A favorable variance has a credit balance and is a contra expense. An unfavorable variance means more expense and has a debit balance.

2.	Work in process inventory (10,000 square feet × $2.00) (A+)	20,000	
	Direct materials efficiency variance (E+)	4,000	
	Materials inventory (12,000 × $2.00) (A−)		24,000
	To record use of direct materials.		

Smart Touch debits Work in process inventory for the *standard cost* of the 10,000 square feet of direct materials that should have been used to make 10,000 DVDs. This maintains Work in process inventory at standard cost. Materials inventory is credited for the *actual quantity* of materials put into production (12,000 square feet) costed at the *standard price.*

Smart Touch's direct materials efficiency variance was $4,000 unfavorable. An unfavorable variance has a debit balance, which increases expense and decreases profits.

3.	Manufacturing wages (3,800 hours × $10.50) (E+)	39,900	
	Direct labor price variance (E+)	1,900	
	Wages payable (3,800 × $11.00) (L+)		41,800
	To record direct labor costs incurred.		

Manufacturing wages is debited for the *standard price* ($10.50) of direct labor hours actually used (3,800). Wages payable is credited for the *actual cost* (the *actual* hours worked at the *actual* wage rate) because this is the amount Smart Touch must pay the workers. The direct labor price variance is $1,900 unfavorable, a debit amount.

4.	Work in process inventory (4,000 hours × $10.50) (A+)	42,000	
	Direct labor efficiency variance (CE+)		2,100
	Manufacturing wages (3,800 × $10.50) (E–)		39,900
	To allocate direct labor cost to production.		

Smart Touch debits Work in process inventory for the standard cost per direct labor hour ($10.50) that should have been used for 10,000 DVDs (4,000 hours), like direct materials entry 2. Manufacturing wages is credited to close its prior debit balance from journal entry 3. The Direct labor efficiency variance is credited for the $2,100 favorable variance. This maintains Work in process inventory at standard cost.

5.	Manufacturing overhead (actual cost) (E+)	21,300	
	Accounts payable, Accumulated depreciation, etc.		21,300
	To record actual overhead costs incurred (Exhibit 8-11).		

This entry records Smart Touch's actual overhead cost for June.

6.	Work in process inventory (4,000 hours × $5.00) (A+)	20,000	
	Manufacturing overhead (E–)		20,000
	To allocate overhead to production (See Exhibit 8-11).		

In standard costing, the overhead allocated to Work in process inventory is computed as the standard overhead rate ($5.00 per hour) × standard quantity of the allocation base allowed for actual output (4,000 hours for 10,000 DVDs).

7.	Finished goods inventory (A+)	82,000	
	Work in process inventory (A–)		82,000
	To record completion of 10,000 DVDs ($20,000 of materials +		
	$42,000 of labor + $20,000 of manufacturing overhead),		
	all at standard cost.		

This entry transfers the standard cost of the 10,000 DVDs completed during June from Work in process inventory to Finished goods.

8.	Cost of goods sold (E+)	82,000	
	Finished goods inventory (A–)		82,000
	To record the cost of sales of 10,000 DVDs at standard cost.		

Entry 9 closes the Manufacturing overhead account and records the overhead variances.

9.	Overhead flexible budget variance (E+)	3,700	
	Overhead production volume variance (CE+)		2,400
	Manufacturing overhead (E–)		1,300
	To record overhead variances and close the Manufacturing		
	Overhead account. (Exhibit 8-11)		

Exhibit 8-12 shows the relevant Smart Touch accounts after posting these entries.

EXHIBIT 8-12 | **Smart Touch's Flow of Costs in a Standard Costing System**

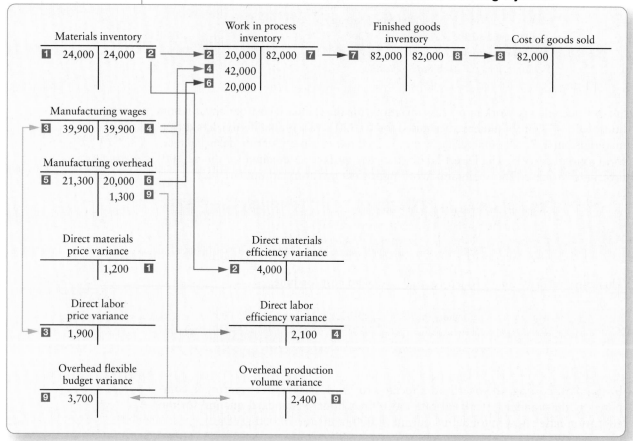

Standard Cost Income Statement for Management

Smart Touch's top management needs to know about the company's cost variances. Exhibit 8-13 shows a standard cost income statement that highlights the variances for management.

The statement starts with sales revenue at standard and adds the favorable sales revenue variance of $1,000 (Exhibit 8-4) to yield actual sales revenue. Next, the statement shows the cost of goods sold at standard cost. Then the statement separately lists each manufacturing cost variance, followed by cost of goods sold at actual cost. At the end of the period, all the variance accounts are closed to zero out their balances. Operating income is then closed to Income summary.

The income statement shows that the net effect of all the manufacturing cost variances is $3,900 unfavorable. Therefore, June's operating income is $3,900 lower than it would have been if all the actual manufacturing costs had been equal to their standard costs.

EXHIBIT 8-13 | **Standard Cost Income Statement**

SMART TOUCH LEARNING, INC.
Standard Cost Income Statement
Month Ended June 30, 2011

Sales revenue at standard (10,000 × $12)			$120,000
Sales revenue variance			1,000
Sales revenue at actual			121,000
Cost of goods sold at standard cost		$82,000	
Manufacturing cost variances (parentheses denote a credit balance):			
Direct materials price variance	$(1,200)		
Direct materials efficiency variance	4,000		
Direct labor price variance	1,900		
Direct labor efficiency variance	(2,100)		
Overhead flexible budget variance	3,700		
Overhead production volume variance	(2,400)		
Total manufacturing variance		3,900	
Cost of goods sold at actual cost			85,900
Gross profit			35,100
Marketing and administrative expense*			(19,100)
Operating income			$ 16,000

*$9,400 + $9,700 from Exhibit 8-8, Panel A.

The Decision Guidelines summarize standard costing and variance analysis.

Decision Guidelines

STANDARD COSTS AND VARIANCE ANALYSIS

Now you have seen how managers use standard costs and variances to identify potential problems. Variances help managers see *why* actual costs differ from the budget. This is the first step in determining how to correct problems. Let us review how Smart Touch Learning made some key decisions in setting up and using its standard cost system.

Decision	Guidelines
• How to set standards?	• Historical performance data • Engineering analysis/time-and-motion studies • Continuous improvement standards • Benchmarking
• How to compute a price variance for materials or labor?	$$\text{Price variance} = \left(\begin{array}{c} \text{Actual price} \\ \text{per input unit} \end{array} - \begin{array}{c} \text{Standard price} \\ \text{per input unit} \end{array} \right) \times \begin{array}{c} \text{Actual quantity} \\ \text{of input} \end{array}$$
• How to compute an efficiency variance for materials or labor?	$$\text{Efficiency variance} = \left(\begin{array}{c} \text{Actual} \\ \text{quantity} \\ \text{of input} \end{array} - \begin{array}{c} \text{Standard} \\ \text{quantity of input} \\ \text{for actual output} \end{array} \right) \times \begin{array}{c} \text{Standard price} \\ \text{per input unit} \end{array}$$
• Who is best able to explain a • sales volume variance? • sales revenue variance? • direct material price variance? • direct material efficiency variance? • direct labor price variance? • direct labor efficiency variance?	 The Marketing Department The Marketing Department The Purchasing Department The Production Department The Human Resources Department The Production Department
• How do you allocate manufacturing overhead in a standard costing system?	$$\begin{array}{c} \text{Manufacturing} \\ \text{overhead} \\ \text{allocated} \end{array} = \left(\begin{array}{c} \text{Standard} \\ \text{overhead} \\ \text{rate} \end{array} \right) \times \left(\begin{array}{c} \text{Standard quantity of} \\ \text{allocation base allowed} \\ \text{for actual output} \end{array} \right)$$
• How do you analyze over- or underallocated overhead?	Split over- or underallocated overhead into $$\begin{array}{c} \text{Flexible} \\ \text{budget} \\ \text{variance} \end{array} = \begin{array}{c} \text{Actual} \\ \text{overhead} \end{array} - \begin{array}{c} \text{Flexible budget} \\ \text{overhead for} \\ \text{actual output} \end{array}$$ $$\begin{array}{c} \text{Production} \\ \text{volume} \\ \text{variance} \end{array} = \begin{array}{c} \text{Flexible budget} \\ \text{overhead for} \\ \text{actual output} \end{array} - \begin{array}{c} \text{Standard overhead} \\ \text{allocated to} \\ \text{actual output} \end{array}$$
• How do you record standard costs in the accounts?	• Materials Inventory: Actual quantity at standard price • Work in process inventory (and Finished goods inventory and Cost of goods sold): Standard quantity of inputs allowed for actual outputs, at standard price of inputs
• How do you analyze cost variances?	• Debit balance → more expense • Credit balance → less expense

Summary Problem 2

Exhibit 8-8 indicates that Smart Touch Learning sold 10,000 DVDs in June. Suppose Smart Touch had sold 7,000 DVDs instead of 10,000 and that *actual costs* were as follows:

Direct materials (vinyl)...............	7,400 square feet @ $2.00 per square foot
Direct labor................................	2,740 hours @ $10.00 per hour
Variable overhead	$5,400
Fixed overhead...........................	$11,900

Requirements

1. Given these new data, prepare an exhibit similar to Exhibit 8-8. Ignore marketing and administrative expense.
2. Compute price and efficiency variances for direct materials and direct labor.
3. Compute the total variance, the flexible budget variance, and the production volume variance for manufacturing overhead. Standard total overhead allocated to production is $5.00 per direct labor hour.

Solution

Requirement 1

PANEL A—Comparison of Actual Results with Flexible Budget for 7,000 DVDs

SMART TOUCH LEARNING, INC.
Revised Data for Standard Costing Example
Month Ended June 30, 2011

	Actual Results at Actual Prices	Flexible Budget for 7,000 DVDs	Flexible Budget Variance
Variable costs:			
Direct materials	$14,800*	$14,000†	$ 800 U
Direct labor	27,400*	29,400†	2,000 F
Variable overhead	5,400	5,600†	200 F
Total variable costs	47,600	49,000	1,400 F
Fixed costs:			
Fixed overhead	11,900	9,600‡	2,300 U
Total costs	$59,500	$58,600	$ 900 U

*See Panel C.
†See Panel B.
‡Fixed overhead was budgeted at $9,600 per month from page 372

PANEL B—Computation of Flexible Budget for Direct Materials, Direct Labor, and Variable Overhead for 7,000 DVDs—Based on Standard Costs

	(1) Standard Quantity of Inputs Allowed for 7,000 DVDs	(2) Standard Price per Unit of Input	(3) (1) × (2) Flexible Budget for 7,000 DVDs
Direct materials	1 square foot per DVD × 7,000 DVDs = 7,000 square feet	$ 2.00	$14,000
Direct labor	.40 hours per DVD × 7,000 DVDs = 2,800 hours	$10.50	29,400
Variable overhead	.40 hours per DVD × 7,000 DVDs = 2,800 hours	$ 2.00	5,600

PANEL C—Computation of Actual Costs for Direct Materials and Direct Labor for 7,000 DVDs

	(1) Actual Quantity of Inputs Used for 7,000 DVDs	(2) Actual Price per Unit of Input	(3) (1) × (2) Actual Cost for 7,000 DVDs
Direct materials	7,400 square feet actually used	$2.00 actual cost/square foot	$14,800
Direct labor	2,740 hours actually used	$10.00 actual cost/hour	27,400

Requirement 2

$$\text{Price variance} = \left(\begin{array}{c} \text{Actual price} \\ \text{per input unit} \end{array} - \begin{array}{c} \text{Standard price} \\ \text{per input unit} \end{array} \right) \times \text{Actual quantity of input}$$

Direct materials:

$$\text{Price variance} = (\$2.00 - \$2.00) \times 7,400 \text{ square feet} = \$0$$

Direct labor:

$$\text{Rate variance} = (\$10.00 - \$10.50) \times 2,740 \text{ hours} = \$1,370 \text{ F}$$

$$\text{Efficiency variance} = \left(\begin{array}{c} \text{Actual quantity} \\ \text{of input} \end{array} - \begin{array}{c} \text{Standard quantity} \\ \text{of input} \end{array} \right) \times \text{Standard price per input unit}$$

Direct materials:

$$\text{Efficiency variance} = (7,400 \text{ square feet} - 7,000 \text{ square feet}) \times \$2.00 \text{ per square foot} = \$800 \text{ U}$$

Direct labor:

$$\text{Efficiency variance} = (2,740 \text{ hours} - 2,800 \text{ hours}) \times \$10.50 \text{ per hours} = \$630 \text{ F}$$

Requirement 3

Total overhead variance:	
Actual overhead cost ($5,400 variable + $11,900 fixed)..................	$17,300
Standard overhead allocated to actual output (2,800 standard direct labor hours × $5.00)	14,000
Total overhead variance	$ 3,300 U
Overhead flexible budget variance:	
Actual overhead cost ($5,400 + $11,900)	$17,300
Flexible budget overhead for actual output (($2.00 x 2,800 standard direct labor hours) + $9,600)...	15,200
Overhead flexible budget variance...	$2,100 U
Overhead production volume variance:	
Flexible budget overhead for actual output ($5,600 + $9,600)	$15,200
Standard overhead allocated to actual output (2,800 standard direct labor hours × $5.00).................................	14,000
Overhead production volume variance	$ 1,200 U

Review *Flexible Budgets and Standard Costs*

■ Accounting Vocabulary

Efficiency (Quantity) Variance (p. 374)
Measures whether the quantity of materials or labor used to make the actual number of outputs is within the standard allowed for that number of outputs. Computed as the difference in quantities (actual quantity of input used minus standard quantity of input allowed for the actual number of outputs) multiplied by the standard price per unit of the input.

Flexible Budget (p. 365)
A summarized budget that managers can easily compute for several different volume levels; separates variable costs from fixed costs.

Flexible Budget Variance (p. 366)
The difference arising because the company actually earned more or less revenue, or incurred more or less cost, than expected for the actual level of output. Equals the difference between the actual amount and a flexible budget amount.

Overhead Flexible Budget Variance (p. 381)
Shows how well management has controlled overhead costs. The difference between the actual overhead cost and the flexible budget overhead for the actual number of outputs.

Price (Rate) Variance (p. 374)
Measures how well the business keeps unit prices of material and labor inputs within standards. Computed as the difference in prices (actual price per unit minus standard price per unit) of an input multiplied by the actual quantity of the input.

Production Volume Variance (p. 381)
Arises when actual production differs from expected production. The difference between: (1) the manufacturing overhead cost in the flexible budget or actual outputs, and (2) the standard overhead allocated to production.

Sales Volume Variance (p. 366)
The difference arising only because the number of units actually sold differs from the static budget units. Equals the difference between a static budget amount and a flexible budget amount.

Standard Cost (p. 371)
A budget for a single unit.

Static Budget (p. 364)
The budget prepared for only one level of sales volume. Also called the **master budget**.

Variance (p. 364)
The difference between an actual amount and the budget. Labeled as favorable if it increases operating income and unfavorable if it decreases operating income.

■ Quick Check

Questions 1–4 rely on the following data. FastNet Systems is a start-up company that makes connectors for high-speed Internet connections. The company has budgeted variable costs of $120 for each connector and fixed costs of $7,000 per month.

FastNet's static budget predicted production and sales of 100 connectors in August, but the company actually produced and sold only 76 connectors at a total cost of $25,000.

1. FastNet's total flexible budget cost for 76 connectors per month is
   a. $16,120.
   b. $7,120.
   c. $12,000.
   d. $9,120.

2. FastNet's sales volume variance for total costs is
   a. $2,880 U.
   b. $2,880 F.
   c. $8,880 F.
   d. $8,880 U.

3. FastNet's flexible budget variance for total costs is
   a. $2,880 U.
   b. $2,880 F.
   c. $8,880 F.
   d. $8,880 U.

4. FastNet Systems' managers could set direct labor standards based on

    a. continuous improvement.

    b. time-and-motion studies.

    c. benchmarking.

    d. past actual performance.

    e. Any of the above

Questions 5–7 rely on the following data. ProNet Systems has budgeted 3 hours of direct labor per connector, at a standard cost of $15 per hour. During January, technicians actually worked 198 hours completing 76 connectors. ProNet paid the technicians $15.50 per hour.

5. What is ProNet's direct labor price variance for January?

    a. $99.00 U

    b. $114.00 U

    c. $106.50 U

    d. $38.00 U

6. What is ProNet's direct labor efficiency variance for January?

    a. $605.00 F

    b. $77.50 F

    c. $1,386.00 F

    d. $450.00 F

7. The journal entry to record ProNet's *use* of direct labor in January is which of the following?

    a.
Work in process inventory		
Direct labor efficiency variance		
Manufacturing wages		

    b.
Work in process inventory		
Direct labor efficiency variance		
Manufacturing wages		

    c.
Manufacturing wages		
Direct labor efficiency variance		
Work in process inventory		

    d.
Manufacturing wages		
Direct labor efficiency variance		
Work in process inventory		

8. BackFill Systems allocates manufacturing overhead based on machine hours. Each connector should require 11 machine hours. According to the static budget, BackFill expected to incur:

    1,045 machine hours per month (95 connectors × 11 machine hours per connector)

    $5,650 in variable manufacturing overhead costs

    $7,900 in fixed manufacturing overhead costs

    During August, BackFill actually used 865 machine hours to make the 78 connectors. BackFill's predetermined standard *total* manufacturing overhead rate is

    a. $12.97 per machine hour.

    b. $15.66 per machine hour.

    c. $7.56 per machine hour.

    d. $5.41 per machine hour.

9. The total manufacturing overhead variance is composed of
   a. price variance and production volume variance.
   b. flexible budget variance and production volume variance.
   c. efficiency variance and production volume variance.
   d. price variance and efficiency variance.

10. When a company *uses* direct materials, the amount of the debit to Work in process inventory is based on which of the following:
    a. Standard quantity of the materials allowed for actual production × Standard price per unit of the materials
    b. Actual quantity of the materials used × Actual price per unit of the materials
    c. Actual quantity of the materials used × Standard price per unit of the materials
    d. Standard quantity of the materials allowed for actual production × Actual price per unit of the materials

Answers are given after Apply Your Knowledge (p. 407).

Assess Your Progress

■ Short Exercises

S8-1 *(L. OBJ. 1)* **Matching terms [10 min]**
Consider the following terms:

a. Flexible Budget
b. Flexible Budget Variance
c. Sales Volume Variance
d. Static Budget
e. Variance

Consider the following definitions:

_____ 1. The budget prepared for only one level of sales volume.

_____ 2. The difference between an actual amount and the budget.

_____ 3. A summarized budget for several levels of volume that separates variable costs from fixed costs.

_____ 4. The difference arising only because the number of units actually sold differs from the static budget units.

_____ 5. The difference arising because the company actually earned more or less revenue, or incurred more or less cost, than expected for the actual level of output.

Requirement

   1. Match each term to the correct definition.

S8-2 *(L. OBJ. 1)* **Matching terms [10 min]**
Consider the following terms:

a. Benchmarking
b. Efficiency Variance
c. Overhead Flexible Budget Variance
d. Price Variance
e. Production Volume Variance
f. Standard Cost

Consider the following definitions:

_____ 1. A budget for a single unit.

_____ 2. Using standards based on "best practice."

_____ 3. Measures how well the business keeps unit prices of material and labor inputs within standards.

_____ 4. Measures whether the quantity of materials or labor used to make the actual number of outputs is within the standard allowed for that number of outputs.

_____ 5. Shows how well management has controlled overhead costs.

_____ 6. Arises when actual production differs from expected production.

Requirement

1. Match each term to the correct definition.

S8-3 *(L. OBJ. 1)* **Flexible budget preparation [10 min]**
Tik-a-Lock, Inc., manufactures travel locks. The budgeted selling price is $18 per lock, the variable cost is $12 per lock, and budgeted fixed costs are $12,000.

Requirement

1. Prepare a flexible budget for output levels of 6,000 locks and 9,000 locks for the month ended April 30, 2011.

S8-4 *(L. OBJ. 2)* **Flexible budget variance [10–15 min]**
Consider the following partially completed income statement performance report for Woje, Inc.

	WOJE, INC.		
	Income Statement Performance Report (partial)		
	Month Ended April 30, 2011		
	Actual Results at Actual Prices	Flexible Budget Variance	Flexible Budget for Actual Number of Output Units
Output units	10,000		10,000
Sales revenue	$ 170,000		$ 150,000
Variable costs	52,100		49,700
Fixed costs	15,700		14,600
Total costs	67,800		64,300
Operating income	$ 102,200		$ 85,700

Requirement

1. Complete the flexible budget variance analysis by filling in the blanks in the partial Income Statement Performance Report for 10,000 travel locks.

S8-5 *(L. OBJ. 3)* **Identifying the benefits of standard costs [5 min]**

Setting standards for a product may involve many employees of the company.

Requirement

1. Identify some of the employees who may be involved in setting the standard costs and describe what their role might be in setting those standards.

S8-6 *(L. OBJ. 4)* **Calculate materials variances [10–15 min]**

Smithson, Inc., is a manufacturer of lead crystal glasses. The standard materials quantity is .9 pound per glass at a price of $0.45 per pound. The actual results for the production of 7,100 glasses was 1.3 pounds per glass, at a price of $0.55 per pound.

Requirement

1. Calculate the materials price variance and the materials efficiency variance.

S8-7 *(L. OBJ. 4)* **Calculate labor variances [10–15 min]**

Smithson, Inc., manufactures lead crystal glasses. The standard direct labor time is 1/4 hour per glass, at a price of $15 per hour. The actual results for the production of 6,800 glasses were 1/3 hour per glass, at a price of $14 per hour.

Requirement

1. Calculate the labor price variance and the labor efficiency variance.

Note: Short Exercises 8-6 and 8-7 should be completed before attempting Short Exercise 8-8.

S8-8 *(L. OBJ. 4)* **Interpreting material and labor variances [5–10 min]**

Refer to your results from S8-6 and S8-7.

Requirements

1. For each variance, who in Smithson's organization is most likely responsible?
2. Interpret the direct materials and direct labor variances for Smithson's management.

S8-9 *(L. OBJ. 5)* **Standard overhead rates [5 min]**

Smithson, Inc., manufactures lead crystal glasses. The following information relates to the company's overhead costs:

Static budget variable overhead	$ 7,500
Static budget fixed overhead	$ 3,000
Static budget direct labor hours	1,500 hours
Static budget number of glasses	4,800

Smithson allocates manufacturing overhead to production based on standard direct labor hours. Last month, Smithson reported the following actual results for the production of 7,500 glasses: actual variable overhead, $10,500; actual fixed overhead, $2,760.

Requirement

1. Compute the standard variable overhead rate and the standard fixed overhead rate.

Note: Short Exercise 8-9 should be completed before attempted Short Exercise 8-10.

S8-10 *(L. OBJ. 6)* **Computing overhead variances [10 min]**
Refer to the Smithson data in S8-9.

Requirement

1. Compute the overhead variances.

S8-11 *(L. OBJ. 6)* **Materials journal entries [5–10 min]**
The following materials variance analysis was performed for Goldman.

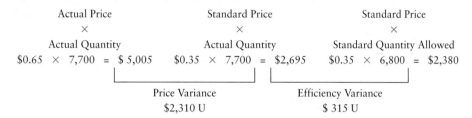

Actual Price	Standard Price	Standard Price
×	×	×
Actual Quantity	Actual Quantity	Standard Quantity Allowed
$0.65 × 7,700 = $ 5,005	$0.35 × 7,700 = $2,695	$0.35 × 6,800 = $2,380

Price Variance $2,310 U   Efficiency Variance $ 315 U

Requirement

1. Record Goldman's direct materials journal entries.

S8-12 *(L. OBJ. 6)* **Labor journal entries [5–10 min]**
The following labor variance analysis was performed for Goldman.

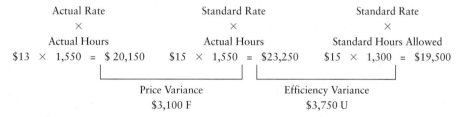

Actual Rate	Standard Rate	Standard Rate
×	×	×
Actual Hours	Actual Hours	Standard Hours Allowed
$13 × 1,550 = $ 20,150	$15 × 1,550 = $23,250	$15 × 1,300 = $19,500

Price Variance $3,100 F   Efficiency Variance $3,750 U

Requirement

1. Record Goldman's direct labor journal entries.

S8-13 *(L. OBJ. 6)* **Journal entries for goods completed and sold [5–10 min]**
Goldman completed 70,000 glasses in 2011, at a standard cost of $360,000. The company sold all of them on account at a sale price of $8.00 each. There were no beginning or ending inventories of any kind.

Requirement

1. Record the journal entries for the completion and sale of the 70,000 glasses.

S8-14 *(L. OBJ. 6)* **Standard cost income statement [10–15 min]**
Consider the following information:

Cost of goods sold	$362,000	Direct labor efficiency variance	$16,500 F
Sales revenue	$530,000	Overhead flexible budget variance	$3,300 U
Direct materials price variance	$7,200 U	Production volume variance	$11,700 F
Direct materials efficiency variance	$2,200 U	Marketing and administrative costs were	$71,000
Direct labor price variance	$45,000 U		

Requirement

1. Use the previous information to prepare a standard cost income statement for Goldman, using Exhibit 8-13 as a guide. Remember that unfavorable variances are added to cost of goods sold.

E8-15 *(L. OBJ. 1)* **Preparing a flexible budget [10–15 min]**
ErgoNow sells its main product, ergonomic mouse pads, for $13 each. Its variable cost is $5.60 per pad. Fixed costs are $200,000 per month for volumes up to 60,000 pads. Above 60,000 pads, monthly fixed costs are $255,000.

Requirement

1. Prepare a monthly flexible budget for the product, showing sales revenue, variable costs, fixed costs, and operating income for volume levels of 30,000, 45,000, and 80,000 pads.

E8-16 *(L. OBJ.2)* **Preparing an income statement performance report [15–20 min]**
White Pro Company managers received the following incomplete performance report:

	Actual Results at Actual Prices	Flexible Budget Variance	Flexible Budget for Actual Number of Output Units	Sales Volume Variance		Static (Master) Budget
WHITE PRO COMPANY						
Income Statement Performance Report						
Year Ended July 31, 2011						
Output units	41,000	——	41,000	7,000	F	——
Sales revenue	$ 215,000	——	$ 215,000	$ 19,000	F	——
Variable costs	85,000	——	79,000	9,000	U	——
Fixed costs	107,000	——	101,000	0		——
Total costs	192,000	——	180,000	9,000	U	——
Operating income	$ 23,000	——	$ 35,000	$ 10,000	F	——

Requirement

1. Complete the performance report. Identify the employee group that may deserve praise and the group that may be subject to criticism. Give your reasoning.

E8-17 *(L. OBJ. 2)* **Preparing an income statement performance report [20–25 min]**
Top managers of Root Industries predicted 2010 sales of 15,000 units of its product at a unit price of $7.50 Actual sales for the year were 14,100 units at $9.00 each. Variable costs were budgeted at $2.60 per unit, and actual variable costs were $2.70 per unit. Actual fixed costs of $46,000 exceeded budgeted fixed costs by $2,000.

Requirement

1. Prepare Root's income statement performance report. What variance contributed most to the year's favorable results? What caused this variance?

E8-18 *(L. OBJ. 3, 4)* **Defining the benefits of setting cost standards, and calculating materials and labor variances [10–15 min]**
Quality, Inc., produced 1,000 units of the company's product in 2011. The standard quantity of materials was three yards of cloth per unit at a standard price of $1.10 per yard. The accounting records showed that 2,900 yards of cloth were used and the company paid $1.15 per yard. Standard time was one direct labor hour per unit at a standard rate of $10 per direct labor hour. Employees worked 650 hours and were paid $9.50 per hour.

Requirements

1. What are the benefits of setting cost standards?
2. Calculate the materials price variance and the materials efficiency variance, as well as the labor price and efficiency variances.

E8-19 *(L. OBJ. 4)* **Calculating materials variances [10–15 min]**
The following direct materials variance computations are incomplete:

1. Price variance = ($? – $2) × 9,800 pounds = $4,900 U
2. Efficiency variance = (? – 15,800 pounds) × $2 = ? F
3. Flexible budget variance = $?

Requirement

1. Fill in the missing values, and identify the flexible budget variance as favorable or unfavorable.

E8-20 *(L. OBJ. 4)* **Calculating materials and labor variances [20–30 min]**
All-Star Fender, which uses a standard cost accounting system, manufactured 20,000 boat fenders during the year, using 146,000 feet of extruded vinyl purchased at $1.15 per square foot. Production required 480 direct labor hours that cost $15.00 per hour. The materials standard was 7 feet of vinyl per fender, at a standard cost of $1.20 per square foot. The labor standard was 0.026 direct labor hour per fender, at a standard price of $14.00 per hour.

Requirement

1. Compute the price and efficiency variances for direct materials and direct labor. Does the pattern of variances suggest All-Star Fender's managers have been making trade-offs? Explain.

E8-21 *(L. OBJ. 5)* **Computing overhead variances [20–30 min]**
Houston Paint Company's budgeted production volume for the month was 30,000 gallons of paint. The standard overhead cost included a $0.55 variable overhead per gallon and fixed overhead costs of $30,000.

Houston Paint actually produced 33,000 gallons of paint. Actual variable overhead was $16,400, and fixed overhead was $32,000.

Requirement

1. Compute the total overhead variance, the overhead flexible budget variance, and the production volume variance.

E8-22 *(L. OBJ. 5)* **Preparing a standard cost income statement [15 min]**
The May 2010 revenue and cost information for Boise Outfitters, Inc., follows:

Sales revenue	$ 580,000	
Cost of goods sold (standard)	344,000	
Direct materials price variance	900	F
Direct materials efficiency variance	6,500	F
Direct labor price variance	4,500	U
Direct labor efficiency variance	2,200	F
Overhead flexible budget variance	3,100	U
Production volume variance	8,400	F

Requirement

1. Prepare a standard cost income statement for management through gross profit. Report all standard cost variances for management's use. Has management done a good or poor job of controlling costs? Explain.

Note: Exercise 8-20 should be completed before attempting Exercise 8-23.

E8-23 *(L. OBJ. 6)* **Preparing journal entries [20–30 min]**
Review the results from E8-20.

Requirement

1. Make the journal entries to record the purchase and use of direct materials and direct labor from E8-20.

E8-24 *(L. OBJ. 6)* **Preparing a standard cost income statement [15–20 min]**
The managers of Johnson DVD, Co., a contract manufacturer of DVD drives, are seeking explanations for the variances in the following report.

JOHNSON DVD CO. Standard Cost Income Statement Year Ended December 31, 2011		
Sales revenue		$1,200,000
Cost of goods sold at standard cost		$700,000
Manufacturing cost variances:		
Direct materials price variance	$ 10,000 F	
Direct materials efficiency variance	32,000 U	
Direct labor price variance	24,000 F	
Direct labor efficiency variance	10,000 U	
Overhead flexible budget variance	28,000 U	
Production volume variance	8,000 F	
Total manufacturing variances		28,000
Cost of goods sold at actual cost		728,000
Gross profit		472,000
Marketing and administrative costs		418,000
Operating income		$ 54,000

Requirement

1. Explain the meaning of each of Johnson's materials, labor, and overhead variances.

■ Problems (Group A)

P8-25A *(L. OBJ. 1, 3, 4, 5)* **Preparing a flexible budget and computing standard cost variances [60–75 min]**
Root Recliners manufactures leather recliners and uses flexible budgeting and a standard cost system. Root allocates overhead based on yards of direct materials. The company's performance report includes the following selected data:

	Static Budget (1,025 recliners)	Actual Results (1,005 recliners)
Sales (1,025 recliners × $ 505)	$ 517,625	
(1,005 recliners × $ 485)		$ 487,425
Variable manufacturing costs:		
Direct materials (6,150 yds @ $8.90)	54,735	
(6,300 yds @ $8.70)		54,810
Direct labor (10,250 hrs @ $9.40)	96,350	
(9,850 hrs @ $9.55)		94,068
Variable overhead (6,150 yds @ $5.10)	31,365	
(6,300 yds @ $6.50)		40,950
Fixed manufacturing costs:		
Fixed overhead	62,730	64,730
Total cost of goods sold	245,180	254,558
Gross profit	$ 272,445	$ 232,867

Requirements

1. Prepare a flexible budget based on the actual number of recliners sold.

2. Compute the price variance and the efficiency variance for direct materials and for direct labor. For manufacturing overhead, compute the total variance, the flexible budget variance, and the production volume variance.

3. Have Root's managers done a good job or a poor job controlling materials and labor costs? Why?

4. Describe how Root's managers can benefit from the standard costing system.

P8-26A *(L. OBJ. 2)* **Preparing an income statement performance report [30 min]**
CellBase Technologies manufactures capacitors for cellular base stations and other communications applications. The company's December 2011 flexible budget income statement shows output levels of 7,500, 9,000, and 11,000 units. The static budget was based on expected sales of 9,000 units.

CELLBASE TECHNOLOGIES Flexible Budget Income Statement Month Ended December 31, 2011				
	Flexible Budget per Output Unit	Output Units (Capacitors)		
		7,500	9,000	11,000
Sales revenue	23	$ 172,500	$ 207,000	$ 253,000
Variable costs	11	82,500	99,000	121,000
Fixed costs		57,000	57,000	57,000
Total costs		139,500	156,000	178,000
Operating income		$ 33,000	$ 51,000	$ 75,000

The company sold 11,000 units during December, and its actual operating income was as follows:

CELLBASE TECHNOLOGIES
Income Statement
Month Ended December 31, 2011

Sales revenue	$ 260,000
Variable costs	$ 126,000
Fixed costs	58,500
Total costs	184,500
Operating income	$ 75,500

Requirements

1. Prepare an income statement performance report for December.

2. What was the effect on CellBase Technologies' operating income of selling 2,000 units more than the static budget level of sales?

3. What is CellBase Technologies' static budget variance? Explain why the income statement performance report provides more useful information to CellBase Technologies' managers than the simple static budget variance. What insights can CellBase Technologies' managers draw from this performance report?

P8-27A *(L. OBJ. 4)* **Using incomplete cost and variance information to determine the number of direct labor hours worked [30–35 min]**

Abby's Shades manufactures lamp shades. Abby Sanders, the manager, uses standard costs to judge performance. Recently, a clerk mistakenly threw away some of the records, and Sanders has only partial data for October. She knows that the direct labor flexible budget variance for the month was $1,385 U, the standard labor rate was $10 per hour, and the actual labor rate was $10.50 per hour. The standard direct labor hours for the actual October output were 4,450.

Requirements

1. Find the actual number of direct labor hours worked during October. First, calculate the standard labor cost. Next, calculate the actual labor cost by adding the unfavorable flexible budget variance of $1,385 to the standard labor cost. Finally, divide the actual labor cost by the actual labor rate per hour.

2. Compute the direct labor price and efficiency variances. Do these variances suggest the manager may have made a trade-off? Explain.

P8-28A *(L. OBJ. 4, 5, 6)* **Computing and journalizing standard cost variances [45 min]**

Stenback manufactures coffee mugs that it sells to other companies for customizing with their own logos. Stenback prepares flexible budgets and uses a standard cost system to control manufacturing costs. The standard unit cost of a coffee mug is based on static budget volume of 59,900 coffee mugs per month:

Direct materials (0.2 lbs @ $0.25 per lb)		$ 0.05
Direct labor (3 minutes @ $0.10 per minute)		0.30
Manufacturing overhead:		
Variable (3 minutes @ $0.05 per minute)	$ 0.15	
Fixed (3 minutes @ $0.13 per minute)	0.39	0.54
Total cost per coffee mug		$ 0.89

Actual cost and production information for July follow:

a. Actual production and sales were 62,600 coffee mugs.
b. Actual direct materials usage was 12,000 lbs., at an actual price of $0.18 per lb.
c. Actual direct labor usage of 199,000 minutes at a total cost of $25,870.
d. Actual overhead cost was $40,500.

Requirements

1. Compute the price and efficiency variances for direct materials and direct labor.
2. Journalize the usage of direct materials and the assignment of direct labor, including the related variances.
3. For manufacturing overhead, compute the total variance, the flexible budget variance, and the production volume variance. (*Hint:* Remember that the fixed overhead in the flexible budget equals the fixed overhead in the static budget.)
4. Stenback intentionally hired more-skilled workers during July. How did this decision affect the cost variances? Overall, was the decision wise?

P8-29A *(L. OBJ. 4, 5, 6)* **Computing standard cost variances and reporting to management [45–60 min]**
SmartSound manufactures headphone cases. During September 2011, the company produced and sold 105,000 cases and recorded the following cost data:

Standard Cost Information:

	Quantity	Price
Direct materials	2 parts	$ 0.15 per part
Direct labor	0.02 hours	$ 9.00 per hour
Variable manufacturing overhead	0.02 hours	$ 9.00 per hour
Fixed manufacturing overhead ($28,500 for static budget volume of 95,000 units and 1,900 hours, or $ 15 per hour)		

Actual Information:

Direct materials (235,000 parts @ $0.20 per part = $47,000)
Direct labor (1,700 hours @ $9.15 per hour = $15,555)
Manufacturing overhead $61,000

Requirements

1. Compute the price and efficiency variances for direct materials and direct labor.
2. For manufacturing overhead, compute the total variance, the flexible budget variance, and the production volume variance.
3. Prepare a standard cost income statement through gross profit to report all variances to management. The sale price of the headset cases was $1.50 each.
4. SmartSound's management used more-experienced workers during September. Discuss the trade-off between the two direct labor variances.

P8-30B *(L. OBJ. 1, 3, 4, 5)* **Preparing a flexible budget and computing standard cost variances [60–75 min]**

McKnight Recliners manufactures leather recliners and uses flexible budgeting and a standard cost system. McKnight allocates overhead based on yards of direct materials. The company's performance report includes the following selected data:

	Static Budget (1,000 recliners)	Actual Results (980 recliners)
Sales (1,000 recliners × $ 505)	$ 505,000	
(980 recliners × $ 485)		$ 475,300
Variable manufacturing costs:		
Direct materials (6,000 yds @ $8.90)	53,400	
(6,150 yds @ $8.65)		53,198
Direct labor (10,000 hrs @ $9.40)	94,000	
(9,600 hrs @ $9.60)		92,160
Variable overhead (6,000 yds @ $5.20)	31,200	
(6,150 yds @ $6.60)		40,590
Fixed manufacturing costs:		
Fixed overhead	60,600	62,600
Total cost of goods sold	239,200	248,548
Gross profit	$ 265,800	$ 226,752

Requirements

1. Prepare a flexible budget based on the actual number of recliners sold.
2. Compute the price variance and the efficiency variance for direct materials and for direct labor. For manufacturing overhead, compute the total variance, the flexible budget variance, and the production volume variance.
3. Have McKnight's managers done a good job or a poor job controlling materials and labor costs? Why?
4. Describe how McKnight's managers can benefit from the standard costing system.

P8-31B *(L. OBJ. 2)* **Preparing an income statement performance report [30 min]**

AllTalk Technologies manufactures capacitors for cellular base stations and other communication applications. The company's January 2011 flexible budget income statement shows output levels of 6,500, 8,000, and 10,000 units. The static budget was based on expected sales of 8,000 units.

ALLTALK TECHNOLOGIES				
Flexible Budget Income Statement				
Month Ended January 31, 2011				
	Flexible Budget per Output Unit	Output Units (Capacitors)		
		6,500	8,000	10,000
Sales revenue	21	$ 136,500	$ 168,000	$ 210,000
Variable costs	11	71,500	88,000	110,000
Fixed costs		57,000	57,000	57,000
Total costs		128,500	145,000	167,000
Operating income		$ 8,000	$ 23,000	$ 43,000

The company sold 10,000 units during January, and its actual operating income was as follows:

ALLTALK TECHNOLOGIES
Income Statement
Month Ended January 31, 2011

Sales revenue	$ 217,000
Variable costs	$ 115,100
Fixed costs	58,500
Total costs	173,600
Operating income	$ 43,400

Requirements

1. Prepare an income statement performance report for January 2011.
2. What was the effect on AllTalk Technologies' operating income of selling 2,000 units more than the static budget level of sales?
3. What is AllTalk Technologies' static budget variance? Explain why the income statement performance report provides more useful information to AllTalk Technologies' managers than the simple static budget variance. What insights can AllTalk Technologies' managers draw from this performance report?

P8-32B *(L. OBJ. 4)* **Using incomplete cost and variance information to determine the number of direct labor hours worked [30–35 min]**

Lilly's Shades manufactures lamp shades. Lilly Sanders, the manager, uses standard costs to judge performance. Recently, a clerk mistakenly threw away some of the records, and Sanders has only partial data for October. She knows that the direct labor flexible budget variance for the month was $1,585 U, the standard labor rate was $9 per hour, and the actual labor rate was $9.50 per hour. The standard direct labor hours for the actual October output were 4,500.

Requirements

1. Find the actual number of direct labor hours worked during October. First, calculate the standard labor cost. Next, calculate the actual labor cost by adding the unfavorable flexible budget variance of $1,585 to the standard labor cost. Finally, divide the actual labor cost by the actual labor rate per hour.
2. Compute the direct labor price and efficiency variances. Do these variances suggest the manager may have made a trade-off? Explain.

P8-33B *(L. OBJ. 4, 5, 6)* **Computing and journalizing standard cost variances [45 min]**

Smith manufactures coffee mugs that it sells to other companies for customizing with their own logos. Smith prepares flexible budgets and uses a standard cost system to control manufacturing costs. The standard unit cost of a coffee mug is based on static budget volume of 59,700 coffee mugs per month:

Direct materials (0.2 lbs @ $0.25 per lb)		$ 0.05
Direct labor (3 minutes @ $0.12 per minute)		0.36
Manufacturing overhead:		
Variable (3 minutes @ $0.05 per minute)	$ 0.15	
Fixed (3 minutes @ $0.14 per minute)	0.42	0.57
Total cost per coffee mug		$ 0.98

Actual cost and production information for July:

a. Actual production and sales were 62,400 coffee mugs.
b. Actual direct materials usage was 12,000 lbs., at an actual price of $0.18 per lb.
c. Actual direct labor usage of 203,000 minutes at a total cost of $28,420.
d. Actual overhead cost was $40,900.

Requirements

1. Compute the price variance and efficiency variance for direct materials and direct labor.
2. Journalize the usage of direct materials and the assignment of direct labor, including the related variances.
3. For manufacturing overhead, compute the total variance, the flexible budget variance, and the production volume variance. (*Hint:* Remember that the fixed overhead in the flexible budget equals the fixed overhead in the static budget.)
4. Smith intentionally hired more-skilled workers during July. How did this decision affect the cost variances? Overall, was the decision wise?

P8-34B *(L. OBJ. 4, 5, 6)* **Computing standard cost variances and reporting to management [45–60 min]**

HeadSmart manufactures headphone cases. During September 2011, the company produced 106,000 cases and recorded the following cost data:

Standard Cost Information:

	Quantity		Price	
Direct materials	2	parts	$ 0.17	per part
Direct labor	0.02	hours	$ 9.00	per hour
Variable manufacturing overhead	0.02	hours	$10.00	per hour
Fixed manufacturing overhead ($32,640 for static budget volume of				
96,000 units and 1,920 hours, or	$ 17	per hour)		

Actual Information:

Direct materials (215,000 parts @ $0.22 per part = $47,300)
Direct labor (1,720 hours @ $9.10 per hour = $15,652)
Manufacturing overhead $60,500

Requirements

1. Compute the price variance and efficiency variance for direct materials and direct labor.
2. For manufacturing overhead, compute the total variance, the flexible budget variance, and the production volume variance.
3. Prepare a standard cost income statement through gross profit to report all variances to management. The sale price of the headset cases was $1.60 each.
4. HeadSmart's management used more-experienced workers during September. Discuss the trade-off between the two direct labor variances.

▪ Continuing Exercise

E8-35 This exercise continues the Sherman Lawn Service, Inc., situation from Exercise 7-32 of Chapter 7. Sherman Lawn Service budgeted production volume for the month was 500 lawns. The standard overhead cost included $20.00 variable cost per lawn and fixed overhead costs of $5,000.

Sherman actually mowed 550 lawns in October. Actual variable overhead was $12,400, and fixed overhead was $5,600.

1. Compute the total overhead variance, the overhead flexible budget variance, and the production volume variance.

■ Continuing Problem

P8-36 This problem continues the Haupt Consulting, Inc., situation from Problem 7-33 of Chapter 7. Assume Haupt Consulting has created a standard cost card for each job. Standard direct materials include 10 software packages at a cost of $1,000 per package. Standard direct labor costs per job include 100 hours at $100 per hour. Haupt plans on completing 10 jobs during October.

Actual direct materials costs for October included 95 software packages at a total cost of $97,000. Actual direct labor costs included 110 hours at an average rate of $105 per hour. Haupt completed all 10 jobs in October.

Requirements

1. Calculate direct materials price and efficiency variances.
2. Calculate direct labor rate and efficiency variances.
3. Prepare journal entries to record the use of both materials and labor for October for the company.

Apply Your Knowledge

■ Decision Cases

Case 1. Movies Galore distributes DVDs to movie retailers, including dot.coms. Movies Galore's top management meets monthly to evaluate the company's performance. Controller Allen Walsh prepared the following performance report for the meeting:

MOVIES GALORE Income Statement Performance Report Month Ended July 31, 2012	Actual Results	Static Budget	Variance
Sales revenue	$1,640,000	$1,960,000	$320,000 U
Variable costs:			
Cost of goods sold	775,000	980,000	205,000 F
Sales commisions	77,000	107,800	30,800 F
Shipping cost	43,000	53,900	10,900 F
Fixed costs:			
Salary cost	311,000	300,500	10,500 U
Depreciation cost	209,000	214,000	5,000 F
Rent cost	129,000	108,250	20,750 U
Advertising cost	81,000	68,500	12,500 U
Total costs	1,625,000	1,832,950	207,950 F
Operating income	$ 15,000	$ 127,050	$112,050 U

Walsh also revealed that the actual sale price of $20 per movie was equal to the budgeted sale price and that there were no changes in inventories for the month.

Management is disappointed by the operating income results. CEO Jilinda Robinson exclaims, "How can actual operating income be roughly 12% of the static budget amount when there are so many favorable variances?"

Requirements

1. Prepare a more informative performance report. Be sure to include a flexible budget for the actual number of DVDs bought and sold.
2. As a member of Movies Galore's management team, which variances would you want investigated? Why?
3. Robinson believes that many consumers are postponing purchases of new movies until after the introduction of a new format for recordable DVD players. In light of this information, how would you rate the company's performance?

Case 2. Suppose you manage the local Scoopy's ice cream parlor. In addition to selling ice-cream cones, you make large batches of a few flavors of milk shakes to sell throughout the day. Your parlor is chosen to test the company's "Made-for-You" system. This new system enables patrons to customize their milk shakes by choosing different flavors.

Customers like the new system and your staff appears to be adapting, but you wonder whether this new made-to-order system is as efficient as the old system in which you just made a few large batches. Efficiency is a special concern because your performance is evaluated in part on the restaurant's efficient use of materials and labor. Your superiors consider efficiency variances greater than 5% to be unacceptable.

You decide to look at your sales for a typical day. You find that the parlor used 390 lbs. of ice cream and 72 hours of direct labor to produce and sell 2,000 shakes. The standard quantity allowed for a shake is 0.2 pound of ice cream and 0.03 hour (1.8 minutes) of direct labor. The standard prices are $1.50 per pound for ice cream and $8 an hour for labor.

Requirements

1. Compute the efficiency variances for direct labor and direct materials.
2. Provide likely explanations for the variances. Do you have reason to be concerned about your performance evaluation? Explain.
3. Write a memo to Scoopy's national office explaining your concern and suggesting a remedy.

■ Ethical Issues

Rita Lane is the accountant for Outdoor Living, a manufacturer of outdoor furniture that is sold through specialty stores and Internet companies. Lane is responsible for reviewing the standard costs. While reviewing the standards for the coming year, two ethical issues arise. Use the IMA's ethical guidelines (https://www.imanet.org/about_ethics_statement.asp) to identify the ethical dilemma in each situation. Identify the relevant factors in each situation and suggest what Lane should recommend to the controller.

Requirements

Issue 1. Lane has been approached by Casey Henderson, a former colleague who worked with Lane when they were both employed by a public accounting firm. Henderson has recently started his own firm, Henderson Benchmarking Associates, which collects and sells data on industry benchmarks. He offers to provide Lane with benchmarks for the outdoor furniture industry free of charge if she will provide him with the last three years of Outdoor Living's standard and actual costs. Henderson explains that this is how he obtains most of his firm's benchmarking data. Lane always has a difficult time with the standard-setting process and believes that the benchmark data would be very useful.

Issue 2. Outdoor Living's management is starting a continuous improvement policy that requires a 10% reduction in standard costs each year for the next three years. Dan Jacobs, manufacturing foreman of the Teak furniture line, asks Lane to set loose standard costs this year before the continuous improvement policy is implemented. Jacobs argues that there is no other way to meet the tightening standards while maintaining the high quality of the Teak line.

Financial Statement Case—Amazon.com

This case is based on the **Amazon.com** annual report in Appendix A at the end of the book. Use it to answer the following questions.

Requirements

1. Review the data for **Amazon.com**. Consider your Chapter 7 Financial case budgets and prepare a performance report comparing their actual results to the first budget you prepared for Chapter 7.

2. What do the results tell you and why?

Team Project

Lynx, Corp., manufactures wood windows and doors. Lynx has been using a standard cost system that bases price and quantity standards on Lynx's historical long-run average performance. Suppose Lynx's controller has engaged your team of management consultants to advise him or her whether Lynx should use some basis other than historical performance for setting standards.

Requirements

1. List the types of variances you recommend that Lynx compute (for example, direct materials price variance for glass). For each variance, what specific standards would Lynx need to develop? In addition to cost standards, do you recommend that Lynx develop any nonfinancial standards?

2. There are many approaches to setting standards other than simply using long-run average historical prices and quantities.
   a. List three alternative approaches that Lynx could use to set standards, and explain how Lynx could implement each alternative.
   b. Evaluate each alternative method of setting standards, including the pros and cons of each method.
   c. Write a memo to Lynx's controller detailing your recommendations. First, should Lynx retain its historical data-based standard cost approach? If not, which of the alternative approaches should it adopt?

Quick Check Answers

1. *a* 2. *b* 3. *d* 4. *e* 5. *a* 6. *d* 7. *b* 8. *a* 9. *b* 10. *a*

For online homework, exercises, and problems that provide you immediate feedback, please visit www.myaccountinglab.com.

Big Picture

Ch 1 Introduction to Management Accounting

- Distinguish management accounting from financial accounting
- The role and responsibilities of management accountants
- Classify costs and prepare income statements for merchandising companies
- Classify costs and prepare income statements and statements of cost of goods manufactured for manufacturing companies

Ch 2 Job Order Costing

- Distinguish between job order and process costing
- Record materials, labor, and overhead in a job order costing system
- Record completion and sales of finished goods and adjust for under-/overallocated overhead
- Calculate unit costs for service companies

Ch 3 Activity-Based Costing and Other Cost Management Tools

- Develop activity-based costs and used activity-based management to determine target product costs
- Record transactions in JIT systems
- Use the four types of quality costs to make management decisions

Ch 4 Process Costing

- Calculate equivalent units and conversion costs
- Prepare cost of production reports and the related journal entries using the weighted-average costing method
- Prepare cost of production reports and the related journal entries using the FIFO costing method

Ch 5 Cost Behavior and Cost-Volume-Profit Analysis

- Identify how changes in volume affect cost
- Distinguish among variable, mixed, and fixed cost
- Split mixed cost into fixed and variable components by using the high-low method and by using regression analysis
- Use CVP to compute breakeven points, to plan profits, to graph relationships, and to perform sensitivity analysis

Ch 6 Absorption and Variable Costing

- Distinguish between absorption costing and variable costing
- Prepare absorption costing and variable costing income statements and explained the differences between the two costing techniques
- Illustrate the pros and cons of absorption and variable costing

Ch 7 The Master Budget: Profit Planning

- Understand and prepare all components of the master budget for manufacturers
- Use sensitivity analysis to adjust budget preparations

Ch 8 Flexible Budgets and Standard Costs

- Prepare flexible income statement budgets and income statement performance reports
- Compute standard cost variances for direct materials, direct labor, and overhead
- Record transactions using standard costs and prepare standard cost income statements

Chapter 8: Demo Doc

▪ Standard Costs

Learning Objectives 3–6

Bumpy Road Maps manufactures road maps. Bumpy uses a standard cost system to control manufacturing costs.

The following standard unit cost information is based on the static budget volume of 120,000 road maps per month:

Direct materials (40 sq. yards @ $0.015 per sq. yard)		$0.60
Direct labor (0.10 hours @ $12.00 per hour)		1.20
Manufacturing overhead:		
Variable (0.10 hours @ $3.00 per hour)	0.30	
Fixed (0.10 hours @ $8.00 per hour)	0.80	1.10
Total cost per map		$2.90

In this example, total budgeted fixed manufacturing overhead = $0.80 × 120,000 road maps = $96,000.

Actual cost and production volume information is as follows:

- Actual production was 118,000 maps.
- Actual direct materials usage was 41 square yards per map, at an actual cost of $0.016 per square yard.
- Actual direct labor usage of 11,600 hours at $12.10 per hour, total cost of $140,360.
- Total actual overhead was $126,000.

Requirements

1. Bumpy has developed their standards. What are the five benefits of standard costing?

2. Compute the price and efficiency variances for direct materials and direct labor. Are these variances favorable or unfavorable? Why?

3. Journalize the usage of direct materials, including the related variance.

4. For manufacturing overhead, compute the total variance, the flexible variance, and the production volume variance. Are these variances favorable or unfavorable? Why?

Demo Doc Solutions

Requirement 1

3 Identify the benefits of standard costs and learn how to set standards

Bumpy has developed their standards. What are the five benefits of standard costing?

Part 1	Part 2	Part 3	Part 4	Part 5	Part 6	Part 7	Demo Doc Complete

A **standard cost** is a budget for a single unit. A standard is developed for the quantity and price of direct materials, direct labor, and manufacturing overhead.

Material price standards consider the cost of purchases plus freight in and receiving costs less discounts. Direct labor cost standards include the labor rates, payroll taxes, and fringe benefits. Overhead cost standards are developed by dividing estimated variable and fixed overhead costs by an appropriate allocation base. The quantity standards are usually developed using the input from knowledgeable employees taking into account an expected amount of spoilage, waste, and downtime.

Standards help managers in five areas:

1. Plan by providing unit amounts for budgeting

2. Control by setting target levels of performance

3. Motivate employees by serving as performance benchmarks

4. Set sales prices of products or services by providing unit costs

5. Simplify record keeping and reduce clerical costs

Requirement 2

4 Compute standard cost variances for direct materials and direct labor

Compute the price and efficiency variances for direct materials and direct labor. Are these variances favorable or unfavorable? Why?

Part 1	Part 2	Part 3	Part 4	Part 5	Part 6	Part 7	Demo Doc Complete

Direct Materials Price Variance

The actual quantity of direct materials used was the total number of maps produced (118,000) multiplied by the amount of direct materials used per map. Actual direct materials usage was 41 square yards per map, for an actual quantity of 4,838,000 square yards of materials.

To compute the variance, multiply the difference between the actual and standard costs per unit by the actual quantity. Bumpy estimated a cost of $0.015 per square yard, but the actual cost was $0.016 per square yard, for a difference of $0.001, which multiplied by 4,838,000 yields a variance of $4,838:

Direct materials price variance = (Actual price − Standard price) × Actual quantity of **material** for maps produced

= ($0.016 − $0.015) × (41 sq. yards usage per unit × 118,000 units)

= $0.001 × 4,838,000

= $4,828U

This variance is unfavorable because the actual price is greater than the standard price.

Direct Materials Quantity Variance

This variance measures whether the quantity of materials actually used to produce the *actual* number of output units is within the *standard* allowed for that number of outputs. This is calculated by multiplying the difference between quantities of material (actual vs. standard) by the *standard* price per unit of material.

We know from computing the direct materials price variance that the actual quantity of direct materials used was 41 square yards per map × 118,000 maps = 4,838,000 square yards. From this, we subtract the standard quantity (40 square yards per map × 118,000 maps = 4,720,000 square yards) for a difference of 118,000 square yards.

We then multiply that difference in quantity by the standard price per unit. Remember, efficiency variance is measured against the standard (flexible budget, not actual costs), for a total variance of 118,000 × $0.015 = $1,770:

$$
\begin{aligned}
\text{Direct materials quantity variance} &= (\text{Actual quantity} - \text{Standard quantity}) \times \text{Standard price} \\
&= [(41 \times 118,000) - (40 \times 118,000)] \times \$0.015 \\
&= (4,838,000 - 4,720,000) \times \$0.015 \\
&= 118,000 \times \$0.015 \\
&= \$1,770\text{U}
\end{aligned}
$$

This variance is unfavorable because the actual material used per map, 41 square yards, was greater than the standard per map, 40 square yards.

Part 1	Part 2	**Part 3**	Part 4	Part 5	Part 6	Part 7	Demo Doc Complete

Direct Labor Rate Variance

This variance measures the difference between the actual price per unit (in this case, rate per hour for labor) and the standard price per unit, multiplied by the actual quantity of input (that is, hours worked).

In this case, Bumpy estimated a rate of $12.00 per hour for labor, and actual costs were $12.10, so the difference is $0.10 per hour, which multiplied by the actual hours of 11,600 yields a variance of $1,160:

$$
\begin{aligned}
\text{Direct labor rate variance} &= (\text{Actual rate} - \text{Standard rate}) \times \text{Actual hours} \\
&= (\$12.10 - \$12.00) \times 11,600 \\
&= \$0.10 \times 11,600 \\
&= \$1,160\text{U}
\end{aligned}
$$

This variance is unfavorable because the actual hourly rate for labor, $12.10, was greater than the standard rate for labor, $12.00.

Direct Labor Efficiency Variance

This variance measures the difference between the actual quantity of input (in this case, the number of hours Bumpy actually purchased) and the standard quantity of input, multiplied by the standard price per input unit (hourly cost of the labor).

In this case, we know that the actual number of hours purchased was 11,600. To compute standard hours, multiply the standard rate per map, 0.10, by the actual number of maps produced, 118,000 = 11,800. So the difference between actual and standard hours is 200, multiplied by the standard price per hour of $12.00 = $2,400:

$$
\begin{aligned}
\text{Direct labor efficiency variance} &= (\text{Actual hours} - \text{Standard hours}) \times \text{Standard price} \\
&= [11,600 - (0.10 \times 118,000)] \times \$12.00 \\
&= (11,600 - 11,800) \times \$12.00 \\
&= -200 \times \$12.00 \\
&= \$2,400\text{F}
\end{aligned}
$$

This variance is favorable because the number of actual hours used was less than standard hours.

Requirement 3

Journalize the usage of direct materials, including the related variance.

Part 1	Part 2	Part 3	**Part 4**	Part 5	Part 6	Part 7	Demo Doc Complete

Usage of Direct Materials

Bumpy debits (increases) Work in process inventory for the standard price multiplied by the standard quantity of direct materials that should have been used for the actual output of 118,000 maps. This maintains inventory at standard cost. Materials inventory is credited (decreased) for the actual quantity of materials put into production multiplied by the standard price:

Work in process inventory (118,000 × 40 × $0.015) (A+)	70,800	
???	1,770	
Materials inventory (118,000 × 41 × $0.015) (A-)		72,570

So where does the rest of the debit side of this entry come from?

We learned in requirement 2 that because Bumpy used more materials than the standard, its direct materials quantity variance was $1,770 unfavorable. This unfavorable variance increases the cost of production. Unfavorable variances will always be debited (increased).

Work in process inventory (118,000 × 40 × $0.015) A+)	70,800	
Direct materials quantity variance (118,000 × $0.015) (E+)	1,770	
Materials inventory (118,000 × 41 × $0.015) (A-)		72,570

Record transactions at standard cost and prepare a standard cost income statement

Requirement 4

For manufacturing overhead, compute the total variance, the flexible variance, and the production volume variance. Are these variances favorable or unfavorable? Why?

5 Analyze manufacturing overhead in a standard cost system

| Part 1 | Part 2 | Part 3 | Part 4 | **Part 5** | Part 6 | Part 7 | Demo Doc Complete |

Total Overhead Variance

Total overhead variance is the difference between actual overhead cost and standard overhead allocated to production.

The standard overhead allocated to production is the standard cost of the overhead per map times the number of maps actually produced. We know from the question that the standard overhead cost per map is $0.30 (variable cost) + $0.80 (fixed cost) = $1.10. So the standard overhead allocated to production = 118,000 × $1.10 = $129,800. Actual overhead cost as given in the question is $126,000, the difference being $3,800:

> Total overhead variance = Actual overhead cost – Standard overhead allocated to production
> = $126,000 – (118,000 × $1.10)
> = $126,000 – $129,800
> = $3,800F

The variance is favorable because the actual overhead is less than the standard overhead. Overapplied overhead is favorable because enough cost was put into production.

| Part 1 | Part 2 | Part 3 | Part 4 | Part 5 | **Part 6** | Part 7 | Demo Doc Complete |

Overhead Flexible Budget Variance

The flexible budget variance is equal to the difference between the actual overhead cost and the flexible budget overhead for the actual number of maps produced.

To compute the flexible budget overhead variance, the fixed portion of the overhead must be separated from the variable part. The variable part of the overhead is flexible, therefore the variable cost of overhead per map ($0.30) is multiplied by the actual number of maps produced (118,000); the variable part of overhead is thus $35,400.

The fixed portion of the overhead is not flexible within the relevant range, so to compute the full fixed part of the overhead, the fixed cost of overhead per map ($0.80) must be multiplied by the static expected budget output of 120,000 maps. The fixed part of overhead is thus $96,000, the same as the original budgeted amount. Total flexible budget overhead is $35,400 + $96,000 = $131,400.

We know that the actual overhead cost was \$126,000, the difference between actual and flexible thus being \$5,400:

Overhead flexible budget variance = Actual overhead cost − Flexible budget overhead for the actual number of outputs

$$= \$126,000 - [(118,000 \times \$0.30) + (120,000 \times \$0.80)]$$

$$= \$126,000 - (\$35,400 + \$96,000)$$

$$= \$126,000 - \$131,400$$

$$= \$5,400F$$

The flexible budget variance is favorable because the actual overhead cost is less than the flexible budget.

Part 1	Part 2	Part 3	Part 4	Part 5	Part 6	**Part 7**	Demo Doc Complete

Production Volume Variance

The production volume variance arises when actual production differs from expected production. It is calculated as the difference between the flexible budget overhead for the actual number of outputs and the standard overhead allocated to actual production.

Standard overhead allocated to actual production is calculated by multiplying the number of maps actually produced, 118,000, by the standard overhead per unit, \$1.10, which equals \$129,800.

We know from calculating the overhead flexible budet variance that the flexible budget overhead for the

$$\text{Actual number of outputs} = [(118,000 \times \$0.30) + (120,000 \times \$0.80)]$$

$$= \$35,400 + \$96,000$$

$$= \$131,400$$

So the difference is calculated as \$131,400 − \$129,800 = \$1,600:

$$\text{Production volume variance} = \frac{\text{Flexible budget overhead for}}{\text{the actual number of outputs}} - \frac{\text{Standard overhead allocated}}{\text{to actual production}}$$

$$= \$131,400 - (\$1.10 \times 118,000)$$

$$= \$131,400 - \$129,800$$

$$= \$1,600U$$

This variance accounts for Bumpy producing fewer maps, 118,000, than expected output, 120,000. Bumpy didn't use their production capacity as efficiently as possible. Whenever a business produces less than expected, the production volume variance will be unfavorable.

Part 1	Part 2	Part 3	Part 4	Part 5	Part 6	Part 7	**Demo Doc Complete**

9 Decentralization: Allocating Service Department Costs and Responsibility Accounting

Learning Objectives/ Success Keys

1. Learning about shared resources and service departments

2. Allocating service department costs

3. Decentralization and responsibility center accounting

I t is common for large companies to have one department that handles all employees' paychecks and payroll filing requirements. The Payroll Department at Smart Touch Learning operates this way. It generates no revenue, but acts as support for departments, such as the Excel DVD Department and the Specialty DVD Department. This chapter addresses ways that Smart Touch can allocate its payroll or other shared costs to the departments that use their services. Additionally, the chapter explains responsibility accounting.

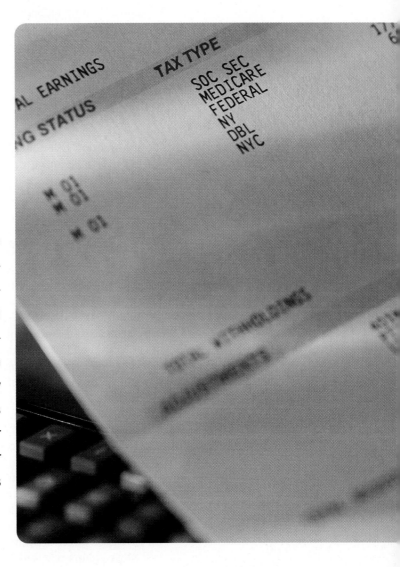

Learn About Resources and Service Departments

<table>
<tr>
<td>1</td>
<td>Learning about shared resources and service departments</td>
</tr>
</table>

In most companies, there are departments that provide services to multiple departments or divisions for the company. These shared resources are often called **service departments** because they provide *services* to other departments at the same company. Another common characteristic of service departments is that they usually do not generate revenues. Some examples of service departments follow:

- Payroll and Human Resources
- Accounting
- Copying/Graphic Services
- Physical Plant (repairs and maintains administrative and production facilities)
- Advertising (companywide, not specific products)
- Mail and Shipping Services
- Shared Facilities (such as meeting rooms used by various departments)
- Legal Services
- Travel Booking Services

This list is not all-inclusive, but merely some common centralized functions. For example at your college or university, there are many similar shared services that support academic departments such as the library, admissions, counseling center and information technology. The key is that a service department is a centralized, non-revenue generating department that provides services to many departments within a company.

Allocating Service Department Costs

<table>
<tr>
<td>2</td>
<td>Allocating service department costs</td>
</tr>
</table>

So, how do companies charge various departments for their use of service departments? Let's start with an example. Suppose Smart Touch Learning incurs $30,000 per month to operate the Centralized Payroll Department. To simplify the illustration, let us assume the company only has three division allocations: CDs, DVDs, and e-Learning. How should the company split, or allocate, the $30,000 cost among the three divisions? Splitting the cost equally—charging each division $10,000—may not be fair, especially if the three units do not use the services equally. Smart Touch's data for allocation follows in Exhibit 9-1, showing not only the three divisions, but also a further separation of information, for the DVD Division.

Ideally, the company should allocate the $30,000 based on each division's use of centralized payroll services. The company should use the primary activity that drives (increases or decreases) the cost of central payroll services as the allocation base. As you may recall from Chapter 3, companies identify cost drivers when they implement ABC. Therefore, a company that has already implemented ABC should know what cost drivers would be suitable for allocating service department charges. For example, payroll processing cost may be driven by the number of employee payroll checks or direct deposits processed.

Most companies will use some type of usage-related cost driver to allocate Service Department costs. Exhibit 9-2 provides several examples of centralized services and common allocation bases.

EXHIBIT 9-1 | **Smart Touch Learning's Data for Allocation**

Divisions Sharing Central Payroll Services	Number of Employees (allocation base)	Operating Income Before Allocation of Shared Service Costs
CD	100	$ 560,000
DVD	140	350,000
e-Learning	160	490,000
Total	400	$1,400,000

Departments in the DVD Division Sharing Central Payroll Services	Number of Employees (allocation base)	Operating Income Before Allocation of Shared Service Costs
Excel DVDs	84	$280,000
Specialty DVDs	56	70,000
Total	140	$350,000

EXHIBIT 9-2 | **Common Service Departments**

Centralized Service Departments	Examples of Departments' cost	Typical allocation base
Payroll and Human Resources	Payroll and human resources' salaries depreciation on equipment and facilities, payroll software	Number of employees
Accounting	Accounting personnel salaries, depreciation on equipment and facilities used by accounting staff, accounting software costs	Number of reports prepared
Copying/Graphic Services	Copier depreciation, toner and paper; salaries of Copying/Graphic Services	Number of copies made for department
Physical Plant	Salaries of physical plant employees, depreciation on physical plant equipment, cost of repair and maintenance parts, plant supplies (glue, bolts, small tools)	Number of repairs made
Advertising	Cost of advertising spots on TV/Radio/Internet and cost advertising employee salaries	Allocation based on percent of sales or product mix
Mail and Shipping Services	Cost of shipping/mailing, salaries of shipping personnel, depreciation on equipment and facilities used by mail personnel	Pieces of mail processed
Shared Facilities	Depreciation on furniture and fixtures and utilities cost	Allocation based on hours of use
Legal	Salaries of legal department personnel, depreciation on legal department equipment, software costs	Number of hours spent on legal matters
Travel	Salaries of travel department personnel, depreciation on travel department equipment, software costs	Number of business trips booked

Based on the data in Exhibit 9-1, Smart Touch Learning would probably chose the "number of employees" as the cost driver for allocating the $30,000 in payroll costs as this would closely match how much each division uses the Centralized Payroll Department. Smart Touch's data is in Exhibit 9-1. Exhibit 9-3 shows the allocation of the $30,000 based on the total number of employees in each division.

EXHIBIT 9-3 | Smart Touch Learning's Allocation of Central Payroll Services (Three Divisions) Using Allocation Base

Divisions Sharing Central Payroll Services	Number of Employees (allocation base)	Percentage of Total Employees	Service Department Charge ($30,000 × %)
CD	100	25.00%	$ 7,500
DVD	140	35.00%	10,500
e-Learning	160	40.00%	12,000
Total	400	100.00%	$30,000

There are other cost drivers or allocation bases that could be used that may reveal a different result. For example, when usage data are not available or are too costly to collect, companies will resort to allocating Service Department costs based on each division's "ability to bear" the cost. In such cases, companies allocate the Service Department cost based on the amount of revenue or operating income one division generates compared to others. Look at Smart Touch again, and allocate the shared payroll costs using operating income as the allocation base. Exhibit 9-4 illustrates this type of allocation.

EXHIBIT 9-4 | Smart Touch Learning's Allocation of Central Payroll Services (Three Divisions) Using Income

Divisions Sharing Central Payroll Services	Unit Operating Income Before Payroll Service Department Charges	Percentage of Total Operating Income	Service Department Charge ($30,000 × %)
CD	$ 560,000	40.00%	$12,000
DVD	350,000	25.00%	7,500
e-Learning	490,000	35.00%	10,500
Total	$1,400,000	100.00%	$30,000

This type of allocation is similar to a tax: The higher the division's income, the higher the charge. Consider the CD Department at Smart Touch. Its charge for actual usage in Exhibit 9-3 was $7,500, but the Payroll Service Department charge using operating income in Exhibit 9-4 allocates $12,000 to the CD Department. Using operating income as an allocator of shared costs serves to penalize the successful departments (such as Smart Touch's CD Department) and rewards the departments that are not as successful (such as Smart Touch's DVD Department).

The allocation of the payroll department for Smart Touch can be further broken down by product line. We determined in Exhibit 9-3, that the DVD Division was allocated $10,500 of the total $30,000 shared Payroll Service Department costs, when we used employees as an allocation base. From earlier chapters we know that Smart Touch's DVD Division mainly produces two types of DVDs—Excel DVDs and Specialty DVDs. We need to allocate the $10,500 in shared payroll costs for the DVD Division to the two product lines within the DVD Division to determine the profit from each product line. Step one would allocate the $10,500 shared payroll costs between Excel and Specialty DVDs as before and as shown in Exhibit 9-5 on the next page.

EXHIBIT 9-5	Smart Touch Learning's Allocation of Central Payroll Services (DVD Division) Using Allocation Base			
Divisions Sharing Central Payroll Services		Number of Employees (allocation base)	Percentage of Total Employees	Service Department Charge ($30,000 × %)
Excel DVD		84	60.00%	$ 6,300
Specialty DVD		56	40.00%	4,200
Total		140	100.00%	$10,500

Step two would calculate income by division and by product line after allocating the shared service department costs. This is illustrated in Exhibit 9-6 for the divisions and the whole company, and in Exhibit 9-7 for the DVD Division only.

EXHIBIT 9-6	Income Statement—All Divisions—Service Department Charges Allocated by Employee

SMART TOUCH LEARNING, INC.
Income Statement
For the year ended December 31, 2012

	CD	DVD	e-Learning	Total
Sales revenue	$3,600,000	$1,200,000	$3,840,000	$8,640,000
Less: variable expense	3,040,000	850,000	3,350,000	7,240,000
Contribution margin	560,000	350,000	490,000	1,400,000
Less: allocated service department charges (Exhibit 9-3)	7,500	10,500	12,000	30,000
Net operating income (loss)	552,500	339,500	478,000	1,370,000

EXHIBIT 9-7	Income Statement—DVD Division—Service Department Charges Allocated by Employee

SMART TOUCH LEARNING, INC.
Income Statement—DVD Division
For the year ended December 31, 2012

	Excel DVD	Specialty DVD	DVD Division
Sales revenue	$960,000	$240,000	$1,200,000
Less: variable expense	680,000	170,000	850,000
Contribution margin	280,000	70,000	350,000
Less: allocated service department charges (Exhibit 9-4)	6,300	4,200	10,500
Net operating income (loss)	273,700	65,800	339,500

Even usage-related allocation systems have limitations. What if the cost of running the service department is fixed rather than variable? Then, much of the cost cannot be attributed to a specific cost driver. In our payroll example, suppose $20,000 of the total $30,000 is straight-line depreciation on the equipment and software. Should the company still use the number of employees to allocate the entire $30,000 of cost? Probably not.

As another example, suppose the e-Learning Division downsizes and its number of employees drops to 80, while the number of employees in each of the other two divisions stays constant. If that happens, the CD and DVD Divisions will be charged higher costs even though they did nothing to cause an increase. These changes are shown in blue highlighting in Exhibit 9-8 on the following page.

EXHIBIT 9-8	Smart Touch Learning's Allocation of Central Payroll Services (Three Divisions) Using Allocation Base After e-Leaning Employee Reduction		

Divisions Sharing Central Payroll Services	Number of Employees (allocation base)	Percentage of Total Employees	Service Department Charge ($30,000 × %)
CD	100	31.25%	$ 9,375
DVD	140	43.75%	13,125
e-Learning	80	25.00%	7,500
Total	320	100.00%	$30,000

Notice that now the DVD Division is allocated $13,125 of the total payroll cost, whereas before the reduction in the e-Learning Division workforce, the DVD Division was only allocated $10,500 of the shared payroll cost (Exhibit 9-3). In short, the DVD Division did nothing to increase overall payroll costs, yet it received a higher cost allocation. This is an example of why mixed costs allocation can be challenging. There is no one perfect allocation formula.

Consider that the two examples of cost allocations (number of employees in Exhibit 9-3 and operating income in Exhibit 9-4) are just two of many methods to allocate shared cost. Even the best allocation systems are subject to inherent flaws. More complex service department allocation systems, such as the step-down and reciprocal methods, are discussed in advanced accounting texts.

Stop & Think...

Say you and your roommates share groceries at your apartment. The last grocery trip was $200. How do you split up the costs? There are many ways you could divide the grocery bill. You could split the total grocery cost between the two of you evenly, $100 each. You could split the bill based on the number of meals each of you eats a week. If you eat at the apartment 5 times a week, but your roommate eats at the apartment 15 times a week, then your roommate would rightfully pay a bigger part of the grocery bill ($200 × 15/20 meals, or $150). Your roommate may balk at this arguing that your meals are larger than hers. Then how do you split the bill? This is the same logic we use in allocating shared cost. No system is perfect, but you aim for the allocation that best measures the true usage of the shared expense.

Summary Problem 1

Wilke's Tool-a-Rama manufactures small tools and tool sets. The company utilizes a shared Accounting Department that handles reports needed by the operations managers. The Small Tools Division requested 150 reports and the Tool Set Division requested 100 reports during August. The total cost of the Accounting Department's services was $5,000. Additionally, the operating income by division before allocating the shared cost was $20,000 for Small Tools and $5,000 for the Tool Set Division.

Requirements

1. Prepare an allocation of shared Accounting Department costs based on the number of reports prepared for August, 2011.
2. Prepare an allocation of shared Accounting Department costs based on operating income for August, 2011.

Solution

Requirements

1.

Divisions Sharing Accounting Services	Number of Reports (allocation base)	Percentage of Total Reports	Service Department Charge ($5,000 × %)
Small Tools	150	60.00%	$3,000
Tools Sets	100	40.00%	2,000
Total	250	100.00%	$5,000

2.

Divisions Sharing Accounting Services	Unit Operating Income Before Accounting Service Department Changes	Percentage of Total Operating Income	Service Department Charge ($5,000 × %)
Small Tools	$20,000	80.00%	$4,000
Tools Sets	5,000	20.00%	1,000
Total	$25,000	100.00%	$5,000

Decentralization and Responsibility Accounting

3 Decentralization and responsibility center accounting

In Chapter 8, you learned about how managers set strategic goals and then develop plans and budget resources for activities that will help reach those goals. **Decentralization** allows decision making to occur at many levels throughout the organization. This means that managers working directly within a division are empowered to make decisions for their division. In order for decentralization to work most effectively, managers must *use* budgets and other reports to control operations.

Each manager is responsible for planning and controlling some part of the firm's activities. A **responsibility center** is a part or subunit of an organization whose manager is accountable for specific activities. Lower-level managers are often responsible for budgeting and controlling costs of a single value-chain function. For example, one manager is responsible for planning and controlling the *production* of Greg's Groovy Tunes CDs at the plant, while another is responsible for planning and controlling the *distribution* of the product to customers. Lower-level managers report to higher-level managers, who have broader responsibilities. Managers in charge of production and distribution report to senior managers that are responsible for profits (revenues minus costs) earned by an entire product line.

Four Types of Responsibility Centers

Responsibility accounting is a system for evaluating the performance of each responsibility center and its manager. Responsibility accounting reports compare plans (budgets) with actions (actual results) for each center. Upper-level management then evaluates how well each manager (1) used the budgeted resources to achieve the responsibility center's goals, and thereby (2) controlled the operations for which he or she was responsible. Recall that budgets are prepared before an accounting period occurs to use as a management tool that ensures that the company's objectives are met. Actual results are later compared with amounts budgeted to calculate the difference or variance. This variance is then used by management to determine whether corrective action should be taken or not.

Exhibit 9-9 illustrates four types of responsibility centers.

EXHIBIT 9-9 | **Four Types of Responsibility Centers**

In a **cost center**, such as a production line for CDs, managers are responsible for costs.

In a **revenue center**, such as the Midwest sales region, managers are responsible for generating sales revenue.

In a **profit center**, such as a line of products, managers are responsible for generating income.

In an **investment center**, such as the CD & DVD division, managers are responsible for income and invested capital.

1. **In a cost center, managers are accountable for costs (expenses) only.** Manufacturing operations, such as the CD production lines, are cost centers. The line foreman controls costs by ensuring that employees work efficiently. The foreman is *not* responsible for generating revenues because he or she is not involved in selling the product. The plant manager evaluates the foreman on his or her ability to control *costs* by comparing actual costs to budgeted costs. All else being equal (for example, holding quality constant), the foreman is likely to receive a more favorable evaluation if actual costs are less than budgeted costs.

2. **In a revenue center, managers are primarily accountable for revenues.** Examples include the Midwest and Southeast sales regions of businesses that carry Greg's Groovy Tunes products, such as CDs and DVDs. Revenue center performance reports compare actual with budgeted revenues. The manager is likely to receive a more favorable evaluation if actual revenues exceed the budget.

3. **In a profit center, managers are accountable for both revenues and costs (expenses) and, therefore, profits.** The (higher-level) manager responsible for the entire CD product line would be accountable for increasing sales revenue *and* controlling costs to achieve the profit goals. Profit center reports include both revenues and expenses to show the profit center's income. Superiors evaluate the manager's performance by comparing actual revenues, expenses, and profits to the budget. All else being equal, the manager is likely to receive a more favorable evaluation if actual profits exceed the budget.

4. **In an investment center, managers are accountable for investments, revenues, and costs (expenses).** Examples include the **Saturn** Division of **General Motors** and the North American CD and DVD Division (which includes CDs) of Greg's Groovy Tunes. Managers of investment centers are responsible for (1) generating sales, (2) controlling expenses, and (3) managing the amount of investment required to earn the income (revenues minus expenses). Investments include assets and cash necessary to run the company. Management must ensure that all company investments are being used wisely and are aligned with the company goals to provide a strong profit.

Top management often evaluates investment center managers based on return on investment (ROI), residual income, or economic value added (EVA). Chapter 12 explains how these measures are calculated and used. All else being equal, the manager will receive a more favorable evaluation if the division's actual ROI, residual income, or EVA exceeds the amount budgeted.

Stop & Think...

Consider your personal "budget" is an investment responsibility center. You are responsible for generating revenue (from your job), controlling expenses (for food, school, rent, gas, etc.) and managing the amount of asset investments required (maybe you need to buy a personal computer or increase your savings) to earn the income you desire (revenues minus expenses).

Responsibility Accounting Performance Reports

Exhibit 9-10 on the following page shows how an organization like Greg's Groovy Tunes might assign responsibility.

At the top level, the CEO oversees each of the four divisions. Division managers generally have broad responsibility, including deciding how to use assets to maximize ROI. Most companies consider divisions as *investment centers*.

EXHIBIT 9-10 | **Partial Organization Chart**

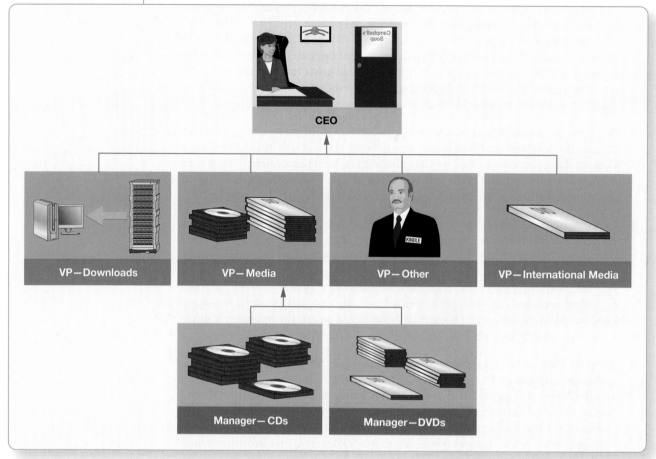

Each division manager supervises all the product lines in that division. Exhibit 9-10 shows that the VP of Media oversees the CD and DVD lines. Product lines are generally considered *profit centers*. Thus, the manager of the CD product line is responsible for evaluating lower-level managers of both

- *cost centers* (such as plants that make CD products) and
- *revenue centers* (such as managers responsible for CD products sales).

Exhibit 9-11 illustrates responsibility accounting performance reports for each level of management shown in Exhibit 9-10 for Greg's Groovy Tunes. Note that the performance report contains both budgeted and actual amounts. Generally budgets are prepared before the accounting period begins and the actual results are calculated at the end of the period, after all service costs are allocated. A variance is determined by comparing budgeted with actual.

Exhibit 9-11 illustrates the many uses of responsibility accounting performance reports as follows:

- the CEO may use to evaluate divisions.
- the divisional VPs may use to evaluate individual product lines.
- the product-line managers may use to evaluate the development, production, marketing, and distribution of their products.
- the budget director may use to modify future budgets.
- the board of directors may use to examine overall corporate fiscal responsibility.

At each level, the reports compare actual results with the budget and display a favorable or unfavorable variance to use for performance evaluation at each level of responsibility.

EXHIBIT 9-11	Responsibility Accounting Performance Reports at Various Levels

CEO'S QUARTERLY RESPONSIBILITY REPORT
(in millions of dollars)

Operating Income of Divisions and Corporate Headquarters Expense	Budget	Actual	Variance Favorable/ (Unfavorable)
Downloads	$218	$209	$ (9)
Media	70	84	14
Other	79	87	8
International Media	35	34	(1)
Corporate Headquarters Expense	(33)	(29)	4
Operating Income	$369	$385	$16

VP—MEDIA QUARTERLY RESPONSIBILITY REPORT
(in millions of dollars)

Operating Income of Product Lines	Budget	Actual	Variance Favorable/ (Unfavorable)
CDs	25	38	13
DVDs	45	46	1
Operating Income	$70	$84	$14

MANAGER—CDs QUARTERLY RESPONSIBILITY REPORT
(in millions of dollars)

Revenue and Expenses	Budget	Actual	Variance Favorable/ (Unfavorable)
Sales revenue	$ 80	$ 84	$ 4
Cost of goods sold	(36)	(30)	6
Gross profit	44	54	10
Marketing expenses	(12)	(9)	3
Research and development expenses	(2)	(3)	(1)
Other expenses	(5)	(4)	1
Operating income	$ 25	$ 38	$13

Start with the lowest level and move to the top. Follow the $25 million budgeted operating income from the CDs product-line report to the report for the VP—Media. The VP's report summarizes the budgeted and actual operating incomes for each of the two product lines he or she supervises.

Now, trace the $70 million budgeted operating income from the VP's report to the CEO's report. The CEO's report includes a summary of each division's budgeted and actual profits, as well as the costs incurred by corporate headquarters, which are not assigned to any of the divisions.

Management by Exception

The variances reported in Exhibit 9-11 aid **management by exception**, which directs executives' attention to important differences between actual and budgeted amounts. For example in the CEO's Quarterly Responsibility Report, The International Media Division's actual operating income of $34 million is very close to the budgeted $35 million. Unless there are other signs of trouble, the CEO will not waste time investigating such a small variance.

In contrast, the Media Division earned much more profit than budgeted, with a positive variance of $14 million. The CEO will want to know why. Suppose the VP of the division believes a national sales promotion was especially effective. That specific promotion may be repeated or adapted by other divisions. To identify the reason for exceptional results, so that other parts of the organization may benefit, is one reason why managers investigate large favorable variances (not just large unfavorable ones). Another reason is to ensure that employees are not skimping on production ingredients, marketing, or R&D, which could hurt the company's long-term success.

The CEO who received the report at the top of Exhibit 9-11 would likely concentrate on improving the Downloads Division because its actual income fell $9 million below budget. The CEO will want to see which product lines caused the shortfall and work with the VP of the Downloads Division to correct any problems.

Exhibit 9-11 also shows how summarized data may hide problems. Although according to the CEO's report, the Media Division as a whole performed well, the DVD lines did not perform as well as the CD lines. This information, found on the VP-Media Quarterly Responsibility Report, shows the importance of division managers and the need for them to spot and correct problems in individual product lines.

Not a Question of Blame

Responsibility accounting assigns managers responsibility for their unit's actions and provides a way to evaluate both their individual and their unit's performance. But superiors should not misuse responsibility accounting to find fault or place blame. The question is not "Who is to blame for an unfavorable variance?" Instead, the question is "Who can best *explain* why a specific variance occurred?"

Consider the Downloads Division in Exhibit 9-11. Suppose a tornado devastated the primary production plant. It may be that the remaining plants operated very efficiently, and this efficiency kept the income variance down to $9 million. If so, the Downloads Division and its VP may actually have done a good job.

Keep in mind that not all costs are allocateable/traceable. There is often a portion of costs that are not properly allocated to any divisions. These are called **untraceable costs** and are shown as a deduction to the company totals as Corporate Headquarters Expense, but not to any specific division.

Stop & Think...

Reconsider your personal budget discussed in the previous Stop & Think. Assume that you budgeted personal expenses for the month of $100, but your actual expenses were $140. Management by exception would dictate that you dig a bit deeper to discover why you did not meet your $100 goal. It could be that you spent $40 more on new iTunes downloads than you budgeted. Alternately, it could be that your literature class textbook cost $40 more than you budgeted. Investigating the "why" allows you to be accountable to your long-term budget plans for your personal investment center.

Other Performance Measures

Top management uses responsibility accounting performance reports to assess each responsibility center's *financial* performance. Top management also often assesses each responsibility center's nonfinancial *operating* performance. Typical nonfinancial performance measures include customer satisfaction ratings, delivery time, product quality, employee expertise, and so forth. Chapter 12 discusses the broader view of performance evaluation, known as the "balanced scorecard." In that chapter, we will look at how managers use both financial and nonfinancial performance measures to form a "balanced view" of each responsibility center's performance.

The "Decision Guidelines" review budgets and how managers use them in responsibility accounting. Study these guidelines before working on Summary Problem 2.

Decision Guidelines

DECENTRALIZATION ALLOCATING SERVICE DEPARTMENT COSTS AND RESPONSIBILITY ACCOUNTING

Amazon.com's initial strategy was to "get big fast." The company has many shared resources, such as accounting services and human resources. **Amazon.com** made many financial decisions when setting up its budgeting process.

Decision	Guidelines
• How might **Amazon.com** allocate its human resource costs?	• The company could allocate shared resource costs by number of employees, operating income, payroll costs or some other method that best reflects the base that drives the human resource costs.
• What kind of a responsibility center does each manager supervise?	• *Cost center*: The manager is responsible for costs. • *Revenue center*: The manager is responsible for revenues. • *Profit center*: The manager is responsible for both revenues and costs, and, therefore, profits. • *Investment center*: The manager is responsible for revenues, costs, and the amount of the investment required to earn the income.
• How should **Amazon.com** evaluate managers?	Typically the company would compare actual performance with the budget for the manager's responsibility center. *Management by exception* focuses on large differences between budgeted and actual results and is a management style used by many companies.

Summary Problem 2

Continue the Wilke's Tool-a-Rama illustration from Summary Problem 1 earlier in the chapter. Recall that their shared resources included an accounting department with shared service fees of $5,000. Relevant data follows, showing all budgeted items, as well as actual revenues and expenses before allocation of shared resources:

Divisions Sharing Accounting Services	Number of Reports (allocation base)		Budget Sales Revenue		Variable Expenses		Service Dept Charges		Actual Sales Revenue		Variable Expenses	
Small Tools	150	A	$120,000	E	$ 90,000	I	$2,500	M	$120,000	Q	$100,000	U
Tool Set	100	B	110,000	F	98,000	J	2,500	N	100,000	R	95,000	V
Total	250	A+B	$230,000	E+F	$188,000	I+J	$5,000	M+N	$220,000	Q+R	$195,000	U+V

Departments in the Tool Set Division Sharing Accounting Services	Number of Reports (allocation base)		Budget Sales Revenue		Variable Expenses		Service Dept Charges		Actual Sales Revenue		Variable Expenses	
Wrench Tool Set	20	C	$ 40,000	G	$38,000	K	$ 500	O	$ 30,000	S	$27,000	W
Screwdriver Tool Set	80	D	70,000	H	60,000	L	2,000	P	70,000	T	68,000	X
Total	100	B=C+D	$110,000	F=G+H	$98,000	J=K+L	$2,500	N=O+P	$100,000	R=S+T	$95,000	V=W+X

Requirements

1. Prepare Tool Set Division responsibility income reports, using the number of reports as the allocation base for shared services.
2. Prepare companywide responsibility income reports for the company.

Solution

Requirement 1

First, figure the shared cost that will be allocated to the two product lines of the Tool Set Division

Divisions Sharing Accounting Services	Number of Reports (allocation base)		Percentage of Total Reports	Service Department Charge ($5,000 × %)	
Small Tools	150	A	60.00%	$3,000	Y
Tool Set	100	B	40.00%	2,000	Z
Total	250	A+B	100.00%	$5,000	Y+Z
Product Lines Sharing Accounting Services	**Number of Reports (allocation base)**		**Percentage of Total Reports**	**Service Department Charge ($2,000 × %)**	
Wrench Tool Set	20	C	20.00%	$ 400	a
Screwdriver Tool Set	80	D	80.00%	1,600	b
Total	100	B	100.00%	$2,000	Z=a+b

From there, calculate operating income for the Tool Set Division after all costs as follows:

Wilke's Tool-a-Rama—Calculation of Actual Operating Income

Actual Results										
Product Lines	Sales Revenue		Variable Expenses		Service Dept Charge		Operating Income			
Wrench Tool Set	$ 30,000	S	27,000	W	400	a	$2,600		c=S-W-a	
Screwdriver Tool Set	$ 70,000	T	68,000	X	1,600	b	400		d=T-X-b	
Total	$100,000	R=S+T	$95,000	V=W+X	$2,000	Z=a+b	$3,000		e=c+d	

Finally, prepare the Tool Set Division responsibility income report.

WILKE'S TOOL-A-RAMA
Tool Set Division Responsibility Report
For the month ended August 31, 2011

Operating Income of Product Lines	Budget		Actual		Variance Favorable/ (Unfavorable)	
Wrench Tool Set	$1,500*	f=G–K–O	$2,600	c	$ 1,100	i=c–f
Screwdriver Tool Set	8,000~	g=H–L–P	400	d	(7,600)	j=d–g
Operating Income	$9,500	h=f+g	$3,000	e=c+d	$(6,500)	k=i+j
*$40,000 G – 38,000 K – 500 O = $1,500 f						
~$70,000 H – 60,000 L – 2,000 P = $8,000 g						

Requirement 2

WILKE'S TOOL-A-RAMA
CEO's Responsibility Report
For the month ended August 31, 2011

Operating Income of Divisions	Budget		Actual		Variance Favorable/ (Unfavorable)	
Small Tools	$27,500*	l=E–I–M	$17,000~	n=Q–U–Y	$(10,500)	p=n–i
Tool Set	9,500	h	3,000	e	(6,500)	q=e–h
Operating Income	$37,000	m=l+h	$20,000	o=n+e	$(17,000)	r=p+q
*$120,000 E – 90,000 I – 2,500 M = $27,500 l						
~$120,000 Q – 100,000 U – 3,000 Y = $17,000 n						

Review *Decentralization: Allocating Service Department Costs and Responsibility Accounting*

■ Accounting Vocabulary

Decentralization (p. 422)
A process that allows decision making to occur at many levels throughout the organization.

Management by Exception (p. 426)
A management strategy that directs management's attention to relevant differences between actual and budgeted amounts.

Responsibility Accounting (p. 422)
A system for evaluating the performance of each responsibility center and its manager.

Responsibility Center (p. 422)
A part or subunit of an organization whose manager is accountable for specific activities.

Service Departments (p. 416)
A part or subunit of an organization whose manager is accountable for specific activities that provide a service for other divisions, but that do not generate revenue. Such areas are generally cost centers and should be allocated to other divisions within a company.

Untraceable Costs (p. 426)
Costs that a company incurs that cannot be properly allocated to any company divisions or products that instead belong to the company as a whole.

■ Quick Check

1. Which of the following is most likely a shared department?
   a. Payroll
   b. Accounting
   c. Legal
   d. All of the above

2. Assume that Human Resources is a shared department for a particular company. Which is the best way to allocate the Human Resources Department's cost to divisions that use its services?
   a. Number of employees
   b. Number of payroll returns filed
   c. Amount of operating income
   d. Total division sales

3. Shared resource departments are typically
   a. centralized functions that are used by many departments in a company.
   b. decentralized functions that are used by many departments in a company.
   c. centralized functions that are used by only two departments in a company.
   d. decentralized functions that are used by only two departments in a company.

Use the following information about Dahl Computers to answer Questions 4 through 10.

		Budget			Actual	
Divisions Sharing Accounting Services	**Number of Reports (allocation base)**	**Sales Revenue**	**Variable Expense**	**Service Dept Charges**	**Sales Revenue**	**Variable Expense**
Desktop Computers	250	$ 300,000	$250,000	$ 3,000	$ 310,000	$262,000
Laptop Computers	150	450,000	$350,000	$ 4,500	$ 450,000	$355,000
Servers	100	250,000	200,000	$ 2,500	245,000	190,000
Total	500	$1,000,000	$800,000	$10,000	$1,005,000	$807,000

		Budget			Actual	
Departments in the Laptop Division Sharing Accounting Services	**Number of Reports (allocation base)**	**Sales Revenue**	**Variable Expense**	**Service Dept Charges**	**Sales Revenue**	**Variable Expense**
Customized Laptops	105	$150,000	$120,000	$ 900	$100,000	$ 80,000
Standard Laptops	45	300,000	230,000	3,600	350,000	275,000
Total	150	$450,000	$350,000	$4,500	$450,000	$355,000

4. If allocation is based on the number of reports prepared by Accounting Services, and accounting services are $10,000 for the period, how much accounting service cost will be assigned to the Desktop Computers Division?

a. $5,000

b. $3,000

c. $4,500

d. $10,000

5. If the number of reports is the allocation base used to assign Accounting Services, and accounting services are $10,000 for the period, how much of accounting service cost will be allocated to the Laptop Computers Division?

a. $2,500

b. $3,000

c. $4,500

d. $10,000

6. If the number of reports is the allocation base used to allocate Accounting Services, and accounting services are $10,000 for the period, how much of accounting service cost will be allocated to the Server Division?

a. $2,000

b. $3,000

c. $4,500

d. $10,000

7. If the number of reports is the allocation base used to assign Accounting Services from division allocation to product line, how much of accounting service cost will be allocated to the customized laptop product line?

a. $2,100

b. $500

c. $2,500

d. Cannot be determined

8. Consider your answers from Questions 4, 5, and 6. What is the amount of actual operating income after shared accounting service allocations for the Laptop Computer Division? Assume total actual accounting services are the same as total budgeted accounting services.
   a. $43,000
   b. $53,000
   c. $92,000
   d. $95,000

9. Consider your answers from Questions 4, 5, 6, and 7. What is the amount of actual operating income after shared accounting service allocations for the customized laptop product line? Assume total actual accounting services are the same as total budgeted accounting services.
   a. $2,100
   b. $17,900
   c. $74,100
   d. $92,000

10. Assume total actual accounting services are the same as total budgeted accounting services. If shared accounting services are allocated based on the number of reports, were the operating income results favorable or unfavorable for the Server Division?
    a. $5,000 unfavorable
    b. $5,000 favorable
    c. $5,500 favorable
    d. $5,500 unfavorable

Answers are given after Apply Your Knowledge (p. 448).

Assess Your Progress

■ Short Exercises

S9-1 *(L.OBJ. 1)* **Learning about shared resources and service departments (5–10 min)**
The following data are available:

Centralized Service Departments	Typical Allocation Base
Payroll and Human Resources	Number of reports prepared
Accounting	Number of buisness trips booked
Copying/Graphic Services	Number of copies made for department
Physical Plant	Allocation based on hours of use
Advertising	Number of employees
Mail and Shipping Services	Number of hours spent on legal matters
Shared Facilities	Number of repairs made
Legal	Pieces of mail processed
Travel	Allocation based on percent of sales or product mix

Requirement

1. Match the method of cost allocation that would be best for each of the shared division costs.

S9-2 *(L.OBJ. 2)* **Allocating shared costs among divisions using an allocation base (5–10 min)**

Zaps-it Exterminators have three departments using the services of the Payroll Department. Total monthly payroll shared cost is $5,000.

The following data are available:

Divisions Sharing Payroll Services	Number of Employees	Number of Employee Requests	Operating Income Before Shared Cost Allocation
Annual Inspections	7	100	$ 10,000
Emergency Services	3	60	50,000
Rodent Division	10	40	40,000
Total	20	200	$100,000

Requirements

1. Allocate the cost to each division using total number of employees as the allocation cost base.

2. Allocate the cost to each division using total number of employee requests as the allocation cost base.

Note: Short Exercise 9-2 must be completed before attempting Short Exercise 9-3.

S9-3 *(L.OBJ. 2)* **Allocating shared costs among divisions using operating income (10–15 min)**

Refer to S9-2.

Requirements

1. Allocate the cost to each division using operating income before shared cost allocation as the allocation cost base.

2. Evaluate the results between S9-2 and S9-3. Which allocation cost base would you recommend?

Note: Short Exercise 9-2 must be completed before attempting Short Exercise 9-4.

S9-4 *(L.OBJ. 3)* **Preparing performance reports for responsibility centers (10–15 min)**

Refer to S9-2. Assume that Zaps-it budgeted operating income before shared cost of $50,000 and shared cost allocation of $1,000 for the Rodent Division. All division managers report to the CEO.

Requirement

1. Prepare a performance report that shows the performance of the Rodent Division to the company as a whole, using the number of employee requests as the allocation base for shared payroll costs. Follow the format of Exhibit 9-11.

S9-5 *(L.OBJ. 2)* **Allocating shared costs among divisions using an allocation base (5–10 min)**

Fruit Paradise grows, packages, and ships fresh fruit countrywide. Some shipments are made to an individual customer and some are made on bulk orders that are mailed to multiple addresses. The company is considering how to best allocate the cost of shipping. Three alternatives were suggested by the Accounting Department: charge based on each address processed (parcel), charge based on the total number of requests (bulk shipments to multiple addresses would be assessed as one request), or allocate based on operating income. Total monthly shared cost for the department is $12,000.

The following data are available:

Divisions Sharing Shipping Services	Number of Parcels Processed	Number of Requests Processed	Operating Income Before Shared Cost Allocation
Apple Division	6,000	400	$ 10,000
Lime Division	3,000	200	50,000
Orange Division	4,000	800	150,000
Tangerine Division	7,000	200	40,000
Total	20,000	1,600	$250,000

Requirements

1. Allocate the cost of shipping to each division using total number of parcels as the allocation cost base.

2. Allocate the cost of shipping to each division using total number of requests as the allocation cost base.

Note: Short Exercise 9-5 must be completed before attempting Short Exercise 9-6.

S9-6 *(L.OBJ. 2)* Allocating shared costs among divisions using operating income (10–15 min)

Refer to S9-5.

Requirements

1. Allocate the cost of shipping to each division using operating income as the allocation cost base.

2. Evaluate the results between S9-4 and S9-5. Which allocation cost base would you recommend?

Note: Short Exercise 9-5 must be completed before attempting Short Exercise 9-7.

S9-7 *(L.OBJ. 3)* Preparing performance reports for responsibility centers (10–15 min)

Refer to S9-5. Assume that Fruit Paradise budgeted its operating income before allocation of shared cost to be $55,000 and its budgeted shared cost allocation for the Lime Division was $4,000. The Lime Division manager reports to the CEO.

Requirement

1. Prepare a performance report, similar to the one in Exhibit 9-11 that shows the performance for the Lime Division as compared to the company as a whole using number of parcels as the allocation base for shared shipping costs. Is this variance favorable or unfavorable?

S9-8 *(L.OBJ. 3)* Preparing performance reports for responsibility centers [5 min]

Consider the following list of responsibility centers and phrases.

A cost center   A revenue center

An investment center   Lower

A profit center   Higher

A responsibility center

Requirement

1. Fill in the blanks with the phrase that best completes the sentence.

   a. The Maintenance Department at the San Diego Zoo is _____.

   b. The concession stand at the San Diego Zoo is _____.

   c. The Menswear Department at Bloomingdale's, which is responsible for buying and selling merchandise, is _____.

   d. A production line at an iPod plant is _____.

   e. _____ is any segment of the business whose manager is accountable for specific activities.

   f. Gatorade, a division of Quaker Oats, is _____.

   g. The sales manager in charge of Nike's northwest sales territory oversees _____.

   h. Managers of cost and revenue centers are at _____ levels of the organization than are managers of profit and investment centers.

S9-9 *(L.OBJ. 3)* **Preparing performance reports for responsibility centers [5–10 min]**
Look at the following performance report:

MANAGER—MEXICAN SAUCES Quarterly Responsibility Report (in millions of dollars)			
Revenues and Expenses	Budget	Actual	Variance Favorable/ (Unfavorable)
Sales revenue	$ 79	$ 84	$ 5
Cost of goods sold	(36)	(29)	7
Gross profit	43	55	12
Marketing expenses	(12)	(10)	2
Research and development expenses	(3)	(4)	(1)
Other expenses	(4)	(2)	2
Operating income	$ 24	$ 39	$ 15

Requirement

1. On which variances should the manager of the Mexican sauces product line focus his or her efforts, according to the management by exception principle? For these variances, compute the variance as a percent of the budgeted amount, and suggest some questions the manager may want to ask during their investigation.

■ Exercises

E9-10 *(L.OBJ. 1, 2)* **Learning about shared costs and allocating shared costs among divisions (10–15 min)**

Integrity Company has three departments using the services of the Payroll Department. The following data are available:

Subunits Sharing Central Payroll Services	Number of Employees	Number of Employee Requests
Division A	100	200
Division B	140	400
Division C	160	400
Total	400	1,000

Requirements

1. Is the payroll department a shared service department for Integrity? Why?
2. Allocate the $20,000 payroll cost to each division using total number of employees as the allocation cost base.
3. Allocate the $20,000 payroll cost to each division using total number of employee requests as the allocation cost base.
4. Evaluate the results. Which allocation cost base would you recommend?

E9-11 *(L.OBJ. 2)* **Allocating shared costs among divisions using an allocation base (5–10 min)**

Career College is a private college located in Independence, MS. It provides instruction in five divisions: Creative Arts, Business, Computer Science, Math, and Science. The college shares copy services with a total monthly cost of $15,000, of which $12,500 of those costs are considered traceable. The college is considering allocating the traceable portion of costs using either number of copies or operating income as its allocation base. Data for the month of June 2012 follows:

Divisions Sharing Copy Services	Number of Copies	Budgeted Operating Income Before Shared Cost Allocation	Budgeted Traceable Costs Allocated	Actual Operating Income Before Shared Cost Allocation
Creative Arts Division	6,000	2,000	2,500	$ 1,000
Buisness Division	3,000	5,000	2,500	5,000
Computer Science Division	6,000	4,500	2,500	4,000
Math Division	12,000	7,700	2,500	7,000
Science Division	3,000	3,300	2,500	3,000
Total	30,000	$22,500	$12,500	$20,000

Requirements

1. Allocate the cost to each division using the total number of copies actually printed at the end of the year as the allocation cost base.
2. Allocate the cost to each division using total actual operating income before shared cost allocation as the allocation cost base.

Note: Exercise 9-11 must be completed before attempting Exercise 9-12.

E9-12 *(L.OBJ. 3)* **Preparing performance reports for responsibility centers (10–15 min)**
Refer to E9-11. All divisions report to the President of the College.

Requirement

1. Prepare a performance report that shows the performance of the Math Division to the college as a whole, using the number of copies as the allocation base for shared copy costs. Follow the format of Exhibit 9-11. Be sure to deduct the untraceable costs on the performance report for the total college.

E9-13 *(L.OBJ. 2)* **Allocating shared costs among divisions using an allocation base (5–10 min)**
Soy Delite products has two product divisions: Dairy and Meat-Alternatives. The Dairy Division products budgeted an average sales price of $4 and budget variable costs of $2 per unit. The Meat-Alternatives Division budgets an average sales price of $7 and budget variable costs of $3 per unit. Both divisions use the Accounting Department, which incurs a monthly cost of $12,000, of which $10,000 is traceable to the two divisions based on the number of reports requested. Data for the month of September 2012 follows:

	Divisions	
	Dairy Division	Meat-Alternatives Division
Budgeted number of units sold	6,000	2,000
Actual number of units sold	7,000	1,900
Actual average sales price per unit	$ 4.00	$ 8.00
Actual average variable cost per unit	$ 2.10	$ 2.90
Budgeted traceable accounting costs	$5,000	$5,000
Actual reports requested from accounting	300	200

Requirement

1. Allocate the cost to each division using the actual reports requested from accounting as the allocation cost base.

Note: Exercise 9-13 must be completed before attempting Exercise 9-14.

E9-14 *(L.OBJ. 3)* **Preparing performance reports for responsibility centers (20–30 min)**
Refer to E9-13. Both division managers report to the CEO.

Requirement

1. Prepare a performance report that shows the performance of the Meat Alternatives Division to the company as a whole, using the number of reports requested as the allocation base for shared accounting costs. Follow the format of Exhibit 9-11. Be sure to deduct the untraceable costs from the company total.

E9-15 *(L.OBJ. 3)* **Preparing performance reports for responsibility centers [5 min]**
Consider the following:

a. The bakery department of a **Publix** supermarket reports income for the current year.

b. **Pace Foods** is a subsidiary of **Campbell Soup Company**.

c. The personnel department of **State Farm Insurance Companies** prepares its budget and subsequent performance report on the basis of its expected expenses for the year.

d. The shopping section of **Burpee.com** reports both revenues and expenses.

e. **Burpee.com**'s investor relations Web site provides operating and financial information to investors and other interested parties.

f. The manager of a **BP** service station is evaluated based on the station's revenues and expenses.

g. A charter airline records revenues and expenses for each airplane each month. Each airplane's performance report shows its ratio of operating income to average book value.

h. The manager of the Southwest sales territory is evaluated based on a comparison of current period sales against budgeted sales.

1. Identify each responsibility center as a cost center (C), a revenue center (R), a profit center (P), or an investment center (R).

E9-16 *(L.OBJ. 3)* **Preparing performance reports for responsibility centers [15–20 min]**
Web Touch is a Fresno company that sells cell phones and MP3s on the Web. Web Touch has assistant managers for its digital and video cell phone operations. These assistant managers report to the manager of the total cell phone product line, who, with the manager of MP3s, reports to the manager for all sales of handheld devices, Mary Burton. Burton received the following data for September 2011 operations:

	Cell Phones		
	Digital	Video	PDAs
Revenues, budget	$ 202,000	$ 800,000	$ 400,000
Expenses, budget	143,000	420,000	275,000
Revenues, actual	213,000	890,000	350,000
Expenses, actual	130,000	440,000	260,000

Requirement

1. Arrange the data in a performance report similar to Exhibit 9-11. Show September results, in thousands of dollars, for digital cell phones, for the total cell phone product line, and for all devices. Which product line should Burton investigate and why?

■ Problems (Group A)

P9-17A *(L.OBJ. 1, 2, 3)* **Service departments, allocating shared costs, and preparing performance reports for responsibility centers [50–60 min]**
Doggy World operates a chain of pet stores in the Midwest. The manager of each store reports to the regional manager, who, in turn, reports to the headquarters in Milwaukee, Wisconsin. The income statement includes *actual* figures for three separate reporting segments as of July 2011:

1. The Dayton Store
2. The Ohio region (which includes the Dayton store)
3. Companywide—the entire company (which includes the Ohio region)

DOGGY WORLD Income Statement For the month ended July 31, 2011			
	Dayton	Ohio	Companywide
Revenue	$ 158,400	$ 1,760,000	$ 4,400,000
Expenses:			
Regional manager/headquarters office	$ –	$ 58,000	$ 122,000
Cost of materials	85,536	880,000	1,760,000
Salary expense	41,184	440,000	1,100,000
Depreciation expense	7,800	91,000	439,000
Utilities expense	4,000	46,600	264,000
Rent expense	2,500	34,500	178,000
Total expenses	141,020	1,550,100	3,863,000
Operating income	$ 17,380	$ 209,900	$ 537,000

Budgeted amounts for July were as follows:

DOGGY WORLD Budgeted Income Statement For the month ended July 31, 2011			
	Dayton	Ohio	Companywide
Revenue	$ 173,400	$ 1,883,000	$ 4,650,000
Expenses:			
Regional manager/headquarters office	$ –	$ 64,600	$ 124,000
Cost of materials	91,902	1,035,650	2,092,500
Salary expense	41,616	470,750	1,162,500
Depreciation expense	7,800	87,500	446,000
Utilities expense	4,900	54,600	274,000
Rent expense	3,400	32,700	169,000
Total expenses	149,618	1,745,800	4,268,000
Operating income	$ 23,782	$ 137,200	$ 382,000

Additionally, the company incurs shared Payroll Service Department cost of $20,000, which it allocates based on the number of employees. The company currently employs a total of 1,000 employees, including 200 in Ohio and 20 in Dayton. The company originally budgeted $22,000 in monthly shared payroll cost for 1,000 total employees. This budget included 250 employees in Ohio and 25 in Dayton.

Requirements

1. What kind of responsibility center is the Dayton center? What kind of center is the Payroll Services Department?

2. Prepare a report showing the allocation of payroll costs for Ohio compared to the payroll costs allocated companywide. Prepare another allocation showing payroll costs for Dayton compared to the payroll costs allocated companywide. Follow the format of Exhibit 9-5.

3. Prepare a report for July 2011 that shows the performance of the Dayton store, the Ohio region, and the company as a whole. Follow the format of Exhibit 9-11.

4. If you were the companywide manager, which of these performance reports would you investigate?

P9-18A *(L.OBJ. 1, 2, 3)* **Service departments, allocating shared costs, and preparing performance reports for responsibility centers (45–55 min)**
Submarines Unlimited provides submarine adventures in various locations around the world. The company's headquarters are located in Sugarland, TX. The company headquarters provide two main services: accounting and reservation services. Both shared service departments provide services to all four tourist locations. All locations report to the CEO.

Budget and actual data for the four tourist locations are as follows:

	Maui	Orlando	San Diego	Juneau	Total
			Locations		
Budgeted number of dives sold	6,000	2,000	2,000	2,000	12,000
Actual number of dives sold	7,000	1,900	1,900	1,900	12,700
Budgeted average sales revenue per dive	$120.00	$90.00	$100.00	$110.00	
Actual average sales revenue per dive	$115.00	$88.00	$110.00	$110.00	
Budgeted average variable cost per dive	$ 50.00	$30.00	$ 35.00	$ 40.00	
Actual average variable cost per dive	$ 48.00	$32.00	$ 36.00	$ 41.00	
Budgeted fixed costs by location	$11,000	$9,000	$10,000	$10,000	$40,000
Actual fixed costs by location	$11,000	$9,000	$10,000	$10,000	$40,000
Budgeted traceable accounting costs	$ 5,500	$5,500	$ 5,500	$ 5,500	$22,000
Actual reports requested from accounting	70	40	60	30	200
Budgeted traceable reservation costs	$ 9,000	$5,500	$ 3,500	$ 3,500	$21,500
Actual calls by location	24,000	12,000	18,000	6,000	60,000

The Accounting Services Department actually incurred $11,000 in costs for May 2012. These costs are allocated based on the number of reports requested. The Reservation Department incurred $23,000 in actual costs, of which $20,000 were traceable to the four locations based on actual calls by location.

Requirements

1. What kind of responsibility center is each location? What kind of responsibility center is corporate headquarters?

2. Prepare a report allocating the traceable shared cost to each division using the respective allocation base given.

3. Prepare a performance report that shows the performance of the Maui location to the company as a whole, using the allocation bases prepared in Requirement 2 for both shared costs. Follow the format of Exhibit 9-11. Be sure to deduct the untraceable portion of the Reservation Department costs from the company total.

P9-19A *(L.OBJ. 2, 3)* **Allocating shared costs, and preparing performance reports for responsibility centers (45–55 min)**
Musical Notes, Inc., manufactures and sells two different types of guitars: Blastercaster and Cool Blues. The two product lines share physical plant resource costs of $7,000 of which $1,000 is not traceable to either product line.
Budget and actual data for each of the two product lines are as follows:

	Blastercaster	Cool Blues
	Product Lines	
Budgeted number of units sold	3,000	2,000
Actual number of units sold	3,400	2,100
Budgeted average sales price per unit	$ 400	$ 600
Actual average sales price per unit	$ 390	$ 560
Actual standard variable cost per unit	$ 250	$ 300
Budgeted traceable physical plant costs	$3,000	$3,000
Actual number of repair orders	20	10
Actual hours on repair jobs	150	250

Budgeted variable cost per unit were the same as actual for the month. The company is considering two methods of allocating the physical plant resource costs: number of repair orders or number of hours on job. Both guitar line managers report to the CEO of Musical Notes, Inc.

Requirements

1. Prepare a report allocating the traceable shared cost to each product line using the number of repair orders as the allocation base.

2. Prepare a report allocating the traceable shared cost to each product line using the number of hours on the job as the allocation base.

3. Prepare a performance report that shows the performance of the Blastercaster Guitar Division to the company as a whole, using the allocation bases prepared in Requirement 2 for shared costs. Follow the format of Exhibit 9-11. Be sure to deduct the untraceable portion of the physical plant costs from the company total.

■ Problems (Group B)

P9-20B *(L.OBJ. 1, 2, 3)* **Service departments, allocating shared costs, and preparing performance reports for responsibility centers [50–60 min]**
Winnie's World operates a chain of pet stores in the Midwest. The manager of each store reports to the regional manager, who in turn, reports to headquarters in Milwaukee, Wisconsin. The income statement includes *actual* figures for three separate reporting segments as of July 2011:

1. The Kansas City Store
2. The Kansas region (which includes the Kansas City store)
3. Companywide—the entire company (which includes the Kansas region)

	Winnie's World Income Statement For the month ended July 31, 2011		
	Kansas City	**Kansas**	**Companywide**
Revenue	$147,600	$1,640,000	$4,100,000
Expenses:			
Regional manager/headquarters office	$ –	$ 57,000	$ 118,000
Cost of materials	79,704	820,000	1,640,000
Salary expense	38,376	410,000	1,025,000
Depreciation expense	7,700	95,000	438,000
Utilities expense	4,000	46,600	264,000
Rent expense	2,500	34,500	174,000
Total expenses	132,280	1,463,100	3,659,000
Operating income	$ 15,320	$ 176,900	$ 441,000

Budgeted amounts for July were as follows:

Winnie's World Budgeted Income Statement For the month ended July 31, 2011	Kansas City	Kansas	Companywide
Revenue	$160,600	$1,763,000	$4,350,000
Expenses:			
Regional manager/headquarters office	$ –	$ 63,600	$ 120,000
Cost of materials	85,118	969,650	1,957,500
Salary expense	38,544	440,750	1,087,500
Depreciation expense	7,700	87,500	449,000
Utilities expense	4,500	54,900	274,000
Rent expense	3,600	32,500	171,000
Total expenses	139,462	1,648,900	4,059,000
Operating income	$ 21,138	$ 114,100	$ 291,000

Additionally, the company incurs shared Payroll Service Department costs of $30,000, which it allocates based on the number of employees. The company employs a total of 2,000 employees, of which 500 are employed in Kansas and 100 are employed in Kansas City. The company originally budgeted $28,000 in monthly shared payroll cost for 2,000 total employees with 400 employees in Kansas and 80 in Kansas City.

Requirements

1. What kind of responsibility center is the Kansas City center? What kind of center is the Payroll Services Department?

2. Prepare a report showing the allocation of payroll costs for Kansas compared to other company locations. Prepare another allocation showing payroll costs for Kansas City compared to other locations in Kansas. Follow the format of Exhibit 9-5.

3. Prepare a report for July 2011 that shows the performance of the Kansas City store, the Kansas region, and the company as a whole. Follow the format of Exhibit 9-11.

4. As the Kansas region manager, would you investigate the Kansas City store on the basis of this report? Why or why not?

P9-21B *(L.OBJ. 1, 2, 3)* **Service departments, allocating shared costs, and preparing performance reports for responsibility centers (45–55 min)**

Deep Sea Dive provides submarine adventures in various locations around the world. The company headquarters are located in Sugarland, TX. The headquarters provide two main services: accounting and reservation services. Both shared service departments provide services to all four tourist locations. All locations report to the CEO. Budget and actual data for their four tourist locations are as follows:

	Maui	Orlando	San Diego	Juneau	Total
			Locations		
Budgeted number of dives sold	7,000	2,700	2,800	2,100	14,600
Actual number of dives sold	6,000	2,200	3,000	2,600	13,800
Budgeted average sales revenue per dive	$ 115	75	90	105	
Actual average sales revenue per dive	$ 105	70	95	103	
Budgeted average variable cost per dive	$ 45	25	35	35	
Actual average variable cost per dive	$ 43	27	38	36	
Budgeted fixed costs by location	$13,000	9,000	8,500	10,000	40,500
Actual fixed costs by location	$13,000	10,000	8,500	10,000	41,500
Budgeted traceable accounting costs	$ 7,000	7,000	7,000	7,000	28,000
Actual reports requested from accounting	120	75	90	15	300
Budgeted traceable reservation costs	$ 8,500	5,000	3,500	2,500	19,500
Actual calls by location	27,500	5,500	16,500	5,500	55,000

The Accounting Services Department actually incurred $13,500 in costs for May 2012, which are allocated based on accounting reports requested. The Reservation Department incurred $20,600 in actual costs of which $17,600 were traceable to the locations. These costs are allocated based on actual calls by location.

Requirements

1. What kind of responsibility center is each location? What kind of responsibility center is corporate headquarters?

2. Prepare a report allocating the traceable shared cost to each division using the appropriate allocation base.

3. Prepare a performance report that shows the performance of the Maui location to the company as a whole, using the allocation bases prepared in Requirement 2 for both shared costs. Follow the format of Exhibit 9-11. Be sure to deduct the untraceable portion of the reservation department costs from the company total.

P9-22B *(L.OBJ. 2, 3)* **Allocating shared costs, and preparing performance reports for responsibility centers (45–55 min)**

Smooth Sounds, Inc., manufactures and sells two different types of guitars: Rock Z100 and Cool Strings. The two product lines share physical plant resource costs of $8,500 of which $500 is not traceable to either product line. Budget and actual data for each of the two product lines are as follows:

	Rock Z100	Cool Strings
	Product Lines	
Budgeted number of units sold	3,800	1,900
Actual number of units sold	3,600	1,700
Budgeted average sales price per unit	$ 350	$ 640
Actual average sales price per unit	$ 330	$ 630
Actual standard variable cost per unit	$ 300	$ 340
Budgeted traceable physical plant costs	$4,000	$4,000
Actual number of repair orders	35	15
Actual hours on repair jobs	160	340

Budgeted variable costs per unit were the same as actual for the month. The company is considering two methods of allocating the physical plant resource costs: number of repair orders or number of hours on job. Both guitar line managers report to the CEO of Smooth Sounds, Inc.

Requirements

1. Prepare a report allocating the traceable shared cost to each product line using the number of repair orders as the allocation base.

2. Prepare a report allocating the traceable shared cost to each product line using the number of hours on the repair job as the allocation base.

3. Prepare a performance report that shows the performance of the Rock Z100 Guitar Division to the company as a whole, using the allocation bases prepared in Requirement 2 for shared costs. Follow the format of Exhibit 9-11. Be sure to deduct the untraceable portion of the physical plant costs from the company total.

■ Continuing Exercise

E9-23 This exercise continues the Sherman Lawn Service, Inc., situation from Exercise 8-35 of Chapter 8. In addition to the budget and actual data presented in Exercise 8-35, consider that Sherman also must allocate office resources to the lawn and landscaping divisions. Sherman thinks that the best allocation base or cost driver would be the number of jobs. Sherman budgeted $1,200 for the cost of office resources to the lawn divisions and $800 of the cost of office resources to landscaping. Actual jobs for the month were 550 lawns and 200 landscaping jobs.

Requirement

1. Prepare a report allocating the traceable shared cost to each product line using the number of jobs as the allocation base.

2. Prepare a performance report for the lawn division.

■ Continuing Problem

P9-24 This problem continues the Haupt Consulting, Inc., situation from P8-36 of Chapter 8. Consider the standard and budgeted cost presented for each package in P8-36. Consider that budgeted sales revenue for the 10 jobs completed in October was $30,000 per job. Actual total sales revenue for October was $315,000.

Requirements

1. Prepare Haupt Consulting's performance report for October.

2. Which variances would most concern management and why?

Apply Your Knowledge

▪ Decision Case

Case 1. Luxury Loom weaves comforters that are sold through various distributors. The Economy Comforters sell for $100 each and the Deluxe Comforters sell for $150 each. The company has woven and sold 2,500 each of both types of comforters each month. The direct materials cost per Economy Comforter is $45 and per Deluxe Comforter is $70. Conversion costs are $20 per set, regardless of the comforter type.

Luxury Loom has two shared resources providing services to the both product lines: the Human Resources Department, $3,000 per month, and the Graphic Services Department, $2,000 per month. The following table presents usage data for each department:

	Product Lines	
	Economy	Deluxe
Human resources—Actual number of employees	15	15
Human resources—Number of employees' requests	60	40
Plant—Actual number of graphic designs	10	20
Plant—Actual hours spent on designs	150	50

Requirements

1. Prepare allocation reports for each of the shared resource costs.
2. Which allocation method best allocates the shared resource costs of the Human Resources Department? Of the Graphic Services Department? Give your reason.
3. What other allocation methods might Luxury Loom consider?

▪ Ethical Issue

Kaitlyn's Karate, owned by Kaitlyn Stump, operates regional karate centers for all ages. Each center is operated by an onsite manager/controller. Each center has two full-time instructors who teach classes and many contract instructors who are independent contractors.

The various operations sites share human resource functions at the corporate headquarters in Keller, TX based on the sum of the following:

- a $2,000 flat rate per center plus
- an allocation of the remaining shared cost based on the number of independent contractors hired at the center.

The Sugarland, TX location has experienced high contractor turnover. The center manager is concerned about the effect this will have on sales at the center as well as center profitability. The center manager receives a significant annual bonus based on center profitability. The manager has been moving some of the contractor costs into various expense accounts to reduce the number of registered independent contractors that corporate headquarters will use to allocate Sugarland's share of human resource costs at year end.

Requirements

Put yourself in Stump's position. In deciding how to deal with the situation, answer the following questions:

1. What is the ethical issue?
2. What are my options?

3. What are the possible consequences?
4. What should I do?

■ Financial Statement Case—Amazon.com

This case is based on the **Amazon.com** annual report in Appendix A at the end of the book. Use it to answer the following questions.

Requirement

1. Review the data for **Amazon.com**.
   a. What shared services departments might **Amazon.com** have? Given the company departments noted, what method could the company use to fairly allocate the shared costs to the various divisions and/or product lines at the company.
   b. Evaluate the options and draft a report recommending a specific allocation method for each shared cost center you identify.

■ Team Project

Xellnet provides e-commerce software for the pharmaceuticals industry. Xellnet is organized into several divisions. A companywide planning committee sets general strategy and goals for the company and its divisions, but each division develops its own budget.

Lonnie Draper is the new division manager of wireless communications software. His division has two departments: Development and Sales. Chad Sanchez manages the 20 or so programmers and systems specialists typically employed in the Development Department to create and update the division's software applications. Liz Smith manages the Sales Department.

Xellnet considers the divisions to be investment centers. To earn his bonus next year, Draper must achieve a 30% return on the $3 million invested in his division. Within the Wireless Division, development is considered a cost center, and sales is categorized as a revenue center.

Budgeting is in progress for 2011. Sanchez met with his staff and is now struggling with two sets of numbers. Alternative A is his best estimate of next year's costs. However, unexpected problems can arise when writing software, and finding competent programmers is an ongoing challenge. Sanchez knows that Draper, the new manager, was a programmer before he earned an MBA so he should understand the challenges within the division. Consequently, he is thinking of increasing his budgeted costs (Alternative B). His department's bonuses largely depend on whether the department meets its budgeted costs.

XELLNET Wireless Division Development Budget 2011	Alternative A	Alternative B
Salaries expense (including overtime and part time)	$2,400,000	$2,640,000
Software expense	120,000	132,000
Travel expense	65,000	71,500
Depreciation expense	255,000	255,000
Miscellaneous expense	100,000	110,000
Total expense	$2,940,000	$3,208,500

Liz Smith is also struggling with her sales budget. Prospective customers appear to have made their initial investments in communications software so it is harder to obtain new clients. If things go well, she believes her sales team can maintain the level of growth achieved over the last few years. This is Alternative A in the sales budget. However, if Smith is too optimistic, sales may fall short of the budget. If this happens, her team will not receive bonuses. Therefore, Smith is considering reducing the sales numbers and submitting Alternative B.

XELLNET Wireless Division Sales Budget 2011		
	Alternative A	Alternative B
Sales revenue	$5,000,000	$4,500,000
Salaries expense	360,000	360,000
Travel expense	240,000	210,500

Neither Chad nor Liz's budgets contain an allocation for the $100,000 shared human resource costs that the Wireless Division uses, yet these are required for their budgets to be complete. The Wireless Division has historically employed 1,000 of the company total 5,000 employees. Additionally, its employee requests in pasts years averaged 800 of the total 8,000 requests made each year. Unfortunately, the Wireless Division has experienced a lot of turnover and anticipates its requests will probably triple next year.

Chad and Liz are struggling with how to allocate the shared costs. Split your team into three groups. Each group should meet separately before the entire team meets.

Requirements

1. The first team plays the role of development manager Chad Sanchez. Before meeting with the entire team, determine which set of budget numbers you are going to present to Lonnie Draper, as well as which allocation of shared cost you will advocate for the division's share of human resource costs. Write a memo supporting your decision. Use the format shown in Decision Case 1. Give this memo to the third group before the team meeting.

2. The second group plays the role of sales manager Liz Smith. Before meeting with the entire team, determine which set of budget numbers you are going to present to Lonnie Draper, as well as the suggested allocation of shared human resource cost you will advocate as the sale's division share. Write a memo supporting your decision. Use the format shown in Decision Case 1. Give this memo to the third group before the team meeting.

3. The third group plays the role of division manager Lonnie Draper. Before meeting with the entire team, use the memos that Sanchez and Smith have provided to prepare a total division budget based on the sales and development budgets Your divisional overhead costs (additional costs beyond those incurred by the development and sales departments) are approximately $390,000. Determine whether the Wireless Division can meet its targeted 30% return on assets given the budgeted alternatives submitted by your department managers. During the meeting of the entire team, group three playing Draper presents the division budget and considers its implications. Each group should take turns discussing concerns with the proposed budget. The team as a whole should consider whether the division budget must be revised. The team should prepare a report that includes the division budget and a summary of the issues covered in the team meeting.

Quick Check Answers

1. *d.* 2. *a.* 3. *a.* 4. *a.* 5. *b.* 6. *a.* 7. *a.* 8. *c.* 9. *b.* 10. *c.*

For online homework, exercises, and problems that provide you immediate feedback, please visit www.myaccountinglab.com.

Big Picture

Ch 1 Introduction to Management Accounting

- Distinguish management accounting from financial accounting
- The role and responsibilities of management accountants
- Classify costs and prepare income statements for merchandising companies
- Classify costs and prepare income statements and statements of cost of goods manufactured for manufacturing companies

Ch 2 Job Order Costing

- Distinguish between job order and process costing
- Record materials, labor, and overhead in a job order costing system
- Record completion and sales of finished goods and adjust for under-/overallocated overhead
- Calculate unit costs for service companies

Ch 3 Activity-Based Costing and Other Cost Management Tools

- Develop activity-based costs and used activity-based management to determine target product costs
- Record transactions in JIT systems
- Use the four types of quality costs to make management decisions

Ch 4 Process Costing

- Calculate equivalent units and conversion costs
- Prepare cost of production reports and the related journal entries using the weighted-average costing method
- Prepare cost of production reports and the related journal entries using the FIFO costing method

Ch 5 Cost Behavior and Cost-Volume-Profit Analysis

- Identify how changes in volume affect cost
- Distinguish among variable, mixed, and fixed cost
- Split mixed cost into fixed and variable components by using the high-low method and by using regression analysis
- Use CVP to compute breakeven points, to plan profits, to graph relationships, and to perform sensitivity analysis

Ch 6 Absorption and Variable Costing

- Distinguish between absorption costing and variable costing
- Prepare absorption costing and variable costing income statements and explained the differences between the two costing techniques
- Illustrate the pros and cons of absorption and variable costing

Ch 7 The Master Budget: Profit Planning

- Understand and prepare all components of the master budget for manufacturers
- Use sensitivity analysis to adjust budget preparations

Ch 8 Flexible Budgets and Standard Costs

- Prepare flexible income statement budgets and income statement performance reports
- Compute standard cost variances for direct materials, direct labor, and overhead
- Record transactions using standard costs and prepare standard cost income statements

Ch 9 Decentralization: Allocating Service Department Costs and Responsibility Accounting

- Identify a shared resource or service department
- Allocate service department costs to the departments that use its services utilizing various allocation methods
- Learn the four types of responsibility centers and prepared responsibility reports they utilize

Chapter 9: Demo Doc

■ Preparing Performance Reports for Responsibility Centers

Learning Objective 3

The Better Bagel Company operates a chain of bakeries that are located throughout the United States. The company is divided into regions with four to six states per region. A regional manager oversees each region, and there is a store manager in each store who is responsible for the day-to-day operations of the store. The income statements for the Spokane, Washington, store, all stores located in the Pacific Northwest Region (including Spokane), and all of the U.S stores combined are presented as follows for the month of June 2012:

	Spokane Store	Pacific Northwest Region Stores	U.S. Stores
Sales revenue	$166,200	$778,700	$4,793,400
Cost of goods sold	48,500	260,300	1,442,100
Gross profit	117,700	518,400	3,351,300
Operating expenses:			
Salaries and wages expense	37,600	182,000	1,062,200
Rent expense	18,000	81,800	484,000
Depreciation expense	12,000	58,000	510,000
Office supplies expense	8,200	43,200	328,700
Utilities expense	6,100	30,300	337,300
Total operating expenses	81,900	395,300	2,722,200
Operating income	$ 35,800	$123,100	$ 629,100

The budgeted financial statements for June are presented as follows:

	Spokane Store	Pacific Northwest Region Stores	U.S. Stores
Sales revenue	$155,000	$796,500	$4,750,000
Cost of goods sold	46,000	262,400	1,450,600
Gross profit	109,000	534,100	3,299,400
Operating expenses:			
Salaries and wages expense	36,000	178,000	1,085,000
Rent expense	16,800	82,900	490,200
Depreciation expense	12,600	56,000	512,000
Office supplies expense	8,500	39,800	330,300
Utilities expense	6,400	28,700	332,400
Total operating expenses	80,300	385,400	2,749,900
Operating income	$ 28,700	$148,700	$ 549,500

Requirements

1. Prepare reports for June 2012 that show the performance for the Spokane store, for all of the stores in the Pacific Northwest Region, and for all the stores in the United States. Follow the format of the exhibits in the textbook.

2. Based on the report for the Spokane store, what areas should the manager of the store investigate?

Demo Doc Solution

Requirement 1

3 Decentralization and responsibility accounting

Prepare reports for June 2012 that show the performance for the Spokane store, for all of the stores in the Pacific Northwest Region, and for all the stores in the United States. Follow the format below.

Part 1	Part 2	Demo Doc Complete

In the performance report, we will show the actual results of operations and the budgeted amounts and then show whether a favorable or unfavorable variance was achieved. We will start with the Spokane store. The format for the report should look like this:

Manager—Spokane Store
June 2012 Responsibility Report

Revenue and Expenses	Actual	Budget	Variance Favorable/ (Unfavorable)

The next step is to insert the actual revenues and expenses given in the problem for the Spokane store as follows:

Manager—Spokane Store
June 2012 Responsibility Report

Revenue and Expenses	Actual	Budget	Variance Favorable/ (Unfavorable)
Sales revenue	$166,200		
Cost of goods sold	48,500		
Gross profit	117,700		
Operating expenses:			
Salaries and wages expense	37,600		
Rent expense	18,000		
Depreciation expense	12,000		
Office supplies expense	8,200		
Utilities expense	6,100		
Total operating expenses	81,900		
Operating income	$ 35,800		

Next, we need to insert the budgeted data that was given for the Spokane store as follows:

Manager—Spokane Store
June 2012 Responsibility Report

Revenue and Expenses	Actual	Budget	Variance Favorable/ (Unfavorable)
Sales revenue	$166,200	$155,000	
Cost of goods sold	48,500	46,000	
Gross profit	117,700	109,000	
Operating expenses:			
Salaries and wages expense	37,600	36,000	
Rent expense	18,000	16,800	
Depreciation expense	12,000	12,600	
Office supplies expense	8,200	8,500	
Utilities expense	6,100	6,400	
Total operating expenses	81,900	80,300	
Operating income	$ 35,800	$ 28,700	

Now we calculate the variance for each item by subtracting the greater amount (budgeted amount or actual amount) from the lesser amount. Then we need to label the variance as favorable or unfavorable. For revenues, gross profit, and operating income, a favorable variance exists when the actual amount exceeds the budgeted amount. An unfavorable variance will exist if the actual amount is less than the budgeted amount. For expenses (including cost of goods sold), a favorable variance exists when the actual amount is less than what was budgeted. If the actual amount is greater than the budgeted amount, then an unfavorable variance exists.

The sales revenue variance would be calculated by subtracting the greater amount (actual) from the lesser amount (budgeted) to get $11,200 ($166,200 – $155,000). Because the actual revenue amount is greater than the budgeted amount, this would be a favorable variance. The remaining items can be calculated in the same manner and the report can be completed as follows:

Manager—Spokane Store
June 2012 Responsibility Report

Revenue and Expenses	Actual	Budget	Variance Favorable/ (Unfavorable)	
Sales revenue	$166,200	$155,000	$11,200	F
Cost of goods sold	48,500	46,000	(2,500)	U
Gross profit	117,700	109,000	8,700	F
Operating expenses:				
Salaries and wages expense	37,600	36,000	(1,600)	U
Rent expense	18,000	16,800	(1,200)	U
Depreciation expense	12,000	12,600	600	F
Office supplies expense	8,200	8,500	300	F
Utilities expense	6,100	6,400	300	F
Total operating expenses	81,900	80,300	(1,600)	U
Operating income	$ 35,800	$ 28,700	$ 7,100	F

Now that we have completed the report for the Spokane store, we can create a performance report for the Pacific Northwest Region in the same manner.

First, we need to format the report and insert the actual and budgeted amounts for the Pacific Northwest Region as follows:

Regional Manager—Pacific Northwest Region
June 2012 Responsibility Report

Revenue and Expenses	Actual	Budget	Variance Favorable/ (Unfavorable)
Sales revenue	$778,700	$796,500	
Cost of goods sold	260,300	262,400	
Gross profit	518,400	534,100	
Operating expenses:			
Salaries and wages expense	182,000	178,000	
Rent expense	81,800	82,900	
Depreciation expense	58,000	56,000	
Office supplies expense	43,200	39,800	
Utilities expense	30,300	28,700	
Total operating expenses	395,300	385,400	
Operating income	$123,100	$148,700	

Next, we can compute and label the variances the same way that we did for the Spokane store. The completed regional performance report should look like this:

Regional Manager—Pacific Northwest Region
June 2012 Responsibility Report

Revenue and Expenses	Actual	Budget	Variance Favorable/ (Unfavorable)	
Sales revenue	$778,700	$796,500	$(17,800)	U
Cost of goods sold	260,300	262,400	2,100	F
Gross profit	518,400	534,100	(15,700)	U
Operating expenses:				
Salaries and wages expense	182,000	178,000	(4,000)	U
Rent expense	81,800	82,900	1,100	F
Depreciation expense	58,000	56,000	(2,000)	U
Office supplies expense	43,200	39,800	(3,400)	U
Utilities expense	30,300	28,700	(1,600)	U
Total operating expenses	395,300	385,400	(9,900)	U
Operating income	$123,100	$148,700	$(25,600)	U

The final performance report we need to complete is for all of the stores in the United States. As we did when we created the other two reports, we first need to insert the actual and budgeted amounts as follows:

CEO
June 2012 Responsibility Report

Revenue and Expenses	Actual	Budget	Variance Favorable/ (Unfavorable)
Sales revenue	$4,793,400	$4,750,000	
Cost of goods sold	1,442,100	1,450,600	
Gross profit	3,351,300	3,299,400	
Operating expenses:			
Salaries and wages expense	1,062,200	1,085,000	
Rent expense	484,000	490,200	
Depreciation expense	510,000	512,000	
Office supplies expense	328,700	330,300	
Utilities expense	337,300	332,400	
Total operating expenses	2,722,200	2,749,900	
Operating income	$ 629,100	$ 549,500	

We can complete the report by finding the variances between the actual and budgeted amounts and labeling them in the same manner as we did for the Spokane store and the Pacific Northwest Region. The completed report should look like this:

CEO
June 2012 Responsibility Report

Revenue and Expenses	Actual	Budget	Variance Favorable/ (Unfavorable)	
Sales revenue	$4,793,400	$4,750,000	$43,400	F
Cost of goods sold	1,442,100	1,450,600	8,500	F
Gross profit	3,351,300	3,299,400	51,900	F
Operating expenses:				
Salaries and wages expense	1,062,200	1,085,000	22,800	F
Rent expense	484,000	490,200	6,200	F
Depreciation expense	510,000	512,000	2,000	F
Office supplies expense	328,700	330,300	1,600	F
Utilities expense	337,300	332,400	(4,900)	U
Total operating expenses	2,722,200	2,749,900	27,700	F
Operating income	$ 629,100	$ 549,500	$79,600	F

Requirement 2

Based on the report for the Spokane store, what areas should the manager of the store investigate?

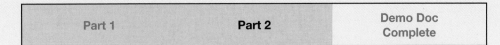

When investigating variances, it is often tempting to focus only on unfavorable variances. However, it is just as important to investigate favorable variances in order to try to determine the cause of the variance so that whatever caused the variance can be repeated and shared with other areas of the company when appropriate.

The manager of the Spokane store should investigate the large favorable variance in sales revenue. If the manager can determine what caused the increased sales (perhaps a new advertising campaign), the store will have a better chance of achieving increased sales in the months to come. Although the store had an unfavorable cost of goods sold variance, this should be expected because of the significant increase in sales revenue.

The manager should also look at the unfavorable variances in the salaries and wages expense and the rent expense. The manager may find that the increase in these expenses was required to support the increased sales. If not, he or she can try to hold these expenses closer to what was budgeted and increase the store's operating income.

| Part 1 | Part 2 | **Demo Doc Complete** |

10 Short-Term Business Decisions

Learning Objectives/
Success Keys

1 Describe and identify information relevant to business decisions

2 Make special order and pricing decisions

3 Make dropping a product and product-mix decisions

4 Make outsourcing and sell as is or process further decisions

Most major companies outsource work as they grow. As Smart Touch Learning, Inc., expands, it is considering subcontracting its call center operations. But why would Smart Touch consider hiring other people to handle such an important function? Primarily it would do so to save money. Most companies are experiencing financial difficulties due to rising fuel costs and tight competition so they need to find ways to reduce their costs. One way to reduce costs is through outsourcing. Companies can save 20% or more by outsourcing call center work to English-speaking workers in developing countries.

Outsourcing also enables companies to concentrate on their core competencies—the operating activities in which they are experts. When companies focus on just their core competencies, they often outsource the activities that do not give them a competitive advantage. For example, call center operations require expertise that can be purchased through outsourcing, leaving Smart Touch to focus on its core competency—developing learning solutions.

In Chapter 5, we saw how managers use cost behavior to determine the company's breakeven point and to estimate the sales volume needed to achieve target profits. In this chapter, we will see how managers use their knowledge of cost behavior to make six special business decisions, such as whether or not to outsource operating activities. The decisions we will discuss in this chapter pertain to short periods of time so managers do not need to worry about the time value of money. In other words, they do not need to compute the present value of the revenues and expenses relating to the decision. In Chapter 11 we will discuss longer-term decisions (such as plant expansions) in which the time value of money becomes important. Before we look at the six business decisions in detail, let us consider a manager's decision-making process and the information managers need to evaluate their options.

How Managers Make Decisions

Exhibit 10-1 illustrates how managers make decisions among alternative courses of action. Management accountants help with the third step: gathering and analyzing *relevant information* to compare alternatives.

1 Describe and identify information relevant to business decisions

EXHIBIT 10-1 | **How Managers Make Decisions**

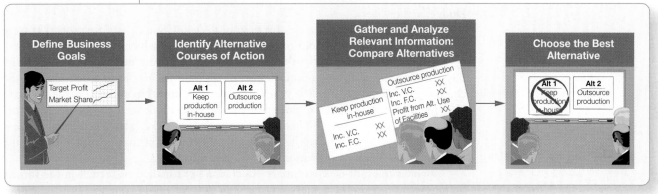

Relevant Information

When managers make decisions, they focus on costs and revenues that are relevant to the decisions. Exhibit 10-2 on the following page shows that **relevant information** is

1. expected *future* data that

2. *differs* among alternatives.

Relevant costs are those costs that are relevant to a particular decision. To illustrate, if Smart Touch were considering purchasing a Dodge or a Chevy delivery truck, the cost of the truck, the sales tax, and the insurance premium costs would all be relevant because these costs

- are incurred in the *future* (after Smart Touch decides which truck to buy), and
- *differ between alternatives* (each truck has a different invoice price, sales tax, and insurance premium).

These costs are *relevant* because they can affect the decision of which truck to purchase.

EXHIBIT 10-2 | **Relevant Information**

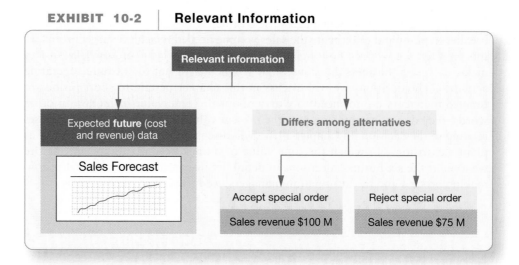

Irrelevant costs are costs that *do not* affect the decision. For example, because the Dodge and Chevy both have similar fuel efficiency and maintenance ratings, we do not expect the truck operating costs to differ between those two alternatives. Because these costs do not differ, they do not affect Smart Touch's decision. In other words, they are *irrelevant* to the decision. Similarly, the cost of an annual license tag is also irrelevant because the tag costs the same whether Smart Touch buys the Dodge or the Chevy.

Sunk costs are always irrelevant to your decision. Sunk costs are costs that were incurred in the *past* and cannot be changed regardless of which future action is taken. Perhaps Smart Touch wants to trade in its current Ford truck when the company buys the new truck. The amount Smart Touch paid for the Ford truck—which the company bought for $15,000 a year ago—is a sunk cost. No decision made *now* can alter the past. Smart Touch already bought the Ford truck so *the price the company paid for it is a sunk cost.* All Smart Touch can do *now* is keep the Ford truck, trade it in, or sell it for the best price the company can get, even if that price is substantially less than what Smart Touch originally paid for the truck.

What *is* relevant is what Smart Touch can get for the Ford truck in the future. Suppose that the Dodge dealership offers $8,000 for the Ford truck, but the Chevy dealership offers $10,000. Because the amounts differ and the transaction will take place in the future, the trade-in cost *is* relevant to Smart Touch's decision. Why? Because the trade-in value alternatives are different.

The same principle applies to all situations—*only relevant data affect decisions.* Let us consider another application of this general principle.

Suppose Smart Touch is deciding whether to use non-recycled DVDs or DVDs made from recycled materials for its Excel Learning DVDs. Assume Smart Touch predicts the following costs under the two alternatives:

	New Materials	Recycled Materials	Cost Difference
Manufacturing cost per DVD:			
Direct materials	$2.40	$2.60	$0.20
Direct labor	$4.00	$4.00	$0.00

The cost of direct materials is relevant because this cost differs between alternatives (the recycled DVDs cost $0.20 more per DVD than the non-recycled DVDs). The labor cost is irrelevant because that cost is the same for both.

Stop & Think...

You are considering replacing your Pentium IV computer with the latest model. Is the $1,200 you spent in 2005 on the Pentium relevant to your decision about buying the new model?

Answer: The $1,200 cost of your Pentium is irrelevant. It is a *sunk* cost that you incurred in the past so it is the same whether or not you buy the new computer.

Relevant Nonfinancial Information

Nonfinancial, or qualitative factors, also play a role in managers' decisions. For example, closing manufacturing plants and laying off employees can seriously hurt employee morale. **Outsourcing,** the decision to buy or subcontract a product or service rather than produce it in-house, can reduce control over delivery time or product quality. Offering discounted prices to select customers can upset regular customers and tempt them to take their business elsewhere. Managers must always fully consider the likely quantitative *and* qualitative effects of their decisions.

Managers who ignore qualitative factors can make serious mistakes. For example, the City of Nottingham, England, spent $1.6 million on 215 solar-powered parking meters after seeing how well the parking meters worked in countries along the Mediterranean Sea. However, they did not consider that British skies are typically overcast. The result was that the meters did not always work because of the lack of sunlight. The city *lost* money because people ended up parking for free! Relevant qualitative information has the same characteristics as relevant financial information: The qualitative factor occurs in the *future* and it *differs* between alternatives. In the example, the amount of *future* sunshine required *differed* between alternatives. The mechanical meters did not require any sunshine, but the solar-powered meters needed a lot of sunshine.

Keys to Making Short-Term Special Decisions

Our approach to making short-term special decisions is called the **relevant information approach,** or the **incremental analysis approach.** Instead of looking at the company's *entire* income statement under each decision alternative, we will just look at how operating income would *change or differ* under each alternative. Using this approach, we will leave out irrelevant information—the costs and revenues that will not differ between alternatives. We will consider six kinds of decisions in this chapter:

1. Special sales orders

2. Pricing

3. Dropping products, departments, and territories

4. Product mix

5. Outsourcing (make or buy)

6. Selling as is or processing further

As you study these decisions, keep in mind the two keys in analyzing short-term special business decisions shown in Exhibit 10-3:

1. **Focus on relevant revenues, costs, and profits.** Irrelevant information only clouds the picture and creates information overload.

2. **Use a contribution margin approach that separates variable costs from fixed costs.** Because fixed costs and variable costs behave differently, they must be analyzed separately. Traditional (absorption costing) income statements, which

blend fixed and variable costs together, can mislead managers. Contribution margin income statements, which isolate costs by behavior (variable or fixed), help managers gather the cost-behavior information they need. Keep in mind that unit manufacturing costs are mixed costs, too, so they can also mislead managers. If you use unit manufacturing costs in your analysis, be sure to first separate the cost's fixed and variable components.

We will use these two keys in each decision.

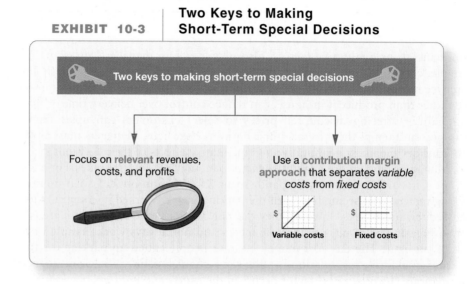

EXHIBIT 10-3 | **Two Keys to Making Short-Term Special Decisions**

Special Sales Order and Regular Pricing Decisions

2 Make special order and pricing decisions

We will start our discussion by looking at special sales order decisions and regular pricing decisions. In the past, managers did not consider pricing to be a short-term decision. However, product life cycles are shrinking in most industries. Companies often sell products for only a few months before replacing them with an updated model, even if the updating is barely noticeable. The clothing and technology industries have always had short life cycles. Even auto and housing styles change frequently. Pricing has become a shorter-term decision than it was in the past.

Let us examine a special sales order in detail, and then we will discuss regular pricing decisions.

When to Accept a Special Sales Order

A special order occurs when a customer requests a one-time order at a *reduced* sale price. Before agreeing to the special deal, management must consider the questions shown in Exhibit 10-4.

EXHIBIT 10-4 | **Special Order Considerations**

- Does the company have excess capacity available to fill this order?

- Will the reduced sales price be high enough to cover the *incremental* costs of filling the order (the variable costs and any additional fixed costs)?

- Will the special order affect regular sales in the long run?

First, managers must consider available capacity. If the company is already making as many units as possible with its existing manufacturing capacity and selling them all at its *regular* sales price, it would not make sense to fill a special order at a *reduced* sales price. Therefore, available excess capacity that is not being used is almost a necessity for accepting a special order. This is true for service firms (law firms, hair salons, and so forth) as well as manufacturers.

Second, managers need to consider whether the special reduced sales price is high enough to cover the incremental costs of filling the order. The special price *must* exceed the variable costs of filling the order or the company will lose money on the deal. In other words, the special order must provide a *positive* contribution margin.

Next, the company must consider fixed costs. If the company has excess capacity, fixed costs probably will not be affected by producing more units (or delivering more service). However, in some cases, management may have to incur some other fixed cost to fill the special order, for example, additional insurance premiums. If so, it will need to consider whether the special sales price is high enough to generate a positive contribution margin *and* cover the additional fixed costs.

Finally, managers need to consider whether the special order will affect regular sales in the long run. Will regular customers find out about the special order and demand a lower price or take their business elsewhere? Will the special order customer come back *again and again*, asking for the same reduced price? Will the special order price start a price war with competitors? Managers should determine the answers to these questions and/or consider how customers will respond. Managers may decide that any profit from the special sales order is not worth these risks.

Let us consider a special sales order example. We learned in Chapter 3 that Smart Touch normally sells its Excel DVDs for $12.00 each. Assume that a company has offered Smart Touch $67,500 for 10,000 DVDs, or $6.75 per DVD. This sale

- will use manufacturing capacity that would otherwise be idle (excess capacity).
- will not change fixed costs.
- will not require any variable *nonmanufacturing* expenses because no extra marketing costs are incurred with this special order.
- will not affect regular sales.

We have addressed every consideration except one: Is the special sales price high enough to cover the variable *manufacturing* costs associated with the order? Let us first take a look at the *wrong* way and then the *right* way to figure out the answer to this question.

Suppose Smart Touch made and sold 100,000 DVDs before considering the special order. Using the traditional (absorption costing) income statement on the left-hand side of Exhibit 10-5, the ABC manufacturing cost per unit is $7.00 (as calculated in Exhibit 3-9). A manager who does not examine these numbers carefully may believe that Smart Touch should *not* accept the special order at a sale price of $6.75 because each DVD costs $7.00 to manufacture. But appearances can be deceiving! Remember that the unit manufacturing cost of a product, $7.00, is a *mixed* cost, containing both fixed and variable cost components. To correctly answer our question, we need to find only the *variable* portion of the manufacturing unit cost.

The right-hand side of Exhibit 10-5 shows the contribution margin income statement that separates variable expenses from fixed expenses. The contribution margin income statement allows us to see that the *variable* manufacturing cost per unit is only $6.50 ($650,000 ÷ 100,000). The special sales price of $6.75 per DVD is *higher* than the variable manufacturing cost of $6.50. Therefore, the special order will provide a positive contribution margin of $0.25 per unit ($6.75 – $6.50). Since the special order is for 10,000 units, Smart Touch's total contribution margin should increase by $2,500 (10,000 units × $0.25 per unit) if it accepts this order.

EXHIBIT 10-5	Traditional (Absorption Costing) Format and Contribution Margin Format Income Statements

SMART TOUCH LEARNING, INC.
Income Statement (at a production and sales level of 100,000 Excel DVDs)
Year Ended December 31, 2011

Traditional (Absorption Costing) Format			Contribution Margin Format			
Sales revenue		$1,200,000	Sales revenue			$1,200,000
Less cost of goods sold		(700,000)	Less variable expenses:			
Gross profit		$ 500,000	Manufacturing		$(640,000)	
Less marketing and administrative expenses		(110,000)	Marketing and administrative		(10,000)	(650,000)
			Contribution margin			$ 550,000
			Less fixed expenses:			
			Manufacturing		$ (60,000)	
			Marketing and administrative		(100,000)	(160,000)
Operating income (loss)		$ 390,000	Operating income			$ 390,000

Using an incremental analysis approach, Smart Touch compares the additional revenues from the special order with the incremental expenses to see if the special order will contribute to profits. Exhibit 10-6 shows that the special sales order will increase revenue by $67,500 (10,000 × $6.75), but will also increase variable manufacturing cost by $65,000 (10,000 × $6.50). As a result, Smart Touch's contribution margin will increase by $2,500, as previously anticipated. The other costs seen in Exhibit 10-5 are irrelevant. Variable marketing and administrative expenses will be the same whether or not Smart Touch accepts the special order, because Smart Touch made no special efforts to get this sale. Fixed manufacturing expenses will not change because Smart Touch has enough idle capacity to produce 10,000 extra Excel DVDs without requiring additional facilities. Fixed marketing and administrative expenses will not be affected by this special order either. Because there are no additional fixed costs, the total increase in contribution margin flows directly to operating income. As a result, the special sales order will increase operating income by $2,500.

EXHIBIT 10-6	Incremental Analysis of Special Sales Order of 10,000 Excel DVDs

Expected increase in revenues (10,000 DVDs × $6.50)	$ 67,500
Expected increase in variable manufacturing costs (10,000 DVDs × $6.50)	(65,000)
Expected increase in operating income	$ 2,500

Notice that the analysis follows the two keys to making short-term special business decisions discussed earlier: (1) Focus on relevant data (revenues and costs that *will change* if Smart Touch accepts the special order) and (2) use of a contribution margin approach that separates variable costs from fixed costs.

To summarize, for special sales orders, the decision rule is as follows:

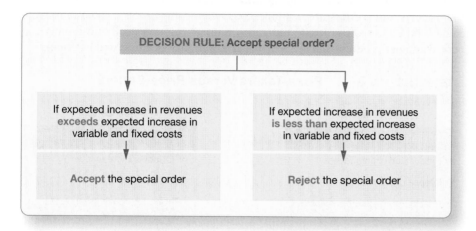

DECISION RULE: Accept special order?

If expected increase in revenues
exceeds expected increase in
variable and fixed costs

→ Accept the special order

If expected increase in revenues
is less than expected increase
in variable and fixed costs

→ Reject the special order

How to Set Regular Prices

In the special order decision, Smart Touch decided to sell a limited quantity of DVDs for $6.75 each, even though the normal price was $12.00 per unit. But how did Smart Touch decide to set its regular price at $12.00 per DVD? Exhibit 10-7 shows that managers start with three basic questions when setting regular prices for their products or services.

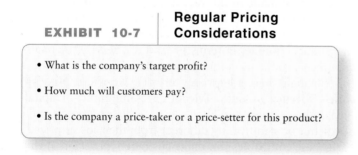

EXHIBIT 10-7 | **Regular Pricing Considerations**

- What is the company's target profit?

- How much will customers pay?

- Is the company a price-taker or a price-setter for this product?

The answers to these questions are often complex and ever-changing. Stockholders expect the company to achieve certain profits. Economic conditions, historical company earnings, industry risk, competition, and new business developments all affect the level of profit that stockholders expect. Stockholders usually tie their profit expectations to the amount of assets invested in the company. For example, stockholders may expect a 10% annual return on their investment. A company's stock price tends to decline if it does not meet target profits, so managers must keep costs low while generating enough revenue to meet target profits.

This leads to the second question: How much will customers pay? Managers cannot set prices above what customers are willing to pay or sales will decline. The amount customers will pay depends on the competition, the product's uniqueness, the effectiveness of marketing campaigns, general economic conditions, and so forth.

To address the third pricing question, imagine a horizontal line with price-takers at one end and price-setters at the other end. A company's products and services fall somewhere along this line, shown in Exhibit 10-8. Companies are price-takers when they have little or no control over the prices of their products or services. This occurs when their products and services are *not* unique or when competition is intense. Examples include food commodities (milk and corn), natural resources (oil and lumber), and generic consumer products and services (paper towels, dry cleaning, and banking).

EXHIBIT 10-8   Price-Takers Versus Price-Setters

Price-Takers ←	→ Price-Setters
Characteristics of price-takers	**Characteristics of price-setters**
• Product lacks uniqueness	• Product is more unique
• Intense competition	• Less competition
• Pricing approach emphasizes target pricing	• Pricing approach emphasizes cost-plus pricing

Companies are price-setters when they have more control over pricing—in other words, they can "set" the price to some extent. Companies are price-setters when their products are unique, which results in less competition. Unique products, such as original art and jewelry, specially manufactured machinery, patented perfume scents, and custom-made furniture, can command higher prices.

Obviously, managers would rather be price-setters than price-takers. To gain more control over pricing, companies try to differentiate their products. They want to make their products unique, in terms of features, service, or quality, or at least make you *think* their product is unique or somehow better—companies achieve this differentiation through their advertising efforts. Consider **Nike**'s tennis shoes, **Starbucks**' coffee, **Kleenex**'s tissues, **Tylenol**'s acetaminophen, **Capital One**'s credit cards, **Shell**'s gas, **Abercrombie and Fitch**'s jeans—the list goes on and on. Are these products really better or significantly different from their lower-priced competitors? It is possible. If these companies can make customers *believe* that this is true, they have gained more control over their pricing because customers are willing to pay *more* for their product or service. What is the downside? These companies must charge higher prices or sell more just to cover their advertising costs.

A company's approach to pricing depends on whether its product or service is on the price-taking or price-setting side of the spectrum. Price-takers emphasize a target-pricing approach. Price-setters emphasize a cost-plus pricing approach. Keep in mind that many products fall somewhere along the horizontal line in Exhibit 10-8. Therefore, managers tend to use both approaches to some extent. We will now discuss each approach in turn.

Stop & Think...

It is lunchtime....you are hungry for a hamburger. Where do you go—**Wendy**'s, **McDonald**'s, or your college's cafeteria? Why? A hamburger is the same wherever you go, right? The answer to that question is the key to changing a product (a hamburger) from a commodity to a unique product (a **Wendy**'s hamburger). The advertising, conditioning of your family, etc. have possibly made you think that the three companies' hamburgers are different. The perceived uniqueness of the hamburger helps the company (say **Wendy**'s) be a price-setter instead of a price-taker.

Target Pricing

When a company is a price-taker, it emphasizes a target pricing approach to pricing. Target pricing starts with the market price of the product (the price customers are willing to pay) and then subtracts the company's desired profit to determine the product's **target full cost**—the *full* cost to develop, produce, and deliver the product or service.

> Revenue at market price
> Less: Desired profit
> Equals: Target full cost

In this relationship, the market price is "taken." Recall from Chapter 1 that a product's *full* cost contains all elements from the value chain—both inventoriable costs and period costs. It also includes both fixed and variable costs. If the product's current cost is higher than the target cost, the company must find ways to reduce costs or it will not meet its profit goals. Managers often use ABC costing along with value engineering (as discussed in Chapter 3) to find ways to cut costs. Let us look at an example of target pricing.

Let us assume that Excel Learning DVDs are a commodity, and that the current market price is $11.00 per DVD (not the $12.00 sales price assumed in the earlier Smart Touch example). Because the DVDs are a commodity, Smart Touch will emphasize a target-pricing approach. Let us assume Smart Touch's stockholders expect a 10% annual return on the company's assets. If the company has $3,000,000 of assets, the desired profit is $300,000 ($3,000,000 × 10%). Exhibit 10-9 calculates the target full cost at the current sales volume (100,000 units). Once we know the target full cost, we can analyze the fixed and variable cost components separately.

EXHIBIT 10-9 | **Calculating Target Full Cost**

	Calculations	
Revenue at market price	100,000 DVDs × $11.00 price	$1,100,000
Less: Desired profit	10% × $3,000,000 average assets	(300,000)
Target full cost		$ 800,000

Can Smart Touch make and sell 100,000 Excel Learning DVDs at a full cost of $800,000? We know from Smart Touch's contribution margin income statement (Exhibit 10-5) that the company's variable costs are $6.50 per unit ($650,000 ÷ 100,000 units). This variable cost per unit includes both manufacturing costs ($6.40 per unit) and marketing and administrative costs ($0.10 per unit). We also know the company incurs $160,000 in fixed costs in its current relevant range. Again, some fixed costs stem from manufacturing and some from marketing and administrative activities. *In setting regular sales prices, companies must cover all of their costs—whether inventoriable or period, fixed or variable.*

Making and selling 100,000 DVDs currently costs the company $810,000 [(100,000 units × $6.50 variable cost per unit) + $160,000 of fixed costs], which is more than the target full cost ($800,000). So, what are Smart Touch's options?

1. Accept a lower profit (an operating income of $290,000, which is a 9.67% return, not the 10% target return required by stockholders).

2. Reduce fixed costs by $10,000 or more.

3. Reduce variable costs by $10,000 or more.

4. Use other strategies. For example, Smart Touch could attempt to increase sales volume. Recall that the company has excess capacity so making and selling more units would only affect variable costs; however, it would mean that current fixed costs are spread over more units. The company could also consider changing or adding to its product mix. Finally, it could attempt to differentiate its Excel Learning DVDs from the competition to gain more control over sales prices (be a price-setter).

Let us look at some of these options. Smart Touch may first try to cut fixed costs. As shown in Exhibit 10-10, the company would have to reduce fixed costs to $150,000 to meet its target profit level.

EXHIBIT 10-10 | **Calculating Target Fixed Cost**

	Calculations	
Target full cost	(From Exhibit 10-9)	$ 800,000
Less: Current variable costs	100,000 DVDs × $6.50	(650,000)
Target fixed cost		$ 150,000

If the company cannot reduce its fixed costs by $10,000 ($160,000 current fixed costs – $150,000 target fixed costs), it would have to lower its variable cost to $6.40 per unit, as shown in Exhibit 10-11.

EXHIBIT 10-11 | **Calculating Target DVD Variable Cost**

	Calculations	
Target full cost	(From Exhibit 10-9)	$ 800,000
Less: Current fixed costs	(From Exhibit 10-5)	(160,000)
Target total variable costs		$ 640,000
Divided by the number of DVDs		÷ 100,000
Target variable cost per unit		$ 6.40

If Smart Touch cannot reduce variable costs to that level either, could it meet its target profit through a combination of lowering both fixed costs and variable costs?

Another strategy would be to increase sales. Smart Touch's managers can use CVP analysis, as you learned in Chapter 5, to figure out how many Excel Learning DVDs the company would have to sell to achieve its target profit. How could the company increase demand for the Excel Learning DVDs? Perhaps it could reach new markets or advertise. How much would advertising cost—and how many extra Excel Learning DVDs would the company have to sell to cover the cost of advertising? These are only some of the questions managers must ask. As you can see, managers do not have an easy task when the current cost exceeds the target full cost. Sometimes companies just cannot compete given the current market price. If that is the case, they may have no other choice than to exit the market for that product.

Cost-Plus Pricing

When a company is a price-setter, it emphasizes a cost-plus approach to pricing. This pricing approach is essentially the *opposite* of the target-pricing approach. Cost-plus pricing starts with the company's full costs (as a given) and *adds* its desired profit to determine a cost-plus price.

Full cost
Plus: Desired profit
Equals: Cost-plus price

When the product is unique, the company has more control over pricing. The company still needs to make sure that the cost-plus price is not higher than what customers are willing to pay. Let us go back to our original Smart Touch example. This time, let us say the Excel Learning DVDs benefit from brand recognition so the company has some control over the price it charges for its DVDs. Exhibit 10-12 takes a cost-plus pricing approach, assuming the current level of sales:

EXHIBIT 10-12 | **Calculating Cost-Plus Price**

	Calculations	
Current variable costs	100,000 DVDs × $6.50	$ 650,000
Plus: Current fixed costs	(From Exhibit 10-5)	160,000
Full product cost		$ 810,000
Plus: Desired profit	10% of $3,000,000 average assets	300,000
Target revenue		$1,110,000
Divided by the number of DVDs		÷ 100,000
Cost-plus price per DVD		$ 11.10

If the current market price for generic Excel Learning DVDs is $11.00, as we assumed earlier, can Smart Touch sell its brand-name filters for $11.10, or more, apiece? The answer depends on how well the company has been able to differentiate its product or brand name. The company may use focus groups or marketing surveys to find out how customers would respond to its cost-plus price. The company may find out that its cost-plus price is too high, or it may find that it could set the price even higher without jeopardizing sales.

Notice how pricing decisions used our two keys to decision making: (1) focus on relevant information and (2) use a contribution margin approach that separates variable costs from fixed costs. In pricing decisions, all cost information is relevant because the company must cover *all* costs along the value chain before it can generate a profit. However, we still need to consider variable costs and fixed costs separately because they behave differently at different volumes.

Our pricing decision rule is as follows:

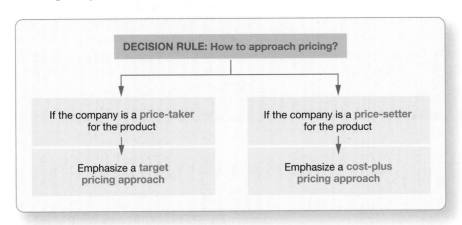

Decision Guidelines

RELEVANT INFORMATION FOR BUSINESS DECISIONS

Nike makes special order and regular pricing decisions. Even though it sells mass-produced tennis shoes and sport clothing, **Nike** has differentiated its products with advertising and with athlete endorsements. **Nike**'s managers consider both quantitative and qualitative factors as they make pricing decisions. Here are key guidelines **Nike**'s managers follow in making their decisions.

Decision	Guidelines
• What information is relevant to a short-term special business decision?	Relevant data 1. are expected *future* data. 2. *differ* between alternatives.
• What are two key guidelines in making short-term special business decisions?	1. Focus on *relevant* data 2. Use a *contribution margin* approach that separates variable costs from fixed costs
• Should **Nike** accept a lower sale price than the regular price for a large order from a customer in Roatan Bay, Honduras?	If the revenue from the order exceeds the extra variable and fixed costs incurred to fill the order, then accepting the order will increase operating income.
• What should **Nike** consider in setting its regular product prices?	**Nike** considers 1. the profit stockholders expect it to make. 2. the price customers will pay. 3. whether it is a price-setter or a price-taker.
• What approach should **Nike** take to pricing?	**Nike** has differentiated its products by advertising. Thus, **Nike** tends to be a price-setter. **Nike**'s managers can emphasize a cost-plus approach to pricing.
• What approach should discount shoe stores, such as **Payless Shoes,** take to pricing?	**Payless Shoes** sells generic shoes (no-name brands) at low prices. **Payless** is a price-taker so managers use a target-pricing approach to pricing.

Summary Problem 1

MC Alexander Industries makes tennis balls. Its only plant can produce up to 2.5 million cans of balls per year. Current production is 2 million cans. Annual manufacturing, selling, and administrative fixed costs total $700,000. The variable cost of making and selling each can of balls is $1.00. Stockholders expect a 12% annual return on the company's $3 million of assets.

Requirements

1. What is MC Alexander's current full cost of making and selling 2 million cans of tennis balls? What is the current full *unit* cost of each can of tennis balls?
2. Assume MC Alexander is a price-taker, and the current market price is $1.45 per can of balls (this is the price at which manufacturers sell to retailers). What is the *target* full cost of producing and selling 2 million cans of balls? Given MC Alexander Industries' current costs, will the company reach stockholders' profit goals?
3. If MC Alexander cannot change its fixed costs, what is the target variable cost per can of balls?
4. Suppose MC Alexander could spend an extra $100,000 on advertising to differentiate its product so that it could be a price-setter. Assuming the original volume and costs, plus the $100,000 of new advertising costs, what cost-plus price will MC Alexander want to charge for a can of balls?
5. **Nike** has just asked MC Alexander to supply the company with 400,000 cans of balls at a special order price of $1.20 per can. **Nike** wants MC Alexander to package the balls under the **Nike** label (MC Alexander will imprint the **Nike** logo on each ball and can). MC Alexander will have to spend $10,000 to change the packaging machinery. Assuming the original volume and costs, should MC Alexander Industries accept this special order? (Unlike the chapter problem, assume MC Alexander will incur variable selling costs as well as variable manufacturing costs related to this order.)

Solutions

Requirement 1

The full unit cost is as follows:

Fixed costs	$ 700,000
Plus: Total variable costs (2 million cans × $1.00 per unit)	+ 2,000,000
Total full costs	$2,700,000
Divided by the number of cans..	÷ 2,000,000
Full cost per can...	$ 1.35

Requirement 2

The target full cost is as follows:

	Calculations	Total
Revenue at market price	2,000,000 units × $1.45 price =	$2,900,000
Less: Desired profit	12% × $3,000,000 of assets	(360,000)
Target *full* cost		$2,540,000

MC Alexander's current total full costs ($2,700,000 from requirement 1) are $160,000 higher than the target full cost ($2,540,000). If MC Alexander cannot reduce costs, it will not be able to meet stockholders' profit expectations.

Requirement 3

Assuming MC Alexander cannot reduce its fixed costs, the target variable cost per can is as follows:

	Total
Target *full* cost (from requirement 2)	$2,540,000
Less: Fixed costs	(700,000)
Target total variable cost	$1,840,000
Divided by the number of units	÷2,000,000
Target variable cost per unit	$ 0.92

Since MC Alexander cannot reduce its fixed costs, it needs to reduce variable costs by $0.08 per can ($1.00 – $0.92) to meet its profit goals. This would require an 8% cost reduction, which may not be possible.

Requirement 4

If MC Alexander can differentiate its tennis balls, it will gain more control over pricing. The company's new cost-plus price would be as follows:

Current total costs (from requirement 1)	$2,700,000
Plus: Additional cost of advertising	+ 100,000
Plus: Desired profit (from requirement 2)	+ 360,000
Target revenue	$3,160,000
Divided by the number of units	÷ 2,000,000
Cost-plus price per unit	$ 1.58

MC Alexander must study the market to determine whether retailers would pay $1.58 per can of balls.

Requirement 5

Nike's special order price ($1.20) is less than the current full cost of each can of balls ($1.35 from requirement 1). However, this should not influence management's decision. MC Alexander could fill **Nike**'s special order using existing excess capacity. MC Alexander takes an incremental analysis approach to its decision: comparing the extra revenue with the incremental costs of accepting the order. Variable costs will increase if MC Alexander accepts the order, so the variable costs are relevant. Only the *additional* fixed costs of changing the packaging machine ($10,000) are relevant since all other fixed costs will remain unchanged.

Revenue from special order (400,000 × $1.20 per unit)	$ 480,000
Less: Variable cost of special order (400,000 × $1.00)	(400,000)
Contribution margin from special order	$ 80,000
Less: Additional fixed costs of special order	(10,000)
Operating income provided by special order	$ 70,000

MC Alexander should accept the special order because it will increase operating income by $70,000. However, MC Alexander also needs to consider whether its regular customers will find out about the special price and demand lower prices too.

When to Drop Products, Departments, or Territories

Managers must often decide whether to drop products, departments, or territories that are not as profitable as desired. How do managers make these decisions? Exhibit 10-13 lists some of the questions managers must consider when deciding whether to drop a product line, department, or territory.

3 Make dropping a product and product-mix decisions

EXHIBIT 10-13	Considerations for Dropping Products, Departments, or Territories

- Does the product provide a positive contribution margin?

- Will fixed costs continue to exist, even if the company drops the product?

- Are there any direct fixed costs that can be avoided if the company drops the product?

- Will dropping the product affect sales of the company's other products?

- What could the company do with the freed capacity?

Once again, we follow the two key guidelines for special business decisions: (1) focus on relevant data and (2) use a contribution margin approach. The relevant financial data are still the changes in revenues and expenses, but now we are considering a *decrease* in volume rather than an *increase*, as we did in the special sales order decision. In the following example, we will consider how managers decide to drop a product. Managers would use the same process in deciding whether to drop a department or territory.

Earlier, we focused on only one of Smart Touch's products—Excel Learning DVDs. Now let us focus on both of its products—the Excel Learning DVDs and the specialty DVDs we covered in Chapter 3. Exhibit 10-14 shows the company's

EXHIBIT 10-14	Contribution Margin Income Statements by Product Line

SMART TOUCH LEARNING, INC.			
Income Statement			
For the month ended January 31, 2012			
		Product Line	
		Excel DVDs **(100,000 DVDs)**	**Specialty DVDs** **(350 DVDs)**
	Total	**(From Exhibit 10-5)**	
Sales revenue	$1,224,500	$1,200,000	$ 24,500
Less: Variable expenses			
Manufacturing	(652,740)	(640,000)	(12,740)
Marketing and administrative	(10,035)	(10,000)	(35)
Total variable expenses	(662,775)	(650,000)	(12,775)
Contribution margin	561,725	550,000	11,725
Less: Fixed expenses:			
Manufacturing	(71,795)	(60,000)	(11,795)
Marketing and administrative	(100,350)	(100,000)	(350)
Total fixed expenses	(172,145)	(160,000)	(12,145)
Operating income (loss)	$ 389,580	$ 390,000	$ (420)

contribution margin income statement by product line, assuming fixed costs are shared by both products. Because the specialty DVD line has an operating *loss* of $420, management is considering dropping the line.

The first question management should ask is "Does the product provide a positive contribution margin?" If the product line has a negative contribution margin, then the product is not even covering its variable costs. Therefore, the company should drop the product line. However, if the product line has a positive contribution margin, then it is *helping* to cover at least some of the company's fixed costs. In Smart Touch's case, the specialty DVDs provide a positive contribution margin of $11,725. Smart Touch's managers now need to consider fixed costs.

Suppose Smart Touch allocates fixed costs using the ABC costs per unit calculated in Chapter 3, Exhibit 3-9 ($7.00 per unit). Smart Touch could allocate fixed costs in many different ways, and each way would have allocated a different amount of fixed costs to each product line. Therefore, allocated fixed costs are *irrelevant* because they are arbitrary in amount. What is relevant, however, are the following:

1. Will the fixed costs continue to exist *even if* the product line is dropped?

2. Are there any *direct* fixed costs of the specialty DVDs that can be avoided if the product line is dropped?

Dropping Products Under Various Assumptions

Fixed Costs Continue to Exist and Will Not Change

Fixed costs that will continue to exist even after a product is dropped are often called unavoidable fixed costs. Unavoidable fixed costs are *irrelevant* to the decision because they *will not change* if the company drops the product line—they will be incurred either way. Let us assume that all of Smart Touch's fixed costs ($172,145) will continue to exist even if the company drops the specialty DVDs. Assume that Smart Touch makes the specialty DVDs in the same plant using the same machinery as the Excel Learning DVDs. Since this is the case, only the contribution margin the specialty DVDs provide is relevant. If Smart Touch drops the specialty DVDs, it will lose the $11,725 contribution margin.

The incremental analysis shown in Exhibit 10-15 verifies the loss. If Smart Touch drops the specialty DVDs, revenue will decrease by $24,500, but variable expenses will decrease by only $12,775, resulting in a net $11,725 decrease in operating income. Because fixed costs are unaffected, they are not included in the analysis. This analysis suggests that management should *not* drop specialty DVDs. It is actually more beneficial for Smart Touch to lose $475 than to drop the specialty DVDs and lose $11,725 in operating income.

EXHIBIT 10-15	**Incremental Analysis for Dropping a Product When Fixed Costs Will *Not* Change**

Expected decrease in revenues (350 specialty DVDs × $70.00)	$(24,500)
Expected decrease in variable costs (From Exhibit 10-14)	12,775
Expected *decrease* in operating income	$(11,725)

Direct Fixed Costs That Can Be Avoided

Since Smart Touch allocates its fixed costs using ABC costing, some of the fixed costs *belong* only to the specialty DVD product line. These would be direct fixed costs of the specialty DVDs only.[1] Assume that $12,000 of the fixed costs will be avoidable if Smart Touch drops the specialty DVD line. The $12,000 are then avoidable fixed costs and *are relevant* to the decision because they would change (go away) if the product line is dropped.

Exhibit 10-16 shows that, in this situation, operating income will *increase* by $275 if Smart Touch drops the specialty DVDs. Why? Because revenues will decline by $24,500 but expenses will decline even more—by $24,775. The result is a net increase to operating income of $275. This analysis suggests that management should drop specialty DVDs.

EXHIBIT 10-16	**Incremental Analysis for Dropping a Product When Fixed Costs *Will* Change**		
Expected decrease in revenues (350 specialty DVDs × $70.00)			$(24,500)
Expected decrease in variable costs (From Exhibit 10-14)	12,775		
Expected decrease in fixed costs	12,000		
Expected decrease in total expenses			24,775
Expected increase in operating income			$ 275

Other Considerations

Management must also consider whether dropping the product line, department, or territory would hurt other sales. In the examples given so far, we assumed that dropping the specialty DVDs would not affect Smart Touch's other product sales. However, think about a grocery store. Even if the produce department is not profitable, would managers drop it? Probably not, because if they did, they would lose customers who want one-stop shopping. In such situations, managers must also include the loss of contribution margin from *other* departments affected by the change when deciding whether or not to drop a department.

Management should also consider what it could do with freed capacity. In the Smart Touch example, we assumed that the company produces both Excel Learning DVDs and specialty DVDs using the same manufacturing equipment. If Smart Touch drops the specialty DVDs, could it make and sell another product using the freed machine hours? Managers should consider whether using the machinery to produce a different product would be more profitable than using the machinery to produce specialty DVDs.

Special decisions should take into account all costs affected by the choice of action. Managers must ask, "What total costs—variable and fixed—will change?" As Exhibits 10-15 and 10-16 show, the key to deciding whether to drop products, departments, or territories is to compare the lost revenue against the costs that can

---

[1]To aid in decision-making, companies should separate direct fixed costs from indirect fixed costs on their contribution margin income statements. Companies should *trace direct fixed costs* to the appropriate product line and only *allocate indirect fixed costs* among product lines.

be saved and to consider what would be done with the freed capacity. The decision rule is as follows:

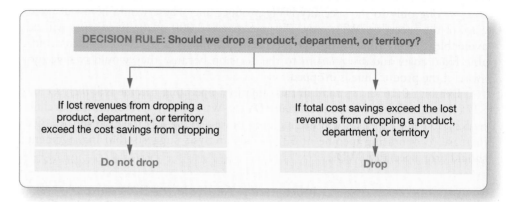

Product Mix: Which Product to Emphasize?

Companies do not have unlimited resources. **Constraints** that restrict production or sale of a product vary from company to company. For a manufacturer like Smart Touch Learning, the production constraint may be labor hours, machine hours, or available materials. For a merchandiser like **Wal-Mart**, the primary constraint is cubic feet of display space. Other companies are constrained by sales demand. Competition may be stiff, and so the company may be able to sell only a limited number of units. In such cases, the company produces only as much as it can sell. However, if a company can sell all the units it can produce, which products should it emphasize? For which items should production be increased? Companies facing constraints consider the questions shown in Exhibit 10-17.

EXHIBIT 10-17 | Product Mix Considerations

- What constraint(s) stops the company from making (or displaying) all the units the company can sell?

- Which products offer the highest contribution margin per unit of the constraint?

- Would emphasizing one product over another affect fixed costs?

Let us return to our Smart Touch example. Assume the company can sell all the Excel DVDs and all the specialty DVDs it produces, but it only has 2,000 machine hours of capacity. The company uses the same machines to produce both types of DVDs. In this case, machine hours is the constraint. Note that this is a short-term decision because in the long run, Smart Touch could expand its production facilities to meet sales demand, if it made financial sense to do so. The following data in Exhibit 10-18 suggest that specialty DVDs are more profitable than Excel DVDs:

EXHIBIT 10-18 | Smart Touch's Contribution Margin per Unit

	Excel DVD	Specialty DVD
Sale price per DVD	$12.00	$70.00
Less: Variable cost per DVD:	(6.50)	(36.50)
Contribution margin	5.50	33.50
Contribution margin ratio:		
Excel DVDs $5.50/$12.00	46%	
Specialty DVDs $33.50/$70.00		48%

However, an important piece of information is missing—the time it takes to make each product. Let us assume that Smart Touch can produce either 80 Excel DVDs *or* 10 specialty DVDs per machine hour. *The company will incur the same fixed costs either way so fixed costs are irrelevant.* Which product should it emphasize?

To maximize profits when fixed costs are irrelevant, follow the decision rule:

> **DECISION RULE: Which product to emphasize?**
>
> ↓
>
> Emphasize the product with the highest
> contribution margin per unit of the constraint.

Because *machine hours* is the constraint, Smart Touch needs to figure out which product has the *highest contribution margin per machine hour*. Exhibit 10-19 determines the contribution margin per machine hour for each product.

EXHIBIT 10-19	**Smart Touch's Contribution Margin per Machine Hour**		
		Excel DVD	Specialty DVD
(1) DVDs that can be produced each machine hour		80	10
(2) Contribution margin per DVD from Exhibit 10-18		$ 5.50	$ 33.50
Contribution margin per machine hour (1) × (2)		$ 440	$ 335
Available capacity—number of machine hours		2,000	2,000
Total contribution margin at full capacity		$880,000	$670,000

Excel DVDs have a higher contribution margin per machine hour, $440, than specialty DVDs, $335. Smart Touch will earn more profit by producing Excel DVDs. Why? Because even though Excel DVDs have a lower contribution margin *per unit*, Smart Touch can make eight times as many Excel DVDs as specialty DVDs in the 2,000 available machine hours. Exhibit 10-19 also proves that Smart Touch earns more total profit by making Excel DVDs. Multiplying the contribution margin per machine hour by the available number of machine hours shows that Smart Touch can earn $880,000 of contribution margin by producing Excel DVDs, but only $670,000 by producing specialty DVDs.

To maximize profit, Smart Touch should make 160,000 Excel DVDs (2,000 machine hours × 80 Excel DVDs per hour) and zero specialty DVDs. Why should Smart Touch make zero specialty DVDs? Because for every machine hour spent making specialty DVDs, Smart Touch would *give up* $105 of contribution margin ($440 per hour for Excel DVDs versus $335 per hour for specialty DVDs).

We made two assumptions here: (1) Smart Touch's sales of other products, if any, will not be hurt by this decision and (2) Smart Touch can sell as many Excel DVDs as it can produce. Let us challenge these assumptions. First, how could making only Excel DVDs hurt sales of other products? By producing the specialty DVDs, Smart Touch also sells many of its standard offerings like the Excel DVDs that coordinate with the specialty DVDs. Other DVD sales might fall if Smart Touch no longer offers specialty DVDs.

Let us challenge our second assumption. Suppose that a new competitor has decreased the demand for Smart Touch's Excel DVDs. Now the company can only sell 120,000 Excel DVDs. Smart Touch should only make as many Excel DVDs as it can sell, and use the remaining machine hours to produce specialty DVDs. Let us see how this constraint in sales demand changes profitability.

Recall from Exhibit 10-19 that Smart Touch will make $880,000 of contribution margin from using all 2,000 machine hours to produce Excel DVDs. However, if Smart Touch only makes 120,000 Excel DVDs, it will only use 1,500 machine hours (120,000 Excel DVDs ÷ 80 Excel DVDs per machine hour). That leaves 500 machine hours available for making specialty DVDs. Smart Touch's new contribution margin will be as shown in Exhibit 10-20.

EXHIBIT 10-20	Smart Touch's Contribution Margin per Machine Hour—Limited Market for Product		
	Excel DVD	Specialty DVD	Total
(1) DVDs that can be produced each machine hour	80	10	
(2) Contribution margin per DVD from Exhibit 10-18	$ 5.50	$ 33.50	
Contribution margin per machine hour (1) × (2)	$ 440	$ 335	
Machine hours devoted to product	1,500	500	
Total contribution margin at full capacity	$660,000	$167,500	$827,500

Because of the change in product mix, Smart Touch's total contribution margin will fall from $880,000 to $827,500, a $52,500 decline. Smart Touch had to give up $105 of contribution margin per machine hour ($440 – $335) on the 500 hours it spent producing specialty DVDs rather than Excel DVDs. However, Smart Touch had no choice—the company would have incurred an *actual loss* from producing Excel DVDs that it could not sell. If Smart Touch had produced 160,000 Excel DVDs but only sold 120,000, the company would have spent $220,000 to make the unsold DVDs (40,000 Excel DVDs × $5.50 variable cost per Excel DVD), yet received no sales revenue from them.

What about fixed costs? In most cases, changing the product mix emphasis in the short run will not affect fixed costs, so fixed costs are irrelevant. However, it is possible that fixed costs could differ by emphasizing a different product mix. What if Smart Touch had a month-to-month lease on a production camera used only for making specialty DVDs? If Smart Touch only made Excel DVDs, it could *avoid* the lease cost. However, if Smart Touch makes any specialty DVDs, it needs the camera. In this case, the fixed costs become relevant because they differ between alternative product mixes (specialty DVDs only *versus* Excel DVDs only, or Excel DVDs and specialty DVDs).

Notice that the analysis again follows the two guidelines for special business decisions: (1) focus on relevant data (only those revenues and costs that differ) and (2) use a contribution margin approach, which separates variable from fixed costs.

Outsourcing and Sell As Is or Process Further Decisions

4 Make outsourcing and sell as is or process further decisions

When to Outsource

Delta outsources much of its reservation work and airplane maintenance. **IBM** outsources most of its desktop production of personal computers. Make-or-buy decisions are often called outsourcing decisions because managers must decide whether to buy a component product or service, or produce it in-house. The heart of these decisions is *how best to use available resources.*

Let us see how managers make outsourcing decisions. Greg's Groovy Tunes, a manufacturer of music CDs, is deciding whether to make the paper liners for the CD cases in-house or whether to outsource them to Becky's Box Designs, a company that specializes in producing paper liners. Greg's Groovy Tunes' cost to produce 250,000 liners is as follows:

	Total Cost (250,000 liners)
Direct materials...	$ 40,000
Direct labor...	20,000
Variable manufacturing overhead	15,000
Fixed manufacturing overhead..............................	50,000
Total manufacturing cost	$125,000
Number of liners..	÷ 250,000
Cost per liner	$ 0.50

Becky's Box Designs offers to sell Greg's Groovy Tunes the liners for $0.37 each. Should Greg's Groovy Tunes make the liners or buy them from Becky's Box Designs? Greg's Groovy Tunes' $0.50 cost per unit to make the liner is $0.13 higher than the cost of buying it from Becky's Box Designs. It appears that Greg's Groovy Tunes should outsource the liners. But the correct answer is not so simple. Why? Because manufacturing unit costs contain both fixed and variable components. In deciding whether or not to outsource, managers must assess fixed and variable costs separately. Exhibit 10-21 shows some of the questions managers must consider when deciding whether or not to outsource.

EXHIBIT 10-21 | **Outsourcing Considerations**

- How do the company's variable costs compare to the outsourcing cost?

- Are any fixed costs avoidable if the company outsources?

- What could the company do with the freed capacity?

Let us see how these considerations apply to Greg's Groovy Tunes. By purchasing the liners, Greg's Groovy Tunes can avoid all variable manufacturing costs—$40,000 of direct materials, $20,000 of direct labor, and $15,000 of variable manufacturing overhead. In total, the company will save $75,000 in variable manufacturing costs, or $0.30 per liner ($75,000 ÷ 250,000 liners). However, Greg's Groovy Tunes will have to pay the variable outsourcing price of $0.37 per unit, or $92,500 for the 250,000 liners. Based only on variable costs, the lower cost alternative is to manufacture the liners in-house. However, managers must still consider fixed costs.

Assume first, that Greg's Groovy Tunes cannot avoid any of the fixed costs by outsourcing. In this case, the company's fixed costs are irrelevant to the decision because Greg's Groovy Tunes would continue to incur $50,000 of fixed costs either way (the fixed costs do not differ between alternatives). Greg's Groovy Tunes should continue to make its own liners because the variable cost of outsourcing the liners, $92,500, exceeds the variable cost of making the liners, $75,000.

However, what if Greg's Groovy Tunes can avoid some fixed costs by outsourcing the liners? Let us assume that management can reduce fixed overhead cost by $10,000 by outsourcing the liners. Greg's Groovy Tunes will still incur $40,000 of fixed overhead ($50,000 − $10,000) even if it outsources the liners. In this case, fixed costs become relevant to the decision because they differ between alternatives.

Exhibit 10-22 shows the differences in costs between the make and buy alternatives under this scenario.

EXHIBIT 10-22 | **Incremental Analysis for Outsourcing Decision**

Liner Costs	Make Liners	Buy Liners	Difference
Variable costs:			
Direct materials	$ 40,000	—	$40,000
Direct labor	20,000	—	20,000
Variable overhead	15,000	—	15,000
Purchase cost from Becky's			
(250,000 × $0.37)	—	$ 92,500	(92,500)
Fixed overhead	50,000	40,000	10,000
Total cost of liners	$125,000	$132,500	$ (7,500)

Exhibit 10-22 shows that it would still cost Greg's Groovy Tunes less to make the liners than to buy them from Becky's Box Designs, even with the $10,000 reduction in fixed costs. The net savings from making 250,000 liners is $7,500. Exhibit 10-22 also shows that outsourcing decisions follow our two key guidelines for special business decisions: (1) Focus on relevant data (differences in costs in this case) and (2) use a contribution margin approach that separates variable costs from fixed costs.

Note how the unit cost—which does *not* separate costs according to behavior—can be deceiving. If Greg's Groovy Tunes' managers made their decision by comparing the total manufacturing cost per liner ($0.50) to the outsourcing unit cost per liner ($0.37), they would have incorrectly decided to outsource. Recall that the manufacturing unit cost ($0.50) contains both fixed and variable components, whereas the outsourcing cost ($0.37) is strictly variable. To make the correct decision, Greg's Groovy Tunes had to separate the two cost components and analyze them separately.

Our decision rule for outsourcing is as follows:

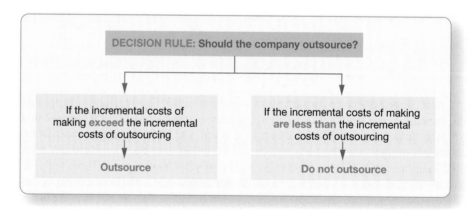

We have not considered what Greg's Groovy Tunes could do with the freed capacity it would have if it outsourced the liners. The analysis in Exhibit 10-22 assumes there is no other use for the production facilities if Greg's Groovy Tunes buys the liners from Becky's Box Designs. But suppose Greg's Groovy Tunes has an opportunity to use its freed-up facilities to make more CDs, which have an expected profit of $18,000. Now, Greg's Groovy Tunes must consider its **opportunity cost**—the benefit forgone by not choosing an alternative course of action. In this case, Greg's Groovy Tunes' opportunity cost of making the liners is the $18,000 profit it forgoes if it does not free its production facilities to make the additional CDs.

Let us see how Greg's Groovy Tunes' managers decide among three alternatives:

1. Use the facilities to make the liners.

2. Buy the liners and leave facilities idle (continue to assume $10,000 of avoidable fixed costs from outsourcing liners).

3. Buy the liners and use facilities to make more CDs (continue to assume $10,000 of avoidable fixed costs from outsourcing liners).

The alternative with the lowest *net* cost is the best use of Greg's Groovy Tunes' facilities. Exhibit 10-23 compares the three alternatives.

EXHIBIT 10-23 | **Best Use of Facilities, Given Opportunity Costs**

		Buy Liners	
	Make Liners	Facilities Idle	Make Additional CDs
Expected cost of 250,000 liners (from Exhibit 10-22)	$125,000	$132,500	$132,500
Expected *profit* from additional CDs	—	—	(18,000)
Expected net cost of obtaining 250,000 liners	$125,000	$132,500	$114,500

Greg's Groovy Tunes should buy the liners from Becky's Box Designs and use the vacated facilities to make more CDs. If Greg's Groovy Tunes makes the liners, or if it buys the liners from Becky's Box Designs but leaves its production facilities idle, it will forgo the opportunity to earn $18,000.

Greg's Groovy Tunes' managers should consider qualitative factors as well as revenue and cost differences in making their final decision. For example, Greg's Groovy Tunes' managers may believe they can better control quality by making the liners themselves. This is an argument for Greg's to continue making the liners.

Stop & Think...

Assume you and two of your friends are working on a team project for a class. The project has three equal portions to it. The visual portion requires the team to develop a **PowerPoint** presentation. The written portion requires the team to write a group report of the results of the team's research. The auditory portion requires the team to present its findings. You all contribute equally to the research, but you will divide the other three portions. Which part will you do—the visual, written, or auditory portion? Because you are the best at **PowerPoint**, the team would want you to prepare the visual portion. This is similar to the outsourcing decision—focus on doing what jobs you do best.

Outsourcing decisions are increasingly important in today's globally wired economy. In the past, make-or-buy decisions often ended up as "make" because coordination, information exchange, and paperwork problems made buying from suppliers too inconvenient. Now, companies can use the Internet to tap into information systems of suppliers and customers located around the world. Paperwork vanishes, and information required to satisfy the strictest JIT delivery schedule is available in real time. As a result, companies are focusing on their core competencies and are outsourcing more functions.

Sell As Is or Process Further?

At what point in processing should a company sell its product? Many companies, especially in the food processing and natural resource industries, face this business decision. Companies in these industries process a raw material (milk, corn, livestock, crude oil, lumber, to name a few) to a point before it is saleable. For example, **Kraft** pasteurizes raw milk before it is saleable. **Kraft** must then decide whether it should sell the pasteurized milk "as is," or process it further into other dairy products (reduced-fat milk, butter, sour cream, cottage cheese, yogurt, blocks of cheese, shredded cheese, and other dairy products). Managers consider the questions shown in Exhibit 10-24 when deciding whether to sell as is or process further.

EXHIBIT 10-24 | **Sell As Is or Process Further Considerations**

- How much revenue will the company receive if we sell the product as is?

- How much revenue will the company receive if the company sells the product after processing it further?

- How much will it cost to process the product further?

Let us look at one of **Chevron**'s sell as is or process further decisions. Suppose **Chevron** spent $125,000 to process crude oil into 50,000 gallons of regular gasoline, as shown in Exhibit 10-25. After processing crude oil into regular gasoline, should **Chevron** sell the regular gas as is or should it spend more to process the gasoline into premium grade? In making the decision, **Chevron**'s managers consider the following relevant information:

EXHIBIT 10-25 | **Sell As Is or Process Further Decision**

Sell as is

Regular gasoline: $190,000 sales revenue

($125,000) Sunk cost of producing 50,000 gallons of regular gasoline

($7,500) Cost of further processing

Premium gasoline: $200,000 sales revenue

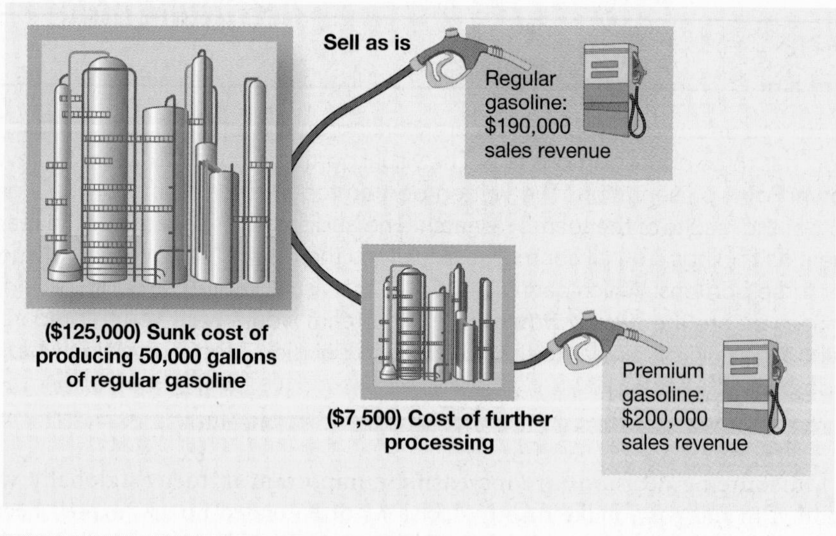

- **Chevron** could sell premium gasoline for $4.00 per gallon, for a total of $200,000 (50,000 × $4.00).

- **Chevron** could sell regular gasoline for $3.80 per gallon, for a total of $190,000 (50,000 × $3.80).

- **Chevron** would have to spend $0.15 per gallon, or $7,500 (50,000 gallons × $0.15) to further process regular gasoline into premium-grade gas.

Notice that **Chevron**'s managers do *not* consider the $125,000 spent on processing crude oil into regular gasoline. Why? It is a *sunk* cost. Recall from our previous discussion that a sunk cost is a past cost that cannot be changed regardless of which future action the company takes. **Chevron** has incurred $125,000—regardless of whether it sells the regular gasoline as is or processes it further into premium gasoline. Therefore, the cost is *not* relevant to the decision.

By analyzing only the relevant costs in Exhibit 10-26, managers see that they can increase profit by $2,500 if they convert the regular gasoline into premium gasoline. The $10,000 extra revenue ($200,000 − $190,000) outweighs the incremental $7,500 cost of the extra processing.

EXHIBIT 10-26 | **Incremental Analysis for Sell As Is or Process Further Decision**

	Sell As Is	Process Further	Difference
Expected revenue from selling 50,000 gallons of regular gasoline at $3.80 per gallon	$190,000		
Expected revenue from selling 50,000 gallons of premium gasoline at $4.00 per gallon		$200,000	$10,000
Additional costs of $0.15 per gallon to convert 50,000 gallons of regular gasoline into premium gasoline		(7,500)	(7,500)
Total net revenue	$190,000	$192,500	$ 2,500

Thus, the decision rule is as follows:

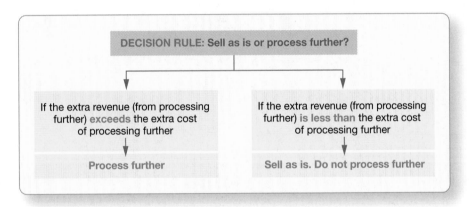

Recall that our keys to decision making include (1) focusing on relevant information and (2) using a contribution margin approach that separates variable costs from fixed costs. The analysis in Exhibit 10-26 includes only those *future* costs and revenues that *differ* between alternatives. We assumed **Chevron** already has the equipment and labor necessary to convert regular gasoline into premium grade gasoline. Because fixed costs would not differ between alternatives, they were irrelevant. However, if **Chevron** has to acquire equipment, or hire employees to convert the gasoline into premium grade gasoline, the extra fixed costs would be relevant. Once again, we see that fixed costs are only relevant if they *differ* between alternatives.

Decision Guidelines

SHORT-TERM SPECIAL BUSINESS DECISIONS

Amazon.com has confronted most of the special business decisions we have covered. Here are the key guidelines **Amazon.com**'s managers follow in making their decisions.

Decision	Guidelines
• Should **Amazon.com** drop its electronics product line?	If the cost savings exceed the lost revenues from dropping the electronics product line, then dropping will increase operating income.
• Given limited warehouse space, which products should **Amazon.com** focus on selling?	**Amazon.com** should focus on selling the products with the highest contribution margin per unit of the constraint, which is cubic feet of warehouse space.
• Should **Amazon.com** outsource its warehousing operations?	If the incremental costs of operating its own warehouses exceed the costs of outsourcing, then outsourcing will increase operating income.
• How should **Amazon.com** decide whether to sell a product as is or process further?	It should process further only if the extra sales revenue (from processing further) exceeds the extra costs of additional processing.

Summary Problem 2

Shelly's Shades produces standard and deluxe sunglasses:

	Per Pair	
	Standard	**Deluxe**
Sale price...	$20	$30
Variable expenses..................................	16	21

The company has 15,000 machine hours available. In one machine hour, Shelly's Shades can produce either 70 pairs of the standard model or 30 pairs of the deluxe model.

Requirements

1. Which model should Shelly's Shades emphasize?
2. Shelly's Shades incurs the following costs for 20,000 of its high-tech hiking shades:

Direct materials...	$ 20,000
Direct labor...	80,000
Variable manufacturing overhead	40,000
Fixed manufacturing overhead.......................................	80,000
Total manufacturing cost	$220,000
Cost per pair ($220,000 ÷ 20,000)................................	$ 11

Another manufacturer has offered to sell Shelly's Shades similar shades for $10, a total purchase cost of $200,000. If Shelly's Shades outsources *and* leaves its plant idle, it can save $50,000 of fixed overhead cost. Or, the company can use the released facilities to make other products that will contribute $70,000 to profits. In this case, the company will not be able to avoid any fixed costs. Identify and analyze the alternatives. What is the best course of action?

Solutions

Requirement 1

	Style of Sunglasses	
	Standard	**Deluxe**
Sale price per pair...........................	$ 20	$ 30
Variable expense per pair	(16)	(21)
Contribution margin per pair	$ 4	$ 9
Units produced each machine hour	× 70	× 30
Contribution margin per machine hour.........	$ 280	$ 270
Capacity—number of machine hours	× 15,000	× 15,000
Total contribution margin at full capacity	$4,200,000	$4,050,000

Decision: Emphasize the standard model because it has the higher contribution margin per unit of the constraint—machine hours—resulting in a higher contribution margin for the company.

Requirement 2

	Make Shades	Buy Shades	
		Facilities Idle	Make Other Products
Relevant costs:			
Direct materials	$ 20,000	—	—
Direct labor	80,000	—	—
Variable overhead.....................	40,000	—	—
Fixed overhead	80,000	$ 30,000	$ 80,000
Purchase cost from outsider (20,000 × $10)	—	200,000	200,000
Total cost of obtaining shades	220,000	230,000	280,000
Profit from other products.........	—	—	(70,000)
Net cost of obtaining 20,000 shades	$220,000	$230,000	$210,000

Decision: Shelly's Shades should buy the shades from the outside supplier and use the released facilities to make other products.

Review *Short-Term Business Decisions*

■ Accounting Vocabulary

Constraint (p. 476)
A factor that restricts production or sale of a product.

Incremental Analysis Approach (p. 461)
A method that looks at how operating income would *change or differ* under each decision alternative. Leaves out irrelevant information—the costs and revenues that will not differ between alternatives. Also called the **relevant information approach**.

Irrelevant costs (p. 460)
Costs that *do not* affect a decision.

Opportunity Cost (p. 480)
The benefit forgone by not choosing an alternative course of action.

Outsourcing (p. 461)
The decision to buy or subcontract a component product or service rather than produce it in-house.

Relevant costs (p. 459)
Costs that *do* affect a decision.

Relevant Information (p. 459)
Expected *future* data that *differs* among alternatives.

Relevant Information Approach (p. 461)
A method that looks at how operating income would *change or differ* under each decision alternative. Leaves out irrelevant information—the costs and revenues that will not differ between alternatives. Also called the **incremental analysis approach**.

Sunk Cost (p. 460)
A past cost that cannot be changed regardless of which future action is taken.

Target Full Cost (p. 467)
The total cost in developing, producing, and delivering a product or service.

■ Quick Check

1. In making short-term special decisions, you should
   a. separate variable from fixed costs.
   b. use a traditional absorption costing approach.
   c. only focus on quantitative factors.
   d. focus on total costs.

2. Which of the following is relevant to Bookworm.com's decision to accept a special order at a lower sale price from a large customer in China?
   a. The cost of Bookworm.com's warehouses in the United States
   b. The cost of shipping the order to the customer
   c. Founder Leon Lyons's salary
   d. Bookworm.com's investment in its Web site

3. Which of the following costs are irrelevant to business decisions?
   a. Variable costs
   b. Sunk costs
   c. Avoidable costs
   d. Costs that differ between alternatives

4. When making decisions, managers should
   a. consider revenues that differ between alternatives.
   b. consider costs that do not differ between alternatives.
   c. consider sunk costs in their decisions.
   d. consider only variable costs.

5. When pricing a product or service, managers must consider which of the following?

 a. Only variable costs

 b. Only manufacturing costs

 c. Only period costs

 d. All costs

6. When companies are price-setters, their products and services

 a. are priced by managers using a target-pricing emphasis.

 b. tend to be unique.

 c. tend to be commodities.

 d. tend to have a lot of competitors.

7. In deciding whether to drop its electronics product line, Bookworm.com would consider

 a. how dropping the electronics product line would affect sales of its other products like CDs.

 b. the revenues it would lose from dropping the product line.

 c. the costs it could save by dropping the product line.

 d. All of the above

8. In deciding which product lines to emphasize, Bookworm.com should focus on the product line that has the highest

 a. contribution margin per unit of the constraining factor.

 b. contribution margin per unit of product.

 c. profit per unit of product.

 d. contribution margin ratio.

9. When making outsourcing decisions

 a. avoidable fixed costs are irrelevant.

 b. expected use of the freed capacity is irrelevant.

 c. the variable cost of producing the product in-house is relevant.

 d. the manufacturing unit cost of making the product in-house is relevant.

10. When deciding whether to sell as is or process a product further, managers should ignore which of the following?

 a. The revenue if the product is processed further

 b. The costs of processing the product thus far

 c. The cost of processing further

 d. The revenue if the product is sold as is

Answers are given after Apply Your Knowledge (p. 506).

Assess Your Progress

■ Short Exercises

S10-1 *(L.OBJ. 1)* **Describing and identifying information relevant to business decisions [5 min]**
You are trying to decide whether to trade in your inkjet printer for a more recent model. Your usage pattern will remain unchanged, but the old and new printers use different ink cartridges.

1. Indicate if the following items are relevant or irrelevant to your decision:

   a. The price of the new printer
   b. The price you paid for the old printer
   c. The trade-in value of the old printer
   d. Paper costs
   e. The difference between ink cartridges' costs

S10-2 *(L.OBJ. 2)* **Making special order and pricing decisions [10 min]**
SnowDelight operates a Rocky Mountain ski resort. The company is planning its lift ticket pricing for the coming ski season. Investors would like to earn a 13% return on the company's $105 million of assets. The company primarily incurs fixed costs to groom the runs and operate the lifts. SnowDelight projects fixed costs to be $34,250,000 for the ski season. The resort serves about 650,000 skiers and snowboarders each season. Variable costs are about $11 per guest. Currently, the resort has such a favorable reputation among skiers and snowboarders that it has some control over the lift ticket prices.

Requirements

1. Would SnowDelight emphasize target pricing or cost-plus pricing. Why?
2. If other resorts in the area charge $82 per day, what price should SnowDelight charge?

Note: Short Exercise 10-2 must be completed before attempting Short Exercise 10-3.

S10-3 *(L.OBJ. 2)* **Making special order and pricing decisions [10 min]**
Consider SnowDelight from Short Exercise 10-2. Assume that SnowDelight's reputation has diminished and other resorts in the vicinity are only charging $75 per lift ticket. SnowDelight has become a price-taker and will not be able to charge more than its competitors. At the market price, SnowDelight managers believe they will still serve 650,000 skiers and snowboarders each season.

Requirements

1. If SnowDelight cannot reduce its costs, what profit will it earn? State your answer in dollars and as a percent of assets. Will investors be happy with the profit level?
2. Assume SnowDelight has found ways to cut its fixed costs to $28 million. What is its new target variable cost per skier/snowboarder?

S10-4 *(L.OBJ. 3)* **Making dropping a product and product-mix decisions [5–10 min]**
Linda Fashions operates three departments: Men's, Women's, and Accessories. Departmental operating income data for the third quarter of 2011 are as follows:

LINDA FASHIONS					
Income Statement					
For the quarter ended September 30, 2011					
		Department			
		Men's	Women's	Accessories	Total
Sales revenue		$ 109,000	$ 53,000	$ 102,000	$ 264,000
Variable expenses		61,000	32,000	89,000	182,000
Fixed expenses		24,000	20,000	24,000	68,000
Total expenses		85,000	52,000	113,000	250,000
Operating income (loss)		$ 24,000	$ 1,000	$ (11,000)	$ 14,000

Assume that the fixed expenses assigned to each department include only direct fixed costs of the department:

- Salary of the department's manager
- Cost of advertising directly related to that department
  If Linda Fashions drops a department, it will not incur these fixed expenses.

Requirement

1. Under these circumstances, should Linda Fashions drop any of the departments? Give your reasoning.

Note: Short Exercise 10-4 must be completed before attempting Short Exercise 10-5.

S10-5 *(L.OBJ. 3)* **Making dropping a product and product-mix decisions [10 min]**
Consider Linda Fashions from Short Exercise 10-4. Assume that Linda Fashions allocates all fixed costs based on square footage. If Linda Fashions drops one of the current departments, it plans to replace the dropped department with a shoe department. The company expects the shoe department to produce $76,000 in sales and have $54,000 of variable costs. Because the shoe business would be new to Linda Fashions, the company would have to incur an additional $7,100 of fixed costs (advertising, depreciation on new shoe display racks, and so forth) per period related to the department.

Requirements

1. What is the potential profit from the new shoe department?
2. Should Linda Fashions consider replacing one of its existing departments with a new shoe department?

S10-6 *(L.OBJ. 3)* **Making dropping a product and product-mix decisions [15 min]**
Store-It produces plastic storage bins for household storage needs. The company makes two sizes of bins: large (50 gallon) and regular (35 gallon). Demand for the product is so high that Store-It can sell as many of each size as it can produce. The company uses the same machinery to produce both sizes. The machinery can only be run for 3,400 hours per period. Store-It can produce 10 large bins every hour, whereas it can produce 17 regular bins in the same amount of time. Fixed costs amount to $105,000 per period. Sales prices and variable costs are as follows:

	Regular	Large
Sales price per unit	$8.50	$10.50
Variable cost per unit	$3.50	$ 4.30

Requirements

1. Which product should Store-It emphasize? Why?
2. To maximize profits, how many of each size bin should Store-It produce?
3. Given this product mix, what will the company's operating income be?

Note: Short Exercise 10-6 must be completed before attempting Short Exercise 10-7.

S10-7 *(L.OBJ. 3)* **Making dropping a product and product-mix decisions [15 min]**
Consider Store-It in Short Exercise 10-6. Assume demand for regular bins is limited to 32,000 units and demand for large bins is limited to 27,000 units.

Requirements

1. How many of each size bin should Store-It make now?
2. Given this product mix, what will the company's operating income be?
3. Explain why the operating income is less than it was when Store-It was producing its optimal product mix in 10-6.

S10-8 *(L.OBJ. 4)* **Making outsourcing and sell as is or process further decisions [10 min]**

Suppose an Olive Tree restaurant is considering whether to (1) bake bread for its restaurant in-house or (2) buy the bread from a local bakery. The chef estimates that variable costs of making each loaf include $0.56 of ingredients, $0.22 of variable overhead (electricity to run the oven), and $0.76 of direct labor for kneading and forming the loaves. Allocating fixed overhead (depreciation on the kitchen equipment and building) based on direct labor assigns $1.00 of fixed overhead per loaf. None of the fixed costs are avoidable. The local bakery would charge $1.74 per loaf.

Requirements

1. What is the unit cost of making the bread in-house (use absorption costing)?
2. Should Olive Tree bake the bread in-house or buy from the local bakery? Why?
3. In addition to the financial analysis, what else should Olive Tree consider when making this decision?

S10-9 *(L.OBJ. 4)* **Making outsourcing decisions [10–15 min]**

Rita Riley manages a fleet of 200 delivery trucks for Greely, Corp. Riley must decide if the company should outsource the fleet management function. If she outsources to Fleet Management Services (FMS), FMS will be responsible for maintenance and scheduling activities. This alternative would require Riley to lay off her five employees. However, her own job would be secure; she would be Greely's liaison with FMS. If she continues to manage the fleet she will need fleet-management software that costs $8,000 a year to lease. FMS offers to manage this fleet for an annual fee of $280,000. Rita performed the following analysis:

GREELY CORPORATION Outsourcing Decision Analysis			
	Retain In-House	Outsource to FMS	Difference
Annual leasing fee for software	$ 8,000	$ —	$ 8,000
Annual maintenance of trucks	145,000	—	145,000
Total annual salaries of five other fleet management employees	150,000	—	150,000
Fleet Management Services' annual fee	—	280,000	(280,000)
Total cost / cost savings	$ 303,000	$ 280,000	$ 23,000

Requirements

1. Which alternative will maximize Greely's short-term operating income?
2. What qualitative factors should Riley consider before making a final decision?

S10-10 *(L.OBJ. 4)* **Sell as is or process further decisions [10 min]**

Chocolicious processes cocoa beans into cocoa powder at a processing cost of $9,800 per batch. Chocolicious can sell the cocoa powder as is or it can process the cocoa powder further into either chocolate syrup or boxed assorted chocolates. Once processed, each batch of cocoa beans would result in the following sales revenue:

Cocoa powder..	$ 14,500
Chocolate syrup	$100,000
Boxed assorted chocolates.......................	$200,000

The cost of transforming the cocoa powder into chocolate syrup would be $72,000. Likewise, the company would incur a cost of $178,000 to transform the cocoa powder into boxed assorted chocolates. The company president has decided to make boxed assorted chocolates owing to its high sales value and to the fact that the cocoa bean processing cost of $9,800 eats up most of the cocoa powder profits.

Requirement

1. Has the president made the right or wrong decision? Explain your answer. Be sure to include the correct financial analysis in your response.

■ Exercises

E10-11 *(L.OBJ. 1)* **Describing and identifying information relevant to business decisions [5–10 min]**

Joe Roberts, production manager for Fabricut, invested in computer-controlled production machinery last year. He purchased the machinery from Advanced Design at a cost of $2 million. A representative from Advanced Design has recently contacted Joe because the company has designed an even more efficient piece of machinery. The new design would double the production output of the year-old machinery but cost Fabricut another $3 million. Roberts is afraid to bring this new equipment to the company president's attention because he convinced the president to invest $2 million in the machinery last year.

Requirement

1. Explain what is relevant and irrelevant to Roberts's dilemma. What should he do?

E10-12 *(L.OBJ. 2)* **Making special order and pricing decisions [10–15 min]**

Suppose the Baseball Hall of Fame in Cooperstown, New York, has approached Active-Cardz with a special order. The Hall of Fame wishes to purchase 50,000 baseball card packs for a special promotional campaign and offers $0.37 per pack, a total of $18,500. Active-Cardz's total production cost is $0.57 per pack, as follows:

Variable costs:	
Direct materials	$ 0.14
Direct labor	0.07
Variable overhead	0.11
Fixed overhead	0.25
Total cost	$ 0.57

Active-Cardz has enough excess capacity to handle the special order.

Requirements

1. Prepare an incremental analysis to determine whether Active-Cardz should accept the special sales order.
2. Now assume that the Hall of Fame wants special hologram baseball cards. Active-Cardz will spend $5,800 to develop this hologram, which will be useless after the special order is completed. Should Active-Cardz accept the special order under these circumstances?

E10-13 *(L.OBJ. 2)* **Making special order and pricing decisions [20–25 min]**

Maui Smith Sunglasses sell for about $150 per pair. Suppose that the company incurs the following average costs per pair:

Direct materials	$	42
Direct labor		10
Variable manufacturing overhead		6
Variable marketing expenses		4
Fixed manufacturing overhead		16*
Total cost	$	78

* $2,100,000 total fixed manufacturing overhead ÷ 131,250 pairs of sunglasses

Maui Smith has enough idle capacity to accept a one-time-only special order from Montana Glasses for 18,000 pairs of sunglasses at $70 per pair. Maui Smith will not incur any variable marketing expenses for the order.

Requirements

1. How would accepting the order affect Maui Smith's operating income? In addition to the special order's effect on profits, what other (longer-term qualitative) factors should Maui Smith's managers consider in deciding whether to accept the order?

2. Maui Smith's marketing manager, Jim Revo, argues against accepting the special order because the offer price of $70 is less than Maui Smith's $78 cost to make the sunglasses. Revo asks you, as one of Maui Smith's staff accountants, to explain whether his analysis is correct.

E10-14 *(L.OBJ. 2)* **Making special order and pricing decisions [10–15 min]**

White Builders builds 1,500 square-foot starter tract homes in the fast-growing suburbs of Atlanta. Land and labor are cheap, and competition among developers is fierce. The homes are "cookie-cutter," with any upgrades added by the buyer after the sale. White Builders' costs per developed sub-lot are as follows:

Land	$ 54,000
Construction	$ 122,000
Landscaping	$ 5,000
Variable marketing costs	$ 3,000

White Builders would like to earn a profit of 15% of the variable cost of each home sale. Similar homes offered by competing builders sell for $206,000 each.

Requirements

1. Which approach to pricing should White Builders emphasize? Why?
2. Will White Builders be able to achieve its target profit levels?
3. Bathrooms and kitchens are typically the most important selling features of a home. White Builders could differentiate the homes by upgrading the bathrooms and kitchens. The upgrades would cost $20,000 per home, but would enable White Builders to increase the selling prices by $35,000 per home. (Kitchen and bathroom upgrades typically add about 150% of their cost to the value of any home.) If White Builders makes the upgrades, what will the new cost-plus price per home be? Should the company differentiate its product in this manner?

E10-15 *(L.OBJ. 3)* **Making dropping a product and product-mix decisions [10 min]**

Top managers of Movie Plus are alarmed by their operating losses. They are considering dropping the VCR-tape product line. Company accountants have prepared the following analysis to help make this decision:

		DVD	VCR
	Total	**Discs**	**Tapes**
Sales revenue	$ 438,000	$ 309,000	$ 129,000
Variable expenses	250,000	157,000	93,000
Contribution margin	188,000	152,000	36,000
Fixed expenses:			
Manufacturing	134,000	76,000	58,000
Marketing and administrative	70,000	59,000	11,000
Total fixed expenses	204,000	135,000	69,000
Operating income (loss)	$ (16,000)	$ 17,000	$ (33,000)

MOVIE PLUS
Income Statement
For the year ended December 31, 2010

Total fixed costs will not change if the company stops selling VCR tapes.

Requirement

1. Prepare an incremental analysis to show whether Movie Plus should drop the VCR-tape product line. Will dropping VCR tapes add $33,000 to operating income? Explain.

Note: Exercise 10-15 must be completed before attempting Exercise 10-16.

E10-16 *(L.OBJ. 3)* **Making dropping a product and product-mix decisions [10 min]**

Refer to Exercise 10-15. Assume that Movie Plus can avoid $26,000 of fixed expenses by dropping the VCR-tape product line (these costs are direct fixed costs of the VCR product line).

Requirement

1. Prepare an incremental analysis to show whether Movie Plus should stop selling VCR tapes.

E10-17 *(L.OBJ. 3)* **Product mix under production constraints [15 min]**

ExerLight produces two types of exercise treadmills: regular and deluxe. The exercise craze is such that ExerLight could use all its available machine hours to produce either model. The two models are processed through the same production departments. Data for both models is as follows:

	Per Unit	
	Deluxe	**Regular**
Sale price	$ 1,000	$ 580
Costs:		
Direct materials	310	110
Direct labor	80	184
Variable manufacturing overhead	252	84
Fixed manufacturing overhead*	108	36
Variable operating expenses	113	69
Total cost	863	483
Operating income	$ 137	$ 97

*Allocated on the basis of machine hours.

Requirements

1. What is the constraint?
2. Which model should ExerLight produce? (*Hint:* Use the allocation of fixed manufacturing overhead to determine the proportion of machine hours used by each product.)
3. If ExerLight should produce both models, compute the mix that will maximize operating income.

E10-18 *(L.OBJ. 3)* **Making dropping a product and product-mix decisions [10–15 min]**
Cole sells both designer and moderately priced fashion accessories. Top management is deciding which product line to emphasize. Accountants have provided the following data:

	Per Item	
	Designer	Moderately Priced
Average sale price	$ 195	$ 83
Average variable expenses	95	22
Average contribution margin	100	61
Average fixed expenses (allocated)	20	15
Average operating income	$ 80	$ 46

The Cole store in Reno, Nevada, has 8,000 square feet of floor space. If Cole emphasizes moderately priced goods, it can display 560 items in the store. If Cole emphasizes designer wear, it can only display 240 designer items. These numbers are also the average monthly sales in units.

Requirement

1. Prepare an analysis to show which product the company should emphasize.

E10-19 *(L.OBJ. 3)* **Making dropping a product and product-mix decisions [15–20 min]**
Each morning, Mike Smith stocks the drink case at Mike's Beach Hut in Myrtle Beach, South Carolina. Mike's Beach Hut has 100 linear feet of refrigerated display space for cold drinks. Each linear foot can hold either five 12-ounce cans or four 20-ounce plastic or glass bottles.

Mike's Beach Hut sells three types of cold drinks:
1. Grand – Cola in 12-oz. cans, for $1.55 per can
2. Grand – Cola in 20-oz. plastic bottles, for $1.65 per bottle
3. Right – Cola in 20-oz. glass bottles, for $2.25 per bottle

Mike's Beach Hut pays its suppliers:
1. $0.25 per 12-oz. can of Grand – Cola
2. $0.30 per 20-oz. bottle of Grand – Cola
3. $0.70 per 20-oz. bottle of Right – Cola

Mike's Beach Hut's monthly fixed expenses include:

Hut rental	$	375
Refrigerator rental		60
Mike's salary		1,600
Total fixed expenses	$	2,035

Mike's Beach Hut can sell all the drinks stocked in the display case each morning.

Requirements

1. What is Mike's Beach Hut's constraining factor? What should Mike stock to maximize profits?
2. Suppose Mike's Beach Hut refuses to devote more than 65 linear feet to any individual product. Under this condition, how many linear feet of each drink should Mike's stock? How many units of each product will be available for sale each day?

E10-20 *(L.OBJ. 4)* **Making outsourcing decisions [10–15 min]**

Opti Systems manufactures an optical switch that it uses in its final product. The switch has the following manufacturing costs per unit:

Direct materials	$ 11.00
Direct labor	2.00
Variable overhead	3.00
Fixed overhead	7.00
Manufacturing product cost	$ 23.00

Another company has offered to sell Opti Systems the switch for $17.50 per unit. If Opti Systems buys the switch from the outside supplier, the manufacturing facilities that will be idled cannot be used for any other purpose, yet none of the fixed costs are avoidable.

Requirement

1. Prepare an outsourcing analysis to determine if Opti Systems should make or buy the switch.

Note: Exercise 10-20 must be completed before attempting Exercise 10-21.

E10-21 *(L.OBJ. 4)* **Making outsourcing decisions [10–15 min]**

Refer to Exercise 10-20. Opti Systems needs 82,000 optical switches. By outsourcing them, Opti Systems can use its idle facilities to manufacture another product that will contribute $223,000 to operating income.

Requirements

1. Identify the *incremental* costs that Opti Systems will incur to acquire 82,000 switches under three alternative plans.
2. Which plan makes the best use of Opti System's facilities? Support your answer.

E10-22 *(L.OBJ. 4)* **Making sell as is or process further decisions [10 min]**

Organicmaid processes organic milk into plain yogurt. Organicmaid sells plain yogurt to hospitals, nursing homes, and restaurants in bulk, one-gallon containers. Each batch, processed at a cost of $820, yields 540 gallons of plain yogurt. Organicmaid sells the one-gallon tubs for $6 each, and spends $0.12 for each plastic tub. Organicmaid has recently begun to reconsider its strategy. Organicmaid wonders if it would be more profitable to sell individual-size portions of fruited organic yogurt at local food stores. Organicmaid could further process each batch of plain yogurt into 11,520 individual portions (3/4 cup each) of fruited yogurt. A recent market analysis indicates that demand for the product exists. Organicmaid would sell each individual portion for $0.56. Packaging would cost $0.06 per portion, and fruit would cost $0.10 per portion. Fixed costs would not change.

Requirement

1. Should Organicmaid continue to sell only the gallon-size plain yogurt (sell as is), or convert the plain yogurt into individual-size portions of fruited yogurt (process further)? Why?

■ Problems (Group A)

P10-23A *(L.OBJ. 1, 2)* **Identifying which information is relevant and making special order and pricing decisions [15–20 min]**

Maritime manufactures flotation vests in Tampa, Florida. Maritime's contribution-margin income statement for the month ended December 31, 2010, contains the following data:

MARITIME Income Statement For the month ended December 31, 2010	
Sales in units	30,000
Sales revenue	$ 480,000
Variable expenses:	
Manufacturing	90,000
Marketing and administrative	105,000
Total variable expenses	195,000
Contribution margin	285,000
Fixed expenses:	
Manufacturing	126,000
Marketing and administrative	89,000
Total fixed expenses	215,000
Operating income	$ 70,000

Suppose Overton wishes to buy 4,500 vests from Maritime. Acceptance of the order will not increase Maritime's variable marketing and administrative expenses. The Maritime plant has enough unused capacity to manufacture the additional vests. Overton has offered $11.00 per vest, which is below the normal sale price of $16.

Requirements

1. Identify each cost in the income statement as either relevant or irrelevant to Maritime's decision.

2. Prepare an incremental analysis to determine whether Maritime should accept this special sales order.

3. Identify long-term factors Maritime should consider in deciding whether to accept the special sales order.

P10-24A *(L.OBJ. 2)* **Making special order and pricing decisions [15–20 min]**

Garden House operates a commercial plant nursery where it propagates plants for garden centers throughout the region. Garden House has $5,000,000 in assets. Its yearly fixed costs are $625,000 and the variable costs for the potting soil, container, label, seedling, and labor for each gallon-size plant total $1.70. Garden House's volume is currently 500,000 units. Competitors offer the same plants, at the same quality, to garden centers for $4.00 each. Garden centers then mark them up to sell to the public for $8 to $10, depending on the type of plant.

Requirements

1. Garden House's owners want to earn a 12% return on the company's assets. What is Garden House's target full cost?

2. Given Garden House's current costs, will its owners be able to achieve their target profit?

3. Assume Garden House has identified ways to cut its variable costs to $1.55 per unit. What is its new target fixed cost? Will this decrease in variable costs allow the company to achieve its target profit?

4. Garden House started an aggressive advertising campaign strategy to differentiate its plants from those grown by other nurseries. Monrovia Plants made this strategy work so Garden House has decided to try it, too. Garden House does not expect volume to be affected, but it hopes to gain more control over pricing. If Garden House has to spend $120,000 this year to advertise, and its variable costs continue to be $1.55 per unit, what will its cost-plus price be? Do you think Garden House will be able to sell its plants to garden centers at the cost-plus price? Why or why not?

P10-25A (*L.OBJ. 3*) **Making dropping a product and product-mix decisions [20–25 min]**
Members of the board of directors of Security Force have received the following operating income data for the year ended December 31, 2010:

	Industrial Systems	Household Systems	Total
SECURITY FORCE			
Income Statement			
For the year ended December 31, 2010			
	Product Line		
	Industrial Systems	Household Systems	Total
Sales revenue	$ 320,000	$ 340,000	$ 660,000
Cost of goods sold:			
Variable	38,000	45,000	83,000
Fixed	250,000	67,000	317,000
Total cost of goods sold	288,000	112,000	400,000
Gross profit	32,000	228,000	260,000
Marketing and administrative expenses:			
Variable	67,000	70,000	137,000
Fixed	42,000	23,000	65,000
Total marketing and administrative exp.	109,000	93,000	202,000
Operating income (loss)	$ (77,000)	$ 135,000	$ 58,000

Members of the board are surprised that the industrial systems product line is losing money. They commission a study to determine whether the company should drop the line. Company accountants estimate that dropping industrial systems will decrease fixed cost of goods sold by $85,000 and decrease fixed marketing and administrative expenses by $13,000.

Requirements

1. Prepare an incremental analysis to show whether Security Force should drop the industrial systems product line.

2. Prepare contribution margin income statements to show Security Force's total operating income under the two alternatives: (a) with the industrial systems line and (b) without the line. Compare the *difference* between the two alternatives' income numbers to your answer to requirement 1.

3. What have you learned from the comparison in requirement 2?

P10-26A (*L.OBJ. 3*) **Making dropping a product and product-mix decisions [10–15 min]**
Britt, located in St. Cloud, Minnesota, produces two lines of electric toothbrushes: deluxe and standard. Because Britt can sell all the toothbrushes it can produce, the

owners are expanding the plant. They are deciding which product line to emphasize. To make this decision, they assemble the following data:

	Per Unit	
	Deluxe Toothbrush	Standard Toothbrush
Sale price	$ 80	$ 58
Variable expenses	21	19
Contribution margin	$ 59	$ 39
Contribution margin ratio	73.8%	67.2%

After expansion, the factory will have a production capacity of 4,300 machine hours per month. The plant can manufacture either 65 standard electric toothbrushes or 23 deluxe electric toothbrushes per machine hour.

Requirements

1. Identify the constraining factor for Britt.
2. Prepare an analysis to show which product line to emphasize.

P10-27A *(L.OBJ. 4)* **Making outsourcing decisions [20–30 min]**
Wild Ride manufactures snowboards. Its cost of making 1,800 bindings is as follows:

Direct materials	$ 17,530
Direct labor	2,700
Variable overhead	2,120
Fixed overhead	7,100
Total manufacturing costs for 1,800 bindings	$ 29,450

Suppose Lewis will sell bindings to Wild Ride for $15 each. Wild Ride would pay $1 per unit to transport the bindings to its manufacturing plant, where it would add its own logo at a cost of $0.60 per binding.

Requirements

1. Wild Ride's accountants predict that purchasing the bindings from Lewis will enable the company to avoid $2,600 of fixed overhead. Prepare an analysis to show whether Wild Ride should make or buy the bindings.
2. The facilities freed by purchasing bindings from Lewis can be used to manufacture another product that will contribute $2,600 to profit. Total fixed costs will be the same as if Wild Ride had produced the bindings. Show which alternative makes the best use of Wild Ride's facilities: (a) make bindings, (b) buy bindings and leave facilities idle, or (c) buy bindings and make another product.

P10-28A *(L.OBJ. 4)* **Making sell as is or process further decisions [20–25 min]**
Rouse Petroleum has spent $201,000 to refine 64,000 gallons of petroleum distillate, which can be sold for $6.00 a gallon. Alternatively, Rouse can process the distillate further and produce 57,000 gallons of cleaner fluid. The additional processing will cost $1.70 per gallon of distillate. The cleaner fluid can be sold for $9.20 a gallon. To sell the cleaner fluid, Rouse must pay a sales commission of $0.12 a gallon and transportation charge of $0.17 a gallon.

Requirements

1. Diagram Rouse's decision alternatives, using Exhibit 10-25 as a guide.
2. Identify the sunk cost. Is the sunk cost relevant to Rouse's decision?
3. Should Rouse sell the petroleum distillate or process it into cleaner fluid? Show the expected net revenue difference between the two alternatives.

■ Problems (Group B)

P10-29B *(L.OBJ. 1, 2)* **Identifying which information is relevant and making special order and pricing decisions [15–20 min]**

Buoy manufactures flotation vests in Tampa, Florida. Buoy's contribution-margin income statement for the month ended January 31, 2010, contains the following data:

BUOY Income Statement For the month ended January 31, 2010	
Sales in units	32,000
Sales revenue	$ 448,000
Variable expenses:	
Manufacturing	96,000
Marketing and administrative	112,000
Total variable expenses	208,000
Contribution margin	240,000
Fixed expenses:	
Manufacturing	125,000
Marketing and administrative	94,000
Total fixed expenses	219,000
Operating income	$ 21,000

Suppose Overton wishes to buy 5,300 vests from Buoy. Acceptance of the order will not increase Buoy's variable marketing and administrative expenses. The Buoy plant has enough unused capacity to manufacture the additional vests. Overton has offered $9.00 per vest, which is below the normal sale price of $14.

Requirements

1. Identify each cost in the income statement as either relevant or irrelevant to Buoy's decision.
2. Prepare an incremental analysis to determine whether Buoy should accept this special sales order.
3. Identify long-term factors Buoy should consider in deciding whether to accept the special sales order.

P10-30B *(L.OBJ. 2)* **Making special order and pricing decisions [15–20 min]**

Green Thumb operates a commercial plant nursery, where it propagates plants for garden centers throughout the region. Green Thumb has $5,000,000 in assets. Its yearly fixed costs are $600,000 and the variable costs for the potting soil, container, label, seedling, and labor for each gallon-size plant total $1.35. Green Thumb's volume is currently 500,000 units. Competitors offer the same plants, at the same quality, to garden centers for $3.60 each. Garden centers then mark them up to sell to the public for $8 to $10, depending on the type of plant.

Requirements

1. Green Thumb's owners want to earn a 12% return on the company's assets. What is Green Thumb's target full cost?
2. Given Green Thumb's current costs, will its owners be able to achieve their target profit?

3. Assume Green Thumb has identified ways to cut its variable costs to $1.20 per unit. What is its new target fixed cost? Will this decrease in variable costs allow the company to achieve its target profit?

4. Green Thumb started an aggressive advertising campaign strategy to differentiate its plants from those grown by other nurseries. Monrovia Plants made this strategy work so Green Thumb has decided to try it, too. Green Thumb does not expect volume to be affected, but it hopes to gain more control over pricing. If Green Thumb has to spend $120,000 this year to advertise, and its variable costs continue to be $1.20 per unit, what will its cost-plus price be? Do you think Green Thumb will be able to sell its plants to garden centers at the cost-plus price? Why or why not?

P10-31B *(L.OBJ. 3)* **Making dropping a product and product-mix decisions [20–25 min]**
Members of the board of directors of Security First have received the following operating income data for the year ended August 31, 2010:

	Product Line		
SECURITY FIRST **Income Statement** For the year ended August 31, 2010			
	Industrial Systems	Household Systems	Total
Sales revenue	$ 340,000	$ 360,000	$ 700,000
Cost of goods sold:			
Variable	33,000	45,000	78,000
Fixed	250,000	63,000	313,000
Total cost of goods sold	283,000	108,000	391,000
Gross profit	57,000	252,000	309,000
Marketing and administrative expenses:			
Variable	68,000	75,000	143,000
Fixed	42,000	24,000	66,000
Total marketing and administrative exp.	110,000	99,000	209,000
Operating income (loss)	$ (53,000)	$ 153,000	$ 100,000

Members of the board are surprised that the industrial systems product line is losing money. They commission a study to determine whether the company should drop the line. Company accountants estimate that dropping industrial systems will decrease fixed cost of goods sold by $84,000 and decrease fixed marketing and administrative expenses by $12,000.

Requirements

1. Prepare an incremental analysis to show whether Security First should drop the industrial systems product line.

2. Prepare contribution margin income statements to show Security First's total operating income under the two alternatives: (a) with the industrial systems line and (b) without the line. Compare the *difference* between the two alternatives' income numbers to your answer to requirement 1.

3. What have you learned from this comparison?

P10-32B *(L.OBJ. 3)* **Making dropping a product and product-mix decisions [10–15 min]**

Brett, located in Rochester, New York, produces two lines of electric toothbrushes: deluxe and standard. Because Brett can sell all the toothbrushes it can produce, the owners are expanding the plant. They are deciding which product line to emphasize. To make this decision, they assemble the following data:

	Per Unit	
	Deluxe Toothbrush	Standard Toothbrush
Sale price	$ 80	$ 52
Variable expenses	24	16
Contribution margin	$ 56	$ 36
Contribution margin ratio	70.0%	69.2%

After expansion, the factory will have a production capacity of 4,100 machine hours per month. The plant can manufacture either 55 standard electric toothbrushes or 23 deluxe electric toothbrushes per machine hour.

Requirements

1. Identify the constraining factor for Brett.
2. Prepare an analysis to show which product line the company should emphasize.

P10-33B *(L.OBJ. 4)* **Making outsourcing decisions [20–30 min]**

X-Perience manufactures snowboards. Its cost of making 1,700 bindings is as follows:

Direct materials	$ 17,600
Direct labor	3,100
Variable overhead	2,080
Fixed overhead	6,600
Total manufacturing costs for 1,700 bindings	$ 29,380

Suppose Livingston will sell bindings to X-Perience for $14 each. X-Perience would pay $2 per unit to transport the bindings to its manufacturing plant, where it would add its own logo at a cost of $0.60 per binding.

Requirements

1. X-Perience's accountants predict that purchasing the bindings from Livingston will enable the company to avoid $1,800 of fixed overhead. Prepare an analysis to show whether X-Perience should make or buy the bindings.
2. The facilities freed by purchasing bindings from Livingston can be used to manufacture another product that will contribute $2,800 to profit. Total fixed costs will be the same as if X-Perience had produced the bindings. Show which alternative makes the best use of X-Perience's facilities: (a) make bindings, (b) buy bindings and leave facilities idle, or (c) buy bindings and make another product.

P10-34B *(L.OBJ. 4)* **Make sell as is or process further decisions [20–25 min]**

Castillo Petroleum has spent $205,000 to refine 64,000 gallons of petroleum distillate, which can be sold for $6.10 a gallon. Alternatively, Castillo can process the distillate further and produce 56,000 gallons of cleaner fluid. The additional processing will cost $1.70 per gallon of distillate. The cleaner fluid can be sold for $9.30 a gallon. To sell the cleaner fluid, Castillo must pay a sales commission of $0.11 a gallon and transportation charge of $0.18 a gallon.

1. Diagram Castillo's decision alternatives, using Exhibit 10-25 as a guide.
2. Identify the sunk cost. Is the sunk cost relevant to Castillo's decision?
3. Should Castillo sell the petroleum distillate or process it into cleaner fluid? Show the expected net revenue difference between the two alternatives.

■ Continuing Exercise

E10-35 This exercise continues the Sherman Lawn Service, Inc., situation from Exercise 9-23 of Chapter 9. Sherman Lawn Service currently charges $50 for a standard lawn service and incurs $20 in variable cost. Assume fixed costs are $1,200 per month. Sherman has been offered a special contract for $35 each for 10 lawns in one subdivision. This special contract will not affect Sherman's other business.

Requirements

1. Should Sherman take the special contract?
2. What will Sherman's incremental profit be on the special contract?

■ Continuing Problem

P10-36 This problem continues the Haupt Consulting, Inc., situation from Problem 9-24 of Chapter 9. Haupt Consulting provides consulting service at an average price of $100 per hour and incurs variable costs of $40 per hour. Assume average fixed costs are $4,000 a month.

Haupt has developed new software that will revolutionize billing for companies. Haupt has already invested $300,000 in the software. It can market the software as is at $50,000 a client and expects to sell to eight clients. Haupt can develop the software further, adding integration to Microsoft products at an additional development cost of $150,000. The additional development will allow Haupt to sell the software for $60,000 each, but to ten clients.

Requirement

1. Should Haupt sell the software as is or develop it further?

Apply Your Knowledge

■ Decision Cases

Case 1. BKFin.com provides banks access to sophisticated financial information and analysis systems over the Web. The company combines these tools with benchmarking data access, including e-mail and wireless communications, so that banks can instantly evaluate individual loan applications and entire loan portfolios.

BKFin.com's CEO Jon Wise is happy with the company's growth. To better focus on client service, Wise is considering outsourcing some functions. CFO Jenny Lee suggests that the company's e-mail may be the place to start. She recently attended a conference and learned that companies like **Continental Airlines, DellNet, GTE,** and **NBC** were outsourcing their e-mail function. Wise asks Lee to identify costs related to BKFin.com's in-house Microsoft Exchange mail application, which has 2,300 mailboxes. This information follows:

Variable costs:	
E-mail license...	$7 per mailbox per month
Virus protection license	$1 per mailbox per month
Other variable costs..	$8 per mailbox per month
Fixed costs:	
Computer hardware costs...	$94,300 per month
$8,050 monthly salary for two information technology	
staff members who work only on e-mail	$16,100 per month

Requirements

1. Compute the *total cost* per mailbox per month of BKFin.com's current e-mail function.
2. Suppose Mail.com, a leading provider of Internet messaging outsourcing services, offers to host BKFin.com's e-mail function for $9 per mailbox per month. If BKFin.com outsources its e-mail to Mail.com, BKFin.com will still need the virus protection software, its computer hardware, and one information technology staff member, who would be responsible for maintaining virus protection, quarantining suspicious e-mail, and managing content (e.g., screening e-mail for objectionable content). Should CEO Wise accept Mail.com's offer?
3. Suppose for an additional $5 per mailbox per month, Mail.com will also provide virus protection, quarantine, and content-management services. Outsourcing these additional functions would mean that BKFin.com would not need either an e-mail information technology staff member or the separate virus protection license. Should CEO Wise outsource these extra services to Mail.com?

■ Ethical Issue

Mary Tan is the controller for Duck Associates, a property management company in Portland, Oregon. Each year Tan and payroll clerk Toby Stock meet with the external auditors about payroll accounting. This year, the auditors suggest that Tan consider outsourcing Duck Associates' payroll accounting to a company specializing in payroll processing services. This would allow Tan and her staff to focus on their primary responsibility: accounting for the properties under management. At present, payroll requires 1.5 employee positions—payroll clerk Toby Stock and a bookkeeper who spends half her time entering payroll data in the system.

Tan considers this suggestion, and she lists the following items relating to outsourcing payroll accounting:

a. The current payroll software that was purchased for $4,000 three years ago would not be needed if payroll processing were outsourced.
b. Duck Associates' bookkeeper would spend half her time preparing the weekly payroll input form that is given to the payroll processing service. She is paid $450 a week.
c. Duck Associates would no longer need payroll clerk Toby Stock, whose annual salary is $42,000.
d. The payroll processing service would charge $2,000 a month.

Requirements

1. Would outsourcing the payroll function increase or decrease Duck Associates' operating income?
2. Tan believes that outsourcing payroll would simplify her job, but she does not like the prospect of having to lay off Stock, who has become a close personal friend. She does not believe there is another position available for Stock at his current salary. Can you think of other factors that might support keeping Stock, rather than outsourcing payroll processing? How should each of the factors affect Tan's decision if she wants to do what is best for Duck Associates and act ethically?

Financial Statement Case—Amazon.com

This case is based on the **Amazon.com** annual report in Appendix A at the end of the book. Use it to answer the following questions.

Requirements

1. **Amazon.com** is considering marketing functions. Consider the amount the company spent for marketing in 2008 on its Consolidated statements of operations as its only marketing costs. Fifty million dollars of these costs are fixed and thus will remain if the outsourcing occurs. The outsourcer has offered to handle all marketing functions for $300 million. Should **Amazon.com** outsource? If so, why? If not, why not?

Team Project

John Menard is the founder and sole owner of **Menards**. Analysts have estimated that his chain of home improvement stores scattered around nine midwestern states generate about $3 billion in annual sales. But how can **Menards** compete with giant **Home Depot**?

Suppose Menard is trying to decide whether to invest $45 million in a state-of-the-art manufacturing plant in Eau Claire, Wisconsin. Menard expects the plant would operate for 15 years, after which it would have no residual value. The plant would produce **Menards'** own line of Formica countertops, cabinets, and picnic tables.

Suppose **Menards** would incur the following unit costs in producing its own product lines:

	Per Unit		
	Countertops	Cabinets	Picnic Tables
Direct materials..	$15	$10	$25
Direct labor..	10	5	15
Variable manufacturing overhead	5	2	6

Rather than making these products, assume that **Menards** could buy them from outside suppliers. Suppliers would charge **Menards** $40 per countertop, $25 per cabinet, and $65 per picnic table.

Whether Menard makes or buys these products, assume that he expects the following annual sales:

- Countertops—487,200 at $130 each
- Picnic tables—100,000 at $225 each
- Cabinets—150,000 at $75 each

If "making" is sufficiently more profitable than outsourcing, Menard will build the new plant. John Menard has asked your consulting group for a recommendation. Menard uses the straight-line depreciation method.

Requirements

1. Are the following items relevant or irrelevant in Menard's decision to build a new plant that will manufacture his own products?
   a. The unit sale prices of the countertops, cabinets, and picnic tables (the sale prices that **Menards** charges its customers)
   b. The prices outside suppliers would charge **Menards** for the three products, if **Menards** decides to outsource the products rather than make them
   c. The $45 million to build the new plant
   d. The direct materials, direct labor, and variable overhead **Menards** would incur to manufacture the three product lines
   e. John Menard's salary

2. Determine whether **Menards** should make or outsource the countertops, cabinets, and picnic tables, *assuming that the company has already built the plant and, therefore, has the manufacturing capacity to produce these products.* In other words, what is the annual difference in cash flows if **Menards** decides to make rather than outsource each of these three products?

3. Write a memo giving your recommendation to John Menard. The memo should clearly state your recommendation, along with a brief summary of the reasons for your recommendation.

Quick Check Answers

1. *a* 2. *b* 3. *b* 4. *a* 5. *d* 6. *b* 7. *d* 8. *a* 9. *c* 10. *b*

For online homework, exercises, and problems that provide you immediate feedback, please visit www.myaccountinglab.com.

Big Picture

Ch 1 Introduction to Management Accounting
- O⊓ Distinguish management accounting from financial accounting
- O⊓ The role and responsibilities of management accountants
- O⊓ Classify costs and prepare income statements for merchandising companies
- O⊓ Classify costs and prepare income statements and statements of cost of goods manufactured for manufacturing companies

Ch 2 Job Order Costing
- O⊓ Distinguish between job order and process costing
- O⊓ Record materials, labor, and overhead in a job order costing system
- O⊓ Record completion and sales of finished goods and adjust for under-/overallocated overhead
- O⊓ Calculate unit costs for service companies

Ch 3 Activity-Based Costing and Other Cost Management Tools
- O⊓ Develop activity-based costs and used activity-based management to determine target product costs
- O⊓ Record transactions in JIT systems
- O⊓ Use the four types of quality costs to make management decisions

Ch 4 Process Costing
- O⊓ Calculate equivalent units and conversion costs
- O⊓ Prepare cost of production reports and the related journal entries using the weighted-average costing method
- O⊓ Prepare cost of production reports and the related journal entries using the FIFO costing method

Ch 5 Cost Behavior and Cost-Volume-Profit Analysis
- O⊓ Identify how changes in volume affect cost
- O⊓ Distinguish among variable, mixed, and fixed cost
- O⊓ Split mixed cost into fixed and variable components by using the high-low method and by using regression analysis
- O⊓ Use CVP to compute breakeven points, to plan profits, to graph relationships, and to perform sensitivity analysis

Ch 6 Absorption and Variable Costing
- O⊓ Distinguish between absorption costing and variable costing
- O⊓ Prepare absorption costing and variable costing income statements and explained the differences between the two costing techniques
- O⊓ Illustrate the pros and cons of absorption and variable costing

Ch 7 The Master Budget: Profit Planning

- Understand and prepare all components of the master budget for manufacturers
- Use sensitivity analysis to adjust budget preparations

Ch 8 Flexible Budgets and Standard Costs

- Prepare flexible income statement budgets and income statement performance reports
- Compute standard cost variances for direct materials, direct labor, and overhead
- Record transactions using standard costs and prepare standard cost income statements

Ch 9 Decentralization: Allocating Service Department Costs and Responsibility Accounting

- Identify a shared resource or service department
- Allocate service department costs to the departments that use its services utilizing various allocation methods
- Learn the four types of responsibility centers and prepared responsibility reports they utilize

Ch 10 Short-Term Business Decisions

- Distinguish between relevant, irrelevant, and sunk costs
- Evaluate special order, pricing, product profitability, and product-mix decisions
- Make outsourcing and sell as is or process further decisions

Chapter 10: Demo Doc

■ Capital Investment Decisions

Learning Objectives 3, 4

Pattie's Tea Pots makes two types of teapots. The Deluxe pot requires more machine hours to produce than the Standard one. Due to increased demand for both pots, Pattie is wondering whether she should be producing more of the Deluxe or Standard type.

			Standard	Deluxe
	Sales price		$30	$40
	Variable expenses		15	24

Each year, 10,000 machine hours are available. The Standard pot takes 5 minutes to produce while the Deluxe pot takes 10 minutes.

Requirements

1. What should Pattie do to maximize her net income assuming sufficient demand to sell either type exclusively?

2. Pattie is purchasing another factory to manufacture teapots. This site will produce teapots that will be hand painted and trimmed in gold. Pattie is considering whether she should produce the basic ceramic pot and sell it to another company to do the hand painting and trim or have her company complete the processing. She plans on producing 36,000 pots this year. She can sell the unfinished pots at $26 per unit (the cost per unit is $17) or she can finish the painting and trim at a cost of $8 per unit and sell them for $45. What should Pattie do?

Demo Doc Solution

Requirement 1

What should Pattie do to maximize her net income assuming sufficient demand to sell either type exclusively?

3 Make dropping a product and product-mix decisions

Part 1	Part 2	Demo Doc Complete

Even though Pattie has sufficient demand for both the standard and deluxe teapots, the constraint on this company is the 10,000 machine hours available. In the *long run*, the company could expand its facilities, but for now Pattie faces a short-run business decision.

The product that should be produced, given sufficient demand as we have in this case, is the one that generates the *greatest contribution margin per unit of constraint*. This approach will result in the largest net income for the company.

First the calculation of the contribution margin (sales price less variable expenses) must be made.

		Per Unit	
		Standard	Deluxe
Sales price		$30	$40
Less: Variable expenses		15	24
Contribution margin		$15	$16

As shown, the Deluxe pots have a higher contribution margin, $16 per unit. However, we cannot assume that the Deluxe pots should be produced exclusively. The *contribution margin per unit of constraint (machine hours)* must now be calculated.

	Standard	Deluxe
Units that can be produced each machine hour*	12	6
Contribution margin per unit	$ 15	$ 16
Contribution margin per machine hour	$ 180	$ 96
Available capacity (number of machine hours)	10,000	10,000
Total contribution margin at full capacity	$1,800,000	$960,000

*A Standard pot requires 5 minutes to produce. 60 minutes/5 minutes = 12 pots per hour.
*A Deluxe pot requires 10 minutes to produce. 60 minutes/10 minutes = 6 pots per hour.

The Standard pots will generate the most contribution margin. Even though the Deluxe pot has a contribution margin of $16, $1 greater than the Standard pot, twice as many Standard pots can be produced within an hour than the Deluxe. Based on ample customer demand, the increased level of production will result in a much greater contribution margin for Pattie.

Requirement 2

4 Make outsourcing and sell as is or process further decisions

Pattie is purchasing another factory to manufacture teapots. This site will produce teapots that will be hand painted and trimmed in gold. Pattie is considering whether she should produce the basic ceramic pot and sell it to another company to do the hand painting and trim or have her company complete the processing. She plans on producing 36,000 pots this year. She can sell the unfinished pots at $26 per unit (the cost per unit is $17) or she can finish the painting and trim at a cost of $8 per unit and sell them for $45. What should Pattie do?

Part 1	Part 2	Demo Doc Complete

Again, short-run business decisions require that the relevant information and a contribution margin approach be used. The relevant information includes the following:

1. Sales price for the pot as is, $26

2. Future costs of processing, $8

3. Sales price of the fully processed pot, $45

Sell as Is or Process Further Decision	Sell as Is	Process Further	Difference
Expected revenue from selling 36,000 pots as is (36,000 × $26)	$936,000		
Expected revenue from selling 36,000 fully processed pots (36,000 × $45)		$1,620,000	684,000
Additional costs to paint and trim pots (36,000 × $8)		(288,000)	(288,000)
Total net revenue	$936,000	$1,332,000	
Differrence in net revenue			$396,000

The decision rule states that if the extra revenue from processing further exceeds the extra cost of processing, then the decision should be to process further. Pattie should process the teapots further.

Part 1	Part 2	Demo Doc Complete

11 Capital Investment Decisions and the Time Value of Money

Learning Objectives/ Success Keys

1 Describe the importance of capital investments and the capital budgeting process

2 Use the payback and accounting rate of return methods to make capital investment decisions

3 Use the time value of money to compute the present and future values of single lump sums and annuities

4 Use discounted cash flow models to make capital investment decisions

Music DVDs and learning DVDs seem to have little or nothing to do with accounting. But every part of the growth and expansion of Smart Touch Learning and Greg's Groovy Tunes began first with the decision—do we spend the money to expand the business?

In this chapter, we will see how companies like Smart Touch and Greg's Groovy Tunes use capital investment analysis techniques to decide which long-term capital investments to make.

Capital Budgeting

Describe the importance of capital investments and the capital budgeting process

The process of making capital investment decisions is often referred to as **capital budgeting**. Companies make capital investments when they acquire *capital assets*— assets used for a long period of time. Capital investments include buying new equipment, building new plants, automating production, and developing major commercial Web sites. In addition to affecting operations for many years, capital investments usually require large sums of money.

Capital investment decisions affect all businesses as they try to become more efficient by automating production and implementing new technologies. Grocers and retailers, such as **Wal-Mart**, have invested in expensive self-scan check-out machines, while airlines, such as **Delta** and **Continental**, have invested in self check-in kiosks. These new technologies cost money. How do managers decide whether these expansions in plant and equipment will be good investments? They use capital budgeting analysis. Some companies, such as **Georgia Pacific**, employ staff solely dedicated to capital budgeting analysis. They spend thousands of hours a year determining which capital investments to pursue.

Four Popular Methods of Capital Budgeting Analysis

In this chapter, we discuss four popular methods of analyzing potential capital investments:

1. Payback period
2. Accounting rate of return (ARR)
3. Net present value (NPV)
4. Internal rate of return (IRR)

The first two methods, payback period and accounting rate of return, are fairly quick and easy and work well for capital investments that have a relatively short life span, such as computer equipment and software that may have a useful life of only three to five years. Payback period and accounting rate of return are also used to screen potential investments from those that are less desirable. The payback period provides management with valuable information on how fast the cash invested will be recouped. The accounting rate of return shows the effect of the investment on the company's accrual-based income. However, these two methods are inadequate if the capital investments have a longer life span. Why? Because these methods do not consider the time value of money. The last two methods, net present value and internal rate of return, factor in the time value of money so they are more appropriate for longer-term capital investments, such as Smart Touch's expansion to manufacturing DVDs. Management often uses a combination of methods to make final capital investment decisions.

Capital budgeting is not an exact science. Although the calculations these methods require may appear precise, remember that they are based on predictions about an uncertain future—estimates. These estimates must consider many unknown factors, such as changing consumer preferences, competition, the state of the economy, and government regulations. The further into the future the decision extends, the more likely that actual results will differ from predictions. Long-term decisions are riskier than short-term decisions.

Focus on Cash Flows

Generally accepted accounting principles (GAAP) are based on accrual accounting, but capital budgeting focuses on cash flows. The desirability of a capital asset depends on its ability to generate net cash inflows—that is, inflows in excess of outflows—over the asset's useful life. Recall that operating income based on accrual accounting contains noncash expenses, such as depreciation expense and bad-debt expense. The capital investment's *net cash inflows,* therefore, will differ from its operating income. Of the four capital budgeting methods covered in this chapter, only the accounting rate of return method uses accrual-based accounting income. The other three methods use the investment's projected *net cash inflows.*

What do the projected *net cash inflows* include? Cash *inflows* include future cash revenue generated from the investment, any future savings in ongoing cash operating costs resulting from the investment, and any future residual value of the asset. To determine the investment's *net* cash inflows, the inflows are *netted* against the investment's *future cash outflows*, such as the investment's ongoing cash operating costs and refurbishment, repairs, and maintenance costs. The initial investment itself is also a significant cash outflow. However, in our calculations, *we will always consider the amount of the investment separately from all other cash flows related to the investment.* The projected net cash inflows are "given" in our examples and in the assignment material. In reality, much of capital investment analysis revolves around projecting these figures as accurately as possible using input from employees throughout the organization (production, marketing, and so forth, depending on the type of capital investment).

Capital Budgeting Process

The first step in the capital budgeting process is to identify potential investments—for example, new technology and equipment that may make the company more efficient, competitive, and/or profitable. Employees, consultants, and outside sales vendors often offer capital investment proposals to management. After identifying potential capital investments, managers project the investments' net cash inflows and then analyze the investments using one or more of the four capital budgeting methods previously described. Sometimes the analysis involves a two-stage process. In the first stage, managers screen the investments using one or both of the methods that do *not* incorporate the time value of money: payback period or accounting rate of return. These simple methods quickly weed out undesirable investments. Potential investments that "pass stage one" go on to a second stage of analysis. In the second stage, managers further analyze the potential investments using the net present value and/or internal rate of return methods. Because these methods consider the time value of money, they provide more accurate information about the potential investment's profitability.

Some companies can pursue all of the potential investments that meet or exceed their decision criteria. However, because of limited resources, other companies must engage in **capital rationing**, and choose among alternative capital investments. Based on the availability of funds, managers determine if and when to make specific capital investments. For example, management may decide to wait three years to buy a certain piece of equipment because it considers other investments more important. In the intervening three years, the company will reassess whether it should still invest in the equipment. Perhaps technology has changed, and even better equipment is available. Perhaps consumer tastes have changed so the company no longer needs the equipment. Because of changing factors, long-term capital budgets are rarely set in stone.

Most companies perform **post-audits** of their capital investments. After investing in the assets, they compare the actual net cash inflows generated from the investment to the projected net cash inflows. Post-audits help companies determine whether the investments are going as planned and deserve continued support, or whether they should abandon the project and sell the assets. Managers also use feedback from post-audits to better estimate net cash flow projections for future projects. If managers expect routine post-audits, they will more likely submit realistic net cash flow estimates with their capital investment proposals.

Using Payback and Accounting Rate of Return to Make Capital Investment Decisions

2 Use the payback and accounting rate of return methods to make capital investment decisions

Payback Period

Payback is the length of time it takes to recover, in net cash inflows, the cost of the capital outlay. The payback model measures how quickly managers expect to recover their investment dollars. All else being equal, the shorter the payback period the more attractive the asset. Computing the payback period depends on whether net cash inflows are equal each year, or whether they differ over time. We consider each in turn.

Payback with Equal Annual Net Cash Inflows

Smart Touch Learning is considering investing $240,000 in hardware and software to upgrade its Web site to provide a business-to-business (B2B) portal. Employees throughout the company will use the B2B portal to access company-approved suppliers. Smart Touch expects the portal to save $60,000 a year for each of the six years of its useful life. The savings will arise from reducing the number of purchasing personnel the company employs and from lower prices on the goods and services purchased. Net cash inflows arise from an increase in revenues, a decrease in expenses, or both. In Smart Touch's case, the net cash inflows result from lower expenses.

When net cash inflows are equal each year, managers compute the payback period as shown in Exhibit 11-1.

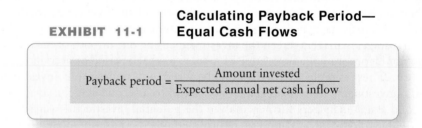

EXHIBIT 11-1 | **Calculating Payback Period— Equal Cash Flows**

$$\text{Payback period} = \frac{\text{Amount invested}}{\text{Expected annual net cash inflow}}$$

Smart Touch computes the investment's payback as follows:

$$\text{Payback period for B2B portal} = \frac{\$240,000}{\$60,000} = 4 \text{ years}$$

Exhibit 11-2 verifies that Smart Touch expects to recoup the $240,000 investment in the B2B portal by the end of year 4, when the accumulated net cash inflows total $240,000.

Smart Touch is also considering investing $240,000 to upgrade its Web site. The company expects the upgraded Web site to generate $80,000 in net cash inflows each year of its three-year life. The payback period is computed as follows:

$$\text{Payback period for Web site development} = \frac{\$240,000}{\$80,000} = 3 \text{ years}$$

Exhibit 11-2 verifies that Smart Touch will recoup the $240,000 investment for the Web site upgrade by the end of year 3, when the accumulated net cash inflows total $240,000.

| EXHIBIT 11-2 | Payback—Equal Annual Net Cash Inflows |

| | | Net Cash Inflows | | | |
| | | B2B Portal | | Web Site Upgrade | |
Year	Amount Invested	Annual	Accumulated	Annual	Accumulated
0	240,000	—	—	—	—
1	—	$60,000	$ 60,000	$80,000	$ 80,000
2	—	60,000	120,000	80,000	160,000
3	—	60,000	180,000	80,000	240,000
4	—	60,000	240,000		
5	—	60,000	300,000		
6	—	60,000	360,000		

Payback with Unequal Net Cash Inflows

The payback equation in Exhibit 11-1 only works when net cash inflows are the same each period. When periodic cash flows are unequal, you must total net cash inflows until the amount invested is recovered. Assume that Smart Touch is considering an alternate investment, the Z80 portal. The Z80 portal differs from the B2B portal and the Web site in two respects: (1) It has *unequal* net cash inflows during its life and (2) it has a $30,000 residual value at the end of its life. The Z80 portal will generate net cash inflows of $100,000 in year 1, $80,000 in year 2, $50,000 each year in years 3 through 5, $30,000 in year 6, and $30,000 when it is sold at the end of its life. Exhibit 11-3 shows the payback schedule for these unequal annual net cash inflows.

| EXHIBIT 11-3 | Payback: Unequal Annual Net Cash Inflows |

| | | Net Cash Inflows Z80 Portal | |
Year	Amount Invested	Annual	Accumulated
0	$240,000	—	—
1	—	100,000	$100,000
2	—	80,000	180,000
3	—	50,000	230,000
4	—	50,000	280,000
5	—	50,000	330,000
6	—	30,000	360,000
6–Residual Value		30,000	390,000

By the end of year 3, the company has recovered $230,000 of the $240,000 initially invested, so it is only $10,000 short of payback. Because the expected net cash inflow in year 4 is $50,000, by the end of year 4 the company will have recovered *more* than the initial investment. Therefore, the payback period is somewhere between three and four years. Assuming that the cash flow occurs evenly throughout the fourth year, the payback period is calculated as follows:

$$\text{Payback} = 3 \text{ years} + \frac{\$10,000 \text{ (amount needed to complete recovery in year 4)}}{\$50,000 \text{ (net cash inflow in year 4)}}$$

$$= 3.2 \text{ years}$$

Criticism of the Payback Period Method

A major criticism of the payback method is that it focuses only on time, not on profitability. The payback period considers only those cash flows that occur *during* the payback period. This method ignores any cash flows that occur *after* that period. For example, Exhibit 11-2 shows that the B2B portal will continue to generate net cash inflows for two years after its payback period. These additional net cash inflows amount to $120,000 ($60,000 × 2 years), yet the payback method ignores this extra cash. A similar situation occurs with the Z80 portal. As shown in Exhibit 11-3, the Z80 portal will provide an additional $150,000 of net cash inflows, including residual value, after its payback period of 3.2 years ($390,000 total accumulated cash inflows – $240,000 amount invested). However, the Web site's useful life, as shown in Exhibit 11-2, is the *same* as its payback period (three years). No cash flows are ignored, yet the Web site will merely cover its cost and provide no profit. Because this is the case, the company has no financial reason to invest in the Web site.

Exhibit 11-4 compares the payback period of the three investments. As the exhibit illustrates, the payback method does not consider the asset's profitability. The method only tells management how quickly it will recover the cash. Even though the Web site has the shortest payback period, both the B2B portal and the Z80 portal are better investments because they provide profit. The key point is that the investment with the shortest payback period is best *only if all other factors are the same*. Therefore, managers usually use the payback method as a screening device to "weed out" investments that will take too long to recoup. They rarely use payback period as the sole method for deciding whether to invest in the asset. When using the payback period method, managers are guided by following decision rule:

DECISION RULE: Payback Period

↓

Investments with **shorter** payback periods are more desirable, *all else being equal.*

EXHIBIT 11-4 | **Comparing Payback Periods Between Investments**

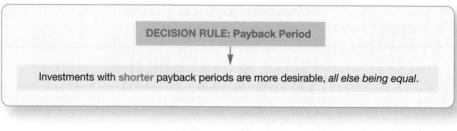

Payback period

Web site—3 years
(but no profit)

Z80 portal—3.2 years
(but $150,000 net cash inflow after payback ignored)

B2B portal—4 years
(but $120,000 net cash inflow after payback ignored)

Stop & Think...

Let us say you loan $50 to a friend today (a Friday). The friend says he will pay you $25 next Friday when he gets paid and another $25 the following Friday. What is your payback period? The friend will pay you back in 2 weeks.

Accounting Rate of Return (ARR)

Companies are in business to earn profits. One measure of profitability is the **accounting rate of return (ARR)** on an asset. The formula for calculating ARR is shown in Exhibit 11-5.

EXHIBIT 11-5 | **Calculating Accounting Rate of Return**

$$\text{Accounting rate of return} = \frac{\text{Average annual operating income from an asset}}{\text{Average amount invested in an asset}}$$

The ARR focuses on the *operating income, not the net cash inflow,* an asset generates. The ARR measures the *average* rate of return over the asset's entire life. Let us first consider investments with no residual value.

Recall the B2B portal, which costs $240,000, has equal annual net cash inflows of $60,000, a six-year useful life, and no (zero) residual value.

Let us look at the average annual operating income in the numerator first. The average annual operating income of an asset is simply the asset's total operating income over the course of its operating life divided by its lifespan (number of years). Operating income is based on *accrual accounting.* Therefore, any noncash expenses, such as depreciation expense, must be subtracted from the asset's net cash inflows to arrive at its operating income. Exhibit 11-6 displays the formula for calculating average annual operating income.

EXHIBIT 11-6 | **Calculating Average Annual Operating Income from Asset**

Total net cash inflows during operating life of the asset	A
Less: Total depreciation during operating life of the asset (Cost – Residual Value)	B
Total operating income during operating life	(A – B)
Divide by: Asset's operating life in years	C
Average annual operating income from asset	[(A – B)/C]

The B2B portal's average annual operating income is as follows:

Total net cash inflows during operating life of the asset ($60,000 × 6 years)	$ 360,000
Less: Total depreciation during operating life of asset (cost – any salvage value)	(240,000)
Total operating income during operating life	$ 120,000
Divide by: Asset's operating life (in years)	÷ 6 years
Average annual operating income from asset	$ 20,000

Now let us look at the denominator of the ARR equation. The *average* amount invested in an asset is its *net book value* at the beginning of the asset's useful life plus the net book value at the end of the asset's useful life divided by two. Another way to say that is the asset's cost plus the asset's residual value divided by two. The net book value of the asset decreases each year because of depreciation, as shown in Exhibit 11-6.

Because the B2B portal does not have a residual value, the *average* amount invested is $120,000 [($240,000 cost + 0 residual value) ÷ 2].

We calculate the B2B's ARR as:

$$\text{Accounting rate of return} = \frac{\$20,000}{(\$240,000 - \$0)/2} = \frac{\$20,000}{\$120,000} = 0.167 = 16.70\%$$

Now consider the Z80 portal (data from Exhibit 11-3). Recall that the Z80 portal differed from the B2B portal only in that it had unequal net cash inflows during its life and a $30,000 residual value at the end of its life. Its average annual operating income is calculated as follows:

Total net cash inflows *during* operating life of asset (does not include the residual value at end of life) (Year 1 + Year 2, etc.)	$ 360,000
Less: Total depreciation during operating life of asset (cost – any salvage value) ($240,000 cost – $30,000 residual value)	(210,000)
Total operating income during operating life of asset.................	$ 150,000
Divide by: Asset's operating life (in years)..................................	÷ 6 years
Average annual operating income from asset	$ 25,000

Notice that the Z80 portal's average annual operating income of $25,000 is higher than the B2B portal's operating income of $20,000. Since the Z80 asset has a residual value at the end of its life, less depreciation is expensed each year, leading to a higher average annual operating income.

Now let us calculate the denominator of the ARR equation, the average amount invested in the asset. For the Z80, the average asset investment is as follows:

Average amount invested	=	(Amount invested in asset	+	Residual value)/2
$135,000	=	($240,000	+	$30,000) /2

We calculate the Z80's ARR as follows:

$$\text{Accounting rate of return} = \frac{\$25,000}{(\$240,000 + \$30,000)/2} = \frac{\$25,000}{\$135,000} = 0.185 = 18.5\%$$

Companies that use the ARR model set a minimum required accounting rate of return. If Smart Touch requires an ARR of at least 20%, then its managers would not approve an investment in the B2B portal or the Z80 portal because the ARR for both investments is less than 20%.

The decision rule is as follows:

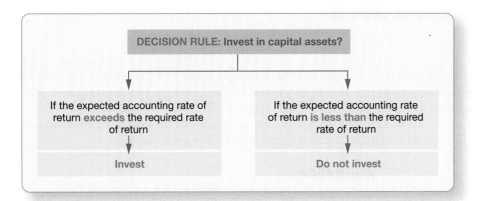

In summary, the payback period focuses on the time it takes for the company to recoup its cash investment but ignores all cash flows occurring after the payback period. Because it ignores any additional cash flows (including any residual value), the method does not consider the profitability of the project.

The ARR, however, measures the profitability of the asset over its entire life using accrual accounting figures. It is the only method that uses accrual accounting rather than net cash inflows in its computations. The payback period and ARR methods are simple and quick to compute so managers often use them to screen out undesirable investments. However, both methods ignore the time value of money.

Decision Guidelines

CAPITAL BUDGETING

Amazon.com started as a virtual retailer. It held no inventory. Instead, it bought books and CDs only as needed to fill customer orders. As the company grew, its managers decided to invest in their own warehouse facilities. Why? Owning warehouse facilities allows **Amazon.com** to save money by buying in bulk. Also, shipping all items in the customer's order in one package, from one location, saves shipping costs. Here are some of the guidelines **Amazon.com**'s managers used as they made the major capital budgeting decision to invest in building warehouses.

Decision	Guidelines
• Why is this decision important?	Capital budgeting decisions typically require large investments and affect operations for years to come.
• What method shows us how soon we will recoup our cash investment?	The payback method shows managers how quickly they will recoup their investment. This method highlights investments that are too risky due to long payback periods. However, it does not reveal any information about the investment's profitability.
• Does any method consider the impact of the investment on accrual accounting income?	The accounting rate of return is the only capital budgeting method that shows how the investment will affect accrual accounting income, which is important to financial statement users. All other methods of capital investment analysis focus on the investment's net cash inflows.
• How do we compute the payback period if cash flows are *equal*?	$$\text{Payback period} = \frac{\text{Amount invested}}{\text{Expected annual net cash inflow}}$$
• How do we compute the payback period if cash flows are *unequal*?	Accumulate net cash inflows until the amount invested is recovered.
• How do we compute the ARR?	$$\frac{\text{Accounting rate}}{\text{of return}} = \frac{\text{Average annual operating income from asset}}{\text{Average amount invested in asset}}$$

Summary Problem 1

Reality-max is considering buying a new bar-coding machine for its Austin, Texas, plant. The company screens its potential capital investments using the payback period and accounting rate of return methods. If a potential investment has a payback period of less than four years and a minimum 12% accounting rate of return, it will be considered further. The data for the machine follow:

Cost of machine	$48,000
Estimated residual value..	$ 0
Estimated annual net cash inflow (each year for 5 years)	$13,000
Estimated useful life	5 years

Requirements

1. Compute the bar-coding machine's payback period.
2. Compute the bar-coding machine's ARR.
3. Should Reality-max turn down this investment proposal or consider it further?

Solution

Requirement 1

$$\text{Payback period} = \frac{\text{Amount invested}}{\text{Expected annual net cash inflow}} = \frac{\$48,000}{\$13,000} = 3.7 \text{ years (rounded)}$$

Requirement 2

$$\text{Accounting rate of return} = \frac{\text{Average annual operating income from asset}}{\text{Average amount invested in asset}}$$

$$= \frac{\$3,400*}{(\$48,000 + \$0)/2}$$

$$= \frac{\$3,400}{\$24,000}$$

$$= 0.142 \text{ (rounded)}$$

$$= 14.2\%$$

*Total net cash inflows during life ($13,000 × 5 years)	$ 65,000
Less: total depreciation during life	(48,000)
Total operating income during life	$ 17,000
Divided by: life of the asset	÷ 5 years
Average annual operating income	$ 3,400

Requirement 3

The bar-coding machine proposal passes both initial screening tests. The payback period is slightly less than four years, and the accounting rate of return is higher than 12%. Reality-max should further analyze the proposal using a method that incorporates the time value of money.

A Review of the Time Value of Money

3 Use the time value of money to compute the present and future values of single lump sums and annuities

A dollar received today is worth more than a dollar to be received in the future. Why? Because you can invest today's dollar and earn extra income. The fact that invested money earns income over time is called the *time value of money*, and this explains why we would prefer to receive cash sooner rather than later. The time value of money means that the timing of capital investments' net cash inflows is important. Two methods of capital investment analysis incorporate the time value of money: the NPV and IRR. This section reviews time value of money to make sure you have a firm foundation for discussing these two methods.

Factors Affecting the Time Value of Money

The time value of money depends on several key factors:

1. the principal amount (p)
2. the number of periods (n)
3. the interest rate (i)

The principal (p) refers to the amount of the investment or borrowing. Because this chapter deals with capital investments, we will primarily discuss the principal in terms of investments. However, the same concepts apply to borrowings, which you learned in your financial accounting class. We state the principal as either a single lump sum or an annuity. For example, if you win the lottery, you have the choice of receiving all the winnings now (a single lump sum) or receiving a series of equal payments for a period of time in the future (an annuity). An **annuity** is a stream of *equal installments* made at *equal time intervals under the same interest rate*.[1]

The number of periods (n) is the length of time from the beginning of the investment until termination. All else being equal the shorter the investment period the lower the total amount of interest earned. If you withdraw your savings after four years, rather than five years, you will earn less interest. In this chapter, the number of periods is stated in years.[2]

The interest rate (i) is the annual percentage earned on the investment. **Simple interest** means that interest is calculated *only* on the principal amount. **Compound interest** means that interest is calculated on the principal *and* on all interest earned to date. *Compound interest assumes that all interest earned will remain invested and earn additional interest at the same interest rate*. Exhibit 11-7 compares simple interest

EXHIBIT 11-7 | **Simple Versus Compound Interest for a Principal Amount of $10,000, at 6%, over 5 Years**

Year	Simple Interest Calculation	Simple Interest	Compound Interest Calculation	Compound Interest
1	$10,000 × 6% =	$ 600	$10,000 × 6% =	$ 600
2	$10,000 × 6% =	600	($10,000 + 600) × 6% =	636
3	$10,000 × 6% =	600	($10,000 + 600 + 636) × 6% =	674
4	$10,000 × 6% =	600	($10,000 + 600 + 636 + 674) × 6% =	715
5	$10,000 × 6% =	600	($10,000 + 600 + 636 + 674 + 715) × 6% =	758
	Total interest	$3,000	Total interest	$3,383

---

[1]An *ordinary annuity* is an annuity in which the installments occur at the *end* of each period. An *annuity due* is an annuity in which the installments occur at the beginning of each period. Throughout this chapter we use ordinary annuities since they are better suited to capital budgeting cash flow assumptions.
[2]The number of periods can also be stated in days, months, or quarters. If so, the interest rate needs to be adjusted to reflect the number of time periods in the year.

(6%) on a five-year, $10,000 CD with interest compounded yearly (rounded to the nearest dollar). As you can see, the amount of compound interest earned yearly grows as the base on which it is calculated (principal plus cumulative interest to date) grows. Over the life of this investment, the total amount of compound interest is about 10% more than the total amount of simple interest. Most investments yield compound interest so we assume compound interest, rather than simple interest, for the rest of this chapter.

Fortunately, time value calculations involving compound interest do not have to be as tedious as those shown in Exhibit 11-7. Formulas and tables (or proper use of business calculators programmed with these formulas, or spreadsheet software such as Microsoft Excel) simplify the calculations. In the next sections, we will discuss how to use these tools to perform time value calculations.

Future Values and Present Values: Points Along the Time Line

Consider the time line in Exhibit 11-8. The future value or present value of an investment simply refers to the value of an investment at different points in time.

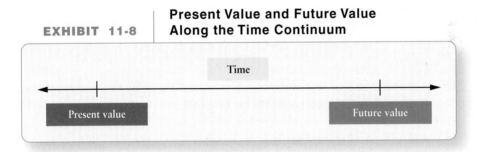

EXHIBIT 11-8 | **Present Value and Future Value Along the Time Continuum**

We can calculate the future value or the present value of any investment by knowing (or assuming) information about the three factors we listed earlier: (1) the principal amount, (2) the period of time, and (3) the interest rate. For example, in Exhibit 11-7, we calculated the interest that would be earned on (1) a $10,000 principal, (2) invested for five years, (3) at 6% interest. The future value of the investment is simply its worth at the end of the five-year time frame—the original principal *plus* the interest earned. In our example, the future value of the investment is as follows:

$$\text{Future value} = \text{Principal} + \text{Interest earned}$$
$$= \$10,000 + \$3,383$$
$$= \$13,383$$

If we invest $10,000 *today*, its *present value* is simply $10,000. So another way of stating the future value is as follows:

$$\text{Future value} = \text{Present value} + \text{Interest earned}$$

We can rearrange the equation as follows:

$$\text{Present value} = \text{Future value} - \text{Interest earned}$$
$$\$10,000 = \$13,383 - \$3,383$$

The only difference between present value and future value is the amount of interest that is earned in the intervening time span.

Future Value and Present Value Factors

Calculating each period's compound interest, as we did in Exhibit 11-7, and then adding it to the present value to figure the future value (or subtracting it from the future value to figure the present value) is tedious. Fortunately, mathematical formulas have been developed that specify future values and present values for unlimited combinations of interest rates (i) and time periods (n). Separate formulas exist for single-lump-sum investments and annuities.

These formulas are programmed into most business calculators so that the user only needs to correctly enter the principal amount, interest rate, and number of time periods to find present or future values. These formulas are also programmed into spreadsheets functions in Microsoft Excel. Because the specific steps to operate business calculators differ between brands, we will use tables instead. These tables contain the results of the formulas for various interest rate and time period combinations.

The formulas and resulting tables are shown in Appendix B at the end of this book:

1. Present Value of $1 (Appendix B, Table A, p. B-1)—*used for lump-sum amounts*

2. Present Value of Annuity of $1 (Appendix B, Table B, p. B-3)—*used for annuities*

3. Future Value of $1 (Appendix B, Table C, p. B-5)—*used for lump-sum amounts*

4. Future Value of Annuity of $1 (Appendix B, Table D, p. B-6)—*used for annuities*

Take a moment to look at these tables because we are going to use them throughout the rest of the chapter. Note that the columns are interest rates (i) and the rows are periods (n).

The data in each table, known as future value factors (FV factors) and present value factors (PV factors), are for an investment (or loan) of $1. To find the future value of an amount other than $1, you simply multiply the FV factor by the present amount. To find the present value of an amount other than $1, you multiply the PV factor by the future amount.

The annuity tables are derived from the lump-sum tables. For example, the Annuity PV factors (in the Present Value of Annuity of $1 table) are the *sums* of the PV factors found in the Present Value of $1 tables for a given number of time periods. The annuity tables allow us to perform "one-step" calculations rather than separately computing the present value of each annual cash installment and then summing the individual present values.

Calculating Future Values of Single Sums and Annuities Using FV Factors

Let us go back to our $10,000 lump-sum investment. If we want to know the future value of the investment five years from now at an interest rate of 6%, we determine the FV factor from the table labeled Future Value of $1 (Appendix B, Table C). We use this table for lump-sum amounts. We look down the 6% column, and across the 5 periods row, and find the future value factor is 1.338. We finish our calculations as follows:

$$\text{Future value} = \text{Principal amount} \times (\text{FV factor for } i = 6\%, n = 5)$$
$$= \$10,000 \times (1.338)$$
$$= \$13,380$$

This figure materially agrees with our earlier calculation of the investment's future value of $13,383 in Exhibit 11-7. (The difference of $3 is due to two facts: (1) The tables round the FV and PV factors to three decimal places and (2) we rounded our earlier yearly interest calculations in Exhibit 11-7 to the nearest dollar.)

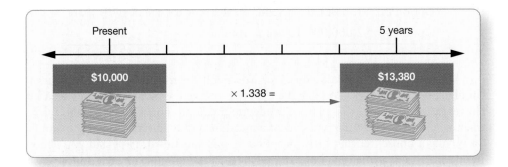

Let us also consider our alternative investment strategy, investing $2,000 at the end of each year for five years. The procedure for calculating the future value of an *annuity* is quite similar to calculating the future value of a lump-sum amount. This time, we use the Future Value of Annuity of $1 table (Appendix B, Table D). Assuming 6% interest, we once again look down the 6% column. Because we will be making five annual installments, we look across the row marked 5 periods. The Annuity FV factor is 5.637. We finish the calculation as follows:

Future value = Amount of each cash installment × (Annuity FV factor for $i = 6\%$, $n = 5$)
= $2,000 × (5.637)
= $11,274

This is considerably less than the future value of $13,380 of the lump sum of $10,000, even though we have invested $10,000 out-of-pocket either way.

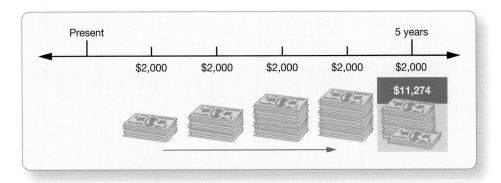

Calculating Present Values of Single Sums and Annuities Using PV Factors

The process for calculating present values—often called discounting cash flows—is similar to the process for calculating future values. The difference is the point in time at which you are assessing the investment's worth. Rather than determining its value at a future date, you are determining its value at an earlier point in time (today). For our example, let us assume you have just won the lottery after purchasing one $5 lottery ticket. The state offers you the following three payout options for your after-tax prize money:

Option #1: $1,000,000 now

Option #2: $150,000 at the end of each year for the next 10 years

Option #3: $2,000,000 10 years from now

Which alternative should you take? You might be tempted to wait 10 years to "double" your winnings. You may be tempted to take the money now and spend it. However, let us assume you plan to prudently invest all money received—no matter when you receive it—so that you have financial flexibility in the future (for example, for buying a house, retiring early, or taking exotic vacations). How can you choose among the three payment alternatives, when the total amount of each option varies ($1,000,000 versus $1,500,000 versus $2,000,000) and the timing of the cash flows varies (now versus some each year versus later)? Comparing these three options is like comparing apples to oranges—we just cannot do it—unless we find some common basis for comparison. Our common basis for comparison will be the prize-money's worth at a certain point in time—namely, today. In other words, if we convert each payment option to its *present value*, we can compare apples to apples.

We already know the principal amount and timing of each payment option, so the only assumption we will have to make is the interest rate. The interest rate will vary, depending on the amount of risk you are willing to take with your investment. Riskier investments (such as stock investments) command higher interest rates; safer investments (such as FDIC-insured bank deposits) yield lower interest rates. Let us say that after investigating possible investment alternatives, you choose an investment contract with an 8% annual return. We already know that the present value of Option #1 is $1,000,000. Let us convert the other two payment options to their present values so that we can compare them. We will need to use the Present Value of Annuity of $1 table (Appendix B, Table B) to convert payment Option #2 (since it is an annuity) and the Present Value of $1 table (Appendix B, Table A) to convert payment Option #3 (since it is a single-lump-sum). To obtain the PV factors, we will look down the 8% column and across the 10 period row. Then, we finish the calculations as follows:

Option #2

Present value = Amount of each cash installment × (Annuity PV factor for $i = 8\%$, $n = 10$)

Present value = $150,000 × (6.710)

Present value = $1,006,500

Option #3

Present value = Principal amount × (PV factor for $i = 8\%$, $n = 10$)

Present value = $2,000,000 × (0.463)

Present value = $926,000

Exhibit 11-9 shows that we have converted each payout option to a common basis—its worth *today*—so we can make a valid comparison among the options. Based on this comparison, we should choose Option #2 because its worth, in today's dollars, is the highest of the three options.

Now that you have reviewed time value of money concepts, we will discuss the two capital budgeting methods that incorporate the time value of money: net present value (NPV) and internal rate of return (IRR).

| EXHIBIT 11-9 | Present Value of Lottery Payout Options |

Payment Options	Present Value of Lottery Payout ($i = 8\%$, $n = 10$)
Option #1	$1,000,000
Option #2	$1,006,500
Option #3	$ 926,000

Using Discounted Cash Flow Models to Make Capital Budgeting Decisions

Neither the payback period nor the ARR recognizes the time value of money. That is, these models fail to consider the *timing* of the net cash inflows an asset generates. *Discounted cash flow models*—the NPV and the IRR—overcome this weakness. These models incorporate compound interest by assuming that companies will reinvest future cash flows when they are received. Over 85% of large industrial firms in the United States use discounted cash-flow methods to make capital investment decisions. Companies that provide services also use these models.

The NPV and IRR methods rely on present value calculations to *compare* the amount of the investment (the investment's initial cost) with its expected net cash inflows. Recall that an investment's *net cash inflows* includes all *future* cash flows related to the investment, such as future increased sales or cost savings netted against the investment's cash operating costs. Because the cash outflow for the investment occurs *now*, but the net cash inflows from the investment occur in the *future*, companies can only make valid "apple-to-apple" comparisons if they convert the cash flows to the *same point in time*—namely the present value. Companies use the present value to make the comparison (rather than the future value) because the investment's initial cost is already stated at its present value.[3]

As shown in Exhibit 11-10, in a favorable investment, the present value of the investment's net cash inflows exceeds the initial cost of the investment. In terms of our earlier lottery example, the lottery ticket turned out to be a "good investment" because the present value of its net cash inflows (the present value of the lottery payout under *any* of the three payout options) exceeded the cost of the investment (the lottery ticket cost $5 to purchase). Let us begin our discussion by taking a closer look at the NPV method.

Net Present Value (NPV)

Greg's Groovy Tunes is considering producing CD players and digital video recorders (DVRs). The products require different specialized machines that each cost $1 million. Each machine has a five-year life and zero residual value. The two products have different patterns of predicted net cash inflows, as shown in Exhibit 11-11.

The CD-player project generates more net cash inflows, but the DVR project brings in cash sooner. To decide how attractive each investment is, we find its **net present value (NPV)**. The NPV is the *net difference* between the present value of the

4   Use discounted cash flow models to make capital investment decisions

---

[3]If the investment is to be purchased through lease payments, rather than a current cash outlay, we would still use the current cash price of the investment as its initial cost. If no current cash price is available, we would discount the future lease payments back to their present value to estimate the investment's current cash price.

EXHIBIT 11-10 | **Comparing the Present Value of an Investment's Net Cash Inflows Against the Investment's Initial Cost**

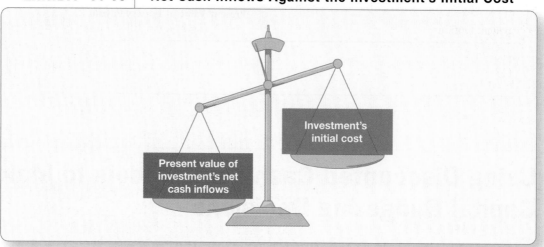

EXHIBIT 11-11 | **Expected Cash Flows for Two Projects**

	Annual Net Cash Inflows	
Year	CD Players	DVRs
1	$ 305,450	$ 500,000
2	$ 305,450	350,000
3	$ 305,450	300,000
4	$ 305,450	250,000
5	$ 305,450	40,000
Total	$1,527,250	$1,440,000

investment's net cash inflows and the investment's cost (cash outflows). We *discount* the net cash inflows—just as we did in the lottery example—using Greg's minimum desired rate of return. This rate is called the **discount rate** because it is the interest rate used for the present value calculations. It is also called the **required rate of return** because the investment must meet or exceed this rate to be acceptable. The discount rate depends on the riskiness of investments. The higher the risk, the higher the discount (interest) rate. Greg's discount rate for these investments is 14%.

We then compare the present value of the net cash inflows to the investment's initial cost to decide which projects meet or exceed management's minimum desired rate of return. In other words, management is deciding whether the $1 million option is worth more (because the company would give it up now to invest in the project) or whether the project's future net cash inflows are worth more. Management can only make a valid comparison between the two sums of money by comparing them at the *same* point in time—namely, at their present value.

NPV with Equal Periodic Net Cash Inflows (Annuity)

Greg's expects the CD-player project to generate $305,450 of net cash inflows each year for five years. Because these cash flows are equal in amount, and occur every year, they are an annuity. Therefore, we use the Present Value of Annuity of $1 table (Appendix B, Table B) to find the appropriate Annuity PV factor for $i = 14\%, n = 5$.

The present value of the net cash inflows from Greg's CD-player project is as follows:

Present value = Amount of each cash net cash inflow × (Annuity PV factor for i = 14%, n = 5)

= \$305,450 × (3.433)

= \$1,048,610

Next, we simply subtract the investment's initial cost of \$1 million (cash out-flows) from the present value of the net cash inflows of \$1,048,610. The difference of \$48,610 is the *net* present value (NPV), as shown in Exhibit 11-12.

EXHIBIT 11-12	**NPV of Equal Net Cash Inflows—CD-Player Project**			
Time		Annuity PV Factor (i = 14%, n = 5)	Net Cash Inflow	Present Value
1–5 yrs	Present value of annuity of equal annual net cash inflows for 5 years at 14%	3.433* ×	\$305,450 =	\$ 1,048,610
0	Investment			(1,000,000)
	Net present value of the CD-player project			\$ 48,610

*Annuity PV Factor is found in Appendix B, Table B.

A *positive* NPV means that the project earns *more* than the required rate of return. A negative NPV means that the project earns less than the required rate of return. This leads to the following decision rule:

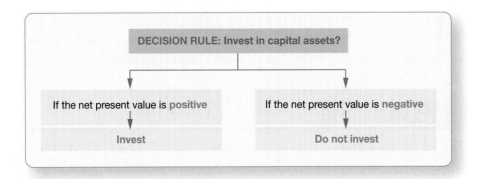

In Greg's Groovy Tunes' case, the CD-player project is an attractive investment. The \$48,610 positive NPV means that the CD-player project earns *more than* Greg's Groovy Tunes' 14% target rate of return.

Another way managers can use present value analysis is to start the capital budgeting process by computing the total present value of the net cash inflows from the project to determine the *maximum* the company can invest in the project and still earn the target rate of return. For Greg's, the present value of the net cash inflows is \$1,048,610. This means that Greg's Groovy Tunes can invest a maximum of \$1,048,610 and still earn the 14% target rate of return (i.e., if Greg's invests \$1,048,610, NPV will be 0 and return will be exactly 14%). Because Greg's Groovy Tunes' managers believe they can undertake the project for \$1 million, the project is an attractive investment.

NPV with Unequal Periodic Net Cash Inflows

In contrast to the CD-player project, the net cash inflows of the DVR project are unequal—$500,000 in year 1, $350,000 in year 2, and so on. Because these amounts vary by year, Greg's Groovy Tunes' managers *cannot* use the annuity table to compute the present value of the DVR project. They must compute the present value of each individual year's net cash inflows *separately (as separate lump sums received in different years)*, using the Present Value of $1 table (Appendix B, Table A). Exhibit 11-13 shows that the $500,000 net cash inflow received in year 1 is discounted using a PV factor of $i = 14\%$, $n = 1$, while the $350,000 net cash inflow received in year 2 is discounted using a PV factor of $i = 14\%$, $n = 2$, and so forth. After separately discounting each of the five year's net cash inflows, we add each result to find that the *total* present value of the DVR project's net cash inflows is $1,078,910. Finally, we subtract the investment's cost of $1 million (cash outflows) to arrive at the DVR project's NPV: $78,910.

EXHIBIT 11-13	**NPV with Unequal Net Cash Inflows—DVR Project**			
Year		PV Factor ($i = 14\%$)	Net Cash Inflow	Present Value
	Present value of each year's net cash inflows discounted at 14%			
1	Year 1 ($n = 1$)	0.877[†] ✕	$500,000 =	$ 438,500
2	Year 2 ($n = 2$)	0.769 ✕	350,000 =	269,150
3	Year 3 ($n = 3$)	0.675 ✕	300,000 =	202,500
4	Year 4 ($n = 4$)	0.592 ✕	250,000 =	148,000
5	Year 5 ($n = 5$)	0.519 ✕	40,000 =	20,760
	Total present value of net cash inflows			1,078,910
0	Investment			(1,000,000)
	Net present value of the DVR project			$ 78,910

[†]PV Factors are found in Appendix B, Table A.

Because the NPV is positive, Greg's Groovy Tunes expects the DVR project to earn more than the 14% target rate of return, making this an attractive investment.

Stop & Think...

Assume you win the lottery today and you have the choice of taking $1,000,000 today or $120,000 a year for the next 10 years. If you think that you can earn 6%, which option should you take? That is the key to NPV. We must find the NPV of the $120,000 annuity at 6% (PV factor is 7.360) to compare. The value of the $120,000 annuity today is $883,200, which is less than the $1,000,000. So, you should take the $1,000,000 payout today rather than the $120,000 annuity.

Capital Rationing and the Profitability Index

Exhibits 11-12 and 11-13 show that both the CD player and DVR projects have positive NPVs. Therefore, both are attractive investments. Because resources are limited, companies are not always able to invest in all capital assets that meet their investment criteria. This is called *capital rationing*. For example, Greg's may not have the funds to invest in both the DVR and CD-player projects at this time. In this case, Greg's should choose the DVR project because it yields a higher NPV. The DVR project should earn an additional $78,910 beyond the 14% required rate of return, while the CD-player project returns an additional $48,610.

This example illustrates an important point. The CD-player project promises more *total* net cash inflows. But the *timing* of the DVR cash flows—loaded near the beginning of the project—gives the DVR investment a higher NPV. The DVR project is more attractive because of the time value of money. Its dollars, which are received sooner, are worth more now than the more-distant dollars of the CD-player project.

If Greg's had to choose between the CD and DVR project, the company would choose the DVR project because it yields a higher NPV ($78,910). However, comparing the NPV of the two projects is *only* valid because both projects require the same initial cost—$1 million. In contrast, Exhibit 11-14 summarizes three capital investment options faced by Smart Touch. Each capital project requires a different initial investment. All three projects are attractive because each yields a positive NPV. Assuming Smart Touch can only invest in one project at this time, which one should it choose? Project B yields the highest NPV, but it also requires a larger initial investment than the alternatives.

EXHIBIT 11-14 | **Smart Touch Capital Investment Options**

Year	Project A	Project B	Project C
Present value of net cash inflows	$ 150,000	$ 238,000	$ 182,000
Investment	(125,000)	(200,000)	(150,000)
Net present value (NPV)	$ 25,000	$ 38,000	$ 32,000

To choose among the projects, Smart Touch computes the **profitability index** (also known as the **present value index**). The profitability index is computed as follows:

Profitability index = Present value of net cash inflows ÷ Investment

The profitability index computes the number of dollars returned for every dollar invested, *with all calculations performed in present value dollars*. It allows us to compare alternative investments in present value terms (like the NPV method), but it also considers differences in the investments' initial cost. Let us compute the profitability index for all three alternatives.

Present value of net cash inflows ÷ Investment = Profitability index			
Project A:	$150,000	÷ $125,000 =	1.20
Project B:	$238,000	÷ $200,000 =	1.19
Project C:	$182,000	÷ $150,000 =	1.21

The profitability index shows that Project C is the best of the three alternatives because it returns $1.21 (in present value dollars) for every $1.00 invested. Projects A and B return slightly less.

Let us also compute the profitability index for Greg's Groovy Tunes' CD-player and DVR projects:

CD-player: $1,048,610 ÷ $1,000,000 = 1.048
DVR: $1,078,910 ÷ $1,000,000 = 1.078

The profitability index confirms our prior conclusion that the DVR project is more profitable than the CD-player project. The DVR project returns $1.078 (in present value dollars) for every $1.00 invested (beyond the 14% return already used to discount the cash flows). We did not need the profitability index to determine that the DVR project was preferable because both projects required the same investment ($1 million).

NPV of a Project with Residual Value

Many assets yield cash inflows at the end of their useful lives because they have residual value. Companies discount an investment's residual value to its present value when determining the *total* present value of the project's net cash inflows. The residual value is discounted as a single lump sum—not an annuity—because it will be received only once, when the asset is sold. In short, it is just another type of cash inflow of the project.

Suppose Greg's expects that the CD project equipment will be worth $100,000 at the end of its five-year life. To determine the CD-player project's NPV, we discount the residual value of $100,000 using the Present Value of $1 table ($i = 14\%$, $n = 5$). (See Appendix B, Table A, page B-1.) We then *add* its present value of $51,900 to the present value of the CD project's other net cash inflows we calculated in Exhibit 11-13 ($1,048,610). This gives the new net present value calculation as shown in Exhibit 11-15 below:

EXHIBIT 11-15 | **NPV of a Project with Residual Value**

Year		PV Factor ($i = 14\%$, $n = 5$)	Net Cash Inflow	Present Value
1–5	Present value of annuity	3.433	× $305,450 =	$ 1,048,610
5	Present value of residual value (single lump sum)	0.519	× $100,000 =	51,900
	Total present value of net cash inflows			$ 1,100,510
0	Investment			$(1,000,000)
	Net present value (NPV)			$ 100,510

Because of the expected residual value, the CD-player project is now more attractive than the DVR project. If Greg's could pursue only the CD or DVR project, it would now choose the CD project, because its NPV of $100,510 is higher than the DVR project's NPV of $78,910, and both projects require the same investment of $1 million.

Sensitivity Analysis

Capital budgeting decisions affect cash flows far into the future. Greg's managers might want to know whether their decision would be affected by any of their major assumptions, for example,

- changing the discount rate from 14% to 12% or to 16%.
- changing the net cash flows by 10%.

After reviewing the basic information for NPV analysis, managers perform sensitivity analyses to recalculate and review the results.

Internal Rate of Return (IRR)

Another discounted cash flow model for capital budgeting is the internal rate of return. The **internal rate of return (IRR)** is the rate of return (based on discounted cash flows) a company can expect to earn by investing in the project. *It is the interest rate that makes the NPV of the investment equal to zero.*

Let us look at this concept in another light by substituting in the definition of NPV:

> Present value of the investment's net cash inflows – Investment's cost (Present value of cash outflows) = 0

In other words, the IRR is the *interest rate* that makes the cost of the investment equal to the present value of the investment's net cash inflows. The higher the IRR, the more desirable the project.

IRR with Equal Periodic Net Cash Inflows (Annuity)

Let us first consider Greg's CD-player project, which would cost $1 million and result in five equal yearly cash inflows of $305,450. We compute the IRR of an investment with equal periodic cash flows (annuity) by taking the following steps:

1. The IRR is the interest rate that makes the cost of the investment *equal to* the present value of the investment's net cash inflows, so we set up the following equation:

> Investment's cost = Present value of investment's net cash inflows
> Investment's cost = Amount of each equal net cash inflow × Annuity PV factor ($i = ?, n =$ given)

2. Next, we plug in the information we do know—the investment cost, $1,000,000, the equal annual net cash inflows, $305,450, no residual value, and the number of periods (five years):

> $1,000,000 = $305,450 × Annuity PV factor ($i = ?, n = 5$)

3. We then rearrange the equation and solve for the Annuity PV factor ($i = ?, n = 5$):

> $1,000,000 ÷ $305,450 = Annuity PV factor ($i = ?, n = 5$)
> 3.274 = Annuity PV factor ($i = ?, n = 5$)

4. Finally, we find the interest rate that corresponds to this Annuity PV factor. Turn to the Present Value of Annuity of $1 table (Appendix B, Table B). Scan the row corresponding to the project's expected life—five years, in our example. Choose the column(s) with the number closest to the Annuity PV factor you calculated in step 3. The 3.274 annuity factor is in the 16% column. Therefore, the IRR of the CD-player project is 16%. Greg's expects the project to earn an internal rate of return of 16% over its life. Exhibit 11-16 confirms this result: Using a 16% discount rate, the project's NPV is zero. In other words, 16% is the discount rate that makes the investment cost equal to the present value of the investment's net cash inflows.

EXHIBIT 11-16 | **IRR—CD-Player Project**

Years		Annuity PV Factor ($i = 16\%, n = 5$)		Net Cash Inflow		Total Present Value
1–5	Present value of annuity of equal annual net cash inflows for 5 years at 16%	3.274	×	$305,450	=	$1,000,000[†]
0	Investment					(1,000,000)
	Net present value of the CD-player project					$ 0[‡]

[†]Slight rounding error.
[‡]The zero difference proves that the IRR is 16%.

To decide whether the project is acceptable, compare the IRR with the minimum desired rate of return. The decision rule is as follows:

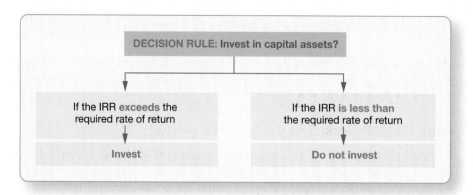

Recall that Greg's Groovy Tunes' required rate of return is 14%. Because the CD project's IRR (16%) is higher than the hurdle rate (14%), Greg's would invest in the project.

In the CD-player project, the exact Annuity PV factor (3.274) appears in the Present Value of an Annuity of $1 table (Appendix B, Table B). Many times, the exact factor will not appear in the table. For example, let us find the IRR of Smart Touch's B2B Web portal. Recall the B2B portal had a six-year life with annual net cash inflows of $60,000. The investment costs $240,000. We find its Annuity PV factor using the same steps:

Investment's cost	= Present value of investment's net cash inflows
Investment's cost	= Amount of each equal net cash inflow × Annuity PV factor (i = ?, n = given)
$240,000	= $60,000 × Annuity PV factor (i = ?, n = 6)
$240,000 ÷ $60,000	= Annuity PV factor (i = ?, n = 6)
4.00	= Annuity PV factor (i = ?, n = 6)

Now look in the Present Value of Annuity of $1 table in the row marked 6 periods (Appendix B, Table B). You will not see 4.00 under any column. The closest two factors are 3.889 (at 14%) and 4.111 (at 12%). Thus, the B2B portal's IRR must be somewhere between 12% and 14%. If we need a more precise figure, we could interpolate, or use a business calculator or Microsoft Excel to find the portal's exact IRR of 12.978%. If Smart Touch had a 14% required rate of return, it would *not* invest in the B2B portal because the portal's IRR is less than 14%.

IRR with Unequal Periodic Cash Flows

Because the DVR project has unequal cash inflows, Greg's cannot use the Present Value of Annuity of $1 table to find the asset's IRR. Rather, Greg's must use a trial-and-error procedure to determine the discount rate making the project's NPV equal to zero. For example, because the company's minimum required rate of return is 14%, Greg's might start by calculating whether the DVR project earns at least 14%. Recall from Exhibit 11-13 that the DVR's NPV using a 14% discount rate is $78,910. Since the NPV is *positive*, the IRR must be *higher* than 14%. Greg's continues the trial-and-error process using *higher* discount rates until the company finds the rate that brings the net present value of the DVR project to *zero*. Exhibit 11-17 shows that at 16%, the DVR has an NPV of $40,390. Therefore, the IRR must be higher than 16%. At 18%, the NPV is $3,980, which is very close to zero. Thus, the IRR must be slightly higher than 18%. If we use a business calculator, rather than the trial-and-error procedure, we would find the IRR is 18.23%.

EXHIBIT 11-17 | **Finding the DVR's IRR Through Trial-and-Error**

Years		Net Cash Inflow	PV Factor (for i = 16%)		Present Value at 16%	Net Cash Inflow	PV Factor (for i = 18%)		Present Value at 18%
1	Inflows	$500,000	× 0.862*	=	$ 431,000	$500,000	× 0.847*	=	$ 423,500
2	Inflows	350,000	× 0.743	=	260,050	350,000	× 0.718	=	251,300
3	Inflows	300,000	× 0.641	=	192,300	300,000	× 0.609	=	182,700
4	Inflows	250,000	× 0.552	=	138,000	250,000	× 0.516	=	129,000
5	Inflows	40,000	× 0.476	=	19,040	40,000	× 0.437	=	17,480
	Total present value of net cash inflows				$ 1,040,390				$ 1,003,980
0	Investment				(1,000,000)				(1,000,000)
	Net present value (NPV)				$ 40,390				$ 3,980

*PV Factors are found in Appendix B, Table A.

The DVR's internal rate of return is higher than Greg's 14% required rate of return so the DVR project is attractive.

Comparing Capital Budgeting Methods

We have discussed four capital budgeting methods commonly used by companies to make capital investment decisions. Two of these methods do not incorporate the time value of money: payback period and ARR. Exhibit 11-18 summarizes the similarities and differences between these two methods.

EXHIBIT 11-18 | **Capital Budgeting Methods That *Ignore* the Time Value of Money**

Payback period	Accounting rate of return
• Simple to compute	• The only method that uses accrual accounting figures
• Focuses on the time it takes to recover the company's cash investment	• Shows how the investment will affect operating income, which is important to financial statement users
• Ignores any cash flows occurring after the payback period, including any residual value	• Measures the profitability of the asset over its entire life
• Highlights risks of investments with longer cash recovery periods	• Ignores the time value of money
• Ignores the time value of money	

The discounted cash-flow methods are superior because they consider both the time value of money and profitability. These methods compare an investment's initial cost (cash outflow) with its future net cash inflows, which are all converted to the *same point in time*—the present value. Profitability is built into the discounted cash-flow methods because they consider *all* cash inflows and outflows over the project's life. Exhibit 11-19 considers the similarities and differences between the two discounted cash-flow methods.

EXHIBIT 11-19	Capital Budgeting Methods That *Incorporate* the Time Value of Money

Net present value	Internal rate of return
• Incorporates the time value of money and the asset's net cash flows over its entire life	• Incorporates the time value of money and the asset's net cash flows over its entire life
• Indicates whether or not the asset will earn the company's minimum required rate of return	• Computes the project's unique rate of return
• Shows the excess or deficiency of the asset's present value of net cash inflows over its initial investment cost	• No additional steps needed for capital rationing decisions
• The profitability index should be computed for capital rationing decisions when the assets require different initial investments	

Managers often use more than one method to gain different perspectives on risks and returns. For example, Smart Touch Learning could decide to pursue capital projects with positive NPVs, provided that those projects have a payback of four years or fewer.

Decision Guidelines

CAPITAL BUDGETING

Here are more of the guidelines **Amazon.com**'s managers used as they made the major capital budgeting decision to invest in building warehouses.

Decision	Guideline
• Which capital budgeting methods are best?	Discounted cash-flow methods (NPV and IRR) are best because they incorporate both profitability and the time value of money.
• Why do the NPV and IRR models use the present value?	Because an investment's cash inflows and cash outflows occur at different points in time, they must be converted to a common point in time to make a valid comparison (that is, to determine whether inflows exceed cash outflows). These methods use the *present* value as the common point in time.
• How do we know if investing in warehouse facilities will be worthwhile?	An investment in warehouse facilities may be worthwhile if the NPV is positive or the IRR exceeds the required rate of return.
• How do we compute the net present value with	
• equal annual cash flows?	Compute the present value of the investment's net cash inflows using the Present Value of an Annuity of $1 table and then subtract the investment's cost.
• unequal annual cash flows?	Compute the present value of each year's net cash inflows using the Present Value of $1 (lump sum) table, sum the present values of the inflows, and then subtract the investment's cost.
• How do we compute the internal rate of return with	
• equal annual cash flows?	Find the interest rate that yields the following PV factor: $$\text{Annuity PV factor} = \frac{\text{Investment cost}}{\text{Expected annual net cash inflow}}$$
• unequal annual cash flows?	Trial and error, spreadsheet software, or business calculator

Summary Problem 2

Recall from Summary Problem 1 that Reality-max is considering buying a new bar-coding machine. The investment proposal passed the initial screening tests (payback period and accounting rate of return) so the company now wants to analyze the proposal using the discounted cash flow methods. Recall that the bar-coding machine costs $48,000, has a five-year life, and no residual value. The estimated net cash inflows are $13,000 per year over its life. The company's required rate of return is 16%.

Requirements

1. Compute the bar-coding machine's NPV.
2. Find the bar-coding machine's IRR (exact percentage is not required).
3. Should Reality-max buy the bar-coding machine? Why?

Solution

Requirement 1

Present value of annuity of equal annual net cash inflows at 16% ($13,000 × 3.274*).....................................	$ 42,562
Investment..	(48,000)
Net present value	$ (5,438)

*Annuity PV factor ($i = 16\%$, $n = 5$)

Requirement 2

Investment's cost = Amount of each equal net cash inflow × Annuity PV factor ($i = ?$, $n = 5$)

$48,000 = $13,000 × Annuity PV factor ($i = ?$, $n = 5$)

$48,000 ÷ $13,000 = Annuity PV factor ($i = ?$, $n = 5$)

3.692 = Annuity PV factor ($i = ?$, $n = 5$)

Because the cash flows occur for five years, we look for the PV factor 3.692 in the row marked $n = 5$ on the Present Value of Annuity of $1 table (Appendix B, Table B). The PV factor is 3.605 at 12% and 3.791 at 10%. Therefore, the bar-coding machine has an IRR that falls between 10% and 12%. (*Optional:* Using a business calculator, we find an 11.038% internal rate of return.)

Requirement 3

Decision: Do not buy the bar-coding machine. It has a negative NPV and its IRR falls below the company's required rate of return. Both methods consider profitability and the time value of money.

Review Capital Investment Decisions and the Time Value of Money

■ Accounting Vocabulary

Accounting Rate of Return (p. 517)
A measure of profitability computed by dividing the average annual operating income from an asset by the average amount invested in the asset.

Annuity (p. 522)
A stream of equal installments made at equal time intervals.

Capital Budgeting (p. 512)
The process of making capital investment decisions. Companies make capital investments when they acquire *capital assets*—assets used for a long period of time.

Capital Rationing (p. 513)
Choosing among alternative capital investments due to limited funds.

Compound Interest (p. 522)
Interest computed on the principal *and* all interest earned to date.

Discount Rate (p. 528)
Management's minimum desired rate of return on an investment. Also called the required rate of return.

Internal Rate of Return (IRR) (p. 532)
The rate of return (based on discounted cash flows) that a company can expect to earn by investing in a capital asset. The interest rate that makes the NPV of the investment equal to zero.

Net Present Value (NPV) (p. 527)
The *difference* between the present value of the investment's net cash inflows and the investment's cost.

Payback (p. 514)
The length of time it takes to recover, in net cash inflows, the cost of a capital outlay.

Post-Audits (p. 513)
Comparing a capital investment's actual net cash inflows to its projected net cash inflows.

Present Value Index (p. 531)
An index that computes the number of dollars returned for every dollar invested, *with all calculations performed in present value dollars*. Computed as present value of net cash inflows divided by investment. Also called **profitability index**.

Profitability Index (p. 531)
An index that computes the number of dollars returned for every dollar invested, *with all calculations performed in present value dollars*. Computed as present value of net cash inflows divided by investment. Also called **present value index**.

Required Rate of Return (p. 528)
The rate an investment must meet or exceed in order to be acceptable.

Simple Interest (p. 522)
Interest computed *only* on the principal amount.

■ Quick Check

1. What is the first step of capital budgeting?
   a. Gathering the money for the investment
   b. Getting the accountant involved
   c. Identifying potential projects
   d. All of the above

2. Which of the following methods uses accrual accounting, rather than net cash flows, as a basis for calculations?
   a. Payback
   b. ARR
   c. NPV
   d. IRR

3. Which of the following methods does not consider the investment's profitability?
   a. ARR
   b. NPV
   c. Payback
   d. IRR

4. Suppose Stephanie Feigenbaum's Sweets is considering investing in warehouse-management software that costs $450,000, has $35,000 residual value, and should lead to cost savings of $120,000 per year for its five-year life. In calculating the ARR, which of the following figures should be used as the equation's denominator (average amount invested in the asset)?

   a. $242,500

   b. $257,500

   c. $272,500

   d. $277,000

5. Your rich aunt has promised to give you $3,000 a year at the end of each of the next four years to help you pay for college. Using a discount rate of 10%, the present value of the gift can be stated as

   a. PV = $3,000 (Annuity PV factor, $i = 10\%$, $n = 4$).

   b. PV = $3,000 (PV factor, $i = 4\%$, $n = 10$).

   c. PV = $3,000 \times 10\% \times 5$.

   d. PV = $3,000 (Annuity FV factor, $i = 10\%$, $n = 4$).

6. Which of the following affects the present value of an investment?

   a. The type of investment (annuity versus single lump sum)

   b. The interest rate

   c. The number of time periods (length of the investment)

   d. All of the above

7. Which of the following is true regarding capital rationing decisions?

   a. Companies should always choose the investment with the shortest payback period.

   b. Companies should always choose the investment with the highest ARR.

   c. Companies should always choose the investment with the highest NPV.

   d. None of the above

8. In computing the IRR on an expansion at Snow Park Lodge, Deer Valley would consider all of the following *except?*

   a. The cost of the expansion

   b. Predicted cash inflows over the life of the expansion

   c. Present value factors

   d. Depreciation on the assets built in the expansion

9. The IRR is

   a. the interest rate at which the NPV of the investment is zero.

   b. the same as the ARR.

   c. the firm's hurdle rate.

   d. None of the above

10. Which of the following is the most reliable method for making capital budgeting decisions?

   a. Post-audit method

   b. NPV method

   c. ARR method

   d. Payback method

Answers are given after Apply Your Knowledge (p. 551).

Assess Your Progress

■ Short Exercises

S11-1 *(L. OBJ. 1)* **The importance of capital investments and the capital budgeting process [10 min]**
Review the following activities of the capital budgeting process:

    a. Budget capital investments
    b. Project investments' cash flows
    c. Perform post-audits
    d. Make investments
    e. Use feedback to reassess investments already made
    f. Identify potential capital investments
    g. Screen/analyze investments using one or more of the methods discussed

Requirement

    1. Place the activities in sequential order as they occur in the capital budgeting process.

S11-2 *(L. OBJ. 2)* **Using the payback and accounting rate of return methods to make capital investment decisions [10 min]**
Consider how White Valley Snow Park Lodge could use capital budgeting to decide whether the $12,500,000 Brook Park Lodge expansion would be a good investment.

    Assume White Valley's managers developed the following estimates concerning the expansion:

Number of additional skiers per day	120
Average number of days per year that weather	
conditions allow skiing at White Valley	149
Useful life of expansion (in years)	12
Average cash spent by each skier per day . . . . $	159
Average variable cost of serving each skier per day . . . $	85
Cost of expansion	$12,500,000
Discount rate	12%

Assume that White Valley uses the straight-line depreciation method and expects the lodge expansion to have a residual value of $600,000 at the end of its 12-year life.

Requirements

    1. Compute the average annual net cash inflow from the expansion.
    2. Compute the average annual operating income from the expansion.

Note: Short Exercise 11-2 must be completed before attempting Short Exercise 11-3.

S11-3 *(L. OBJ. 2)* **Using the payback method to make capital investment decisions [5 min]**
Refer to the White Valley Snow Park Lodge expansion project in S11-2.

Requirement

    1. Compute the payback period for the expansion project.

Note: Short Exercise 11-2 must be completed before attempting Short Exercise 11-4.

S11-4 *(L. OBJ. 2)* **Using the accounting rate of return method to make capital investment decisions [5–10 min]**
Refer to the White Valley Snow Park Lodge expansion project in S11-2.

Requirement

1. Calculate the ARR.

Note: Short Exercise 11-2 must be completed before attempting Short Exercise 11-5.

S11-5 *(L. OBJ. 2)* **Using the payback and accounting rate of return methods to make capital investment decisions [5–10 min]**
Refer to the White Valley Snow Park Lodge expansion project in S11-2. *Assume the expansion has zero residual value.*

Requirements

1. Will the payback period change? Explain your answer and recalculate if necessary.
2. Will the project's ARR change? Explain your answer and recalculate if necessary.
3. Assume White Valley screens its potential capital investments using the following decision criteria:

Maximum payback period	5.4 years
Minimum accounting rate of return	12.0%

Will White Valley consider this project further, or reject it?

S11-6 *(L.OBJ. 2)* **Using the payback and accounting rate of return methods to make capital investment decisions [5–10 min]**
Suppose White Valley is deciding whether to purchase new accounting software. The payback period for the $27,375 software package is five years, and the software's expected life is three years. White Valley's required rate of return is 12.0%.

Requirement

1. Assuming equal yearly cash flows, what are the expected annual cash savings from the new software?

S11-7 *(L.OBJ. 3)* **Using the time value of money to compute the present and future values of single lump sums and annuities [10–15 min]**
Your grandfather would like to share some of his fortune with you. He offers to give you money under one of the following scenarios (you get to choose):

1. $7,550 a year at the end of each of the next eight years
2. $48,350 (lump sum) now
3. $100,050 (lump sum) eight years from now

Requirement

1. Calculate the present value of each scenario using an 8% discount rate. Which scenario yields the highest present value? Would your preference change if you used a 10% discount rate?

S11-8 *(L.OBJ. 3)* **Using the time value of money to compute the present and future values of single lump sums and annuities [5–10 min]**
Assume you make the following investments:

a. You invest $7,250 for three years at 12% interest.
b. In a different account earning 12% interest, you invest $2,500 at the end of each year for three years.

Requirement

1. Calculate the value of each investment at the end of three years.

S11-9 *(L. OBJ. 3)* **Using the time value of money to compute the present and future values of single lump sums and annuities [10–15 min]**

Refer to the lottery payout options summarized in Exhibit 11-9.

Requirement

1. Rather than comparing the payout options at their present values (as done in the chapter), compare the payout options at their future value, 10 years from now.
   a. Using a 8% interest rate, what is the future value of each payout option?
   b. Rank your preference among payout options.
   c. Does computing the future value, rather than the present value of the options, change your preference between payout options? Explain your reasoning.

S11-10 *(L.OBJ. 3)* **Using the time value of money to compute the present and future values of single lump sums and annuities [10–15 min]**

Use the Present Value of $1 table (Appendix B, Table A) to determine the present value of $1 received one year from now. Assume a 14% interest rate. Use the same table to find the present value of $1 received two years from now. Continue this process for a total of five years.

Requirements

1. What is the *total* present value of the cash flows received over the five-year period?
2. Could you characterize this stream of cash flows as an annuity? Why, or why not?
3. Use the Present Value of Annuity of $1 table (Appendix B, Table B) to determine the present value of the same stream of cash flows. Compare your results to your answer to part 1.
4. Explain your findings.

Note: Short Exercise 11-2 must be completed before attempting Short Exercise 11-11.

S11-11 *(L. OBJ. 4)* **Using discounted cash flow models to make capital investment decisions [10–15 min]**

Refer to the White Valley Snow Park Lodge expansion project in S11-2.

Requirement

1. What is the project's NPV? Is the investment attractive? Why?

Note: Short Exercise 11-2 must be completed before attempting Short Exercise 11-12.

S11-12 *(L. OBJ. 4)* **Using discounted cash flow models to make capital investment decisions [10–15 min]**

Refer to S11-2. *Assume the expansion has no residual value.*

Requirement

1. What is the project's NPV? Is the investment still attractive? Why?

Note: Short Exercise 11-12 must be completed before attempting Short Exercise 11-13.

S11-13 *(L. OBJ. 4)* **Using discounted cash flow models to make capital investment decisions [10–15 min]**

Refer to S11-12. *Continue to assume that the expansion has no residual value.*

Requirement

1. What is the project's IRR? Is the investment attractive? Why?

E11-14 *(L. OBJ. 1)* **The importance of capital investments and the capital budgeting process [15–20 min]**
You have just started a business and want your new employees to be well informed about capital budgeting.

Requirement

1. Match each definition with its capital budgeting method.

METHODS
1. Accounting rate of return
2. Internal rate of return
3. Net present value
4. Payback period

DEFINITIONS
A. Is only concerned with the time it takes to get cash outflows returned
B. Considers operating income but not the time value of money in its analyses
C. Compares the present value of cash out to the cash in to determine investment worthiness
D. The true rate of return an investment earns

E11-15 *(L. OBJ. 2)* **Using the payback and accounting rate of return methods to make capital investment decisions [5–10 min]**
Stenback, Co., is considering acquiring a manufacturing plant. The purchase price is $1,300,000. The owners believe the plant will generate net cash inflows of $314,000 annually. It will have to be replaced in seven years.

Requirement

1. Use the payback method to determine whether Stenback should purchase this plant.

E11-16 *(L. OBJ. 2)* **Using the payback and accounting rate of return methods to make capital investment decisions [5–10 min]**
Pace Hardware is adding a new product line that will require an investment of $1,512,000. Managers estimate that this investment will have a 10-year life and generate net cash inflows of $320,000 the first year, $280,000 the second year, and $240,000 each year thereafter for eight years.

Requirement

1. Compute the payback period.

E11-17 *(L. OBJ. 2)* **Using the payback and accounting rate of return methods to make capital investment decisions [10–15 min]**
Transport Design is shopping for new equipment. Managers are considering two investments. Equipment manufactured by Rouse, Inc., costs $1,020,000 and will last for five years, with no residual value. The Rouse equipment will generate annual operating income of $265,000. Equipment manufactured by Vargas Co. costs $1,240,000 and will remain useful for six years. It estimates annual operating income of $230,000, and its expected residual value is $100,000.

Requirement

1. Which equipment offers the higher ARR?

Note: Exercise 11-16 must be completed before attempting Exercise 11-18.

E11-18 *(L. OBJ. 2)* **Using the payback and accounting rate of return methods to make capital investment decisions [10–15 min]**
Refer to the Pace Hardware information in E11-16. Assume the project has no residual value.

Requirement

1. Compute the ARR for the investment.

E11-19 *(L. OBJ. 3)* **Using the time value of money to compute the present and future values of single lump sums and annuities [15–20 min]**
Assume you want to retire early at age 52. You plan to save using one of the following two strategies: (1) save $2,700 a year in an IRA beginning when you are 27 and ending when you are 52 (25 years), or (2) wait until you are 42 to start saving and then save $6,750 per year for the next 10 years. Assume you will earn the historic stock market average of 12% per year.

Requirements

1. How much "out-of-pocket" cash will you invest under the two options?
2. How much savings will you have accumulated at age 52 under the two options?
3. Explain the results.
4. If you were to let the savings continue to grow for 10 more years (with no further out-of-pocket investments), what would the investments be worth when you are age 62?

E11-20 *(L. OBJ. 3)* **Using the time value of money to compute the present and future values of single lump sums and annuities [15–20 min]**
Your best friend just received a gift of $6,000 from his favorite aunt. He wants to save the money to use as "starter" money after college. He can invest it (1) risk-free at 4%, (2) taking on moderate risk at 10%, or (3) taking on high risk at 16%.

Requirement

1. Help your friend project the investment's worth at the end of four years under each investment strategy and explain the results to him.

E11-21 *(L.OBJ. 3)* **Using the time value of money to compute the present and future values of single lump sums and annuities [5–10 min]**
Janet wants to take the next six years off work to travel around the world. She estimates her annual cash needs at $35,000 (if she needs more, she will work odd jobs). Janet believes she can invest her savings at 12% until she depletes her funds.

Requirements

1. How much money does Janet need now to fund her travels?
2. After speaking with a number of banks, Janet learns she will only be able to invest her funds at 6%. How much does she need now to fund her travels?

E11-22 *(L. OBJ. 3)* **Using the time value of money to compute the present and future values of single lump sums and annuities [10–15 min]**
Congratulations! You have won a state lotto. The state lottery offers you the following (after-tax) payout options:

Option #1: $13,000,000 after five years
Option #2: $2,300,000 per year for the next five years
Option #3: $12,000,000 after three years

Requirement

1. Assuming you can earn 6% on your funds, which option would you prefer?

E11-23 *(L. OBJ. 4)* **Using discounted cash flow models to make capital investment decisions [15–20 min]**

Use the NPV method to determine whether Stenback Products should invest in the following projects:

- *Project A*: Costs $290,000 and offers eight annual net cash inflows of $57,000. Stenback Products requires an annual return of 14% on projects like A.
- *Project B*: Costs $380,000 and offers nine annual net cash inflows of $77,000. Stenback Products demands an annual return of 12% on investments of this nature.

Requirements

1. What is the NPV of each project?
2. What is the maximum acceptable price to pay for each project?

E11-24 *(L.OBJ. 4)* **Using discounted cash flow models to make capital investment decisions [15–20 min]**

Bevil Industries is deciding whether to automate one phase of its production process. The manufacturing equipment has a six-year life and will cost $900,000. Projected net cash inflows are as follows:

Year 1	$264,000
Year 2	$251,000
Year 3	$228,000
Year 4	$213,000
Year 5	$202,000
Year 6	$176,000

Requirements

1. Compute this project's NPV using Bevil Industries's 14% hurdle rate. Should Bevil Industries invest in the equipment?
2. Bevil Industries could refurbish the equipment at the end of six years for $106,000. The refurbished equipment could be used one more year, providing $78,000 of net cash inflows in year 7. Additionally, the refurbished equipment would have a $52,000 residual value at the end of year 7. Should Bevil Industries invest in the equipment and refurbishing it after six years? (*Hint:* In addition to your answer to requirement 1, discount the additional cash outflow and inflows back to the present value.)

Note: Exercise 11-23 must be completed before attempting Exercise 11-25.

E11-25 *(L.OBJ. 4)* **Using discounted cash flow models to make capital investment decisions [15 min]**

Refer to Stenback Products in E11-23.

Requirement

1. Compute the IRR of each project, and use this information to identify the better investment.

E11-26 *(L.OBJ. 4)* **Using discounted cash flow models to make capital investment decisions [10–15 min]**

Sheffield Manufacturing is considering three capital investment proposals. At this time, Sheffield Manufacturing only has funds available to pursue one of the three investments.

	Equipment A	Equipment B	Equipment C
Present value of			
net cash inflows	$ 1,775,424	$ 2,004,215	$ 2,242,989
Investment	$ (1,467,293)	$ (1,629,443)	$ (1,808,862)
NPV	$ 308,131	$ 374,772	$ 434,127

Requirement

1. Which investment should Sheffield Manufacturing pursue at this time? Why?

Problems (Group A)

P11-27A *(L. OBJ. 1)* **Describing the importance of capital investments and the capital budgeting process [10–15 min]**

Consider the following statements about capital budgeting.

a. _____ and _____ incorporate the time value of money.

b. _____ focuses on time, not profitability.

c. _____ uses accrual accounting income.

d. _____ finds the discount rate which brings the investment's NPV to zero.

e. In capital rationing decisions, the profitability index must be computed to compare investments requiring different initial investments when the _____ method is used.

f. _____ ignores salvage value.

g. _____ uses discounted cash flows to determine the asset's unique rate of return.

h. _____ highlights risky investments.

i. _____ measures profitability, but ignores the time value of money.

Requirement

1. Fill in each statement with the appropriate capital budgeting method: Payback period, ARR, NPV, or IRR.

P11-28A *(L. OBJ. 2, 4)* **Using the payback and accounting rate of return methods to make capital investment decisions, and using discounted cash flow models to make capital investment decisions [20–30 min]**

Water Nation is considering purchasing a water park in San Antonio, Texas, for $1,850,000. The new facility will generate annual net cash inflows of $440,000 for nine years. Engineers estimate that the facility will remain useful for nine years and have no residual value. The company uses straight-line depreciation, and its stockholders demand an annual return of 12% on investments of this nature.

Requirements

1. Compute the payback period, the ARR, the NPV of this investment, and its IRR.
2. Recommend whether the company should invest in this project.

P11-29A *(L. OBJ. 2, 4)* **Using the payback and accounting rate of return methods to make capital investment decisions, and using discounted cash flow models to make capital investment decisions [30–45 min]**

Locos operates a chain of sandwich shops. The company is considering two possible expansion plans. Plan A would open eight smaller shops at a cost of $8,410,000. Expected annual net cash inflows are $1,650,000, with zero residual value at the end of nine years. Under Plan B, Locos would open three larger shops at a cost of $8,340,000. This plan is expected to generate net cash inflows of $1,120,000 per year for nine years, the estimated useful life of the properties. Estimated residual value for Plan B is $1,300,000. Locos uses straight-line depreciation and requires an annual return of 8%.

Requirements

1. Compute the payback period, the ARR, and the NPV of these two plans. What are the strengths and weaknesses of these capital budgeting models?
2. Which expansion plan should Locos choose? Why?
3. Estimate Plan A's IRR. How does the IRR compare with the company's required rate of return?

P11-30A *(L. OBJ. 3)* **Using the time value of money to compute the present and future values of single lump sums and annuities [15–20 min]**

You are planning for a very early retirement. You would like to retire at age 40 and have enough money saved to be able to draw $225,000 per year for the next 35 years (based on family history, you think you will live to age 75). You plan to save by making 10 equal annual installments (from age 30 to age 40) into a fairly risky investment fund that you expect will earn 14% per year. You will leave the money in this fund until it is completely depleted when you are 75 years old.

Requirements

1. How much money must you accumulate by retirement to make your plan work? (*Hint:* Find the present value of the $225,000 withdrawals.)
2. How does this amount compare to the total amount you will draw out of the investment during retirement? How can these numbers be so different?
3. How much must you pay into the investment each year for the first 10 years? (*Hint:* Your answer from requirement 1 becomes the future value of this annuity.)
4. How does the total "out-of-pocket" savings compare to the investment's value at the end of the 10-year savings period and the withdrawals you will make during retirement?

■ Problems (Group B)

P11-31B *(L. OBJ. 1)* **Describing the importance of capital investments and the capital budgeting process [10–15 min]**

Consider the following statements about capital budgeting.

a. _____ and _____ work well for capital investments with a relatively short life span.

b. _____ highlights risky investments.

c. _____ uses accrual accounting income rather than net cash flows in its computation.

d. _____ uses discounted cash flows to determine the asset's unique rate of return.

e. In capital rationing decisions, management must identify the required rate of return when the _____ method is used.

f. _____ provides management with information on how fast the cash invested will be recouped.

g. _____ finds the discount rate which brings the investment's NPV to zero.

h. _____ does not consider the asset's profitability.

i. _____ is calculated by dividing the average amount invested by the asset's average annual operating income.

Requirement

1. Fill in each statement with the appropriate capital budgeting method: Payback period, ARR, NPV, or IRR.

P11-32B *(L. OBJ. 2, 4)* **Using the payback and accounting rate of return methods to make capital investment decisions, and using discounted cash flow models to make capital investment decisions [20–30 min]**

Water World is considering purchasing a water park in San Antonio, Texas, for $1,910,000. The new facility will generate annual net cash inflows of $481,000 for eight years. Engineers estimate that the facility will remain useful for eight years and have no residual value. The company uses straight-line depreciation, and its stockholders demand an annual return of 12% on investments of this nature.

Requirements

1. Compute the payback period, the ARR, the NPV of this investment, and its IRR.
2. Recommend whether the company should invest in this project.

P11-33B *(L. OBJ. 2, 4)* **Using the payback and accounting rate of return methods to make capital investment decisions, and using discounted cash flow models to make capital investment decisions [30–45 min]**

Lolas operates a chain of sandwich shops. The company is considering two possible expansion plans. Plan A would open eight smaller shops at a cost of $8,500,000. Expected annual net cash inflows are $1,600,000, with zero residual value at the end of ten years. Under Plan B, Lolas would open three larger shops at a cost of $8,100,000. This plan is expected to generate net cash inflows of $1,090,000 per year for ten years, which is the estimated useful life of the properties. Estimated residual value for Plan B is $1,300,000. Lolas uses straight-line depreciation and requires an annual return of 8%.

Requirements

1. Compute the payback period, the ARR, and the NPV of these two plans. What are the strengths and weaknesses of these capital budgeting models?
2. Which expansion plan should Lolas choose? Why?
3. Estimate Plan A's IRR. How does the IRR compare with the company's required rate of return?

P11-34B *(L. OBJ. 3)* **Using the time value of money to compute the present and future values of single lump sums and annuities [15–20 min]**

You are planning for an early retirement. You would like to retire at age 40 and have enough money saved to be able to draw $220,000 per year for the next 45 years (based on family history, you think you will live to age 85). You plan to save by making 20 equal annual installments (from age 20 to age 40) into a fairly risky investment fund that you expect will earn 14% per year. You will leave the money in this fund until it is completely depleted when you are 85 years old.

Requirements

1. How much money must you accumulate by retirement to make your plan work? (*Hint:* Find the present value of the $220,000 withdrawals.)
2. How does this amount compare to the total amount you will draw out of the investment during retirement? How can these numbers be so different?
3. How much must you pay into the investment each year for the first 20 years? (*Hint:* Your answer from requirement 1 becomes the future value of this annuity.)
4. How does the total "out-of-pocket" savings compare to the investment's value at the end of the 20-year savings period and the withdrawals you will make during retirement?

▪ Continuing Exercise

E11-35 This exercise continues the Sherman Lawn Service, Inc., situation from Exercise 10-35 of Chapter 10. Sherman Lawn Service is considering purchasing a mower that will generate cash inflows of $5,000 per year. The mower has a zero residual value and an estimated useful life of three years. The mower costs $10,000. Sherman's required rate of return is 10%.

Requirements

1. Calculate payback period, accounting rate of return, and net present value for the mower investment.
2. Should Sherman invest in the new mower?

▪ Continuing Problem

P11-36 This problem continues the Haupt Consulting, Inc., situation from Problem 10-36 of Chapter 10. Haupt Consulting is considering purchasing two different types of servers. Server A will generate cash inflows of $20,000 per year and has a zero residual value. Server A's estimated useful life is three years and it costs $50,000.

Server B will generate cash inflows of $30,000 in year 1, $15,000 in year 2, and $5,000 in year 3. Server B has a $1,000 residual value and an estimate life of three years. Server B also costs $50,000. Haupt's required rate of return is 8%.

Requirements

1. Calculate payback period, accounting rate of return, and net present value for both server investments.
2. Assuming capital rationing applies, which server should Haupt invest in?

Apply Your Knowledge

▪ Decision Case

Case 1. Dominic Hunter, a second-year business student at the University of Utah, will graduate in two years with an accounting major and a Spanish minor. Hunter is trying to decide where to work this summer. He has two choices: work full-time for a bottling plant or work part-time in the accounting department of a meat-packing plant. He probably will work at the same place next summer as well. He is able to work 12 weeks during the summer.

The bottling plant will pay Hunter $380 per week this year and 7% more next summer. At the meat-packing plant, he could work 20 hours per week at $8.75 per hour. By working only part-time, he could take two accounting courses this summer. Tuition is $225 per hour for each of the four-hour courses. Hunter believes that the experience he gains this summer will qualify him for a full-time accounting position with the meat-packing plant next summer. That position will pay $550 per week.

Hunter sees two additional benefits of working part-time this summer. First, he could reduce his studying workload during the fall and spring semesters by one course each term. Second, he would have the time to work as a grader in the university's accounting department during the 15-week fall term. Grading pays $50 per week.

Requirements

1. Suppose that Hunter ignores the time value of money in decisions that cover this short time period. Suppose also that his sole goal is to make as much money as possible between now and the end of next summer. What should he do? What nonquantitative factors might Dominic consider? What would *you* do if you were faced with these alternatives?

2. Now suppose that Hunter considers the time value of money for all cash flows that he expects to receive one year or more in the future. Which alternative does this consideration favor? Why?

■ Financial Statement Case—Amazon.com

This case is based on the **Amazon.com** annual report in Appendix A at the end of the book. Use it to answer the following questions.

Requirements

1. **Amazon.com** is considering investing in remodeling its distribution facility. The initial cost is estimated to be $970,000 in equipment plus another $130,000 in wages. Amazon.com feels the investment will increase cash flows $150,000 each year for the next 10 years. Amazon.com investors require a 12% rate of return. Using NPV, should **Amazon.com** make the investment? If so, why? If not, why not?

Quick Check Answers

1. *c* 2. *b* 3. *c* 4. *a* 5. *a* 6. *d* 7. *d* 8. *d* 9. *a* 10. *b*

For online homework, exercises, and problems that provide you immediate feedback, please visit www.myaccountinglab.com.

Big Picture

Ch 1   Introduction to Management Accounting

- O‑ Distinguish management accounting from financial accounting
- O‑ The role and responsibilities of management accountants
- O‑ Classify costs and prepare income statements for merchandising companies
- O‑ Classify costs and prepare income statements and statements of cost of goods manufactured for manufacturing companies

Ch 2   Job Order Costing

- O‑ Distinguish between job order and process costing
- O‑ Record materials, labor, and overhead in a job order costing system
- O‑ Record completion and sales of finished goods and adjust for under-/overallocated overhead
- O‑ Calculate unit costs for service companies

Chapter 11: Demo Doc

■ Capital Budgeting

Learning Objectives 2, 3, 4

Better Body Fitness produces exercise equipment. They are considering producing one of two possible new products: either a new type of rowing machine or an upper torso piece of equipment. They would need to purchase new machinery to manufacture these items. Each machine would require an additional investment of $500,000. The rower machine would have a useful life of seven years and the torso machine would have a useful life of four years. Neither has a residual value. The expected annual net cash inflows are as follows:

Net Cash Inflows				
Useful Life	Rower		Torso	
Years	Annual	Accumulated	Annual	Accumulated
1	$120,000	$120,000	$160,000	$160,000
2	120,000	240,000	160,000	320,000
3	120,000	360,000	160,000	480,000
4	120,000	480,000	160,000	640,000
5	120,000	600,000		
6	120,000	720,000		
7	120,000	840,000		

Requirements

1. Determine the payback period for each product. What is the major weakness of payback analysis?
2. Calculate the accounting rate of return. What is the major weakness of the accounting rate of return?
3. If Better Body Fitness requires a 14% return, what is the net present value of each project?
4. Compute the internal rate of return for each project.

Demo Doc Solution

Requirement 1

Determine the payback period for each product. What is the major weakness of payback analysis?

Part 1	Part 2	Part 3	Part 4	Demo Doc Complete

Payback period is a simple approach that is used sometimes to screen potential projects. A company would want to recoup the investment amount as quickly as possible, assuming all other factors are constant.

In this case, payback is the length of time it takes Better Body Fitness to recover, in net cash inflows, the $500,000 initial outlay. The rower and torso have equal cash inflows each year, so the payback period is calculated as:

$$\text{Payback period} = \frac{\text{Amount invested}}{\text{Expected annual net cash inflow}}$$

$$\text{Payback period for rower} = \frac{\$500,000}{\$120,000}$$

$$= \textbf{4.17 years}$$

$$\text{Payback period for torso} = \frac{\$500,000}{\$160,000}$$

$$= \textbf{3.13 years}$$

The payback method favors the torso because it recovers the initial investment more quickly. The major weakness of payback analysis is that it only focuses on time, not on profit. Although the torso recovers the initial investment faster, the rower produces $200,000 more in net cash inflows ($840,000 − $640,000). The payback period must be shorter than the useful life to provide any profit.

Requirement 2

Calculate the accounting rate of return. What is the major weakness of the accounting rate of return?

Part 1	Part 2	Part 3	Part 4	Demo Doc Complete

The accounting rate of return calculated is compared to the required return set by management. The company will invest in the asset if the return is more than that required and will not invest if the return is less than the required return. If several alternatives are being considered, the higher the return, the better it is.

The accounting rate of return is determined by dividing the average operating income from the asset by the average amount invested in the asset.

The average amount invested in the asset is calculated as

$$\frac{\text{Asset cost} - \text{Residual value}}{2}$$

Average amount invested in the rower and torso is

$$\frac{\$500,000 - 0}{2} = \$250,000$$

To determine the average operating income, depreciation must first be calculated. The depreciation associated with the rower is

$$\frac{\$500,000}{\text{7-year life}} = \$71,429$$

Depreciation associated with the torso machine is

$$\frac{\$500,000}{\text{4-year life}} = \$125,000$$

The depreciation expense is now subtracted from the expected annual net cash inflows to calculate the average operating income:

$$\text{Rower average operating income} = \$120,000 - \$71,429$$
$$= \$48,571$$

$$\text{Torso average operating income} = \$160,000 - \$125,000$$
$$= \$35,000$$

The accounting rate of return on the rower and torso machines are

$$\text{Rower} = \frac{\$48,571}{\$250,000}$$
$$= 19.428\%$$

$$\text{Torso} = \frac{\$35,000}{\$250,000}$$
$$= 14.00\%$$

The major weakness of the accounting rate of return is that it does not consider the timing of the income. The accounting rate of return does not consider whether the income is greater early in the life of the asset or near the end of the useful life of the asset. Management would prefer greater income early in the life of the asset so the funds could be used to generate additional income.

Requirement 3

If Better Body requires a 14% return, what is the net present value of each project?

Part 1	Part 2	**Part 3**	Part 4	Demo Doc Complete

3 Use the time value of money to compute the present and future values of single lump sums and annuities

4 Use discounted cash flow models to make capital investment decisions

Net present value brings future cash inflows and future cash outflows to a common time period in order to more easily compare the feasibility of each product.

The net present value (NPV) method compares the present value of the net cash inflows to the initial investment of the capital project. To obtain the present value of the net cash inflows, the minimum desired rate of return is used to find the appropriate discounting factor in the present value tables. If cash flows are equal each year, it is considered to be an annuity and Table B in Appendix B (p. B-3) is used; if the cash flows are unequal, Table A (p. B-1) is used for each year's present value calculation. *If the present value of the inflows to be received is equal or greater to that invested, the project is considered to be desirable.*

Consider the following:

> Net present value = Present value of ALL of the cash flows IN (PVCFI)
>
>   Less: Present value of ALL of the cash flows OUT (PVCFO)

Both of these projects expect a stream of equal periodic cash flows, which is called an annuity. The present value of an annuity is the periodic cash flow multiplied by the present value of an annuity of $1. Table B (reproduced here) shows the present value of annuity factors for various interest rates and numbers of periods:

| | Present Value of Annuity of $1 | | | | | | |
Period	4%	6%	8%	10%	12%	14%	16%
1	0.962	0.943	0.926	0.909	0.893	0.877	0.862
2	1.886	1.833	1.783	1.736	1.690	1.647	1.605
3	2.775	2.673	2.577	2.487	2.402	2.322	2.246
4	3.630	3.465	3.312	3.170	3.037	2.914	2.798
5	4.452	4.212	3.993	3.791	3.605	3.433	3.274
6	5.242	4.917	4.623	4.355	4.111	3.889	3.685
7	6.002	5.582	5.206	4.868	4.564	4.288	4.039
8	6.733	6.210	5.747	5.335	4.968	4.639	4.344
9	7.435	6.802	6.247	5.759	5.328	4.946	4.607
10	8.111	7.360	6.710	6.145	5.650	5.216	4.833

Appendix B-2 provides a more comprehensive table for the present value of an annuity of $1.

As shown in Table B, the present value factor for the rower investment, 14% and 7 periods, is 4.288, and the present value factor for the torso investment, 14% and 4 periods, is 2.914.

The present value of a project is equal to the present value factor multiplied by one period's cash flow.

The net present value is the present value less the cost of the investment, where the investment is made at time zero, or today at an interest factor of 1.0000, for a "present value" approach.

To calculate net present value for each product:

Rower:

PVCFI	$120,000 × 4.288 =	$ 514,560
PVCFO	$500,000 × 1.000 =	(500,000)
Net present value		= $ 14,560

Torso Machine:

PVCFI	$160,000 × 2.914 =	$ 466,240
PVCFO	$500,000 × 1.000 =	(500,000)
Net present value	=	$ (33,760)

The torso machine has a negative net present value and that should not be accepted. The rower has a positive net present value of $14,560. Because the net present value is positive the investment must be earning *more than* a 14% return.

If the net present value of a project is *zero*, the investment is earning exactly the amount desired, 14% in this case.

Requirement 4

Compute the internal rate of return for each project.

Part 1	Part 2	Part 3	**Part 4**	Demo Doc Complete

3 Use the time value of money to compute the present and future values of single lump sums and annuities

4 Use discounted cash flow models to make capital investment decisions

The internal rate of return (IRR) method calculates the estimated rate of return Better Body can expect to earn by investing in the project. The IRR uses the same concepts as the net present value. The net present value uses management's minimum desired rate of return to determine whether the present value of the future net cash inflows equals or exceeds the cost of the initial investment. If they are equal, it means that the project is earning exactly the minimum desired rate of return. If the amount is positive, the project is earning a rate of return in excess of the minimum, but it is unknown. The IRR method *calculates* the projected rate of return in the following way:

a. Identify the projected future cash flows (as is done with the net present value method).

b. Estimate the present value of an annuity factor as

$$\text{Annuity PV factor} = \frac{\text{Investment}}{\text{Expected annual net cash flow}}$$

c. Refer to the present value of an annuity table in Appendix B, Table B. Find the number of cash flow periods in the left column and follow that row to the right until you locate the factor that is closest to the present value of an annuity factor computed in part b. Follow that number up to the interest rate at the top of the column to determine the rate of return. *If the rate of return calculated is equal to or higher than management's minimum desired rate of return, the project is acceptable.*

To determine the internal rate of return, we must find the discount rate that makes the total present value of the cash inflows equal to the present value of the cash outflows. Work backward to find the discount rate that makes the present value of the annuity of cash inflows equal to the amount of the investment by solving the following equation for the annuity present value factor (which is, in reality, the figure obtained when calculating the payback period, as we did in requirement 1):

$$\text{Annuity PV factor for Rower} = \frac{\$500,000}{\$120,000}$$
$$= 4.17$$

$$\text{Annuity PV factor for Torso} = \frac{\$500,000}{\$160,000}$$
$$= 3.13$$

Look at Table B and scan the row corresponding to the project's expected life—period 7 for the rower, period 4 for the torso machine. Choose the column with the number closest to the annuity PV factor previously calculated. The 4.17 annuity factor for the rower is closest to 4.288, the 14% column and the 3.13 annuity factor for the torso machine is closest to 3.17, the 10% column. Therefore, the internal rate of return for the rower is approximately 14% and the internal rate of return for the torso machine is approximately 10%.

Part 1	Part 2	Part 3	Part 4	**Demo Doc Complete**

12 Performance Evaluation and the Balanced Scorecard

Learning Objectives/ Success Keys

1 Explain why and how companies decentralize

2 Explain why companies use performance evaluation systems

3 Describe the balanced scorecard and identify key performance indicators for each perspective

4 Use performance reports to evaluate cost, revenue, and profit centers

5 Use ROI, RI, and EVA to evaluate investment centers

To deliver over 3.6 billion packages a year in over 200 countries, **United Parcel Service (UPS)** employs over 370,000 people. But how does management successfully guide the actions of all of these employees? First, it divides—or decentralizes—the company into three segments: domestic packaging, international packaging, and non-packaging services (such as supply chain and logistics). It further breaks each packaging segment into geographic regions and each region into districts. Management gives each district manager authority to make decisions for his or her own district. Because top management wants *every* employee to know how his or her day-to-day job contributes to the company's goals, it implemented a system, called the balanced scorecard, for communicating strategy to all district managers and employees. Management can also use the balanced scorecard to measure whether each district is meeting its goals and to assess where it should make changes. According to one **UPS** executive, "The balanced scorecard provided a road map—the shared vision of our future goals—with action elements that let *everyone* contribute to our success." After reading this article, Smart Touch's CEO, Sheena Bright, wants to learn more about this managerial tool.

In 2000, *Forbes* named **UPS** the "Company of the Year" and in 2004, *Fortune* rated **UPS** as the "World's Most Admired Company in its Industry" for the sixth consecutive year.[1]

Many companies, like UPS, decentralize their operations into subunits. Decentralization provides large companies with many advantages. Because top management is not directly involved in running the day-to-day operations of each subunit, it needs a system—such as the balanced scorecard—for communicating the company's strategy to subunit managers and for measuring how well the subunits are achieving their goals. Let us first take a look at the advantages and disadvantages of decentralization.

Decentralized Operations

1 Explain why and how companies decentralize

In a small company, the owner or top manager often makes all planning and operating decisions. Small companies are most often considered to be **Centralized companies** because centralizing decision making is easier due to the smaller scope of their operations. However, when a company grows, it is impossible for a single person to manage the entire organization's daily operations. Therefore, most companies decentralize as they grow. These are called **decentralized companies.**

Companies decentralize by splitting their operations into different divisions or operating units. Top management delegates decision-making responsibility to the unit managers. Top management determines the type of decentralization that best suits the company's strategy. For example, decentralization may be based on geographic area, product line, customer base, business function, or some other business characteristic. **Citizen's Bank** segments its operations by state (different geographic areas). **Sherwin-Williams** segments by customer base (commercial and consumer paint divisions). **PepsiCo** segments by brands (**Pepsi, Frito-Lay, Quaker, Gatorade,** and **Tropicana**). And **UPS** segmented first by function (domestic packaging, international packaging, and nonpackaging services), then by geographic area. Smart Touch Learning thinks it will segment by product line (DVDs and Web-based learning).

Sources: Robert Kaplan and David Norton, *The Strategy-Focused Organization: How Balanced Scorecard Companies Thrive in the New Business Environment*, Harvard Business School Press, Boston, 2001, pp. 21–22, 239–241; UPS Web site.

Advantages of Decentralization

What advantages does decentralization offer large companies? Let us take a look.

Frees Top Management Time

By delegating responsibility for daily operations to unit managers, top management can concentrate on long-term strategic planning and higher-level decisions that affect the entire company. Decentralization also naturally places the decision makers (top management) closer to the source of the decisions.

Supports Use of Expert Knowledge

Decentralization allows top management to hire the expertise each business unit needs to excel in its own specific operations. For example, decentralizing by state allows **Citizens Bank** to hire managers with specialized knowledge of the banking laws in each state. Such specialized knowledge can help unit managers make better decisions, than could the company's top managers, about product and business improvements within the business unit (state).

Improves Customer Relations

Unit managers focus on just one segment of the company. Therefore, they can maintain closer contact with important customers than can upper management. Thus, decentralization often leads to improved customer relations and quicker customer response time.

Provides Training

Decentralization also provides unit managers with training and experience necessary to become effective top managers. For example, in politics, presidential candidates often have experience as senators or state governors. Likewise, companies often choose CEOs based on their past performance as division managers.

Improves Motivation and Retention

Empowering unit managers to make decisions increases managers' motivation and retention. This improves job performance and satisfaction.

Disadvantages of Decentralization

Despite its advantages, decentralization can also cause potential problems, including those outlined in this section.

Duplication of Costs

Decentralization may cause the company to duplicate certain costs or assets. For example, each business unit may hire its own payroll department and purchase its own payroll software. Companies can often avoid such duplications by providing centralized services. For example, **Doubletree Hotels** segments its business by property, yet each property shares one centralized reservations office and one centralized Web site.

Problems Achieving Goal Congruence

Goal congruence occurs when unit managers' goals align with top management's goals. Decentralized companies often struggle to achieve goal congruence. Unit managers may not fully understand the "big picture" of the company. They may make decisions that are good for their division but could harm another division or the rest of the company. For example, the purchasing department may buy cheaper components to decrease product cost. However, cheaper components may hurt the product line's quality, and the company's brand, *as a whole*, may suffer. Later in this chapter, we will see how managerial accountants can design performance evaluation systems that encourage goal congruence.

As Exhibit 12-1 illustrates, the many advantages of decentralization usually outweigh the disadvantages.

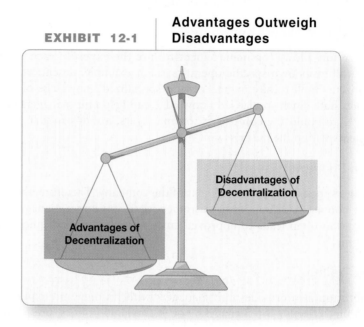

EXHIBIT 12-1 | **Advantages Outweigh Disadvantages**

Disadvantages of Decentralization

Advantages of Decentralization

Responsibility Centers

Decentralized companies delegate responsibility for specific decisions to each sub-unit, creating responsibility centers. Recall from Chapter 9 that a *responsibility center* is a part or subunit of an organization whose manager is accountable for specific activities. Exhibit 12-2 reviews the four most common types of responsibility centers.

EXHIBIT 12-2 | **The Four Most Common Types of Responsibility Centers**

Responsibility Center	Manager is responsible for...	Examples
Cost center	Controlling costs	Production line at Dell Computer; legal department and accounting departments at Nike
Revenue center	Generating sales revenue	Midwest sales region at Pace Foods; central reservation office at Delta
Profit center	Producing profit through generating sales and controlling costs	Product line at Anheuser-Busch; individual Home Depot stores
Investment center	Producing profit and managing the division's invested capital	Company divisions, such as Walt Disney World Resorts and Toon Disney

Performance Measurement

Once a company decentralizes operations, top management is no longer involved in running the subunits' day-to-day operations. Performance evaluation systems provide top management with a framework for maintaining control over the entire organization.

2 Explain why companies use performance evaluation systems

Goals of Performance Evaluation Systems

When companies decentralize, top management needs a system to communicate its goals to subunit managers. Additionally, top management needs to determine whether the decisions being made at the subunit level are effectively meeting company goals. We will now consider the primary goals of performance evaluation systems.

Promoting Goal Congruence and Coordination

As previously mentioned, decentralization increases the difficulty of achieving goal congruence. Unit managers may not always make decisions consistent with the overall goals of the organization. A company will be able to achieve its goals only if each unit moves, in a synchronized fashion, toward the overall company goals. The performance measurement system should provide incentives for coordinating the subunits' activities and direct them toward achieving the overall company goals.

Communicating Expectations

To make decisions that are consistent with the company's goals, unit managers must know the goals and the specific part their unit plays in attaining those goals. The performance measurement system should spell out the unit's most critical objectives. Without a clear picture of what management expects, unit managers have little to guide their daily operating decisions.

Motivating Unit Managers

Unit managers are usually motivated to make decisions that will help to achieve top management's expectations. For additional motivation, upper management may offer bonuses to unit managers who meet or exceed performance targets. Top management must exercise extreme care in setting performance targets. For example, a manager measured solely by his ability to control costs may take whatever actions are necessary to achieve that goal, including sacrificing quality or customer service. But such actions would *not* be in the best interests of the firm as a whole. Therefore, upper management must consider the ramifications of the performance targets it sets for unit managers.

Providing Feedback

In decentralized companies, top management is no longer involved in the day-to-day operations of each subunit. Performance evaluation systems provide upper management with the feedback it needs to maintain control over the entire organization, even though it has delegated responsibility and decision-making authority to unit managers. If targets are not met at the unit level, upper management will take corrective actions, ranging from modifying unit goals (if the targets were unrealistic) to replacing the unit manager (if the targets were achievable, but the manager failed to reach them).

Benchmarking

Performance evaluation results are often used for benchmarking, which is the practice of comparing the company's achievements against the best practices in the industry. Comparing results against industry benchmarks is often more revealing than comparing results against budgets. To survive, a company must keep up with its competitors. Benchmarking helps the company determine whether or not it is performing at least as well as its competitors.

Stop & Think...

Do companies, such as **UPS**, only benchmark subunit performance against competitors and industry standards?

Answer: No. Companies also benchmark performance against the subunit's past performance. Historical trend data (measuring performance over time) helps managers assess whether their decisions are improving, having no effect, or adversely affecting subunit performance. Some companies also benchmark performance against other subunits with similar characteristics.

Limitations of Financial Performance Measurement

In the past, performance measurement revolved almost entirely around *financial* performance. Until 1995, 95% of **UPS's** performance measures were financial. On the one hand, this focus makes sense because the ultimate goal of a company is to generate profit. On the other hand, *current* financial performance tends to reveal the results of *past* actions rather than indicate *future* performance. For this reason, financial measures tend to be **lag indicators** (after the fact), rather than **lead indicators** (future predictors). Management needs to know the results of past decisions, but it also needs to know how current decisions may affect the future. To adequately assess the company, managers need both lead indicators and lag indicators.

Another limitation of financial performance measures is that they tend to focus on the company's short-term achievements, rather than on long-term performance. Why is this the case? Because financial statements are prepared on a monthly, quarterly, or annual basis. To remain competitive, top management needs clear signals that assess and predict the company's performance over longer periods of time.

The Balanced Scorecard

3 Describe the balanced scorecard and identify key performance indicators for each perspective

In the early 1990s, Robert Kaplan and David Norton introduced the **balanced scorecard**.[2] The balanced scorecard recognizes that management must consider *both* financial performance measures (which tend to measure the results of actions already taken—lag indicators) and operational performance measures (which tend to drive future performance—lead indicators) when judging the performance of a company and its subunits. These measures should be linked with the company's goals and its strategy for achieving those goals. The balanced scorecard represents a major shift in corporate performance measurement. Rather than treating financial indicators as the sole measure of performance, companies recognize that they are only one measure among a broader set. Keeping score of operating measures *and* traditional financial measures gives management a "balanced" view of the organization.

---

[2]Robert Kaplan and David Norton, "The Balanced Scorecard—Measures That Drive Performance," *Harvard Business Review on Measuring Corporate Performance*, Boston, 1991, pp. 123–145; Robert Kaplan and David Norton, *Translating Strategy into Action: The Balanced Scorecard*, Boston, Harvard Business School Press, 1996.

Kaplan and Norton use the analogy of an airplane pilot to illustrate the necessity for a balanced scorecard approach to performance evaluation. The pilot of an airplane cannot rely on only one factor, such as wind speed, to fly a plane. Rather, the pilot must consider other critical factors, such as altitude, direction, and fuel level. Likewise, management cannot rely on only financial measures to guide the company. Management needs to consider other critical factors, such as customer satisfaction, operational efficiency, and employee excellence. Similar to the way a pilot uses cockpit instruments to measure critical factors, management uses *key performance indicators*—such as customer satisfaction ratings and revenue growth—to measure critical factors that affect the success of the company. As shown in Exhibit 12-3, **key performance indicators (KPIs)** are summary performance measures that help managers assess whether the company is achieving its goals.

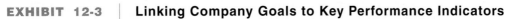

EXHIBIT 12-3 | **Linking Company Goals to Key Performance Indicators**

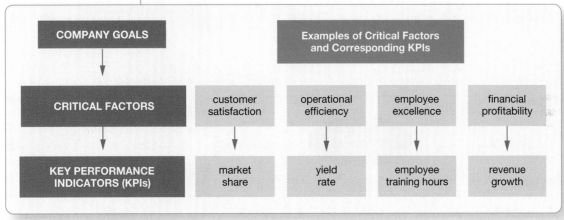

The Four Perspectives of the Balanced Scorecard

The balanced scorecard views the company from four different perspectives, each of which evaluates a specific aspect of organizational performance:

1. Financial perspective
2. Customer perspective
3. Internal business perspective
4. Learning and growth perspective

Exhibit 12-4 on the following page illustrates how the company's strategy affects, and, in turn, is affected by all four perspectives. Additionally, it shows the cause-and-effect relationship linking the four perspectives.

Companies that adopt the balanced scorecard usually have specific objectives they wish to achieve within each of the four perspectives. Once management clearly identifies the objectives, it develops KPIs that will assess how well the objectives are being achieved. To focus attention on the most critical elements and prevent information overload, management should use only a few KPIs for each perspective. Let us now look at each of the perspectives and discuss the links between them.

Financial Perspective

This perspective helps managers answer the question, "How do we look to shareholders?" The ultimate goal of companies is to generate income for their owners. Therefore, company strategy revolves around increasing the company's profits through increasing revenue growth and increasing productivity. Companies grow revenue through introducing new products, gaining new customers, and increasing

EXHIBIT 12-4 | **The Four Perspectives of the Balanced Scorecard**

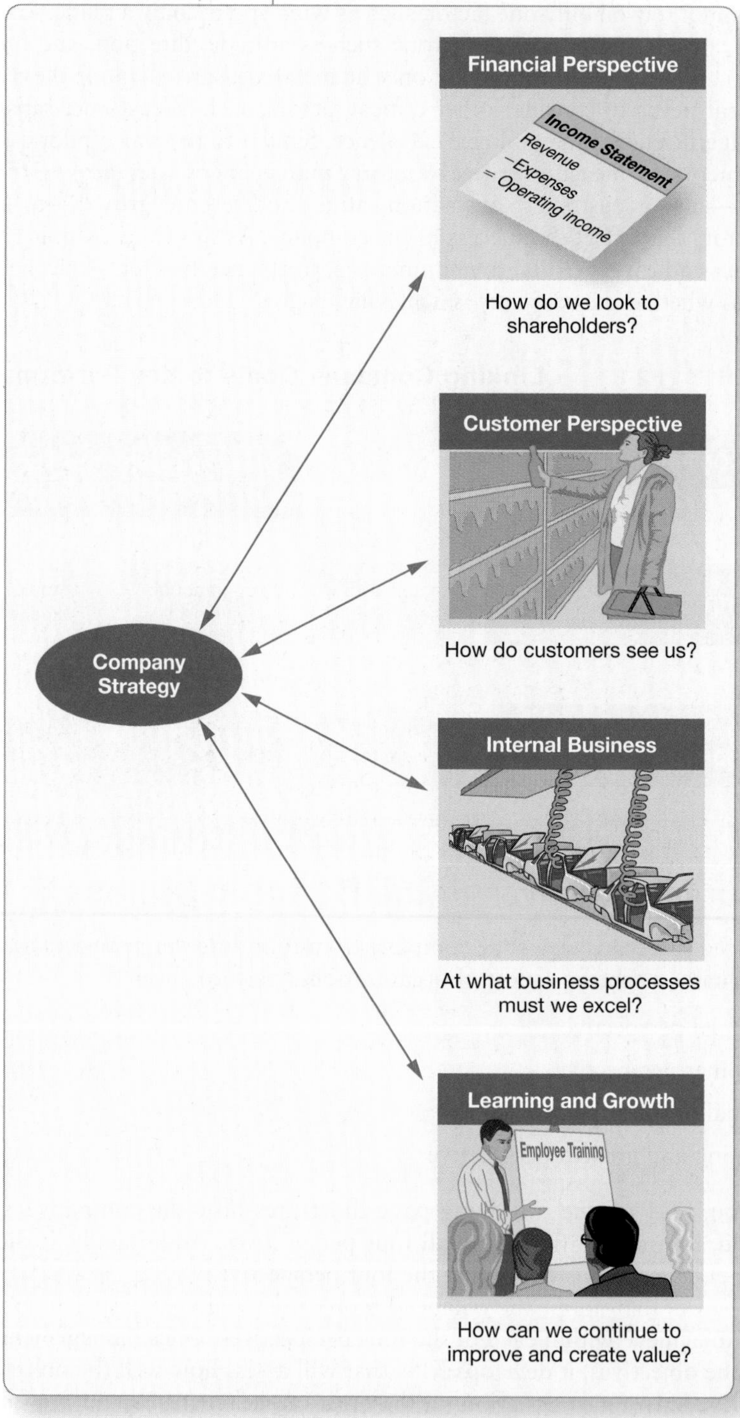

Financial Perspective

Income Statement
Revenue
−Expenses
= Operating income

How do we look to shareholders?

Customer Perspective

How do customers see us?

Company Strategy

Internal Business

At what business processes must we excel?

Learning and Growth

Employee Training

How can we continue to improve and create value?

sales to existing customers. Companies increase productivity through reducing costs and using the company's assets more efficiently. Managers may implement seemingly sensible strategies and initiatives, but the test of their judgment is whether these decisions increase company profits. The financial perspective focuses management's attention on KPIs that assess financial objectives, such as revenue growth and cost cutting. Some commonly used KPIs include: *sales revenue growth, gross margin growth,* and *return on investment.* The latter portion of this chapter discusses in detail the most commonly used financial perspective KPIs.

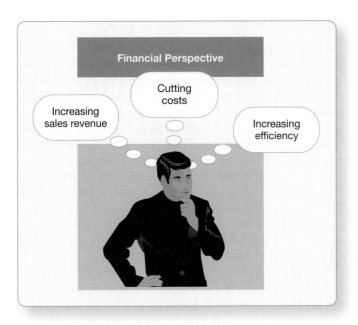

Customer Perspective

This perspective helps managers evaluate the question, "How do customers see us?" Customer satisfaction is a top priority for long-term company success. If customers are not happy, they will not come back. Therefore, customer satisfaction is critical to achieving the company's financial goals outlined in the financial perspective of the balanced scorecard. Customers are typically concerned with four specific product or service attributes: (1) the product's price, (2) the product's quality, (3) the sales service quality, and (4) the product's delivery time (the shorter the better). Since each of these attributes is critical to making the customer happy, most companies have specific objectives for each of these attributes.

Businesses commonly use KPIs, such as *customer satisfaction ratings*, to assess how they are performing on these attributes. No doubt you have filled out a customer satisfaction survey. Because customer satisfaction is crucial, customer satisfaction ratings often determine the extent to which bonuses are granted to restaurant managers. Other typical KPIs include *percentage of market share, increase in the number of customers, number of repeat customers*, and *rate of on-time deliveries*.

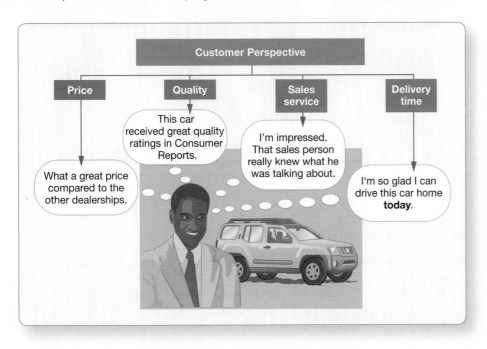

Internal Business Perspective

This perspective helps managers address the question, "At what business processes must we excel to satisfy customer and financial objectives?" The answer to this question incorporates three factors: innovation, operations, and post-sales service. All three factors critically affect customer satisfaction, which will affect the company's financial success.

Satisfying customers once does not guarantee future success, which is why the first important factor of the internal business perspective is innovation. Customers' needs and wants change as the world around them changes. Just a couple of years ago, digital cameras, flat-panel computer monitors, plasma screen televisions, and digital video recorders (DVRs) did not exist. Companies must continually improve existing products (such as adding cameras to cell phones) and develop new products (such as iPods and portable DVD players) to succeed in the future. Companies commonly assess innovation using KPIs, such as the *number of new products developed* or *new-product development time*.

The second important factor of the internal business perspective is operations. Efficient and effective internal operations allow the company to meet customers' needs and expectations. For example, the time it takes to manufacture a product (*manufacturing cycle time*) affects the company's ability to deliver quickly to meet a customer's demand. Production efficiency (*number of units produced per hour*) and product quality (*defect rate*) also affect the price charged to the customer. To remain competitive, companies must be at least as good as the industry leader at those internal operations that are essential to their business.

The third factor of the internal business perspective is post-sales service. How well does the company service customers after the sale? Claims of excellent post-sales service help to generate more sales. Management assesses post-sales service through the following typical KPIs: *number of warranty claims received, average repair time*, and *average wait time on the phone for a customer service representative*.

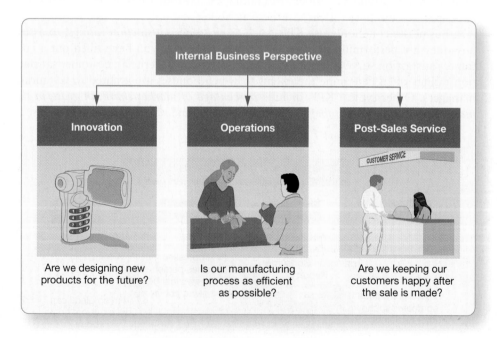

Learning and Growth Perspective

This perspective helps managers assess the question, "How can we continue to improve and create value?" The learning and growth perspective focuses on three factors: (1) employee capabilities, (2) information system capabilities, and (3) the company's "climate for action." The learning and growth perspective lays the foundation needed to improve internal business operations, sustain customer satisfaction, and generate financial success. Without skilled employees, updated technology, and a positive corporate culture, the company will not be able to meet the objectives of the other perspectives.

Let us consider each of these factors. First, because most routine work is automated, employees are freed up to be critical and creative thinkers who, therefore, can help achieve the company's goals. The learning and growth perspective measures employees' skills, knowledge, motivation, and empowerment. KPIs typically include *hours of employee training*, *employee satisfaction*, *employee turnover*, and *number of employee suggestions implemented*. Second, employees need timely and accurate information on customers, internal processes, and finances; therefore, other KPIs measure the maintenance and improvement of the company's information system. For example, KPIs might include the *percentage of employees having online access to information about customers*, and the *percentage of processes with real-time feedback on quality, cycle time, and cost*. Finally, management must create a corporate culture that supports communication, change, and growth. For example, **UPS** used the balanced scorecard to communicate strategy to every employee and to show each employee how his or her daily work contributed to company success.

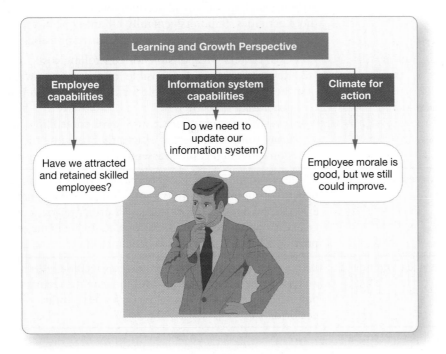

In summary, the balanced scorecard focuses performance measurement on progress toward the company's goals in each of the four perspectives. In designing the scorecard, managers start with the company's goals and its strategy for achieving those goals and then identify the *most* important measures of performance that will predict long-term success. Some of these measures are operational lead indicators, while others are financial lag indicators. Managers must consider the linkages between strategy and operations and how those operations will affect finances now and in the future.

So far, we have looked at why companies decentralize, why they need to measure subunit performance, and how the balanced scorecard can help. In the second half of the chapter, we will focus on how companies measure the financial perspective of the balanced scorecard.

Decision Guidelines

UPS had to make the following types of decisions when it decentralized and developed its balanced scorecard for performance evaluation.

Decision	Guidelines
• On what basis should the company be decentralized?	The manner of decentralization should fit the company's strategy. Many companies decentralize based on geographic region, product line, business function, or customer type.
• Will decentralization have any negative impact on the company?	Decentralization usually provides many benefits; however, decentralization also has potential drawbacks: • Subunits may duplicate costs or assets. • Subunit managers may not make decisions that are favorable to the entire company.
• How can responsibility accounting be incorporated at decentralized companies?	Subunit managers are given responsibility for specific activities and are only held accountable for the results of those activities. Subunits generally fall into one of the following four categories according to their responsibilities: 1. Cost centers—responsible for controlling costs 2. Revenue centers—responsible for generating revenue 3. Profit centers—responsible for controlling costs and generating revenue 4. Investment centers—responsible for controlling costs, generating revenue, and efficiently managing the division's invested capital (assets)
• Is a performance evaluation system necessary?	While not mandatory, most companies will reap many benefits from implementing a well-designed performance evaluation system. Such systems will promote goal congruence, communicate expectations, motivate managers, provide feedback, and enable benchmarking.
• Should the performance evaluation system include lag or lead measures?	Better performance evaluation systems include *both* lag and lead measures. Lag measures indicate the results of past actions, while lead measures a project's future performance.
• What are the four balanced scorecard perspectives?	1. Financial perspective 2. Customer perspective 3. Internal Business perspective 4. Learning and Growth perspective
• Must all four perspectives be included in the company's balanced scorecard?	Every company's balanced scorecard will be unique to its business and strategy. Because each of the four perspectives is causally linked, most companies will benefit from developing performance measures for each of the four perspectives.

Summary Problem 1

The balanced scorecard gives performance perspective from four different viewpoints.

Requirements

1. Each of the following describes a key performance indicator. Determine which of the following balanced scorecard perspectives is being addressed (financial, customer, internal business, or learning and growth):
   a. Employee turnover
   b. Earnings per share
   c. Percentage of on-time deliveries
   d. Revenue growth rate
   e. Percentage of defects discovered during manufacturing
   f. Number of warranties claimed
   g. New product development time
   h. **Number of repeat customers**
   i. **Number of employee suggestions implemented**

2. Read the following company initiatives and determine which of the balanced scorecard perspectives is being addressed (financial, customer, internal business, learning and growth):
   a. Purchasing efficient production equipment
   b. Providing employee training
   c. Updating retail store lighting
   d. Paying quarterly dividends
   e. Updating the company's information system

Solution

Requirement 1
   a. Learning and growth
   b. Financial
   c. Customer
   d. Financial
   e. Internal business
   f. Internal business
   g. Internal business
   h. Customer
   i. Learning and growth

Requirement 2
   a. Internal business
   b. Learning and growth
   c. Customer
   d. Financial
   e. Learning and growth

Measuring the Financial Performance of Cost, Revenue, and Profit Centers

4 Use performance reports to evaluate cost, revenue, and profit centers

In this half of the chapter we will take a more detailed look at how companies measure the financial perspective of the balanced scorecard for different subunits of the company. We will focus now on the financial performance measurement of each type of responsibility center.

Responsibility accounting performance reports capture the financial performance of cost, revenue, and profit centers. Recall from Chapter 7 that responsibility accounting performance reports compare *actual* results with *budgeted* amounts and display a variance, or difference, between the two amounts. Because *cost centers* are only responsible for controlling costs, their performance reports only include information on actual versus budgeted *costs*. Likewise, performance reports for *revenue centers* only contain actual versus budgeted *revenue*. However, *profit centers* are responsible for both controlling costs and generating revenue. Therefore, their performance reports contain actual and budgeted information on both their *revenues and costs*.

Cost center performance reports typically focus on the *flexible budget variance*—the difference between actual results and the flexible budget (as described in Chapter 8). Exhibit 12-5 shows an example of a cost center performance report for a regional payroll processing department of Smart Touch Learning. Because the payroll processing department only incurs expenses and does not generate revenue, it is classified as a cost center.

EXHIBIT 12-5 | **Example of Cost Center Performance Report**

	Actual	Flexible Budget	Flexible Budget Variance (U or F)	% Variance* (U of F)
SMART TOUCH LEARNING, INC.				
Payroll Processing Department Performance Report				
July 2012				
Salary and wages	$18,500	$18,000	$ 500 U	2.8% U
Payroll benefits	6,100	5,000	1,100 U	22.0% U
Equipment depreciation	3,000	3,000	0	0%
Supplies	1,850	2,000	150 F	7.5% F
Other expenses	1,900	2,000	100 F	5.0% F
Total expenses	$31,350	$30,000	$1,350 U	4.5% U

*Flexible budget variance/flexible budget

Managers use management by exception to determine which variances in the performance report are worth investigating. For example, management may only investigate variances that exceed a certain dollar amount (for example, over $1,000) or a certain percentage of the budgeted figure (for example, over 10%). Smaller variances signal that operations are close to target and do not require management's immediate attention. For example, in the cost center performance report illustrated in Exhibit 12-5, management might only investigate "payroll benefits" because the variance exceeds both $1,000 and 10%. Companies that use standard costs can compute price and efficiency variances, as described in Chapter 8, to better understand why significant flexible budget variances occurred.

Revenue center performance reports often highlight both the flexible budget variance and the sales volume variance. The performance report for the specialty DVD department of Smart Touch Learning might look similar to Exhibit 12-6, with detailed sales volume and revenue shown for each brand and type of DVD sold. (For simplicity, the exhibit shows volume and revenue for only one item.) The cash register barcoding system provides management with the sales volume and sales revenue generated by individual products.

EXHIBIT 12-6 | **Example of a Revenue Center Performance Report**

SMART TOUCH LEARNING, INC.
Specialty DVD Department Performance Report
July 2012

Sales revenue	Actual Sales	Flexible Budget Variance	Flexible Budget	Sales Volume Variance	Static (Master) Budget
Number of DVDs	2,480	–0–	2,480	155 (F)	2,325
Specialty DVDs	$40,920	$3,720 (U)	$44,640	$2,790 (F)	$41,850

Recall from Chapter 8 that the sales volume variance is due strictly to volume differences—selling more or fewer units (DVDs) than originally planned. The flexible budget variance, however, is due strictly to differences in the sales price—selling units for a higher or lower price than originally planned. Both the sales volume variance and the flexible budget variance help revenue center managers understand why they have exceeded or fallen short of budgeted revenue.

Managers of profit centers are responsible for both generating revenue and controlling costs so their performance reports include both revenues and expenses. Exhibit 12-7 shows an example of a profit center performance report for the DVD department.

EXHIBIT 12-7 | **Example of a Profit Center Performance Report**

SMART TOUCH LEARNING, INC.
DVD—Performance Report
July 2012

	Actual	Flexible Budget	Flexible Budget Variance	% Variance
Sales revenue	$5,243,600	$5,000,000	$243,600 F	4.9% F
Operating expenses	4,183,500	4,000,000	183,500 U	4.6% U
Income from operations before service				
department charges	1,060,100	1,000,000	60,100 F	6.0% F
Service department charges (allocated)	84,300	75,000	9,300 U	12.4% U
Income from operations	$ 975,800	$ 925,000	$ 50,800 F	5.5% F

Notice how this profit center performance report contains a line called "Service department charges." Recall that one drawback of decentralization is that subunits may duplicate costs or assets. Many companies avoid this problem by providing centralized service departments where several subunits, such as profit centers, share assets or costs. For example, the payroll processing cost center shown in Exhibit 12-5 serves all of Smart Touch Learning. In addition to centralized payroll departments, companies often provide centralized human resource departments, legal departments, and information systems.

When subunits share centralized services, should those services be "free" to the subunits? If they are free, the subunit's performance report will *not* include any charge for using those services. However, if they are not free, the performance report will show a charge, as you see in Exhibit 12-7. Most companies charge subunits for their use of centralized services because the subunit would incur a cost to buy those services on its own. For example, if Smart Touch Learning did not operate a centralized payroll department, the DVD Department would have to hire its own payroll department personnel and purchase computers, payroll software, and supplies necessary to process the department's payroll. As an alternative, it could outsource payroll to a company, such as **Paychex** or **ADP**. In either event, the department would incur a cost for processing payroll. It only seems fair that the department is charged for using the centralized payroll processing department. Chapter 10 describes how companies allocate service department costs between subunits. Because the charges are the result of allocation, rather than a direct cost of the profit center, they are usually shown on a separate line rather than "buried" in the subunit's other operating expenses.

Regardless of the type of responsibility center, performance reports should focus on information, not blame. Analyzing budget variances helps managers understand the underlying *reasons* for the unit's performance. Once management understands these reasons, it may be able to take corrective actions. But some variances are uncontrollable. For example, the 2005 hurricanes in the Gulf Coast increased prices of gasoline (due to damaged oil refineries) and building materials (as people repaired hurricane-damaged homes). These price increases resulted in unfavorable cost variances for many companies. Managers should not be held accountable for conditions they cannot control. Responsibility accounting can help management identify the causes of variances, thereby allowing them to determine what was controllable, and what was not.

We have just looked at the detailed financial information presented in responsibility accounting performance reports. In addition to these *detailed* reports, upper management often uses *summary* measures—financial KPIs—to assess the financial performance of cost, revenue, and profit centers. Examples include the *cost per unit of output* (for cost centers), *revenue growth* (for revenue centers), and *gross margin growth* (for profit centers). KPIs, such as these, are used to address the financial perspective of the balanced scorecard for cost, revenue, and profit centers. In the next section we will look at the most commonly used KPIs for investment centers.

Stop & Think...

We have just seen that companies like Smart Touch Learning use responsibility accounting performance reports to evaluate the financial performance of cost, revenue, and profit centers. Are these types of responsibility reports sufficient for evaluating the financial performance of investment centers? Why or why not?

Answer: Investment centers are responsible not only for generating revenue and controlling costs, but also for efficiently managing the subunit's invested capital. The performance reports we have just seen address how well the subunits control costs and generate revenue, but they do not address how well the subunits manage their assets. Therefore, these performance reports will be helpful but not sufficient for evaluating investment center performance.

Measuring the Financial Performance of Investment Centers

Investment centers are typically large divisions of a company, such as the media division of **Amazon.com** or of Smart Touch Learning. The duties of an investment center manager are similar to those of a CEO. The CEO is responsible for maximizing income, in relation to the company's invested capital, by using company assets efficiently. Likewise, investment center managers are responsible not only for generating profit but also for making the best use of the investment center's assets.

How does an investment center manager influence the use of the division's assets? An investment center manager has the authority to open new stores or close old stores. The manager may also decide how much inventory to hold, what types of investments to make, how aggressively to collect accounts receivable, and whether to invest in new equipment. In other words, the manager has decision-making responsibility over all of the division's assets.

Companies cannot evaluate investment centers the way they evaluate profit centers, based only on operating income. Why? Because income does not indicate how *efficiently* the division is using its assets. The financial evaluation of investment centers must measure two factors: (1) how much income the division is generating and (2) how efficiently the division is using its assets.

Consider Smart Touch Learning. In addition to its DVD Division, it also has an online e-learning Division. Operating income, total assets, and sales for the two divisions follow (in thousands of dollars):

Smart Touch Learning	e-learning	DVD
Operating income	$ 450,000	$ 975,800
Total assets	2,500,000	6,500,000
Sales	7,500,000	5,243,600

Based on operating income alone, the DVD Division (with operating income of $975,800) appears to be more profitable than the e-learning Division (with operating income of $450,000). However, this comparison is misleading because it does not consider the assets invested in each division. The DVD Division has more assets to use for generating income than does the e-learning Division.

To adequately evaluate an investment center's financial performance, companies need summary performance measures—or KPIs—that include *both* the division's operating income *and* its assets. (See Exhibit 12-8 on the following page.) In the next sections, we discuss three commonly used performance measures: return on investment (ROI), residual income (RI), and economic value added (EVA). All three measures incorporate both the division's assets and its operating income. For simplicity, we will leave the word *divisional* out of the equations. However, keep in mind that all of the equations use divisional data when evaluating a division's performance.

5   Use ROI, RI, and EVA to evaluate investment centers

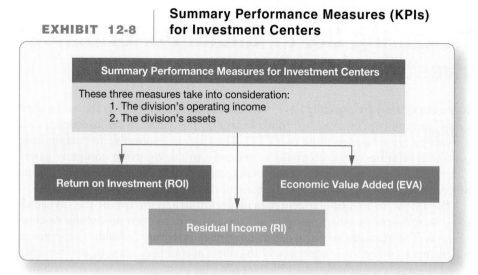

EXHIBIT 12-8 | **Summary Performance Measures (KPIs) for Investment Centers**

Return on Investment (ROI)

Return on Investment (ROI) is one of the most commonly used KPIs for evaluating an investment center's financial performance. Companies typically define ROI as follows:

$$\text{ROI} = \frac{\text{Operating income}}{\text{Total assets}}$$

ROI measures the amount of income an investment center earns relative to the amount of its assets. Let us calculate each division's ROI:

$$\text{e-learning Division ROI} = \frac{\$450,000}{\$2,500,000} = 18\%$$

$$\text{DVD Division ROI} = \frac{975,800}{\$6,500,000} = 15\%$$

Although the DVD Division has a higher operating income than the e-learning Division, the DVD Division is actually *less* profitable than the e-learning Division when we consider that the DVD Division has more assets from which to generate its profit.

If you had $1,000 to invest, would you rather invest it in the DVD Division or the e-learning Division? The DVD Division earns a profit of $0.15 on every $1.00 of assets, but the e-learning Division earns $0.18 on every $1.00 of assets. When top management decides how to invest excess funds, it often considers each division's ROI. A division with a higher ROI is more likely to receive extra funds because it has a history of providing a higher return.

In addition to comparing ROI across divisions, management also compares a division's ROI across time to determine whether the division is becoming more or less profitable in relation to its assets. Additionally, management often benchmarks divisional ROI with other companies in the same industry to determine how each division is performing compared to its competitors.

To determine what is driving a division's ROI, management often restates the ROI equation in its expanded form. Notice that Sales is incorporated in the denominator of the first term, and in the numerator of the second term. When the two terms are multiplied together, Sales cancels out, leaving the original ROI formula.

$$\text{ROI} = \frac{\text{Operating income}}{\text{Sales}} \times \frac{\text{Sales}}{\text{Total assets}} = \frac{\text{Operating income}}{\text{Total assets}}$$

Why do managers rewrite the ROI formula this way? Because it helps them better understand how they can improve their ROI. The first term in the expanded equation is called the **profit margin**:

$$\text{Profit margin} = \frac{\text{Operating income}}{\text{Sales}}$$

The profit margin shows how much operating income the division earns on every $1.00 of sales, so this term focuses on profitability. Let us calculate each division's sales margin:

$$\text{e-learning Division's profit margin} = \frac{\$450,000}{\$7,500,000} = 6\%$$

$$\text{DVD Division's profit margin} = \frac{\$975,800}{\$5,243,600} = 19\%$$

The e-learning Division has a profit margin of 6%, meaning that it earns a profit of $0.06 on every $1.00 of sales. The DVD Division, however, is much more profitable with a profit margin of 19%, earning $0.19 on every $1.00 of sales.

Capital turnover is the second term of the expanded ROI equation:

$$\text{Capital turnover} = \frac{\text{Sales}}{\text{Total assets}}$$

Capital turnover shows how efficiently a division uses its assets to generate sales. Rather than focusing on profitability, capital turnover focuses on efficiency. Let us calculate each division's capital turnover:

$$\text{e-learning Division's capital turnover} = \frac{\$7,500,000}{\$2,500,000} = 3$$

$$\text{DVD Division's capital turnover} = \frac{\$5,243,600}{\$6,500,000} = 0.80$$

The e-learning Division has a capital turnover of 3. This means that the e-learning Division generates $3.00 of sales with every $1.00 of assets. The DVD Division's capital turnover is only 0.80. The DVD Division generates only $0.80 of sales with every $1.00 of assets. The e-learning Division uses its assets much more efficiently in generating sales than the DVD Division.

Let us put the two terms back together in the expanded ROI equation:

	Profit margin	×	Capital turnover	= ROI
e-learning Division:	6%	×	3	= 18%
DVD Division:	19%	×	0.80	= 15%

As you can see, the expanded ROI equation gives management more insight into the division's ROI. Management can now see that the DVD is more profitable on its sales (19%) than the e-learning Division, but the e-learning Division is doing a better job of generating sales with its assets (capital turnover of 3) than the DVD Division (capital turnover of 0.80). Consequently, the e-learning Division has a higher ROI of 18%.

If a manager is not satisfied with his or her division's capital turnover rate, how can he or she improve it? He or she might try to eliminate nonproductive assets, for example, by being more aggressive in collecting accounts receivables or decreasing inventory levels. He or she might decide to change retail-store layout to generate sales.

What if management is not satisfied with the current profit margin? To increase the profit margin, management must increase the operating income earned on every dollar of sales. Management may cut product costs or selling and administrative costs, but it needs to be careful when trimming costs. Cutting costs in the short term can hurt long-term ROI. For example, sacrificing quality or cutting back on research and development could decrease costs in the short run, but may hurt long-term sales. The balanced scorecard helps management carefully consider the consequences of cost-cutting measures before acting on them.

ROI has one major drawback. Evaluating division managers based solely on ROI gives them an incentive to adopt *only* projects that will maintain or increase their current ROI. Let us say that top management has set a company-wide target ROI of 16%. Both divisions are considering investing in in-store video display equipment that shows customers how to use featured products. This equipment will increase sales because customers are more likely to buy the products when they see these infomercials. The equipment would cost each division $100,000 and is expected to provide each division with $17,000 of annual income. The *equipment's* ROI is as follows:

$$\text{Equipment ROI} = \frac{\$17,000}{\$100,000} = 17\%$$

Upper management would want the divisions to invest in this equipment since the equipment will provide a 17% ROI, which is higher than the 16% target rate. But what will the managers of the divisions do? Because the DVD Division currently has an ROI of 15%, the new equipment (with its 17% ROI) will *increase* the division's *overall* ROI. Therefore, the DVD Division manager will buy the equipment. However, the e-learning Division currently has an ROI of 18%. If the e-learning Division invests in the equipment, its *overall* ROI will *decrease*. Therefore, the manager of the e-learning Division will probably turn down the investment. In this case, goal congruence is *not* achieved—only one division will invest in equipment. Yet top management wants both divisions to invest in the equipment because the equipment return exceeds the 16% target ROI. Next, we discuss a performance measure that overcomes this problem with ROI.

Residual Income (RI)

Residual income (RI) is another commonly used KPI for evaluating an investment center's financial performance. Similar to ROI, RI considers both the division's operating income and its total assets. RI measures the division's profitability and the efficiency with which the division uses its assets. RI also incorporates another piece of information: top management's target rate of return (such as the 16% target return in the previous example). The target rate of return is the minimum acceptable rate of return that top management expects a division to earn with its assets.

RI compares the division's operating income with the minimum operating income expected by top management *given the size of the division's assets*. A positive RI means that the division's operating income exceeds top management's target rate of return. A negative RI means the division is not meeting the target rate of return. Let us look at the RI equation and then calculate the RI for both divisions using the 16% target rate of return from the previous example.

$$RI = \text{Operating income} - \text{Minimum acceptable income}$$

In this equation, the minimum acceptable income is defined as top management's target rate of return multiplied by the division's total assets. Therefore,

$$RI = \text{Operating income} - (\text{Target rate of return} \times \text{Total assets})$$

$$
\begin{aligned}
\text{e-learning Division RI} &= \$450,000 - (16\% \times \$2,500,000) \\
&= \$450,000 - \$400,000 \\
&= \$50,000
\end{aligned}
$$

The positive RI indicates that the e-learning Division exceeded top management's 16% target return expectations. The RI calculation also confirms what we learned about the e-learning Division's ROI. Recall that the e-learning Division's ROI was 18%, which is higher than the targeted 16%.

Let us also calculate the RI for the DVD Division:

$$
\begin{aligned}
\text{DVD Division RI} &= \$975,800 - (16\% \times \$6,500,000) \\
&= \$975,800 - \$1,040,000 \\
&= \$(64,200)
\end{aligned}
$$

The DVD Division's RI is negative. This means that the DVD Division did not use its assets as effectively as top management expected. Recall that the DVD Division's ROI of 15% fell short of the target rate of 16%.

Why would a company prefer to use RI over ROI for performance evaluation? The answer is that RI is more likely to lead to goal congruence than ROI. Let us once again consider the video display equipment that both divisions could buy. In both divisions, the equipment is expected to generate a 17% return. If the divisions are evaluated based on ROI, we learned that the DVD Division will buy the equipment because it will increase the division's ROI. The e-learning Division, on the other hand, will probably not buy the equipment because it will lower the division's ROI.

However, if management evaluates divisions based on RI rather than ROI, what will the divisions do? The answer depends on whether the project yields a positive or negative RI. Recall that the equipment would cost each division $100,000, but will provide $17,000 of operating income each year. The RI provided by *just* the equipment would be as follows:

$$\text{Equipment RI} = \$17,000 - (\$100,000 \times 16\%)$$
$$= \$17,000 - \$16,000$$
$$= \$1,000$$

If purchased, this equipment will *improve* each division's current RI by $1,000. As a result, both divisions will be motivated to invest in the equipment. Goal congruence is achieved because both divisions will take the action that top management desires. That is, both divisions will invest in the equipment.

Another benefit of RI is that management may set different target returns for different divisions. For example, management might require a higher target rate of return from a division operating in a riskier business environment. If the DVD industry were riskier than the e-learning industry, top management might decide to set a higher target return—perhaps 17%—for the DVD Division.

Economic Value Added (EVA)

Economic Value Added (EVA) is a special type of RI calculation. Unlike the RI calculation we have just discussed, EVA looks at a division's RI through the eyes of the company's primary stakeholders: its investors and long-term creditors (such as bondholders). Since these stakeholders provide the company's capital, management often wishes to evaluate how efficiently a division is using its assets from these two stakeholders' viewpoints. EVA calculates RI for these stakeholders by specifically considering the following:

1. The income available to these stakeholders

2. The assets used to generate income for these stakeholders

3. The minimum rate of return required by these stakeholders (referred to as the **weighted average cost of capital**, or WACC)

Let us compare the EVA equation with the RI equation and then explain the differences in more detail:

RI = Operating income   – (Total assets   × Target rate of return)
EVA = After-tax operating income – [(Total assets – Current liabilities) × WACC%]

Both equations calculate whether any income was created by the division above and beyond expectations. They do this by comparing actual income with the minimum acceptable income. But note the differences in the EVA calculation:

1. The EVA calculation uses *after-tax operating income*, which is the income left over after subtracting income taxes. Why? Because the portion of income paid to the government is not available to investors and long-term creditors.

2. *Total assets is reduced by current liabilities.* Why? Because funds owed to short-term creditors, such as suppliers (accounts payable) and employees (wages payable), will be paid in the immediate future and will not be available for generating income in the long run. The division is not expected to earn a

return for investors and long-term creditors on those funds that will soon be paid out to short-term creditors.

3. The *WACC* replaces management's target rate of return. Since EVA focuses on investors and creditors, it is *their* expected rate of return that should be used, not management's expected rate of return. The WACC, which represents the minimum rate of return expected by *investors and long-term creditors*, is based on the company's cost of raising capital from both groups of stakeholders. The riskier the business, the higher the expected return. Detailed WACC computations are discussed in advanced accounting and finance courses.

In summary, EVA incorporates all the elements of RI from the perspective of investors and long-term creditors. Now that we have walked through the equation's components, let us calculate EVA for the e-learning and DVD Divisions discussed earlier. We will need the following additional information:

Effective income tax rate	30%
WACC	13%
e-learning Division's current liabilities	$150,000
DVD Division's current liabilities	$250,000

The 30% effective income tax rate means that the government takes 30% of the company's income, leaving only 70% to the company's stakeholders. Therefore, we calculate *after-tax operating income* by multiplying the division's operating income by 70% (100% – effective tax rate of 30%).

EVA = After-tax operating income – [(Total assets – Current liabilities) × WACC%]

e-learning Division EVA = ($450,000 × 70%) – [($2,500,000 – $150,000) × 13%]
= $315,000 – ($2,350,000 × 13%)
= $315,000 – $305,500
= $9,500

DVD Division EVA = ($975,800 × 70%) – [($6,500,000 – 250,000) × 13%]
= $683,060 – ($6,250,000 × 13%)
= $683,060 – $812,500
= $(129,440)

These EVA calculations show that the e-learning Division has generated income in excess of expectations for its investors and long-term debt-holders, whereas the DVD Division has not.

Many firms, such as **Coca-Cola, Amazon.com,** and **J.C. Penney,** measure the financial performance of their investment centers using EVA. EVA promotes goal congruence, just as RI does. Additionally, EVA looks at the income generated by the division in excess of expectations, solely from the perspective of investors and long-term creditors. Therefore, EVA specifically addresses the financial perspective of the balanced scorecard that asks, "How do we look to shareholders?"

Exhibit 12-9 on the following page summarizes the three performance measures and some of their advantages.

EXHIBIT 12-9 | **Three Investment Center Performance Measures: A Summary**

	ROI:
Equation	$$ROI = \frac{Operating\ income}{Sales} \times \frac{Sales}{Total\ assets} = \frac{Operating\ income}{Total\ assets}$$
Advantages	• The expanded equation provides management with additional information on profitability and efficiency • Management can compare ROI across divisions and with other companies • ROI is useful for resource allocation

	RI:
Equation	RI = Operating income − (Total assets × Target rate of return)
Advantages	• Promotes goal congruence better than ROI • Incorporates management's minimum required rate of return • Management can use different target rates of return for divisions with different levels of risk

	EVA:
Equation	EVA = (After-tax operating income) − [(Total assets − Current liabilities) × WACC%]
Advantages	• Considers income generated for investors and long-term creditors in excess of their expectations • Promotes goal congruence

Limitations of Financial Performance Measures

We have just finished looking at three KPIs (ROI, RI, and EVA) commonly used to evaluate the financial performance of investment centers. As discussed in the following sections, all of these measures have drawbacks that management should keep in mind when evaluating the financial performance of investment centers.

Measurement Issues

The ROI, RI, and EVA calculations appear to be very straightforward; however, management must make some decisions before these calculations can be made. For example, all three equations use the term *total assets*. Recall that total assets is a balance sheet figure, which means that it is a snapshot at any given point in time. Because the total assets figure will be *different* at the beginning of the period and at the end of the period, most companies choose to use a simple average of the two figures in their ROI, RI, and EVA calculations.

Management must also decide if it really wants to include *all* assets in the total asset figure. Many firms, such as **Wal-mart,** are continually buying land on which to build future retail outlets. Until those stores are built and opened, the land (including any construction in progress) is a nonproductive asset, which is not adding to the company's operating income. Including nonproductive assets in the total asset figure will naturally drive down the ROI, RI, and EVA figures. Therefore, some firms will not include nonproductive assets in these calculations.

Another asset measurement issue is whether to use the gross book value of assets (the historical cost of the assets), or the net book value of assets (historical cost less accumulated depreciation). Many firms will use the net book value of assets because the figure is consistent with and easily pulled from the balance sheet. Because depreciation expense factors into the firm's operating income, the net book value concept is also consistent with the measurement of operating income. However, using the net book value of assets has a definite drawback. Over time, the net book value of assets decreases because accumulated depreciation continues to grow until the assets are fully depreciated. Therefore, ROI, RI, and EVA get *larger* over time *simply because of depreciation* rather than from actual improvements in operations. In addition, the rate of this depreciation effect will depend on the depreciation method used.

In general, calculating ROI based on the net book value of assets gives managers incentive to continue using old, outdated equipment because its low net book value results in a higher ROI. However, top management may want the division to invest in new technology to create operational efficiency (internal business perspective of the balanced scorecard) or to enhance its information systems (learning and growth perspective). The long-term effects of using outdated equipment may be devastating, as competitors use new technology to produce and sell at lower cost. Therefore, to create *goal congruence*, some firms prefer calculating ROI based on the gross book value of assets. The same general rule holds true for RI and EVA calculations: All else being equal, using net book value will increase RI and EVA over time.

Short-Term Focus

One serious drawback of financial performance measures is their short-term focus. Companies usually prepare performance reports and calculate ROI, RI, and EVA figures over a one-year time frame or less. If upper management uses a short time frame, division managers have an incentive to take actions that will lead to an immediate increase in these measures, even if such actions may not be in the company's long-term interest (such as cutting back on R&D or advertising). On the other hand, some potentially positive actions considered by subunit managers may take longer than one year to generate income at the targeted level. Many product life cycles start slow, even incurring losses in the early stages, before generating profit. If managers are measured on short-term financial performance only, they may not introduce new products because they are not willing to wait several years for the positive effect to show up in their financial performance measures.

As a potential remedy, management can measure financial performance using a longer time horizon, such as three to five years. Extending the time frame gives subunit managers the incentive to think long term rather than short term and make decisions that will positively impact the company over the next several years.

The limitations of financial performance measures confirm the importance of the balanced scorecard. The deficiencies of financial measures can be overcome by taking a broader view of performance—including KPIs from all four balanced scorecard perspectives rather than concentrating on only the financial measures.

Decision Guidelines

When managers at **UPS** developed the financial perspective of their balanced scorecard, they had to make decisions such as the examples that follow.

Decision	Guidelines
• How should the financial section of the balanced scorecard be measured for cost, revenue, and profit centers?	Responsibility accounting performance reports measure the financial performance of cost, revenue, and profit centers. These reports typically highlight the variances between budgeted and actual performance.
• How should the financial section of the balanced scorecard be measured for investment centers?	Investment centers require measures that take into account the division's operating income *and* the division's assets. Typical measures include the following: • Return on investment (ROI) • Residual income (RI) • Economic value added (EVA)
• How is ROI computed and interpreted?	$$\text{ROI} = \text{Operating income} \div \text{Total assets}$$ ROI measures the amount of income earned by a division relative to the size of its assets—the higher, the better.
• Can managers learn more by writing the ROI formula in its expanded form?	In its expanded form, ROI is written as follows: $$\text{ROI} = \text{Profit margin} \times \text{Capital turnover}$$ where, $$\text{Profit margin} = \text{Operating income} \div \text{Sales}$$ $$\text{Capital turnover} = \text{Sales} \div \text{Total assets}$$ Profit margin focuses on profitability (the amount of income earned on every dollar of sales), while capital turnover focuses on efficiency (the amount of sales generated with every dollar of assets).
• How is RI computed and interpreted?	$$\text{RI} = \text{Operating income} - \left(\text{Target rate of return} \times \text{Total assets} \right)$$ If RI is positive, the division is earning income at a rate that exceeds management's minimum expectations.
• How does EVA differ from RI?	EVA is a special type of RI calculation that focuses on the income (in excess of expectations) created by the division for two specific stakeholders: investors and long-term creditors.
• When calculating ROI, RI, or VA, are there any measurement issues of concern?	If the net book value of assets is used to measure total assets, ROI, RI, and EVA will "artificially" rise over time due to the depreciation of the assets. Using gross book value to measure total assets eliminates this measurement issue. Many firms use the average balance of total assets, rather than the beginning or ending balance of assets, when they calculate ROI, RI, and EVA.

Summary Problem 2

Assume Smart Touch Learning expects each division to earn a 16% target rate of return. Smart Touch Learning's weighted average cost of capital (WACC) is 13%, and its effective tax rate is 30%. Assume the company's original CD Division had the following results last year (in millions of dollars):

Operating income	$ 1,450
Total assets	16,100
Current liabilities	3,600
Sales	26,500

Requirements

1. Compute the CD Division's profit margin, capital turnover, and ROI. Round your results to three decimal places. Interpret the results in relation to the e-learning and DVD Divisions discussed in the chapter.
2. Compute and interpret the CD Division's RI.
3. Compute the CD Division's EVA. What does this tell you?
4. What can you conclude based on all three financial performance KPIs?

Solution

Requirement 1

$$
\begin{aligned}
\text{ROI} = \quad & \text{Profit margin} \quad \times \quad \text{Capital turnover} \\
= \ & (\text{Operating income} \div \text{Sales}) \times (\text{Sales} \div \text{Total assets}) \\
= \ & (\$1,450 \div \$26,500) \times (\$26,500 \div \$16,100) \\
= \ & \quad\quad 0.055 \quad\quad \times \quad\quad 1.646 \\
= \ & \quad\quad 0.091
\end{aligned}
$$

The original CD Division is far from meeting top management's expectations. Its ROI is only 9.1%. The profit margin of 5.5% is slightly lower than the e-learning Division and significantly lower than both Divisions (6% for e-learning and 19% for the DVD division). The capital turnover (1.646) is much lower than the e-learning Division (3.0 capital turnover) but much higher than the DVD capital turnover of 0.80. This means that the original CD Division is not generating sales from its assets as efficiently as the e-learning Division, but is more efficient than the DVD Division. Division management needs to consider ways to increase the efficiency with which it uses divisional assets.

Requirement 2

$$
\begin{aligned}
\text{RI} = \ & \text{Operating income} - (\text{Target rate of return} \times \text{Total assets}) \\
= \ & \quad \$1,450 \quad\quad - \quad\quad (16\% \times \$16,100) \\
= \ & \quad \$1,450 \quad\quad - \quad\quad \$2,576 \\
= \ & \quad \$(1,126)
\end{aligned}
$$

The negative RI confirms the ROI results: The division is not meeting management's target rate of return.

Requirement 3

$$\begin{aligned}
\text{EVA} &= \text{After-tax operating income} - [(\text{Total assets} - \text{Current liabilities}) \times \text{WACC\%}] \\
&= (\$1{,}450 \times 70\%) \quad - \quad [(\$16{,}100 - \$3{,}600) \times 13\%] \\
&= \$1{,}015 \quad - \quad (\$12{,}500) \times 13\% \\
&= \$1{,}015 \quad - \quad \$1{,}625 \\
&= \$(610)
\end{aligned}$$

The negative EVA means that the division is not generating income for investors and long-term creditors at the rate desired by these stakeholders.

Requirement 4

All three investment center performance measures (ROI, RI, and EVA) point to the same conclusion: The original CD Division is not meeting financial expectations. Either top management and stakeholders' expectations are unrealistic or the division is not *currently* performing up to par. Recall, however, that financial performance measures tend to be lag indicators—measuring the results of decisions made in the past. The division's managers may currently be implementing new initiatives to improve the division's future profitability. Lead indicators should be used to project whether such initiatives are pointing the company in the right direction.

Review *Performance Evaluation and the Balanced Scorecard*

■ Accounting Vocabulary

Balanced Scorecard (p. 564)
Recognition that management must consider both financial performance measures and operational performance measures when judging the performance of a company and its subunits.

Capital Turnover (p. 577)
The amount of sales revenue generated for every dollar of invested assets; a component of the ROI calculation, computed as sales divided by total assets.

Centralized Companies (p. 560)
Companies in which all major planning and operating decisions are made by top management.

Cost Center (p. 562)
A subunit responsible only for controlling costs.

Decentralized Companies (p. 560)
Companies that are segmented into smaller operating units; unit managers make planning and operating decisions for their unit.

Economic Value Added (EVA) (p. 580)
A residual income measure calculating the amount of income generated by the company or its divisions in excess of stockholders' and long-term creditors' expectations.

Goal Congruence (p. 561)
Aligning the goals of subunit managers with the goals of top management.

Investment Center (p. 562)
A subunit responsible for generating profits and efficiently managing the division's invested capital (assets).

Key Performance Indicator(s) (KPIs) (p. 565)
Summary performance measures that help managers assess whether the company is achieving its long-term and short-term goals.

Lag Indicators (p. 564)
Performance measures that indicate past performance.

Lead Indicators (p. 564)
Performance measures that forecast future performance.

Profit Center (p. 562)
A subunit responsible for generating revenue and controlling costs.

Profit Margin (p. 577)
The amount of income earned on every dollar of sales; a component of the ROI calculation, computed as operating income divided by sales.

Residual Income (RI) (p. 579)
A measure of profitability and efficiency, computed as the excess of actual income over a specified minimum acceptable income.

Return on Investment (ROI) (p. 576)
A measure of profitability and efficiency, computed as operating income divided by total assets.

Revenue Center (p. 562)
A subunit responsible only for generating revenue.

Weighted Average Cost of Capital (WACC) (p. 580)
The company's cost of capital; the target return used in EVA calculations to denote the return expected by stockholders and long-term creditors.

■ Quick Check

1. Which is *not* one of the potential advantages of decentralization?
   a. Improves motivation and retention
   b. Increases goal congruence
   c. Supports use of expert knowledge
   d. Improves customer relations

2. The **Quaker Foods** division of **PepsiCo** is most likely treated as a
   a. revenue center.
   b. cost center.
   c. profit center.
   d. investment center.

3. Decentralization is often based on all the following except

   a. geographic region.

   b. product line.

   c. business function.

   d. revenue size.

4. Manufacturing yield rate (number of units produced per unit of time) would be a typical measure for which of the following balanced scorecard perspectives?

   a. Learning and growth

   b. Internal business

   c. Financial

   d. Customer

5. Which of the following balanced scorecard perspectives essentially asks, "Can we continue to improve and create value?"

   a. Financial

   b. Learning and growth

   c. Customer

   d. Internal business

The following data applies to Questions 6 through 9. Assume the Residential Division of Krandell Faucets had the following results last year (in thousands of dollars):

Sales..................... $	4,648,000	Management's Target Rate of return..........	17%
Operating income...........	1,208,480	WACC.................................	10%
Total assets................	5,600,000		
Current liabilities...........	250,000		

6. What is the division's profit margin?

   a. 26%

   b. 83%

   c. 4%

   d. 22%

7. What is the division's capital turnover?

   a. 117%

   b. 17%

   c. 83%

   d. 21%

8. What is the division's ROI?

   a. 18%

   b. 5.83%

   c. 22%

   d. 81%

9. What is the division's RI?

   a. ($407,080)

   b. $407,080

   c. ($256,480)

   d. $256,480

10. The performance evaluation of a cost center is typically based on its

   a. static budget variance.

   b. ROI.

   c. sales volume variance.

   d. flexible budget variance.

Answers are given after Apply Your Knowledge (p. 599).

Assess Your Progress

▪ Short Exercises

S12-1 *(L. OBJ. 1)* **Explaining why and how companies decentralize [5 min]**
Decentralization divides company operations into various reporting units.

Requirement

1. Explain why companies decentralize. Describe some typical methods of decentralization.

S12-2 *(L. OBJ. 1)* **Explaining why and how companies decentralize [5 min]**
Most decentralized subunits can be described as one of four different types of responsibility centers.

Requirement

1. List the four most common types of responsibility centers and describe their responsibilities.

S12-3 *(L. OBJ. 1)* **Explaining why and how companies decentralize [5 min]**
Each of the following managers has been given certain decision-making authority:

   1. Manager of Holiday Inn's Central Reservation Office
   2. Managers of various corporate-owned Holiday Inn locations
   3. Manager of the Holiday Inn Corporate Division
   4. Manager of the Housekeeping Department at a Holiday Inn
   5. Manager of the Holiday Inn Express Corporate Division
   6. Manager of the complimentary breakfast buffet at a Holiday Inn Express

Requirement

1. Classify each of the managers according to the type of responsibility center they manage.

S12-4 *(L. OBJ. 2)* **Explaining why companies use performance evaluation systems [5 min]**
Well-designed performance evaluation systems accomplish many goals. Consider the following actions:

   a. Comparing targets to actual results
   b. Providing subunit managers with performance targets
   c. Comparing actual results with industry standards
   d. Providing bonuses to subunit managers who achieve performance targets
   e. Aligning subunit performance targets with company strategy
   f. Comparing actual results to the results of competitors
   g. Taking corrective actions
   h. Using the adage, "you get what you measure," when designing the performance evaluation system

Requirement

1. State which goal is being achieved by the action.

S12-5 *(L. OBJ. 3)* **Describing the balanced scorecard and identifying key performance indicators for each perspective [5–10 min]**

Consider the following key performance indicators:

a. Number of employee suggestions implemented
b. Revenue growth
c. Number of on-time deliveries
d. Percentage of sales force with access to real-time inventory levels
e. Customer satisfaction ratings
f. Number of defects found during manufacturing
g. Number of warranty claims
h. ROI
i. Variable cost per unit
j. Percentage of market share
k. Number of hours of employee training
l. Number of new products developed
m. Yield rate (number of units produced per hour)
n. Average repair time
o. Employee satisfaction
p. Number of repeat customers

Requirement

1. Classify each of the preceding key performance indicators according to the balanced scorecard perspective it addresses. Choose from financial perspective, customer perspective, internal business perspective, or learning and growth perspective.

S12-6 *(L. OBJ. 4)* **Using performance reports to evaluate cost, revenue, and profit centers [5 min]**

Management by exception is a term often used in performance evaluation.

Requirement

1. Describe management by exception and how it is used in the evaluation of cost, revenue, and profit centers.

S12-7 *(L. OBJ. 5)* **Using ROI, RI, and EVA to evaluate investment centers [5–10 min]**

Consider the following data:

	Domestic	International
Operating income	$ 9 million	$ 11 million
Total assets	$ 24 million	$ 36 million

Requirement

1. Which of the corporate divisions is more profitable? Explain.

S12-8 *(L. OBJ. 5)* **Using ROI, RI, and EVA to evaluate investment centers [5–10 min]**

Speedy Sports Company makes snowboards, downhill skis, cross-country skis, skateboards, surfboards, and in-line skates. The company has found it beneficial to split operations into two divisions based on the climate required for the sport: Snow sports and Non-snow sports. The following divisional information is available for the past year:

	Sales	Operating Income	Total Assets	Current Liabilities	ROI
Snow sports	$ 5,700,000	$ 1,083,000	$ 4,700,000	$ 410,000	23.0%
Non-snow sports	8,900,000	1,691,000	6,800,000	660,000	24.9%

Speedy's management has specified a 13% target rate of return. The company's weighted average cost of capital (WACC) is 11% and its effective tax rate is 33%.

Requirement

1. Calculate each division's profit margin. Interpret your results.

Note: Short Exercise 12-8 should be completed before attempting Short Exercise 12-9.

S12-9 *(L. OBJ. 5)* **Using ROI, RI, and EVA to evaluate investment centers [10 min]**
Refer to the information in S12-8.

Requirements

1. Compute each division's capital turnover (round to two decimal places). Interpret your results.

2. Use your answers to question 1, along with the profit margin, to recalculate ROI using the expanded formula. Do your answers agree with the basic ROI in S12-8?

Note: Short Exercise 12-8 should be completed before attempting Short Exercise 12-10.

S12-10 *(L. OBJ. 5)* **Using ROI, RI, and EVA to evaluate investment centers [5–10 min]**
Refer to the information in S12-8.

Requirement

1. Compute each division's RI. Interpret your results. Are your results consistent with each division's ROI?

Note: Short Exercise 12-8 should be completed before attempting Short Exercise 12-11.

S12-11 *(L. OBJ. 5)* **Using ROI, RI, and EVA to evaluate investment centers [10–15 min]**
Refer to the information in S12-8.

Requirement

1. Compute each division's EVA. Interpret your results.

■ Exercises

E12-12 *(L. OBJ. 1)* **Explaining why and how companies decentralize [10–15 min]**
Grandma Jones Cookie Company sells homemade cookies made with organic ingredients. Her sales are strictly Web-based. The business is taking off more than Grandma Jones ever expected, with orders coming from across the country from both consumers and corporate event planners. Even by employing a full-time baker and a Web designer, Grandma Jones can no longer handle the business on her own. She wants your advice on whether she should decentralize and, if so, how she should do it.

Requirement

1. Explain some of the advantages and disadvantages of decentralization and offer her three ways she might decentralize her company.

E12-13 *(L. OBJ. 2)* **Explaining why companies use performance evaluation systems [5–10 min]**
Financial performance is measured in many ways.

Requirement

1. Explain the difference between lag and lead indicators. Are financial performance measures typically referred to as lag or lead indicators? Are operational measures (such as customer satisfaction ratings, defect rates, number of on-time deliveries, and so forth) typically referred to as lag or lead indicators? Explain why, using **L.L.Bean** (a catalog clothing merchandiser) as an example.

E12-14 *(L. OBJ. 2)* **Explaining why companies use performance evaluation systems [10 min]**

Well-designed performance evaluation systems accomplish many goals.

Requirement

1. Describe the potential benefits performance evaluation systems offer.

E12-15 *(L. OBJ. 3)* **Describing the balanced scorecard and identifying key performance indicators for each perspective [10–15 min]**

Consider the following key performance indicators:

a. Number of customer complaints
b. Number of information system upgrades completed
c. EVA
d. New product development time
e. Employee turnover rate
f. Percentage of products with online help manuals
g. Customer retention
h. Percentage of compensation based on performance
i. Percentage of orders filled each week
j. Gross margin growth
k. Number of new patents
l. Employee satisfaction ratings
m. Manufacturing cycle time (average length of production process)
n. Earnings growth
o. Average machine setup time
p. Number of new customers
q. Employee promotion rate
r. Cash flow from operations
s. Customer satisfaction ratings
t. Machine downtime
u. Finished products per day per employee
v. Percentage of employees with access to upgraded system
w. Wait time per order prior to start of production

Requirement

1. Classify each indicator according to the balanced scorecard perspective it addresses. Choose from the financial perspective, customer perspective, internal business perspective, or the learning and growth perspective.

E12-16 *(L. OBJ. 4)* **Using performance reports to evaluate cost, revenue, and profit centers [10–15 min]**

One subunit of Racer Sports Company had the following financial results last month:

Racer – Subunit X	Actual	Flexible Budget	Flexible Budget Variance (U or F)	% Variance (U or F)
Direct materials	$ 28,600	$ 26,800		
Direct labor	13,100	13,900		
Indirect labor	26,300	23,000		
Utilities	12,300	11,200		
Depreciation	30,000	30,000		
Repairs and maintenance	4,500	5,600		
Total	$ 114,800	$ 110,500		

Requirements

1. Complete the performance evaluation report for this subunit. Enter the variance percent as a percentage rounded to two decimal places.
2. Based on the data presented, what type of responsibility center is this subunit?
3. Which items should be investigated if part of management's decision criteria is to investigate all variances exceeding $3,000 or 10%?
4. Should only unfavorable variances be investigated? Explain.

E12-17 *(L. OBJ. 4)* **Using performance reports to evaluate cost, revenue, and profit centers [15–20 min]**
The accountant for a subunit of Racer Sports Company went on vacation before completing the subunit's monthly performance report. This is as far as she got:

Racer – Subunit X Revenue by Product	Actual	Flexible Budget Variance	Flexible Budget	Sales Volume Variance	Static (Master) Budget
Downhill Model RI	$ 330,000			$ 16,000 F	$ 305,000
Downhill Model RII	150,000		$ 163,000		144,000
Cross-Country Model EXI	285,000	$ 2,000 U	287,000		302,000
Cross-Country Model EXII	256,000		251,000	15,500 U	266,500
Snowboard Model LXI	429,000	7,000 F			406,000
Total	$ 1,450,000				$ 1,423,500

Requirements

1. Complete the performance evaluation report for this subunit.
2. Based on the data presented, what type of responsibility center is this subunit?
3. Which items should be investigated if part of management's decision criteria is to investigate all variances exceeding $15,000?

E12-18 *(L. OBJ. 5)* **Using ROI, RI, and EVA to evaluate investment centers [10–15 min]**
Zuds, a national manufacturer of lawn-mowing and snow-blowing equipment, segments its business according to customer type: professional and residential. The following divisional information was available for the past year (in thousands of dollars):

	Sales	Operating Income	Total Assets	Current Liabilities
Residential	$ 580,000	$ 63,700	$ 196,000	$ 66,000
Professional	1,100,000	162,400	406,000	147,000

Management has a 27% target rate of return for each division. Zuds' weighted average cost of capital is 15% and its effective tax rate is 30%.

Requirements

1. Calculate each division's ROI. Round all of your answers to four decimal places.
2. Calculate each division's profit margin. Interpret your results.
3. Calculate each division's capital turnover. Interpret your results.
4. Use the expanded ROI formula to confirm your results from requirement 1. What can you conclude?

Note: Exercise 12-18 should be completed before attempting Exercise 12-19.

E12-19 *(L. OBJ. 5)* **Using ROI, RI, and EVA to evaluate investment centers [10–15 min]**
Refer to the data in E12-18.

Requirements

1. Calculate each division's RI. Interpret your results.
2. Calculate each division's EVA. Interpret your results.
3. Describe the conceptual and computational similarities and differences between RI and EVA.

■ Problems (Group A)

P12-20A *(L. OBJ. 1, 2, 3, 4)* **Explaining why and how companies decentralize and why they use performance evaluation systems [30–45 min]**
One subunit of Field Sports Company had the following financial results last month:

Subunit X	Flexible Budget	Actual	Flexible Budget Variance (U or F)	Percentage Variance
Sales	$ 451,000	$ 480,000		
Cost of goods sold	256,000	266,000		
Gross margin	$ 195,000	$ 214,000		
Operating expenses	48,000	55,000		
Operating income before service department charges	$ 147,000	$ 159,000		
Service department charges (allocated)	31,000	41,000		
Operating income	$ 116,000	$ 118,000		

Requirements

1. Complete the performance evaluation report for this subunit (round to two decimal places).
2. Based on the data presented and your knowledge of the company, what type of responsibility center is this subunit?
3. Which items should be investigated if part of management's decision criteria is to investigate all variances equal to or exceeding $10,000 *and* exceeding 10% (both criteria must be met)?
4. Should only unfavorable variances be investigated? Explain.
5. Is it possible that the variances are due to a higher-than-expected sales volume? Explain.
6. Will management place equal weight on each of the $10,000 variances? Explain.
7. Which balanced scorecard perspective is being addressed through this performance report? In your opinion, is this performance report a lead or lag indicator? Explain.
8. List one key performance indicator for the three other balanced scorecard perspectives. Make sure to indicate which perspective is being addressed by the indicators you list. Are they lead or lag indicators? Explain.

P12-21A *(L. OBJ. 5)* **Using ROI, RI, and EVA to evaluate investment centers [30–45 min]**

Benjamin Doore is a national paint manufacturer and retailer. The company is segmented into five divisions: Paint stores (branded retail locations), Consumer (paint sold through stores like **Sears, Home Depot,** and **Lowe's**), Automotive (sales to auto manufacturers), International, and Administration. The following is selected divisional information for its two largest divisions: Paint stores and Consumer (in thousands of dollars).

	Sales	Operating Income	Total Assets	Current Liabilities
Paint stores	$ 4,020,000	$ 478,000	$ 1,385,000	$ 335,000
Consumer	1,310,000	193,000	1,585,000	607,000

Management has specified a 22% target rate of return. The company's weighted average cost of capital is 17%. The company's effective tax rate is 33%.

Requirements

1. Calculate each division's ROI.

2. Calculate each division's profit margin. Interpret your results.

3. Calculate each division's capital turnover. Interpret your results.

4. Use the expanded ROI formula to confirm your results from requirement 1. Interpret your results.

5. Calculate each division's RI. Interpret your results and offer a recommendation for any division with negative RI.

6. Calculate each division's EVA. Interpret your results.

7. Describe the conceptual and computational similarities and differences between RI and EVA.

8. Total asset data was provided in this problem. If you were to gather this information from an annual report, how would you measure total assets? Describe your measurement choices and some of the pros and cons of those choices.

9. Describe some of the factors that management considers when setting its minimum target rate of return.

10. Explain why some firms prefer to use RI rather than ROI for performance measurement.

11. Explain why budget versus actual performance reports are insufficient for evaluating the performance of investment centers.

P12-22B *(L. OBJ. 1, 2, 3, 4)* **Explaining why and how companies decentralize and why they use performance evaluation systems [30–45 min]**

One subunit of Athlete Sports Company had the following financial results last month:

Subunit X	Flexible Budget	Actual	Flexible Budget Variance (U or F)	Percentage Variance
Sales	$ 454,000	$ 479,000		
Cost of goods sold	252,000	262,000		
Gross margin	$ 202,000	$ 217,000		
Operating expenses	51,000	54,000		
Operating income before service department charges	$ 151,000	$ 163,000		
Service department charges (allocated)	27,000	37,000		
Operating income	$ 124,000	$ 126,000		

Requirements

1. Complete the performance evaluation report for this subunit (round to two decimal places).
2. Based on the data presented and your knowledge of the company, what type of responsibility center is this subunit?
3. Which items should be investigated if part of management's decision criteria is to investigate all variances equal to or exceeding $10,000 *and* exceeding 10% (both criteria must be met)?
4. Should only unfavorable variances be investigated? Explain.
5. Is it possible that the variances are due to a higher-than-expected sales volume? Explain.
6. Will management place equal weight on each of the $10,000 variances? Explain.
7. Which balanced scorecard perspective is being addressed through this performance report? In your opinion, is this performance report a lead or lag indicator? Explain.
8. List one key performance indicator for the three other balanced scorecard perspectives. Make sure to indicate which perspective is being addressed by the indicators you list. Are they lead or lag indicators? Explain.

P12-23B *(L. OBJ. 5)* **Using ROI, RI, and EVA to evaluate investment centers [30–45 min]**

Ralph Laurel is a national paint manufacturer and retailer. The company is segmented into five divisions: Paint stores (branded retail locations), Consumer (paint sold through stores like **Sears, Home Depot,** and **Lowe's**), Automotive (sales to auto manufacturers), International, and Administration. The following is selected divisional information for its two largest divisions: Paint stores and Consumer (in thousands of dollars):

	Sales	Operating Income	Total Assets	Current Liabilities
Paint stores	$ 3,970,000	$ 478,000	$ 1,390,000	$ 355,000
Consumer	1,275,000	184,000	1,585,000	610,000

Management has specified a 20% target rate of return. The company's weighted average cost of capital is 17%. The company's effective tax rate is 36%.

Requirements

1. Calculate each division's ROI.
2. Calculate each division's profit margin. Interpret your results.
3. Calculate each division's capital turnover. Interpret your results.
4. Use the expanded ROI formula to confirm your results from requirement 1. Interpret your results.
5. Calculate each division's RI. Interpret your results and offer a recommendation for any division with negative RI.
6. Calculate each division's EVA. Interpret your results.
7. Describe the conceptual and computational similarities and differences between RI and EVA.
8. Total asset data was provided for this problem. If you were to gather this information from an annual report, how would you measure total assets? Describe your measurement choices and some of the pros and cons of those choices.
9. Describe some of the factors that management considers when setting its minimum target rate of return.
10. Explain why some firms prefer to use RI rather than ROI for performance measurement.
11. Explain why budget versus actual performance reports are insufficient for evaluating the performance of investment centers.

■ Continuing Exercise

E12-24 This exercise continues the Sherman Lawn Service, Inc., situation from Exercise 11-35 of Chapter 11. Sherman Lawn Service experienced Sales of $400,000 and Operating income of $75,000 for 2011. Total assets were $200,000 and total liabilities were $20,000 at the end of 2011. Sherman's target rate of return is 14% and WACC is 10%. Its 2011 tax rate was 30%.

Requirement

1. Calculate Sherman's profit margin for 2011.

■ Continuing Problem

P12-25 This problem continues the Haupt Consulting, Inc., situation from Problem 11-36 of Chapter 11. Haupt Consulting reported 2011 Sales of $2,500,000 and Operating income of $250,000. Total assets were $700,000 and total liabilities were $200,000 at the end of 2011. Haupt's target rate of return is 16% and WACC is 8%. Its 2011 tax rate was 35%.

Requirement

1. Calculate Haupt's profit margin, capital turnover, and EVA for 2011.

Apply Your Knowledge

■ Decision Case

Case 1. Colgate-Palmolive operates two product segments. Using the company Web site, locate segment information for 2007 in the company's 2007 annual report. (*Hint*: Look under investor relations on the company Web site.)

Requirements

1. What are the two segments? Gather data about each segment's net sales, operating income, and identifiable assets.
2. Calculate ROI for each segment.
3. Which segment has the highest ROI? Explain why.
4. If you were on the top management team and could allocate extra funds to only one division, which division would you choose? Why?

■ Ethical Issue

Dixie Irwin is the department manager for Religious Books, a manufacturer of religious books that are sold through Internet companies. Irwin's bonus is based on reducing production costs.

Requirement

Issue 1. Irwin has identified a supplier, Cheap Paper, that can provide paper products at a 10% cost reduction. The paper quality is not the same as that of the current paper used in production. If Irwin uses the supplier, he will certainly achieve his personal bonus goals; however, other company goals may be in jeopardy. Identify the key performance issues at risk and recommend a plan of action for Irwin.

■ Financial Statement Case—Amazon

This case is based on the **Amazon.com** annual report in Appendix A at the end of the book. Use it to answer the following questions.

Requirements

1. Considering **Amazon.com**'s business, create key performance indicators from the four perspectives of the balanced scorecard. Describe reasons why you selected the KPIs and how it will help the organization measure performance.
2. Calculate ROI, RI and EVA for the company for 2008. What does this tell you, as a potential investor?

▪ Team Project

Each group should identify one public company's product that it wishes to evaluate. The team should gather all the information it can about the product.

Requirement

1. Develop a list of key performance indicators for the product.

Big Picture

Ch 1   Introduction to Management Accounting

- Distinguish management accounting from financial accounting
- The role and responsibilities of management accountants
- Classify costs and prepare income statements for merchandising companies
- Classify costs and prepare income statements and statements of cost of goods manufactured for manufacturing companies

Ch 2   Job Order Costing

- Distinguish between job order and process costing
- Record materials, labor, and overhead in a job order costing system
- Record completion and sales of finished goods and adjust for under-/overallocated overhead
- Calculate unit costs for service companies

Ch 3   Activity-Based Costing and Other Cost Management Tools

- Develop activity-based costs and used activity-based management to determine target product costs
- Record transactions in JIT systems
- Use the four types of quality costs to make management decisions

Ch 4   Process Costing

- Calculate equivalent units and conversion costs
- Prepare cost of production reports and the related journal entries using the weighted-average costing method
- Prepare cost of production reports and the related journal entries using the FIFO costing method

Ch 5   Cost Behavior and Cost-Volume-Profit Analysis

- Identify how changes in volume affect cost
- Distinguish among variable, mixed, and fixed cost
- Split mixed cost into fixed and variable components by using the high-low method and by using regression analysis
- Use CVP to compute breakeven points, to plan profits, to graph relationships, and to perform sensitivity analysis

Ch 6   Absorption and Variable Costing

- Distinguish between absorption costing and variable costing
- Prepare absorption costing and variable costing income statements and explained the differences between the two costing techniques
- Illustrate the pros and cons of absorption and variable costing

Chapter 12: Demo Doc

■ ROI, RI, and EVA to Evaluate Investment Centers

Learning Objective 5

The Vas Company has two large divisions with separate facilities that produce specialty coffees and teas. Some key financial information for the past year is shown for these two divisions:

Division	Sales	Operating Income	Total Assets	Current Liabilities
Coffee	$3,800,000	$ 750,000	$2,700,000	$250,000
Tea	5,200,000	1,200,000	4,000,000	500,000

Vas's management has specified a target 10% minimum rate of return. The company's weighted average cost of capital is 7% and its effective tax rate is 25%.

Requirements

1. Calculate each division's ROI.
2. Top management has extra funds to invest. Which division will most likely receive those funds? Why?
3. Can you explain why one division's ROI is higher? How could management gain more insight?
4. Compute each division's RI. Interpret your results.
5. Compute each division's EVA. Interpret your results.

Demo Doc Solution

Requirement 1

Calculate each division's ROI.

Part 1	Part 2	Part 3	Part 4	Part 5	Demo Doc Complete

$$\text{ROI} = \frac{\text{Operating income}}{\text{Sales}} \times \frac{\text{Sales}}{\text{Total assets}} = \frac{\text{Operating income}}{\text{Total assets}}$$

Coffee Division = ($750,000/$2,700,000)

= 27.8%

Tea Division = ($1,200,000/$4,000,000)

= 30.0%

Requirement 2

Top management has extra funds to invest. Which division will most likely receive those funds? Why?

Part 1	Part 2	Part 3	Part 4	Part 5	Demo Doc Complete

Top management would invest extra funds in the tea division. The higher the ROI the better. The tea division has a higher ROI, 30.0%; the coffee division is 27.8%.

Requirement 3

Can you explain why one division's ROI is higher? How could management gain more insight?

Part 1	Part 2	Part 3	Part 4	Part 5	Demo Doc Complete

The tea division ROI may be higher because they may earn more operating income for every dollar of sales. The ROI may also be higher for the tea division because it is operating more efficiently than the coffee division, generating more sales per dollar of assets.

Requirement 4

Compute each division's RI. Interpret your results.

Part 1	Part 2	Part 3	**Part 4**	Part 5	Demo Doc Complete

$$RI = \text{Operating income} - (\text{Target rate of return} \times \text{Total assets})$$

$$\text{Coffee Divsion RI} = \$750,000 - (0.10 \times \$2,700,00)$$
$$= \$480,000$$

$$\text{Tea Division RI} = \$1,200,000 - (0.10 \times \$4,000,000)$$
$$= \$800,000$$

A positive amount indicates that the divisions have met the minimum required return. The tea division has a higher RI than the coffee division.

Requirement 5

Compute each division's EVA. Interpret your results.

Part 1	Part 2	Part 3	Part 4	**Part 5**	Demo Doc Complete

$$EVA = \text{After-tax operating income} - [(\text{Total assets} - \text{Current liabilities}) \times \text{WACC \%}]$$

$$\text{Coffee Division EVA} = [(\$750,000 \times (100\% - 25\%)] - [(\$2,700,000 - \$250,000) \times 0.07\%]$$
$$= \$562,500 - \$171,500$$
$$= \$391,000$$

$$\text{Tea Division EVA} = [(\$1,200,000 \times (100\% - 25\%))] - [(\$4,000,000 - \$500,000) \times 0.07\%]$$
$$= \$900,000 - \$245,000$$
$$= \$655,000$$

These EVA calculations show that both divisions have generated wealth in excess of expectations for the company's investors and long-term debt-holders. The tea division has the higher EVA.

Part 1	Part 2	Part 3	Part 4	Part 5	**Demo Doc Complete**

13 The Statement of Cash Flows

Learning Objectives/Success Keys

1 Identify the purposes of the Statement of Cash Flows

2 Distinguish among operating, investing, and financing cash flows

3 Prepare the Statement of Cash Flows by the indirect method

4 Prepare the Statement of Cash Flows by the direct method (Appendix 13A)

Why is cash so important? You can probably answer that question from your own experience: It takes cash to pay the bills. You have some income and you have expenses; and these events create cash receipts and payments.

Businesses, including Smart Touch Learning, Inc., and Greg's Groovy Tunes, Inc., work the same way. Net income is a good thing, but Smart Touch and Greg's both need enough cash to pay the bills and run their operations.

This chapter covers cash flows—cash receipts and cash payments. We will see how to prepare the Statement of Cash Flows, starting with the format used by the vast majority of non-public companies; it is called the *indirect method*. Chapter Appendix 13A covers the alternate format of the Statement of Cash Flows, the *direct method*.

The chapter has four distinct sections:

- Introduction: The Statement of Cash Flows
- Preparing the Statement of Cash Flows by the Indirect Method
- Chapter Appendix 13A: Preparing the Statement of Cash Flows by the Direct Method
- Chapter Appendix 13B: Preparing the Statement of Cash Flows Using a Spreadsheet

The focus company throughout the chapter once again is Smart Touch Learning.

Chapter Appendix 13B shows how to use a spreadsheet to prepare the Statement of Cash Flows. This appendix presents the indirect-method spreadsheet first, and the direct-method spreadsheet last—to maintain consistency with the order in which these topics are covered in the chapter.

Introduction: The Statement of Cash Flows

The Balance Sheet reports financial position. When a comparative Balance Sheet for two periods is presented, it shows whether cash increased or decreased. For example, Smart Touch Learning's comparative Balance Sheet reported the following:

1 Identify the purposes of the Statement of Cash Flows

	2012	2011	Increase (Decrease)
Cash.........	$22,000	$42,000	$(20,000)

Smart Touch's cash decreased by $20,000 during 2012. But the Balance Sheet does not show *why* cash decreased. We need the cash-flow statement for that.

The Statement of Cash Flows reports **cash flows**—cash receipts and cash payments. It:

- shows where cash came from (receipts) and how cash was spent (payments).
- reports why cash increased or decreased during the period.
- covers a span of time and is dated the same as the Income Statement—"Year Ended December 31, 2012," for example.

The Statement of Cash Flows explains why net income as reported on the Income Statement does not equal the change in the cash balance. In essence the cash flow statement is the communicating link between the accrual based Income Statement and the cash reported on the Balance Sheet.

Exhibit 13-1 illustrates the relationships among the Balance Sheet, the Income Statement, and the Statement of Cash Flows.

How do people use cash-flow information? The Statement of Cash Flows helps:

1. **predict future cash flows.** Past cash receipts and payments help predict future cash flows.

2. **evaluate management decisions.** Wise investment decisions help the business prosper, while unwise decisions cause problems. Investors and creditors use cash-flow information to evaluate managers' decisions.

3. **predict ability to pay debts and dividends.** Lenders want to know whether they will collect on their loans. Stockholders want dividends on their investments. The Statement of Cash Flows helps make these predictions.

Cash Equivalents

On a Statement of Cash Flows, *Cash* means more than cash on hand and cash in the bank. *Cash* includes **cash equivalents**, which are highly liquid investments that can be converted into cash quickly. As the name implies, cash equivalents are so close to cash that they are treated as "equals." Examples of cash equivalents are money-market accounts and investments in U.S. government securities. Throughout this chapter, the term *cash* refers to both cash and cash equivalents.

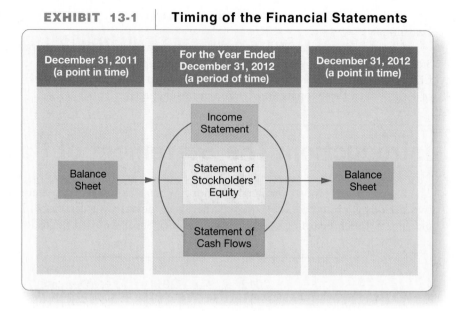

EXHIBIT 13-1 | **Timing of the Financial Statements**

Operating, Investing, and Financing Activities

2 | Distinguish among operating, investing, and financing cash flows

There are three basic types of cash-flow activities and the Statement of Cash Flows has a section for each:

- Operating activities
- Investing activities
- Financing activities

Each section reports cash flows coming into the company and cash flowing going out of the company based on these three divisions.

Operating Activities:

- Is the most important category of cash flows because it reflects the day-to-day operations that determine the future of an organization
- Create revenues, expenses, gains, and losses
- Affect net income on the Income Statement
- Affect current assets and current liabilities on the Balance Sheet

Investing Activities:

- Increase and decrease long-term assets, such as computers, software, land, buildings, and equipment
- Include purchases and sales of these assets, plus loans receivable from others and collections of those loans

Financing Activities:

- Increase and decrease long-term liabilities and equity
- Include issuing stock, paying dividends, and buying and selling treasury stock
- Include borrowing money and paying off loans

Exhibit 13-2 shows the relationship between operating, investing, and financing cash flows and the various parts of the Balance Sheet.

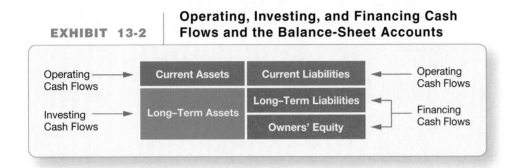

| EXHIBIT 13-2 | Operating, Investing, and Financing Cash Flows and the Balance-Sheet Accounts |

As you can see, operating cash flows affect the current accounts. Investing cash flows affect the long-term assets. Financing cash flows affect long-term liabilities and equity.

Two Formats for Operating Activities

There are two ways to format operating activities on the Statement of Cash Flows:

- The **indirect method** starts with net income and adjusts it to net cash provided by operating activities.
- The **direct method** restates the Income Statement in terms of cash. The direct method shows all the cash receipts and all the cash payments from operating activities.

    The indirect and direct methods:

- use different computations but produce the same amount of cash flow from operations.
- have no effect on investing activities or financing activities.

    We will begin with the indirect method because most companies use it. To focus on the direct method, go to Appendix 13A.

Preparing the Statement of Cash Flows by the Indirect Method

To prepare the Statement of Cash Flows, you need the Income Statement and both the current year and the prior year's Balance Sheets. Consider Smart Touch Learning's financial statements on page 610. To prepare the Statement of Cash Flows by the indirect method follow Steps 1–4:

3 Prepare the Statement of Cash Flows by the indirect method

> STEP 1: Lay out the statement format as shown in Exhibit 13-3. Steps 2–4 will complete the Statement of Cash Flows.

EXHIBIT 13-3 | **Format of the Statement of Cash Flows: Indirect Method**

SMART TOUCH LEARNING, INC.
Statement of Cash Flows
Year Ended December 31, 2012

± Cash flows from operating activities:		
Net income		
Adjustments to reconcile net income to net cash provided by operating activities:		
+ Depreciation / amortization expense		
+ Loss on sale of long-term assets		
– Gain on sale of long-term assets		
– Increases in current assets other than cash		
+ Decreases in current assets other than cash		
+ Increases in current liabilities		
– Decreases in current liabilities		
Net cash provided by (used for) operating activities		
± Cash flows from investing activities:		
+ Cash receipts from sales of long-term (plant) assets (investments, land, building, equipment, and so on)		
– Acquisition of long-term (plant) assets		
Net cash provided by (used for) investing activities		
± Cash flows from financing activities:		
+ Cash receipts from issuance of stock		
+ Cash receipts from sale of treasury stock		
– Purchase of treasury stock		
+ Cash receipts from issuance of notes or bonds payable (borrowing)		
– Payment of notes or bonds payable		
– Payment of dividends		
Net cash provided by (used for) financing activities		
= Net increase (decrease) in cash during the year		
+ Cash at December 31, 2011		
= Cash at December 31, 2012		

STEP 2: Compute the change in cash from the comparative Balance Sheet. The change in cash is the "key reconciling figure" for the Statement of Cash Flows. Exhibit 13-5 is the comparative Balance Sheet of Smart Touch Learning, where the top line shows that cash decreased by $20,000 during 2012.

STEP 3: Take net income, depreciation, and any gains or losses from the Income Statement. Exhibit 13-6 gives the 2012 Income Statement of Smart Touch Learning, with the relevant items highlighted.

STEP 4: Complete the Statement of Cash Flows, using data from the Income Statement and the Balance Sheet. The statement is complete only after you have explained all the year-to-year changes in all the accounts on the Balance Sheet.

Let us apply these steps to show the operating activities of Smart Touch Learning. Exhibit 13-4 depicts the Statement of Cash Flows. All lettered items are tied to either a balance sheet or income statement item. That makes it easy to trace the data from one statement to the other.

EXHIBIT 13-4 | **Indirect Method Cash Flow Statement**

	SMART TOUCH LEARNING, INC. Statement of Cash Flows Year Ended December 31, 2012		
	Cash flows from operating activities:		*(Thousands)*
A	Net income		$ 40
	Adjustments to reconcile net income to net cash provided by operating activities:		
B	Depreciation	$ 20	
C	Gain on sale of plant assets	(10)	
	Increase in accounts receivable	(17)	
D	Decrease in inventory	2	
	Increase in accounts payable	40	
	Decrease in accrued liabilities	(5)	30
	Net cash provided by operating activities		70
	Cash flows from investing activities:		
E	Acquisition of plant assets	$(310)	
F	Cash receipt from sale of plant asset	50	
	Net cash used for investing activities		(260)
	Cash flows from financing activities:		
I	Cash receipt from issuance of common stock	120	
G	Cash receipt from issuance of notes payable	90	
H	Payment of notes payable	(10)	
J	Purchase of treasury stock	(20)	
K	Payment of dividends	(10)	
	Net cash provided by financing activities		170
L	Net decrease in cash		$ (20)
L	Cash balance, December 31, 2011		42
L	Cash balance, December 31, 2012		$ 22

Cash Flows from Operating Activities

Operating cash flows begin with net income, taken from the Income Statement.

A Net Income

The Statement of Cash Flows—indirect method—begins with net income because revenues and expenses, which affect net income, produce cash receipts and cash payments. Revenues bring in cash receipts, and expenses must be paid. But net income is accrual based and the cash flows (cash basis net income) do not always equal the accrual basis revenues and expenses. For example, sales *on account* are revenues that increase net income, but the company has not yet collected cash from those sales. Accrued expenses decrease net income, but the company has not paid cash *if the expenses are accrued.*

To go from net income to cash flow from operations, we must make some adjustments to net income on the Statement of Cash Flows. These additions and subtractions follow net income and are labeled *Adjustments to reconcile net income to net cash provided by operating activities.*

EXHIBIT 13-5 | **Comparative Balance Sheet**

SMART TOUCH LEARNING, INC.
Comparative Balance Sheet
December 31, 2012 and 2011

(In thousands)	2012	2011	Increase (Decrease)	
Assets				
Current:				
Cash	$ 22	$ 42	$ (20)	L
Accounts receivable	90	73	17	D
Inventory	143	145	(2)	
Plant assets, net	460	210	250	E/F
Total assets	$715	$470	$245	
Liabilities				
Current:			—	
Accounts payable	$ 90	$ 50	$ 40	D
Accrued liabilities	5	10	(5)	
Long-term notes payable	160	80	80	G/H
Stockholders' Equity				
Common stock	370	250	120	I
Retained earnings	110	80	30	A/K
Less: Treasury stock	(20)	0	(20)	J
	$715	$470	$245	

EXHIBIT 13-6 | **Income Statement**

SMART TOUCH LEARNING, INC.
Income Statement
Year Ended December 31, 2012

		(In thousands)	
Revenues and gains:			
	Sales revenue	$286	
	Interest revenue	12	
	Dividend revenue	9	
C	Gain on sale of plant assets	10	
	Total revenues and gains		$317
Expenses:			
	Cost of goods sold	$156	
	Salary and wage expense	56	
B	Depreciation expense	20	
	Other operating expense	16	
	Interest expense	15	
	Income tax expense	14	
	Total expenses		277
A	Net income		$ 40

B Depreciation, Depletion, and Amortization Expenses

These expenses are added back to net income to reconcile from net income to cash flow from operations. Let us see why this occurs. Depreciation is recorded as follows:

Depreciation expense (E+)		20,000	
Accumulated depreciation (CA+)			20,000

You can see that depreciation does not affect cash because there is no Cash account in the journal entry. However, depreciation, like all the other expenses, decreases net income. Therefore, to go from net income to cash flows, we must remove depreciation by adding it back to net income.

Example: Suppose you had only two transactions during the period:

- $40,000 cash sale
- Depreciation expense of $20,000

Accrual basis net income is $20,000 ($40,000 – $20,000). But cash flow from operations is $40,000. To reconcile from net income, $20,000, to cash flow from operations, $40,000, add back depreciation, $20,000. Also add back depletion and amortization expenses because they are similar to depreciation.

C Gains and Losses on the Sale of Assets

Sales of long-term assets such as land and buildings are investing activities, and these sales usually create a gain or a loss. The gain or loss is included in net income, which is already in the operating section of the cash flow statement. Gains and losses require an adjustment to cash flow from operating activities: The gain or loss must be removed from net income on the Statement of Cash Flows so the total cash from the transaction can be shown in the investing section.

Exhibit 13-4 includes an adjustment for a gain. During 2012 Smart Touch sold equipment and there was a gain of $10,000 on the sale. The gain was included in the calculation of net income on the Income Statement, so the gain must be removed from operating cash flows. The gain made net income bigger, so it is deducted from the operating section. On the other hand, a loss on the sale of plant assets would make net income smaller, so it would be added back to net income.

D Changes in the Current Assets and the Current Liabilities

Most current assets and current liabilities result from operating activities. For example,

- accounts receivable result from sales,
- inventory relates to cost of goods sold, and so on.

Changes in the current accounts create adjustments to net income on the cash-flow statement, as follows:

1. **An increase in a current asset other than cash causes a decrease in cash.** It takes cash to acquire assets. If Accounts receivable, Inventory, or Prepaid expenses increased, then cash decreased. Therefore, subtract the increase in the current asset from net income to get cash flow from operations. For example, Smart Touch's Accounts receivable went up by $17,000. That increase in the current asset shows as a decrease in cash on the cash flow statement (Exhibit 13-4).

↑ **Current assets** ↓ **Cash**

↓ Current assets   ↑ Cash

↓ Current liabilities   ↓ Cash

↑ Current liabilities   ↑ Cash

2. **A decrease in a current asset other than cash causes an increase in cash.** Smart Touch's Inventory decreased by $2,000. What caused the decrease? Smart Touch must have sold some inventory, and collected cash. Therefore, we add the decrease in Inventory of $2,000 in the cash flow statement (Exhibit 13-4).

3. **A decrease in a current liability causes a decrease in cash.** The payment of a current liability decreases cash. Therefore, we subtract decreases in current liabilities from net income to get cash flow from operations. Smart Touch's Accrued liabilities went down $5,000. That change shows up as a $5,000 decrease in cash flows in Exhibit 13-4.

4. **An increase in a current liability causes an increase in cash.** Smart Touch's Accounts payable increased by $40,000. This means that cash was not spent at the time the expense was incurred, but rather it will be paid at a later time—resulting in a liability. Accordingly, even though net income was reduced by the expense, cash was not reduced. However, cash will be reduced later when Smart Touch pays off its liability. Therefore, an increase in a current liability is *added* to net income in the Statement of Cash Flows (Exhibit 13-4).

Evaluating Cash Flows from Operating Activities

During 2012, Smart Touch Learning's operations provided net cash flow of $70,000. This amount exceeds net income (due to the various adjustments discussed in sections B, C, and D). However, to fully evaluate a company's cash flows, we must also examine its investing and financing activities. Exhibit 13-4 shows the completed operating activities section.

Stop & Think...

The operating activities represent the core of the day to day results of any business. Remember when we learned the difference between accrual and cash basis accounting? All the operating activities section represents is a cash basis income statement. With the indirect method, we indirectly back into cash basis—that is, we start with accrual basis net income and adjust it back to cash basis "operating" cash flows (cash basis net income).

Cash Flows from Investing Activities

Investing activities affect long-term assets, such as Plant assets and Investments. These are shown for Smart Touch in Exhibit 13-5. Let us see how to compute the investing cash flows.

Computing Acquisitions and Sales of Plant Assets

Companies keep a separate account for each asset. But for computing investing cash flows, it is helpful to combine all the plant assets into a single Plant assets account. We subtract Accumulated depreciation from the assets' cost in order to work with a single net figure for plant assets, such as Plant assets, net—$460,000. This simplifies the computations.

To illustrate, observe that Smart Touch Learning's

- Balance Sheet reports plant assets, net of depreciation, of $460,000 at the end of 2012 and $210,000 at the end of 2011 (Exhibit 13-5).
- Income Statement shows depreciation expense of $20,000 and a $10,000 gain on sale of plant assets (Exhibit 13-6).

Also, assume that Smart Touch's acquisitions of plant assets during 2012 totaled $310,000. **E**

This gives us an incomplete T-account as follows:

Plant assets, net

12/31/11 Bal	210,000			
		Depreciation (from Inc Stmt)	20,000	**B**
E Acquisitions	310,000	Cost of sold assets (COSA)	?	
12/31/12 Bal	460,000			

We also know that Smart Touch sold some older plant assets because there was a gain on sale of assets reported on the Income Statement. We don't care about the gain itself, we need to know the cash amount of the sale. Remember, we are looking for cash movement. How much cash did the business receive from the sale of plant assets? First, let us look at the cost of the sold assets. This will be the missing value in our Plant assets, net T-account.

$$12/31/11 \text{ Bal} + \text{Acquisitions} - \text{Depreciation} - \text{COSA?} = 12/31/12 \text{ Bal}$$
$$210,000 + 310,000 - 20,000 - \text{COSA?} = 460,000$$
$$500,000 - \text{COSA?} = 460,000$$
$$\text{Sales} = 40,000$$

So our completed T-account is as follows:

Plant assets, net

12/31/11 Bal	210,000			
		Depreciation (from Inc Stmt)	20,000	**B**
E Acquisitions	310,000	Cost of sold assets (COSA)	40,000	
12/31/12 Bal	460,000			

Cash received from selling plant assets can be computed by using the journal entry approach:

			?????
Cash			
	Gain on sale of plant assets (from the Income Statement) **C**		10,000
	Plant assets (from the T-account)		40,000

The book-value information comes from the Plant assets (Net) account on the Balance Sheet. The gain or loss comes from the Income Statement. The missing amount must be the cash received from the sale.

So, we compute the cash receipt from the sale as follows:

Cash = $10,000 Gain + $40,000 Plant assets, net
Cash = $50,000

The cash receipt from the sale of plant assets of $50,000 is shown as item **F** in the investing activities section of the Statement of Cash Flows (see Exhibit 13-4).

Exhibit 13-7 summarizes the computation of the investing cash flows. Items to be computed are shown in color.

EXHIBIT 13-7 | **Computing Cash Flows from Investing Activities**

Cash Receipts

| From sale of plant assets | Beginning plant assets (net) | + | Acquisition | − | Depreciation expense | − | Book value of assets sold | = | Ending plant assets (net) |

$$\text{Cash receipt} = \text{Book value of assets sold} \begin{cases} + & \text{Gain on sale} \\ \text{or} & \\ - & \text{Loss on sale} \end{cases}$$

Cash Payments

| For acquisition of plant assets | Beginning plant assets (net) | + | Acquisition | − | Depreciation expense | − | Book value of assets sold | = | Ending plant assets (net) |

Cash Flows from Financing Activities

Financing activities affect the liability and owners' equity accounts, such as Long-Term notes payable, Bonds payable, Common stock, and Retained earnings. These are shown for Smart Touch in Exhibit 13-5.

Computing Issuances and Payments of Long-Term Notes Payable

The beginning and ending balances of Notes payable or Bonds payable are taken from the Balance Sheet. If either the amount of new issuances or payments is known, the other amount can be computed. For Smart Touch Learning, new issuances of notes payable total $90,000 (Shown as item **G** in Exhibit 13-4). The computation of note payments uses the Long-Term notes payable account, with amounts from Smart Touch Learning's Balance Sheet in Exhibit 13-5 to create the following incomplete T-account:

Long-Term notes payable

Notes payments	?	12/31/11 Bal	80,000
		New notes issued	90,000 **G**
		12/31/12 Bal	160,000

Then, solve for the missing payments value:

12/31/11 Bal + New Notes Issued − Payments? = 12/31/12 Bal

80,000 + 90,000 − Payments? = 160,000

170,000 − Payments? = 160,000

Payments = 10,000

Complete the T-Account:

Long-Term notes payable

H Notes payments	10,000	12/31/11 Bal	80,000
		New notes issued	90,000 **G**
		12/31/12 Bal	160,000

The payment of $10,000 as an outflow of cash is shown on the Statement of Cash Flows. (See item **H** in Exhibit 13-4).

Computing Issuances of Stock and Purchases of Treasury Stock

Cash flows for these financing activities can be determined by analyzing the stock accounts. For example, the amount of a new issuance of common stock is determined from Common stock. Using data from Exhibit 13-5, the incomplete Common stock T-account is as follows:

Common stock

		12/31/11 Bal	250,000
Retirements	?	Issuance	?
		12/31/12 Bal	370,000

We would have to be told if there were any stock retirements. Since there were not, we know the balance change must be represented by new stock issuances. Solving for the missing value is completed as follows:

> 12/31/11 Bal + Issuance of Stock? – Retirements? = 12/31/12 Bal
> 250,000   + Issuance of Stock? –   0   = 370,000
> Issuance of Stock = 120,000

The completed T-Account for Common stock is as follows:

Common stock

		12/31/11 Bal	250,000	
Retirements	0	Issuance	120,000	**I**
		12/31/12 Bal	370,000	

Therefore, the new stock issuance shows as $120,000 positive cash flows in the financing section of the statement (item **I** in Exhibit 13-4).

The last item that changed on Smart Touch Learning's Balance Sheet was Treasury stock. The T-account balances from the Treasury stock account on the Balance sheet show the following:

Treasury stock

12/31/11 Bal	0		
Purchases	?	Sales	?
12/31/12 Bal	20,000		

Since we were not told that any Treasury stock was sold, we must assume that 100% of the account change represents new acquisitions of Treasury stock. Solving for the amount, the equation follows:

> 12/31/11 Bal + Purchases? – Sales? = 12/31/12 Bal
> 0   + Purchases? – 0   = 20,000
> Purchases = 20,000

Completing the T-account, we have the following:

Treasury stock

	12/31/11 Bal	0		
J	Purchases	20,000	Sales	0
	12/31/12 Bal	20,000		

So, $20,000 is shown as a cash outflow in the financing section of the cash flow statement for purchase of treasury stock (item **J** in Exhibit 13-4).

Computing Dividend Payments

The amount of dividend payments can be computed by analyzing the Retained earnings account. First we input the balances from the Balance Sheet:

Retained earnings			
		12/31/11 Bal	80,000
Net loss	?	Net income	?
Dividend declarations	?		
		12/31/12 Bal	110,000

Retained earnings increases when companies earn net income. Retained earnings decreases when companies have a net loss and when they declare dividends. We know that Smart Touch earned net income of $40,000 from the Income Statement in Exhibit 13-6.

Retained earnings				
		12/31/11 Bal	80,000	
Net loss	?	Net income	40,000	A
Dividend declarations	?			
		12/31/12 Bal	110,000	

Therefore, the missing value must be the amount of dividends Smart Touch declared. Solving for the value is as follows:

$$12/31/11 \text{ Bal} + \text{Net Income} - \text{Dividends Declared} = 12/31/12 \text{ Bal}$$
$$80,000 + 40,000 - \text{Dividends Declared} = 110,000$$
$$120,000 - \text{Dividends Declared} = 110,000$$
$$\text{Dividends Declared} = 10,000$$

So our final Retained earnings T-account shows the following:

Retained earnings					
			12/31/11 Bal	80,000	
			Net income	40,000	A
K	Dividend declarations	10,000			
			12/31/12 Bal	110,000	

A stock dividend has *no* effect on Cash and is *not* reported on the cash-flow statement. Smart Touch had no stock dividends—only cash dividends. Exhibit 13-8 on the next page summarizes the computation of cash flows from financing activities, highlighted in color.

Net Change in Cash and Cash Balances L

The next line of the cash flow statement (underneath Net cash provided by financing activities in Exhibit 13-4) represents the total change in cash for the period. In the case of Smart Touch Learning, it is the net decrease in cash balances of $20,000 for the year. The decrease in cash of $20,000 is also represented by the following:

(amounts in thousands)							
Net cash provided by Operating activities	−	Net cash used by Investing activities	+	Net cash provided by Financing activities		Net decrease in Cash	
70	−	260	+	170	=	−20	

EXHIBIT 13-8 | **Computing Cash Flows from Financing Activities**

Cash Receipts

From issuance of notes payable	Beginning notes payable	+	Cash receipt from issuance of notes payable	−	Payment of notes payable	=	Ending notes payable	
From issuance of stock	Beginning stock	+	Cash receipt from issuance of new stock	=	Ending stock			

Cash Payments

Of notes payable	Beginning notes payable	+	Cash receipt from issuance of notes payable	−	Payment of notes payable	=	Ending notes payable	
To purchase treasury stock	Beginning treasury stock	+	Cost of treasury stock purchased	=	Ending treasury stock			
Of dividends	Beginning retained earnings	+	Net income	−	Dividends declared	=	Ending retained earnings	

Next, the beginning cash from December 31, 2011, is listed at $42,000. The net decrease of $20,000 from beginning cash of $42,000 equals the ending cash balance on December 31, 2012, of $22,000. This is the key to the Statement of Cash Flows—it explains why the cash balance for Smart Touch decreased by $20,000, even though the company reported net income for the year.

Stop & Think...

Most of you probably have a checking or savings account. Think about how the balance changes from month to month. It does not always change because you have earned revenues or incurred expenses (operating). Sometimes it changes because you buy a long-lasting asset, such as a TV (investing). Sometimes it changes because you make a payment on your car note (financing). It is the same with business; business bank accounts do not change only because they earn revenue or incur expenses (operating). The cash flow statement explains all the reasons that cash changed (operating, investing, and financing).

Noncash Investing and Financing Activities

Companies make investments that do not require cash. They also obtain financing other than cash. Such transactions are called noncash investing and financing activities, and appear in a separate part of the cash flow statement. Our Smart Touch example did not include transactions of this type because the company did not have any noncash transactions during the year. So, to illustrate them, let us consider the three noncash transactions for Greg's Groovy Tunes. How would they be reported? First, we gather the noncash activity for the company:

1	Acquired $300,000 building by issuing stock
2	Acquired $70,000 land by issuing note payable
3	Paid $100,000 note payable by issuing common stock

Now, we consider each transaction individually.

1. Greg's Groovy Tunes issued common stock of $300,000 to acquire a building. The journal entry to record the purchase would be as follows:

Building	(A+)		300,000	
	Common stock	(Q+)		300,000

This transaction would not be reported on the cash-flow statement because no cash was paid. But the building and the common stock are important.

The purchase of the building is an investing activity. The issuance of common stock is a financing activity. Taken together, this transaction is a *noncash investing and financing activity*.

2. The second transaction listed indicates that Greg's Groovy Tunes acquired $70,000 of land by issuing a note. The journal entry to record the purchase would be as follows:

Land	(A+)		70,000	
	Notes payable	(L+)		70,000

This transaction would not be reported on the cash-flow statement because no cash was paid. But the land and the notes payable are important.

The purchase of the land is an investing activity. The issuance of the note is a financing activity. Taken together, this transaction is a *noncash investing and financing activity*.

3. The third transaction listed indicates that Greg's Groovy Tunes exchanged $100,000 of debt by issuing common stock. The journal entry to record the purchase would be as follows:

Notes payable	(L–)		100,000	
	Common stock	(Q+)		100,000

This transaction would not be reported on the cash-flow statement because no cash was paid. But the notes payable and the stock issuance are important.

The payment on the note and the issuance of the common stock are both financing activities. Taken together, this transaction, even though it is two financing transactions, is reported in the *noncash investing and financing activities*.

Noncash investing and financing activities can be reported in a separate schedule that accompanies the Statement of Cash Flows. Exhibit 13-9 on the next page illustrates noncash investing and financing activities for Greg's Groovy Tunes (all amounts are assumed). This information either follows the cash-flow statement or can be disclosed in a note.

EXHIBIT 13-9 | **Noncash Investing & Financing Activities**

GREG'S GROOVY TUNES Statement of Cash Flows—partial Year Ended December 31, 2012	
	(In thousands)
Noncash investing and financing activities:	
Acquisition of building by issuing common stock	$300
Acquisition of land by issuing note payable	70
Payment of note payable by issuing common stock	100
Total noncash investing and financing activities	$470

Measuring Cash Adequacy: Free Cash Flow

Throughout this chapter we have focused on cash flows from operating, investing, and financing activities. Some investors want to know how much cash a company can "free up" for new opportunities. **Free cash flow** is the amount of cash available from operations after paying for planned investments in long-term assets. Free cash flow can be computed as follows:

$$\text{Free cash flow} = \begin{array}{c}\text{Net cash provided}\\\text{by operating}\\\text{activities}\end{array} - \begin{array}{c}\text{Cash payments planned for}\\\text{investments in plant, equipment,}\\\text{and other long-term assets}\end{array}$$

Many companies use free cash flow to manage their operations. Suppose Greg's Groovy Tunes expects net cash provided by operations of $200,000. Assume Greg's Groovy Tunes plans to spend $160,000 to modernize its production facilities. In this case, Greg's Groovy Tunes' free cash flow would be $40,000 ($200,000 – $160,000). If a good investment opportunity comes along, Greg's Groovy Tunes should have $40,000 to invest.

Now we will put into practice what you have learned about the Statement of Cash Flows prepared by the indirect method.

Decision Guidelines

USING CASH-FLOW AND RELATED INFORMATION TO EVALUATE INVESTMENTS

Ann Browning is a private investor. Through the years, she has devised some guidelines for evaluating investments. Here are some of her guidelines.

Question	Financial Statement	What to Look For
• Where is most of the company's cash coming from?	Statement of cash flows	Operating activities → Good sign Investing activities → Bad sign Financing activities → Okay sign
• Do high sales and profits translate into more cash?	Statement of cash flows	Usually, but cash flows from *operating* activities must be the main source of cash for long-term success.
• If sales and profits are low, how is the company generating cash?	Statement of cash flows	If *investing* activities are generating the cash, the business may be in trouble because it is selling off its long-term assets. If *financing* activities are generating the cash, that cannot go on forever. Sooner or later, investors will demand cash flow from operating activities.
• Is the cash balance large enough to provide for expansion?	Balance sheet	The cash balance should be growing over time. If not, the company may be in trouble.
• Can the business pay its debts?	Income statement	Does the trend indicate increasing net income?
	Statement of cash flows	Cash flows from operating activities should be the main source of cash.
	Balance sheet	Are the current ratio and debt ratio adequate?

Summary Problem

The Adams Corporation reported the following Income Statement and comparative Balance Sheet for 2012 and 2011, along with transaction data for 2012:

ADAMS CORPORATION
Income Statement
Year Ended December 31, 2012

Sales revenue		$662,000
Cost of goods sold		560,000
Gross profit		102,000
Operating expenses:		
Salary expense	$46,000	
Depreciation expense	10,000	
Rent expense	2,000	
Total operating expenses		58,000
Income from operations		44,000
Other items:		
Loss on sale of equipment		(2,000)
Income before income tax		42,000
Income tax expense		(16,000)
Net income		$ 26,000

ADAMS CORPORATION
Balance Sheet
December 31, 2012 and 2011

Assets	2012	2011	Liabilities	2012	2011
Current:			Current:		
Cash and equivalents	$ 22,000	$ 3,000	Accounts payable	$ 35,000	$ 26,000
Accounts receivable	22,000	23,000	Accrued liabilities	7,000	9,000
Inventories	35,000	34,000	Income tax payable	10,000	10,000
Total current assets	79,000	60,000	Total current liabilities	52,000	45,000
Equipment, net	126,000	72,000	Bonds payable	84,000	53,000
			Stockholders' Equity		
			Common stock	52,000	20,000
			Retained earnings	27,000	19,000
			Less: Treasury stock	(10,000)	(5,000)
Total assets	$205,000	$132,000	Total liabilities and equity	$205,000	$132,000

Transaction Data for 2012:

Purchase of equipment..	$140,000
Payment of dividends..	18,000
Issuance of common stock to retire bonds payable	13,000
Issuance of bonds payable to borrow cash..	44,000
Cash receipt from issuance of common stock	19,000
Cash receipt from sale of equipment (book value, $76,000)	74,000
Purchase of treasury stock	5,000

Requirement

1. Prepare Adams Corporation's Statement of Cash Flows for the year ended December 31, 2012. Format operating cash flows by the indirect method. Follow the four steps outlined below.

   STEP 1. Lay out the format of the Statement of Cash Flows.

   STEP 2. From the comparative Balance Sheet, compute the increase in cash during the year.

   STEP 3. From the Income Statement, take net income, depreciation, and the loss on sale of equipment to the Statement of Cash Flows.

   STEP 4. Complete the Statement of Cash Flows. Account for the year-to-year change in each Balance Sheet account. Prepare a T-account to show the transaction activity in each long-term balance-sheet account.

Solution

ADAMS CORPORATION
Statement of Cash Flows
Year Ended December 31, 2012

Cash flows from operating activities:		
Net income		$26,000
Adjustments to reconcile net income to net cash		
provided by operating activities:		
Depreciation	$ 10,000	
Loss on sale of equipment	2,000	
Decrease in accounts receivable	1,000	
Increase in inventories	(1,000)	
Increase in accounts payable	9,000	
Decrease in accrued liabilities	(2,000)	19,000
Net cash provided by operating activities		45,000
Cash flows from investing activities:		
Purchase of equipment	(140,000)	
Sale of equipment	74,000	
Net cash used for investing activities		(66,000)
Cash flows from financing activities:		
Issuance of common stock	19,000	
Payment of dividends	(18,000)	
Issuance of bonds payable	44,000	
Purchase of treasury stock	(5,000)	
Net cash provided by financing activities		40,000
Net increase in cash		19,000
Cash balance, December 31, 2011		3,000
Cash balance, December 31, 2012		$22,000
Noncash investing and financing activities:		
Issuance of common stock to retire bonds payable		$13,000
Total noncash investing and financing activities		$13,000

Relevant T-Accounts:

Equipment, net			
Bal	72,000		
	140,000	10,000	
		76,000	
Bal	126,000		

Bonds payable			
		Bal	53,000
13,000			44,000
		Bal	84,000

Common stock			
		Bal	20,000
			13,000
			19,000
		Bal	52,000

Retained earnings			
		Bal	19,000
18,000			26,000
		Bal	27,000

Treasury stock		
Bal	5,000	
	5,000	
Bal	10,000	

Review *The Statement of Cash Flows*

■ Accounting Vocabulary

Cash Equivalents (p. 605)
Highly liquid short-term investments that can be readily converted into cash.

Cash Flows (p. 605)
Cash receipts and cash payments.

Direct Method (p. 607)
Format of the operating activities section of the Statement of Cash Flows; lists the major categories of operating cash receipts and cash payments.

Financing Activities (p. 606)
Activities that obtain the cash needed to launch and sustain the business; a section of the Statement of Cash Flows.

Free Cash Flow (p. 619)
The amount of cash available from operations after paying for planned investments in plant, equipment, and other long-term assets.

Indirect Method (p. 607)
Format of the operating activities section of the Statement of Cash Flows; starts with

net income and reconciles to net cash provided by operating activities.

Investing Activities (p. 606)
Activities that increase or decrease long-term assets; a section of the Statement of Cash Flows.

Operating Activities (p. 606)
Activities that create revenue or expense in the entity s major line of business; a section of the Statement of Cash Flows. Operating activities affect the Income Statement.

■ Quick Check

1. The purposes of the cash-flow statement are to
   a. evaluate management decisions.
   b. determine ability to pay liabilities and dividends.
   c. predict future cash flows.
   d. All of the above

2. The main categories of cash-flow activities are
   a. direct and indirect.
   b. operating, investing, and financing.
   c. current and long-term.
   d. noncash investing and financing.

3. Operating activities are most closely related to
   a. long-term assets.
   b. long-term liabilities and owners' equity.
   c. current assets and current liabilities.
   d. dividends and treasury stock.

4. Which item does *not* appear on a Statement of Cash Flows prepared by the indirect method?
   a. Collections from customers
   b. Depreciation
   c. Net income
   d. Gain on sale of land

5. Hobby Gas Station earned net income of $73,000 after deducting depreciation of $7,000 and all other expenses. Current assets decreased by $6,000, and current liabilities increased by $9,000. How much was Hobby Gas Station's cash provided by operating activities (indirect method)?
   a. $95,000
   b. $51,000
   c. $83,000
   d. $63,000

6. The Plant assets account of Vacation Club shows the following:

Plant assets, net

Beg	99,000	Depr	27,000
Purchase	437,000	Sale	54,000
End	455,000		

Vacation Club sold plant assets at a $16,000 loss. Where on the Statement of Cash Flows should Vacation Club report the sale of plant assets? How much should the business report for the sale?

a. Investing cash flows—cash receipt of $54,000

b. Investing cash flows—cash receipt of $38,000

c. Financing cash flows—cash receipt of $70,000

d. Investing cash flows—cash receipt of $70,000

7. Rock Music, Corp., borrowed $36,000, issued common stock of $15,000, and paid dividends of $21,000. What was Rock Music's net cash provided (used) by financing activities?

a. $0

b. ($21,000)

c. $30,000

d. $72,000

8. Which item appears on a Statement of Cash Flows prepared by the indirect method?

a. Payments to suppliers

b. Payments of income tax

c. Depreciation

d. Collections from customers

9. (**Appendix 13A: Direct Method**) Sun Copy Center had accounts receivable of $23,000 at the beginning of the year and $51,000 at year-end. Revenue for the year totaled $103,000. How much cash did the business collect from customers?

a. $75,000

b. $131,000

c. $177,000

d. $126,000

10. (**Appendix 13A: Direct Method**) Cell Call Company had operating expense of $44,000. At the beginning of the year, Cell Call owed $7,000 on accrued liabilities. At year-end, accrued liabilities were $3,500. How much cash did Cell Call pay for operating expenses?

a. $37,000

b. $47,500

c. $48,500

d. $40,500

Answers are given after Apply Your Knowledge (p. 643).

Assess Your Progress

▪ Short Exercises

S13-1   *(L.OBJ. 1)* **Purposes of the Statement of Cash Flows [10 min]**
Financial statements all have a goal. The cash flow statement does as well.

Requirement

1. Describe how the Statement of Cash Flows helps investors and creditors perform each of the following functions:
   a. Predict future cash flows
   b. Evaluate management decisions
   c. Predict the ability to make debt payments to lenders and pay dividends to stockholders

S13-2   *(L.OBJ. 2)* **Classifying cash-flow items [10 min]**
Cash-flow items must be categorized into one of four categories.

Requirement

1. Answer the following questions about the Statement of Cash Flows:
   a. List the categories of cash flows in order of presentation.
   b. What is the "key reconciling figure" for the Statement of Cash Flows? Where do you get this figure?
   c. What is the first dollar amount to report for the indirect method?

S13-3   *(L.OBJ. 3)* **Classifying items on the indirect Statement of Cash Flows [10 min]**
Triumph Corporation is preparing its Statement of Cash Flows by the *indirect* method. Triumph has the following items for you to consider in preparing the statement:

_____ a. Increase in accounts payable   _____ g. Depreciation expense

_____ b. Payment of dividends   _____ h. Increase in inventory

_____ c. Decrease in accrued liabilities   _____ i. Decrease in accounts receivable

_____ d. Issuance of common stock   _____ j. Purchase of equipment

_____ e. Gain on sale of building

_____ f. Loss on sale of land

Requirement

1. Identify each item as an
   • Operating activity—addition to net income (O+), or subtraction from net income (O–)
   • Investing activity—addition to cash flow (I+), or subtraction from cash flow (I–)
   • Financing activity—addition to cash flow (F+), or subtraction from cash flow (F–)
   • Activity that is not used to prepare the indirect cash-flow statement (N)

S13-4   *(L.OBJ. 3)* **Computing cash flows from operating activities—indirect method [10 min]**
DVR Equipment, Inc., reported the following data for 2011:

Income Statement	
Net income	$ 40,000
Depreciation	10,000
Balance sheet	
Increase in Accounts receivable	9,000
Decrease in Accounts payable	6,000

Requirement

1. Compute DVR's net cash provided by operating activities—indirect method.

S13-5 *(L.OBJ. 3)* **Computing cash flows from operating activities—indirect method [10 min]**

Street Cellular accountants have assembled the following data for the year ended June 30, 2012:

Cash receipt from sale of land	$ 29,000	Net income	$ 64,000
Depreciation expense	19,000	Purchase of equipment	44,000
Payment of dividends	5,700	Decrease in current liabilities	7,000
Cash receipt from issuance of		Increase in current assets	
common stock	16,000	other than cash	13,000

Requirement

1. Prepare the *operating* activities section using the indirect method for Street Cellular's Statement of Cash Flows for the year ended June 30, 2012.

Note: Short Exercise 13-5 data is used to complete Short Exercise 13-6.

S13-6 *(L.OBJ. 3)* **Computing cash flows—indirect method [15 min]**

Use the data in Short Exercise 13-5 to complete this exercise.

Requirement

1. Prepare Street Cellular's Statement of Cash Flows using the indirect method for the year ended June 30, 2012. Stop after determining the net increase (or decrease) in cash.

S13-7 *(L.OBJ. 3)* **Computing investing and financing cash flows [10 min]**

White Media Corporation had the following Income Statement and Balance Sheet for 2011:

WHITE MEDIA CORPORATION	
Income Statement	
Year Ended December 31, 2011	
Service revenue	$ 79,000
Depreciation expense	6,000
Other expenses	54,000
Net income	$ 19,000

WHITE MEDIA CORPORATION					
Comparative Balance Sheet					
December 31, 2011 and 2010					
Assets	2011	2010	Liabilities	2011	2010
Current:			Current:		
Cash	$ 5,100	$ 4,200	Accounts payable	$ 6,500	$ 4,500
Accounts receivable	10,100	8,100	Long–term notes payable	7,000	10,000
Equipment, net	76,000	68,000	**Stockholders' Equity**		
			Common stock	27,000	18,000
			Retained earnings	50,700	47,800
Total assets	$ 91,200	$ 80,300	Total liabilities and stockholders' equity	$ 91,200	$ 80,300

1. Compute for White Media Corporation during 2011 the
   a. Acquisition of equipment. The business sold no equipment during the year.
   b. Payment of a long-term note payable. During the year the business issued a $5,100 note payable.

Note: Short Exercise 13-8 should be used only after completing Short Exercise 13-7.

S13-8 *(L.OBJ. 3)* **Preparing the Statement of Cash Flows—indirect method [15-20 min]**
Use the White Media Corporation data in Short Exercise 13-7 and the results you calculated from the requirements.

Requirement

1. Prepare White Media's Statement of Cash Flows—indirect method—for the year ended December 31, 2011.

S13-9 *(L.OBJ. 3)* **Computing the change in cash [5 min]**
Brianna's Wedding Shops earned net income of $76,000, which included depreciation of $17,000. Brianna's paid $122,000 for a building and borrowed $63,000 on a long-term note payable.

Requirement

1. How much did Brianna's cash balance increase or decrease during the year?

S13-10 *(L.OBJ. 3)* **Computing the change in cash [5 min]**
Roberta McLeary Company expects the following for 2011:

- Net cash provided by operating activities of $156,000
- Net cash provided by financing activities of $63,000
- Net cash used for investing activities of $78,000 (no sales of long-term assets)

Requirement

1. How much free cash flow does McLeary expect for 2011?

■ Exercises

E13-11 *(L.OBJ. 1)* **Predicting future cash flows [10 min]**
Magnuson's Magnets reported net loss for the year of $10,000; however, they reported an increase in cash balance of $20,000. The CFO states "Magnuson's Magnets would have shown a profit were it not for the depreciation expense recorded this year."

Requirements

1. Can the CFO be right? Why?
2. Based on the information provided, what would you predict future cash flows to be?

E13-12 *(L.OBJ. 2)* **Classifying cash-flow items [10 min]**
Consider the following transactions:

- a. Purchased Building for $200,000 cash
- b. Issued $10 par preferred stock for cash
- c. Cash received from sales to customers of $20,000
- d. Cash paid to vendors, $10,000
- e. Sold Building for $5,000 gain for cash
- f. Purchased common treasury shares for $15,000
- g. Paid a notes payable with 1,000 of the company's common shares

Requirement

1. Identify the category of the Statement of Cash Flows in which each transaction would be reported.

E13-13 *(L.OBJ. 3)* **Classifying items on the indirect Statement of Cash Flows [5-10 min]**
The cash flow statement categorizes like transactions for optimal reporting.

Requirement

1. Identify each of the following transactions as an (a)
   - Operating activity (O),
   - Investing activity (I),
   - Financing activity (F),
   - Noncash investing and financing activity (NIF), or
   - transaction that is not reported on the Statement of Cash Flows (N).

   For each cash flow, indicate whether the item increases (+) or decreases (–) cash. The *indirect* method is used to report cash flows from operating activities.

_____ a. Loss on sale of land		_____ i. Cash sale of land
_____ b. Acquisition of equipment by issuance of note payable		_____ j. Issuance of long-term note payable to borrow cash
_____ c. Payment of long-term debt		_____ k. Depreciation
_____ d. Acquisition of building by issuance of common stock		_____ l. Purchase of treasury stock
_____ e. Accrual of salary expense		_____ m. Issuance of common stock
_____ f. Decrease in inventory		_____ n. Increase in accounts payable
_____ g. Increase in prepaid expenses		_____ o. Net income
_____ h. Decrease in accrued liabilities		_____ p. Payment of cash dividend

E13-14 *(L.OBJ. 3)* **Classifying transactions on the Statement of Cash Flows—indirect method [5–10 min]**
Consider the following transactions:

a. Cash	81,000			g. Land	18,000	
Common stock		81,000		Cash		18,000
b. Treasury stock	13,000			h. Cash	7,200	
Cash		13,000		Equipment		7,200
c. Cash	60,000			i. Bonds payable	45,000	
Sales revenue		60,000		Cash		45,000
d. Land	87,700			j. Building	164,000	
Cash		87,700		Note payable, long–term		164,000
e. Depreciation expense	9,000			k. Loss on disposal of equipment	1,400	
Accumulated depreciation		9,000		Equipment, net		1,400
f. Dividends payable	16,500					
Cash		16,500				

1. Indicate whether each transaction would result in an operating activity, an investing activity, or a financing activity for an indirect method Statement of Cash Flows and the accompanying schedule of noncash investing and financing activities.

E13-15 *(L.OBJ. 3)* **Computing operating acitivites cash flow—indirect method [10–15 min]**

The records of Paramount Color Engraving reveal the following:

Net income	$ 42,000	Depreciation	$ 11,000
Sales revenue	12,000	Decrease in current liabilities	20,000
Loss on sale of land	7,000	Increase in current assets	
Acquisition of land	36,000	other than cash	8,000

Requirements

1. Compute cash flows from operating activities by the indirect method.
2. Evaluate the operating cash flow of Paramount Color Engraving. Give the reason for your evaluation.

E13-16 *(L.OBJ. 3)* **Computing operating activities cash flow—indirect method [15–20 min]**

The accounting records of CD Sales, Inc., include the following accounts:

Cash			Accounts receivable			Inventory	
Mar 1	7,000		Mar 1	19,000		Mar 1	21,000
	????			????			????
Mar 31	5,000		Mar 31	14,000		Mar 31	24,000

Accounts payable			Accumulated depr.—equipment			Retained earnings		
		Mar 1	13,000		Mar 1	50,000		Mar 1	66,000
			????		Depr	4,000	Dividend 16,000	Net Inc	81,000
		Mar 31	17,500		Mar 31	54,000		Mar 31	131,000

Requirement

1. Compute CD's net cash provided by (used for) operating activities during March. Use the indirect method.

E13-17 *(L.OBJ. 3)* **Preparing the Statement of Cash Flows—indirect method [20–30 min]**

The Income Statement and additional data of Minerals Plus, Inc., follow:

MINERALS PLUS, INC.		
Income Statement		
Year Ended June 30, 2010		
Revenues:		
Service revenue		$ 236,000
Expenses:		
Cost of goods sold	$ 96,000	
Salary expense	54,000	
Depreciation expense	27,000	
Income tax expense	9,000	186,000
Net income		$ 50,000

Additional data follow:

a. Acquisition of plant assets is $120,000. Of this amount, $103,000 is paid in cash and $17,000 by signing a note payable.

b. Cash receipt from sale of land totals $24,000. There was no gain or loss.

c. Cash receipts from issuance of common stock total $32,000.

d. Payment of note payable is $17,000.

e. Payment of dividends is $11,000.

f. From the balance sheet:

	June 30,	
	2010	2009
Current Assets:		
Cash	$ 32,000	$ 15,000
Accounts receivable	38,000	55,000
Inventory	92,000	86,000
Current Liabilities:		
Accounts payable	$ 36,000	$ 22,000
Accrued liabilities	15,000	25,000

Requirement

1. Prepare Minerals Plus' Statement of Cash Flows for the year ended June 30, 2010, using the indirect method. Include a separate section for noncash investing and financing activities.

E13-18 *(L.OBJ. 3)* **Computing operating activities cash flow—indirect method [10–15 min]**

Consider the following facts for Java Jolt:

a. Beginning and ending Retained earnings are $48,000 and $69,000, respectively. Net income for the period is $64,000.

b. Beginning and ending Plant assets, net, are $102,000 and $106,000, respectively. Depreciation for the period is $19,000, and acquisitions of new plant assets total $26,000. Plant assets were sold at a $4,000 gain.

Requirements

1. How much are cash dividends?

2. What was the amount of the cash receipt from the sale of plant assets?

E13-19 *(L.OBJ. 3)* **Computing the cash effect of acquiring assets [10 min]**

Cole Gymnastics Equipment, Inc., reported the following financial statements for 2011:

COLE GYMNASTICS EQUIPMENT, INC.		
Income Statement		
Year Ended December 31, 2011		
		(In thousands)
Sales revenue		$ 711
Cost of goods sold	$ 343	
Depreciation expense	49	
Other expenses	210	
Total expenses		602
Net income		$ 109

(In thousands)						
COLE GYMNASTICS EQUIPMENT, INC. **Comparative Balance Sheet** **December 31, 2011 and 2010**						
Assets	2011	2010	Liabilities	2011	2010	
Current:			Current:			
Cash	$ 20	$ 16	Accounts payable	$ 75	$ 73	
Accounts receivable	56	50	Salary payable	3	4	
Inventory	80	87	Long–term notes payable	58	69	
Long–term investments	91	74	**Stockholders' Equity**			
Plant assets, net	225	185	Common stock	45	32	
			Retained earnings	291	234	
Total	$ 472	$ 412	Total	$ 472	$ 412	

Requirement

1. Compute the amount of Cole Gymnastics' acquisition of plant assets. Cole Gymnastics sold no plant assets.

E13-20 *(L.OBJ. 3)* **Computing the cash effect of transactions [15 min]**
Use the Cole Gymnastics data in Exercise 13-19.

Requirement

1. Compute the following:

   a. New borrowing or payment of long-term notes payable, with Cole Gymnastics having only one long-term note payable transaction during the year
   b. Issuance of common stock, with Cole Gymnastics having only one common stock trans-action during the year
   c. Payment of cash dividends

Note: Exercise 13-21 should be used only after completing Exercises 13-19 and 13-20.

E13-21 *(L.OBJ. 3)* **Computing the cash effect of transactions [15 min]**
Use the Cole Gymnastics data in Exercises 13-19 and 13-20.

Requirement

1. Prepare the company's Statement of Cash Flows—indirect method—for the year ended December 31, 2011. Show all amounts in thousands.

Problems (Group A)

P13-22A *(L.OBJ. 1, 2, 3)* **Purpose of the statement and preparing the Statement of Cash Flows—indirect method [40–50 min]**

North American Reserve Rare Coins (NARRC) was formed on January 1, 2010, when NARRC issued its common stock for $475,000. Additional data for the year follows:

a. On January 1, 2010, NARRC issued common stock for $475,000.

b. Early in January, NARRC made the following cash payments:
   1. For store fixtures, $46,000
   2. For inventory, $330,000
   3. For rent expense on a store building, $11,000

c. Later in the year, NARRC purchased inventory on account for $235,000. Before year-end, NARRC paid $135,000 of this account payable.

d. During 2010, NARRC sold 2,900 units of inventory for $300 each. Before year-end, the company collected 85% of this amount. Cost of goods sold for the year was $310,000, and ending inventory totaled $255,000.

e. The store employs three people. The combined annual payroll is $96,000, of which NARRC still owes $5,000 at year-end.

f. At the end of the year, NARRC paid income tax of $16,000.

g. Late in 2010, NARRC paid cash dividends of $43,000.

h. For equipment, NARRC uses the straight-line depreciation method, over five years, with zero residual value.

Requirements

1. What is the purpose of the cash flow statement?
2. Prepare NARRC's Income Statement for the year ended December 31, 2010. Use the single-step format, with all revenues listed together and all expenses together.
3. Prepare NARRC's Balance Sheet at December 31, 2010.
4. Prepare NARRC's Statement of Cash Flows using the indirect method for the year ended December 31, 2010.

P13-23A *(L.OBJ. 3)* **Preparing the Statement of Cash Flows—indirect method [35–45 min]**

Accountants for Smithson, Inc., have assembled the following data for the year ended December 31, 2011:

	December 31,	
	2011	2010
Current Accounts:		
Current assets:		
Cash and cash equivalents	$105,600	$ 26,000
Accounts receivable	64,200	69,300
Inventories	85,000	83,000
Current liabilities:		
Accounts payable	57,800	56,000
Income tax payable	15,000	16,700

Transaction Data for 2011:

Issuance of common stock			Payment of note payable	$45,100
for cash	$ 37,000		Payment of cash dividends	51,000
Depreciation expense	18,000		Issuance of note payable	
Purchase of equipment	71,000		to borrow cash	60,000
Acquisition of land by issuing			Gain on sale of building	4,500
long–term note payable	118,000		Net income	72,500
Cost basis of building sold	56,000			

Requirement

1. Prepare Smithson's Statement of Cash Flows using the *indirect* method. Include an accompanying schedule of noncash investing and financing activities.

P13-24A *(L.OBJ. 3)* **Preparing the Statement of Cash Flows—indirect method—and evaluating cash flows [35–45 min]**

The comparative Balance Sheet of Morston Medical Supply at December 31, 2012, reported the following:

	December 31,	
	2012	2011
Current assets:		
Cash and cash equivalents	$ 87,800	$ 23,500
Accounts receivable	14,800	21,300
Inventories	63,200	60,000
Current Liabilities:		
Accounts payable	30,100	30,100
Accrued liabilities	10,500	11,100

Morston's transactions during 2012 included the following:

Payment of cash dividend	$ 14,200	Depreciation expense	$ 16,800
Purchase of equipment	54,600	Purchase of building	105,000
Issuance of long–term note payable		Net income	60,600
to borrow cash	49,000	Issuance of common stock for cash	109,000

Requirements

1. Prepare the Statement of Cash Flows of Morston Medical Supply for the year ended December 31, 2012. Use the *indirect* method to report cash flows from operating activities.

2. Evaluate Morston's cash flows for the year. Mention all three categories of cash flows and give the reason for your evaluation.

P13-25A *(L.OBJ. 3)* **Preparing the Statement of Cash Flows—indirect method [35-45 min]**
The 2012 comparative Balance Sheet and Income Statement of Cobbs Hill, Inc., follow:

COBBS HILL, INC.			
Comparative Balance Sheet			
December 31, 2012 and 2011			
	2012	2011	Increase (Decrease)
Current assets:			
Cash and cash equivalents	$ 26,000	$ 15,300	$ 10,700
Accounts receivable	26,700	25,000	1,700
Inventories	79,000	91,800	(12,800)
Plant assets:			
Land	34,700	10,000	24,700
Equipment, net	100,900	92,700	8,200
Total assets	$ 267,300	$ 234,800	$ 32,500
Current liabilities:			
Accounts payable	$ 35,600	$ 30,700	$ 4,900
Accrued liabilities	28,200	30,000	(1,800)
Long–term liabilities:			
Notes payable	77,000	104,000	(27,000)
Stockholders' equity:			
Common stock	88,200	64,400	23,800
Retained earnings	38,300	5,700	32,600
Total liabilities and stockholders' equity	$ 267,300	$ 234,800	$ 32,500

COBBS HILL, INC.		
Income Statement		
Year Ended December 31, 2012		
Revenues:		
Sales revenue		$ 443,000
Interest revenue		8,700
Total revenues		451,700
Expenses:		
Cost of goods sold	$ 200,200	
Salary expense	73,400	
Depreciation expense	14,200	
Other operating expense	10,000	
Interest expense	21,800	
Income tax expense	19,700	
Total expenses		339,300
Net income		$ 112,400

Cobbs Hill had no noncash investing and financing transactions during 2012. During the year, there were no sales of land or equipment, no issuances of notes payable, no retirements of stock, and no treasury stock transactions.

Requirements

1. Prepare the 2012 Statement of Cash Flows, formatting operating activities by the *indirect* method.
2. How will what you learned in this problem help you evaluate an investment?

P13-26B *(L.OBJ. 1, 2, 3)* **Purpose of the statement and preparing the Statement of Cash Flows—indirect method [40–50 min]**

Official Reserve Rare Coins (ORRC) was formed on January 1, 2010, when ORRC issued its common stock for $475,000. Additional data for the year follows:

---

a. On January 1, 2010, ORRC issued common stock for $475,000.

b. Early in January, ORRC made the following cash payments:
   1. For store fixtures, $46,000
   2. For inventory, $310,000
   3. For rent expense on a store building, $10,000

c. Later in the year, ORRC purchased inventory on account for $237,000. Before year-end, ORRC paid $137,000 of this account payable.

d. During 2010, ORRC sold 2,800 units of inventory for $225 each. Before year end, the company collected 80% of this amount. Cost of goods sold for the year was $340,000, and ending inventory totaled $207,000.

e. The store employs three people. The combined annual payroll is $94,000, of which ORRC still owes $2,000 at year-end.

f. At the end of the year, ORRC paid income tax of $22,000.

g. Late in 2010, ORRC paid cash dividends of $44,000.

h. For equipment, ORRC uses the straight-line depreciation method, over 5 years, with zero residual value.

Requirements

1. What is the purpose of the cash flow statement?

2. Prepare ORRC's Income Statement for the year ended December 31, 2010. Use the single-step format, with all revenues listed together and all expenses together.

3. Prepare ORRC's Balance Sheet at December 31, 2010.

4. Prepare ORRC's Statement of Cash Flows using the *indirect* method for the year ended December 31, 2010.

P13-27B *(L.OBJ. 3)* **Preparing the Statement of Cash Flows—indirect method [35-45 min]**

Accountants for Carlson, Inc., have assembled the following data for the year ended December 31, 2011:

	December 31,	
	2011	2010
Current Accounts:		
Current assets:		
Cash and cash equivalents	$ 60,100	$ 19,000
Accounts receivable	64,500	69,000
Inventories	86,000	84,000
Current liabilities:		
Accounts payable	57,600	56,200
Income tax payable	14,700	16,400

Transaction Data for 2011:

Issuance of common stock for cash	$ 42,000	Payment of note payable	$44,100
		Payment of cash dividends	48,000
Depreciation expense	21,000	Issuance of note payable	
Purchase of equipment	66,000	to borrow cash	59,000
Acquisition of land by issuing		Gain on sale of building	4,500
long–term note payable ...	118,000	Net income	69,500
		Cost basis of building sold	$ 5,500

1. Prepare Carlson's Statement of Cash Flows using the *indirect* method. Include an accompanying schedule of noncash investing and financing activities.

P13-28B *(L.OBJ. 3)* **Preparing the Statement of Cash Flows—indirect method—and evaluating cash flows [35–45 min]**

The comparative Balance Sheet of Smithson Medical Supply at December 31, 2012, reported the following:

	December 31,	
	2012	2011
Current assets:		
Cash and cash equivalents	$ 78,600	$ 19,500
Accounts receivable	14,700	21,400
Inventories	62,600	60,400
Current liabilities:		
Accounts payable	28,100	27,100
Accrued liabilities	10,300	11,300

Smithson's transactions during 2012 included the following:

Payment of cash dividend	$ 22,200	Depreciation expense	$ 16,800
Purchase of equipment	54,600	Purchase of building	109,000
Issuance of long–term note payable		Net income	61,600
to borrow cash	50,000	Issuance of common stock for cash	112,000

Requirements

1. Prepare the Statement of Cash Flows of Smithson Medical Supply for the year ended December 31, 2012. Use the *indirect* method to report cash flows from operating activities.
2. Evaluate Smithson's cash flows for the year. Mention all three categories of cash flows and give the reason for your evaluation.

P13-29B *(L.OBJ. 3)* **Preparing the statement of cash flow—indirect method [35–45 min]**

The 2012 comparative Balance Sheet and Income Statement of Digital Subscriptions, Inc., follow:

	DIGITAL SUBSCRIPTIONS, INC. Comparative Balance Sheet December 31, 2012 and 2011		
	2012	**2011**	**Increase (Decrease)**
Current assets:			
Cash and cash equivalents	$ 26,800	$ 15,800	$ 11,000
Accounts receivable	26,500	25,000	1,500
Inventories	79,500	91,100	(11,600)
Plant assets:			
Land	34,700	10,000	24,700
Equipment, net	96,900	88,700	8,200
Total assets	$ 264,400	$ 230,600	$ 33,800
Current liabilities:			
Accounts payable	$ 35,500	$ 30,000	$ 5,500
Accrued liabilities	28,500	30,100	(1,600)
Long–term liabilities:			
Notes payable	73,000	102,000	(29,000)
Stockholders' equity:			
Common stock	88,700	64,300	24,400
Retained earnings	38,700	4,200	34,500
Total liabilities and stockholders' equity	$ 264,400	$ 230,600	$ 33,800

	DIGITAL SUBSCRIPTIONS, INC. Income Statement Year Ended December 31, 2012	
Revenues:		
Sales revenue		$ 441,000
Interest revenue		8,100
Total revenues		449,100
Expenses:		
Cost of goods sold	$ 205,200	
Salary expense	79,400	
Depreciation expense	14,800	
Other operating expense	10,300	
Interest expense	21,900	
Income tax expense	19,900	
Total expenses		351,500
Net income		$ 97,600

Digital Subscriptions had no noncash investing and financing transactions during 2012. During the year, there were no sales of land or equipment, no issuances of notes payable, no retirements of stock, and no treasury stock transactions.

1. Prepare the 2012 Statement of Cash Flows, formatting operating activities by the *indirect* method.
2. How will what you learned in this problem help you evaluate an investment?

■ Continuing Exercise

E13-30 This exercise continues the Sherman Lawn Service, Inc., situation from Exercise 12-24 of Chapter 12. Refer to the Comparative Balance Sheet for Sherman Lawn Service.

SHERMAN LAWN SERVICE, INC. Comparative Balance Sheet As of December 31, 2012 and 2011		
Assets	2012	2011
Cash	$ 5,000	$ 1,480
Accounts receivable	2,200	150
Lawn supplies	150	70
Equipment	1,400	1,400
(Less Accumulated depreciation)	(495)	(146)
Total Assets	$ 8,255	$ 2,954
Liabilities		
Accounts payable	$ 350	$ 1,400
Stockholders' Equity		
Common stock	2,000	1,000
Retained earnings	5,905	554
Total liabilities and stockholders' equity	$ 8,255	$ 2,954

Requirement

1. Prepare the Statement of Cash Flows using the *indirect* method. Assume no dividends were declared or paid during the year.

■ Continuing Problem

P13-31 This problem continues the Haupt Consulting, Inc., situation from Problem 12-25 of Chapter 12. Refer to the balance sheet and income statement for Haupt Consulting.

HAUPT CONSULTING, INC. Comparative Balance Sheet As of December 31, 2012 and 2011		
Assets	2012	2011
Cash	$ 5,000	$ 8,100
Accounts receivable	2,200	1,700
Supplies	420	300
Equipment	10,000	2,000
Furniture	3,600	3,600
Building	75,000	—
(Less Accumulated depreciation)	(2,753)	(93)
Total Assets	$ 93,467	$ 15,607
Liabilities		
Accounts payable	$ 350	$ 3,900
Salary payable	2,500	0
Notes payable	40,000	0
Stockholders' Equity		
Common stock	20,000	10,000
Retained earnings	30,617	1,707
Total liabilities and stockholders' equity	$ 93,467	$ 15,607

Requirement

1. Prepare the Statement of Cash Flows using the indirect method.

Apply Your Knowledge

■ Decision Cases

Case 1. The 2010 comparative Income Statement and the 2010 comparative Balance Sheet of Golf America, Inc., have just been distributed at a meeting of the company's board of directors. The members of the board of directors raise a fundamental question: Why is the cash balance so low? This question is especially hard to understand because 2010 showed record profits. As the controller of the company, you must answer the question.

GOLF AMERICA, INC.
Comparative Income Statement
Years Ended December 31, 2010 and 2009

(In thousands)	2010	2009
Revenues and gains:		
Sales revenue	$444	$310
Gain on sale of equipment (sale price, $33)	—	18
Total revenues and gains	$444	$328
Expenses and losses:		
Cost of goods sold	$221	$162
Salary expense	48	28
Depreciation expense	46	22
Interest expense	13	20
Amortization expense on patent	11	11
Loss on sale of land (sale price, $61)	—	35
Total expenses and losses	339	278
Net income	$105	$ 50

GOLF AMERICA, INC.
Comparative Balance Sheet
December 31, 2010 and 2009

(In thousands)	2010	2009
Assets		
Cash	$ 25	$ 63
Accounts receivable, net	72	61
Inventories	194	181
Long-term investments	31	0
Property, plant, and equipment, net	125	61
Patents	177	188
Totals	$624	$554
Liabilities and Owners' Equity		
Accounts payable	$ 63	$ 56
Accrued liabilities	12	17
Notes payable, long-term	179	264
Common stock	149	61
Retained earnings	221	156
Totals	$624	$554

Requirements

1. Prepare a Statement of Cash Flows for 2010 in the format that best shows the relationship between net income and operating cash flow. The company sold no plant assets or long-term investments and issued no notes payable during 2010. There were *no* noncash investing and financing transactions during the year. Show all amounts in thousands.

2. Considering net income and the company's cash flows during 2010, was it a good year or a bad year? Give your reasons.

Case 2. Showcase Cinemas and Theater by Design are asking you to recommend their stock to your clients. Because Showcase and Theater by Design earn about the same net income and have similar financial positions, your decision depends on their cash-flow statements, summarized as follows:

	Theater by Design		Showcase Cinemas	
Net cash provided by operating activities		$ 30,000		$ 70,000
Cash provided by (used for) investing activities:				
Purchase of plant assets	$(20,000)		$(100,000)	
Sale of plant assets	40,000	20,000	10,000	(90,000)
Cash provided by (used for) financing activities:				
Issuance of common stock		—		30,000
Paying off long-term debt		(40,000)		—
Net increase in cash		$ 10,000		$ 10,000

Requirement

1. Based on their cash flows, which company looks better? Give your reasons.

■ Ethical Issue

Moss Exports is having a bad year. Net income is only $60,000. Also, two important overseas customers are falling behind in their payments to Moss, and Moss's accounts receivable are ballooning. The company desperately needs a loan. The Moss Exports board of directors is considering ways to put the best face on the company's financial statements. Moss's bank closely examines cash flow from operations. Daniel Peavey, Moss's controller, suggests reclassifying as long-term the receivables from the slow-paying clients. He explains to the board that removing the $80,000 rise in accounts receivable from current assets will increase net cash provided by operations. This approach may help Moss get the loan.

Requirements

1. Using only the amounts given, compute net cash provided by operations, both without and with the reclassification of the receivables. Which reporting makes Moss look better?
2. Under what condition would the reclassification of the receivables be ethical? Unethical?

■ Financial Statement Case—Amazon.com

Use the **Amazon.com** Statement of Cash Flows, along with the company's other financial statements at the end of this book, to answer the following questions.

Requirements

1. Which method does **Amazon.com** use to report net cash flows from *operating* activities? How can you tell?
2. **Amazon.com** earned net income during 2008. Did operations *provide* cash or *use* cash during 2008? Give the amount. How did operating cash during 2008 compare with 2007? Be specific, and state the reason for your answer.

3. Suppose **Amazon.com** reported net cash flows from operating activities by the direct method. Compute these amounts for the year ended December 31, 2008:
   a. Collections from customers (Assume other current assets were $116 million at December 31, 2008, and $20 million at December 31, 2007.)
   b. Payments for inventory
4. Evaluate 2008 in terms of net income, cash flows, Balance Sheet position, and overall results. Be specific.

■ Team Projects

Project 1. Each member of the team should obtain the annual report of a different company. Select companies in different industries. Evaluate each company's trend of cash flows for the most recent two years. In your evaluation of the companies' cash flows, you may use any other information that is publicly available: for example, the other financial statements (Income Statement, Balance Sheet, statement of stockholders' equity, and the related notes) and news stories from magazines and newspapers. Rank the companies' cash flows from best to worst and write a two-page report on your findings.

Project 2. Select a company and obtain its annual report, including all the financial statements. Focus on the Statement of Cash Flows and, in particular, the cash flows from operating activities. Specify whether the company uses the *direct* method or the *indirect* method to report operating cash flows. As necessary, use the other financial statements (Income Statement, Balance Sheet, and Statement of Retained Earnings) and the notes to prepare the company's cash flows from operating activities by the *other* method.

Quick Check Answers

1. *d* 2. *b* 3. *c* 4. *a* 5. *a* 6. *b* 7. *c* 8. *c* 9. *a* 10. *b*

For online homework, exercises, and problems that provide you immediate feedback, please visit www.myaccountinglab.com.

Big Picture

Ch 1 Introduction to Management Accounting

- Distinguish management accounting from financial accounting
- The role and responsibilities of management accountants
- Classify costs and prepare income statements for merchandising companies
- Classify costs and prepare income statements and statements of cost of goods manufactured for manufacturing companies

Ch 2 Job Order Costing

- Distinguish between job order and process costing
- Record materials, labor, and overhead in a job order costing system
- Record completion and sales of finished goods and adjust for under-/overallocated overhead
- Calculate unit costs for service companies

Ch 3 **Activity-Based Costing and Other Cost Management Tools**

- Develop activity-based costs and used activity-based management to determine target product costs
- Record transactions in JIT systems
- Use the four types of quality costs to make management decisions

Ch 4 **Process Costing**

- Calculate equivalent units and conversion costs
- Prepare cost of production reports and the related journal entries using the weighted-average costing method
- Prepare cost of production reports and the related journal entries using the FIFO costing method

Ch 5 **Cost Behavior and Cost-Volume-Profit Analysis**

- Identify how changes in volume affect cost
- Distinguish among variable, mixed, and fixed cost
- Split mixed cost into fixed and variable components by using the high-low method and by using regression analysis
- Use CVP to compute breakeven points, to plan profits, to graph relationships, and to perform sensitivity analysis

Ch 6 **Absorption and Variable Costing**

- Distinguish between absorption costing and variable costing
- Prepare absorption costing and variable costing income statements and explained the differences between the two costing techniques
- Illustrate the pros and cons of absorption and variable costing

Ch 7 **The Master Budget: Profit Planning**

- Understand and prepare all components of the master budget for manufacturers
- Use sensitivity analysis to adjust budget preparations

Ch 8 **Flexible Budgets and Standard Costs**

- Prepare flexible income statement budgets and income statement performance reports
- Compute standard cost variances for direct materials, direct labor, and overhead
- Record transactions using standard costs and prepare standard cost income statements

Ch 9 **Decentralization: Allocating Service Department Costs and Responsibility Accounting**

- Identify a shared resource or service department
- Allocate service department costs to the departments that use its services utilizing various allocation methods
- Learn the four types of responsibility centers and prepared responsibility reports they utilize

Ch 10 **Short-Term Business Decisions**

- Distinguish between relevant, irrelevant, and sunk costs
- Evaluate special order, pricing, product profitability, and product-mix decisions
- Make outsourcing and sell as is or process further decisions

Ch 11 **Capital Investment Decisions and the Time Value of Money**

- Evaluate capital investments using payback, accounting rate of return, net present value, and internal rate of return as measures of investment performance
- Apply time value of money analysis to single lump sums and annuities

Ch 12 **Performance Evaluation and the Balanced Scorecard**

- Apply the balanced scorecard as performance indicators for reporting centers
- Evaluate investments using ROI, RI, and EVA

Ch 13 **The Statement of Cash Flows**

- Identify the purposes of the Statement of Cash Flows and distinguished among operating, investing, and financing cash flows
- Prepare the Statement of Cash Flows using the indirect and direct methods

Appendix 13A

Preparing the Statement of Cash Flows by the Direct Method

The Financial Accounting Standards Board (FASB) prefers the direct method of reporting cash flows from operating activities. The direct method provides clearer information about the sources and uses of cash than does the indirect method. However, very few non-public companies use the direct method because it takes more computations than the indirect method. Investing and financing cash flows are exactly the same presentation under both direct and indirect methods. Since only the preparation of the operating section differs, it is all we discuss in this Appendix.

> **4** Prepare the Statement of Cash Flows by the direct method

To illustrate how the operating section of the Statement of Cash Flows differs for the direct method , we will be using the Smart Touch Learning data we used within the main chapter. The steps to prepare the Statement of Cash Flows by the direct method are as follows:

STEP 1: Lay out the operating section format of the Statement of Cash Flows by the direct method, as shown in Exhibit 13A-1.

EXHIBIT 13A-1 | **Format of the Statement of Cash Flows: Direct Method**

SMART TOUCH LEARNING, INC.
Statement of Cash Flows
Year Ended December 31, 2012

± Cash flows from operating activities:
  Receipts:
    Collections from customers
    Interest received
    Dividends received on investments
      Total cash receipts
  Payments:
    To suppliers
    To employees
    For interest and income tax
      Total cash payments
  Net cash provided by (used for) operating activities
± Cash flows from investing activities:
  + Cash receipts from sales of long-term (plant) assets (investments,
    land, building, equipment, and so on)
  − Acquisitions of long-term (plant) assets
  Net cash provided by (used for) investing activities
± Cash flows from financing activities:
  + Cash receipts from issuance of stock
  + Cash receipts from sale of treasury stock
  − Purchase of treasury stock
  + Cash receipts from issuance of notes or bonds payable (borrowing)
  − Payment of notes or bonds payable
  − Payment of dividends
  Net cash provided by (used for) financing activities
= Net increase (decrease) in cash during the year
  + Cash at December 31, 2011
  = Cash at December 31, 2012

STEP 2: Use the comparative Balance Sheet to determine the increase or decrease in cash during the period. The change in cash is the "reconciling key figure" for the Statement of Cash Flows. Smart Touch's comparative Balance Sheet shows that cash decreased by $20,000 during 2012. (See Exhibit 13A-2.)

EXHIBIT 13A-2 | **Comparative Balance Sheet**

SMART TOUCH LEARNING, INC.
Comparative Balance Sheet
December 31, 2012 and 2011

(In thousands)	2012	2011	Increase (Decrease)
Assets			
Current:			
Cash	$ 22	$ 42	$ (20)
Accounts receivable	90	73	17
Inventory	143	145	(2)
Plant assets, net	460	210	250
Total assets	$715	$470	$245
Liabilities			
Current:			
Accounts payable	$ 90	$ 50	$ 40
Accrued liabilities	5	10	(5)
Long-term notes payable	160	80	80
Stockholders' Equity			
Common stock	370	250	120
Retained earnings	110	80	30
Less: Treasury stock	(20)	0	(20)
Total	$715	$470	$245

Operating { Accounts receivable, Inventory
Investing { Plant assets, net
Operating { Accounts payable, Accrued liabilities
Financing { Long-term notes payable
Net income—Operating { Retained earnings
Dividends Financing

EXHIBIT 13A-3 | **Income Statement**

SMART TOUCH LEARNING, INC.
Income Statement
Year Ended December 31, 2012

	(In thousands)	
Revenues and gains:		
Sales revenue	$286	
Interest revenue	12	
Dividend revenue	9	
Gain on sale of plant assets	10	
Total revenues and gains		$317
Expenses:		
Cost of goods sold	$156	
Salary and wage expense	56	
Depreciation expense	20	
Other operating expense	16	
Interest expense	15	
Income tax expense	14	
Total expenses		277
Net income		$ 40

STEP 3: Use the available data to prepare the Statement of Cash Flows. In the case of Smart Touch Learning, there was no additional data outside of the Balance Sheet and Income Statement data in Exhibit 13A-3 that affected the operating activities section.

The Statement of Cash Flows reports only transactions with cash effects. Exhibit 13A-4 shows Smart Touch Learning's completed direct method Statement of Cash Flows for 2012.

EXHIBIT 13A-4 | **Statement of Cash Flows—Direct Method**

SMART TOUCH LEARNING, INC.
Statement of Cash Flows
Year Ended December 31, 2012

	(In thousands)	
Cash flows from operating activities:		
Receipts:		
Collections from customers	$ 269	
Interest received	12	
Dividends received	9	
Total cash receipts		$ 290
Payments:		
To suppliers	$(135)	
To employees	(56)	
For interest	(15)	
For income tax	(14)	
Total cash payments		(220)
Net cash provided by operating activities		70
Cash flows from investing activities:		
Acquisition of plant assets	$(310)	
Cash receipts from sale of plant assets	50	
Net cash used for investing activities		(260)
Cash flows from financing activities:		
Cash receipts from issuance of common stock	$ 120	
Cash receipts from issuance of notes payable	90	
Payment of notes payable	(10)	
Purchase of treasury stock	(20)	
Payment of dividends	(10)	
Net cash provided by financing activities		170
Net decrease in cash		$ (20)
Cash balance, December 31, 2011		42
Cash balance, December 31, 2012		$ 22

Next, we will explain how we calculated each number.

Cash Flows from Operating Activities

In the indirect method, we start with net income and then adjust it to "cash-basis" through a series of adjusting items. We take each line item of the Income Statement and convert it from accrual to cash basis. So, in essence, the operating activities section of the direct-method cash flows statement is really just a cash-basis Income Statement. We can do this using the T-account method (review the Demo Doc for this chapter in myaccountinglab.com) or we can modify the account change chart used earlier in the chapter as seen in Exhibit 13A-5 on the following page.

Direct Method: How Changes in Account Balances Affect Cash Receipts and Cash Payments

> Asset ↑ Cash Flow ↓ Cash Receipts ↓ or Cash Payments ↑
> Asset ↓ Cash Flow ↑ Cash Receipts ↑ or Cash Payments ↓
> Liability ↑ Cash Flow ↑ Cash Receipts ↑ or Cash Payments ↓
> Liability ↓ Cash Flow ↓ Cash Receipts ↓ or Cash Payments ↑
> Equity ↑ Cash Flow ↑ Cash Receipts ↑ or Cash Payments ↓
> Equity ↓ Cash Flow ↓ Cash Receipts ↓ or Cash Payments ↑

Notice that we have added the Cash Receipts and Payments to the existing chart. An increase in Cash is either going to arise from increasing cash receipts or decreasing cash payments. Now let us apply this information to Smart Touch Learning.

Cash Collections from Customers

The first item on the Income Statement is Sales revenue. Sales revenue represents the total of all sales, whether for cash or on account. The Balance Sheet account related to Sales revenue is Accounts receivable. Accounts receivable went from $73,000 at 12/31/11 to $90,000 at 12/31/12, an increase of $17,000. Applying our chart appears as follows:

> Sales Revenue − Increase in Accounts receivable = Cash Collections from Customers
> $286,000 − $17,000 = $269,000
> Asset ↑ Cash Flow ↓ Cash Receipts ↓ or Cash Payments ↑

So, the cash Smart Touch received from customers is $269,000. This is the first item in the operating activities section of the direct-method cash flow statement. You can verify this by looking at Exhibit 13A-4 on page 647.

Cash Receipts of Interest

The second item on the Income Statement is interest revenue. The Balance Sheet account related to Interest revenue is Interest receivable. Since there is no Interest receivable account on the Balance Sheet, the interest revenue must have all been received in cash. So, the cash flow statement shows Interest received of $12,000 (Exhibit 13A-4 on page 647).

Cash Receipts of Dividends

Dividend revenue is the third item reported on the Income Statement. The Balance Sheet account related to Dividend revenue is Dividends receivable. As with the interest, there is no Dividends receivable account on the Balance Sheet. Therefore, the dividend revenue must have all been received in cash. So, the cash flow statement shows cash received from dividends of $9,000 in Exhibit 13A-4 on page 647.

Gain on Sale of Plant Assets

The next item on the Income Statement is the gain on sale of plant assets. However, the cash received from the sale of the assets is reported in the investing section, not the operating section. As noted earlier, there is no difference in the investing section between the indirect method and direct method of the Statement of Cash Flows.

Payments to Suppliers

Payments to suppliers include all payments for

- inventory and
- operating expenses except employee compensation, interest, and income taxes.

   Suppliers are those entities that provide the business with its inventory and essential services. The accounts related to supplier payments for inventory are Cost of goods sold, Inventory, and Accounts payable. Cost of goods sold on the Income statement was $156,000. Inventory decreased from $145,000 at 12/31/11 to $143,000 at 12/31/12. Accounts payable increased from $50,000 at 12/31/11 to $90,000 at 12/31/12. Applying our formula, we can calculate cash paid for inventory as follows:

Cost of goods sold – Decrease in Inventory – Increase in Accounts payable = Cash paid for Inventory
$156,000 – $2,000 – 40,000 = $114,000
Asset ↓ Cash Flow ↑ Cash Receipts ↑ or Cash Payments ↓ Liability ↑ Cash Flow ↑ Cash Receipts ↑ or Cash Payments ↓

   The accounts related to supplier payments for operating expenses are Operating expenses and Accrued liabilities. Operating expenses on the Income statement were $16,000. Accrued liabilities decreased from $10,000 at 12/31/11 to $5,000 at 12/31/12. Applying our formula, we can calculate cash paid for operating expenses as follows:

Operating expenses + Decrease in Accrued liabilities = Cash paid for operating
$16,000 + 5,000 = $21,000
Liability ↓ Cash Flow ↓ Cash Receipts ↓ or Cash Payments ↑

   Adding them together, we get total cash paid to suppliers of $135,000. (Confirm in Exhibit 13A-4 on page 647).

Cash paid for Inventory + Cash paid for operating = Cash paid to suppliers
$114,000 + 21,000 = $135,000

Payments to Employees

This category includes payments for salaries, wages, and other forms of employee compensation. Accrued amounts are not cash flows because they have not yet been paid. The accounts related to employee payments are Salary and wage expense from the Income Statement and Salary and wage payable from the Balance Sheet. Since there is not a Salary payable account on the Balance Sheet, the salary and wage expense account must represent all amounts paid in cash to employees. So, the cash flow statement shows cash payments to employees of $56,000 (Exhibit 13A-4 on page 647).

Depreciation, Depletion, and Amortization Expense

These expenses are *not* reported on the direct method Statement of Cash Flows because they do not affect cash.

Payments for Interest Expense

These cash payments are reported separately from the other expenses. The accounts related to interest payments are Interest expense from the Income Statement and Interest payable from the Balance Sheet. Since there is no Interest payable account on the Balance Sheet, the interest expense account from the Income Statement must represent all amounts paid in cash for interest. So, the cash flow statement shows cash payments for interest of $15,000 (Exhibit 13A-4 on page 647).

Payments for Income Tax Expense

Like interest expense, these cash payments are reported separately from the other expenses. The accounts related to income tax payments are Income tax expense from the Income Statement and Income tax payable from the Balance Sheet. Since there is no Income tax payable account on the Balance Sheet, the income tax expense account from the Income Statement must represent all amounts paid in cash for income tax. So, the cash flow statement shows cash payments for income tax of $14,000 (Exhibit 13A-4 on page 647).

Net Cash Provided by Operating Activities

To calculate net cash provided by operating activities using the direct method, we add all the cash receipts and cash payments described previously and find the difference. For Smart Touch Learning, total Cash receipts were $290,000. Total Cash payments were $220,000. So, net cash provided by operating activities is $70,000. If you refer back to the indirect-method cash flow statement shown in Exhibit 13-4 on page 609, you will find that it showed the same $70,000 for net cash provided by operating activities—only the method by which it was calculated was different.

The remainder of Smart Touch's cash flow statement is exactly the same as what we calculated using the indirect method. (See Exhibit 13-4 on page 609).

Summary Problem

Assume that **Berkshire Hathaway** is considering buying Granite Shoals Corporation. Granite Shoals reported the following comparative Balance Sheet and Income Statement for 2012:

GRANITE SHOALS CORPORATION
Balance Sheet
December 31, 2012 and 2011

	2012	2011	Increase (Decrease)
Cash	$ 19,000	$ 3,000	$16,000
Accounts receivable	22,000	23,000	(1,000)
Inventory	34,000	31,000	3,000
Prepaid expenses	1,000	3,000	(2,000)
Equipment (net)	90,000	79,000	11,000
Intangible assets	9,000	9,000	—
Total assets	$175,000	$148,000	$27,000
Accounts payable	$ 14,000	$ 9,000	$ 5,000
Accrued liabilities	16,000	19,000	(3,000)
Income tax payable	14,000	12,000	2,000
Long-term note payable	45,000	50,000	(5,000)
Common stock	31,000	20,000	11,000
Retained earnings	64,000	40,000	24,000
Treasury stock	(9,000)	(2,000)	(7,000)
Total liabilities and stockholders' equity	$175,000	$148,000	$27,000

GRANITE SHOALS CORPORATION
Income Statement
Year Ended December 31, 2012

Sales revenue	$190,000
Gain on sale of equipment	6,000
Total revenue and gains	196,000
Cost of goods sold	$ 85,000
Depreciation expense	19,000
Other operating expenses	36,000
Total expenses	140,000
Income before income tax	56,000
Income tax expense	18,000
Net income	$ 38,000

1. Compute the following cash-flow amounts for 2012.
   a. Collections from customers
   b. Payments for inventory
   c. Payments for other operating expenses
   d. Payment of income tax
   e. Acquisition of equipment. Granite Shoals sold equipment that had book value of $15,000.
   f. Cash receipt from sale of plant assets
   g. Issuance of long-term note payable. Granite Shoals paid off $10,000 of long-term notes payable.
   h. Issuance of common stock
   i. Payment of dividends
   j. Purchase of treasury stock
2. Prepare Granite Shoals Corporation's Statement of Cash Flows (*direct* method) for the year ended December 31, 2012. There were no noncash investing and financing activities.

Solution

1. Cash-flow amounts:

1. Cash-flow amounts:

a.
$$\begin{array}{ccc} \text{Collections} \\ \text{from} \\ \text{customers} \end{array} = \begin{array}{c} \text{Sales} \\ \text{revenue} \end{array} + \begin{array}{c} \text{Decrease in} \\ \text{accounts} \\ \text{receivables} \end{array}$$

$$\$191{,}000 = \$190{,}000 + \$1{,}000$$

b.
$$\begin{array}{c} \text{Payments} \\ \text{for} \\ \text{inventory} \end{array} = \begin{array}{c} \text{Cost of} \\ \text{goods} \\ \text{sold} \end{array} + \begin{array}{c} \text{Increase} \\ \text{in} \\ \text{inventory} \end{array} - \begin{array}{c} \text{Increase in} \\ \text{accounts} \\ \text{payable} \end{array}$$

$$\$83{,}000 = \$85{,}000 + \$3{,}000 - \$5{,}000$$

c.
$$\begin{array}{c} \text{Payments} \\ \text{for other} \\ \text{operating expenses} \end{array} = \begin{array}{c} \text{Other} \\ \text{Operating} \\ \text{expenses} \end{array} - \begin{array}{c} \text{Decrease} \\ \text{in prepaid} \\ \text{expenses} \end{array} + \begin{array}{c} \text{Decrease in} \\ \text{accrued} \\ \text{liabilities} \end{array}$$

$$\$37{,}000 = \$36{,}000 - \$2{,}000 + \$3{,}000$$

d.
$$\begin{array}{c} \text{Payment of} \\ \text{income tax} \end{array} = \begin{array}{c} \text{Income tax} \\ \text{expense} \end{array} - \begin{array}{c} \text{Increase in} \\ \text{income tax payable} \end{array}$$

$$\$16{,}000 = \$18{,}000 - \$2{,}000$$

e. Equipment, Net (let X = Acquisitions)

Beginning	+	Acquisitions	−	Depreciation expense	−	Book value sold	=	Ending
$79,000	+	X	−	$19,000	−	$15,000	=	$90,000
		X	=	$45,000				

f. Sale of plant assets

$$\begin{array}{c} \text{Cash} \\ \text{received} \end{array} = \begin{array}{c} \text{Book value of} \\ \text{assets sold} \end{array} + \text{Gain on sale}$$

$$\$21{,}000 = \$15{,}000 + \$6{,}000$$

g. Long-term Note payable (let X = Issuance)

Beginning	+	Issuance	−	Payment	=	Ending
$50,000	+	X	−	$10,000	=	$45,000
		X	=	$ 5,000		

h. Common stock (let X = Issuance)

Beginning	+	Issuance	=	Ending
$20,000	+	X	=	$31,000
		X	=	$11,000

i. Retained earnings (let X = Dividends)

Beginning	+	Net income	−	Dividends	=	Ending
$40,000	+	$38,000	−	X	=	$64,000
				X	=	$14,000

j. Treasury stock (let X = Purchases)

Beginning	+	Purchases	=	Ending
$2,000	+	X	=	$9,000
		X	=	$7,000

2.

GRANITE SHOALS CORPORATION		
Statement of Cash Flows		
Year Ended December 31, 2012		
Cash flows from operating activities:		
Receipts:		
Collections from customers	$ 191,000	
Payments:		
To suppliers ($83,000 + $37,000)	(120,000)	
For income tax	(16,000)	
Net cash provided by operating activities		$ 55,000
Cash flows from investing activities:		
Acquisition of plant assets	$ (45,000)	
Sale of plant assets ($15,000 + $6,000)	21,000	
Net cash used for investing activities		(24,000)
Cash flows from financing activities:		
Payment of dividends	$ (14,000)	
Issuance of common stock	11,000	
Payment of note payable	(10,000)	
Purchase of treasury stock	(7,000)	
Issuance of note payable	5,000	
Net cash used for financing activities		(15,000)
Net increase in cash		$ 16,000
Cash balance, December 31, 2011		3,000
Cash balance, December 31, 2012		$ 19,000

Appendix 13A Assignments

■ Short Exercises

S13A-1 *(L.OBJ. 4)* **Preparing the direct method Statement of Cash Flows [15 min]**
White Chocolate, Inc., began 2011 with cash of $52,000. During the year White Chocolate earned revenue of $591,000 and collected $624,000 from customers. Expenses for the year totaled $423,000, of which White Chocolate paid $413,000 in cash to suppliers and employees. White Chocolate also paid $143,000 to purchase equipment and a cash dividend of $49,000 to its stockholders during 2011.

Requirement

1. Prepare the company's Statement of Cash Flows for the year ended December 31, 2011. Format operating activities by the direct method.

S13A-2 *(L.OBJ. 4)* **Preparing operating activities using the direct method [5 min]**
Stella's Learning Center has assembled the following data for the year ended June 30, 2011:

Payments to suppliers	$ 110,000
Purchase of equipment	37,000
Payments to employees	68,000
Payment of note payable	34,000
Payment of dividends	4,000
Cash receipt from issuance of stock	20,000
Collections from customers	196,000
Cash receipt from sale of land	61,000

Requirement

1. Prepare the *operating* activities section of the business' Statement of Cash Flows for the year ended June 30, 2011, using the direct method for operating cash flows.

Note: Short Exercise 13A-3 should be used only after completing Short Exercise 13A-2.

S13A-3 *(L.OBJ. 4)* **Preparing the direct method Statement of Cash Flows [15 min]**
Use the data in Short Exercise 13A-2 and your results.

Requirement

1. Prepare the business's complete Statement of Cash Flows for the year ended June 30, 2011, using the *direct* method for operating activities. Stop after determining the net increase (or decrease) in cash.

S13A-4 (L.OBJ. 4) Preparing the direct method Statement of Cash Flows [15 min]

White Toy Company reported the following comparative Balance Sheet:

Assets	2011	2010	Liabilities	2011	2010
WHITE TOY COMPANY					
Comparative Balance Sheet					
December 31, 2011 and 2010					
Current:			Current:		
Cash	$ 20,000	$ 16,000	Accounts payable	$ 46,000	$ 42,000
Accounts receivable	50,000	44,000	Salary payable	21,000	18,000
Inventory	75,000	82,000	Accrued liabilities	4,000	13,000
Prepaid expenses	2,500	1,500	Long–term notes payable	61,000	69,000
Long–term investments	72,000	88,000	**Stockholders' Equity**		
Plant assets, net	228,000	187,000	Common stock	36,000	30,000
			Retained earnings	279,500	246,500
Total assets	$447,500	$418,500	Total liabilities and stockholders' equity	$447,500	$418,500

Requirement

1. Compute the following for White Toy Company:
   a. Collections from customers during 2011. Sales totaled $142,000.
   b. Payments for inventory during 2011. Cost of goods sold was $79,000.

■ Exercises

E13A-5 (L.OBJ. 4) Identifying activity categories—direct method [10–15 min]

Consider the following transactions:

_____	a. Collection of account receivable	_____	i. Purchase of treasury stock
_____	b. Issuance of note payable to borrow cash	_____	j. Issuance of common stock for cash
_____	c. Depreciation	_____	k. Payment of account payable
_____	d. Issuance of preferred stock for cash	_____	l. Acquisition of building by issuance of common stock
_____	e. Payment of cash dividend	_____	m. Purchase of equipment
_____	f. Sale of land	_____	n. Payment of wages to employees
_____	g. Acquisition of equipment by issuance of note payable	_____	o. Collection of cash interest
_____	h. Payment of note payable	_____	p. Sale of building

Requirement

1. Identify each of the transactions as a(n)
   - Operating activity (O),
   - Investing activity (I),
   - Financing activity (F),
   - Noncash investing and financing activity (NIF), or
   - transaction that is not reported on the Statement of Cash Flows (N).

   For each cash flow, indicate whether the item increases (+) or decreases (–) cash. The *direct* method is used for cash flows from operating activities.

E13A-6 *(L. OBJ. 4)* **Identifying activity categories of transactions—direct method [5–10 min]**

Consider the following transactions:

a. Land	18,000		g. Salary expense	4,300	
Cash		18,000	Cash		4,300
b. Cash	7,200		h. Cash	81,000	
Equipment		7,200	Common stock		81,000
c. Bonds payable	45,000		i. Treasury stock	13,000	
Cash		45,000	Cash		13,000
d. Building	164,000		j. Cash	2,000	
Note payable		164,000	Interest revenue		2,000
e. Cash	1,400		k. Land	87,700	
Accounts receivable		1,400	Cash		87,700
f. Dividends payable	16,500		l. Accounts payable	8,300	
Cash		16,500	Cash		8,300

Requirement

1. Indicate where, if at all, each of the transactions would be reported on a Statement of Cash Flows prepared by the *direct* method and the accompanying schedule of noncash investing and financing activities.

E13A-7 *(L. OBJ. 4)* **Preparing operating activities cash flow—direct method [10–15 min]**

The accounting records of Value Auto Parts reveal the following:

Payment of salaries and wages	$ 36,000	Net income	$ 23,000
Depreciation	12,000	Payment of income tax	13,000
Payment of interest	15,000	Collection of dividend revenue	5,000
Payment of dividends	5,000	Payment to suppliers	56,000
Collections from customers	118,000		

Requirement

1. Compute cash flows from operating activities by the *direct* method.

E13A-8 *(L. OBJ. 4)* **Identifying activity categories of transactions—direct method [5–10 min]**

Selected accounts of Routing Networks, Inc., show the following:

Accounts receivable

Beginning balance	9,300	Cash collections	36,000
Service revenue	38,000		
Ending balance	11,300		

Land

Beginning balance	93,000	
Acquisition	16,000	
Ending balance	109,000	

Long–term notes payable

		Beginning balance	277,000
Payments	69,000	Issuance for cash	85,000
		Ending balance	293,000

Requirement

1. For each account, identify the item or items that should appear on a Statement of Cash Flows prepared by the *direct* method. Also state each item's amount and where to report the item.

E13A-9 *(L. OBJ. 4)* **Preparing the Statement of Cash Flows—direct method [20–30 min]**

The Income Statement and additional data of Rolling Hills Corporation follow:

ROLLING HILLS CORPORATION		
Income Statement		
Year Ended June 30, 2010		
Revenues:		
Sales revenue	$ 228,000	
Dividend revenue	7,000	$ 235,000
Expenses:		
Cost of goods sold	$ 105,000	
Salary expense	42,000	
Depreciation expense	22,000	
Advertising expense	13,500	
Income tax expense	9,500	
Interest expense	2,500	194,500
Net income		$ 40,500

Additional data follow:

a. Collections from customers are $14,500 more than sales.
b. Dividend revenue, interest expense, and income tax expense equal their cash amounts.
c. Payments to suppliers are the sum of cost of goods sold plus advertising expense.
d. Payments to employees are $1,500 more than salary expense.
e. Acquisition of plant assets is $100,000.
f. Cash receipts from sale of land total $21,000.
g. Cash receipts from issuance of common stock total $38,000.
h. Payment of long-term note payable is $11,000.
i. Payment of dividends is $10,500.
j. Cash balance, June 30, 2009, was $20,000; June 30, 2010 was $33,000.

Requirement

1. Prepare Rolling Hills Corporation's Statement of Cash Flows for the year ended June 30, 2010. Use the *direct* method.

E13A-10 *(L. OBJ. 4)* **Computing cash flow items—direct method [10–15 min]**
Consider the following facts:

a. Beginning and ending Accounts receivable are $22,000 and $18,000, respectively. Credit sales for the period total $60,000.
b. Cost of goods sold is $75,000. Beginning Inventory balance is $25,000, and ending Inventory balance is $21,000. Beginning and ending Accounts payable are $11,000 and $8,000, respectively.

Requirements

1. Compute cash collections from customers.
2. Compute cash payments for inventory.

E13A-11 *(L. OBJ. 4)* **Computing cash flow items—direct method [20–30 min]**
TipTop Mobile Homes reported the following in its financial statements for the year ended December 31, 2011 (adapted, in millions):

	2011	2010
Income Statement		
Net sales	$ 24,859	$ 21,674
Cost of sales	18,121	15,497
Depreciation	270	234
Other operating expenses	4,432	4,221
Income tax expense	532	486
Net income	$ 1,504	$ 1,236
Balance Sheet		
Cash and cash equivalents ...	$ 17	$ 16
Accounts receivable	798	621
Inventories	3,483	2,830
Property and equipment, net ..	4,342	3,428
Accounts payable	1,546	1,362
Accrued liabilities	938	848
Long–term liabilities	477	467
Common stock	678	446
Retained earnings	5,001	3,772

1. Determine the following for TipTop Mobile Homes during 2011:

   a. Collections from customers
   b. Payments for inventory
   c. Payments of operating expenses
   d. Acquisitions of property and equipment (no sales of property during 2011)
   e. Borrowing, with TipTop paying no long-term liabilities
   f. Cash receipt from issuance of common stock
   g. Payment of cash dividends

■ Problem (Group A)

P13A-12A *(L. OBJ. 4)* **Preparing the Statement of Cash Flows—direct method [35–45 min]**

KTG, Inc., accountants have developed the following data from the company's accounting records for the year ended November 30, 2011:

   a. Purchase of plant assets, $58,400
   b. Cash receipt from issuance of notes payable, $48,100
   c. Payments of notes payable, $49,000
   d. Cash receipt from sale of plant assets, $22,500
   e. Cash receipt of dividends, $4,200
   f. Payments to suppliers, $371,300
   g. Interest expense and payments, $13,500
   h. Payments of salaries, $94,000
   i. Income tax expense and payments, $39,000
   j. Depreciation expense, $57,000
   k. Collections from customers, $605,300
   l. Payment of cash dividends, $50,400
   m. Cash receipt from issuance of common stock, $68,900
   n. Cash balance: November 30, 2010, $39,700; November 30, 2011, $113,100

Requirement

1. Prepare KTG's Statement of Cash Flows for the year ended November 30, 2011. Use the *direct* method for cash flows from operating activities.

P13A-13A *(L.OBJ. 4)* **Preparing the Statement of Cash Flows—direct method [40 min]**

Use the North American Reserve Rare Coins data from Problem 13-22A.

Requirements

1. Prepare North American Reserve Rare Coins' Income Statement for the year ended December 31, 2010. Use the single-step format, with all revenues listed together and all expenses together.
2. Prepare North American Reserve's Balance Sheet at December 31, 2010.
3. Prepare North American Reserve's Statement of Cash Flows for the year ended December 31, 2010. Format cash flows from operating activities by the *direct* method.

P13A-14A *(L. OBJ. 4)* **Preparing the Statement of Cash Flows—direct method [30–40 min]**

Use the Cobbs Hill data from Problem 13-25A.

Requirements

1. Prepare the 2012 Statement of Cash Flows by the *direct* method.
2. How will what you learned in this problem help you evaluate an investment?

P13A-15A (L. OBJ. 4) Preparing the Statement of Cash Flows—direct method [45–60 min]

To prepare the Statement of Cash Flows, accountants for I-M-Mobile, Inc., have summarized 2010 activity in the Cash account as follows:

Cash

Beginning balance	87,300	Payments of operating expenses	46,200
Issuance of common stock	60,700	Payments of salaries and wages	65,500
Receipts of interest revenue	17,100	Payment of note payable	82,000
Collections from customers	308,600	Payment of income tax	6,000
		Payments on accounts payable	101,100
		Payments of dividends	1,500
		Payments of interest	21,100
		Purchase of equipment	54,500
Ending balance	95,800		

Requirement

1. Prepare I-M-Mobile's Statement of Cash Flows for the year ended December 31, 2010, using the *direct* method to report operating activities.

■ Problem (Group B)

P13A-16B (L. OBJ. 4) Preparing the Statement of Cash Flows—direct method [35–45 min]

SKG, Inc., accountants have developed the following data from the company's accounting records for the year ended November 30, 2011:

a. Purchase of plant assets, $55,400
b. Cash receipt from issuance of notes payable, $43,100
c. Payments of notes payable, $48,000
d. Cash receipt from sale of plant assets, $25,500
e. Cash receipt of dividends, $4,400
f. Payments to suppliers, $374,800
g. Interest expense and payments, $12,500
h. Payments of salaries, $95,000
i. Income tax expense and payments, $40,000
j. Depreciation expense, $56,500
k. Collections from customers, $605,500
l. Payment of cash dividends, $50,400
m. Cash receipt from issuance of common stock, $60,900
n. Cash balance: November 30, 2010, $40,000; November 30, 2011, $103,300

Requirement

1. Prepare SKG's Statement of Cash Flows for the year ended November 30, 2011. Use the *direct* method for cash flows from operating activities.

P13A-17B (L. OBJ. 4) Preparing the Statement of Cash Flows—direct method [40 min]

Use the Official Reserve Rare Coins data from Problem 13-26B.

Requirements

1. Prepare Official Reserve Rare Coins' Income Statement for the year ended December 31, 2010. Use the single-step format, with all revenues listed together and all expenses together.
2. Prepare Official Reserve's Balance Sheet at December 31, 2010.
3. Prepare Official Reserve's Statement of Cash Flows for the year ended December 31, 2010. Format cash flows from operating activities by the *direct* method.

P13A-18B *(L. OBJ. 4)* **Preparing the Statement of Cash Flows—direct method [30–40 min]**

Use the Digital Subscriptions data from Problem 13-29B.

Requirements

1. Prepare the 2012 Statement of Cash Flows by the *direct* method.
2. How will what you learned in this problem help you evaluate an investment?

P13A-19B *(L. OBJ.4)* **Preparing the Statement of Cash Flows—direct method [45–60 min]**

To prepare the Statement of Cash Flows, accountants for B-Mobile, Inc., have summarized 2010 activity in the Cash account as follows:

Cash

Beginning balance	87,400	Payments of operating expenses	46,700
Issuance of common stock	60,100	Payments of salaries and wages	69,500
Receipts of interest revenue	14,600	Payment of note payable	75,000
Collections from customers	308,900	Payment of income tax	9,500
		Payments on accounts payable	101,100
		Payments of dividends	1,300
		Payments of interest	21,100
		Purchase of equipment	49,500
Ending balance	97,300		

Requirement

1. Prepare B-Mobile's Statement of Cash Flows for the year ended December 31, 2010, using the *direct* method to report operating activities.

Preparing the Indirect Statement of Cash Flows Using a Spreadsheet

The body of this chapter discusses the uses of the Statement of Cash Flows in decision making and shows how to prepare the statement using T-accounts. The T-account approach works well as a learning device. In practice, however, most companies face complex situations. In these cases, a spreadsheet can help in preparing the Statement of Cash Flows.

The spreadsheet starts with the beginning Balance Sheet and concludes with the ending Balance Sheet. Two middle columns—one for debit amounts and the other for credit amounts—complete the spreadsheet. These columns, labeled "Transaction Analysis," hold the data for the Statement of Cash Flows. Accountants can prepare the statement directly from the lower part of the spreadsheet. This appendix is based on the Smart Touch Learning data used in the chapter. We illustrate this approach only with the indirect method for operating activities. This method could be used for the direct method as well.

The *indirect* method reconciles net income to net cash provided by operating activities. Exhibit 13B-1 on the following page is the spreadsheet for preparing the Statement of Cash Flows by the *indirect* method. Panel A shows the transaction analysis, and Panel B gives the Statement of Cash Flows.

Transaction Analysis on the Spreadsheet—Indirect Method

a. Net income of $40,000 is the first operating cash inflow. Net income is entered on the spreadsheet (Panel B) as a debit to Net Income under Cash flows from operating activities and as a credit to Retained earnings on the Balance Sheet (Panel A).

b. Next come the adjustments to net income, starting with depreciation of $20,000—transaction (b)—which is debited to Depreciation and credited to Plant assets, net.

c. This transaction is the sale of plant assets. The $10,000 gain on the sale is entered as a credit to Gain on sale of plant assets—a subtraction from net income—under operating cash flows. This credit removes the $10,000 gain from operations because the cash proceeds from the sale were $50,000, not $10,000. The $50,000 sale amount is then entered on the spreadsheet under investing activities. Entry (c) is completed by crediting the plant assets' book value of $40,000 to the Plant assets, net account.

d. Entry (d) debits Accounts receivable for its $17,000 increase during the year. This amount is credited to Increase in accounts receivable under operating cash flows.

e. This entry credits Inventory for its $2,000 decrease during the year. This amount is debited to Decrease in inventory under operating cash flows.

f. This entry credits Accounts payable for its $40,000 increase during the year. Then, it is debited to show as Increase in accounts payable under operating cash flows.

g. This entry debits Accrued liabilities for its $5,000 decrease during the year. Then, it is credited to show as Decrease in accrued liabilities under operating cash flows.

h. This entry debits Plant assets, net for their purchase ($310,000) and credits Acquisition of plant assets under investing cash flows.

i. This entry debits Cash receipts from issuance of common stock ($120,000) under financing cash flows. The offsetting credit is to Common stock.

j. This entry is represented by a credit to Long-term notes payable and a debit under cash flows from financing activities of $90,000 (Cash receipt from issuance of notes payable).

1	SMART TOUCH LEARNING, INC.				
2	Spreadsheet for Statement of Cash Flows				
3	Year Ended December 31, 2012				

	(In thousands)	Balance 12/31/2011	Transaction Analysis		Balance 12/31/2012
5	**Panel A—Balance Sheet**				
6	Cash	42		20 (n)	22
7	Accounts receivable	73	(d) 17		90
8	Inventory	145		2 (e)	143
9	Plant assets, net	210	(h) 310	20 (b)	
10				40 (c)	460
11	Total Assets	470			715
12					
13	Accounts payable	50		40 (f)	90
14	Accrued liabilities	10	(g) 5		5
15	Long-term notes payable	80	(k) 10	90 (j)	160
16	Common stock	250		120 (i)	370
17	Retained earnings	80	(m) 10	40 (a)	110
18	Less: Treasury stock	0	(l) 20		–20
19	Total liabilities & stockholders' equity	470	372	372	715
20					
21					
22	**Panel B—Statement of Cash Flows**				
23	Cash flows from operating activities:				
24	Net income		(a) 40		
25	Adjustments to reconcile net income to net cash provided by operating activities:				
26	Depreciation		(b) 20		
27	Gain on sale of plant assets			10 (c)	
28	Increase in accounts receivable			17 (d)	
29	Decrease in inventory		(e) 2		
30	Increase in accounts payable		(f) 40		
31	Decrease in accrued liabilities			5 (g)	
32	Net cash provided by operating activities				
33	Cash flows from investing activities:				
34	Acquisition of plant assets			310 (h)	
35	Cash receipt from sale of plant asset		(c) 50		
36	Net cash used for investing activities				
37	Cash flows from financing activities:				
38	Cash receipt from issuance of common stock		(i) 120		
39	Cash receipt from issuance of notes payable		(j) 90		
40	Payment of notes payable			10 (k)	
41	Purchase of treasury stock			20 (l)	
42	Payment of dividends			10 (m)	
43	Net cash provided by financing activities				
44			362	382	
45			(n) 20		
46	Net decrease in cash		382	382	

k. This entry is the opposite of (j). It is represented by a debit (reduction) of $10,000 to Long-term notes payable and a credit under cash flows from financial activities for Payment of notes payable.

l. The purchase of treasury stock debited the Treasury stock account on the Balance Sheet $20,000. The corresponding cash flow entry "Purchase of treasury stock" credits $20,000 to reduce cash flow.

m. The $10,000 reduction (debit) to the Retained earnings account is the result of dividends declared and paid by the company. So, we show "Payment of dividends" as a credit in the financing section.

n. The final item in Exhibit 13B-1 on page 664 is the Net decrease in cash. It is shown as a credit to Cash and a debit to Net decrease in cash of $20,000.

Appendix 13B Assignments

■ Problem (Group A)

P13B-1A *(L. OBJ. 3)* **Preparing the Statement of Cash Flows—indirect method [45–60 min]**
The 2012 comparative Balance Sheet and Income Statement of Alden Group, Inc., follow. Alden had no noncash investing and financing transactions during 2012.

ALDEN GROUP, INC. Comparative Balance Sheet December 31, 2012 and 2011			
	2012	**2011**	**Increase (Decrease)**
Current assets:			
Cash and cash equivalents	$ 13,700	$ 15,600	$ (1,900)
Accounts receivable	41,500	43,100	(1,600)
Inventories	96,600	93,000	3,600
Plant assets:			
Land	35,100	10,000	25,100
Equipment, net	100,900	93,700	7,200
Total assets	$ 287,800	$ 255,400	$ 32,400
Current liabilities:			
Accounts payable	$ 24,800	$ 26,000	$ (1,200)
Accrued liabilities	24,400	22,500	1,900
Long-term liabilities:			
Notes payable	55,000	65,000	(10,000)
Stockholders' equity:			
Common stock	131,100	122,300	8,800
Retained earnings	52,500	19,600	32,900
Total liabilities and stockholders' equity	$ 287,800	$ 255,400	$ 32,400

ALDEN GROUP, INC.
Income Statement
Year Ended December 31, 2012

Revenues:		
Sales revenue		$ 438,000
Interest revenue		11,700
Total revenues		449,700
Expenses:		
Cost of goods sold	$ 205,200	
Salary expense	76,400	
Depreciation expense	15,300	
Other operating expense	49,700	
Interest expense	24,600	
Income tax expense	16,900	
Total expenses		388,100
Net income		$ 61,600

Requirement

1. Prepare the spreadsheet for the 2012 Statement of Cash Flows. Format cash flows from operating activities by the *indirect* method.

P13B-2A *(L. OBJ. 3)* **Preparing the Statement of Cash Flows—indirect method [45–60 min]**
Review the data from P13-25A.

Requirement

1. Prepare the spreadsheet for Cobbs Hill's 2012 Statement of Cash Flows. Format cash flows from operating activities by the *indirect* method.

■ Problem (Group B)

P13B-3B *(L. OBJ. 3)* **Preparing the Statement of Cash Flows—indirect method [45–60 min]**
The 2012 comparative Balance Sheet and Income Statement of Alden Group follow. Alden had no noncash investing and financing transactions during 2012.

ALDEN GROUP, INC.
Comparative Balance Sheet
December 31, 2012 and 2011

	2012	2011	Increase (Decrease)
Current assets:			
Cash and cash equivalents	$ 10,700	$ 15,800	$ (5,100)
Accounts receivable	41,800	43,400	(1,600)
Inventories	96,600	93,200	3,400
Plant assets:			
Land	41,400	16,000	25,400
Equipment, net	100,500	93,800	6,700
Total assets	$ 291,000	$ 262,200	$ 28,800
Current liabilities:			
Accounts payable	$ 25,400	$ 26,500	$ (1,100)
Accrued liabilities	24,000	22,700	1,300
Long-term liabilities:			
Notes payable	54,000	66,000	(12,000)
Stockholders' equity:			
Common stock	136,200	127,900	8,300
Retained earnings	51,400	19,100	32,300
Total liabilities and stockholders' equity	$ 291,000	$ 262,200	$ 28,800

ALDEN GROUP, INC.
Income Statement
Year Ended December 31, 2012

Revenues:		
Sales revenue		$ 438,000
Interest revenue		11,900
Total revenues		449,900
Expenses:		
Cost of goods sold	$ 205,800	
Salary expense	76,700	
Depreciation expense	15,600	
Other operating expense	49,600	
Interest expense	24,800	
Income tax expense	16,700	
Total expenses		389,200
Net income		$ 60,700

1. Prepare the spreadsheet for the 2012 Statement of Cash Flows. Format cash flows from operating activities by the *indirect* method.

P13B-4B *(L. OBJ. 3)* **Preparing the Statement of Cash Flows—indirect method [45–60 min]**
Review the data from P13-29B.

Requirement

1. Prepare the spreadsheet for Digital Subscription's 2012 Statement of Cash Flows. Format cash flows from operating activities by the *indirect* method.

Chapter 13: Demo Doc

■ Statement of Cash Flows (Indirect Method)

Learning Objectives 2, 3

Indirect Method

Tanker, Inc., had the following information at December 31, 2011:

TANKER, INC.
Balance Sheet
December 31, 2011

Assets	2011	2010	Change	Liabilities	2011	2010	Change
Current:				Current:			
Cash	$ 700	$1,160	$(460)	Accounts payable	$ 680	$ 530	$150
Accounts receivable	300	420	(120)				
Inventory	800	750	50	Long-term notes payable	660	815	
Prepaid insurance	120	90	30				
				Total liabilities	$1,340	$1,345	
Furniture	1,500	1,400					
Less acc. depn.	(400)	(475)		**Stockholders' Equity**			
Net	1,100	925		Common stock (no par)	$1,800	$1,800	
				Retained earnings	880	200	
Total assets	$3,020	$3,345		Less treasury stock	(1,000)	0	
				Total equity	$1,680	$2,000	
				Total liabilities and equity	$3,020	$3,345	

TANKER, INC.
Income Statement
Year Ended December 31, 2011

Sales revenue	$3,400
Less cost of goods sold	(1,750)
Gross margin	$1,650
Depreciation expense	$ (110)
Insurance expense	(230)
Other operating expenses	(390)
Gain on sale of furniture	80
Net income	$1,000

Other Information

- Every year, Tanker declares and pays cash dividends.
- During 2011, Tanker sold old furniture for $90 cash. Tanker also bought new furniture by making a cash down payment and signing a $200 note payable.
- During 2011, Tanker repaid $500 of notes payable in cash and borrowed new long-term notes payable for cash.
- During 2011, Tanker purchased treasury stock for cash. No treasury stock was sold.

Requirement

1. Prepare Tanker's statement of cash flows for the year ended December 31, 2011, using the indirect method.

Demo Doc Solution

Requirement 1

Prepare Tanker's statement of cash flows for the year ended December 31, 2011.

| Part 1 | Part 2 | Part 3 | Demo Doc Complete |

2   Distinguish among operating, investing, and financing cash flows

3   Prepare the statement of cash flows by the indirect method

Operating Activities

We first set up the statement of cash flows with the proper title and then start with operating activities.

Net Income

The first item is net income. Because net income is positive, it is added to the Cash balance. Therefore, we add (that is, positive number) $1,000 on our cash-flow statement.

Depreciation Expense

Net income includes depreciation expense, which must be removed because it is a 100% noncash item. Remember, no cash was "spent" for depreciation, yet it was still deducted to arrive at the net income number. Because depreciation expense was *subtracted* to calculate net income, we *add* it back to remove it.

Gain on Sale of Furniture

After depreciation, we must look for gains and losses on disposal of long-term assets. These are treated in a manner similar to the depreciation. No cash was "earned" for the gain, yet it was still added to arrive at the net income number. The gain on sale of furniture was *added* to calculate net income, so we *subtract* it to remove it.

Accounts Receivable

After looking at net income and the depreciation and gain adjustments, we need to incorporate the changes in current assets and current liabilities.

The increases and decreases in these accounts do not tell us whether to add or subtract these items on the cash-flow statement.

The first current asset (other than cash) is Accounts receivable. On the balance sheet we see:

Assets	2011	2010	Change
Current:			
Cash	$700	$1,160	$(460)
Accounts receivable	300	420	(120)

We must add the $120 decrease in Accounts receivable. There are two ways to reason this out:

1. Accounts receivable went down. Why? Tanker is collecting more of the cash that its customers owe. How does this affect Cash? It increases Cash; therefore, we should add the number on the cash-flow statement.

2. Accounts receivable went down. This is a decrease in an asset, which is a credit. If this credit is balanced out by the Cash account, that will be a debit to Cash, which is an increase. If Cash is increased, we should add the number on the cash-flow statement.

Notice that in both of these cases, we are adding or subtracting on the cash-flow statement because of the item's effect on *cash flow. It does not matter if Accounts receivable went up or down; what matters is how that affects cash flow.*

Inventory

Let us try the two ways with the next current asset: Inventory. On the balance sheet, we see:

Assets	2011	2010	Change
Current:			
Cash	$700	$1,160	$(460)
Accounts receivable	300	420	(120)
Inventory	800	750	50

During the year, Inventory increased by $50.

1. Why did Inventory increase? Tanker is purchasing inventory with cash. Therefore, this has a negative effect on cash flow.

2. If Inventory is increased, this is an increase in an asset, which is a debit. If this is balanced out by Cash, then Cash is credited, which is a negative effect on cash flow.

Prepaid Insurance

The last current asset is Prepaid insurance. On the balance sheet, we see:

Assets	2011	2010	Change
Current:			
Cash	$700	$1,160	$(460)
Accounts receivable	300	420	(120)
Inventory	800	750	50
Prepaid insurance	120	90	30

During the year, Prepaid insurance increased by $30.

1. Why did Prepaid insurance increase? Tanker paid more insurance costs in advance. This has a negative effect on cash flow.

2. If Prepaid insurance is increased, this is an increase in an asset, which is a debit. If this is balanced out by Cash, then Cash is credited, which is a negative effect on cash flow.

Accounts Payable

The last part of operating activities is to look at the changes in current liabilities. The only current liability in this question is Accounts payable. On the balance sheet, we see:

Liabilities	2011	2010	Change
Current:			
Accounts payable	$680	$530	$150

During the year, Accounts payable increased by $150.

1. Why did Accounts payable increase? Tanker is not paying all of its bills. This means that it is holding onto its cash, which is a positive effect on cash flow.

2. If Accounts payable is increased, this is an increase in a liability, which is a credit. If this is balanced out by Cash, then Cash is debited, which is a positive effect on cash flow.

We total these numbers, and we are finished with operating activities. The completed operating activities section would appear as:

Operating activities	
Net income	$1,000
Depreciation expense	110
Gain on sale of furniture	(80)
Decrease in accounts receivable	120
Increase in inventory	(50)
Increase in prepaid insurance	(30)
Increase in accounts payable	150
Total cash flow provided by operating activities	$1,220

Investing Activities

Part 1	Part 2	Part 3	Demo Doc Complete

2 Distinguish among operating, investing, and financing cash flows

3 Prepare the statement of cash flows by the indirect method

Investing activities looks at cash purchases and cash disposals of long-term assets. This means that we need to know how much cash was paid to purchase new furniture and how much cash was received when Tanker sold some of the old furniture. Do we have any of these numbers right away? Yes, we are told in the question that Tanker signed a $200 note payable to purchase new furniture. We also know that the old furniture was sold for $90 cash.

Before we do anything else, we should point out that the $200 note payable is a *noncash transaction*. Although we will *need* to use it in our analysis, it will *not* appear on the main body of the cash-flow statement. Instead, it will appear in a note for noncash investing and financing activities:

Noncash investing and financing activities	
Purchase of furniture with note payable	$200

We need to calculate the *cash* Tanker paid to purchase new furniture. To do this, we need to analyze the Furniture (net) T-account:

Furniture (net)

Bal 12/31/10	925		
	increases	decreases	
Bal 12/31/11	1,100		

We know that the Furniture (net) account increased and decreased. What caused that account to increase? Well, it would increase if Tanker bought new furniture. So obviously the cash paid *and* the note signed for new furniture went into this account.

What would cause the Furniture (net) account to decrease?

If Tanker sold furniture, we would decrease the account, *but* it would be decreased by the *book* value (that is, the *net* amount) of the furniture sold. Remember, the book value is another term for *net* value. We are looking at net value in the T-account, so the Furniture (net) account decreases by its *net/book* value.

We know that some furniture was sold, so obviously this decrease occurred.

We know that this furniture was sold for $90 cash, but this is *not* the net book value (NBV) of the furniture sold. This amount is still unknown.

However, we can calculate this amount using the gain/loss formula:

Gain or loss on sale of fixed assets = Cash received on sale of fixed assets − NBV of fixed assets sold

For this example, this becomes

Gain on sale of furniture = Cash received on sale of furniture − NBV of furniture sold

So: $80 = $90 − NBV of furniture sold.

Therefore, the NBV of furniture sold is $10.

What else would decrease Furniture (net)? Well, when Tanker takes depreciation expense, do we not decrease the net value of its assets? We know from the income statement that depreciation expense is $110. Let us now put all of the numbers in and see what comes out:

Furniture (net)

Bal 12/31/10	925		
Cash purchases	X		
Noncash purchases	200		
		NBV furniture sold	10
		Depreciation expense	110
Bal 12/31/11	1,100		

So X = Cash paid to purchase furniture = $95.

To summarize, this is how we find missing information for long-term assets:

1. Set up a T-account for the net value of the asset.

2. Fill in as much information as you can in the T-account (such as beginning and ending balances, depreciation expense, and purchases or net book value of disposals).

3. Solve for any missing information.

4. If there is more than one number missing, or if the missing information is not the number you need, use the gain/loss formula to calculate any remaining information.

Now we can put our two numbers, $90 and $95, into the statement of cash flows. *Cash* purchases of equipment were $95. Did this cause Cash to increase or decrease? Obviously, it is a decrease because Tanker *paid* cash, so we will subtract it. Cash received on sale of equipment is $90, which is an increase to Cash, so we will add it.

Remember that for investing activities, we *cannot* combine these two items. They *must* be listed separately because they are two separate transactions.

Totaling these numbers completes investing activities.

The completed investing activities section would appear as

Investing activities	
Cash paid to purchase new furniture	$(95)
Cash proceeds from sale of furniture	90
Total cash flow provided by investing activities	$ (5)

Financing Activities

Part 1	Part 2	**Part 3**	Demo Doc Complete

2   Distinguish among operating, investing, and financing cash flows

3   Prepare the statement of cash flows by the indirect method

Financing activities deal with long-term liabilities (debt) and equity accounts. First, we will look at long-term liabilities.

There are new notes payable (for which Tanker received cash) and Tanker repaid some other notes.

Notes Payable

We need the cash numbers involved so that we can put them into the cash-flow statement. Do we have any of them immediately available to us?

Yes, we are told that Tanker repaid $500 of notes payable.

We also know that Tanker took out a noncash note (to purchase furniture) of $200. This noncash transaction has already been recorded in the note to the cash-flow statement (discussed under investing activities).

Knowing this, let us analyze the Notes Payable T-account:

Notes payable		
	Bal 12/31/10	815
decreases	increases	
	Bal 12/31/11	660

What would cause this account to increase? Well, it would increase if Tanker took out new notes payable. What would cause it to decrease? It would decrease if Tanker paid off some of the notes. Let us put in that information:

Notes payable			
		Bal 12/31/10	815
Note repayments	500		
		New cash notes	X
		New noncash notes	200
		Bal 12/31/11	660

So we calculate that new cash notes = X = $145.

Now we put these numbers into the cash-flow statement. *Cash* received from new notes was $145. This increased Cash, so it has a positive effect on cash flow. Cash paid to repay old notes was $500. This decreased Cash, so it has a negative effect on cash flow.

Treasury Stock

Now we must analyze the changes in Tanker's equity. Tanker had some activity with treasury stock during the year. We know that Tanker purchased treasury stock.

Treasury stock			
Bal 12/31/10	0		
	increases	decreases	
Bal 12/31/11	1,000		

What could cause this account to go up? It would go up if Tanker purchased treasury stock. What could cause it to go down? It would go down if treasury stock were sold. We know that there was no treasury stock sold, so looking at this again

Treasury stock			
Bal 12/31/10	0		
Treasury stock			
Purchased	X		
		Treasury stock sold	0
Bal 12/31/11	1,000		

So we calculate that treasury stock purchased = X = $1,000. This means that cash was paid by Tanker, which is a negative effect on cash flow.

Dividends

The other account in equity is Retained earnings. The two major transactions impacting Retained earnings are net income and dividends.

Net income was already listed in the operating activities section, so all that remains to be included in the financing activities section is dividend activity.

The Retained earnings account looks like this:

Retained earnings

	Bal 12/31/10	200
decreases	increases	
	Bal 12/31/11	880

What makes Retained earnings go up? It goes up when Tanker earns net income. What makes it go down? It goes down when Tanker pays dividends. Putting this information in

Retained earnings

	Bal 12/31/10	200
Cash dividends paid X	Net income	1,000
	Bal 12/31/11	880

So cash dividends paid = X = $320. These were paid in cash so this has a negative effect on Cash.

Totaling these numbers completes financing activities. The completed financing activities section would appear as

Financing activities	
Cash proceeds from new notes	$ 145
Cash repayment of old notes	(500)
Cash purchase of treasury stock	(1,000)
Cash dividends paid	(320)
Total cash flow provided by financing activities	$(1,675)

Now we must combine operating activities, investing activities, and financing activities to get the total cash flow (the change in cash during the year).

Next, we show the Cash balance from the prior year (December 31, 2010) and add it to total cash flow to get this year's Cash balance (December 31, 2011).

TANKER, INC.
Statement of Cash Flows
Year Ended December 31, 2011

Operating activities	
Net income	$ 1,000
+ Depreciation expense	110
– Gain on sale of furniture	(80)
+ Decrease in accounts receivable	120
– Increase in inventory	(50)
– Increase in prepaid insurance	(30)
+ Increase in accounts payable	150
Total cash flow provided by operating activities	$ 1,220
Investing activities	
Cash paid to purchase new furniture	$ (95)
Cash proceeds from sale of furniture	90
Total cash flow provided by investing activities	$ (5)
Financing activities	
Cash proceeds from new notes	$ 145
Cash repayment of old notes	(500)
Cash purchase of treasury stock	(1,000)
Cash dividends paid	(320)
Total cash flow provided by financing activities	$(1,675)
Total cash flow (change in Cash balance)	$ 460
Cash, December 31, 2010	$ 1,160
Cash, December 31, 2011	$ 700
Noncash investing and financing activities	
Purchase of furniture with note payable	$ 200

Part 1	Part 2	Part 3	**Demo Doc Complete**

14 Financial Statement Analysis

Learning Objectives/Success Keys

1. Perform a horizontal analysis of financial statements

2. Perform a vertical analysis of financial statements

3. Prepare and use common-size financial statements

4. Compute the standard financial ratios

Now that you have learned some of the "how-to's" of financial statement preparation, we are going to show you how to analyze financial statements. We will be using our Smart Touch Learning, Inc., company for the first half of this chapter. Then in the second part of the chapter we will shift over to Greg's Groovy Tunes, Inc., to round out your introduction to financial statement analysis.

To get started, take a look at Smart Touch Learning's comparative income statement, as shown in Exhibit 14-1 on the following page.

You can see that 2015 was an incredible year for the company. Net income was over three times the net income of 2014, and investors were very happy.

Investors and creditors cannot evaluate a company by examining only one year's data. This is why most financial statements cover at least two periods, like the Smart Touch Learning income statement. In fact, most financial analysis covers trends of three to five years. This chapter shows you how to use some of the analytical tools for charting a company's progress through time.

To do that, we need some way to compare a company's performance

a. from year to year.

b. with a competing company, like **Learning Tree**.

c. with the education and training industry.

EXHIBIT 14-1 | **Comparative Income Statement, Smart Touch Learning, Inc.**

SMART TOUCH LEARNING, INC.* Income Statement (Adapted) Year Ended December 31, 2015 and 2014		
(*In millions*)	**2015**	**2014**
Revenues (same as Net sales)	$3,189	$1,466
Expenses:		
Cost of revenues (same as Cost of goods sold)	1,458	626
Sales and marketing expense	246	120
General and administrative expense	140	57
Research and development expense	225	91
Other expense	470	225
Income before income tax	650	347
Income tax expense	251	241
Net income	$ 399	$ 106

*All values are assumed.

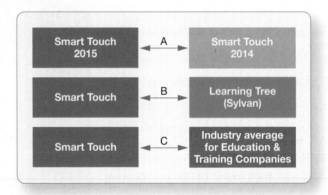

Then we will have a better idea of how to judge Smart Touch Learning's present situation and predict what might happen in the near future.

There are two main ways to analyze financial statements:

- Horizontal analysis provides a year-to-year comparison of a company's performance in different periods.

- Another technique, vertical analysis, is the standard way to compare different companies. Let us begin with horizontal analysis.

Horizontal Analysis

1 Perform a horizontal analysis of financial statements

Many decisions hinge on whether the numbers—in sales, expenses, and net income—are increasing or decreasing. Have sales and other revenues risen from last year? By how much? Sales may have increased by $20,000, but considered alone, this fact is not very helpful. The *percentage change* in sales over time is more relative and, therefore, more helpful. It is better to know that sales increased by 20% than to know that sales increased by $20,000.

The study of percentage changes in comparative statements is called **horizontal analysis**. Computing a percentage change in comparative statements requires two steps:

1. Compute the dollar amount of the change from the earlier period to the later period.

2. Divide the dollar amount of change by the earlier period amount. We call the earlier period the base period.

Illustration: Smart Touch Learning, Inc.

Horizontal analysis is illustrated for Smart Touch Learning as follows (dollar amounts in millions):

	2015	2014	Increase (Decrease) Amount	Percentage
Revenues (same as net sales)……….	$3,189	$1,466	$1,723	117.5%

Sales increased by an incredible 117.5% during 2015, computed as follows:

STEP 1: Compute the dollar amount of change in sales from 2015 to 2014:

> 2015   2014   Increase
> $3,189 − $1,466 = $1,723

STEP 2: Divide the dollar amount of change by the base-period amount. This computes the percentage change for the period:

$$\text{Percentage change} = \frac{\text{Dollar amount of change}}{\text{Base-year amount}}$$

$$= \frac{\$1,723}{\$1,466} = 1.175 = 117.5\%$$

Completed horizontal analyses for Smart Touch's financial statements are shown in the following exhibits:

- Exhibit 14-2 Income Statement
- Exhibit 14-3 Balance Sheet

EXHIBIT 14-2 | **Comparative Income Statement—Horizontal Analysis**

SMART TOUCH LEARNING, INC.*
Income Statement (Adapted)
Year Ended December 31, 2015 and 2014

(Dollar amounts in millions)	2015	2014	Increase (Decrease) Amount	Percentage
Revenues	$3,189	$1,466	$1,723	117.5%
Cost of revenues	1,458	626	832	132.9
Gross profit	1,731	840	891	106.1
Operating expenses:				
Sales and marketing expense	246	120	126	105.0
General and administrative expense	140	57	83	145.6
Research and development expense	225	91	134	147.3
Other expense	470	225	245	108.9
Income before income tax	650	347	303	87.3
Income tax expense	251	241	10	4.1
Net income	$ 399	$ 106	$ 293	276.4

*All values are assumed.

EXHIBIT 14-3 | **Comparative Balance Sheet—Horizontal Analysis**

SMART TOUCH LEARNING, INC.*
Balance Sheet (Adapted)
December 31, 2015 and 2014

(Dollar amounts in millions)	2015	2014	Increase (Decrease) Amount	Percentage
Assets				
Current Assets:				
Cash and cash equivalents	$ 427	$149	$ 278	186.6%
Other current assets	2,266	411	1,855	451.3
Total current assets	2,693	560	2,133	380.9
Property, plant, and equipment, net	379	188	191	101.6
Intangible assets, net	194	106	88	83.0
Other assets	47	17	30	176.5
Total assets	$3,313	$871	$2,442	280.4
Liabilities				
Current Liabilities:				
Accounts payable	$ 33	$ 46	$ (13)	(28.3)%
Other current liabilities	307	189	118	62.4
Total current liabilities	340	235	105	44.7
Long-term liabilities	44	47	(3)	(6.4)
Total liabilities	384	282	102	36.2
Stockholders' Equity				
Capital stock	1	45	(44)	(97.8)
Retained earnings and other equity	2,928	544	2,384	438.2
Total stockholders' equity	2,929	589	2,340	397.3
Total liabilities and equity	$3,313	$871	$2,442	280.4

*All values are assumed.

Horizontal Analysis of the Income Statement

Smart Touch's comparative income statement reveals exceptional growth during 2015. An increase of 100% occurs when an item doubles, so Smart Touch's 117.5% increase in revenues means that revenues more than doubled.

The item on Smart Touch's income statement with the slowest growth rate is income tax expense. Income taxes increased by only 4.1%. On the bottom line, net income grew by an incredible 276.4%. That is real progress!

Horizontal Analysis of the Balance Sheet

Smart Touch's comparative balance sheet also shows rapid growth in assets, with total assets increasing by 280.4%. That means total assets almost tripled in one year. Very few companies grow that fast.

Smart Touch's liabilities grew more slowly. Total liabilities increased by 36.2%, and Accounts payable actually decreased, as indicated by the liability figures in parentheses. This is another indicator of positive growth for Smart Touch.

Trend Percentages

Trend percentages are a form of horizontal analysis. Trends indicate the direction a business is taking. How have sales changed over a five-year period? What trend does net income show? These questions can be answered by trend percentages over a period, such as three to five years.

Trend percentages are computed by selecting a base year. The base-year amounts are set equal to 100%. The amounts for each subsequent year are expressed as a percentage of the base amount. To compute trend percentages, divide each item for the following years by the base-year amount.

$$\text{Trend \%} = \frac{\text{Any year \$}}{\text{Base year \$}} \times 100$$

Let us assume Smart Touch's total revenues were $1,000 million in 2011 and rose to $3,189 million in 2015. To illustrate trend analysis, let us review the trend of net sales during 2011–2015, with dollars in millions. The base year is 2011, so that year's percentage is set equal to 100.

(In millions)	2015	2014	2013	2012	2011
Net sales....................	$3,189	1,466	1,280	976	1,000
Trend percentages	318.9%	146.6%	128%	97.6%	100%

We want trend percentages for the five-year period 2011–2015. We compute these by dividing each year's amount by the 2011 net sales amount.

Net sales decreased a little in 2012 and then the rate of growth increased from 2013–2015.

You can perform a trend analysis on any one or multiple item(s) you consider important. Trend analysis is widely used to predict the future.

Vertical Analysis

As we have seen, horizontal analysis and trend percentages highlight changes in an item from year to year, or over *time*. But no single technique gives a complete picture of a business, so we also need vertical analysis.

2 Perform a vertical analysis of financial statements

Vertical analysis of a financial statement shows the relationship of each item to its base amount, which is the 100% figure. Every other item on the statement is then reported as a percentage of that base. For the income statement, net sales is the base.

$$\text{Vertical analysis \%} = \frac{\text{Each income-statement item}}{\text{Revenues (net sales)}} \times 100$$

Exhibit 14-4 on the following page shows the completed vertical analysis of Smart Touch Learning's 2015 income statement.

In this case, the vertical-analysis percentage for Smart Touch's cost of revenues is 45.7% of net sales ($1,458/$3,189 = 0.457). This means that for every $1 in net sales, almost 46 cents is spent on cost of revenue.

On the bottom line, Smart Touch's net income is 12.5% of revenues. That is extremely good. Suppose under normal conditions a company's net income is 10% of revenues. A drop to 4% may cause the investors to be alarmed and sell their stock.

Exhibit 14-5 on the following page the vertical analysis of Smart Touch's balance sheet.

The base amount (100%) is total assets. The base amount is also total liabilities and equity, because they are exactly the same number, $3,313. (Recall that they should always be the same number because of the accounting equation.)

EXHIBIT 14-4	Comparative Income Statement—Vertical Analysis

SMART TOUCH LEARNING, INC.*
Income Statement (Adapted)
Year Ended December 31, 2015

(Dollar amounts in millions)	Amount	Percent of Total
Revenues	$3,189	100.0%
Cost of revenues	1,458	45.7
Gross profit	1,731	54.3
Operating expenses:		
Sales and marketing expense	246	7.7
General and administrative expense	140	4.4
Research and development expense	225	7.1
Other expense	470	14.7
Income before income tax	650	20.4
Income tax expense	251	7.9
Net income	$ 399	12.5%

*All values are assumed.

EXHIBIT 14-5	Comparative Balance Sheet—Vertical Analysis

SMART TOUCH LEARNING, INC.*
Balance Sheet (Adapted)
December 31, 2015

(Dollar amount in millions)	Amount	Percent of Total
Assets		
Current Assets:		
Cash and cash equivalents	$ 427	12.9%
Other current assets	2,266	68.4
Total current assets	2,693	81.3
Property, plant, and equipment, net	379	11.4
Intangible assets, net	194	5.9
Other assets	47	1.4
Total assets	$3,313	100.0%
Liabilities		
Current Liabilities:		
Accounts payable	$ 33	1.0%
Other current liabilities	307	9.3
Total current liabilities	340	10.3
Long-term liabilities	44	1.3
Total liabilities	384	11.6
Stockholders' Equity		
Common stock	1	0.0
Retained earnings and other equity	2,928	88.4
Total stockholders' equity	2,929	88.4
Total liabilities and equity	$3,313	100.0%

*All values are assumed.

The vertical analysis of Smart Touch's balance sheet reveals several interesting things:

- Current assets make up 81.3% of total assets. For most companies this percentage is closer to 30%. The 81.3% of current assets represent a great deal of liquidity.

- Property, plant, and equipment make up only 11.4% of total assets. This percentage is low because of the nature of Smart Touch's business. Smart Touch's Web-based operations do not require lots of buildings and equipment.

- Total liabilities are only 11.6% of total assets, and stockholders' equity makes up 88.4% of total assets. Most of Smart Touch's equity is retained earnings and other equity—signs of a strong company because most of the equity is internally generated rather than externally generated (through stock share sales).

How Do We Compare One Company with Another?

Horizontal analysis and vertical analysis provide lots of useful data about a company. As we have seen, Smart Touch's percentages depict a very successful company. But the data apply only to one business.

3 Prepare and use common-size financial statements

To compare Smart Touch Learning to another company we can use a common-size statement. A **common-size statement** reports only percentages—the same percentages that appear in a vertical analysis. By only reporting percentages, it removes dollar value bias when comparing the companies. **Dollar value bias** is the bias one sees from comparing numbers in absolute (dollars) rather than relative (percentage) terms. For us, $1 million seems like a lot. For some large companies, it is immaterial. For example, Smart Touch's common-size income statement comes directly from the percentages in Exhibit 14-4.

We can use a common-size income statement to compare Smart Touch Learning and Learning Tree on profitability. The companies compete in the service-learning industry. Which company earns a higher percentage of revenues as profits for its shareholders? Exhibit 14-6 gives both companies' common-size income statements for 2015 so that we may compare them on a relative, not absolute basis.

EXHIBIT 14-6 | **Common-Size Income Statement**
| **Smart Touch vs. Learning Tree**

SMART TOUCH vs. LEARNING TREE* Common-Size Income Statement Year ended Dec. 31, 2015		
	Smart Touch	Learning Tree
Revenues	100.0%	100.0%
Cost of revenues	45.7	36.3
Gross profit	54.3	63.7
Sales and marketing expense	7.7	21.8
General and administrative expense	4.4	7.3
Research and development expense	7.1	10.3
Other expense (income)	14.7	(11.5)
Income before income tax	20.4	35.8
Income tax expense	7.9	12.3
Net income	12.5%	23.5%

*All values are assumed.

Exhibit 14-6 shows that Learning Tree was more profitable than Smart Touch in 2015. Learning Tree's gross profit percentage is 63.7%, compared to Smart Touch's 54.3%. This means that Learning Tree is getting more profit from every dollar than Smart Touch. And, most importantly, Learning Tree's percentage of net income to revenues is 23.5%. That means almost one-fourth of Learning Tree's revenues end up as profits for the company's stockholders. Smart Touch's percentage of net income to revenues, on the other hand, is 12.5%. Both are excellent percentages; however, the common-size statement highlights Learning Tree's advantages over Smart Touch.

Benchmarking

Benchmarking is the practice of comparing a company with other leading companies. There are two main types of benchmarks in financial statement analysis.

Benchmarking Against a Key Competitor

Exhibit 14-6 uses a key competitor, Learning Tree, to compare Smart Touch's profitability. The two companies compete in the same industry, so Learning Tree serves as an ideal benchmark for Smart Touch. The graphs in Exhibit 14-7 highlight the profitability difference between the companies. Focus on the segment of the graphs showing net income. Learning Tree is clearly more profitable than Smart Touch.

EXHIBIT 14-7 | **Graphical Analysis of Common-Size Income Statement Smart Touch Learning vs. Learning Tree**

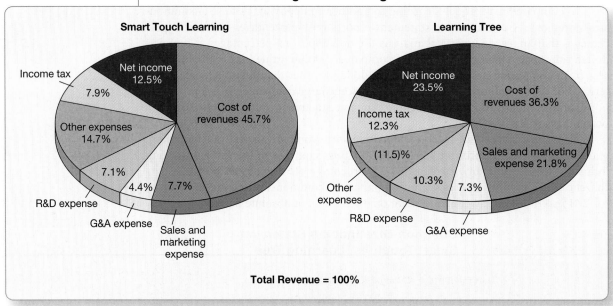

Benchmarking Against the Industry Average

The industry average can also serve as a very useful benchmark for evaluating a company. An industry comparison would show how Smart Touch is performing alongside the average for the e-learning industry. *Annual Statement Studies*, published by The Risk Management Association, provides common-size statements for most industries. To compare Smart Touch to the industry average, simply insert the industry-average common-size income statement in place of Learning Tree in Exhibit 14-6.

Stop & Think...

When you are driving down any road, how do you know how fast you can travel? The speed limit sign. You compare the speed at which you are traveling in your car to that speed limit sign. That is the same concept as benchmarking. The industry averages, for example, are the "sign" and your company results are the "speed at which you are traveling." Sometimes your company is going faster than other companies. Sometimes it is going slower.

Now let us put your learning to practice. Work the summary problem, which reviews the concepts from the first half of this chapter.

Summary Problem 1

Requirements

Perform a horizontal analysis and a vertical analysis of the comparative income statement of Kimball Corporation, which makes iPod labels. State whether 2012 was a good year or a bad year, and give your reasons.

KIMBALL CORPORATION
Comparative Income Statement
Years Ended December 31, 2012 and 2011

	2012	2011
Net sales	$275,000	$225,000
Expenses:		
Cost of goods sold	$194,000	$165,000
Engineering, selling, and administrative expenses	54,000	48,000
Interest expense	5,000	5,000
Income tax expense	9,000	3,000
Other expense (income)	1,000	(1,000)
Total expenses	263,000	220,000
Net income	$ 12,000	$ 5,000

Solution

KIMBALL CORPORATION
Horizontal Analysis of Comparative Income Statement
Years Ended December 31, 2012 and 2011

	2012	2011	Increase (Decrease) Amount	Increase (Decrease) Percent
Net sales	$275,000	$225,000	$50,000	22.2%
Expenses:				
Cost of goods sold	$194,000	$165,000	$29,000	17.6
Engineering, selling, and administrative expenses	54,000	48,000	6,000	12.5
Interest expense	5,000	5,000	—	—
Income tax expense	9,000	3,000	6,000	200.0
Other expense (income)	1,000	(1,000)	2,000	—*
Total expenses	263,000	220,000	43,000	19.5
Net income	$ 12,000	$ 5,000	$ 7,000	140.0%

*Percentage changes are typically not computed for shifts from a negative to a positive amount, and vice versa.

The horizontal analysis shows that total revenues increased 22.2%. Total expenses increased by 19.5%, and net income rose by 140%.

KIMBALL CORPORATION
Vertical Analysis of Comparative Income Statement
Years Ended December 31, 2012 and 2011

		2012		2011	
		Amount	Percent	Amount	Percent
Net sales		$275,000	100.0%	$225,000	100.0%
Expenses:					
Cost of goods sold		$194,000	70.5	$165,000	73.3
Engineering, selling, and administrative expenses		54,000	19.6	48,000	21.3
Interest expense		5,000	1.8	5,000	2.2
Income tax expense		9,000	3.3	3,000	1.4**
Other expense (income)		1,000	0.4	(1,000)	(0.4)
Total expenses		263,000	95.6	220,000	97.8
Net income		$ 12,000	4.4%	$ 5,000	2.2%

**Number is rounded up.

The vertical analysis shows decreases in the percentages of net sales consumed by

- cost of goods sold (from 73.3% to 70.5%);
- engineering, selling, and administrative expenses (from 21.3% to 19.6%).

These two items are Kimball's largest dollar expenses, so their percentage decreases are important.

The 2012 net income rose to 4.4% of sales, compared with 2.2% the preceding year. The analysis shows that 2012 was significantly better than 2011.

Using Ratios to Make Decisions

Online financial databases, such as **Lexis/Nexis** and the **Dow Jones News Retrieval Service,** provide data on thousands of companies. Suppose you want to compare some companies' recent earnings histories. You might want to compare companies' returns on stockholders' equity. The computer could then search the databases and give you the names of the 20 companies with the highest return on equity. You can use any ratio for searching that is relevant to a particular decision.

4 Compute the standard financial ratios

Remember, however, that no single ratio tells the whole picture of any company's performance. Different ratios explain different aspects of a company. The ratios we discuss in this chapter may be classified as follows:

1. Measuring ability to pay current liabilities

2. Measuring ability to sell inventory and collect receivables

3. Measuring ability to pay long-term debt

4. Measuring profitability

5. Analyzing stock as an investment

Measuring Ability to Pay Current Liabilities

Working capital is defined as follows:

> **Working capital = Current assets – Current liabilities**

Working capital measures the ability to meet short-term obligations with current assets. Two decision tools based on working-capital data are the *current ratio* and the *acid-test ratio*.

Current Ratio

The most widely used ratio is the *current ratio*, which is current assets divided by current liabilities. The current ratio measures ability to pay current liabilities with current assets.

Exhibit 14-8 on the following page gives the comparative income statement and balance sheet of Greg's Groovy Tunes, which we will be using in the remainder of this chapter.

The current ratios of Greg's Groovy Tunes, at December 31, 2013 and 2012, follow, along with the average for the entertainment industry:

		Greg's Groovy Tunes' Current Ratio		Industry
	Formula	2013	2012	Average
Current ratio =	$\dfrac{\text{Current assets}}{\text{Current liabilities}}$	$\dfrac{\$262,000}{\$142,000} = 1.85$	$\dfrac{\$236,000}{\$126,000} = 1.87$	.60

A high current ratio indicates that the business has sufficient current assets to maintain normal business operations. Compare Greg's Groovy Tunes' current ratio of 1.85 for 2013 with the industry average of .60.

What is an acceptable current ratio? The answer depends on the industry. The norm for companies in most industries is around 1.50, as reported by The Risk Management Association. Greg's Groovy Tunes' current ratio of 1.85 is strong. Keep in mind that we would not want to see a current ratio that is too high, say 25.0. This would indicate that the company is too liquid and, therefore, is not using its assets effectively.

EXHIBIT 14-8 | **Comparative Financial Statements**

GREG'S GROOVY TUNES, INC.
Comparative Income Statement
Years Ended December 31, 2013 and 2012

	2013	2012
Net sales	$858,000	$803,000
Cost of goods sold	513,000	509,000
Gross profit	345,000	294,000
Operating expenses:		
Selling expenses	126,000	114,000
General expenses	118,000	123,000
Total operating expenses	244,000	237,000
Income from operations	101,000	57,000
Interest revenue	4,000	—
Interest (expense)	(24,000)	(14,000)
Income before income taxes	81,000	43,000
Income tax expense	33,000	17,000
Net income	**$ 48,000**	**$ 26,000**

GREG'S GROOVY TUNES, INC.
Comparative Balance Sheet
December 31, 2013 and 2012

	2013	2012
Assets		
Current Assets:		
Cash	$ 29,000	$ 32,000
Accounts receivable, net	114,000	85,000
Inventories	113,000	111,000
Prepaid expenses	6,000	8,000
Total current assets	262,000	236,000
Long-term investments	18,000	9,000
Property, plant, and equipment, net	507,000	399,000
Total assets	**$787,000**	**$644,000**
Liabilities		
Current Liabilities:		
Notes payable	$ 42,000	$ 27,000
Accounts payable	73,000	68,000
Accrued liabilities	27,000	31,000
Total current liabilities	142,000	126,000
Long-term notes payable	289,000	198,000
Total liabilities	431,000	324,000
Stockholders' Equity		
Common stock, no par	186,000	186,000
Retained earnings	170,000	134,000
Total stockholders' equity	356,000	320,000
Total liabilities and equity	$787,000	$644,000

Acid-Test Ratio

The *acid-test* (or *quick*) *ratio* tells us whether the entity could pay all its current liabilities if they came due immediately. That is, could the company pass this *acid test*?

To compute the acid-test ratio, we add cash, short-term investments, and net current receivables (accounts and notes receivable, net of allowances) and divide this sum by current liabilities. Inventory and prepaid expenses are *not* included in the acid test because they are the least-liquid current assets. Greg's Groovy Tunes' acid-test ratios for 2013 and 2012 follow:

	Formula	Greg's Groovy Tunes' Acid-Test Ratio		Industry Average
		2013	2012	
Acid-test ratio	$\dfrac{\text{Cash + Short-term investments + Net current receivables}}{\text{Current liabilities}}$	$\dfrac{\$29,000 + \$0 + \$114,000}{\$142,000} = 1.01$	$\dfrac{\$32,000 + \$0 + \$85,000}{\$126,000} = 0.93$	.46

The company's acid-test ratio improved during 2013 and is significantly better than the industry average. The norm for the acid-test ratio ranges from 0.20 for shoe retailers to 1.00 for manufacturers of equipment, as reported by The Risk Management Association. An acid-test ratio of 0.90 to 1.00 is acceptable in most industries.

Measuring Ability to Sell Inventory and Collect Receivables

The ability to sell inventory and collect receivables is fundamental to business. In this section, we discuss three ratios that measure the company's ability to sell inventory and collect receivables.

Inventory Turnover

The inventory turnover ratio measures the number of times a company sells its average level of inventory during a year. A high rate of turnover indicates ease in selling inventory; a low rate indicates difficulty. A value of 4 means that the company sold its average level of inventory four times—once every three months—during the year. If the company were a seasonal company, this would be a good ratio because it would mean it turned its inventory over each season, on average.

To compute inventory turnover, we divide cost of goods sold by the average inventory for the period. We use the cost of goods sold—not sales—because both cost of goods sold and inventory are stated *at cost*. Sales at *retail* are not comparable with inventory at *cost*.

Greg's Groovy Tunes' inventory turnover for 2013 is as follows:

Formula	Greg's Groovy Tunes' Inventory Turnover	Industry Average
Inventory turnover = $\dfrac{\text{Cost of goods sold}}{\text{Average inventory}}$	$\dfrac{\$513,000}{\$112,000} = 4.6$	27.65

Cost of goods sold comes from the income statement (Exhibit 14-8). Average inventory is figured by adding the beginning inventory ($111,000) to the ending inventory ($113,000) and dividing by two. (See the balance sheet, Exhibit 14-8.)

Inventory turnover varies widely with the nature of the business. For example, most manufacturers of farm machinery have an inventory turnover close to three times a year. In contrast, companies that remove natural gas from the ground hold their inventory for a very short period of time and have an average turnover of 30.

Greg's Groovy Tunes' turnover of 4.6 times a year is very low for its industry, which has an average turnover of 27.65 times per year. This ratio has identified an area that Greg's Groovy Tunes needs to improve.

Accounts Receivable Turnover

The **accounts receivable turnover ratio** measures the ability to collect cash from credit customers. The higher the ratio, the faster the cash collections. But a receivable turnover that is too high may indicate that credit is too tight, causing the loss of sales to good customers.

To compute accounts receivable turnover, divide net credit sales by average net accounts receivable. Average net accounts receivable is figured by adding the beginning accounts receivable balance ($85,000) and the ending balance ($114,000), then dividing by 2:

$$($85,000 + $114,000)/2 = $99,500$$

Greg's Groovy Tunes' accounts receivable turnover ratio for 2013 is computed as follows:

Formula		Greg's Groovy Tunes' Accounts Receivable Turnover	Industry Average
Accounts receivable turnover	$= \dfrac{\text{Net credit sales}}{\text{Average net accounts receivable}}$	$\dfrac{\$858,000}{\$99,500} = 8.6$	29.10

Greg's receivable turnover of 8.6 times per year is much slower than the industry average of 29.1. Why the difference? Greg's is a fairly new business that sells to established people who pay their accounts over time. Further, this turnover coincides with the lower than average inventory turnover. So, Greg's may achieve a higher receivable turnover by increasing its inventory turnover ratio.

Days' Sales in Receivables

The *days'-sales-in-receivables* ratio also measures the ability to collect receivables. Days' sales in receivables tell us how many days' sales remain in Accounts receivable. To compute the ratio, we can follow a logical two-step process:

1. Divide net sales by 365 days to figure average sales for one day.

2. Divide this average day's sales amount into average net accounts receivable.

The data to compute this ratio for Greg's Groovy Tunes for 2013 are taken from the income statement and the balance sheet (Exhibit 14-8):

Formula		Greg's Groovy Tunes' Days' Sales in Accounts Receivable	Industry Average
Days' sales in *average* Accounts receivable:			
1. One day's sales	$= \dfrac{\text{Net sales}}{365 \text{ days}}$	$\dfrac{\$858,000}{365 \text{ days}} = \$2,351$	
2. Days' sales in average accounts receivable	$= \dfrac{\text{Average net accounts receivable}}{\text{One day's sales}}$	$\dfrac{\$99,500}{\$2,351} = 42 \text{ days}$	25

Average accounts receivable was calculated in the previous ratio example at $99,500.

Greg's Groovy Tunes' ratio tells us that 42 average days' sales remain in Accounts receivable and need to be collected. The company's days'-sales-in-receivables ratio is much higher (worse) than the industry average of 25 days. This is probably because Greg's collects its own receivables rather than paying a collection agency to collect for the company. Without the customers' good paying habits, the company's cash flow would suffer.

Measuring Ability to Pay Long-Term Debt

The ratios discussed so far yield insight into current assets and current liabilities. They help us measure ability to sell inventory, collect receivables, and pay current liabilities. Most businesses also have long-term debt. Two key indicators of a business's ability to pay long-term liabilities are the *debt ratio* and the *times-interest-earned ratio*.

Debt Ratio

A loan officer at Metro Bank is evaluating loan applications from two companies. Both companies have asked to borrow $500,000 and have agreed to repay the loan over a five-year period. The first firm already owes $600,000 to another bank. The second owes only $100,000. If all else is equal, the bank is more likely to lend money to Company 2 because that company owes less than Company 1.

This relationship between total liabilities and total assets—called the *debt ratio*—shows the proportion of assets financed with debt. If the debt ratio is 1, then all the assets are financed with debt. A debt ratio of 0.50 means that half the assets are financed with debt and the other half is financed by the owners of the business. The higher the debt ratio, the higher the company's financial risk.

The debt ratios for Greg's Groovy Tunes at the ends of 2013 and 2012 follow:

Formula	Greg's Groovy Tunes' Debt Ratio		Industry Average
	2013	2012	
Debt ratio = $\dfrac{\text{Total liabilities}}{\text{Total assets}}$	$\dfrac{\$431,000}{\$787,000} = 0.55$	$\dfrac{\$324,000}{\$644,000} = 0.50$	0.69

Greg's debt ratio in 2013 of 0.55 is not very high. The Risk Management Association reports that the average debt ratio for most companies ranges from 0.57 to 0.67, with relatively little variation from company to company. Greg's debt ratio indicates a fairly low-risk position compared with the industry average debt ratio of 0.69.

Times-Interest-Earned Ratio

The debt ratio says nothing about the ability to pay interest expense. Analysts use the **times-interest-earned ratio** to relate income to interest expense. This ratio is also called the **interest-coverage ratio**. It measures the number of times operating income can cover (pay) interest expense. A high interest-coverage ratio indicates ease in paying interest expense; a low ratio suggests difficulty.

To compute this ratio, we divide income from operations (operating income) by interest expense. Calculation of Greg's times-interest-earned ratio follows:

Formula	Greg's Groovy Tunes' Times-Interest-Earned Ratio		Industry Average
	2013	2012	
Times-interest-earned ratio = $\dfrac{\text{Income from operations}}{\text{Interest expense}}$	$\dfrac{\$101,000}{\$24,000} = 4.21$	$\dfrac{\$57,000}{\$14,000} = 4.07$	7.80

The company's times-interest-earned ratio of around 4.00 is significantly lower than the average for the industry of 7.80 times but is slightly better than the average U.S. business. The norm for U.S. business, as reported by The Risk Management Association, falls in the range of 2.0 to 3.0. When you consider Greg's debt ratio and its times-interest-earned ratio, Greg's Groovy Tunes appears to have little difficulty *servicing its debt*, that is, paying liabilities.

Measuring Profitability

The fundamental goal of business is to earn a profit. Ratios that measure profitability are reported in the business press. We will examine four profitability measures.

Rate of Return on Net Sales

In business, the term *return* is used broadly as a measure of profitability. Consider a ratio called the **rate of return on net sales**, or simply **return on sales**. (The word *net* is usually omitted for convenience, even though net sales is used to compute the ratio.) This ratio shows the percentage of each sales dollar earned as net income. Greg's Groovy Tunes' rate of return on sales follows:

| | | Greg's Groovy Tunes' Rate of Return on Sales | | Industry |
	Formula	2013	2012	Average
Rate of return on sales	$= \dfrac{\text{Net income}}{\text{Net sales}}$	$\dfrac{\$48,000}{\$858,000} = 0.056$	$\dfrac{\$26,000}{\$803,000} = 0.032$	.017

Companies strive for a high rate of return on sales. The higher the rate of return, the more sales dollars end up as profit. The increase in Greg's return on sales from 2012 to 2013 is significant and identifies the company as more successful than the average education service provider whose rate of return is .017.

Rate of Return on Total Assets

The *rate of return on total assets*, or simply *return on assets*, measures a company's success in using assets to earn a profit. Two groups finance a company's assets.

- Creditors have loaned money to the company, and they earn interest.
- Shareholders have invested in stock, and their return is net income.

The sum of interest expense and net income divided by total assets is the return to the two groups that have financed the company's assets. Average total assets is the average of beginning and ending total assets from the comparative balance sheet:

$$(\$644,000 + \$787,000)/2 = \$715,500$$

Computation of the return-on-assets ratio for Greg's Groovy Tunes follows:

| | | Greg's Groovy Tunes' 2013 | Industry |
	Formula	Rate of Return on Total Assets	Average
Rate of return on assets	$= \dfrac{\text{Net income} + \text{Interest expense}}{\text{Average total assets}}$	$\dfrac{\$48,000 + \$24,000}{\$715,500} = 0.101$	.0599

Greg's Groovy Tunes' return-on-assets ratio of .101 is much better than the industry average of .0599.

Rate of Return on Common Stockholders' Equity

A popular measure of profitability is *rate of return on common stockholders' equity*, often shortened to *return on equity*. This ratio shows the relationship between net income and common stockholders' equity—how much income is earned for each $1 invested by the common shareholders.

To compute this ratio, we first subtract preferred dividends from net income to get net income available to the common stockholders. (Greg's does not have any preferred stocks issued, so preferred dividends are zero.) Then divide net income available to common stockholders by average common equity during the year. Common equity is total stockholders' equity minus preferred equity. Average equity is the average of the beginning and ending balances.

$$($356,000 + $320,000)/2 = $338,000$$

The 2013 rate of return on common stockholders' equity for Greg's Groovy Tunes follows:

	Formula	Greg's Groovy Tunes' 2013 Rate of Return on Common Stockholders' Equity	Industry Average
Rate of return on common stockholders' equity	$= \dfrac{\text{Net income} - \text{Preferred dividends}}{\text{Average common stockholders' equity}}$	$\dfrac{\$48,000 - \$0}{\$338,000} = 0.142$	.105

Greg's return on equity of 0.142 is higher than its return on assets of 0.101. This difference results from borrowing at one rate—say, 8%—and investing the money to earn a higher rate, such as the firm's 14.2% return on equity. This practice is called **trading on the equity**, or using *leverage*. It is directly related to the debt ratio. The higher the debt ratio, the higher the leverage. Companies that finance operations with debt are said to *leverage* their positions.

During good times, leverage increases profitability. But leverage can have a negative impact on profitability as well. Therefore, leverage is a double-edged sword, increasing profits during good times but compounding losses during bad times. Compare Greg's Groovy Tunes' return on equity with the industry average of 0.105. Once again, Greg's Groovy Tunes is performing much better than the average company in its industry. A return on equity of 15% to 20% year after year is considered good in most industries. At 14.2%, Greg's is doing well.

Earnings per Share of Common Stock

Earnings per share of common stock, or simply *earnings per share (EPS)*, is perhaps the most widely quoted of all financial statistics. EPS is the only ratio that must appear on the face of the income statement. EPS is the amount of net income earned for each share of the company's outstanding *common* stock. Recall that

Outstanding stock = Issued stock − Treasury stock

Earnings per share is computed by dividing net income available to common stockholders by the number of common shares outstanding during the year. Preferred dividends are subtracted from net income because the preferred stockholders have the first claim to dividends. Greg's Groovy Tunes has no preferred stock outstanding and, therefore, paid no preferred dividends.

The firm's EPS for 2013 and 2012 follow. (Note that Greg's had 10,000 shares of common stock outstanding throughout both years.)

| | | Earnings per Share | | Industry |
	Formula	2013	2012	Average
Earnings per share of common stock	$= \dfrac{\text{Net income} - \text{Preferred dividends}}{\text{Number of shares of common stock outstanding}}$	$\dfrac{\$48,000 - \$0}{10,000} = \$4.80$	$\dfrac{\$26,000 - \$0}{10,000} = \$2.60$	$9.76

Greg's Groovy Tunes' EPS increased significantly in 2013 (by almost 85%). Its stockholders should not expect this big a boost in EPS every year. Most companies strive to increase EPS by 10%–15% annually, and leading companies do so. But even the most successful companies have an occasional bad year. EPS for the industry at $9.76 is a little over twice Greg's Groovy Tunes' 2013 EPS. Therefore, Greg's Groovy Tunes needs to work on continuing to increase EPS so that it is more competitive with other companies in its industry.

Analyzing Stock Investments

Investors purchase stock to earn a return on their investment. This return consists of two parts: (1) gains (or losses) from selling the stock at a price above or below purchase price and (2) dividends. The ratios we examine in this section help analysts evaluate stock investments.

Price/Earnings Ratio

The **price/earnings ratio** is the ratio of the market price of a share of common stock to the company's earnings per share. It shows the market price of $1 of earnings. This ratio, abbreviated P/E, appears in *The Wall Street Journal* stock listings.

Calculations for the P/E ratios of Greg's Groovy Tunes follow. The market price of its common stock was $60 at the end of 2013 and $35 at the end of 2012. These prices for real companies can be obtained from a financial publication, a stockbroker, or the company's Web site.

| | | Greg's Groovy Tunes' Price/Earnings Ratio | | Industry |
	Formula	2013	2012	Average
P/E ratio	$= \dfrac{\text{Market price per share of common stock}}{\text{Earnings per share}}$	$\dfrac{\$60.00}{\$4.80} = 12.5$	$\dfrac{\$35.00}{\$2.60} = 13.5$	17.79

Greg's P/E ratio of 12.5 means that the company's stock is selling at 12.5 times one year's earnings. The decline from the 2012 P/E ratio of 13.5 is no cause for alarm because the market price of the stock is not under Greg's Groovy Tunes' control. Net income is more controllable, and net income increased during 2013.

Greg's would like to see this ratio increase in future years in order to be more in line with the industry average P/E of 17.79.

Dividend Yield

Dividend yield is the ratio of dividends per share to the stock's market price per share. This ratio measures the percentage of a stock's market value that is returned annually as dividends. *Preferred* stockholders, who invest primarily to receive dividends, pay special attention to dividend yield.

Greg's paid annual cash dividends of $1.20 per share of common stock in 2013 and $1.00 in 2012. As noted previously, market prices of the company's common stock were $60 in 2013 and $35 in 2012. The firm's dividend yields on common stock follow:

Formula	Dividend Yield on Greg's Groovy Tunes' Common Stock		Industry Average
	2013	2012	
Dividend yield on common stock* $= \dfrac{\text{Dividend per share of common stock}}{\text{Market price per share of common stock}}$	$\dfrac{\$1.20}{\$60.00} = .020$	$\dfrac{\$1.00}{\$35.00} = .029$	.0356

*Dividend yields may also be calculated for preferred stock.

An investor who buys Greg's Groovy Tunes' common stock for $60 can expect to receive 2% of the investment annually in the form of cash dividends. The industry, however, is paying out 3.56% annually.

Book Value per Share of Common Stock

Book value per share of common stock is common equity divided by the number of common shares outstanding. Common equity equals total stockholders' equity less preferred equity. Greg's has no preferred stock outstanding. Its book-value-per-share-of-common-stock ratios follow. (Note that 10,000 shares of common stock were outstanding.)

Formula	Book Value per Share of Greg's Groovy Tunes' Common Stock	
	2013	2012
Book value per share of common stock $= \dfrac{\text{Total stockholders' equity} - \text{Preferred equity}}{\text{Number of shares of common stock outstanding}}$	$\dfrac{\$356,000 - \$0}{10,000} = \$35.60$	$\dfrac{\$320,000 - \$0}{10,000} = \$32.00$

Many experts argue that book value is not useful for investment analysis. It bears no relationship to market value and provides little information beyond stockholders' equity reported on the balance sheet. But some investors base their investment decisions on book value. For example, some investors rank stocks on the basis of the ratio of market price to book value. To these investors, the lower the ratio, the more attractive the stock.

Stop & Think...

If you have ever baked cookies from scratch, you know that you have to measure the ingredients properly to make the cookies taste "right." So say you are making peanut butter cookies and the recipe calls for 2/3 cup of peanut butter. If you only have 1/2 cup, it will not be enough to make the cookies taste like they should. If you put in 3/4; cup, it would be too much and again, the cookies will not taste as they should. Ratio analysis is like this. It measures performance of certain key figures that give you either a result you wanted (good peanut butter cookies) or a result you did not want (peanut butter cookies that do not taste like peanut butter).

Red Flags in Financial Statement Analysis

Analysts look for *red flags* that may signal financial trouble. Recent accounting scandals highlight the importance of these red flags. The following conditions may reveal that the company is too risky.

- **Movement of Sales, Inventory, and Receivables.** Sales, receivables, and inventory generally move together. Increased sales lead to higher receivables and require more inventory to meet demand. Unexpected or inconsistent movements among sales, inventory, and receivables make the financial statements look suspect.
- **Earnings Problems.** Has net income decreased significantly for several years in a row? Has income turned into a loss? Most companies cannot survive consecutive losses year after year.
- **Decreased Cash Flow.** Cash flow validates net income. Is cash flow from operations consistently lower than net income? If so, the company is in trouble. Are the sales of plant assets a major source of cash? If so, the company may face a cash shortage.
- **Too Much Debt.** How does the company's debt ratio compare to that of major competitors? If the debt ratio is too high, the company may be unable to pay its debts.
- **Inability to Collect Receivables.** Are days' sales in receivables growing faster than for competitors? A cash shortage may be looming.
- **Buildup of Inventories.** Is inventory turnover too slow? If so, the company may be unable to sell goods, or it may be overstating inventory.

Do any of these red flags apply to either Smart Touch Learning or Greg's Groovy Tunes from the analysis we did in the chapter? No, the financial statements of both companies depict strong and growing companies. Will both Smart Touch Learning and Greg's Groovy Tunes continue to grow? Time will tell.

The Decision Guidelines summarize the most widely used ratios.

Decision Guidelines

USING RATIOS IN FINANCIAL STATEMENT ANALYSIS

Mike and Roberta Robinson operate a financial-services firm. They manage other people's money and do most of their own financial-statement analysis. How do they measure companies' ability to pay bills, sell inventory, collect receivables, and so on? They use the standard ratios discussed in this chapter.

Ratio	Computation	Information Provided
Measuring ability to pay current liabilities:		
1. Current ratio	$$\frac{\text{Current assets}}{\text{Current liabilities}}$$	Measures ability to pay current liabilities with current assets
2. Acid-test (quick) ratio	$$\frac{\text{Cash} + \text{Short-term investments} + \text{Net current receivables}}{\text{Current liabilities}}$$	Shows ability to pay all current liabilities if they came due immediately
Measuring ability to sell inventory and collect receivables:		
3. Inventory turnover	$$\frac{\text{Cost of goods sold}}{\text{Average inventory}}$$	Indicates salability of inventory—the number of times a company sells its average inventory during a year
4. Accounts receivable turnover	$$\frac{\text{Net credit sales}}{\text{Average net accounts receivable}}$$	Measures ability to collect cash from customers
5. Days' sales in receivables	$$\frac{\text{Average net accounts receivable}}{\text{One day's sales}}$$	Shows how many days' sales remain in Accounts receivable—how many days it takes to collect the average level of receivables
Measuring ability to pay long-term debt:		
6. Debt ratio	$$\frac{\text{Total liabilities}}{\text{Total assets}}$$	Indicates percentage of assets financed with debt
7. Times-interest-earned ratio	$$\frac{\text{Income from operations}}{\text{Interest expense}}$$	Measures the number of times operating income can cover interest expense
Measuring profitability:		
8. Rate of return on net sales	$$\frac{\text{Net income}}{\text{Net sales}}$$	Shows the percentage of each sales dollar earned as net income
9. Rate of return on total assets	$$\frac{\text{Net income} + \text{Interest expense}}{\text{Average total assets}}$$	Measures how profitably a company uses its assets

Ratio	Computation	Information Provided
10. Rate of return on common stock-holders' equity	$$\frac{\text{Net income} - \text{Preferred dividends}}{\text{Average common stockholders' equity}}$$	Gauges how much income is earned for each dollar invested by the common shareholders
11. Earnings per share of common stock	$$\frac{\text{Net income} - \text{Preferred dividends}}{\text{Number of shares of common stock outstanding}}$$	Gives the amount of net income earned for each share of the company's common stock

Analyzing stock as an investment:

Ratio	Computation	Information Provided
12. Price/earnings ratio	$$\frac{\text{Market price per share of common stock}}{\text{Earnings per share}}$$	Indicates the market price of $1 of earnings
13. Dividend yield	$$\frac{\text{Annual dividend per share of common (or preferred) stock}}{\text{Market price per share of common (or preferred) stock}}$$	Shows the percentage of a stock's market value returned as dividends to stockholders each year
14. Book value per share of common stock	$$\frac{\text{Total stockholders' equity} - \text{Preferred equity}}{\text{Number of shares of common stock outstanding}}$$	Indicates the recorded accounting amount for each share of common stock outstanding

Summary Problem 2

JAVA, INC. Four-Year Selected Financial Data (adapted) Years Ended January 31, 2014–2011				
Operating Results*	**2014**	**2013**	**2012**	**2011**
Net sales	$13,848	$13,673	$11,635	$ 9,054
Cost of goods sold	9,704	8,599	6,775	5,318
Interest expense	109	75	45	46
Income from operations	338	1,455	1,817	1,333
Net income (net loss)	(8)	877	1,127	824
Cash dividends	76	75	76	77
Financial Position				
Merchandise inventory	1,677	1,904	1,462	1,056
Total assets	7,591	7,012	5,189	3,963
Current ratio	1.48:1	0.95:1	1.25:1	1.20:1
Stockholders' equity	3,010	2,928	2,630	1,574
Average number of shares of common stock outstanding (in thousands)	860	879	895	576

*Dollar amounts are in thousands.

Requirements

Compute the following ratios for 2012–2014, and evaluate Java's operating results. Are operating results strong or weak? Did they improve or deteriorate during this period? Your analysis should include the following:

1. Net income as a percentage of sales
2. Earnings per share
3. Inventory turnover
4. Times-interest-earned ratio
5. Rate of return on stockholders' equity

Solution

	2014	2013	2012
1. Net income as a percentage of sales	$\dfrac{\$(8)}{\$13,848} = (.06\%)$	$\dfrac{\$877}{\$13,673} = 6.4\%$	$\dfrac{\$1,127}{\$11,635} = 9.7\%$
2. Earnings per share	$\dfrac{\$(8)}{860} = \$(0.01)$	$\dfrac{\$877}{879} = \$1.00$	$\dfrac{\$1,127}{895} = \$1.26$
3. Inventory turnover	$\dfrac{\$9,704}{(\$1,677 + \$1,904)/2} = 5.4 \text{ times}$	$\dfrac{\$8,599}{(\$1,904 + \$1,462)/2} = 5.1 \text{ times}$	$\dfrac{\$6,775}{(\$1,462 + \$1,056)/2} = 5.4 \text{ times}$
4. Times-interest-earned ratio	$\dfrac{\$338}{\$109} = 3.1 \text{ times}$	$\dfrac{\$1,455}{\$75} = 19.4 \text{ times}$	$\dfrac{\$1,817}{\$45} = 40.4 \text{ times}$
5. Rate of return on stockholders' equity	$\dfrac{\$(8)}{(\$3,010 + \$2,928)/2} = (0.3\%)$	$\dfrac{\$877}{(\$2,928 + \$2,630)/2} = 31.6\%$	$\dfrac{\$1,127}{(\$2,630 + \$1,574)/2} = 53.6\%$

Evaluation: During this period, Java's operating results deteriorated on all these measures except inventory turnover. The times-interest-earned ratio and return on equity percentages are down sharply. From these data it is clear that Java could sell its coffee, but not at the markups the company enjoyed in the past. The final result, in 2014, was a net loss for the year.

Review Financial Statement Analysis

■ Accounting Vocabulary

Accounts Receivable Turnover Ratio (p. 692)
Measures a company's ability to collect cash from credit customers. To compute accounts receivable turnover, divide net credit sales by average net accounts receivable.

Benchmarking (p. 686)
The practice of comparing a company with other companies that are leaders.

Common-Size Statement (p. 685)
A financial statement that reports only percentages (no dollar amounts).

Dividend Yield (p. 697)
Ratio of dividends per share of stock to the stock's market price per share. Tells the percentage of a stock's market value that the company returns to stockholders annually as dividends.

Dollar Value Bias (p. 685)
The bias one sees from comparing numbers in absolute (dollars) rather than relative (percentages) terms.

Horizontal Analysis (p. 680)
Study of percentage changes in comparative financial statements.

Interest-Coverage Ratio (p. 693)
Ratio of income from operations to interest expense. Measures the number of times that operating income can cover interest expense. Also called the **times-interest-earned ratio**.

Price/Earnings Ratio (p. 696)
Ratio of the market price of a share of common stock to the company's earnings per share. Measures the value that the stock market places on $1 of a company's earnings.

Rate of Return on Net Sales (p. 694)
Ratio of net income to net sales. A measure of profitability. Also called **return on sales**.

Return on Sales (p. 694)
Ratio of net income to net sales. A measure of profitability. Also called **rate of return on net sales**.

Times-Interest-Earned Ratio (p. 693)
Ratio of income from operations to interest expense. Measures the number of times that operating income can cover interest expense. Also called the **interest-coverage ratio**.

Trading on the Equity (p. 695)
Earning more income on borrowed money than the related interest expense, thereby increasing the earnings for the owners of the business. Also called **leverage**.

Trend Percentages (p. 682)
A form of horizontal analysis in which percentages are computed by selecting a base year as 100% and expressing amounts for following years as a percentage of the base amount.

Vertical Analysis (p. 683)
Analysis of a financial statement that reveals the relationship of each statement item to a specified base, which is the 100% figure.

Working Capital (p. 689)
Current assets minus current liabilities. Measures a business's ability to meet its short-term obligations with its current assets.

Atlantic Corporation reported the following figures:

Account	2011	2010
Cash and cash equivalents	$ 2,106	$ 1,706
Receivables	1,872	1,708
Inventory	1,299	1,042
Prepaid expenses	1,616	2,300
Total current assets	6,893	6,756
Other assets	17,149	15,246
Total assets	24,042	22,002
Total current liabilities	7,120	8,284
Long–term liabilities	5,360	2,622
Common equity	11,562	11,096
Total liabilities and equity	$ 24,042	$ 22,002

Sales	$ 20,015
Cost of sales	6,875
Operating expenses	7,001
Operating income	6,139
Interest expense	202
Other expenses	2,209
Net income	$ 3,728

1. Horizontal analysis of Atlantic's balance sheet for 2011 would report
   a. Cash as 8.76% of total assets.
   b. 23% increase in Cash.
   c. Current ratio of 0.97.
   d. Inventory turnover of 6 times.

2. Vertical analysis of Atlantic's balance sheet for 2011 would report
   a. Cash as 8.76% of total assets.
   b. Current ratio of 1.04.
   c. Inventory turnover of 6 times.
   d. 22% increase in Cash.

3. A common-size income statement for Atlantic would report (amounts rounded)
   a. Cost of sales at 34%.
   b. Net income of 19%.
   c. Sales of 100%.
   d. All of the above

4. Which statement best describes Atlantic's acid-test ratio?
   a. Greater than 1
   b. Equal to 1
   c. Less than 1
   d. None of the above

5. Atlantic's inventory turnover during 2011 was
   a. 7 times.
   b. 6 times.
   c. 8 times.
   d. Not determinable from the data given

6. During 2011, Atlantic's days' sales in receivables ratio was
   a. 37 days.
   b. 33 days.
   c. 43 days.
   d. 41 days.

7. Which measure expresses Atlantic's times-interest-earned ratio?
   a. 30 times
   b. 16 times
   c. 52.6%
   d. 35 times

8. Atlantic's return on common stockholders' equity can be described as
   a. weak.
   b. strong.
   c. average.
   d. normal.

9. The company has 2,300 shares of common stock outstanding. What is Atlantic's earnings per share?
   a. $4.89
   b. 5.16 times
   c. $1.62
   d. $2.39

10. Atlantic's stock has traded recently around $41 per share. Use your answer to question 9 to measure the company's price/earnings ratio.
    a. 0.94
    b. 25
    c. 41
    d. 86

Answers are given after Apply Your Knowledge (p. 723).

Assess Your Progress

■ Short Exercises

S14-1 *(L. OBJ. 1)* **Horizontal Analysis [5–10 min]**

Hooser, Corp., reported the following on its comparative income statement:

(In millions)	2012	2011	2010
Revenue	$9,610	$9,355	$9,050
Cost of sales	5,800	5,600	5,500

Requirement

1. Perform a horizontal analysis of revenues and gross profit—both in dollar amounts and in percentages—for 2012 and 2011.

S14-2   *(L. OBJ. 1)* **Trend Analysis [5–10 min]**

Muscateer, Corp., reported the following revenues and net income amounts:

(In millions)	2013	2012	2011	2010
Revenue	$9,610	$9,355	$9,050	$8,950
Net Income	7,290	6,790	5,020	4,300

Requirements

1. Show Muscateer's trend percentages for revenues and net income. Use 2010 as the base year, and round to the nearest percent.
2. Which measure increased faster during 2011–2013?

S14-3   *(L. OBJ. 2)* **Vertical Analysis [10–15 min]**

Milatin Optical Company reported the following amounts on its balance sheet at December 31, 2010:

	2010
Cash and receivables	$ 48,285
Inventory	39,220
Property, plant, and equipment, net	97,495
Total assets	$ 185,000

Requirement

1. Perform a vertical analysis of Milatin assets at the end of 2010.

S14-4   *(L. OBJ. 3)* **Common-size income statement [10 min]**

Data for Sanchez, Inc., and Bajo, Corp., follow:

	Sanchez	Bajo
Net sales	$ 10,900	$ 17,650
Cost of goods sold	6,769	12,708
Other expenses	3,466	4,007
Net income	$ 665	$ 935

Requirements

1. Prepare common size income statements.
2. Which company earns a higher percentage net income?
3. Which company's cost of goods sold is a higher percentage of its net sales?

S14-5   *(L. OBJ. 4)* **Evaluating current ratio [5–10 min]**

Low's Companies, a home-improvement-store chain, reported the following summarized figures (in billions):

LOW'S COMPANIES	
Income Statement	
Year Ended January 31, 2011	
Net sales	$ 40.6
Cost of goods sold	22.5
Interest expense	0.4
All other expenses	6.9
Net income	$ 10.8

LOW'S COMPANIES					
Balance Sheet					
January 31, 2011 and 2010					
Assets	2011	2010	Liabilities	2011	2010
Cash	$ 2.2	$ 1.2	Total current liabilities	$ 24.0	$ 13.2
Short term investments	24.0	13.0	Long term liabilities	13.7	11.6
Accounts receivable	7.5	5.4	Total liabilities	37.7	24.8
Inventory	7.3	7.2	Stockholder's Equity		
Other current assets	9.0	1.5	Common stock	10.0	10.0
Total current assets	50.0	28.3	Retained earnings	35.3	21.5
All other assets	33.0	28.0	Total equity	45.3	31.5
Total assets	$ 83.0	$ 56.3	Total liabilities and equity	$ 83.0	$ 56.3

Requirements

1. Compute Low's Companies' current ratio at January 31, 2011 and 2010.
2. Did Low's Companies' current ratio improve, deteriorate, or hold steady during 2011?

S14-6 *(L. OBJ. 4)* **Computing inventory turnover and days sales in receivables [10–15 min]**
Use the Low's Companies data in Short Exercise 14-5 to complete the following requirements (amounts in billions).

Requirements

1. Compute the rate of inventory turnover for 2011.
2. Compute days' sales in average receivables during 2011. Round dollar amounts to three decimal places.

S14-7 *(L. OBJ. 4)* **Measuring ability to pay liabilities [5 min]**
Use the financial statements of Low's Companies in Short Exercise 14-5.

Requirements

1. Compute the debt ratio at December 31, 2011.
2. Is Low's ability to pay its liabilities strong or weak? Explain your reasoning.

S14-8 *(L. OBJ. 4)* **Measuring profitability [10 min]**
Use the financial statements of Low's Companies in Short Exercise 14-5 to complete the following profitability measures for 2011.

Requirements

1. Compute the rate of return on net sales.
2. Compute the rate of return on total assets. Interest expense for 2011 was $0.4 billion.
3. Compute the rate of return on common stockholders' equity.
4. Are these rates of return strong or weak? Explain your reasoning.

S14-9 *(L. OBJ. 4)* **Computing EPS and P/E ratio [5–10 min]**
Use the financial statements of Low's Companies in Short Exercise 14-5. Additionally, Low's has issued 0.8 billion common shares.

Requirements

1. Compute earnings per share (EPS) for Low's. Round to the nearest cent.
2. Compute Low's Companies' price/earnings ratio. The price of a share of Low's stock is $67.50.

S14-10 *(L. OBJ. 4)* **Using ratios to reconstruct an income statement [10 min]**

A skeleton of Heirloom Mills' income statement appears as follows (amounts in thousands):

Income Statement	
Net sales	$ 7,000
Cost of goods sold	(a)
Selling and admin expenses	1,700
Interest expense	(b)
Other expenses	135
Income before taxes	1,200
Income tax expense	(c)
Net income	(d)

Requirement

1. Use the following ratio data to complete Heirloom Mills' income statement:
   a. Inventory turnover was 4.50 (beginning inventory was $790; ending inventory was $750).
   b. Rate of return on sales is 0.09.

S14-11 *(L. OBJ. 4)* **Using ratios to reconstruct a balance sheet [15–20 min]**

A skeleton of Heirloom Mills' balance sheet appears as follows (amounts in thousands):

Balance Sheet			
Cash	$ 100	Total current liabilities	$ 2,250
Receivables	(a)	Long–term note payable	(e)
Inventories	600	Other long term	
Prepaid expenses	(b)	liabilities	920
Total current assets . .	(c)	Stockholder's equity	2,700
Plant assets, net	(d)		
Other assets	2,100	Total liabilities and	
Total assets	$ 7,300	equity	$ (f)

Requirement

1. Use the following ratio data to complete Heirloom Mills' balance sheet:
   a. Current ratio is 0.70
   b. Acid-test ratio is 0.20

■ Exercises

E14-12 *(L. OBJ. 1)* **Computing working capital changes [5–15 min]**

Data for Media Enterprises follows:

	2009	2008	2007
Total current assets	$370,000	$310,000	$280,000
Total current liabilities	175,000	155,000	140,000

Requirement

1. Compute the dollar amount of change and the percentage of change in Media Enterprises' working capital each year during 2008 and 2009. Is this trend favorable or unfavorable?

E14-13 *(L. OBJ. 1)* **Horizontal analysis-income statement [10–15 min]**

Data for Verifine Designs, Inc., follow:

VERIFINE DESIGNS, INC. Comparative Income Statement Years Ended December 31, 2011 and 2010		
	2011	2010
Net sales revenue	$ 428,950	$ 371,000
Expenses:		
Cost of goods sold	$ 203,850	$ 189,350
Selling and general expenses	99,350	93,000
Other expense	6,750	5,000
Total expenses	309,950	287,350
Cash and cash equivalents	$ 119,000	$ 83,650

Requirements

1. Prepare a horizontal analysis of the comparative income statement of Verifine Designs, Inc. Round percentage changes to the nearest one-tenth percent (three decimal places).
2. Why did 2011 net income increase by a higher percentage than net sales revenue?

E14-14 *(L. OBJ. 1)* **Computing trend percentages [5–10 min]**

Thousand Oaks Realty's net revenue and net income for the following five-year period, using 2010 as the base year, follow:

(In thousands)	2014	2013	2012	2011	2010
Net revenue	$1,314	$1,183	$1,006	$1,007	$1,043
Net income	120	115	81	71	85

Requirements

1. Compute trend percentages for net revenue and net income. Round to the nearest full percent.
2. Which grew faster during the period, net revenue or net income?

E14-15 *(L. OBJ. 2)* **Vertical analysis of a balance sheet [10–15 min]**
Eta Graphics, Inc., has the following data:

ETA GRAPHICS, INC. Balance Sheet December 31, 2010	
Assets	
Total current assets	$ 41,870
Property, plant, and equipment, net	206,870
Other assets	34,870
Total assets	$ 283,610
Liabilities	
Total current liabilities	$ 47,870
Long–term debt	107,870
Total liabilities	155,740
Stockholders' Equity	
Total stockholders' equity	127,870
Total liabilities and stockholders' equity	$ 283,610

Requirement

1. Perform a vertical analysis of Eta's balance sheet.

E14-16 *(L. OBJ. 3)* **Preparing common-size income statements [10–15 min]**
Consider the data presented in Exercise 14-13.

Requirements

1. Prepare a comparative common-size income statement for Verifine Designs, Inc., using the 2011 and 2010 data. Round percentages to one-tenth percent (three decimal places).

2. To an investor, how does 2011 compare with 2010? Explain your reasoning.

E14-17 *(L. OBJ. 4)* **Computing 4 key ratios [10–15 min]**
The financial statements of Jim's Health Foods include the following items:

	Current Year	Preceding Year
Balance sheet:		
Cash . . . . $	18,000 $	22,000
Short–term investments	10,000	24,000
Net receivables	53,000	75,000
Inventory	75,000	73,000
Prepaid expenses	17,000	10,000
Total current assets . . . . $	173,000 $	204,000
Total current liabilities . . . . $	129,000 $	91,000
Income statement:		
Net credit sales . . . . $	463,000	
Cost of goods sold	319,000	

Requirement

1. Compute the following ratios for the current year:

   a. Current ratio

   b. Acid-test ratio

   c. Inventory turnover

   d. Days' sales in average receivables

E14-18 *(L. OBJ. 4)* **Analyzing the ability to pay liabilities [15–20 min]**

Big Bend Picture Frames has asked you to determine whether the company's ability to pay current liabilities and total liabilities improved or deteriorated during 2009. To answer this question, you gather the following data:

	2009	2008
Cash	$ 50,000	$ 47,000
Short–term investments	27,000	—
Net receivables	128,000	124,000
Inventory	237,000	272,000
Total assets	480,000	490,000
Total current liabilities	295,000	202,000
Long–term note payable	44,000	56,000
Income from operations	170,000	168,000
Interest expense	46,000	33,000

Requirement

1. Compute the following ratios for 2009 and 2008:

   a. Current ratio
   b. Acid-test ratio
   c. Debt ratio
   d. Times-interest-earned ratio

E14-19 *(L. OBJ. 4)* **Analyzing profitability [10–15 min]**

The Micatin, Inc., comparative income statement follows. The 2010 data are given as needed.

MICATIN, INC. Comparative Income Statement Years Ended December 31, 2012 and 2011			
(Dollars in thousands)	2012	2011	2010
Net sales	$177,000	$159,000	
Cost of goods sold	93,200	86,100	
Selling and general expenses	46,500	41,600	
Interest expense	9,700	10,400	
Income tax expense	10,800	9,300	
Net income	$ 16,800	$ 11,600	
Additional data:			
Total assets	$202,000	$192,000	$174,000
Common stockholders' equity	$ 96,700	$ 89,600	$ 79,700
Preferred dividends	$ 3,900	$ 3,900	$ 0
Common shares outstanding during the year	19,000	19,000	17,500

Requirements

1. Calculate the rate of return on net sales.
2. Calculate the rate of return on total assets.
3. Calculate the rate of return on common stockholders' equity.
4. Calculate the EPS.
5. Did the company's operating performance improve or deteriorate during 2012?

E14-20 *(L. OBJ. 4)* **Evaluating a stock as an investment [10–15 min]**

Data for McNight State Bank follows:

	2011	2010
Net income	$ 62,000	$ 54,000
Dividends–common	22,000	22,000
Dividends–preferred	11,400	11,400
Total stockholders' equity at year–end		
(includes 80,000 shares of common stock)	780,000	620,000
Preferred stock, 6%	190,000	190,000
Market price per share of common stock	$ 17.50	$ 12

Requirement

1. Evaluate the common stock of McNight State Bank as an investment. Specifically, use the three stock ratios to determine whether the common stock has increased or decreased in attractiveness during the past year.

E14-21 *(L. OBJ. 4)* **Using ratios to reconstruct a balance sheet [20–30 min]**

The following data (dollar amounts in millions) are adapted from the financial statements of Virginia's Stores, Inc.:

Total current assets	$ 10,800
Accumulated depreciation	$ 1,700
Total liabilities	$ 15,200
Preferred stock	$ 0
Debt ratio	65%
Current ratio	1.60

Requirement

1. Complete Virginia's condensed balance sheet.

Current assets		
Property, plant, and equipment		
Less Accumulated depreciation		
Total assets		
Current liabilities		
Long–term liabilities		
Stockholders' equity		
Total liabilities and stockholders' equity		

Problems (Group A)

P14-22A *(L. OBJ. 1, 4)* **Trend percentages, return on common equity, and comparison with the industry [20–30 min]**

Net sales revenue, net income, and common stockholders' equity for Accurate Mission Corporation, a manufacturer of contact lenses, follow for a four-year period.

(In thousands)	2013	2012	2011	2010
Net sales revenue	$ 766	$ 700	$ 639	$ 661
Net income	63	39	33	47
Ending common				
stockholders' equity . .	360	348	328	302

Requirements

1. Compute trend percentages for each item for 2011–2013. Use 2010 as the base year, and round to the nearest whole percent.

2. Compute the rate of return on common stockholders' equity for 2011–2013, rounding to three decimal places.

P14-23A *(L. OBJ. 2, 3)* **Common-size statements, analysis of profitability and financial position, and comparison with the industry [20–30 min]**

The Russell Department Stores, Inc., chief executive officer (CEO) has asked you to compare the company's profit performance and financial position with the average for the industry. The CEO has given you the company's income statement and balance sheet, as well as the industry average data for retailers.

RUSSELL DEPARTMENT STORES, INC.		
Income Statement Compared with Industry Average		
Year Ended December 31, 2010		
	Russell	Industry Average
Net sales	$ 777,000	100.0%
Cost of goods sold	523,698	65.8
Gross profit	253,302	34.2
Operating expenses	162,393	19.7
Operating income	90,909	14.5
Other expenses	7,770	0.4
Net income	$ 83,139	14.1%

RUSSELL DEPARTMENT STORES, INC.		
Balance Sheet Compared with Industry Average		
December 31, 2010		
	Russell	Industry Average
Current assets	$ 330,750	70.9%
Fixed assets, net	123,480	23.6
Intangible assets, net	9,800	0.8
Other assets	25,970	4.7
Total assets	$ 490,000	100.0%
Current liabilities	$ 227,360	48.1%
Long–term liabilities	111,720	16.6
Stockholders' equity	150,920	35.3
Total liabilities and stockholders' equity	$ 490,000	100.0%

Requirements

1. Prepare a common-size income statement and balance sheet for Russell. The first column of each statement should present Russell's common-size statement, and the second column, the industry averages.
2. For the profitability analysis, compute Russell's (a) ratio of gross profit to net sales, (b) ratio of operating income to net sales, and (c) ratio of net income to net sales. Compare these figures with the industry averages. Is Russell's profit performance better or worse than the industry average?
3. For the analysis of financial position, compute Russell's (a) ratio of current assets to total assets and (b) ratio of stockholders' equity to total assets. Compare these ratios with the industry averages. Is Russell's financial position better or worse than the industry averages?

P14-24A *(L. OBJ. 4)* **Effects of business transactions on selected ratios [30–40 min]**

Financial statement data of Off Road Traveler Magazine include the following items (dollars in thousands):

Cash	$ 18,000
Accounts receivable, net	82,000
Inventories	183,000
Total assets	635,000
Short–term notes payable	48,000
Accounts payable	100,000
Accrued liabilities	41,000
Long–term liabilities	227,000
Net income	71,000
Common shares outstanding ...	40,000

Requirements

1. Compute Off Road Traveler's current ratio, debt ratio, and earnings per share. Round all ratios to two decimal places, and use the following format for your answer:

Current Ratio	Debt Ratio	Earnings Per Share

2. Compute the three ratios after evaluating the effect of each transaction that follows. Consider each transaction *separately*.

   a. Purchased inventory of $43,000 on account
   b. Borrowed $123,000 on a long-term note payable
   c. Issued 4,000 shares of common stock, receiving cash of $106,000
   d. Received cash on account, $6,000

P14-25A *(L. OBJ. 4)* **Using ratios to evaluate a stock investment [40–50 min]**

Comparative financial statement data of Sanfield, Inc., follow:

SANFIELD, INC. Comparative Income Statement Years Ended December 31, 2011 and 2010		
	2011	**2010**
Net sales	$ 458,000	$ 427,000
Cost of goods sold	240,000	216,000
Gross profit	218,000	211,000
Operating expenses	134,000	132,000
Income from operations	84,000	79,000
Interest expense	13,000	14,000
Income before income tax	71,000	65,000
Income tax expense	19,000	23,000
Net income	$ 52,000	$ 42,000

SANFIELD, INC. Comparative Balance Sheet December 31, 2011 and 2010			
	2011	**2010**	**2009***
Current assets:			
Cash	$ 98,000	$ 95,000	
Current receivables, net	107,000	118,000	$ 100,000
Inventories	149,000	165,000	207,000
Prepaid expenses	15,000	8,000	
Total current assets	369,000	386,000	
Property, plant, and equipment, net	213,000	180,000	
Total assets	$ 582,000	$ 566,000	602,000
Total current liabilities	$ 229,000	$ 243,000	
Long–term liabilities	117,000	98,000	
Total liabilities	346,000	341,000	
Preferred stock, 4%	106,000	106,000	
Common stockholders' equity, no par	130,000	119,000	93,000
Total liabilities and stockholders' equity	$ 582,000	$ 566,000	

* Selected 2009 amounts

1. Market price of Sanfield's common stock: $81.26 at December 31, 2011, and $67.20 at December 31, 2010.

2. Common shares outstanding: 10,000 during 2011 and 9,000 during 2010.

3. All sales on credit.

Requirements

1. Compute the following ratios for 2011 and 2010:

   a. Current ratio
   b. Times-interest-earned ratio
   c. Inventory turnover
   d. Return on common stockholders' equity
   e. Earnings per share of common stock
   f. Price/earnings ratio

2. Decide (a) whether Sanfield's ability to pay debts and to sell inventory improved or deteriorated during 2011 and (b) whether the investment attractiveness of its common stock appears to have increased or decreased.

P14-26A *(L. OBJ. 4)* **Using ratios to decide between two stock investments [45–60 min]**
Assume that you are purchasing an investment and have decided to invest in a company in the digital phone business. You have narrowed the choice to Best Digital, Corp., and Every Zone, Inc., and have assembled the following data:

Selected income-statement data for the current year

	Best Digital	Every Zone
Net sales (all on credit) . . . . $	419,000 $	494,000
Cost of goods sold	210,000	256,000
Interest expense	——	14,000
Net income	46,000	74,000

Selected balance-sheet and market-price data at the *end* of the current year

	Best Digital	Every Zone
Current assets:		
Cash .... $	26,000 $	16,000
Short–term investments	41,000	17,000
Current receivables, net	35,000	47,000
Inventories	66,000	100,000
Prepaid expenses	18,000	17,000
Total current assets .... $	186,000 $	197,000
Total assets .... $	263,000 $	328,000
Total current liabilities	101,000	97,000
Total liabilities	101,000	134,000
Common stock, $1 par (10,000 shares)	10,000	
$2 par (15,000 shares)		30,000
Total stockholders' equity	162,000	194,000
Market price per share of common stock .. $	69.00 $	118.32

Selected balance-sheet data at the *beginning* of the current year

	Best Digital	Every Zone
Balance sheet:		
Current receivables, net .... $	40,000 $	52,000
Inventories	82,000	89,000
Total assets	257,000	270,000
Common stock, $1 par (10,000 shares)	10,000	
$2 par (15,000 shares)		30,000

Your strategy is to invest in companies that have low price/earnings ratios but appear to be in good shape financially. Assume that you have analyzed all other factors and that your decision depends on the results of ratio analysis.

Requirement

1. Compute the following ratios for both companies for the current year, and decide which company's stock better fits your investment strategy.

    a. Acid-test ratio
    b. Inventory turnover
    c. Days' sales in average receivables
    d. Debt ratio
    e. Earnings per share of common stock
    f. Price/earnings ratio

■ Problems (Group B)

P14-27B *(L. OBJ. 1, 4)* **Trend percentages, return on common equity, and comparison with the industry [20–30 min]**

Net sales revenue, net income, and common stockholders' equity for Azbel Mission Corporation, a manufacturer of contact lenses, follow for a four-year period.

(In thousands)	2013	2012	2011	2010
Net sales revenue	$ 766	$ 706	$ 640	$ 663
Net income	58	42	33	46
Ending common stockholders' equity ..	368	350	338	298

Requirements

1. Compute trend percentages for each item for 2011–2013. Use 2010 as the base year, and round to the nearest whole percent.

2. Compute the rate of return on common stockholders' equity for 2011–2013, rounding to three decimal places.

P14-28B *(L. OBJ. 2, 3)* **Common-size statements, analysis of profitability and financial position, and comparison with the industry [20–30 min]**

The Klein Department Stores, Inc., chief executive officer (CEO) has asked you to compare the company's profit performance and financial position with the average for the industry. The CEO has given you the company's income statement and balance sheet, as well as the industry average data for retailers.

KLEIN DEPARTMENT STORES, INC. Income Statement Compared with Industry Average Year Ended December 31, 2010		
	Klein	Industry Average
Net sales	$ 780,000	100.0%
Cost of goods sold	525,720	65.8
Gross profit	254,280	34.2
Operating expenses	161,460	19.7
Operating income	92,820	14.5
Other expenses	6,240	0.4
Net income	$ 86,580	14.1%

KLEIN DEPARTMENT STORES, INC. Balance Sheet Compared with Industry Average December 31, 2010		
	Klein	Industry Average
Current assets	$ 291,540	70.9%
Fixed assets, net	110,940	23.6
Intangible assets, net	6,880	0.8
Other assets	20,640	4.7
Total assets	$ 430,000	100.0%
Current liabilities	$ 200,380	48.1%
Long–term liabilities	96,320	16.6
Stockholders' equity	133,300	35.3
Total liabilities and stockholders' equity	$ 430,000	100.0%

1. Prepare a common-size income statement and balance sheet for Klein. The first column of each statement should present Klein's common-size statement, and the second column, the industry averages.

2. For the profitability analysis, compute Klein's (a) ratio of gross profit to net sales, (b) ratio of operating income to net sales, and (c) ratio of net income to net sales. Compare these figures with the industry averages. Is Klein Department Stores' profit performance better or worse than the industry average?

3. For the analysis of financial position, compute Klein's (a) ratio of current assets to total assets and (b) ratio of stockholders' equity to total assets. Compare these ratios with the industry averages. Is Klein Department Stores' financial position better or worse than the industry averages?

P14-29B *(L.OBJ. 4)* **Effects of business transactions on selected ratios [30–40 min]**
Financial statement data of Yankee Traveler Magazine include the following items (dollars in thousands):

Cash	$ 25,000
Accounts receivable, net	81,000
Inventories	183,000
Total assets	636,000
Short–term notes payable	46,000
Accounts payable	98,000
Accrued liabilities	40,000
Long–term liabilities	227,000
Net income	74,000
Common shares outstanding . . .	70,000

Requirements

1. Compute Yankee Traveler's current ratio, debt ratio, and earnings per share. Round all ratios to two decimal places, and use the following format for your answer:

Current Ratio	Debt Ratio	Earnings Per Share

2. Compute the three ratios after evaluating the effect of each transaction that follows. Consider each transaction, a–d, *separately*.

    a. Purchased inventory of $48,000 on account

    b. Borrowed $121,000 on a long-term note payable

    c. Issued 7,000 shares of common stock, receiving cash of $107,000

    d. Received cash on account, $2,000

P14-30B (L. OBJ. 4) Using ratios to evaluate a stock investment [40–50 min]

Comparative financial statement data of Canfield, Inc., follow:

CANFIELD, INC. Comparative Income Statement Years Ended December 31, 2011 and 2010		
	2011	**2010**
Net sales	$ 459,000	$ 427,000
Cost of goods sold	240,000	215,000
Gross profit	219,000	212,000
Operating expenses	132,000	130,000
Income from operations	87,000	82,000
Interest expense	10,000	11,000
Income before income tax	77,000	71,000
Income tax expense	22,000	25,000
Net income	$ 55,000	$ 46,000

CANFIELD, INC. Comparative Balance Sheet December 31, 2011 and 2010			
	2011	**2010**	**2009***
Current assets:			
Cash	$ 93,000	$ 92,000	
Current receivables, net	108,000	117,000	$ 101,000
Inventories	144,000	162,000	205,000
Prepaid expenses	14,000	9,000	
Total current assets	359,000	380,000	
Property, plant, and equipment, net	211,000	173,000	
Total assets	$ 570,000	$ 553,000	595,000
Total current liabilities	$ 229,000	$ 246,000	
Long–term liabilities	119,000	95,000	
Total liabilities	348,000	341,000	
Preferred stock, 4%	106,000	106,000	
Common stockholders' equity, no par	116,000	106,000	86,000
Total liabilities and stockholders' equity	$ 570,000	$ 553,000	

* Selected 2009 amounts

1. Market price of Canfield's common stock: $54.99 at December 31, 2011, and $50.16 at December 31, 2010.

2. Common shares outstanding: 12,000 during 2011 and 10,000 during 2010.

3. All sales on credit.

Requirements

1. Compute the following ratios for 2011 and 2010:

   a. Current ratio
   b. Times-interest-earned ratio
   c. Inventory turnover
   d. Return on common stockholders' equity
   e. Earnings per share of common stock
   f. Price/earnings ratio

2. Decide (a) whether Canfield's ability to pay debts and to sell inventory improved or deteriorated during 2011 and (b) whether the investment attractiveness of its common stock appears to have increased or decreased.

P14-31B *(L. OBJ. 4)* **Using ratios to decide between two stock investments [45–60 min]**
Assume that you are purchasing an investment and have decided to invest in a company in the digital phone business. You have narrowed the choice to Digital Plus, Corp., and Very Network, Inc., and have assembled the following data:

Selected income-statement data for the current year

	Digital Plus	Very Network
Net sales (all on credit) . . . . $	422,000 $	495,000
Cost of goods sold	209,000	255,000
Interest expense	—	15,000
Net income	52,000	74,000

Selected balance-sheet and market-price data at the *end* of the current year

	Digital Plus	Very Network
Current assets:		
Cash . . . . $	28,000 $	22,000
Short–term investments	41,000	19,000
Current receivables, net	40,000	49,000
Inventories	67,000	102,000
Prepaid expenses	20,000	15,000
Total current assets . . . . $	196,000 $	207,000
Total assets . . . . $	262,000 $	324,000
Total current liabilities	100,000	95,000
Total liabilities	100,000	134,000
Common stock, $1 par (10,000 shares)	10,000	
$1 par (15,000 shares)		15,000
Total stockholders' equity	162,000	190,000
Market price per share of common stock . . $	83.20 $	108.46

Selected balance-sheet data at the *beginning* of the current year

	Digital Plus	Very Network
Balance sheet:		
Current receivables, net . . . . $	43,000 $	51,000
Inventories	84,000	85,000
Total assets	257,000	279,000
Common stock, $1 par (10,000 shares)	10,000	
$1 par (15,000 shares)		15,000

Your strategy is to invest in companies that have low price/earnings ratios but appear to be in good shape financially. Assume that you have analyzed all other factors and that your decision depends on the results of ratio analysis.

Requirement

1. Compute the following ratios for both companies for the current year, and decide which company's stock better fits your investment strategy.

   a. Acid-test ratio
   b. Inventory turnover
   c. Days' sales in average receivables
   d. Debt ratio
   e. Earnings per share of common stock
   f. Price/earnings ratio

■ Continuing Exercise

E14-32 This exercise continues the Sherman Lawn Service, Inc., situation from Exercise 13-30 of Chapter 13.

Requirement

1. Prepare a vertical analysis from the comparative balance sheet presented in Exercise 13-30.

■ Continuing Problem

P14-33 This problem continues the Haupt Consulting, Inc., situation from Problem 13-31 of Chapter 13.

Requirement

1. Using the income statement and comparative balance sheet presented in Problem 13-31 and knowing that the current market price of Haupt's stock is $50 per share, calculate the following ratios for the company:

   a. Current ratio
   b. Debt ratio
   c. Earnings per share
   d. P/E ratio
   e. Return on assets
   f. Return on common stockholders' equity

Apply Your Knowledge

■ Decision Cases

Case 1. General Motors, Inc., and Ford Motor Company both had a bad year in 2007; the companies' auto units suffered net losses. The loss pushed some return measures into the negative column, and the companies' ratios deteriorated. Assume top management of GM and Ford are pondering ways to improve their ratios. In particular, management is considering the following transactions:

1. Borrow $100 million on long-term debt.
2. Purchase treasury stock for $500 million cash.
3. Expense one-fourth of the goodwill carried on the books.
4. Create a new auto-design division at a cash cost of $300 million.
5. Purchase patents from Daimler Chrysler, paying $20 million cash.

Requirement

1. Top management wants to know the effects of these transactions (increase, decrease, or no effect) on the following ratios:
   a. Current ratio
   b. Debt ratio
   c. Return on equity

Case 2. Lance Berkman is the controller of Saturn, a dance club whose year-end is December 31. Berkman prepares checks for suppliers in December and posts them to the appropriate accounts in that month. However, he holds on to the checks and mails them to the suppliers in January.

Requirements

1. What financial ratio(s) is(are) most affected by the action?
2. What is Berkman's purpose in undertaking this activity? (Challenge)

■ Ethical Issue

Betsy Ross Flag Company's long-term debt agreements make certain demands on the business. For example, Ross may not purchase treasury stock in excess of the balance of retained earnings. Also, long-term debt may not exceed stockholders' equity, and the current ratio may not fall below 1.50. If Ross fails to meet any of these requirements, the company's lenders have the authority to take over management of the company.

Changes in consumer demand have made it hard for Ross to attract customers. Current liabilities have mounted faster than current assets, causing the current ratio to fall to 1.47. Before releasing financial statements, Ross management is scrambling to improve the current ratio. The controller points out that an investment can be classified as either long-term or short-term, depending on management's intention. By deciding to convert an investment to cash within one year, Ross can classify the investment as short-term—a current asset. On the controller's recommendation, Ross's board of directors votes to reclassify long-term investments as short-term.

Requirements

1. What effect will reclassifying the investments have on the current ratio? Is Ross's true financial position stronger as a result of reclassifying the investments?
2. Shortly after the financial statements are released, sales improve; so, too, does the current ratio. As a result, Ross management decides not to sell the investments it had reclassified as short-term. Accordingly, the company reclassifies the investments as long-term. Has management behaved unethically? Give the reasoning underlying your answer.

■ Financial Statement Case—Amazon

Amazon.com's financial statements in Appendix A at the end of this book reveal some interesting relationships. Answer these questions about **Amazon.com**:

Requirements

1. What is most unusual about the balance sheet?

2. Compute trend percentages for net sales and net income. Use 2006 as the base year. Which trend percentage looks strange? Explain your answer.

3. Compute inventory turnover for 2008 and 2007. The inventory balance at December 31, 2006, was $877 million. Do the trend of net income from 2007 to 2008 and the change in the rate of inventory turnover tell the same story or a different story? Explain your answer.

■ Team Projects

Project 1. Select an industry you are interested in, and use the leading company in that industry as the benchmark. Then select two other companies in the same industry. For each category of ratios in the Decision Guidelines in the chapter, compute all the ratios for the three companies. Write a two-page report that compares the two companies with the benchmark company.

Project 2. Select a company and obtain its financial statements. Convert the income statement and the balance sheet to common size, and compare the company you selected to the industry average. The Risk Management Association's *Annual Statement Studies*, Dun & Bradstreet's *Industry Norms & Key Business Ratios*, and Prentice Hall's *Almanac of Business and Industrial Financial Ratios*, by Leo Troy, publish common-size statements for most industries.

Quick Check Answers

1. *b* 2. *a* 3. *d* 4. *c* 5. *b* 6. *b* 7. *a* 8. *b* 9. *c* 10. *b*

For online homework, exercises, and problems that provide you immediate feedback, please visit www.myaccountinglab.com.

Big Picture

Ch 1   Introduction to Management Accounting

- Distinguish management accounting from financial accounting
- The role and responsibilities of management accountants
- Classify costs and prepare income statements for merchandising companies
- Classify costs and prepare income statements and statements of cost of goods manufactured for manufacturing companies

Ch 2   Job Order Costing

- Distinguish between job order and process costing
- Record materials, labor, and overhead in a job order costing system
- Record completion and sales of finished goods and adjust for under-/overallocated overhead
- Calculate unit costs for service companies

Ch 3 Activity-Based Costing and Other Cost Management Tools

- ⚷ Develop activity-based costs and used activity-based management to determine target product costs
- ⚷ Record transactions in JIT systems
- ⚷ Use the four types of quality costs to make management decisions

Ch 4 Process Costing

- ⚷ Calculate equivalent units and conversion costs
- ⚷ Prepare cost of production reports and the related journal entries using the weighted-average costing method
- ⚷ Prepare cost of production reports and the related journal entries using the FIFO costing method

Ch 5 Cost Behavior and Cost-Volume-Profit Analysis

- ⚷ Identify how changes in volume affect cost
- ⚷ Distinguish among variable, mixed, and fixed cost
- ⚷ Split mixed cost into fixed and variable components by using the high-low method and by using regression analysis
- ⚷ Use CVP to compute breakeven points, to plan profits, to graph relationships, and to perform sensitivity analysis

Ch 6 Absorption and Variable Costing

- ⚷ Distinguish between absorption costing and variable costing
- ⚷ Prepare absorption costing and variable costing income statements and explained the differences between the two costing techniques
- ⚷ Illustrate the pros and cons of absorption and variable costing

Ch 7 The Master Budget: Profit Planning

- ⚷ Understand and prepare all components of the master budget for manufacturers
- ⚷ Use sensitivity analysis to adjust budget preparations

Ch 8 Flexible Budgets and Standard Costs

- ⚷ Prepare flexible income statement budgets and income statement performance reports
- ⚷ Compute standard cost variances for direct materials, direct labor, and overhead
- ⚷ Record transactions using standard costs and prepare standard cost income statements

Ch 9 Decentralization: Allocating Service Department Costs and Responsibility Accounting

- ⚷ Identify a shared resource or service department
- ⚷ Allocate service department costs to the departments that use its services utilizing various allocation methods
- ⚷ Learn the four types of responsibility centers and prepared responsibility reports they utilize

Ch 10 Short-Term Business Decisions

- ⚷ Distinguish between relevant, irrelevant, and sunk costs
- ⚷ Evaluate special order, pricing, product profitability, and product-mix decisions
- ⚷ Make outsourcing and sell as is or process further decisions

Ch 11 Capital Investment Decisions and the Time Value of Money

- ⚷ Evaluate capital investments using payback, accounting rate of return, net present value, and internal rate of return as measures of investment performance
- ⚷ Apply time value of money analysis to single lump sums and annuities

Ch 12 Performance Evaluation and the Balanced Scorecard

- ⚷ Apply the balanced scorecard as performance indicators for reporting centers
- ⚷ Evaluate investments using ROI, RI, and EVA

Ch 13 The Statement of Cash Flows

- ⚷ Identify the purposes of the Statement of Cash Flows and distinguished among operating, investing, and financing cash flows
- ⚷ Prepare the Statement of Cash Flows using the indirect and direct methods

Ch 14 Financial Statement Analysis

- ⚷ Prepare horizontal and vertical analysis of financial statements
- ⚷ Prepare common-size financial statements to evaluate performance in comparable companies
- ⚷ Compute standard financial ratios and analyzed results

Comprehensive Problem
for Chapters 13 and 14

Analyzing a Company for Its Investment Potential

In its annual report, WRS Athletic Supply, Inc., includes the following five-year financial summary.

WRS ATHLETIC SUPPLY, INC.
5-Year Financial Summary (Partial; adapted)

(Dollar amounts in thousands except per share data)	2015	2014	2013	2012	2011	2010
Net sales	$244,524	$217,799	$191,329	$165,013	$137,634	
Net sales increase	12%	14%	16%	20%	17%	
Domestic comparative store sales increase	5%	6%	5%	8%	9%	
Other income—net	2,001	1,873	1,787	1,615	1,391	
Cost of sales	191,838	171,562	150,255	129,664	108,725	
Operating, selling, and general and administrative expenses	41,043	36,173	31,550	27,040	22,363	
Interest costs:						
Debt	1,063	1,357	1,383	1,045	803	
Interest income	(138)	(171)	(188)	(204)	(189)	
Income tax expense	4,487	3,897	3,692	3,338	2,740	
Net income	8,039	6,671	6,295	5,377	4,430	
Per share of common stock:						
Net income	1.81	1.49	1.41	1.21	0.99	
Dividends	0.30	0.28	0.24	0.20	0.16	
Financial Position						
Current assets	$ 30,483	$ 27,878	$ 26,555	$ 24,356	$ 21,132	
Inventories at LIFO cost	24,891	22,614	21,442	19,793	17,076	$16,497
Net property, plant, and equipment	51,904	45,750	40,934	35,969	25,973	
Total assets	94,685	83,527	78,130	70,349	49,996	
Current liabilities	32,617	27,282	28,949	25,803	16,762	
Long-term debt	19,608	18,732	15,655	16,674	9,607	
Shareholders' equity	39,337	35,102	31,343	25,834	21,112	
Financial Ratios						
Current ratio	0.9	1.0	0.9	0.9	1.3	
Return on assets	9.2%	8.5%	8.7%	9.5%	9.6%	
Return on shareholders' equity	21.6%	20.1%	22.0%	22.9%	22.4%	

Requirements

Analyze the company's financial summary for the fiscal years 2011–2015 to decide whether to invest in the common stock of WRS. Include the following sections in your analysis, and fully explain your final decision.

1. Trend analysis for net sales and net income (use 2011 as the base year)
2. Profitability analysis
3. Measuring ability to sell inventory (WRS uses the LIFO method)
4. Measuring ability to pay debts
5. Measuring dividends

Chapter 14: Demo Doc

■ Financial Statement Analysis

Learning Objectives 1–4

MeMe Co. had the following information at December 31, 2011:

MEME CO.
Balance Sheet
December 31, 2011 and 2010

	2011	2010
Assets		
Cash	$150	$130
Accounts receivable	80	145
Inventory	130	190
Total assets	$360	$465
Liabilities		
Accounts payable	90	140
Loans payable	140	220
Total liabilities	$230	$360
Stockholders' Equity		
Common stock	20	10
Retained earnings	110	95
Total stockholders' equity	$130	$105
Total liabilities and equity	$360	$465

MEME CO.
Income Statement
Years Ended December 31, 2011 and 2010

	2011	2010
Sales revenue	$650	$580
Less cost of goods sold	430	350
Gross profit	$220	$230
Salary expense	120	140
Rent expense	70	80
Net income	$ 30	$ 10

At December 31, 2009, MeMe's inventory was $160 and total equity was $95.

Requirements

1. Prepare horizontal and vertical analyses for MeMe's financial statements.
2. Calculate MeMe's inventory turnover and rate of return on stockholders' equity ratios for both years.

Demo Doc Solution

Requirement 1

1 Perform a horizontal analysis of financial statements

Prepare horizontal and vertical analyses for MeMe's financial statements.

Part 1	Part 2	Part 3	Demo Doc Complete

Horizontal Analysis

As its name implies, horizontal analysis goes *across* the rows of the financial statements, looking at *one* account and how it has changed.

For *each* number on the balance sheet and income statement, we calculate the *dollar change* and the *percent change*.

Dollar change = This year's balance – Last year's balance

So in the dollar change of Accounts receivable and Sales revenue:

Accounts receivable = $80 – $145
= $(65) change

Sales revenue = $650 – $580
= $70 change

Notice that the negative value on the change in Accounts receivable indicates that this account has decreased, whereas the positive value on the change in Sales revenue indicates that this account has increased.

Extra care must be taken when using this calculation on expenses (because they are presented as subtracted/negative numbers on the income statement). The *absolute value* of the expense (that is, ignoring the fact that it is already a negative number) must be used to calculate dollar change. In the dollar change of COGS and Rent expense:

COGS = $430 – $350
= $80 change

Rent expense = $70 – $80
= $(70) change

Again, the positive value indicates that COGS increased and the negative value indicates that Rent expense decreased.

$$\text{Percent change} = \frac{\text{Dollar change}}{\text{Last year's balance}}$$

So in the percent change of Accounts receivable and Sales revenue:

$$\text{Accounts receivable} = \frac{\$(65)}{\$145} \text{ change}$$

$$= (44.8)\% \text{ change}$$

$$\text{Sales revenue} = \frac{\$70}{\$580}$$

$$= 12.1\% \text{ change}$$

Again, the percent change numbers are negative for Accounts receivable (which decreased in 2011) and positive for Sales Revenue (which increased in 2011).

The percent change is calculated the same way for expenses, again using the *absolute value* of the expenses. In the percent change of COGS and Rent Expense:

$$\text{COGS} = \frac{\$80}{\$350}$$

$$= 22.9\% \text{ change}$$

$$\text{Rent expense} = \frac{-\$10}{\$80}$$

$$= (12.5)\% \text{ change}$$

MEME CO.
Horizontal Analysis of Balance Sheet
Years Ended December 31, 2011 and 2010

	2011	2010	Increase (Decrease) Amount	Percent
Assets				
Cash	$150	$130	$ 20	15.4%
Accounts receivable	80	145	(65)	(44.8)
Inventory	130	190	(60)	(31.6)
Total assets	$360	$465	$(105)	(22.6)
Liabilities				
Accounts payable	90	140	(50)	(35.7)%
Loans payable	140	220	(80)	(36.4)
Total liabilities	$230	$360	$(130)	(36.1)
Stockholders' Equity				
Common stock	20	10	10	100.0%
Retained earnings	110	95	15	15.8
Total stockholders' equity	$130	$105	$ 25	23.8%
Total liabilities and equity	$360	$465	$(105)	(22.6)%

MEME CO. Horizontal Analysis of Comparative Income Statement Years Ended December 31, 2011 and 2010				
	2011	**2010**	Increase	(Decrease)
			Amount	Percent
Sales revenue	$650	$580	$ 70	12.1%
Less cost of goods sold	430	350	80	22.9
Gross profit	$220	$230	(10)	(4.3)
Salary expense	120	140	(20)	(14.3)
Rent expense	70	80	(10)	(12.5)
Net income	$ 30	$ 10	$ 20	200.0%

2 Perform a vertical analysis of financial statements

3 Prepare and use common-size financial statements

Vertical Analysis

Part 1	**Part 2**	Part 3	Demo Doc Complete

As its name implies, vertical analysis takes *each* number on the financial statements and compares it to others in the same year (that is, *down* the columns of the financial statements). Vertical analysis is sometimes called *common-size analysis* because it allows two companies of different sizes to be compared (through the use of percentages).

Balance Sheet Vertical Analysis

On the **balance sheet**, each number, whether it is before an asset, a liability, or an equity account is calculated as a percentage of *total assets*.

$$\text{Vertical analysis percent (balance sheet)} = \frac{\text{Account balance}}{\text{Total assets}}$$

So in the case of Accounts receivable:

$$\text{Vertical analysis percent (2011 Accounts receivable)} = \frac{\$80}{\$360}$$
$$= 22.2\%$$

In other words, about 22% of all the assets in 2011 are in Accounts receivable.

Income Statement Vertical Analysis

On the **income statement**, each number is calculated as a percentage of **net** *sales revenues*.

$$\text{Vertical analysis percent (income statement)} = \frac{\text{Account balance}}{\text{Net sales revenues}}$$

So in the case of Gross Profit:

$$\text{Vertical analysis percent (2011 Gross profit)} = \frac{\$220}{\$650}$$
$$= 33.8\%$$

This means that for every dollar in sales revenues, $0.338 went to Gross Profit. For expenses, the calculation is the same. So in the cases of COGS and Rent Expense:

$$\text{Vertical analysis percent (2011 COGS)} = \frac{\$430}{\$650}$$
$$= 66.2\%$$

$$\text{Vertical analysis percent (2011 Rent expense)} = \frac{\$70}{\$650}$$
$$= 10.8\%$$

MEME CO.
Vertical Analysis of Balance Sheet
December 31, 2011 and 2010

	2011	2011 %	2010	2010 %
Assets				
Cash	$150	41.7%	$130	28.0%
Accounts receivable	80	22.2	145	31.1*
Inventory	130	36.1	190	40.9
Total assets	$360	100.0%	$465	100.0%
Liabilities				
Accounts payable	$ 90	25.0%	$140	30.1%
Loans payable	140	38.9	220	47.3
Total liabilities	$230	63.9%	$360	77.4%
Stockholders' Equity				
Common stock	$ 20	5.5*%	$ 10	2.2%
Retained earnings	110	30.6	95	20.4
Total stockholders' equity	$130	36.1%	$105	22.6%
Total liabilities and equity	$360	100.0%	$465	100.0%

*Rounded down to balance.

MEME CO.
Vertical Analysis of Comparative Income Statement
Years Ended December 31, 2011 and 2010

	2011	2011 %	2010	2010 %
Net sales revenue	$650	100.0%	$580	100.0%
Less cost of goods sold	430	66.2	350	60.3
Gross profit	$220	33.8%	$230	39.7%
Salary expense	120	18.4*	140	24.1
Rent expense	70	10.8	80	13.8
Net income	$ 30	4.6%	$ 10	1.7%

*Rounded to balance.

Requirement 2

Calculate MeMe's inventory turnover and rate of return on stockholders' equity ratios for both years.

4 Compute the standard financial ratios

Part 1	Part 2	**Part 3**	Demo Doc Complete

$$\text{Inventory turnover} = \frac{\text{COGS}}{\text{Average inventory}}$$

Remember that "average" (when used in a financial ratio) generally means the beginning balance plus the ending balance divided by two.

$$2011 \text{ Inventory turnover} = \frac{\$430}{[\frac{1}{2}(190+130)]}$$

$$= 2.7 \text{ times}$$

$$2010 \text{ Inventory turnover} = \frac{\$350}{[\frac{1}{2}(160+190)]}$$

$$= 2 \text{ times}$$

$$\text{Rate of return on stockholders' equity} = \frac{\text{Net income} - \text{Preferred dividends}}{\text{Average common stockholders' equity}}$$

$$2011 \text{ Rate of return on stockholders' equity} = \frac{[\$30 - \$0]}{\frac{1}{2}(\$105 + \$130)}$$

$$= 25.5\%$$

$$2010 \text{ Rate of return on stockholders' equity} = \frac{[\$10 - \$0]}{\frac{1}{2}(\$95 + \$105)}$$

$$= 10\%$$

Part 1	Part 2	Part 3	**Demo Doc Complete**

2 0 0 8

ANNUAL REPORT

http://phx.corporate-ir.net/External.File?item=UGFyZW50SUQ9MjAyN3xDaGlsZElEPS0xfFR5cGU9Mw==&t=1

Report of Ernst & Young LLP, Independent Registered Public Accounting Firm

The Board of Directors and Stockholders
Amazon.com, Inc.

We have audited the accompanying consolidated balance sheets of Amazon.com, Inc. as of December 31, 2008 and 2007, and the related consolidated statements of operations, stockholders' equity, and cash flows for each of the three years in the period ended December 31, 2008. Our audits also included the financial statement schedule listed in the Index at Item 15(a)(2). These financial statements and schedule are the responsibility of the Company's management. Our responsibility is to express an opinion on these financial statements and schedule based on our audits.

We conducted our audits in accordance with the standards of the Public Company Accounting Oversight Board (United States). Those standards require that we plan and perform the audit to obtain reasonable assurance about whether the financial statements are free of material misstatement. An audit includes examining, on a test basis, evidence supporting the amounts and disclosures in the financial statements. An audit also includes assessing the accounting principles used and significant estimates made by management, as well as evaluating the overall financial statement presentation. We believe that our audits provide a reasonable basis for our opinion.

In our opinion, the financial statements referred to above present fairly, in all material respects, the consolidated financial position of Amazon.com, Inc. at December 31, 2008 and 2007, and the consolidated results of its operations and its cash flows for each of the three years in the period ended December 31, 2008, in conformity with U.S. generally accepted accounting principles. Also, in our opinion, the related financial statement schedule, when considered in relation to the basic financial statements taken as a whole, presents fairly in all material respects the information set forth therein.

As discussed in Note 1 to the consolidated financial statements, the Company adopted FASB Interpretation No. 48 *Accounting for Uncertainty in Income Taxes*, effective January 1, 2007, and FASB No. 157 *Fair Value Measurements*, effective January 1, 2008.

We also have audited, in accordance with the standards of the Public Company Accounting Oversight Board (United States), the effectiveness of Amazon.com, Inc.'s internal control over financial reporting as of December 31, 2008, based on criteria established in Internal Control—Integrated Framework issued by the Committee of Sponsoring Organizations of the Treadway Commission and our report dated January 29, 2009 expressed an unqualified opinion thereon.

/s/ Ernst & Young LLP

Seattle, Washington
January 29, 2009

AMAZON.COM, INC.

CONSOLIDATED STATEMENTS OF CASH FLOWS
(in millions)

	Year Ended December 31,		
	2008	2007	2006
CASH AND CASH EQUIVALENTS, BEGINNING OF PERIOD	$ 2,539	$1,022	$ 1,013
OPERATING ACTIVITIES:			
Net income	645	476	190
Adjustments to reconcile net income to net cash from operating activities:			
Depreciation of fixed assets, including internal-use software and website development, and other amortization	287	246	205
Stock-based compensation	275	185	101
Other operating expense (income), net	(24)	9	10
Losses (gains) on sales of marketable securities, net	(2)	1	(2)
Other expense (income), net	(34)	12	(6)
Deferred income taxes	(5)	(99)	22
Excess tax benefits from stock-based compensation	(159)	(257)	(102)
Changes in operating assets and liabilities:			
Inventories	(232)	(303)	(282)
Accounts receivable, net and other	(218)	(255)	(103)
Accounts payable	812	928	402
Accrued expenses and other	247	429	241
Additions to unearned revenue	449	244	206
Amortization of previously unearned revenue	(344)	(211)	(180)
Net cash provided by operating activities	1,697	1,405	702
INVESTING ACTIVITIES:			
Purchases of fixed assets, including internal-use software and website development	(333)	(224)	(216)
Acquisitions, net of cash acquired, and other	(494)	(75)	(32)
Sales and maturities of marketable securities and other investments	1,305	1,271	1,845
Purchases of marketable securities and other investments	(1,677)	(930)	(1,930)
Net cash provided by (used in) investing activities	(1,199)	42	(333)
FINANCING ACTIVITIES:			
Proceeds from exercises of stock options	11	91	35
Excess tax benefits from stock-based compensation	159	257	102
Common stock repurchased	(100)	(248)	(252)
Proceeds from long-term debt and other	87	24	98
Repayments of long-term debt and capital lease obligations	(355)	(74)	(383)
Net cash provided by (used in) financing activities	(198)	50	(400)
Foreign-currency effect on cash and cash equivalents	(70)	20	40
Net increase in cash and cash equivalents	230	1,517	9
CASH AND CASH EQUIVALENTS, END OF PERIOD	$ 2,769	$2,539	$ 1,022
SUPPLEMENTAL CASH FLOW INFORMATION:			
Cash paid for interest	$ 64	$ 67	$ 86
Cash paid for income taxes	53	24	15
Fixed assets acquired under capital leases and other financing arrangements	148	74	69
Fixed assets acquired under build-to-suit leases	72	15	—
Conversion of debt	605	1	—

See accompanying notes to consolidated financial statements.

44

AMAZON.COM, INC.

CONSOLIDATED STATEMENTS OF OPERATIONS
(in millions, except per share data)

	Year Ended December 31,		
	2008	2007	2006
Net sales	$19,166	$14,835	$10,711
Cost of sales	14,896	11,482	8,255
Gross profit	4,270	3,353	2,456
Operating expenses (1):			
Fulfillment	1,658	1,292	937
Marketing	482	344	263
Technology and content	1,033	818	662
General and administrative	279	235	195
Other operating expense (income), net	(24)	9	10
Total operating expenses	3,428	2,698	2,067
Income from operations	842	655	389
Interest income	83	90	59
Interest expense	(71)	(77)	(78)
Other income (expense), net	47	(8)	7
Total non-operating income (expense)	59	5	(12)
Income before income taxes	901	660	377
Provision for income taxes	(247)	(184)	(187)
Equity-method investment activity, net of tax	(9)	—	—
Net income	$ 645	$ 476	$ 190
Basic earnings per share	$ 1.52	$ 1.15	$ 0.46
Diluted earnings per share	$ 1.49	$ 1.12	$ 0.45
Weighted average shares used in computation of earnings per share:			
Basic	423	413	416
Diluted	432	424	424

(1) Includes stock-based compensation as follows:

Fulfillment	$ 61	$ 39	$ 24
Marketing	13	8	4
Technology and content	151	103	54
General and administrative	50	35	19

See accompanying notes to consolidated financial statements.

45

AMAZON.COM, INC.

CONSOLIDATED BALANCE SHEETS
(in millions, except per share data)

	December 31,	
	2008	2007

ASSETS

	2008	2007
Current assets:		
Cash and cash equivalents	$2,769	$ 2,539
Marketable securities	958	573
Inventories	1,399	1,200
Accounts receivable, net and other	827	705
Deferred tax assets	204	147
Total current assets	6,157	5,164
Fixed assets, net	854	543
Deferred tax assets	145	260
Goodwill	438	222
Other assets	720	296
Total assets	$8,314	$ 6,485

LIABILITIES AND STOCKHOLDERS' EQUITY

	2008	2007
Current liabilities:		
Accounts payable	$3,594	$ 2,795
Accrued expenses and other	1,093	902
Current portion of long-term debt	59	17
Total current liabilities	4,746	3,714
Long-term debt	409	1,282
Other long-term liabilities	487	292
Commitments and contingencies		
Stockholders' equity:		
Preferred stock, $0.01 par value:		
Authorized shares—500		
Issued and outstanding shares—none	—	—
Common stock, $0.01 par value:		
Authorized shares—5,000		
Issued shares—445 and 431		
Outstanding shares—428 and 416	4	4
Treasury stock, at cost	(600)	(500)
Additional paid-in capital	4,121	3,063
Accumulated other comprehensive income (loss)	(123)	5
Accumulated deficit	(730)	(1,375)
Total stockholders' equity	2,672	1,197
Total liabilities and stockholders' equity	$8,314	$ 6,485

See accompanying notes to consolidated financial statements.

46

AMAZON.COM, INC.

CONSOLIDATED STATEMENTS OF STOCKHOLDERS' EQUITY

(in millions)

	Common Stock Shares	Common Stock Amount	Treasury Stock	Additional Paid-In Capital	Accumulated Other Comprehensive Income (Loss)	Accumulated Deficit	Total Stockholders' Equity
Balance at January 1, 2006	416	4	$—	$2,263	$ 6	$(2,027)	$ 246
Net income	—	—	—	—	—	190	190
Foreign currency translation losses, net of tax	—	—	—	—	(13)	—	(13)
Change in unrealized losses on available-for-sale securities, net of tax	—	—	—	—	4	—	4
Amortization of unrealized loss on terminated Euro Currency Swap, net of tax	—	—	—	—	2	—	2
Comprehensive income							183
Exercise of common stock options	6	—	—	35	—	—	35
Repurchase of common stock	(8)	—	(252)	—	—	—	(252)
Excess tax benefits from stock-based compensation	—	—	—	102	—	—	102
Stock-based compensation and issuance of employee benefit plan stock	—	—	—	117	—	—	117
Balance at December 31, 2006	414	4	(252)	2,517	(1)	(1,837)	431
Net income	—	—	—	—	—	476	476
Foreign currency translation losses, net of tax	—	—	—	—	(3)	—	(3)
Change in unrealized losses on available-for-sale securities, net of tax	—	—	—	—	8	—	8
Amortization of unrealized loss on terminated Euro Currency Swap, net of tax	—	—	—	—	1	—	1
Comprehensive income							482
Change in accounting principle	—	—	—	2	—	(14)	(12)
Unrecognized excess tax benefits from stock-based compensation	—	—	—	4	—	—	4
Exercise of common stock options and conversion of debt	8	—	—	92	—	—	92
Repurchase of common stock	(6)	—	(248)	—	—	—	(248)
Excess tax benefits from stock-based compensation	—	—	—	257	—	—	257
Stock-based compensation and issuance of employee benefit plan stock	—	—	—	191	—	—	191
Balance at December 31, 2007	416	4	(500)	3,063	5	(1,375)	1,197
Net income	—	—	—	—	—	645	645
Foreign currency translation losses, net of tax	—	—	—	—	(127)	—	(127)
Change in unrealized losses on available-for-sale securities, net of tax	—	—	—	—	(1)	—	(1)
Comprehensive income							517
Unrecognized excess tax benefits from stock-based compensation	—	—	—	(8)	—	—	(8)
Exercise of common stock options and conversion of debt	14	—	—	624	—	—	624
Repurchase of common stock	(2)	—	(100)	—	—	—	(100)
Excess tax benefits from stock-based compensation	—	—	—	154	—	—	154
Stock-based compensation and issuance of employee benefit plan stock	—	—	—	288	—	—	288
Balance at December 31, 2008	428	4	$(600)	$4,121	$(123)	$ (730)	$2,672

See accompanying notes to consolidated financial statements.

47

AMAZON.COM, INC.

NOTES TO CONSOLIDATED FINANCIAL STATEMENTS

Note 1—DESCRIPTION OF BUSINESS AND ACCOUNTING POLICIES

Description of Business

Amazon.com opened its virtual doors on the World Wide Web in July 1995 and we offer Earth's Biggest Selection. We seek to be Earth's most customer-centric company for three primary customer sets: consumer customers, seller customers and developer customers. We serve our consumer customers through our retail websites and focus on selection, price, and convenience. We offer programs that enable seller customers to sell their products on our websites and their own branded websites and to fulfill orders through us. We serve developer customers through Amazon Web Services, which provides access to technology infrastructure that developers can use to enable virtually any type of business. In addition, we generate revenue through co-branded credit card agreements and other marketing and promotional services, such as online advertising.

We have organized our operations into two principal segments: North America and International. See "Note 13—Segment Information."

Principles of Consolidation

The consolidated financial statements include the accounts of the Company, its wholly-owned subsidiaries, and those entities (relating primarily to *www.amazon.cn*) in which we have a variable interest. Intercompany balances and transactions have been eliminated.

Use of Estimates

The preparation of financial statements in conformity with U.S. GAAP requires estimates and assumptions that affect the reported amounts of assets and liabilities, revenues and expenses, and related disclosures of contingent liabilities in the consolidated financial statements and accompanying notes. Estimates are used for, but not limited to, valuation of investments, receivables valuation, sales returns, incentive discount offers, inventory valuation, depreciable lives of fixed assets, internally-developed software, valuation of acquired intangibles and goodwill, income taxes, stock-based compensation, and contingencies. Actual results could differ materially from those estimates.

Earnings per Share

Basic earnings per share is calculated using our weighted-average outstanding common shares. Diluted earnings per share is calculated using our weighted-average outstanding common shares including the dilutive effect of stock awards as determined under the treasury stock method.

Our convertible debt instrument is excluded from the calculation of diluted earnings per share as its effect under the if-converted method is anti-dilutive. See "Note 5—Long-Term Debt."

The following table shows the calculation of diluted shares (in millions):

	Year Ended December 31,		
	2008	2007	2006
Shares used in computation of basic earnings per share	423	413	416
Total dilutive effect of outstanding stock awards (1)	9	11	8
Shares used in computation of diluted earnings per share	432	424	424

(1) Calculated using the treasury stock method that assumes proceeds available to reduce the dilutive effect of outstanding stock awards, which include the exercise price of stock options, the unrecognized deferred compensation of stock awards, and assumed tax proceeds from excess stock-based compensation deductions.

Treasury Stock

We account for treasury stock under the cost method and include treasury stock as a component of stockholders' equity.

Cash and Cash Equivalents

We classify all highly liquid instruments, including money market funds that comply with Rule 2a-7 of the Investment Company Act of 1940, with an original maturity of three months or less at the time of purchase as cash equivalents.

Inventories

Inventories, consisting of products available for sale, are accounted for using the FIFO method, and are valued at the lower of cost or market value. This valuation requires us to make judgments, based on currently-available information, about the likely method of disposition, such as through sales to individual customers, returns to product vendors, or liquidations, and expected recoverable values of each disposition category. Based on this evaluation, we adjust the carrying amount of our inventories to lower of cost or market value.

We provide fulfillment-related services in connection with certain of our sellers' programs. In those arrangements, as well as all other product sales by other sellers, the seller maintains ownership of the related products. As such, these amounts are not included in our consolidated balance sheets.

Accounts Receivable, Net, and Other

Included in "Accounts receivable, net, and other" on our consolidated balance sheets are amounts primarily related to vendor receivables and customer receivables. At December 31, 2008 and 2007, vendor receivables, net, were $400 million and $280 million, and customer receivables, net, were $311 million and $296 million.

Allowance for Doubtful Accounts

We estimate losses on receivables based on known troubled accounts, if any, and historical experience of losses incurred. The allowance for doubtful customer and vendor receivables was $81 million and $64 million at December 31, 2008 and 2007.

Internal-use Software and Website Development

Costs incurred to develop software for internal use are required to be capitalized and amortized over the estimated useful life of the software in accordance with Statement of Position (SOP) 98-1, *Accounting for the Costs of Computer Software Developed or Obtained for Internal Use.* Costs related to design or maintenance of internal-use software are expensed as incurred. For the years ended 2008, 2007, and 2006, we capitalized $187 million (including $27 million of stock-based compensation), $129 million (including $21 million of stock-based compensation), and $123 million (including $16 million of stock-based compensation) of costs associated with internal-use software and website development. Amortization of previously capitalized amounts was $143 million, $116 million, and $86 million for 2008, 2007, and 2006.

Depreciation of Fixed Assets

Fixed assets include assets such as furniture and fixtures, heavy equipment, technology infrastructure, internal-use software and website development. Depreciation is recorded on a straight-line basis over the estimated useful lives of the assets (generally two years or less for assets such as internal-use software, two or three years for our technology infrastructure, five years for furniture and fixtures, and ten years for heavy equipment). Depreciation expense is generally classified within the corresponding operating expense categories on our consolidated statements of operations, and certain assets are amortized as "Cost of sales."

Leases and Asset Retirement Obligations

We account for our lease agreements pursuant to Statement of Financial Accounting Standards (SFAS) No. 13, *Accounting for Leases*, which categorizes leases at their inception as either operating or capital leases depending on certain defined criteria. On certain of our lease agreements, we may receive rent holidays and other incentives. We recognize lease costs on a straight-line basis without regard to deferred payment terms, such as rent holidays that defer the commencement date of required payments. Additionally, incentives we receive are treated as a reduction of our costs over the term of the agreement. Leasehold improvements are capitalized at cost and amortized over the lesser of their expected useful life or the life of the lease, without assuming renewal features, if any, are exercised. We account for build-to-suit lease arrangements in accordance with EITF 97-10, *The Effect of Lessee Involvement in Asset Construction,* to the extent we are involved in the construction of structural improvements prior to commencement of a lease.

In accordance with SFAS No. 143, *Accounting for Asset Retirement Obligations,* we establish assets and liabilities for the present value of estimated future costs to return certain of our leased facilities to their original condition. Such assets are depreciated over the lease period into operating expense, and the recorded liabilities are accreted to the future value of the estimated restoration costs.

Goodwill

We evaluate goodwill for impairment annually and when an event occurs or circumstances change to suggest that the carrying amount may not be recoverable. Impairment of goodwill is tested at the reporting unit level by comparing the reporting unit's carrying amount, including goodwill, to the fair value of the reporting unit. The fair values of the reporting units are estimated using discounted projected cash flows. If the carrying amount of the reporting unit exceeds its fair value, goodwill is considered impaired and a second step is performed to measure the amount of impairment loss, if any. We conduct our annual impairment test as of October 1 of each year, and have determined there to be no impairment in 2008 or 2007. There were no events or circumstances from the date of our assessment through December 31, 2008 that would impact this conclusion.

See "Note 4—Acquisitions, Goodwill, and Acquired Intangible Assets."

Other Assets

Included in "Other assets" on our consolidated balance sheets are amounts primarily related to marketable securities restricted for longer than one year, the majority of which are attributable to collateralization of bank guarantees and debt related to our international operations; acquired intangible assets, net of amortization; deferred costs; certain equity investments; and intellectual property rights.

AMAZON.COM, INC.

NOTES TO CONSOLIDATED FINANCIAL STATEMENTS—(Continued)

Investments

The initial carrying cost of our investments is the price we paid. Investments are accounted for using the equity method of accounting if the investment gives us the ability to exercise significant influence, but not control, over an investee. The total of these investments in equity-method investees, including identifiable intangible assets, deferred tax liabilities and goodwill, are classified on our consolidated balance sheets as "Other assets" and our share of the investees' earnings or losses along with amortization of the related intangible assets, if any, as "Equity-method investment activity, net of tax" on our consolidated statements of operations.

All other equity investments consist of investments for which we do not have the ability to exercise significant influence. Under the cost method of accounting, investments in private companies are carried at cost and are adjusted only for other-than-temporary declines in fair value, distributions of earnings, and additional investments. For public companies that have readily determinable fair values, we classify our equity investments as available-for-sale and, accordingly, record these investments at their fair values with unrealized gains and losses, net of tax, included in "Accumulated other comprehensive income (loss)," a separate component of stockholders' equity.

We generally invest our excess cash in investment grade short to intermediate term fixed income securities and AAA-rated money market funds. Such investments are included in "Cash and cash equivalents," or "Marketable securities" on the accompanying consolidated balance sheets, are classified as available-for-sale, and reported at fair value with unrealized gains and losses included in "Accumulated other comprehensive income (loss)." The weighted average method is used to determine the cost of Euro-denominated securities sold, and the specific identification method is used to determine the cost of all other securities.

We periodically evaluate whether declines in fair values of our investments below their cost are other-than-temporary. This evaluation consists of several qualitative and quantitative factors regarding the severity and duration of the unrealized loss as well as our ability and intent to hold the investment until a forecasted recovery occurs. Factors considered include quoted market prices; recent financial results and operating trends; other publicly available information; implied values from any recent transactions or offers of investee securities; or other conditions that may affect the value of our investments.

Long-Lived Assets

Long-lived assets, other than goodwill, are reviewed for impairment whenever events or changes in circumstances indicate that the carrying amount of the assets might not be recoverable. Conditions that would necessitate an impairment assessment include a significant decline in the observable market value of an asset, a significant change in the extent or manner in which an asset is used, or any other significant adverse change that would indicate that the carrying amount of an asset or group of assets may not be recoverable.

For long-lived assets used in operations, impairment losses are only recorded if the asset's carrying amount is not recoverable through its undiscounted, probability-weighted future cash flows. We measure the impairment loss based on the difference between the carrying amount and estimated fair value.

Long-lived assets are considered held for sale when certain criteria are met, including when management has committed to a plan to sell the asset, the asset is available for sale in its immediate condition, and the sale is probable within one year of the reporting date. Assets held for sale are reported at the lower of cost or fair value less costs to sell. Assets held for sale were not significant at December 31, 2008 or 2007.

51

AMAZON.COM, INC.

NOTES TO CONSOLIDATED FINANCIAL STATEMENTS—(Continued)

Accrued Expenses and Other

Included in "Accrued expenses and other" at December 31, 2008 and 2007 were liabilities of $270 million and $230 million for unredeemed gift certificates. We recognize revenue from a gift certificate when a customer redeems it. If a gift certificate is not redeemed, we recognize revenue when it expires or, for a certificate without an expiration date, when the likelihood of its redemption becomes remote, generally two years from date of issuance.

Unearned Revenue

Unearned revenue is recorded when payments are received in advance of performing our service obligations and is recognized over the service period. Current unearned revenue is included in "Accrued expenses and other" and non-current unearned revenue is included in "Other long-term liabilities" on our consolidated balance sheets. Current unearned revenue was $191 million and $91 million at December 31, 2008 and 2007. Non-current unearned revenue was $46 million and $19 million at December 31, 2008 and 2007.

Income Taxes

Income tax expense includes U.S. and international income taxes. We do not provide for U.S. taxes on our undistributed earnings of foreign subsidiaries, totaling $328 million at December 31, 2008, since we intend to invest such undistributed earnings indefinitely outside of the U.S. If such amounts were repatriated, determination of the amount of U.S. income taxes that would be incurred is not practicable due to the complexities associated with this calculation.

Deferred income tax balances reflect the effects of temporary differences between the carrying amounts of assets and liabilities and their tax bases and are stated at enacted tax rates expected to be in effect when taxes are actually paid or recovered. At December 31, 2008, our deferred tax assets, net of deferred tax liabilities and valuation allowance, were $349 million, which includes $165 million relating to net operating loss carryforwards that were primarily attributed to stock-based compensation. The majority of our net operating loss carryforwards begin to expire in 2021 and thereafter.

SFAS No. 109, *Accounting for Income Taxes,* requires that deferred tax assets be evaluated for future realization and reduced by a valuation allowance to the extent we believe a portion will not be realized. We consider many factors when assessing the likelihood of future realization of our deferred tax assets, including our recent cumulative earnings experience and expectations of future taxable income by taxing jurisdiction, the carry-forward periods available to us for tax reporting purposes, and other relevant factors. In accordance with SFAS No. 109, we allocate our valuation allowance to current and long-term deferred tax assets on a pro-rata basis.

Effective January 1, 2007, we adopted the provisions of FIN No. 48, *Accounting for Uncertainty in Income Taxes—an Interpretation of FASB Statement No. 109.* FIN 48 contains a two-step approach to recognizing and measuring uncertain tax positions (tax contingencies) accounted for in accordance with SFAS No. 109. The first step is to evaluate the tax position for recognition by determining if the weight of available evidence indicates it is more likely than not that the position will be sustained on audit, including resolution of related appeals or litigation processes, if any. The second step is to measure the tax benefit as the largest amount which is more than 50% likely of being realized upon ultimate settlement. We consider many factors when evaluating and estimating our tax positions and tax benefits, which may require periodic adjustments and which may not accurately forecast actual outcomes. Our policy is to include interest and penalties related to our tax contingencies in income tax expense. Implementation of FIN 48 was not material.

52

Fair Value of Financial Instruments

Effective January 1, 2008, we adopted SFAS No. 157, except as it applies to the nonfinancial assets and nonfinancial liabilities subject to FSP No. 157-2. SFAS No. 157 clarifies the definition of fair value, prescribes methods for measuring fair value, establishes a fair value hierarchy based on the inputs used to measure fair value, and expands disclosures about fair value measurements. The three-tier fair value hierarchy, which prioritizes the inputs used in the valuation methodologies, is:

Level 1—Valuations based on quoted prices for identical assets and liabilities in active markets.

Level 2—Valuations based on observable inputs other than quoted prices included in Level 1, such as quoted prices for similar assets and liabilities in active markets, quoted prices for identical or similar assets and liabilities in markets that are not active, or other inputs that are observable or can be corroborated by observable market data.

Level 3—Valuations based on unobservable inputs reflecting our own assumptions, consistent with reasonably available assumptions made by other market participants. These valuations require significant judgment.

Revenue

We recognize revenue from product sales or services rendered when the following four revenue recognition criteria are met: persuasive evidence of an arrangement exists, delivery has occurred or services have been rendered, the selling price is fixed or determinable, and collectability is reasonably assured. Additionally, revenue arrangements with multiple deliverables are divided into separate units of accounting if the deliverables in the arrangement meet the following criteria: the delivered item has value to the customer on a standalone basis; there is objective and reliable evidence of the fair value of undelivered items; and delivery of any undelivered item is probable.

We evaluate the criteria outlined in EITF Issue No. 99-19, *Reporting Revenue Gross as a Principal Versus Net as an Agent,* in determining whether it is appropriate to record the gross amount of product sales and related costs or the net amount earned as commissions. Generally, when we are primarily obligated in a transaction, are subject to inventory risk, have latitude in establishing prices and selecting suppliers, or have several but not all of these indicators, revenue is recorded gross. If we are not primarily obligated and amounts earned are determined using a fixed percentage, a fixed-payment schedule, or a combination of the two, we generally record the net amounts as commissions earned.

Product sales and shipping revenues, net of promotional discounts, rebates, and return allowances, are recorded when the products are shipped and title passes to customers. Retail sales to customers are made pursuant to a sales contract that provides for transfer of both title and risk of loss upon our delivery to the carrier. Return allowances, which reduce product revenue, are estimated using historical experience. Revenue from product sales and services rendered is recorded net of sales taxes. Amounts received in advance for subscription services, including amounts received for Amazon Prime and other membership programs, are deferred and recognized as revenue over the subscription term. For our products with multiple elements, where a standalone value for each element cannot be established, we recognize the revenue and related cost over the estimated economic life of the product.

We periodically provide incentive offers to our customers to encourage purchases. Such offers include current discount offers, such as percentage discounts off current purchases, inducement offers, such as offers for future discounts subject to a minimum current purchase, and other similar offers. Current discount offers, when accepted by our customers, are treated as a reduction to the purchase price of the related transaction, while inducement offers, when accepted by our customers, are treated as a reduction to purchase price based on estimated future redemption rates. Redemption rates are estimated using our historical experience for similar inducement offers. Current discount offers and inducement offers are presented as a net amount in "Net sales."

Commissions and per-unit fees received from sellers and similar amounts earned through other seller sites are recognized when the item is sold by seller and our collectability is reasonably assured. We record an allowance for estimated refunds on such commissions using historical experience.

Shipping Activities

Outbound shipping charges to customers are included in "Net sales" and were $835 million, $740 million, and $567 million for 2008, 2007, and 2006. Outbound shipping-related costs are included in "Cost of sales" and totaled $1.5 billion, $1.2 billion, and $884 million for 2008, 2007, and 2006. The net cost to us of shipping activities was $630 million, $434 million, and $317 million for 2008, 2007 and 2006.

Cost of Sales

Cost of sales consists of the purchase price of consumer products and content sold by us, inbound and outbound shipping charges, packaging supplies, and costs incurred in operating and staffing our fulfillment and customer service centers on behalf of other businesses. Shipping charges to receive products from our suppliers are included in our inventory, and recognized as "Cost of sales" upon sale of products to our customers. Payment processing and related transaction costs, including those associated with seller transactions, are classified in "Fulfillment" on our consolidated statements of operations.

Vendor Agreements

We have agreements to receive cash consideration from certain of our vendors, including rebates and cooperative marketing reimbursements. We generally presume amounts received from our vendors are a reduction of the prices we pay for their products and, therefore, we reflect such amounts as either a reduction of "Cost of sales" on our consolidated statements of operations, or, if the product inventory is still on hand, as a reduction of the carrying value of inventory. Vendor rebates are typically dependent upon reaching minimum purchase thresholds. We evaluate the likelihood of reaching purchase thresholds using past experience and current year forecasts. When volume rebates can be reasonably estimated, we record a portion of the rebate as we make progress towards the purchase threshold.

When we receive direct reimbursements for costs incurred by us in advertising the vendor's product or service, the amount we receive is recorded as an offset to "Marketing" on our consolidated statements of operations.

Fulfillment

Fulfillment costs represent those costs incurred in operating and staffing our fulfillment and customer service centers, including costs attributable to buying, receiving, inspecting, and warehousing inventories; picking, packaging, and preparing customer orders for shipment; payment processing and related transaction costs, including costs associated with our guarantee for certain seller transactions; and responding to inquiries from customers. Fulfillment costs also include amounts paid to third parties that assist us in fulfillment and customer service operations. Certain of our fulfillment-related costs that are incurred on behalf of other businesses are classified as cost of sales rather than fulfillment.

AMAZON.COM, INC.

NOTES TO CONSOLIDATED FINANCIAL STATEMENTS—(Continued)

Marketing

Marketing costs consist primarily of online advertising, including through our Associates program, sponsored search, portal advertising, e-mail campaigns, and other initiatives. We pay commissions to participants in our Associates program when their customer referrals result in product sales and classify such costs as "Marketing" on our consolidated statements of operations.

We also participate in cooperative advertising arrangements with certain of our vendors, and other third parties. To the extent co-operative marketing reimbursements decline in future periods, we may incur additional expenses to continue certain promotions or elect to reduce or discontinue them.

Marketing expenses also consist of public relations expenditures; payroll and related expenses for personnel engaged in marketing, business development, and selling activities; and to a lesser extent, traditional advertising such as newspaper inserts.

Advertising and other promotional costs, which consist primarily of online advertising, are expensed as incurred, and were $420 million, $306 million, and $226 million, in 2008, 2007, and 2006. Prepaid advertising costs were not significant at December 31, 2008 and 2007.

Technology and Content

Technology and content expenses consist principally of payroll and related expenses for employees involved in, application development, category expansion, editorial content, buying, merchandising selection, and systems support, as well as costs associated with the compute, storage and telecommunications infrastructure.

Technology and content costs are expensed as incurred, except for certain costs relating to the development of internal-use software and website development, including software used to upgrade and enhance our websites and processes supporting our business, which are capitalized and amortized over two years.

General and Administrative

General and administrative expenses consist of payroll and related expenses for employees involved in general corporate functions, including accounting, finance, tax, legal, and human relations, among others; costs associated with use by these functions of facilities and equipment, such as depreciation expense and rent; professional fees and litigation costs; and other general corporate costs.

Stock-Based Compensation

SFAS No. 123(R) requires measurement of compensation cost for all stock-based awards at fair value on date of grant and recognition of compensation over the service period for awards expected to vest. The fair value of restricted stock and restricted stock units is determined based on the number of shares granted and the quoted price of our common stock. Such value is recognized as expense over the service period, net of estimated forfeitures, using the accelerated method. The estimation of stock awards that will ultimately vest requires judgment, and to the extent actual results or updated estimates differ from our current estimates, such amounts will be recorded as a cumulative adjustment in the period estimates are revised. We consider many factors when estimating expected forfeitures, including types of awards, employee class, and historical experience. Actual results and future estimates may differ substantially from our current estimates.

55

Foreign Currency

We have the following internationally-focused websites: *www.amazon.co.uk, www.amazon.de, www.amazon.fr, www.amazon.co.jp, www.amazon.ca*, and *www.amazon.cn*. Net sales generated from internationally-focused websites, as well as most of the related expenses directly incurred from those operations, are denominated in the functional currencies of the resident countries. Additionally, the functional currency of our subsidiaries that either operate or support these international websites is the same as the local currency of the United Kingdom, Germany, France, Japan, Canada, and China. Assets and liabilities of these subsidiaries are translated into U.S. Dollars at period-end exchange rates, and revenues and expenses are translated at average rates prevailing throughout the period. Translation adjustments are included in "Accumulated other comprehensive income (loss)," a separate component of stockholders' equity, and in the "Foreign currency effect on cash and cash equivalents," on our consolidated statements of cash flows. Transaction gains and losses arising from transactions denominated in a currency other than the functional currency of the entity involved are included in "Other income (expense), net" on our consolidated statements of operations. See "Note 11—Other Income (Expense), Net."

Gains and losses arising from intercompany foreign currency transactions are included in net income. In connection with the remeasurement of intercompany balances, we recorded gains of $23 million, $32 million and $50 million in 2008, 2007 and 2006.

Recent Accounting Pronouncements

In September 2006, the Financial Accounting Standards Board (FASB) issued SFAS No. 157, *Fair Value Measurements*, which defines fair value, establishes a framework for measuring fair value in accordance with generally accepted accounting principles and expands disclosures about fair value measurements. For financial assets and liabilities, SFAS No. 157 was effective for fiscal years beginning after November 15, 2007, and interim periods within those fiscal years. See "Note 2—Cash, Cash Equivalents, and Marketable Securities" for further discussion. In February 2008, the FASB issued Staff Position (FSP) No. 157-2 which delays the effective date of SFAS No. 157 one year for all nonfinancial assets and nonfinancial liabilities, except those recognized or disclosed at fair value in the financial statements on a recurring basis. FSP 157-2 is effective for us beginning January 1, 2009.

Those assets and liabilities measured at fair value under SFAS No. 157 in Q1 2008 did not have a material impact on our consolidated financial statements. In accordance with FSP 157-2, we will measure the remaining assets and liabilities beginning Q1 2009. We do not expect the adoption of SFAS No. 157, as amended by FSP 157-2, will have a material impact on our consolidated financial statements.

In December 2007, the FASB issued SFAS No. 141 (R), *Business Combinations*, and SFAS No. 160, *Noncontrolling Interests in Consolidated Financial Statements*. SFAS No. 141 (R) requires an acquirer to measure the identifiable assets acquired, the liabilities assumed and any noncontrolling interest in the acquired entity at their fair values on the acquisition date, with goodwill being the excess value over the net identifiable assets acquired. SFAS No. 160 clarifies that a noncontrolling interest in a subsidiary should be reported as equity in the consolidated financial statements. The calculation of earnings per share will continue to be based on income amounts attributable to the parent. SFAS No. 141 (R) and SFAS No. 160 are effective for financial statements issued for fiscal years beginning after December 15, 2008. Early adoption is prohibited. We do not expect the adoption of SFAS No. 141 (R) and SFAS No. 160 will have a material impact on our consolidated financial statements.

AMAZON.COM, INC.

NOTES TO CONSOLIDATED FINANCIAL STATEMENTS—(Continued)

In April 2008, the FASB issued FSP No. 142-3, *Determination of the Useful Life of Intangible Assets.* FSP No. 142-3 amends the factors that should be considered in developing renewal or extension assumptions used to determine the useful life of a recognized intangible asset under FASB Statement No. 142, *Goodwill and Other Intangible Assets.* FSP No. 142-3 is effective for financial statements issued for fiscal years beginning after December 15, 2008. Early adoption is prohibited. We do not expect the adoption of FSP No. 142-3 will have a material impact on our consolidated financial statements.

In June 2008, the FASB ratified the consensus reached on EITF Issue No. 07-05, *Determining Whether an Instrument (or Embedded Feature) Is Indexed to an Entity's Own Stock.* EITF Issue No. 07-05 clarifies the determination of whether an instrument (or an embedded feature) is indexed to an entity's own stock, which would qualify as a scope exception under SFAS No. 133, *Accounting for Derivative Instruments and Hedging Activities.* EITF Issue No. 07-05 is effective for financial statements issued for fiscal years beginning after December 15, 2008. Early adoption for an existing instrument is not permitted. We do not expect the adoption of EITF Issue No. 07-05 will have a material impact on our consolidated financial statements.

Note 2—CASH, CASH EQUIVALENTS, AND MARKETABLE SECURITIES

As of December 31, 2008 and 2007 our cash, cash equivalents, and marketable securities primarily consisted of cash, government and government agency securities, AAA-rated money market funds and other investment grade securities. Such amounts are recorded at fair value. The following table summarizes, by major security type, our cash, cash equivalents and marketable securities (in millions):

	December 31, 2008			
	Cost or Amortized Cost	Gross Unrealized Gains	Gross Unrealized Losses (1)	Total Estimated Fair Value
Cash	$ 355	$—	$—	$ 355
Money market funds	1,682	—	—	1,682
Foreign government and agency securities	1,120	8	—	1,128
Corporate debt securities (2)	194	2	(2)	194
U.S. government and agency securities	589	5	—	594
Asset-backed securities	62	—	(4)	58
Other fixed income securities	23	—	—	23
Equity securities	2	—	(1)	1
	$4,027	$ 15	$ (7)	$4,035
Less: Long-term marketable securities (3)				(308)
Total cash, cash equivalents, and marketable securities				$3,727

NOTES TO CONSOLIDATED FINANCIAL STATEMENTS—(Continued)

	December 31, 2007			
	Cost or Amortized Cost	Gross Unrealized Gains	Gross Unrealized Losses (1)	Total Estimated Fair Value
Cash	$ 813	$—	$—	$ 813
Money market funds	1,558	—	—	1,558
Foreign government and agency securities	358	—	(1)	357
Corporate debt securities (2)	128	1	(1)	128
U.S. government and agency securities	326	5	—	331
Asset-backed securities	106	1	(1)	106
Other fixed income securities	4	—	—	4
Equity securities	5	7	—	12
	$3,298	$ 14	$ (3)	$3,309
Less: Long-term marketable securities (3)				(197)
Total cash, cash equivalents, and marketable securities				$3,112

---

(1) As of December 31, 2008, the cost and fair value of investments with loss positions was $761 million and $753 million. As of December 31, 2007, the cost and fair value of investments with loss positions was $550 million and $547 million. We evaluated the nature of these investments, credit worthiness of the issuer, and the duration of these impairments to determine if an other-than-temporary decline in fair value has occurred and concluded that these losses were temporary. Investments that have continuously been in loss positions for more than twelve months have gross unrealized losses of $2 million and $2 million as of December 31, 2008 and 2007.

(2) Corporate debt securities include investments in financial, insurance, and corporate institutions. No single issuer represents a significant portion of the total corporate debt securities portfolio.

(3) We are required to pledge or otherwise restrict a portion of our marketable securities as collateral for standby letters of credit, guarantees, debt, and real estate lease agreements. We classify cash and marketable securities with use restrictions of twelve months or longer as non-current "Other assets" on our consolidated balance sheets. See "Note 7—Commitments and Contingencies."

The following table summarizes contractual maturities of our cash equivalent and marketable fixed-income securities as of December 31, 2008 (in millions):

	Amortized Cost	Estimated Fair Value
Due within one year	$3,089	$3,090
Due after one year through five years	578	589
	$3,667	$3,679

Gross gains of $9 million, $2 million, and $18 million and gross losses of $7 million, $3 million and $16 million were realized on sales of available-for-sale marketable securities, including Euro-denominated securities, for 2008, 2007, and 2006. Realized gains and losses are included in "Other income (expense), net" on our consolidated statements of operations.

AMAZON.COM, INC.

NOTES TO CONSOLIDATED FINANCIAL STATEMENTS—(Continued)

The following table summarizes, by major security type, our assets that are measured at fair value on a recurring basis and are categorized using the fair value hierarchy (in millions):

		December 31, 2008			
	Cash	Level 1 Estimated Fair Value	Level 2 Estimated Fair Value	Level 3 Estimated Fair Value	Total Estimated Fair Value
Cash	$355	$ —	$ —	$—	$ 355
Money market funds	—	1,682	—	—	1,682
Foreign government and agency securities	—	—	1,128	—	1,128
Corporate debt securities	—	—	194	—	194
U.S. government and agency securities	—	—	594	—	594
Asset-backed securities	—	—	58	—	58
Other fixed income securities	—	—	23	—	23
Equity securities	—	1	—	—	1
	$355	$1,683	$1,997	$—	$4,035

		December 31, 2007			
	Cash	Level 1 Estimated Fair Value	Level 2 Estimated Fair Value	Level 3 Estimated Fair Value	Total Estimated Fair Value
Cash	$813	$ —	$—	$—	$ 813
Money market funds	—	1,558	—	—	1,558
Foreign government and agency securities	—	—	357	—	357
Corporate debt securities	—	—	128	—	128
U.S. government and agency securities	—	—	331	—	331
Asset-backed securities	—	—	106	—	106
Other fixed income securities	—	—	4	—	4
Equity securities	—	12	—	—	12
	$813	$1,570	$926	$—	$3,309

Note 3—FIXED ASSETS

Fixed assets, at cost, consisted of the following (in millions):

	December 31,	
	2008	2007
Gross Fixed Assets:		
Fulfillment and customer service	$ 564	$ 464
Technology infrastructure	348	196
Internal-use software, content, and website development	331	285
Construction in progress (1)	87	15
Other corporate assets	79	63
Gross fixed assets	1,409	1,023
Accumulated Depreciation :		
Fulfillment and customer service	254	216
Technology infrastructure	82	74
Internal-use software, content, and website development	159	146
Other corporate assets	60	44
Total accumulated depreciation	555	480
Total fixed assets, net	$ 854	$ 543

59

(1) We capitalize construction in progress and record a corresponding long-term liability for certain lease agreements, including our Seattle, Washington corporate office space subject to leases scheduled to begin in 2010 and 2011. See "Note 6—Other Long-Term Liabilities" and "Note 7—Commitments and Contingencies" for further discussion.

Depreciation expense on fixed assets was $311 million, $258 million, and $200 million, which includes amortization of fixed assets acquired under capital lease obligations of $50 million, $40 million, and $26 million for 2008, 2007, and 2006. Gross assets remaining under capital leases were $304 million and $150 million at December 31, 2008 and 2007. Accumulated depreciation associated with capital leases was $116 million and $64 million at December 31, 2008 and 2007.

Note 4—ACQUISITIONS, GOODWILL, AND ACQUIRED INTANGIBLE ASSETS

In 2008, we acquired certain companies for an aggregate purchase price of $432 million. For each acquisition, the purchase price has been allocated to the tangible assets, liabilities assumed, and identifiable intangible assets acquired based on estimated fair values on the acquisition date. The excess of purchase price over the fair value of the net assets acquired is classified as "Goodwill" on our consolidated balance sheets.

The following summarizes the allocation of the purchase price for companies acquired in 2008 (in millions):

Goodwill	$210
Internal-use software	31
Other assets, net	104
Deferred tax liabilities net	(75)
Intangible assets (1):	
Marketing-related	12
Contract-based	60
Technology and content	2
Customer-related	88
	$432

(1) Acquired intangible assets have estimated useful lives of between 2 and 13 years.

We acquired certain companies during 2007 for an aggregate purchase price of $33 million, resulting in goodwill of $21 million and acquired intangible assets of $18 million. We also made principal payments of $13 million on acquired debt in connection with one of these acquisitions.

We acquired certain companies during 2006 for an aggregate purchase price of $50 million, resulting in goodwill of $33 million and acquired intangible assets of $17 million.

The results of operations of each of the businesses acquired in 2008, 2007, and 2006 have been included in our consolidated results from each transaction closing date forward. The effect of these acquisitions on consolidated net sales and operating income during 2008, 2007, and 2006 was not significant.

At December 31, 2008 and December 31, 2007, approximately 22% and 36% of our acquired goodwill related to our International segment.

AMAZON.COM, INC.

NOTES TO CONSOLIDATED FINANCIAL STATEMENTS—(Continued)

Acquired intangible assets, included within "Other assets" on our consolidated balance sheets, consist of the following:

	December 31,					
	2008			**2007**		
	Acquired Intangibles, Gross (1)	Accumulated Amortization (1)	Acquired Intangibles, Net	Acquired Intangibles, Gross (1)	Accumulated Amortization (1)	Acquired Intangibles, Net
	(in millions)					
Marketing-related	$ 23	$ (4)	$ 19	$16	$ (5)	$11
Contract-based	62	(8)	54	5	(4)	1
Technology and content	10	(5)	5	21	(13)	8
Customer-related	97	(15)	82	13	(6)	7
Acquired intangibles ...	$192	$(32)	$160	$55	$(28)	$27

(1) Excludes the original cost and accumulated amortization of fully-amortized intangibles.

Amortization expense for acquired intangibles was $29 million, $13 million, and $10 million in 2008, 2007, and 2006. Expected future amortization expense of acquired intangible assets as of December 31, 2008 is as follows (in millions):

Year Ended December 31,	
2009	$ 35
2010	33
2011	25
2012	18
2013	18
Thereafter	31
	$160

The weighted-average amortization period is 6.5 years based on useful life assumptions between 2 and 13 years.

Note 5—LONG-TERM DEBT

Our long-term debt is summarized as follows:

	December 31,	
	2008	**2007**
	(in millions)	
6.875% PEACS due February 2010	$335	$ 350
4.75% Convertible Subordinated Notes	—	899
Other long-term debt	133	50
	468	1,299
Less current portion of long-term debt	(59)	(17)
	$409	$1,282

61

AMAZON.COM, INC.

NOTES TO CONSOLIDATED FINANCIAL STATEMENTS—(Continued)

Debt Repurchase Authorization

In February 2008 our Board of Directors authorized a debt repurchase program, replacing our previous debt repurchase authorization in its entirety, pursuant to which we may from time to time repurchase (through open market repurchases or private transactions), redeem, or otherwise retire up to an aggregate of all of our outstanding 6.875% PEACS and 4.75% Convertible Subordinated Notes. In 2008, we called for redemption the remaining principal of our 4.75% Convertible Subordinated Notes. See "4.75% Convertible Subordinated Notes."

6.875% PEACS

In February 2000, we completed an offering of €690 million of our 6.875% PEACS. The 6.875% PEACS are convertible, at the holder's option, into our common stock at a conversion price of €84.883 per share ($118.62, based on the exchange rates as of December 31, 2008). Due to changes in the Euro/U.S. Dollar exchange ratio, our remaining principal debt obligation under this instrument since issuance in February 2000 has increased by $99 million as of December 31, 2008. Total common stock issuable, as of December 31, 2008, upon conversion of our outstanding 6.875% PEACS was 2.8 million shares, which is excluded from our calculation of earnings per share as its effect is currently anti-dilutive. The U.S. Dollar equivalent principal, interest, and conversion price fluctuate based on the Euro/U.S. Dollar exchange ratio. Interest on the 6.875% PEACS is payable annually in arrears in February of each year. The 6.875% PEACS are unsecured and are subordinated to any existing and future senior indebtedness. We have the right to redeem the 6.875% PEACS, in whole or in part, by paying the principal, plus any accrued and unpaid interest. No premium payment is required for early redemption.

Upon the occurrence of a "fundamental change" prior to the maturity of the 6.875% PEACS, each holder thereof has the right to require us to redeem all or any part of such holder's 6.875% PEACS at a price equal to 100% of the principal amount of the notes being redeemed, together with accrued interest. As defined in the indenture, a "fundamental change" is the occurrence of certain types of transactions in which our stockholders do not receive publicly-traded securities.

The indenture governing the 6.875% PEACS contains certain affirmative covenants for us, including making principal and interest payments when due, maintaining our corporate existence and properties, and paying taxes and other claims in a timely manner. We were in compliance with these covenants through December 31, 2008.

In 2006, we redeemed principal amounts of €250 million ($300 million based on the Euro to U.S. Dollar exchange rate on the date of redemption) of our outstanding 6.875% PEACS. As a result of these redemptions, in 2006 we recorded a charge classified in "Other expense (income), net," of approximately $6 million related to the redemption, consisting of $3 million in unamortized deferred issuance charges and $3 million relating to unrealized losses on our terminated currency swap that previously hedged a portion of our 6.875% PEACS.

Based upon quoted market prices, the fair value of the 6.875% PEACS was $332 million and $358 million (outstanding principal of €240 million) as of December 31, 2008 and 2007. Such amounts are determined based on quoted prices in active markets for similar instruments (Level 2 as defined under SFAS No. 157). See "Note 1—Description of Business and Accounting Policies" for further discussion.

4.75% Convertible Subordinated Notes

In February 1999, we completed an offering of $1.25 billion of 4.75% Convertible Subordinated Notes. The 4.75% Convertible Subordinated Notes were convertible into our common stock at the holders' option at a conversion price of $78.0275 per share.

62

AMAZON.COM, INC.

NOTES TO CONSOLIDATED FINANCIAL STATEMENTS—(Continued)

In 2008, we called for redemption of the remaining principal amount of $899 million of our outstanding 4.75% Convertible Subordinated Notes. Holders elected to convert $605 million in principal amount of the 4.75% Convertible Subordinated Notes, and we issued 7.8 million shares of our common stock as a result; we redeemed the remaining $294 million of the called principal amount for cash.

Note 6—OTHER LONG-TERM LIABILITIES

Our other long-term liabilities are summarized as follows:

	December 31,	
	2008	2007
	(in millions)	
Tax contingencies	$144	$ 98
Long-term capital lease obligations	124	62
Construction liabilities	87	15
Other	132	117
	$487	$292

Tax Contingencies

As of December 31, 2008 and 2007, we have provided tax reserves for tax contingencies of approximately $144 million and $98 million for U.S. and foreign income taxes, which primarily relate to restructuring of certain foreign operations and intercompany pricing between our subsidiaries. See "Note 12—Income Taxes" for discussion of tax contingencies.

Capital Leases

Certain of our equipment fixed assets, primarily related to technology, have been acquired under capital leases. Long-term capital lease obligations were as follows:

	December 31, 2008
	(in millions)
Gross capital lease obligations	$219
Less imputed interest	(23)
Present value of net minimum lease payments	196
Less current portion	(72)
Total long-term capital lease obligations	$124

Construction Liabilities

We capitalize construction in progress and record a corresponding long-term liability for certain lease agreements, including our Seattle, Washington corporate office space subject to leases scheduled to begin in 2010 and 2011.

In accordance with EITF No. 97-10, for build-to-suit lease arrangements where we are involved in the construction of structural improvements prior to the commencement of the lease or take some level of construction risk, we are considered the owner of the assets during the construction period under U.S. GAAP.

63

AMAZON.COM, INC.

NOTES TO CONSOLIDATED FINANCIAL STATEMENTS—(Continued)

Accordingly, as the landlord incurs the construction project costs, the assets and corresponding financial obligation are recorded in "Fixed assets, net" and "Other long-term liabilities" on our consolidated balance sheet. Once the construction is completed, if the lease meets certain "sale-leaseback" criteria in accordance with SFAS No. 98, *Accounting for Leases*, we will remove the asset and related financial obligation from the balance sheet and treat the building lease as an operating lease. If upon completion of construction, the project does not meet the "sale-leaseback" criteria, the leased property will be treated as a capital lease for financial reporting purposes.

The remainder of our other long-term liabilities primarily include deferred tax liabilities, unearned revenue, asset retirement obligations, and deferred rental liabilities.

Note 7—COMMITMENTS AND CONTINGENCIES

Commitments

We lease office and fulfillment center facilities and fixed assets under non-cancelable operating and capital leases. Rental expense under operating lease agreements was $158 million, $141 million, and $132 million for 2008, 2007, and 2006.

In December 2007, we entered into a series of leases and other agreements for the lease of corporate office space to be developed in Seattle, Washington with initial terms of up to 16 years commencing on completion of development in 2010 and 2011 and options to extend for two five year periods. At December 31, 2008, under the agreements we committed to occupy approximately 1,360,000 square feet of office space. In addition, we have the right to occupy up to an additional approximately 330,000 square feet subject to a termination fee, estimated to be up to approximately $10 million, if we elect not to occupy the additional space. We also have an option to lease up to an additional approximately 500,000 square feet at rates based on fair market values at the time the option is exercised, subject to certain conditions. In addition, if interest rates exceed a certain threshold, we have the option to provide financing for some of the buildings.

The following summarizes our principal contractual commitments, excluding open orders for inventory purchases that support normal operations, as of December 31, 2008:

| | Year Ended December 31, | | | | | | |
	2009	2010	2011	2012	2013	Thereafter	Total
				(in millions)			
Operating and capital commitments:							
Debt principal (1)	$ 59	$335	$ 41	$ 33	$—	$ —	$ 468
Debt interest (1)	30	28	5	1	—	—	64
Capital leases, including interest	86	77	44	7	4	1	219
Operating leases	146	127	105	93	84	261	816
Other commitments (2)(3)	96	143	88	84	76	1,005	1,492
Total commitments	$417	$710	$283	$218	$164	$1,267	$3,059

(1) Under our 6.875% PEACS, the principal payment due in 2010 and the annual interest payments fluctuate based on the Euro/U.S. Dollar exchange ratio. At December 31, 2008, the Euro to U.S. Dollar exchange rate was 1.3974. Due to changes in the Euro/U.S. Dollar exchange ratio, our remaining principal debt obligation under this instrument since issuance in February 2000 has increased by $99 million as of December 31, 2008. The principal and interest commitments at December 31, 2008 reflect the partial redemption of the 6.875% PEACS and full redemption of the 4.75% Convertible Subordinated Notes.

64

(2) Includes the estimated timing and amounts of payments for rent, operating expenses, and tenant improvements associated with approximately 1,360,000 square feet of corporate office space being developed in Seattle, Washington and also includes the $10 million termination fee related to our right to occupy up to an additional approximately 330,000 square feet. The amount of space available and our financial and other obligations under the lease agreements are affected by various factors, including government approvals and permits, interest rates, development costs and other expenses and our exercise of certain rights under the lease agreements.

(3) Excludes $166 million of such tax contingencies for which we cannot make a reasonably reliable estimate of the amount and period of payment, if at all. See Item 8 of Part II, "Financial Statements and Supplementary Data—Note 12—Income Taxes."

Pledged Securities

We are required to pledge or otherwise restrict a portion of our cash and marketable securities as collateral for standby letters of credit, guarantees, debt, and real estate leases. We classify cash and marketable securities with use restrictions of twelve months or longer as non-current "Other assets" on our consolidated balance sheets. The balance of pledged securities at December 31, 2008 consisted of $308 million included in "Other assets." The amount required to be pledged for certain real estate lease agreements changes over the life of our leases based on our credit rating and changes in our market capitalization (common shares outstanding multiplied by the closing price of our common stock). Information about collateral required to be pledged under these agreements is as follows:

	Standby and Trade Letters of Credit and Guarantees	Debt (1)	Real Estate Leases (2)	Total
		(in millions)		
Balance at December 31, 2007	$138	$ 60	$13	$211
Net change in collateral pledged	—	100	(3)	97
Balance at December 31, 2008	$138	$160	$10	$308

(1) Represents collateral for certain debt related to our international operations.
(2) At December 31, 2007, our market capitalization was $22.0 billion. The required amount of collateral to be pledged will increase by $5 million if our market capitalization is equal to or below $18.0 billion and by an additional $6 million if our market capitalization is equal to or below $13.0 billion.

Legal Proceedings

The Company is involved from time to time in claims, proceedings and litigation, including the following:

In June 2001, Audible, Inc., our subsidiary acquired in March 2008, was named as a defendant in a securities class-action filed in United States District Court for the Southern District of New York related to its initial public offering in July 1999. The lawsuit also named certain of the offering's underwriters, as well as Audible's officers and directors as defendants. Approximately 300 other issuers and their underwriters have had similar suits filed against them, all of which are included in a single coordinated proceeding in the Southern District of New York. The complaints allege that the prospectus and the registration statement for Audible's offering failed to disclose that the underwriters allegedly solicited and received "excessive" commissions from investors and that some investors allegedly agreed with the underwriters to buy additional shares in the aftermarket in order to inflate the price of the Company's stock. Audible and its officers and directors were named in the suits pursuant to Section 11 of the Securities Act of 1933, Section 10(b) of the Securities Exchange Act of 1934, and other related provisions. The complaints seek unspecified damages, attorney and expert fees,

65

and other unspecified litigation costs. The Court has directed that the litigation proceed with a number of "focus cases" rather than all of the consolidated cases at once. Audible's case is not one of these focus cases. We dispute the allegations of wrongdoing in the complaint against Audible and its officers and directors and intend to vigorously defend ourselves in this matter.

Beginning in March 2003, we were served with complaints filed in several different states, including Illinois, by a private litigant, Beeler, Schad & Diamond, P.C., purportedly on behalf of the state governments under various state False Claims Acts. The complaints allege that we (along with other companies with which we have commercial agreements) wrongfully failed to collect and remit sales and use taxes for sales of personal property to customers in those states and knowingly created records and statements falsely stating we were not required to collect or remit such taxes. In December 2006, we learned that one additional complaint was filed in the state of Illinois by a different private litigant, Matthew T. Hurst, alleging similar violations of the Illinois state law. All of the complaints seek injunctive relief, unpaid taxes, interest, attorneys' fees, civil penalties of up to $10,000 per violation, and treble or punitive damages under the various state False Claims Acts. It is possible that we have been or will be named in similar cases in other states as well. We dispute the allegations of wrongdoing in these complaints and intend to vigorously defend ourselves in these matters.

In May 2004, Toysrus.com LLC filed a complaint against us for breach of contract in the Superior Court of New Jersey. The complaint alleged that we breached our commercial agreement with Toysrus.com LLC by selling, and by permitting other third parties to sell, products that Toysrus.com LLC alleged it has an exclusive right to sell on our website. We disputed the allegations in the complaint and brought counterclaims alleging breach of contract and seeking damages and declaratory relief. The trial of both parties' claims concluded in November 2005. In March 2006, the Court entered a judgment in favor of Toysrus.com LLC, terminating the contract but declining to award damages to either party. We are pursuing an appeal of the lower court's rulings terminating the contract, declining to award us damages, and denying our motion to compel Toysrus.com to pay certain fees incurred during the wind-down period.

In December 2005, Registrar Systems LLC filed a complaint against us and Target Corporation for patent infringement in the United States District Court for the District of Colorado. The complaint alleges that our website technology, including the method by which Amazon.com enables customers to use Amazon.com account information on websites that Amazon.com operates for third parties, such as Target.com, infringes two patents obtained by Registrar Systems purporting to cover methods and apparatuses for a "World Wide Web Registration Information Processing System" (U.S. Patent Nos. 5,790,785 and 6,823,327) and seeks injunctive relief, monetary damages in an amount no less than a reasonable royalty, prejudgment interest, costs, and attorneys' fees. We dispute the allegations of wrongdoing in this complaint and intend to vigorously defend ourselves in this matter. In September 2006, the Court entered an order staying the lawsuit pending the outcome of the Patent and Trademark Office's re-examination of the patents in suit.

In August 2006, Cordance Corporation filed a complaint against us for patent infringement in the United States District Court for the District of Delaware. The complaint alleges that our website technology, including our 1-Click ordering system, infringes a patent obtained by Cordance purporting to cover an "Object-Based Online Transaction Infrastructure" (U.S. Patent No. 6,757,710) and seeks injunctive relief, monetary damages in an amount no less than a reasonable royalty, treble damages for alleged willful infringement, prejudgment interest, costs, and attorneys' fees. In response, we asserted a declaratory judgment counterclaim in the same action alleging that a service that Cordance has advertised its intent to launch infringes a patent owned by us entitled "Networked Personal Contact Manager" (U.S. Patent No. 6,269,369). We dispute Cordance's allegations of wrongdoing and intend to vigorously defend ourselves in this matter.

In October 2007, Digital Reg of Texas, LLC filed a complaint against our subsidiary, Audible, Inc., and several other defendants in the United States District Court for the Eastern District of Texas. The complaint alleges that Audible's digital rights management technology infringes a patent obtained by Digital Reg purporting to cover a system for "Regulating Access to Digital Content" (U.S. Patent No. 6,389,541) and seeks injunctive relief, monetary damages, enhanced damages for alleged willful infringement, prejudgment and post-judgment interest, costs and attorneys' fees. We dispute the allegations of wrongdoing and intend to vigorously defend ourselves in the matter.

In December 2008, Quito Enterprises, LLC filed a complaint against us for patent infringement in the United States District Court for the Southern District of Florida. The complaint alleges that our website technology infringes a patent obtained by Quito purporting to cover a "Personal Feedback Browser for Obtaining Media Files" (U.S. Patent No. 5,890,152) and seeks injunctive relief and monetary damages. We dispute the allegations of wrongdoing and intend to vigorously defend ourselves in this matter.

In January 2009, we learned that the United States Postal Service, including the Postal Service Office of Inspector General, is investigating our compliance with Postal Service rules, and we are cooperating.

Depending on the amount and the timing, an unfavorable resolution of some or all of these matters could materially affect our business, results of operations, financial position, or cash flows.

See also "Note 12—Income Taxes."

Inventory Suppliers

During 2008, no vendor accounted for 10% or more of our inventory purchases. We do not have long-term contracts or arrangements with most of our vendors to guarantee the availability of merchandise, particular payment terms, or the extension of credit limits.

Note 8—STOCKHOLDERS' EQUITY

Preferred Stock

We have authorized 500 million shares of $0.01 par value Preferred Stock. No preferred stock was outstanding for any period presented.

Stock Conversion Activity

Holders of our 4.75% Convertible Subordinated Notes elected to convert a total of $605 million in outstanding principal amount under called redemptions during 2008, and we issued 7.8 million shares of common stock as a result of such elections.

Stock Repurchase Activity

We repurchased 2.2 million shares of common stock for $100 million in 2008 under the $1 billion repurchase program authorized by our Board of Directors in February 2008. We repurchased 6.3 million shares of common stock for $248 million in 2007, and 8.2 million shares of common stock for $252 million in 2006, under the $500 million repurchase program authorized by our Board of Directors in August 2006.

Stock Award Plans

Employees vest in restricted stock unit awards and stock options over the corresponding service term, generally between two and five years. Outstanding stock options generally have a term of 10 years from the date of grant. Stock options outstanding have a weighted average exercise life of 3 years, with a weighted average exercise price of $25.44.

Stock Award Activity

We granted stock awards, which consist primarily of restricted stock units, representing 7.3 million, 7.6 million, 9.1 million shares of common stock during 2008, 2007, and 2006 with a per share weighted average fair value of $72.21, $47.04, and $36.48.

Common shares underlying outstanding stock awards were as follows:

	Year Ended December 31,	
	2008	2007
	(in millions)	
Restricted stock units	16.7	16.3
Stock options	1.2	1.9
Total outstanding stock awards	17.9	18.2

Common shares outstanding (which includes restricted stock), plus shares underlying outstanding stock options and restricted stock units totaled 446 million, 435 million, and 436 million at December 31, 2008, 2007 and 2006. These totals include all stock-based awards outstanding, without regard for estimated forfeitures, consisting of vested and unvested awards and in-the-money and out-of-the-money stock options. Common shares outstanding increased in 2008 due to vesting of restricted stock units, exercises of stock options, and matching contributions under our 401(k) savings plan, offset by repurchases of our common stock.

The following summarizes our restricted stock unit activity (in millions):

	Number of Units
Outstanding at January 1, 2006	9.9
Units granted	9.1
Units vested	(1.7)
Units cancelled	(2.8)
Outstanding at December 31, 2006	14.5
Units granted	7.6
Units vested	(3.3)
Units cancelled	(2.5)
Outstanding at December 31, 2007	16.3
Units granted	7.3
Units vested	(5.5)
Units cancelled	(1.4)
Outstanding at December 31, 2008	16.7

AMAZON.COM, INC.

NOTES TO CONSOLIDATED FINANCIAL STATEMENTS—(Continued)

Scheduled vesting for outstanding restricted stock units at December 31, 2008 is as follows (in millions):

| | Year Ended December 31, | | | | | | |
	2009	2010	2011	2012	2013	Thereafter	Total
Scheduled vesting—restricted stock units	6.0	5.3	2.9	1.6	0.6	0.3	16.7

As matching contributions under our 401(k) savings plan, we granted 0.1 million shares of common stock in both 2008 and 2007. Shares granted as matching contributions under our 401(k) plan are included in outstanding common stock when issued.

As of December 31, 2008, there was $357 million of net unrecognized compensation cost related to unvested stock-based compensation arrangements. This compensation is recognized on an accelerated basis resulting in approximately half of the compensation expected to be expensed in the next twelve months, and has a weighted average recognition period of 1.3 years.

During 2008 and 2007, the fair value of restricted stock units vested was $362 million and $224 million.

Common Stock Available for Future Issuance

At December 31, 2008, common stock available for future issuance is as follows (in millions):

	December 31, 2008
Stock awards	138.5
Shares issuable upon conversion of 6.875% PEACS	2.8
Total common stock reserved for future issuance	141.3

Note 9—OTHER COMPREHENSIVE INCOME (LOSS)

The changes in the components of other comprehensive income (loss) were as follows:

| | Year Ended December 31, | | |
| | 2008 | 2007 | 2006 |
	(in millions)		
Net income	$ 645	$476	$190
Net change in unrealized gains/losses on available-for-sale securities	(1)	8	4
Foreign currency translation adjustment, net of tax	(127)	(3)	(13)
Amortization of net unrealized losses on terminated Euro Currency Swap, net of tax	—	1	2
Other comprehensive income (loss)	(128)	6	(7)
Comprehensive income	$ 517	$482	$183

69

Accumulated balances within other comprehensive income (loss) were as follows:

	December 31,	
	2008	**2007**
	(in millions)	
Net unrealized losses on foreign currency translation, net of tax	$(128)	$(1)
Net unrealized gains on available-for-sale securities, net of tax	6	7
Net unrealized losses on terminated Euro Currency Swap, net of tax	(1)	(1)
Total accumulated other comprehensive income (loss)	$(123)	$ 5

Note 10—OTHER OPERATING EXPENSE (INCOME), NET

Other operating expense (income), net, was $(24) million, $9 million and $10 million in 2008, 2007 and 2006. The increase in other operating income in 2008 compared to the comparable prior years is primarily attributable to the $53 million non-cash gain recognized on the sale in 2008 of our European DVD rental assets, partially offset by increased amortization of intangible assets. Other operating expense in 2007 and 2006 was primarily attributable to amortization of intangible assets.

Note 11—OTHER INCOME (EXPENSE), NET

Other income (expense), net, was $47 million, $(8) million, and $7 million in 2008, 2007 and 2006, and consisted primarily of gains and losses on sales of marketable securities, foreign currency transaction gains and losses, and other miscellaneous losses.

Foreign currency transaction gains and losses primarily relate to remeasurement of our 6.875% PEACS and remeasurement of intercompany balances.

Note 12—INCOME TAXES

In 2008, 2007 and 2006 we recorded net tax provisions of $247 million, $184 million, and $187 million. A majority of this provision is non-cash. We have current tax benefits and net operating losses relating to excess stock-based compensation that are being utilized to reduce our U.S. taxable income. As such, cash taxes paid were $53 million, $24 million, and $15 million for 2008, 2007, and 2006.

The components of the provision for income taxes, net were as follows:

	Year Ended December 31,		
	2008	**2007**	**2006**
	(in millions)		
Current taxes:			
U.S. and state	$227	$275	$162
International	25	8	3
Current taxes	252	283	165
Deferred taxes	(5)	(99)	22
Provision for income taxes, net	$247	$184	$187

U.S. and international components of income before income taxes were as follows:

	Year Ended December 31,		
	2008	2007	2006
	(in millions)		
U.S.	$436	$360	$396
International (1)	465	300	(19)
Income before income taxes	$901	$660	$377

(1) Included in 2008 is the impact of the $53 million non-cash gain associated with the sale of our European DVD rental assets. This gain will be taxed at rates substantially below the 35% U.S. federal statutory rate.

The items accounting for differences between income taxes computed at the federal statutory rate and the provision recorded for income taxes are as follows:

	Year Ended December 31,		
	2008	2007	2006
Federal statutory rate	35.0%	35.0%	35.0%
Effect of:			
Impact of international operations and restructuring	(13.8)	(11.7)	15.9
State taxes, net of federal benefits	2.8	2.1	1.6
Tax credits	(2.2)	(1.1)	(2.8)
Nondeductible stock-based compensation	1.7	1.4	1.4
Valuation allowance	2.6	(1.2)	(2.6)
Other, net	1.3	3.4	1.1
Total	27.4%	27.9%	49.6%

The effective tax rate in 2008 and 2007 was lower than the 35% U.S. federal statutory rate primarily due to earnings of our subsidiaries outside of the U.S. in jurisdictions where our effective tax rate is lower than in the U.S. The effective tax rate in 2006 was higher than the 35% U.S. federal statutory rate resulting from establishment of our European headquarters in Luxembourg. Associated with the establishment of our European headquarters, we transferred certain of our operating assets in 2005 and 2006 from the U.S. to international locations. These transfers resulted in taxable income and exposure to additional taxable income assertions by taxing jurisdictions.

71

Deferred income tax assets and liabilities were as follows:

	December 31,	
	2008	2007
	(in millions)	
Deferred tax assets:		
Net operating losses—stock-based compensation (1)	$ 120	$ 120
Net operating losses—other	31	28
Net operating losses—obtained through acquisitions (2)	14	—
Assets held for investment	152	167
Revenue items	53	58
Expense items, including stock-based compensation	253	210
Net tax credits (3)	2	2
Deferred tax assets under FIN 48	28	22
Total gross deferred tax assets	653	607
Less valuation allowance (4)	(199)	(195)
Deferred tax assets, net of valuation allowance	454	412
Deferred tax liabilities:		
Basis difference in intangible assets	(80)	—
Expense items	(13)	(24)
Deferred tax liabilities under FIN 48	(12)	(3)
Deferred tax assets, net of valuation allowance and deferred tax liabilities	$ 349	$ 385

(1) Presented net of fully reserved net operating loss carryforward deferred tax assets of $80 million and $219 million at December 31, 2008 and 2007. The total gross deferred tax assets relating to our excess stock-based compensation net operating loss carryforwards at December 31, 2008 and 2007 were $200 million and $339 million (relating to approximately $797 million and $1.1 billion of our net operating loss carryforwards). We have not fully utilized our net operating loss carryforwards generated in the years 2001 and 2003, so that the statute of limitations for these years remains open for purposes of adjusting the amounts of the losses carried forward from those years. The majority of our net operating loss carryforwards begin to expire in 2021 and thereafter.

(2) The utilization of some of these net operating loss carryforwards is subject to an annual limitation under applicable provisions of the Internal Revenue Code.

(3) Presented net of fully reserved deferred tax assets associated with tax credits of $125 million and $95 million at December 31, 2008 and 2007. Total tax credits available to be claimed in future years are approximately $167 million and $129 million as of December 31, 2008 and 2007.

(4) Relates primarily to deferred tax assets that would only be realizable upon the generation of future capital gains and net income in certain taxing jurisdictions.

Tax Contingencies

We are subject to income taxes in the U.S. and numerous foreign jurisdictions. Significant judgment is required in evaluating our tax positions and determining our provision for income taxes. During the ordinary course of business, there are many transactions and calculations for which the ultimate tax determination is uncertain. We establish reserves for tax-related uncertainties based on estimates of whether, and the extent to which, additional taxes will be due. These reserves are established when we believe that certain positions might be challenged despite our belief that our tax return positions are fully supportable. We adjust these reserves in light of changing facts and circumstances, such as the outcome of tax audit. The provision for income taxes

72

includes the impact of reserve provisions and changes to reserves that are considered appropriate. Accruals for tax contingencies are provided for in accordance with the requirements of FIN 48.

The reconciliation of our tax contingencies is as follows (in millions):

Gross tax contingencies—January 1, 2008	$112
Gross increases to tax positions in prior periods	39
Gross decreases to tax positions in prior periods	(4)
Gross increases to current period tax positions	22
Audit settlements paid during 2008	(3)
Gross tax contingencies—December 31, 2008 (1)	$166

(1)   As of December 31, 2008, we had $166 million of tax contingencies of which $165 million, if fully recognized, would affect our effective tax rate and increase additional paid-in capital by $1 million to reflect the tax benefits of excess stock-based compensation deductions.

The increase to current period tax positions results primarily from acquisition-related activity and new regulations we implemented during Q4 2008, and we do not expect such tax positions to increase significantly in the future. Due to the nature of our business operations we expect the total amount of gross unrecognized tax benefits for prior period tax positions will grow in comparable amounts to our current year increase. We do not believe it is reasonably possible that the total amount of unrecognized tax benefits will significantly decrease within the next 12 months.

Our policy is to include interest and penalties related to our tax contingencies in income tax expense. As of December 31, 2008, we had accrued interest and penalties related to tax contingencies of $14 million, net of related income tax benefits, on our balance sheet. Interest and penalties recognized for the year ended December 31, 2008 was $5 million, net of related income tax benefits.

We are under examination, or may be subject to examination, by the Internal Revenue Service ("IRS") for calendar years 2005 through 2008. Additionally, any net operating losses that were generated in prior years and utilized in these years may also be subject to examination by the IRS. We are under examination, or may be subject to examination, in the following major jurisdictions for the years specified: Kentucky for 2004 through 2008, France for 2005 through 2008, Germany for 2003 through 2008, Luxembourg for 2003 through 2008, and the United Kingdom for 2003 through 2008. In addition, in 2007, Japanese tax authorities assessed income tax, including penalties and interest, of approximately $119 million against one of our U.S. subsidiaries for the years 2003 through 2005. We believe that these claims are without merit and are disputing the assessment. Further proceedings on the assessment will be stayed during negotiations between U.S. and Japanese authorities over the double taxation issues the assessment raises, and we have provided bank guarantees to suspend enforcement of the assessment. We also may be subject to income tax examination by Japanese tax authorities for 2006 through 2008.

Note 13—SEGMENT INFORMATION

We have organized our operations into two principal segments: North America and International. We present our segment information along the same lines that our chief executive reviews our operating results in assessing performance and allocating resources.

We allocate to segment results the operating expenses "Fulfillment," "Marketing," "Technology and content," and "General and administrative," but exclude from our allocations the portions of these expense lines attributable to stock-based compensation. Additionally, we do not allocate the line item "Other operating expense (income), net" to our segment operating results. A significant majority of our costs for "Technology and content" are incurred in the United States and most of these costs are allocated to our North America segment. There are no internal revenue transactions between our reporting segments.

North America

The North America segment consists of amounts earned from retail sales of consumer products (including from sellers) and subscriptions through North America-focused websites such as *www.amazon.com* and *www.amazon.ca*. This segment includes export sales from *www.amazon.com* and *www.amazon.ca*.

International

The International segment consists of amounts earned from retail sales of consumer products (including from sellers) and subscriptions through internationally focused websites such as *www.amazon.co.uk*, *www.amazon.de*, *www.amazon.co.jp*, *www.amazon.fr*, and *www.amazon.cn*. This segment includes export sales from these internationally based sites (including export sales from these sites to customers in the U.S. and Canada), but excludes export sales from *www.amazon.com* and *www.amazon.ca*.

Information on reportable segments and reconciliation to consolidated net income was as follows:

	Year Ended December 31,		
	2008	**2007**	**2006**
	(in millions)		
North America			
Net sales	$10,228	$ 8,095	$ 5,869
Cost of sales	7,733	6,064	4,344
Gross profit	2,495	2,031	1,525
Direct segment operating expenses	2,050	1,631	1,295
Segment operating income	$ 445	$ 400	$ 230
International			
Net sales	$ 8,938	$ 6,740	$ 4,842
Cost of sales	7,163	5,418	3,911
Gross profit	1,775	1,322	931
Direct segment operating expenses	1,127	873	661
Segment operating income	$ 648	$ 449	$ 270
Consolidated			
Net sales	$19,166	$14,835	$10,711
Cost of sales	14,896	11,482	8,255
Gross profit	4,270	3,353	2,456
Direct segment operating expenses	3,177	2,504	1,956
Segment operating income	1,093	849	500
Stock-based compensation	(275)	(185)	(101)
Other operating income (expense), net	24	(9)	(10)
Income from operations	842	655	389
Total non-operating income (expense), net	59	5	(12)
Provision for income taxes	(247)	(184)	(187)
Equity-method investment activity, net of tax	(9)	—	—
Net income	$ 645	$ 476	$ 190

74

AMAZON.COM, INC.

NOTES TO CONSOLIDATED FINANCIAL STATEMENTS—(Continued)

Net sales shipped to customers outside of the U.S. represented approximately half of net sales for 2008, 2007, and 2006. Net sales from *www.amazon.co.uk*, *www.amazon.de*, and *www.amazon.co.jp* each represented 10% or more of consolidated net sales in 2008, 2007 and 2006.

Total assets, by segment, reconciled to consolidated amounts were (in millions):

	December 31,	
	2008	2007
North America	$5,266	$4,227
International	3,048	2,258
Consolidated	$8,314	$6,485

Fixed assets, net, by segment, reconciled to consolidated amounts were (in millions):

	December 31,	
	2008	2007
North America	$666	$404
International	188	139
Consolidated	$854	$543

Depreciation expense, by segment, was as follows (in millions):

	Year Ended December 31,		
	2008	2007	2006
North America	$262	$212	$166
International	49	46	34
Consolidated	$311	$258	$200

75

AMAZON.COM, INC.

NOTES TO CONSOLIDATED FINANCIAL STATEMENTS—(Continued)

Note 14—QUARTERLY RESULTS (UNAUDITED)

The following tables contain selected unaudited statement of operations information for each quarter of 2008 and 2007. The following information reflects all normal recurring adjustments necessary for a fair presentation of the information for the periods presented. The operating results for any quarter are not necessarily indicative of results for any future period. Our business is affected by seasonality, which historically has resulted in higher sales volume during our fourth quarter, which ends December 31.

Unaudited quarterly results were as follows (in millions, except per share data):

	Year Ended December 31, 2008 (1)			
	Fourth Quarter	Third Quarter	Second Quarter	First Quarter
Net sales (2)	$6,704	$4,264	$4,063	$4,135
Gross profit	1,348	999	967	956
Income before income taxes	302	182	208	207
Provision for income taxes	79	59	46	62
Net income	225	118	158	143
Basic earnings per share	$ 0.52	$ 0.28	$ 0.38	$ 0.34
Diluted earnings per share	$ 0.52	$ 0.27	$ 0.37	$ 0.34
Shares used in computation of earnings per share:				
Basic	428	427	420	417
Diluted	436	436	430	426

	Year Ended December 31, 2007 (1)			
	Fourth Quarter	Third Quarter	Second Quarter	First Quarter
Net sales	$5,673	$3,262	$2,886	$3,015
Gross profit	1,170	762	701	719
Income before income taxes	281	124	111	144
Provision for income taxes	74	44	33	33
Net income	207	80	78	111
Basic earnings per share	$ 0.50	$ 0.19	$ 0.19	$ 0.27
Diluted earnings per share	$ 0.48	$ 0.19	$ 0.19	$ 0.26
Shares used in computation of earnings per share:				
Basic	416	414	412	412
Diluted	427	425	423	420

(1) The sum of quarterly amounts, including per share amounts, may not equal amounts reported for year-to-date periods. This is due to the effects of rounding and changes in the number of weighted-average shares outstanding for each period.

(2) Our year-over-year revenue growth was 39% in 2007 and 36% for the first three quarters of 2008. For Q4 2008, our quarterly revenue growth rates declined to 18%, driven primarily by decreased consumer demand following disruptions in the global financial markets and changes in foreign exchange rates (excluding the $320 million unfavorable impact from year-over-year changes in foreign exchange rates throughout the fourth quarter, net sales would have grown 24% compared with Q4 2007).

76

Item 9. *Changes in and Disagreements with Accountants On Accounting and Financial Disclosure*

None.

Item 9A. *Controls and Procedures*

Evaluation of Disclosure Controls and Procedures

We carried out an evaluation required by the 1934 Act, under the supervision and with the participation of our principal executive officer and principal financial officer, of the effectiveness of the design and operation of our disclosure controls and procedures, as defined in Rule 13a-15(e) of the 1934 Act, as of December 31, 2008. Based on this evaluation, our principal executive officer and principal financial officer concluded that, as of December 31, 2008, our disclosure controls and procedures were effective to provide reasonable assurance that information required to be disclosed by us in the reports that we file or submit under the 1934 Act is recorded, processed, summarized, and reported within the time periods specified in the SEC's rules and forms and to provide reasonable assurance that such information is accumulated and communicated to our management, including our principal executive officer and principal financial officer, as appropriate to allow timely decisions regarding required disclosures.

Management's Report on Internal Control over Financial Reporting

Management is responsible for establishing and maintaining adequate internal control over financial reporting, as defined in Rule 13a-15(f) of the 1934 Act. Management has assessed the effectiveness of our internal control over financial reporting as of December 31, 2008 based on criteria established in Internal Control—Integrated Framework issued by the Committee of Sponsoring Organizations of the Treadway Commission. As a result of this assessment, management concluded that, as of December 31, 2008, our internal control over financial reporting was effective in providing reasonable assurance regarding the reliability of financial reporting and the preparation of financial statements for external purposes in accordance with generally accepted accounting principles. Ernst & Young has independently assessed the effectiveness of our internal control over financial reporting and its report is included below.

Changes in Internal Control Over Financial Reporting

There were no changes in our internal control over financial reporting during the quarter ended December 31, 2008 that materially affected, or are reasonably likely to materially affect, our internal control over financial reporting.

Limitations on Controls

Our disclosure controls and procedures and internal control over financial reporting are designed to provide reasonable assurance of achieving their objectives as specified above. Management does not expect, however, that our disclosure controls and procedures or our internal control over financial reporting will prevent or detect all error and fraud. Any control system, no matter how well designed and operated, is based upon certain assumptions and can provide only reasonable, not absolute, assurance that its objectives will be met. Further, no evaluation of controls can provide absolute assurance that misstatements due to error or fraud will not occur or that all control issues and instances of fraud, if any, within the Company have been detected.

Report of Ernst & Young LLP, Independent Registered Public Accounting Firm

The Board of Directors and Stockholders
Amazon.com, Inc.

We have audited Amazon.com, Inc.'s internal control over financial reporting as of December 31, 2008, based on criteria established in Internal Control—Integrated Framework issued by the Committee of Sponsoring Organizations of the Treadway Commission (the COSO criteria). Amazon.com, Inc.'s management is responsible for maintaining effective internal control over financial reporting and for its assessment of the effectiveness of internal control over financial reporting included in the accompanying Management's Report on Internal Control over Financial Reporting. Our responsibility is to express an opinion on the effectiveness of the Company's internal control over financial reporting based on our audit.

We conducted our audit in accordance with the standards of the Public Company Accounting Oversight Board (United States). Those standards require that we plan and perform the audit to obtain reasonable assurance about whether effective internal control over financial reporting was maintained in all material respects. Our audit included obtaining an understanding of internal control over financial reporting, assessing the risk that a material weakness exists, testing and evaluating the design and operating effectiveness of internal control based on the assessed risk, and performing such other procedures as we considered necessary in the circumstances. We believe that our audit provides a reasonable basis for our opinion.

A company's internal control over financial reporting is a process designed to provide reasonable assurance regarding the reliability of financial reporting and the preparation of financial statements for external purposes in accordance with generally accepted accounting principles. A company's internal control over financial reporting includes those policies and procedures that (1) pertain to the maintenance of records that, in reasonable detail, accurately and fairly reflect the transactions and dispositions of the assets of the company; (2) provide reasonable assurance that transactions are recorded as necessary to permit preparation of financial statements in accordance with generally accepted accounting principles, and that receipts and expenditures of the company are being made only in accordance with authorizations of management and directors of the company; and (3) provide reasonable assurance regarding prevention or timely detection of unauthorized acquisition, use, or disposition of the company's assets that could have a material effect on the financial statements.

Because of its inherent limitations, internal control over financial reporting may not prevent or detect misstatements. Also, projections of any evaluation of effectiveness to future periods are subject to the risk that controls may become inadequate because of changes in conditions, or that the degree of compliance with the policies or procedures may deteriorate.

In our opinion, Amazon.com, Inc. maintained, in all material respects, effective internal control over financial reporting as of December 31, 2008, based on the COSO criteria.

We have also audited, in accordance with the standards of the Public Company Accounting Oversight Board (United States), the consolidated balance sheets of Amazon.com, Inc. as of December 31, 2008 and 2007, and the related consolidated statements of operations, stockholders' equity, and cash flows for each of the three years in the period ended December 31, 2008 of Amazon.com, Inc. and our report dated January 29, 2009 expressed an unqualified opinion thereon.

/s/   Ernst & Young LLP

Seattle, Washington
January 29, 2009

Appendix B

Present Value Tables

TABLE A | **Present Value of $1**

					Present Value						
Periods	1%	2%	3%	4%	5%	6%	7%	8%	9%	10%	12%
1	0.990	0.980	0.971	0.962	0.952	0.943	0.935	0.926	0.917	0.909	0.893
2	0.980	0.961	0.943	0.925	0.907	0.890	0.873	0.857	0.842	0.826	0.797
3	0.971	0.942	0.915	0.889	0.864	0.840	0.816	0.794	0.772	0.751	0.712
4	0.961	0.924	0.888	0.855	0.823	0.792	0.763	0.735	0.708	0.683	0.636
5	0.951	0.906	0.883	0.822	0.784	0.747	0.713	0.681	0.650	0.621	0.567
6	0.942	0.888	0.837	0.790	0.746	0.705	0.666	0.630	0.596	0.564	0.507
7	0.933	0.871	0.813	0.760	0.711	0.665	0.623	0.583	0.547	0.513	0.452
8	0.923	0.853	0.789	0.731	0.677	0.627	0.582	0.540	0.502	0.467	0.404
9	0.914	0.837	0.766	0.703	0.645	0.592	0.544	0.500	0.460	0.424	0.361
10	0.905	0.820	0.744	0.676	0.614	0.558	0.508	0.463	0.422	0.386	0.322
11	0.896	0.804	0.722	0.650	0.585	0.527	0.475	0.429	0.388	0.350	0.287
12	0.887	0.788	0.701	0.625	0.557	0.497	0.444	0.397	0.356	0.319	0.257
13	0.879	0.773	0.681	0.601	0.530	0.469	0.415	0.368	0.326	0.290	0.229
14	0.870	0.758	0.661	0.577	0.505	0.442	0.388	0.340	0.299	0.263	0.205
15	0.861	0.743	0.642	0.555	0.481	0.417	0.362	0.315	0.275	0.239	0.183
16	0.853	0.728	0.623	0.534	0.458	0.394	0.339	0.292	0.252	0.218	0.163
17	0.844	0.714	0.605	0.513	0.436	0.371	0.317	0.270	0.231	0.198	0.146
18	0.836	0.700	0.587	0.494	0.416	0.350	0.296	0.250	0.212	0.180	0.130
19	0.828	0.686	0.570	0.475	0.396	0.331	0.277	0.232	0.194	0.164	0.116
20	0.820	0.673	0.554	0.456	0.377	0.312	0.258	0.215	0.178	0.149	0.104
21	0.811	0.660	0.538	0.439	0.359	0.294	0.242	0.199	0.164	0.135	0.093
22	0.803	0.647	0.522	0.422	0.342	0.278	0.226	0.184	0.150	0.123	0.083
23	0.795	0.634	0.507	0.406	0.326	0.262	0.211	0.170	0.138	0.112	0.074
24	0.788	0.622	0.492	0.390	0.310	0.247	0.197	0.158	0.126	0.102	0.066
25	0.780	0.610	0.478	0.375	0.295	0.233	0.184	0.146	0.116	0.092	0.059
26	0.772	0.598	0.464	0.361	0.281	0.220	0.172	0.135	0.106	0.084	0.053
27	0.764	0.586	0.450	0.347	0.268	0.207	0.161	0.125	0.098	0.076	0.047
28	0.757	0.574	0.437	0.333	0.255	0.196	0.150	0.116	0.090	0.069	0.042
29	0.749	0.563	0.424	0.321	0.243	0.185	0.141	0.107	0.082	0.063	0.037
30	0.742	0.552	0.412	0.308	0.231	0.174	0.131	0.099	0.075	0.057	0.033
40	0.672	0.453	0.307	0.208	0.142	0.097	0.067	0.046	0.032	0.022	0.011
50	0.608	0.372	0.228	0.141	0.087	0.054	0.034	0.021	0.013	0.009	0.003

Present Value

14%	15%	16%	18%	20%	25%	30%	35%	40%	45%	50%	Periods
0.877	0.870	0.862	0.847	0.833	0.800	0.769	0.741	0.714	0.690	0.667	1
0.769	0.756	0.743	0.718	0.694	0.640	0.592	0.549	0.510	0.476	0.444	2
0.675	0.658	0.641	0.609	0.579	0.512	0.455	0.406	0.364	0.328	0.296	3
0.592	0.572	0.552	0.516	0.482	0.410	0.350	0.301	0.260	0.226	0.198	4
0.519	0.497	0.476	0.437	0.402	0.328	0.269	0.223	0.186	0.156	0.132	5
0.456	0.432	0.410	0.370	0.335	0.262	0.207	0.165	0.133	0.108	0.088	6
0.400	0.376	0.354	0.314	0.279	0.210	0.159	0.122	0.095	0.074	0.059	7
0.351	0.327	0.305	0.266	0.233	0.168	0.123	0.091	0.068	0.051	0.039	8
0.308	0.284	0.263	0.225	0.194	0.134	0.094	0.067	0.048	0.035	0.026	9
0.270	0.247	0.227	0.191	0.162	0.107	0.073	0.050	0.035	0.024	0.017	10
0.237	0.215	0.195	0.162	0.135	0.086	0.056	0.037	0.025	0.017	0.012	11
0.208	0.187	0.168	0.137	0.112	0.069	0.043	0.027	0.018	0.012	0.008	12
0.182	0.163	0.145	0.116	0.093	0.055	0.033	0.020	0.013	0.008	0.005	13
0.160	0.141	0.125	0.099	0.078	0.044	0.025	0.015	0.009	0.006	0.003	14
0.140	0.123	0.108	0.084	0.065	0.035	0.020	0.011	0.006	0.004	0.002	15
0.123	0.107	0.093	0.071	0.054	0.028	0.015	0.008	0.005	0.003	0.002	16
0.108	0.093	0.080	0.060	0.045	0.023	0.012	0.006	0.003	0.002	0.001	17
0.095	0.081	0.069	0.051	0.038	0.018	0.009	0.005	0.002	0.001	0.001	18
0.083	0.070	0.060	0.043	0.031	0.014	0.007	0.003	0.002	0.001		19
0.073	0.061	0.051	0.037	0.026	0.012	0.005	0.002	0.001	0.001		20
0.064	0.053	0.044	0.031	0.022	0.009	0.004	0.002	0.001			21
0.056	0.046	0.038	0.026	0.018	0.007	0.003	0.001	0.001			22
0.049	0.040	0.033	0.022	0.015	0.006	0.002	0.001				23
0.043	0.035	0.028	0.019	0.013	0.005	0.002	0.001				24
0.038	0.030	0.024	0.016	0.010	0.004	0.001	0.001				25
0.033	0.026	0.021	0.014	0.009	0.003	0.001					26
0.029	0.023	0.018	0.011	0.007	0.002	0.001					27
0.026	0.020	0.016	0.010	0.006	0.002	0.001					28
0.022	0.017	0.014	0.008	0.005	0.002						29
0.020	0.015	0.012	0.007	0.004	0.001						30
0.005	0.004	0.003	0.001	0.001							40
0.001	0.001	0.001									50

TABLE B | Present Value of Annuity of $1

					Present Value						
Periods	1%	2%	3%	4%	5%	6%	7%	8%	9%	10%	12%
1	0.990	0.980	0.971	0.962	0.952	0.943	0.935	0.926	0.917	0.909	0.893
2	1.970	1.942	1.913	1.886	1.859	1.833	1.808	1.783	1.759	1.736	1.690
3	2.941	2.884	2.829	2.775	2.723	2.673	2.624	2.577	2.531	2.487	2.402
4	3.902	3.808	3.717	3.630	3.546	3.465	3.387	3.312	3.240	3.170	3.037
5	4.853	4.713	4.580	4.452	4.329	4.212	4.100	3.993	3.890	3.791	3.605
6	5.795	5.601	5.417	5.242	5.076	4.917	4.767	4.623	4.486	4.355	4.111
7	6.728	6.472	6.230	6.002	5.786	5.582	5.389	5.206	5.033	4.868	4.564
8	7.652	7.325	7.020	6.733	6.463	6.210	5.971	5.747	5.535	5.335	4.968
9	8.566	8.162	7.786	7.435	7.108	6.802	6.515	6.247	5.995	5.759	5.328
10	9.471	8.983	8.530	8.111	7.722	7.360	7.024	6.710	6.418	6.145	5.650
11	10.368	9.787	9.253	8.760	8.306	7.887	7.499	7.139	6.805	6.495	5.938
12	11.255	10.575	9.954	9.385	8.863	8.384	7.943	7.536	7.161	6.814	6.194
13	12.134	11.348	10.635	9.986	9.394	8.853	8.358	7.904	7.487	7.103	6.424
14	13.004	12.106	11.296	10.563	9.899	9.295	8.745	8.244	7.786	7.367	6.628
15	13.865	12.849	11.938	11.118	10.380	9.712	9.108	8.559	8.061	7.606	6.811
16	14.718	13.578	12.561	11.652	10.838	10.106	9.447	8.851	8.313	7.824	6.974
17	15.562	14.292	13.166	12.166	11.274	10.477	9.763	9.122	8.544	8.022	7.120
18	16.398	14.992	13.754	12.659	11.690	10.828	10.059	9.372	8.756	8.201	7.250
19	17.226	15.678	14.324	13.134	12.085	11.158	10.336	9.604	8.950	8.365	7.366
20	18.046	16.351	14.878	13.590	12.462	11.470	10.594	9.818	9.129	8.514	7.469
21	18.857	17.011	15.415	14.029	12.821	11.764	10.836	10.017	9.292	8.649	7.562
22	19.660	17.658	15.937	14.451	13.163	12.042	11.061	10.201	9.442	8.772	7.645
23	20.456	18.292	16.444	14.857	13.489	12.303	11.272	10.371	9.580	8.883	7.718
24	21.243	18.914	16.936	15.247	13.799	12.550	11.469	10.529	9.707	8.985	7.784
25	22.023	19.523	17.413	15.622	14.094	12.783	11.654	10.675	9.823	9.077	7.843
26	22.795	20.121	17.877	15.983	14.375	13.003	11.826	10.810	9.929	9.161	7.896
27	23.560	20.707	18.327	16.330	14.643	13.211	11.987	10.935	10.027	9.237	7.943
28	24.316	21.281	18.764	16.663	14.898	13.406	12.137	11.051	10.116	9.307	7.984
29	25.066	21.844	19.189	16.984	15.141	13.591	12.278	11.158	10.198	9.370	8.022
30	25.808	22.396	19.600	17.292	15.373	13.765	12.409	11.258	10.274	9.427	8.055
40	32.835	27.355	23.115	19.793	17.159	15.046	13.332	11.925	10.757	9.779	8.244
50	39.196	31.424	25.730	21.482	18.256	15.762	13.801	12.234	10.962	9.915	8.305

Present Value

14%	15%	16%	18%	20%	25%	30%	35%	40%	45%	50%	Periods
0.877	0.870	0.862	0.847	0.833	0.800	0.769	0.741	0.714	0.690	0.667	1
1.647	1.626	1.605	1.566	1.528	1.440	1.361	1.289	1.224	1.165	1.111	2
2.322	2.283	2.246	2.174	2.106	1.952	1.816	1.696	1.589	1.493	1.407	3
2.914	2.855	2.798	2.690	2.589	2.362	2.166	1.997	1.849	1.720	1.605	4
3.433	3.352	3.274	3.127	2.991	2.689	2.436	2.220	2.035	1.876	1.737	5
3.889	3.784	3.685	3.498	3.326	2.951	2.643	2.385	2.168	1.983	1.824	6
4.288	4.160	4.039	3.812	3.605	3.161	2.802	2.508	2.263	2.057	1.883	7
4.639	4.487	4.344	4.078	3.837	3.329	2.925	2.598	2.331	2.109	1.922	8
4.946	4.772	4.607	4.303	4.031	3.463	3.019	2.665	2.379	2.144	1.948	9
5.216	5.019	4.833	4.494	4.192	3.571	3.092	2.715	2.414	2.168	1.965	10
5.553	5.234	5.029	4.656	4.327	3.656	3.147	2.752	2.438	2.185	1.977	11
5.660	5.421	5.197	4.793	4.439	3.725	3.190	2.779	2.456	2.197	1.985	12
5.842	5.583	5.342	4.910	4.533	3.780	3.223	2.799	2.469	2.204	1.990	13
6.002	5.724	5.468	5.008	4.611	3.824	3.249	2.814	2.478	2.210	1.993	14
6.142	5.847	5.575	5.092	4.675	3.859	3.268	2.825	2.484	2.214	1.995	15
6.265	5.954	5.669	5.162	4.730	3.887	3.283	2.834	2.489	2.216	1.997	16
6.373	6.047	5.749	5.222	4.775	3.910	3.295	2.840	2.492	2.218	1.998	17
6.467	6.128	5.818	5.273	4.812	3.928	3.304	2.844	2.494	2.219	1.999	18
6.550	6.198	5.877	5.316	4.844	3.942	3.311	2.848	2.496	2.220	1.999	19
6.623	6.259	5.929	5.353	4.870	3.954	3.316	2.850	2.497	2.221	1.999	20
6.687	6.312	5.973	5.384	4.891	3.963	3.320	2.852	2.498	2.221	2.000	21
6.743	6.359	6.011	5.410	4.909	3.970	3.323	2.853	2.498	2.222	2.000	22
6.792	6.399	6.044	5.432	4.925	3.976	3.325	2.854	2.499	2.222	2.000	23
6.835	6.434	6.073	5.451	4.937	3.981	3.327	2.855	2.499	2.222	2.000	24
6.873	6.464	6.097	5.467	4.948	3.985	3.329	2.856	2.499	2.222	2.000	25
6.906	6.491	6.118	5.480	4.956	3.988	3.330	2.856	2.500	2.222	2.000	26
6.935	6.514	6.136	5.492	4.964	3.990	3.331	2.856	2.500	2.222	2.000	27
6.961	6.534	6.152	5.502	4.970	3.992	3.331	2.857	2.500	2.222	2.000	28
6.983	6.551	6.166	5.510	4.975	3.994	3.332	2.857	2.500	2.222	2.000	29
7.003	6.566	6.177	5.517	4.979	3.995	3.332	2.857	2.500	2.222	2.000	30
7.105	6.642	6.234	5.548	4.997	3.999	3.333	2.857	2.500	2.222	2.000	40
7.133	6.661	6.246	5.554	4.999	4.000	3.333	2.857	2.500	2.222	2.000	50

TABLE C | **Future Value of $1**

						Future Value							
Periods	1%	2%	3%	4%	5%	6%	7%	8%	9%	10%	12%	14%	15%
1	1.010	1.020	1.030	1.040	1.050	1.060	1.070	1.080	1.090	1.100	1.120	1.140	1.150
2	1.020	1.040	1.061	1.082	1.103	1.124	1.145	1.166	1.188	1.210	1.254	1.300	1.323
3	1.030	1.061	1.093	1.125	1.158	1.191	1.225	1.260	1.295	1.331	1.405	1.482	1.521
4	1.041	1.082	1.126	1.170	1.216	1.262	1.311	1.360	1.412	1.464	1.574	1.689	1.749
5	1.051	1.104	1.159	1.217	1.276	1.338	1.403	1.469	1.539	1.611	1.762	1.925	2.011
6	1.062	1.126	1.194	1.265	1.340	1.419	1.501	1.587	1.677	1.772	1.974	2.195	2.313
7	1.072	1.149	1.230	1.316	1.407	1.504	1.606	1.714	1.828	1.949	2.211	2.502	2.660
8	1.083	1.172	1.267	1.369	1.477	1.594	1.718	1.851	1.993	2.144	2.476	2.853	3.059
9	1.094	1.195	1.305	1.423	1.551	1.689	1.838	1.999	2.172	2.358	2.773	3.252	3.518
10	1.105	1.219	1.344	1.480	1.629	1.791	1.967	2.159	2.367	2.594	3.106	3.707	4.046
11	1.116	1.243	1.384	1.539	1.710	1.898	2.105	2.332	2.580	2.853	3.479	4.226	4.652
12	1.127	1.268	1.426	1.601	1.796	2.012	2.252	2.518	2.813	3.138	3.896	4.818	5.350
13	1.138	1.294	1.469	1.665	1.886	2.133	2.410	2.720	3.066	3.452	4.363	5.492	6.153
14	1.149	1.319	1.513	1.732	1.980	2.261	2.579	2.937	3.342	3.798	4.887	6.261	7.076
15	1.161	1.346	1.558	1.801	2.079	2.397	2.759	3.172	3.642	4.177	5.474	7.138	8.137
16	1.173	1.373	1.605	1.873	2.183	2.540	2.952	3.426	3.970	4.595	6.130	8.137	9.358
17	1.184	1.400	1.653	1.948	2.292	2.693	3.159	3.700	4.328	5.054	6.866	9.276	10.76
18	1.196	1.428	1.702	2.026	2.407	2.854	3.380	3.996	4.717	5.560	7.690	10.58	12.38
19	1.208	1.457	1.754	2.107	2.527	3.026	3.617	4.316	5.142	6.116	8.613	12.06	14.23
20	1.220	1.486	1.806	2.191	2.653	3.207	3.870	4.661	5.604	6.728	9.646	13.74	16.37
21	1.232	1.516	1.860	2.279	2.786	3.400	4.141	5.034	6.109	7.400	10.80	15.67	18.82
22	1.245	1.546	1.916	2.370	2.925	3.604	4.430	5.437	6.659	8.140	12.10	17.86	21.64
23	1.257	1.577	1.974	2.465	3.072	3.820	4.741	5.871	7.258	8.954	13.55	20.36	24.89
24	1.270	1.608	2.033	2.563	3.225	4.049	5.072	6.341	7.911	9.850	15.18	23.21	28.63
25	1.282	1.641	2.094	2.666	3.386	4.292	5.427	6.848	8.623	10.83	17.00	26.46	32.92
26	1.295	1.673	2.157	2.772	3.556	4.549	5.807	7.396	9.399	11.92	19.04	30.17	37.86
27	1.308	1.707	2.221	2.883	3.733	4.822	6.214	7.988	10.25	13.11	21.32	34.39	43.54
28	1.321	1.741	2.288	2.999	3.920	5.112	6.649	8.627	11.17	14.42	23.88	39.20	50.07
29	1.335	1.776	2.357	3.119	4.116	5.418	7.114	9.317	12.17	15.86	26.75	44.69	57.58
30	1.348	1.811	2.427	3.243	4.322	5.743	7.612	10.06	13.27	17.45	29.96	50.95	66.21
40	1.489	2.208	3.262	4.801	7.040	10.29	14.97	21.72	31.41	45.26	93.05	188.9	267.9
50	1.645	2.692	4.384	7.107	11.47	18.42	29.46	46.90	74.36	117.4	289.0	700.2	1,084

TABLE D | Future Value of Annuity of $1

Periods	1%	2%	3%	4%	5%	6%	7%	8%	9%	10%	12%	14%	15%
1	1.000	1.000	1.000	1.000	1.000	1.000	1.000	1.000	1.000	1.000	1.000	1.000	1.000
2	2.010	2.020	2.030	2.040	2.050	2.060	2.070	2.080	2.090	2.100	2.120	2.140	2.150
3	3.030	3.060	3.091	3.122	3.153	3.184	3.215	3.246	3.278	3.310	3.374	3.440	3.473
4	4.060	4.122	4.184	4.246	4.310	4.375	4.440	4.506	4.573	4.641	4.779	4.921	4.993
5	5.101	5.204	5.309	5.416	5.526	5.637	5.751	5.867	5.985	6.105	6.353	6.610	6.742
6	6.152	6.308	6.468	6.633	6.802	6.975	7.153	7.336	7.523	7.716	8.115	8.536	8.754
7	7.214	7.434	7.662	7.898	8.142	8.394	8.654	8.923	9.200	9.487	10.09	10.73	11.07
8	8.286	8.583	8.892	9.214	9.549	9.897	10.26	10.64	11.03	11.44	12.30	13.23	13.73
9	9.369	9.755	10.16	10.58	11.03	11.49	11.98	12.49	13.02	13.58	14.78	16.09	16.79
10	10.46	10.95	11.46	12.01	12.58	13.18	13.82	14.49	15.19	15.94	17.55	19.34	20.30
11	11.57	12.17	12.81	13.49	14.21	14.97	15.78	16.65	17.56	18.53	20.65	23.04	24.35
12	12.68	13.41	14.19	15.03	15.92	16.87	17.89	18.98	20.14	21.38	24.13	27.27	29.00
13	13.81	14.68	15.62	16.63	17.71	18.88	20.14	21.50	22.95	24.52	28.03	32.09	34.35
14	14.95	15.97	17.09	18.29	19.60	21.02	22.55	24.21	26.02	27.98	32.39	37.58	40.50
15	16.10	17.29	18.60	20.02	21.58	23.28	25.13	27.15	29.36	31.77	37.28	43.84	47.58
16	17.26	18.64	20.16	21.82	23.66	25.67	27.89	30.32	33.00	35.95	42.75	50.98	55.72
17	18.43	20.01	21.76	23.70	25.84	28.21	30.84	33.75	36.97	40.54	48.88	59.12	65.08
18	19.61	21.41	23.41	25.65	28.13	30.91	34.00	37.45	41.30	45.60	55.75	68.39	75.84
19	20.81	22.84	25.12	27.67	30.54	33.76	37.38	41.45	46.02	51.16	63.44	78.97	88.21
20	22.02	24.30	26.87	29.78	33.07	36.79	41.00	45.76	51.16	57.28	72.05	91.02	102.4
21	23.24	25.78	28.68	31.97	35.72	39.99	44.87	50.42	56.76	64.00	81.70	104.8	118.8
22	24.47	27.30	30.54	34.25	38.51	43.39	49.01	55.46	62.87	71.40	92.50	120.4	137.6
23	25.72	28.85	32.45	36.62	41.43	47.00	53.44	60.89	69.53	79.54	104.6	138.3	159.3
24	26.97	30.42	34.43	39.08	44.50	50.82	58.18	66.76	76.79	88.50	118.2	158.7	184.2
25	28.24	32.03	36.46	41.65	47.73	54.86	63.25	73.11	84.70	98.35	133.3	181.9	212.8
26	29.53	33.67	38.55	44.31	51.11	59.16	68.68	79.95	93.32	109.2	150.3	208.3	245.7
27	30.82	35.34	40.71	47.08	54.67	63.71	74.48	87.35	102.7	121.1	169.4	238.5	283.6
28	32.13	37.05	42.93	49.97	58.40	68.53	80.70	95.34	113.0	134.2	190.7	272.9	327.1
29	33.45	38.79	45.22	52.97	62.32	73.64	87.35	104.0	124.1	148.6	214.6	312.1	377.2
30	34.78	40.57	47.58	56.08	66.44	79.06	94.46	113.3	136.3	164.5	241.3	356.8	434.7
40	48.89	60.40	75.40	95.03	120.8	154.8	199.6	259.1	337.9	442.6	767.1	1,342	1,779
50	64.46	84.58	112.8	152.7	209.3	290.3	406.5	573.8	815.1	1,164	2,400	4,995	7,218

Glindex

A Combined Glossary/Subject Index

Company Index

How to Use MyAccountingLab

If you have not yet had a chance to explore the benefits of the MyAccountingLab Web site, I would encourage you to log in now and see what a valuable tool it can be. MyAccountingLab is a terrific tool for helping you grasp the accounting concepts that you are learning. So what exactly is MyAccountingLab? MyAccountingLab is a homework management tool that allows you to complete homework online. ▼

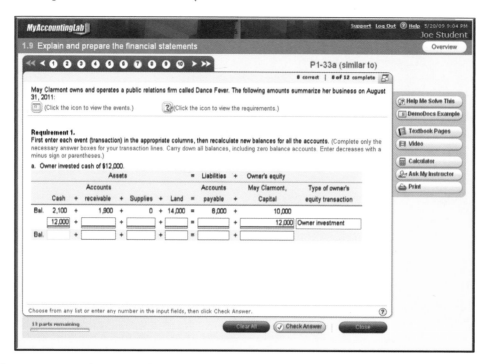

What is so great about completing the homework online, you might wonder?

Well, how about the ability to ask for and receive help *immediately* while you are working the problems? MyAccountingLab allows you to click on a **Help Me Solve This** button at anytime while you are working the problem, and a pop-up window appears with tips to help you solve the specific part of the problem that you are working on. It is similar to having someone standing over your shoulder to help you—right in the middle of the problem—so that you can get through it and understand how to solve it.

MyAccountingLab also has a button that you can click on that will open an **online version of the textbook**—it even takes you right to the section of the textbook that explains the topic related to the problem that you are working on.

Another great feature of MyAccountingLab is the **Ask My Instructor...** button. If your instructor allows you to e-mail questions, you are able to send an e-mail to your instructor in which you can explain what you are having difficulties with. When your instructor receives the e-mail, there will be a link that will take the instructor right to the problem you were working on in MyAccountingLab.

You will also find two different types of problems in MyAccountingLab, **bookmatch** and **algorithmic** problems. The bookmatch problems are the exact problems right out of your textbook (your instructor must make these available in MyAccountingLab). The algorithmic problems are identical to the ones in the textbook, except they have several variables that change in the problem every time it is selected. The algorithmic problems allow you to have an unlimited number of problems you can work in order to master the material. This means that you can see how to do a problem similar to the one in the book.